Lecture Notes in Computer Science 5088

Commenced Publication in 1973
Founding and Former Series Editors:
Gerhard Goos, Juris Hartmanis, and Jan van Leeuwen

T0205285

Andy Schürr   Manfred Nagl
Albert Zündorf (Eds.)

Applications of Graph Transformations with Industrial Relevance

Third International Symposium, AGTIVE 2007
Kassel, Germany, October 10-12, 2007
Revised Selected and Invited Papers

 Springer

Volume Editors

Andy Schürr
TU Darmstadt
Real-Time System Group
Darmstadt, Germany
E-mail: schuerr@es.tu-darmstadt.de

Manfred Nagl
RWTH Aachen
Chair of Computer Science III
Aachen, Germany
E-mail: nagl@i3.informatik.rwth-aachen.de

Albert Zündorf
University of Kassel
Software Engineering Research Group
Kassel, Germany
E-mail: zuendorf@uni-kassel.de

Library of Congress Control Number: Applied for

CR Subject Classification (1998): D.2, F.3, F.4.2, E.1, F.2.1, I.2.8, G.2.2

LNCS Sublibrary: SL 2 – Programming and Software Engineering

ISSN   0302-9743
ISBN-10   3-540-89019-X Springer Berlin Heidelberg New York
ISBN-13   978-3-540-89019-5 Springer Berlin Heidelberg New York

Springer is a part of Springer Science+Business Media

springer.com

© Springer-Verlag Berlin Heidelberg 2008
Printed in Germany

Typesetting: Camera-ready by author, data conversion by Scientific Publishing Services, Chennai, India
Printed on acid-free paper   SPIN: 12550951   06/3180   5 4 3 2 1 0

Preface

This volume compiles all papers presented at the International Symposium on Applications of Graph Transformation with Industrial Relevance (AGTIVE 2007). The submissions first underwent a thorough review process before AGTIVE 2007. A second review round was organized after the symposium for (1) final paper versions of presented contributions, (2) additional short tool surveys, and (3) the results of a separate tool competition satellite event.

AGTIVE 2007 was the third practice-oriented scientific meeting of the graph transformation community. The aim of the AGTIVE series as a whole is to serve as a forum for all those scientists of the graph transformation community that are involved in the development of graph transformation tools and the application of graph transformation techniques—usually in an industrial setting. In more detail, our intentions were and still are to:

1. Bring the practice-oriented Graph Transformation community together
2. Study and integrate different Graph Transformation approaches
3. Build a bridge between academia and industry

In addition, AGTIVE 2007 laid a special emphasis on the role that graph transformation techniques play for model-driven system engineering languages, tools, and methods including the well-known standards of the Object Management Group (OMG).

The first AGTIVE symposium took place at Kerkrade, The Netherlands, in 1999. Its proceedings appeared as vol. 1779 of the Springer LNCS series. The second symposium, AGTIVE 2003, was held in Charlottesville, Virginia, USA. The proceedings were published as LNCS 3062. The conference location for AGTIVE 2007 was a historic site again: the Schlosshotel Bad Wilhelmshöhe, which is next to the Wilhelmshöhe Palace above the city in the famous Bergpark of Kassel, right in the center of Germany. Kassel is a very old city that was first mentioned in 913. In ancient times Castellum Cattorum was a fortification of the German Tribe of the unusually disciplined and well-organized Chatti (cf. Tacitus). In the 19th century it was the home town of the Grimm brothers, who collected and wrote most of their fairy tales in this place. Nowadays it hosts "documenta", an exhibition of modern and contemporary art, which takes place every 5 years during June–September right before AGTIVE 2007.

The symposium's scientific programme—inspired by the historic environment—consisted of more than 30 regular research papers, practice reports, position papers, and system demonstration descriptions. All together these presentations covered an impressive number of different application areas such as business process modeling, ontology engineering, information system design, development of domain-specific languages and tools, embedded system engineering, model and program transformation, and so forth. Furthermore, about half of the submitted contributions proposed new graph transformation concepts and implementation techniques that are urgently needed to solve real-world problems and to deal with different kinds of scaleability problems.

In addition, two invited talks presented at AGTIVE 2007 focused on experiences using model transformation techniques in an industrial setting as well as on the state of the art of the model transformation standard QVT of the OMG.

- J. Koehler (IBM Zuerich): "Combining Quality Assurance and Model Transformations in Business-Driven Development"
- I. Kurtev (University of Twente): "State-of-the-Art of QVT, a Model Transformation Language Standard"

Finally, AGTIVE 2007 had two associated satellite events—one right before and one right after the conference. The 5th International Fujaba Days 2007 aimed at bringing together developers and users of the graph transformation tool Fujaba from all over the world to present their ideas and projects and to discuss them with each other and with the Fujaba core development team.

The other event had a wider scope. It was a Graph Transformation Tools Contest organized by Gabriele Taentzer and Arend Rensink. The aim of this event was to compare the expressiveness, the usability, and the performance of graph transformation tools along a number of selected case studies. It was motivated by the fact that a deeper understanding of the relative merits of different tool features is urgently needed to further improve graph transformation tools and to indicate still open problems. The results of the rather vivid competition are summarized in the form of three contributions in this volume. Furthermore, the participants of the competition as well as the authors of all other AGTIVE 2007 submissions were asked to submit short descriptions of their tools. The resulting last section of this volume thus nicely summarizes the state of the art of today's available graph transformation environments.

To conclude, the AGTIVE 2007 symposium again fulfilled its function of bringing together the growing community of graph transformation tool developers and users to exchange their latest achievements and experiences. The organization of the whole symposium would not have been possible in this form without the help of the Deutsche Forschungsgemeinschaft (German Research Council) DFG. In particular the donations of the DFG allowed 18 young scientists from 8 different countries—in addition to about 70 other participants—to come to Kassel by partially financing their traveling expenses. Furthermore, the grants covered part of the organizational costs of the workshop.

Last but not least the conference Co-chairs would like to thank the local Kassel team, Albert Zündorf and Leif Geiger, for the excellent organization of the AGTIVE 2007 symposium itself including a never-ending tour through the Bergpark of Kassel. They really lived up to the standards of their well-organized Chatti ancestors!

April 2008   Andy Schürr
                                                    Manfred Nagl

Organization

Program Co-chairs   Andy Schürr, TU Darmstadt, Germany
                           Manfred Nagl, RWTH Aachen, Germany
Organizing Chair   Albert Zündorf, University of Kassel
Publicity Chair   Leif Geiger, University of Kassel

Program Committee

Luciano Baresi   Politec. di Milano, Italy
Wim Bast   Compuware, The Netherlands
Paolo Bottoni   University of Rome, Italy
Frank Drewes   University of Umea, Sweden
Heiko Dörr   CARMEQ, Germany
Gregor Engels   University of Paderborn, Germany
Hartmut Ehrig   TU Berlin, Germany
Holger Giese   University of Paderborn, Germany
Pieter van Gorp   University of Antwerp, Belgium
Reiko Heckel   University of Leicester, UK
Jens Jahnke   University of Victoria, Canada
Gabor Karsai   Vanderbilt University, Tennessee, USA
Hans-Jörg Kreowski   University of Bremen, Germany
Jochen Küster   IBM Research GmbH, Switzerland
Juan de Lara   Autonomous University of Madrid, Spain
Tom Mens   University of Mons-Hainaut, Belgium
Mark Minas   University BW Munich, Germany
Jörg Niere   DSPACE, Germany
John L. Pfaltz   University of Virginia, Charlottesville, USA
Rinus Plasmeijer   University of Nijmegen, The Netherlands
Detlef Plump   University of York, UK
Ansgar Radermacher   cea, France
Arend Rensink   University of Twente, The Netherlands
Leila Ribeiro   University of Rio Grande do Sul, Brasil
Gabriele Taentzer   TU Berlin, Germany
Hans Vangheluwe   McGill University, Canada
Daniel Varro   TU Budapest, Hungary
Bernhard Westfechtel   University of Bayreuth, Germany
Edward Willink   Eclipse GMT Project, UK
Kang Zhang   University of Texas at Dallas, USA
Albert Zündorf   University of Kassel, Germany

Additional Referees

Denes Bistray
Pieter De Leenheer
Claudia Ermel
Luciana Foss
Christian Fuß
Leif Geiger
Stefan Henkler
Martin Hirsch
Peter Knirsch
Jun Kong
Rodrigo Machado
Greg Manning
Sonja Maier
Katharina Mehner
Gergely Varró
Robert Wagner
Erhard Weinell
René Woerzberger

Sponsoring Institutions

Deutsche Forschungsgemeinschaft
RWTH Aachen
Technische Universität Darmstadt
University of Kassel

Table of Contents

Graph Transformation Applications

Meta-modeling and Domain-Specific Language

New Graph Transformation Approaches

Program Transformation Applications

Dynamic System Modeling

Model Driven Software Development Applications

Queries, Views, and Model Transformations

New Pattern Matching and Rewriting Concepts

Graph Transformation Tool Contest

Graph Transformation Tools

Combining Quality Assurance and Model Transformations in Business-Driven Development

Jana Koehler, Thomas Gschwind, Jochen Küster,
Cesare Pautasso, Ksenia Ryndina, Jussi Vanhatalo, and Hagen Völzer

IBM Zurich Research Laboratory
8803 Rüschlikon, Switzerland

Abstract. Business-driven development is a methodology for developing IT solutions that directly satisfy business requirements. At its core are business processes, which are usually modeled by combining graphical and textual notations. During business-driven development, business process models are taken to the IT level, where they are implemented in a Service-Oriented Architecture. A major challenge in business-driven development is the semantic gap between models captured at the business and the IT level. Model transformations play a major role in bridging this gap.

This paper presents a transformation framework for IBM WebSphere Business Modeler that enables programmers to quickly develop in-place model transformations, which are then made available to users of this tool. They address various user needs such as quickly correcting modeling errors, refining a process model, or applying a number of refactoring operations. Transformations are combined with quality assurance techniques, which help users to preserve or improve the correctness of their business process models when applying transformations.

1 Introduction

Traditionally, the models of a business process and its implementation in an information system are considered separate artefacts. A business process model, in the best case, serves as documentation for the implemented system. However, as business process models and their implementation evolve independently, they quickly become inconsistent with each other.

Today, an increasing pressure from regulations combined with opportunities provided by new technologies such as those related to Service-Oriented Architecture [1] require models to reflect the reality of the implemented business processes. Furthermore, implementations should be derived more directly from business needs, which is often referred to as business-driven development [2,3,4]. Consequently, modeling tools increasingly address the transition from business to IT and vice versa. We observe two major trends. On the one hand, *quality assurance* strives to enable users to create business process models of higher quality from which correct, executable code can be obtained in a lean development process. On the other hand, *model transformations* aim at automating the transition across the semantic gap between business and IT. Both trends reflect the need to make modeling a less heavy-weight activity with the vision of moving towards more *agile* modeling tools where users can quickly respond to change

A. Schürr, M. Nagl, and A. Zündorf (Eds.): AGTIVE 2007, LNCS 5088, pp. 1–16, 2008.

in processes and systems, where they obtain immediate feedback on the quality of the models and receive help to build software from models in shorter iterations.

The need to constantly adapt and revise process models because of unforeseeable changes leads to an increased interest in providing users with pre-implemented model transformations that enhance the usability of the modeling tools and the productivity of the user. For example, many of the business-level modeling tools available today allow users to generate part of the implementation on the basis of the processes modeled. This comprises the generation of Web service descriptions, usually represented in the Web Service Description Language (WSDL) [5], and of the corresponding service orchestrations represented in the Business Process Execution Language (BPEL) [6]. Many process modeling tools give a lot of freedom to business analysts, which may even include the possibility to define their own extensions to the modeling language. The interpretation of such extensions often lies with the user and is thus not accessible to the modeling tool, making code generation difficult or even impossible. Moreover, technical details that are required at the IT level are usually missing in models drawn by business analysts.

To address this business-IT gap, modeling tools begin to constrain business users by imposing a service-oriented and more technical modeling style so that technical details must be added to the models in a refinement step. Frequently, however, business analysts have difficulties in providing this kind of information. This requires a tool-supported hand-shake between business and IT that is not yet very well understood. It seems that this hand-shake comprises a continuum in which a business process model is refined from an *analysis model* to a *design model* and then further into *executable code*. To develop and provide the necessary refinement, refactoring, and abstraction operations in a modeling tool, a model transformation framework is needed that is seamlessly integrated into the modeling tool's architecture.

In this paper, we discuss such a model transformation framework that we developed for IBM WebSphere Business Modeler [7], an Eclipse-based commercial product for business process modeling and analysis. In Section 2, we relate this framework to other frameworks developed in the academic community and discuss our requirements. In Section 3, an example scenario is introduced and the challenges encountered during the transition from a business process analysis model via a business process design model to executable code are reviewed in more detail. Section 4 explains why linking model transformations with quality assurance is essential for their success in a commercial environment and gives a short overview on our quality assurance techniques. In Section 5, the transformation framework is described in more detail. An overview of a selected set of model transformations that we implemented is given and shortly evaluated in Section 6. Section 7 concludes the paper.

2   Approaches to Model Transformation

Model transformations are key to success of the Model Driven Architecture (MDA) initiative [8] by the Object Management Group. Consequently, a considerable amount of research is devoted to the area of model transformations. Different types of model transformations are distinguished in the literature [9,10,11]: When the source and target models belong to the same metamodel, one usually speaks of *endogenous transformations*, otherwise of *exogenous transformations*. The former is more relevant in our case, because our transformations mostly address the transition from the analysis to the design model of a business process, which we currently consider to be represented by the same metamodel. Exogenous transformations are typically used when mapping models across domains, e.g., when generating code from business process models. Endogenous transformations can be further classified depending on whether the source and target models are physically the same or belong to a separate model. *Out-place* transformations produce a new target model, whereas *in-place* transformations modify the source model. A *vertical* transformation transforms abstract models into more refined models or vice versa, whereas a *horizontal* transformation remains at the same abstraction level. Typical examples of vertical transformations are refinement and abstraction, whereas refactoring is a semantics-preserving horizontal transformation. Research has also distinguished *destructive* and *non-destructive* transformations [10]. A destructive transformation can delete existing model elements, but a non-destructive transformation can only add elements.

For our work, it is important that all types of transformations can be implemented using the framework presented in Section 5. However, in-place transformations play a major role, because they meet our requirements of volatility and rapid execution when transforming models that share the same metamodel. *Rapid execution* is important to provide immediate feedback to users about the results of a transformation. *Volatility* of transformation results enables users to quickly undo (completely or partially) a transformation that was incorrectly applied. Once users are satisfied with the result of a transformation, they can persist the modified model. A transformation should be *applicable to an entire model or to a part thereof*, as indicated by the current user selection. Another requirement for our framework is its *extensibility with new transformations*, i.e., adding new transformations should be easy for developers. The framework should also enable *full integration* of the transformations with the modeling environment so that choosing and running a transformation does not require more than a few mouse clicks and users perceive transformations as being part of the normal editing flow. Finally, to facilitate a possible shipping of the framework in a future version of IBM WebSphere Business Modeler, the product team emphasized the importance of architecting a *lightweight* framework that does not significantly extend the tool's code base.

Several of the Eclipse-based transformation frameworks developed by the academic community provide features that are relevant to our requirements. These are in particular approaches that provide the compilation of transformations and combine declarative with imperative approaches. For example, Biermann et al. [12] present a transformation framework for defining and executing in-place transformations defined visually by graph transformation rules. Transformation execution relies on an interpretation by the AGG graph transformation tool [13] or compilation of the rules into Java. The ATL approach [14] allows developers of transformations to declaratively specify rules in textual form. In addition, it provides imperative constructs to specify the control flow of rule executions. Rules are compiled into byte code for execution on a virtual machine. Mens [15] describes a refactoring plug-in for the Fujaba environment which allows users to interactively call refactorings such as pulling up a method. MATE [16], which is implemented using the Fujaba tool, links model transformations with model analysis to provide users with repair and beautifier operations for MATLAB, Simulink, and Stateflow models. Furthermore, many frameworks provide debugging support specific to transformations.

Our transformation framework does not provide a general solution in the sense of those sophisticated frameworks developed by the academic community, such as for example ATL [14], VIATRA [17], GreAT [18], ATOM3 [19], BOTL [20], Fujaba [21], and SiTRA [22]. Our solution only focuses on transforming business process models given in a specific metamodel used within a specific tool. As such, implementing or using the QVT standard [23] was also not in our focus.

Our transformations are written by specialized developers and currently cannot be composed by business users into larger composite transformations. A simple recording feature that allows them to generate sequences of transformations that require no further user input is nevertheless straightforward. However, providing business users with composition support for iteration and branching as is available in other transformation frameworks seems to require the exposure of transformation rules at the business level. An interesting alternative would be the learning of transformations by observing a user and generalizing her editing operations on a business process model. A first discussion of such an approach has been described by Varró [24].

The example transformations that we discuss in this paper not only illustrate that the entire spectrum of transformations is needed during business-driven development, but also illustrate the necessity to *combine model transformations with quality assurance*. Assuring the quality of the model resulting from the transformation is especially important when transforming models describing complex behavior, because errors such as deadlocks can only occur in behavioral models, but not in static models such as class diagrams. This means that the pre- and postconditions of a transformation involve a very elaborate model analysis, see Section 4. Formulating these conditions declaratively in a transformation framework such as those mentioned above has not yet been achieved, although it would have significant advantages, e.g., in documenting and analyzing transformation code, to study termination and confluence [25,26], or test transformations [27]. To obtain clarity whether the combination of transformations with quality assurance would be possible in transformation frameworks, requires further investigation.

3   A Refinement Scenario

An analysis model of a business process as captured by a business analyst is shown in Fig. 1. The process model describes the (very simplified) handling of claims by an insurance company. First, the claim needs to be recorded, followed by a subprocess during which the coverage of the claim by the insurance policy of the customer is validated. If the customer has no coverage, then she is simply notified of this fact. Otherwise, the company continues to investigate whether the claim can be accepted. If the claim is accepted, a subprocess to offer a benefit is entered, which leads to the final settlement of the claim. If the claim is rejected, three activities take place in parallel: information in the Customer Relationship Management system (CRM) is updated to inform the customer about the rejection, the decision is documented, and the case is sent to product development.

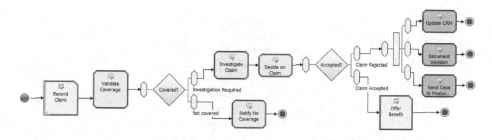

Fig. 1. Analysis model of a simplified claim-handling process in insurance

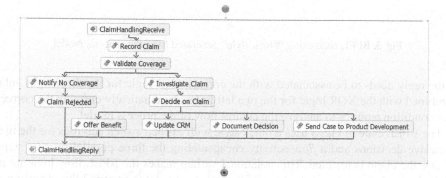

Fig. 2. BPEL code using "link style" generated from the analysis model

Figure 1 only shows the control flow and omits many details of the process such as the data that is involved or the organizations responsible for various activities in the process. We notice that two decisions *Covered?* and *Accepted?* lead to exclusive choices in the process flow. If the claim is covered, but rejected, the process forks into a parallel process fragment containing three activities. This control flow leads in total to five branches in the process model, which consist of a mixture of sequential and parallel execution threads. Each branch ends individually with a single stop node. As soon as one of these stop nodes is reached, the entire process will terminate immediately. This can lead to problems for activities in the process that are executed in parallel as they may not have completely finished when a stop node terminates the process. Although this termination behavior was probably not intended by the business analysist drawing the process model, it can often be observed in real-world process models where it is caused by a modeling practice of not re-joining parallel branches [28].

In the implementing process, this modeling problem should be corrected. The BPEL process must end with a single reply followed by a single stop node to provide the result of the process back to the invoking service. Figure 2 shows an example of BPEL code generated by automatically exporting the process model, i.e., by applying an exogenous transformation from the business-process metamodel to the BPEL metamodel, which we do not consider further in this paper.

A link-based flow is used and the five process branches directly enter the *ClaimHandlingReply* at the end of the process. The join condition that combines these five links

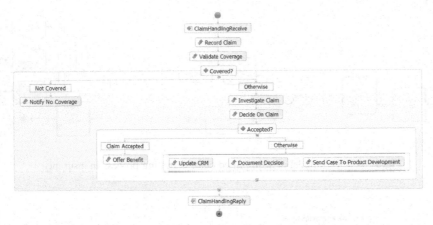

Fig. 3. BPEL code using "block style" generated from the analysis model

at the reply needs to be associated with the correct AND logic for the three right links combined with the XOR logic for the two left links. Automatically deriving the correct join condition requires to analyze the control flow of the process model.

The BPEL code in Fig. 3 uses a block style with explicit *switch* activities for the two exclusive decisions and a *flow* activity encapsulating the three parallel process steps in case the claim is rejected. This notational variant makes the BPEL flow logic more readable. In this variant, an analysis of the process model is required that determines the scope for the *switch* and *flow* activities of the process.

Even in this very simplified example, both BPEL versions already show a slightly changed process model at the IT level, which corrects the termination behavior of the analysis model. Thus, the analysis model is no longer consistent with its implementation. Ideally, changes that have been applied during the business-to-IT transition should be reflected at the analysis level. One possibility is to recompute the analysis model as an abstract view on the BPEL code. However, this leads to two different process models, the one drawn by the business analyst and the other generated from the IT process, which need to be synchronized again. For a general approach to model synchronization see for example [29]. Another possibility is to use the analysis model as input to a business-driven development process in which transformations are applied until a design model is obtained from which BPEL code can be directly generated [3]. In this paper, we concentrate on this second scenario and investigate how a tool can support a user in this activity.

We assume that the user wants to apply transformations to the analysis model of the business process in order to obtain a process design that reflects the desired BPEL block structure. Ideally, the tool should inform the user that the model contains sequential and parallel branches that end in individual stop nodes. Then, it could either automatically apply transformations to make the model structurally aligned to the future BPEL or guide the user in applying the appropriate transformations. Figure 4 illustrates a first possible model transformation that joins the parallel branches of the process model. It takes the three stop nodes ending the branches in the parallel process fragment and replaces them by a join followed by a single stop node.

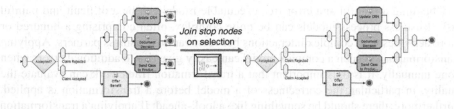

Fig. 4. Joining multiple stop nodes

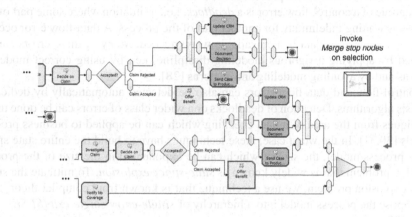

Fig. 5. Merging the remaining stop nodes

In a second transformation, the newly introduced stop node is merged with the two stop nodes ending the exclusive branches, see Fig. 5. A merge is introduced, followed by a single stop node. This yields the desired BPEL block structure, from which also the correct join condition for link-style BPEL code can easily be computed.

If the user had applied a join to a larger selection of stop nodes, an incorrect process model would result that does not terminate correctly. Ideally, a tool should warn or prevent the user from applying transformations that lead to an incorrect model. In the following section, we take a closer look at the structural analysis methods that we use to ensure that users obtain feedback about the correctness of models resulting from a transformation.

4 Ensuring the Quality of Business Process Models

Business process models were traditionally used mainly for documenting and communicating a business process. As they were used only by humans, lack of quality of a model was tolerable to some extent. Today, with the proliferation of business process management systems, many process models are executed by machines. Errors in those models can incur substantial costs. A faithful and error-free model is also important when one tries to obtain realistic business measures from a process model through simulation or analysis, which is also supported by many tools today.

Obtaining a faithful and error-free executable model can be a difficult and painful task. Business process models can be quite complex, often comprising a hundred or more activities with complex interactions between various business partners. Applying transformations to such a complex model can easily give rise to additional errors when done manually. It is thus important that a transformation framework can evaluate the quality, in particular, the correctness of a model before a transformation is applied. Furthermore, there should be something like a look-ahead: If applying a transformation to a correct model yields an incorrect model, the user must be alerted of this issue.

Possible errors in business process models include control-flow and data-flow errors. An example of a control-flow error is a *deadlock*, i.e., a situation where some part of the process is waiting indefinitely for another part of the process. A data-flow error occurs, e.g., when a piece of data is not available when needed. Many of these errors can be avoided by applying a rigorous modeling discipline, i.e., by using correct modeling patterns and by avoiding modeling anti-patterns [28].

Control-flow and data-flow errors can also be detected automatically by dedicated analysis algorithms. Detection of deadlocks or a wider class of errors can be done using techniques from the area of model checking which can be applied to business process models [30,31]. In the worst case, these techniques have to build the entire state space of the process model, the size of which can be exponential in the size of the process model, a problem that is widely known as *state-space explosion*. To mitigate the state-space explosion problem, we use a technique that is known from compiler theory: We decompose the process model into a hierarchy of *single-entry-single-exit (SESE) fragments* [32].

Figure 6 shows a process model and its SESE fragments, which are indicated by dashed boxes. Suppose that this model was derived from the model in Fig. 1 by applying a stop node transformation to the four topmost stop nodes, which were combined by a join, then followed by a second transformation that added a merge. The first of the two transformations introduced a deadlock. For example, if the claim is accepted, the join in fragment F waits in vain for the other three activities in fragment F to finish.

To check for control-flow errors in the overall process model, it is sufficient to check each fragment in isolation, i.e., each error is local to some SESE fragment. For example, the deadlock in Fig. 6 is local to fragment F.

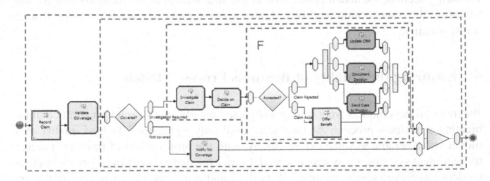

Fig. 6. An erroneous process model and its decomposition into SESE fragments

A SESE fragment is usually much smaller than the overall process. Its size is measured as the number of edges between its direct subfragments. As the decomposition into SESE fragments can be computed in linear time and there are at most twice as many fragments as there are atomic activities in the process model, the time used for the control-flow analysis of all the fragments mainly depends on the size of the largest fragment in the process. In a case study with more than 340 real-world business process models which had an average size of 75 edges with the maximum being 342 edges, we measured that the largest fragment of a process on average had size 25 with a maximum of 82 [32].

As a second technique to mitigate the state-space explosion problem, we use heuristics that can be applied in linear time to sort out many of the error-free and a fair percentage of the erroneous fragments before any state-space generation is applied [32]. This is based on the observation that many error-free and some erroneous fragments in practice have a simple structure that can easily be recognized. For example, the deadlock in fragment F in Fig. 6 can be detected by recognizing that the fragment includes a decision, but no merge [28,32].

Modeling errors are reported to the user, who can then take steps to correct the model by manually editing the model or applying automatic transformations. When interleaving the analysis with model transformations, the user can be warned that the selected transformation is not applicable to the set of selected stop nodes without introducing a deadlock into the model. The decomposition into SESE fragments can also be used to speed up an automatic computation of a correct stop-node merging based on model-checking techniques.

5   In-Place Transformation Framework Architecture

IBM WebSphere Business Modeler is built on top of the Eclipse platform, making it relatively straightforward to plug in custom extensions providing advanced functionality. Whereas a detailed discussion concerning the tool's extension points would exceed the scope of this paper, suffice it to say that the tool has been designed using the model-view-controller pattern and that it is possible to manipulate the model elements using the command pattern [33]. Unfortunately, the command pattern does not support easy programmatic access of a model. For every change, a command object has to be set up with the correct parameters, options and references to the model elements to be modified. With this approach, most of the transformation code would be dedicated to setting up commands and pushing them onto the command execution stack, and the logic of the transformation would become very hard to follow.

Thus, an abstraction layer is needed to enable programmatic access to the in-memory model so that it can be modified with minimal amount of coding, but still without breaking the model-view-controller design of the tool. In this way, the results of a transformation become immediately visible to the user, whereas for the developer the elements of a model are exposed in such a way that it becomes easy to implement transformations using an ordinary programming language, i.e., Java in our case. In this approach, transformations are natively executed because no interpretation is required and the Eclipse infrastructure is reused to package and ship transformation plug-ins as extensions to the product.

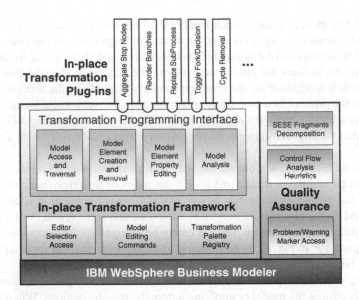

Fig. 7. Architecture of the transformation framework

The main purpose of our transformation framework is to provide such an abstraction layer. It supports the execution of automatic refactoring, refinement and abstraction transformations, and enables their full integration with the existing modeling environment and the quality-assurance functionality. As shown in Fig. 7, the transformation framework extends the IBM WebSphere Business Modeler environment, acting as a container of plug-ins that package the actual transformation code so that the modeling tool can be customized by activating and deactivating the appropriate transformation plug-ins.

The challenge of this approach lies in the design of the "transformation programming interface" (TPI) visible to the developer. It is especially important to add methods to the TPI that make the model efficiently accessible so that it can be traversed, analyzed, and modified by the transformation code.

Table 1 summarizes the main features of the TPI that help in the rapid development of new transformations. Transformations may use the interface to edit models by *creating new elements* and *removing existing ones*. Element *properties can be directly modified*, e.g., to rename an element or to reposition an element in the diagram. Furthermore, the programming interface has been designed to support *different patterns of model traversal*. *Simple transformations* are independently applied once to each target model element and thus do not require the transformation code to deal with model traversal issues. *Complex transformations* may require to filter the elements of a model based on some criteria. In the simplest case, the filter checks the meta-model element type, for example to distinguish stop nodes from start nodes. However, also non-trivial conditions may be required, such as checking whether elements are connected or belong to a SESE fragment. In general, transformations may *traverse* model elements in some specific order, for example, by drilling down the element containment structure or by navigating through the predecessor/successors elements as linked by the control flow. To support

Table 1. Excerpt of the Transformation Programming Interface

TPI Feature	Example
Creation of new model elements	`addStopNode()`
	`addStartNode()`
	`addTask()`
	`addGateway(Type)`
	`addControlEdge()`
	`addDataEdge(Type)`
Removal of existing model elements	`remove(Element)`
Editing of model element properties	`move(Position)`
	`rename(String)`
Random access to model elements	`find(ElementID)`
Access to selected model elements	`selection.getEdges()`
	`selection.getNodes()`
	`selection.getStopNodes()`
Traversal of related model elements	`getInBranch()`
	`getOutBranch()`
	`getPredecessor()`
	`getSuccessor()`
	`getParent()`
	`getChildren()`
Analysis of model elements	`isDisconnected()`
	`isSESE(Fragment)`
Transformation palette registration	`register(Transformation)`
	`unregister(Transformation)`

complex transformations that do not scan elements in a predefined order, the framework offers a direct look-up of elements. Finally, transformations can be registered with a palette or menu of macro-editing buttons displayed to the user, see also Section 6.

To illustrate how the TPI can be used, we show below how to implement the "stop node aggregation" transformation mentioned in Section 1.

```
transformation aggregateSelectedStopNodes(gatewayType) (
    predecessors = [];
    nodes = TPI.selection.getStopNodes();
    if (nodes.length > 1) (
     foreach (node in nodes) (
      predecessors.append(TPI.getPredecessor(node));
      TPI.remove(node);
     )
     gateway = TPI.addGateway(gatewayType, predecessors.length);
     stopNode = TPI.addStopNode();
     TPI.addControlEdge(TPI.getOutBranch(gateway,0), stopNode);
     i = 0;
     foreach (pred in predecessors) (
      TPI.addControlEdge(pred, TPI.getInBranch(gateway,i));
      i++;
    )))
```

This transformation is applied to a set of selected stop nodes and replaces them with a join or merge depending on the user's input, recall Figs. 4 and 5. As shown in the pseudo-code, the transformation first ensures that more than one stop node has been selected. As additional precondition, the transformation could check whether aggregating the selected nodes would not introduce an error, see the discussion in Section 4. Then, the transformation iterates over all selected stop nodes, stores their predecessor element for later use, and subsequently deletes the stop node. Then it adds either a join or a merge to the model and links its outgoing branch with a new stop node. As a last step, it connects each predecessor element to a different incoming branch of the newly added join or merge.

6   Palette-Based Invocation of Transformations

Transformations can be made available to users through a menu or palette. One can imagine that palettes are provided to users with transformations supporting certain development methodologies or industry-specific requirements. Figure 8 shows a possible design of such a palette-based user interface. Users can invoke transformations via a menu or by clicking on the palette button showing a mnemonic picture of the transformation. If no model elements are selected prior to invocation, a transformation is applied to the entire model. An "undo" capability can easily be provided to the user, because transformations are executed as sequences of editor commands. The history of transformed models could be maintained by using version management enhanced with traceability at the model-element level.

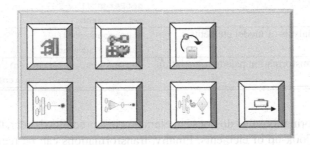

Fig. 8. A palette of model transformations

The palette above shows some of the model transformations that we implemented. Most of these transformations can exist in a simple form without linking to quality assurance and in a more sophisticated form that links to quality assurance to support the user in correctly applying a transformation. In the upper row of the palette, we find (from left to right) the transformations *automatically reorder branches*, *replace subprocess*, and *cycle removal*. In the lower row, we find the transformations *join stop nodes*, *merge stop nodes*, *toggle fork/decision*, and *assign data container*. In addition to these transformations, many others can be imagined.

Automatically reorder branches is a horizontal, non-destructive, semantics-preserving transformation that simply cleans up clutter in the diagram, which can occur when branches are connected to a join or merge. The transformation analyzes the graphical layout and eliminates crossing branches.

Replace subprocess is a horizontal, destructive transformation that replaces a user-selected subprocess by another user-selected subprocess. It prompts the user to select the replacing subprocess from a list of subprocesses that the transformation obtains from the workspace. In the current implementation, this transformation connects the new subprocess only with control-flow edges.

Cycle removal is a vertical, destructive, semantics-preserving transformation that takes a process model with unstructured cycles, i.e., backward edges added to the flow, and produces a model with well-structured loops [34]. The transformation leads to a model with a more technical flavor for many business users—therefore, we consider it as a vertical transformation. Cycle removal relies on the SESE analysis described in Section 4. It can happen that it returns an only partially transformed model. In particular, cycles that spawn parallel branches often cannot be removed.

Join stop nodes and *Merge stop nodes* are horizontal and destructive transformations already known to the reader. While Merge stop nodes is semantics-preserving, Join stop nodes is not due to the semantics of these modeling elements. The two transformations are implemented, but do not link to the quality assurance yet. Hence, it is under the full responsibility of the user whether to apply the transformation.

Toggle fork/decision is a horizontal, destructive transformation that simply flips a selected fork into a decision and vice versa. This version is useful during the editing process, e.g., when correcting modeling errors. However, it can easily introduce control-flow errors, as discussed in Section 4. A more sophisticated version would transform process fragments of sequential branching behavior into fragments of parallel behavior and vice versa, which requires a combination with quality assurance.

A very interesting challenge is the treatment of data flow in transformations. It can be studied in the *Assign data container* transformation, which is a vertical, destructive transformation that takes a model with control flow and refines it into a model with data flow. It can also be applied to models with mixed control and data flow. The transformation leads to a changed interface of model elements.

Several possible solutions exist for how a transformation can modify the interfaces of activities, e.g., it can add only the newly required inputs/outputs or it can in addition remove those inputs/outputs that are no longer needed. Existing data-flow edges can be restored if the old and the new interface of a model element share the inputs and outputs that are required by the data flow. Otherwise, data maps have to be inserted, which will remain abstract in most cases, because the transformation cannot determine what the exact mapping between mismatched data will be. These interface changes usually affect the consistency of other process models that share the same model elements. The resolution of possible inconsistencies is a challenging problem, which may not be amenable to a fully automatic solution and require other transformations to support the user. In addition, beautifier transformations relying on quality assurance may be required to eliminate control and data flow edges that are no longer needed in the transformed models.

At the moment of writing, it is too early to give a comprehensive evaluation of the framework itself. Concerning the performance of the transformations, following an in-place approach has shown its benefits in terms of the speed at which transformations are executed. Users running transformations hardly notice the difference between transformations and normal editing commands, because they see the result of the transformation immediately without having the need to persist the transformed models.

In terms of usability, the transformations are easy to apply and significantly reduce the editing effort for the user. Based on the example scenario in this paper, Fig. 9 shows that model transformations reduce lengthy and error-prone manual editing operations to a few clicks. For example, manually performing the join and merge stop nodes transformations in the example scenario takes 42 mouse clicks. Automating the transformation still requires the user to select the set of nodes (twice three clicks), but then the model is updated with a single mouse click. The chart in Fig. 9 shows two more transformations, *assign data container* and *replace subprocess*, in the context of the example scenario.

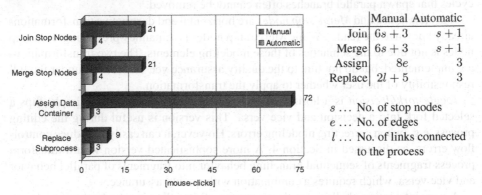

	Manual	Automatic
Join	$6s + 3$	$s + 1$
Merge	$6s + 3$	$s + 1$
Assign	$8e$	3
Replace	$2l + 5$	3

s ... No. of stop nodes
e ... No. of edges
l ... No. of links connected
to the process

Fig. 9. Usability evaluation of selected in-place model transformations

7   Conclusion

Model transformations help significantly in addressing challenges in the business-IT gap encountered during business-driven development, which aims at directly taking business process models to the IT level. In this paper, we report on a transformation framework that adds a lightweight infrastructure to IBM WebSphere Business Modeler for the rapid development of model transformations. Using this framework, in-place transformations are developed that are easily applicable by business users to automate complicated editing steps. By linking them to quality-assurance capabilities provided in modeling tools, the transformations can be made "intelligent" and help users to preserve or re-establish the correctness of their models when going through a sequence of refinement and refactoring operations. The set of transformations implemented significantly increases user productivity as they raise the abstraction level of the model editing palette from a "picture-drawing" tool to a level supporting real business-process modeling.

Acknowledgement.   The work published in this article was partially conducted within the EU project Super (www.ip-super.org) under the EU 6th Framework.

References

1. Newcomer, E., Lomow, G.: Understanding SOA with Web Services. Addison Wesley, Reading (2005)
2. Mitra, T.: Business-driven development. IBM developerWorks article. IBM (2005),
   http://www.ibm.com/developerworks/webservices/library/ws-bdd

3. Koehler, J., Hauser, R., Küster, J., Ryndina, K., Vanhatalo, J., Wahler, M.: The role of visual modeling and model transformations in business-driven development. In: Proceedings of the 5th International Workshop on Graph Transformation and Visual Modeling Techniques, pp. 1–12. Elsevier, Amsterdam (2006)

4. Brahe, S., Bordbar, B.: A Pattern-based Approach to Business Process Modeling and Implementation in Web Services. In: Proceedings of Workshop Modeling the SOA - Business perspective and model mapping, in conjunction with ICSOC (2006)

5. Christensen, E., Curbera, F., Meredith, G., Weerawarana, S.: Web services description language (WSDL) (2001), http://www.w3.org/TR/wsdl

6. Jordan, D., et al.: Web services business process execution language (WSBPEL) 2.0 (2007), http://www.oasis-open.org/committees/wsbpel/

7. IBM: WebSphere Business Modeler, http://www.ibm.com/software/integration/wbimodeler

8. Object Management Group: Model driven architecture (2001), http://www.omg.org/mda

9. Mens, T., van Gorp, P., Karsai, G., Varró, D.: Applying a model transformation taxonomy to graph transformation technology. In: Karsai, G., Taentzer, G. (eds.) GraMot 2005, International Workshop on Graph and Model Transformations. ENTCS, vol. 152, pp. 143–159. Elsevier, Amsterdam (2006)

10. Mens, T., Gorp, P.V.: A Taxonomy of Model Transformation. Electr. Notes Theor. Comput. Sci. 152, 125–142 (2006)

11. Czarnecki, K., Helsen, S.: Feature-based survey of model transformation approaches. IBM Systems Journal, special issue on Model-Driven Software Development 45(3), 621–645 (2006)

12. Biermann, E., Ehrig, K., Köhler, C., Kuhns, G., Taentzer, G., Weiss, E.: Graphical Definition of In-Place Transformations in the Eclipse Modeling Framework. In: Nierstrasz, O., Whittle, J., Harel, D., Reggio, G. (eds.) MoDELS 2006. LNCS, vol. 4199, pp. 425–439. Springer, Heidelberg (2006)

13. Ermel, C., Rudolf, M., Taentzer, G.: The AGG-Approach: Language and Tool Environment. In: Ehrig, H., Engels, G., Kreowski, H.J., Rozenberg, G. (eds.) Handbook of Graph Grammars and Computing by Graph Transformation. Applications, Languages and Tools, vol. 2, pp. 551–603. World Scientific, Singapore (1999)

14. Jouault, F., Kurtev, I.: Transforming Models with ATL. In: Bruel, J.-M. (ed.) MoDELS 2005. LNCS, vol. 3844, pp. 128–138. Springer, Heidelberg (2006)

15. Mens, T.: On the use of graph transformations for model refactoring. In: 2005 Summer School on Generative and Transformational Techniques in Software Engineering, Braga, Portugal, Departamento Informatica, Universidade do Minho, Braga, Portugal, Technical Report TR-CCTC/DI-35, 67–98 (2005)

16. Stürmer, I., Kreuz, I., Schäfer, W., Schürr, A.: Enhanced simulink/stateflow model transformation: The mate approach. In: Proceedings of MathWorks Automotive Conference (MAC 2007), MathWorks (2007)

17. Balogh, A., Németh, A., Schmidt, A., Rath, I., Vágó, D., Varró, D., Pataricza, A.: The VIATRA2 model transformation framework. In: ECMDA 2005 – Tools Track (2005)

18. Karsai, G., Agrawal, A., Shi, F., Sprinkle, J.: On the Use of Graph Transformation in the Formal Specification of Model Interpreters. Journal of Universal Computer Science 9(11), 1296–1321 (2003)

19. de Lara, J., Vangheluwe, H.: $AToM^3$: A Tool for Multi-Formalism and Meta-Modelling. In: Kutsche, R.-D., Weber, H. (eds.) FASE 2002. LNCS, vol. 2306, pp. 174–188. Springer, Heidelberg (2002)

20. Braun, P., Marschall, F.: BOTL - The Bidirectional Objekt Oriented Transformation Language. Technical report, Fakultät für Informatik, Technische Universität München, Technical Report TUM-I0307 (2003)
21. Nickel, U., Niere, J., Zündorf, A.: Tool demonstration: The FUJABA environment. In: Proceedings of the 22nd International Conference on Software Engineering (ICSE), Limerick, Ireland, pp. 742–745. ACM Press, New York (2000)
22. Akehurst, D.H., Bordbar, B., Evans, M.J., Howells, W.G.J., McDonald-Maier, K.D.: SiTra: Simple Transformations in Java. In: Nierstrasz, O., Whittle, J., Harel, D., Reggio, G. (eds.) MoDELS 2006. LNCS, vol. 4199, pp. 351–364. Springer, Heidelberg (2006)
23. Object Management Group (OMG): Meta Object Facility (MOF) 2.0 Query/View/Transformation Specification. Final Adopted Specification ptc/05-11-01 (2005)
24. Varró, D.: Model Transformation by Example. In: Nierstrasz, O., Whittle, J., Harel, D., Reggio, G. (eds.) MoDELS 2006. LNCS, vol. 4199, pp. 410–424. Springer, Heidelberg (2006)
25. Küster, J.M.: Definition and validation of model transformations. Software and Systems Modeling (SoSyM) 5(3), 233–259 (2006)
26. Varró, D., Varró-Gyapay, S., Ehrig, H., Prange, U., Taentzer, G.: Termination Analysis of Model Transformations by Petri Nets. In: Corradini, A., Ehrig, H., Montanari, U., Ribeiro, L., Rozenberg, G. (eds.) ICGT 2006. LNCS, vol. 4178, pp. 260–274. Springer, Heidelberg (2006)
27. Küster, J.M., Abd-El-Razik, M.: Validation of Model Transformations - First Experiences Using a White Box Approach. In: Kühne, T. (ed.) MoDELS 2006. LNCS, vol. 4364, pp. 193–204. Springer, Heidelberg (2007)
28. Koehler, J., Vanhatalo, J.: Process anti-patterns: How to avoid the common traps of business process modeling, part 1 modeling control flow, part 2 modeling data flow. IBM WebSphere Developer Technical Journal 10(2), 10(4) (2007)
29. Giese, H., Wagner, R.: Incremental Model Synchronization with Triple Graph Grammars. In: Nierstrasz, O., Whittle, J., Harel, D., Reggio, G. (eds.) MoDELS 2006. LNCS, vol. 4199, pp. 543–557. Springer, Heidelberg (2006)
30. van der Aalst, W.M.P.: Workflow verification: Finding control-flow errors using Petri-net-based techniques. In: Business Process Management, Models, Techniques, and Empirical Studies, London, UK, pp. 161–183. Springer, Heidelberg (2000)
31. Mendling, J., Moser, M., Neumann, G., Verbeek, H.M.W., Dongen, B.F., van der Aalst, W.M.P.: Faulty EPCs in the SAP reference model. In: Dustdar, S., Fiadeiro, J.L., Sheth, A.P. (eds.) BPM 2006. LNCS, vol. 4102, pp. 451–457. Springer, Heidelberg (2006)
32. Vanhatalo, J., Völzer, H., Leymann, F.: Faster and More Focused Control-Flow Analysis for Business Process Models though SESE Decomposition. In: 5th International Conference on Service-Oriented Computing (ICSOC), Vienna, Austria (September 2007) (to appear)
33. Gamma, E., Helm, R., Johnson, R., Vlissides, J.: Design Patterns: Elements of Reusable Object-Oriented Software. Addison-Wesley, Reading (1994)
34. Koehler, J., Hauser, R., Sendall, S., Wahler, M.: Declarative techniques for model-driven business process integration. IBM Systems Journal 44(1), 47–65 (2005)

Assuring Consistency of Business Process Models and Web Services Using Visual Contracts

Gregor Engels[1,2], Baris Güldali[2], Christian Soltenborn[1], and Heike Wehrheim[1]

[1] Institut für Informatik, Universität Paderborn
[2] Software Quality Lab (s-lab), Universität Paderborn,
33098 Paderborn, Germany
{engels,baris,christian,wehrheim}@upb.de

Abstract. Business process models describe workflows by a set of actions together with their ordering. When implementing business processes within a service-oriented architecture, these actions are mapped to existing IT (web) services, which are then to be executed in the order specified by the business process. However, the execution of a web service can require certain preconditions to be fulfilled. These might not hold at the time of execution specified in the business process model: it can be inconsistent with the web service specification.

In this paper we propose a technique for checking consistency of process models with web service specifications. To this end, both are equipped with a *formal* semantics (in terms of graph transformations). We show how to use an existing model checker for graph transformation systems to carry out the consistency check.

Keywords: Business processes, web services, UML Activities, visual contracts, graph transformations.

1 Introduction

A business process is a real-world activity consisting of a set of logically related actions that, when performed in an appropriate sequence, produces a business outcome. Business process management (BPM) addresses how organizations can identify, model, develop, deploy, and manage their business processes. Business processes can involve IT systems as well as human interactions [1].

Today BPM faces great challenges because of the fast evolving markets. Business processes have to adapt to the steadily changing business needs; they have to be developed efficiently and fast. Service-oriented architectures (SOA) are an enabling technology which can help in improving BPM in order to cope with these challenges. In SOA, the IT functionalities are prepared as *services* which are accessible over open standards. In an SOA-based BPM the actions of a business process are realized by the services. Thus the business process can be adapted to changing requirements just by replacing services with other services or just by changing the service functionality without changing its interface.

A. Schürr, M. Nagl, and A. Zündorf (Eds.): AGTIVE 2007, LNCS 5088, pp. 17–31, 2008.

In this scenario, business processes are (formally or informally) described by *business process models*. Such models represent the handling of certain cases: they determine which actions (or tasks) need to take place in which order to correctly and efficiently process a case. For specifying process models, several modeling languages have been proposed, including Petri Nets [2], Event-driven Process Chains (EPCs) [3], the Business Process Execution Language (BPEL) [4] and UML Activities [5]. All of these modeling languages support basic features like decisions or concurrent handling of cases. In SOA, the actions appearing in the business process model are bound to services (e.g., web services), which realize the functionality of the actions. However, the services are usually not independent of one another: a web service might require certain (data) structures to operate on which might have been build up by a prior invocation of other web services. The essential question is thus: does the business process model manage to achieve this, i.e., are all of the service's preconditions fulfilled when executing them according to the ordering specified in the business process model? If not, the execution of the business process fails.

In this paper, we address this question of *consistency* of business process models and service specifications. Such a consistency analysis requires two prerequisites: we need business process models with precise meanings (to determine the possible orderings of actions) and we need web service specifications precisely stating the requirements and warranties of a service. Thus we need specifications with a *formal semantics*. Here, we use *UML Activities* [6] for modelling business processes and *visual contracts* [7] for specifying web services. Both allow for graphical, visual descriptions, and moreover both are equipped with a formal semantics (in terms of graph transformations). UML Activities have a semantics based on the concept of *dynamic meta modeling* (DMM) [8]; visual contracts (VCs) on the other hand are inspired by the Design by Contract paradigm [9] and specify every service by its pre- and postcondition (the left- and right-hand side of a rule, respectively).

In this setting, consistency checking amounts to proving that all action orderings specified in the business process model (BP) describe executable sequences of corresponding web services (WS), where correspondence is given by a binding b of actions to services. This check is carried out on a graph transformation system *combining* the graph transformation systems which describe the semantics of the business process model (GT_1) and the web services (GT_2): the type graphs as well as the start graphs underlying both transformation systems are conjoined (disjoint union), and the rules are partly kept and partly *synchronized*. More specifically, the DMM rule describing the execution of an action in a business process model has to be synchronized with the VC rule of the corresponding web service (union of left- and right-hand-side). This gives rise to a new graph transformation system $GT_1 \oplus_b GT_2$. In a second step, this new graph transformation system is used to compute a transition system (TS), which is then analyzed for consistency: we determine whether the end-states of the business process model can always be reached (and thus whether the execution of web services in this order is possible). The consistency analysis of business process

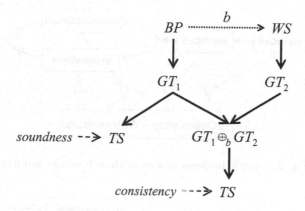

Fig. 1. Overall Approach

models and service specifications requires a structurally correct (*sound*) process model. Therefore the *soundness* of the process model must be analyzed before the combined analysis. The whole approach is illustrated in Fig. 1. The analysis is carried out fully automatically using the GROOVE model checker [10].

The paper is structured as follows: In Sect. 2, we first introduce the foundations of business process modeling and service-oriented architectures with web services. We explain the concepts using a small example. On this basis, in Sect. 3 we define our quality criterion of consistency (for bindings of business process models to web services), and we show how to verify that criterion using model checking techniques. Section 4 shows the tools used to realize our approach, and Sect. 5 concludes, points out related work and gives an outlook on future research.

2   Background

This section explains the concepts which are essential for our approach. The formal semantics of business process models is defined using DMM (Sect. 2.1). Using this formalism we can check some quality aspects of the business process model, e.g. *soundness* (Sect. 2.2). A sound business process may still have problems if the actions of the process are automated in an SOA using web services. Section 2.3 explains the concepts of SOA with web services and visual contracts.

2.1   DMM and UML Activities

The most important prerequisite for automatically analyzing the behavior of models is that the behavior is specified formally. Moreover, to allow advanced language users to understand the precise semantics of their models, the specification should be as easily understandable as possible. Dynamic Meta Modeling (DMM) aims at fulfilling these seemingly contradictory requirements by

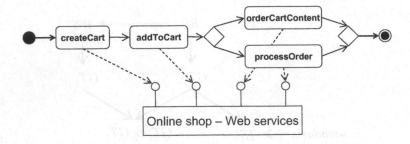

Fig. 2. Sample business process with web service binding

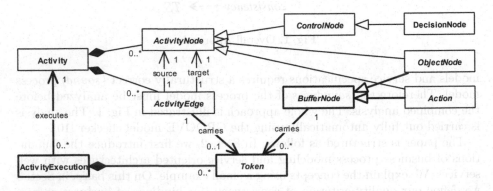

Fig. 3. Enhanced UML Activity meta model

combining two different approaches into one semantics description technique: *denotational modeling* and *operational rules*.

Before we present more details, we first introduce our running example: The upper part of Fig. 2 shows a UML Activity modeling a simple workflow in the context of an online shop. Tasks to be performed are depicted as rounded rectangles and are called **Actions** in the UML terminology. The filled circle marks the start of the workflow (**InitialNode**), and the dotted circle marks the end of the workflow (**ActivityFinalNode**).

DMM is targeted at languages having an abstract syntax which is defined by means of a *meta model* as suggested by the OMG. The static semantics of a language is then specified using *Denotational Meta Modeling*. This means that the meta model of the language is mapped to a semantic domain meta model not only describing the structural, but also the behavioral aspects of the language. That model will often be an enhanced version of the meta model of the language itself.

For example, the UML specification states that "the semantics of Activities is based on token flow". Consequently, the DMM specification for Activities has extended the Activity's meta model with elements like **Token**. Figure 3 shows an excerpt of the enhanced meta model (elements depicted in bold are enhancements to the original meta model). The token concept has been added by means of the

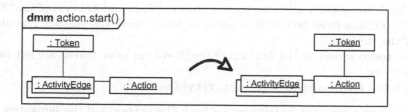

Fig. 4. DMM rule action.start()

token class, having associations to elements which are supposed to carry tokens. Instances of this meta model allow to express states of execution of the modeled Activity.

The dynamic semantics is specified by developing a set of operational rules which describe how instances of the semantic domain meta model change in time. For this, the instances are mapped to *typed graphs* [11], i.e., graphs whose nodes are typed over the enhanced meta model. The operational rules are then defined as *graph transformation rules*, working on the derived typed graphs.

A DMM rule consists of a signature, a left-hand graph, a right-hand graph, and an optional number of invocations of other DMM rules.

Figure 4 shows an example DMM rule implementing the semantics of the Action. Note that for simplicity, the presented rule does not have invocations; in fact, for this paper we have simplified the whole Activity semantics (e.g., the concept of *traverse-to-completion* [6, p. 318] is realized within our Activity semantics, but the details would be out of the scope of this paper). The rule matches if all incoming ActivityEdges of an Action carry a token. If this is the case, all these tokens are deleted, and a new token is created on the Action, corresponding to the fact that the Action is executed.

Since the typed graphs represent states of execution of the Activity, the described specification technique allows for the computation of a transition system representing the precise behavior of the investigated model. The operational rules result in transitions between these states. The resulting transition system can then be verified for certain properties, as we will see in next section.

2.2   Sound Business Processes

When investigating workflow models, one might be interested in properties indicating a certain quality of the models under consideration. Van der Aalst aimed at identifying generic properties for workflows modeled with Petri Nets. For this, he investigated typical flaws of workflows, and he claimed the absence of these flaws to be a sign for good quality [12,13]. In a nutshell, a workflow should always terminate in a well-defined way, and it should not contain any useless elements.

In [14], we have transferred the idea of soundness into the world of UML Activities, and have developed appropriate verification techniques (using the DMM semantics for Activities). A UML Activity is considered to be sound if the following conditions hold:

1. The Activity must have exactly one `InitialNode` and `ActivityFinalNode`.
2. Any `Action` must be executed under at least one of the possible executions of the Activity.
3. If a token arrives at the `ActivityFinalNode`, no more tokens are left in the Activity.
4. A token finally arrives at the `ActivityFinalNode`.

These requirements put restrictions on both the syntax and the semantics of a sound Activity: requirement 1 restricts the structure, and the other requirements restrict how the Activities must behave to be considered sound.

To illustrate the soundness property, let us investigate whether the workflow shown in Fig. 2 is sound. The structural requirement 1 is obviously fulfilled. Now, if the Activity is executed, a token is put on its `InitialNode`. We almost immediately see that this token will eventually end up at the `ActivityFinalNode`. Since the Activity does not contain any concurrency (i.e., at every point in time there is at most one token), requirement 3 is also fulfilled. Finally, since all `Actions` of the Activity sit on the way from the `InitialNode` to the `ActivityFinalNode`, they will all be executed under at least one of the possible executions of the Activity, which makes sure that requirement 2 is also fulfilled. The Activity of Fig. 2 is therefore considered to be sound.

2.3   SOA and Web Services

Having defined a formal semantics for business process models in Sect. 2.1, in this section we show how the business process can be automated using web services (see Fig. 2). In an SOA, the business functionalities are offered as web services building a service layer, which are bound to the actions in the business process. The web services provide well-defined and unambiguous interfaces for accessing the services. Thus, the business process layer does not have to know about the underlying application or technology.

The Web Service Description Language (WSDL) [15] is the widely accepted standard for specifying web service interfaces. Among others, a WSDL description contains information which operations are offered by the web service and how to bind them. However, WSDL lacks a formal description of the services behaviour which is needed for our analysis.

In previous research, we proposed to use *visual contracts* for behavioral desription of web services [16]. Visual contracts are based on the idea of Design-by-Contract [9]. In this technique the requirements and the effects of web services are specified using pre- and postconditions. Preconditions define the web service's requirements in form of a system state which needs to be present before the web service can be executed. Postconditions define the effect of the web service, again by describing the system state after the execution. The changes in the system state represent the behavioral effect of the web service. Thus visual contracts can be used as a behavioral description for web services.

Continuing our running example, the online shop offers some functionalities: a new shopping cart can be created, products can be added to the shopping cart, the order can be sent by the customer, and finally the sent order can

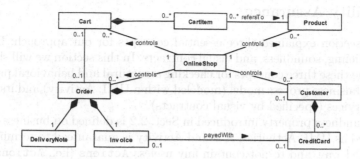

Fig. 5. Service level data model for Online Shop

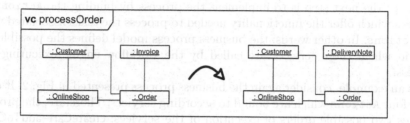

Fig. 6. Visual contract for operation *processOrder*

be processed. These functionalities are offered by the web service operations createCart, addToCart, orderCartContent, and processOrder. Note that for simplicity, the names of the operations correspond to the names of the business process Actions, but this is not a necessary requirement.

Figure 6 shows a visual contract that describes the behavior of the operation processOrder. Before invocation this operation requires that a customer registered in the online shop has given an order and the online shop generated an invoice for this order (*precondition*). After completion of processOrder the contract assures that the invoice is replaced with a deliverynote (*postcondition*). Structurally, a visual contract consists of two graphs, representing pre- and postconditions. The graphs are visualized by UML object diagrams [6]. Each of the graphs is typed over the service level data model defined as UML class diagram shown in Fig. 5. The basic intuition for reading a visual contract is that every model element only present on the right-hand side of the contract (DeliveryNote) is newly created, and every model element which is only present on the left-hand side of the contract is being deleted (Invoice). Elements that are present on both sides are unaffected by the contract. This interpretation is supported by the semantics of graph transformation systems [17].

As stated above visual contracts specify functional behavior of web services. Functional behavior is represented by state changes in object structures before and after the service invocation. For the time being visual contracts can not specify other service qualities like performance, security etc. A detailed evolution of visual contracts in a realistic case study can be found in [16].

3 Quality Assurance

The last section explained three essential concepts for our approach: Dynamic Meta Modeling, soundness, and visual contracts. In this section we will show how to combine these three concepts for checking structural and behavioral properties of both a business process model (modeled with a UML Activity) and its binding to web services (specified by visual contracts).

The soundness property introduced in Sect. 2.2 is defined on business processes modeled as UML Activities. A sound Activity is guaranteed to terminate in a well-defined way, and to not contain any useless Actions (i.e., Actions which, due to the structure of the Activity, can never be executed).

But modeling the business process is just one part of business process management: the next step is to implement the process by binding the Actions to services which offer the functionality needed to process the tasks associated with the Actions. In other words: the business process model defines the possible orders in which these services are called by the workflow engine executing the process.

As an example, consider again the business process presented in Fig. 2. It contains four Actions which are bound to according services. Therefore, the process implies two possible orders of execution of the services: createCart–addToCart–orderCartContent and createCart–addToCart–processOrder.

Now, assume that the workflow engine calls the services, one after the other and according to the underlying business process model, but reaches a point where the next service's precondition is not fulfilled. Assume additionally that the services as well as their visual contracts are "correct". It then seems that the order of the service calls is broken in some sense.

This is exactly the idea of our approach: using the visual contracts, we verify whether the services bound to the Actions can be called in the order determined by the business process model. If this is the case, we consider the process and the services to be *consistent*; otherwise, the process and/or the binding needs to be revised.

Due to the techniques introduced in Sect. 2, verifying the described property turns out to be relatively straight-forward: Since the DMM dynamic semantics as well as the visual contracts are given as graph transformation rules, it suffices to merge the rules representing the execution of an Action (which is part of the semantics specification) with the visual contract of the service the Action is bound to. The effect is that a merged rule can only match an instance graph if the preconditions of the DMM rule *and* the according visual contract are fulfilled.

Now for the details: first, we compute the merged graph transformation rules. To explain this step, we need to get a deeper understanding of our DMM semantics for UML Activities. Obviously, the rules of that specification need to be generic in the sense that one set of DMM rules suffices to describe the semantics of all possible UML Activities.

Consequently, our DMM rule set contains a rule action.start() (which we have already seen in Fig. 4); in Sect. 2.1 we have seen that the execution of this rule corresponds to the execution of a certain Action.

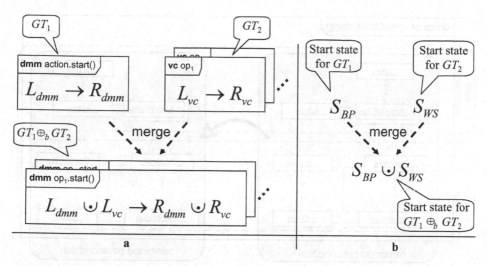

Fig. 7. a) Merging DMM rule action.start() with visual contracts. b) Merging the start states.

Since the given binding maps every Action to a service equipped with a visual contract, we now have two graph transformation rules associated with an Action: the DMM rule action.start() and the visual contract of the service the Action is bound to.

Now, to compute the combined semantics, we need to perform two steps:

1. For every Action op_n of the Activity under consideration, add a merged rule $op_n.start()$ to the DMM rule set (see Fig. 7 a): the left-hand graph of that rule is the disjoint union of the left-hand graph of rule action.start() and the left-hand graph of the visual contract describing the service the Action op_n is bound to (right-hand graph accordingly).
2. Remove the generic rule action.start() from the set of DMM rules.

The derived rules behave exactly as described above: They can only be executed if the precondition of the rule action.start() (i.e., every incoming edge has a token) *and* the precondition of the merged visual contract are fulfilled.

Technically, the merged rules work on a graph containing two subgraphs: one subgraph represents the state of execution of the Activity, and the other subgraph represents the data state for the services. The merged rules perform changes on both graphs. Note that the unchanged rules of the DMM specification only perform changes on the Activity; the data subgraph remains unchanged. Note also that the disjoint union is only possible if the UML Activity metamodel and the data model do not have any concepts in common, e.g., all classes have pairwise different names.

Let us illustrate the merging procedure with our running example: In Sect. 2.1 we have seen the DMM rule action.start() in Fig. 4, and Sect. 2.3 has introduced the visual contract of the service operation processOrder in Fig. 6. Figure 8 shows

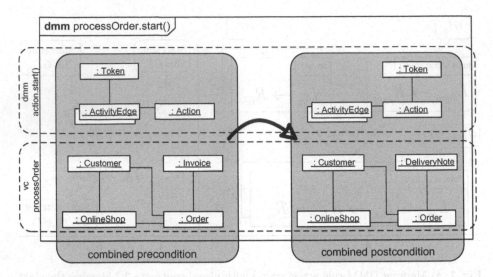

Fig. 8. Combined rule for the web service operation *processOrder*

the result of the merging: the resulting rule contains pre- and postcondition of both the DMM rule and the visual contract.

Recall that we are interested in analyzing the binding of **Actions** to service operations. For this, we need to compute the transition system representing the combined semantics. We have already described how to derive the necessary rule set (recall Fig. 7 a). It remains to show how to derive a combined state which can serve as the start state of the transition system (see Fig. 7 b).

The DMM part (GT_1) of that combined start state is simple: it is the graph S_{BP} representing the given Activity (as it would be used for computing the transition system of the Activity *without* binding). But this graph will not suffice as a start state for the combined rule set: We need to enrich it with object structures (S_{WS}) which (at least) fulfill the precondition of the first service operation to be executed.

Actually, it is more difficult than that. Assume that the first element of the given Activity is a **DecisionNode**, followed by a number of **Actions**. Which **Action** to be executed is then determined at runtime. Therefore, the start graph must be enriched with object structures fulfilling all these **Action**'s preconditions.

Additionally, it might be the case that a part of the precondition of some service operation is not created by another service operation, but needs to be part of the start state (e.g., some "global" object). In this case, even if our Activity has an **Action** to be executed first under all circumstances, it does not suffice to add the precondition of the service bound to that **Action** to the start state.

Finding smart ways of computing a precondition for the combined rule set is therefore not an easy task – in fact, this is one area of our current research (see Sect. 5). For now, it is up to the modeler to equip her business process with a global precondition; that condition is then merged with the Activity's start state giving a start state ($S_{BP} \uplus S_{WS}$) for the combined transition system.

Having said all that, it remains to precisely define our notion of a proper binding. For that, we need to know one more rule of our DMM specification: the semantics of the `ActivityFinalNode` is represented by rule activityFinalNode-.acceptToken(), which matches if the incoming edge of the node carries a token. The rule then just deletes that token.

We are now ready to precisely define consistency of a business process model and its realization. Let $\mathcal{A}$ be a sound Activity describing a business process, let A be the set of `Actions` of that Activity. Let V be the set of graph transformation rules describing the visual contracts of some service operations. Let $b : A \rightarrow V$ be the binding of `Actions` to service operations. Let R be the set of merged rules, and let s_0 be the merged start state as defined above. Let $TS = (S, R, s_0)$ be the transition system computed with that ruleset and start state. $\mathcal{A}$ is consistent with the services described in V iff the following conditions hold:

1. From every state of the transition system, a state can be reached where DMM rule activityFinalNode.acceptToken() can be executed.
2. For every state s of the transition system: if rule activityFinalNode.accept-Token() can be executed in s, then s contains exactly one token.

The rationale behind the definition is that if a token gets stuck in front of an `Action` (because the precondition of the merged service operation is not fulfilled), that token will never arrive at the `ActivityFinalNode`. This means that at least one of the requirements formulated above is not fulfilled: either no token will arrive at the `ActivityFinalNode` at all (violating condition 1), or a token will arrive at the `ActivityFinalNode`, but at that moment, the Activity contains at least one more token (the one being stuck), therefore violating condition 2. Note that since the Activity itself is sound, the token being stuck must be caused by the binding to service operations.

It is straight-forward to formulate these requirements as formulas using temporal logic (see e.g. [14] for details). A model checker can then be used to verify if the conditions hold on the generated transition system (note that the problem of state space explosion can at least partly be avoided by using *decomposition techniques*, as e.g. described in [18]). If this is not the case, the business process and/or the proposed binding needs to be revised.

Let us now discuss whether our sample business process shown in Fig. 2 is consistent with the service operations as partly presented in Fig. 6. In Sect. 2.2 we have seen that the business process model itself is sound. Due to space restrictions, we cannot provide the reader with all visual contracts involved; thus, we ask the reader for an intuitive understanding of the services' meanings by their names.

According to the business process model, a cart will be created, a product will be added to the cart, and then either the content of the cart is ordered, or the order will be processed. This intuitively does not make sense: before an order can be processed, the customer should place that order. Therefore, the business process is not consistent with the service operations its `Actions` are bound to.

Technically, the precondition of service processOrder in Fig. 6 requires that an object of type `Order` must be present (which is created by service orderCartContent).

Therefore, a token reaching the `Action` bound to that service operation will get stuck. Consequently, the model checker will report inconsistency of business process and service operations.

4 Tool Support

Implementing the consistency check as described in the last section requires a couple of tools. First, the UML Activity representing the business process model must be modeled such that the model can be processed automatically. Second, the DMM semantics specification for UML Activities needs to be created. Third, the visual contracts of the services need to be specified. Fourth, the Activity's `Actions` need to be bound to the appropriate service operations. Fifth, a tool for model checking needs to be chosen, i.e., a tool which is able to compute a transition system out of a start graph and a set of graph transformation rules, and which can perform model checking on the computed transition system. Last, the described components need to be glued together. Figure 9 shows the tool environment we use for automating the consistency check.

For the modeling of business processes (BP), we use the Java implementation of UML2 provided by the Eclipse foundation (*UML Activity Editor*) [19]. This implementation has a couple of advantages: it is very close to the original UML2 meta model, has a license which allows to use it cost-free even in commercial products, and allows to traverse models programmatically using the provided Java API.

The DMM specification as well as the visual contracts have been created with tools created by our working group (*UPB Tool Suite*) [14,20]. Based on some frameworks also provided by the Eclipse foundation (EMF, GEF, GMF), we have implemented graphical editors for both formalisms. The *Web Service Binding* tool is pretty simple: we just bind (giving the binding b, also compare with Fig. 1 and Sect. 3) `Actions` to a service operation having the `Action`'s name. We plan to use more sophisticated techniques for this in the future.

For the computation of the transition system and for model checking, we use the *GROOVE Tool Suite*. It has been developed by Arend Rensink [10] and allows for generation of transition systems as well as for the verification of properties on those transition systems. For the latter, GROOVE uses a simple but powerful concept: it allows for the verification of temporal logic formulas over the application of rules. As an example, if the formula $\mathbf{AF}$(activityfinalnode.acceptToken()) holds, we know that on All paths of the transition system under consideration, the rule activityfinalnode.acceptToken() will Finally be executed (which in our case corresponds to the requirement that a token will finally arrive at the `ActivityFinalNode`).

We have then written tools to fill the gaps of our tool chain. First, we have implemented a transformation (*DMM Mapping*) from a UML Activity (BP) into the corresponding GROOVE start graph (S_{BP}). A second tool (*Semantics Merger*) does the merging: It merges the DMM rules (GT_1) and the visual contracts (GT_2) giving the combined rule set ($GT_1 \oplus_b GT_2$). It also takes care of the merging of the start states (S_{BP} and S_{WS}) giving the combined start state ($S_{BP} \uplus S_{WS}$). While doing this, we also generate the needed temporal logic

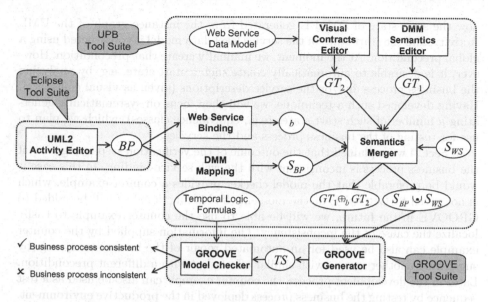

Fig. 9. Tool chain for consistency checking

formulas. Having done all this, we start the *GROOVE Generator* and, having computed the transition system (*TS*), the *GROOVE Model Checker* with the generated formulas. If the outcome of the model checker is positive, then the business process is consistent with the web service binding. Otherwise it is inconsistent. Note that GROOVE does not yet provide counter examples in case the verification of a formula fails.

5 Conclusion

Summary. Aligning business processes with IT services is one of the great challenges of nowadays IT projects. Service-oriented architectures (SOA) are often advocated as a possible solution, while concrete techniques are missing how to glue the business process layer with IT components of a service layer. Our approach addresses this problem and proposes a solution to bind a business process with web services. In particular, we offer an approach where both layers are equipped with a well-defined semantics based on graph transformations. Combining these two graph transformation systems, model checking techniques are deployed to check the consistency of the business process layer with the bound web services. The whole approach is supported by a tool chain which combines editors, transformers and in particular the model checking tool GROOVE.

Outlook. Our approach concentrates mainly on the merging of two sets of graph transformation rules and the properties to be checked on the resulting transition systems. One important prerequisite for generating the transition system is the start state of the combined graph transformation system. Section 3 explained how the start state of DMM is generated from the instance graph of the UML Activity, and the start state of the service level data model is constructed using a global precondition. At the moment, we manually create that precondition. However, it is desirable to automatically create such a start state, e.g. by analyzing the business process and/or the service descriptions (given as visual contracts). Having developed such a technique, we will then focus on systematically generating a number of such start states (e.g., equivalence classes), which we plan to use for testing of the business process and the services.

In Sect. 4 we explained that the outcome of the verification step is negative, if the business process is inconsistent with the web service binding. In this case it would be preferable that the model checker provides a counter example, which is not given by GROOVE at the moment. If this functionality will be added to GROOVE in the future, we will be able to use the counter example to easily localize the cause of the inconsistency. The information supplied by the counter example can also be used for an automated repair of the inconsistency, e.g. by suggesting another service with similar effects but with a different precondition. Later in the development process, the counter example can also be used as a test sequence by testing the business process deployed in the productive environment.

Related Work. Quality assurance for business process modeling and the application of graph transformations for this purpose have been investigated also by other researchers [21,22,23,24]. The usage of visual contracts for web service specifications has been successfully evaluated in a realistic case study with an industrial partner [16]. A continuation of this work within upcoming industrial projects of the Software Quality Lab (s-lab) at the University of Paderborn is envisaged.

References

1. Newcomer, E., Lomow, G.: Understanding SOA with Web Services. Addison-Wesley, Reading (2004)
2. van der Aalst, W., Hofstede, A.: YAWL: Yet Another Workflow Language. Technical report, Queensland University of Technology, Brisbane (2002)
3. Keller, G., Nüttgens, M., Scheer, A.W.: Semantische Prozessmodellierung auf der Grundlage Ereignisgesteuerter Prozessketten (EPK). Technical Report 1989, Institut für Wirtschaftsinformatik, Universität des Saarlandes (1992)
4. Andrews, T., et al.: Business Process Execution Language for Web Services version 1.1 (2003)
5. Dumas, M., Hofstede, A.: UML Activity Diagrams as a Workflow Specification Language. In: UML 2001: Proceedings of the 4th International Conference on The Unified Modeling Language, Modeling Languages, Concepts, and Tools, London, UK, pp. 76–90. Springer, Heidelberg (2001)
6. Object Management Group: UML Specification V2.1.1 (2007), http://www.omg.org/cgi-bin/doc?formal/07-02-05
7. Lohmann, M.: Kontraktbasierte Modellierung, Implementierung und Suche von Komponenten in serviceorientierten Architekturen. PhD thesis, University of Paderborn (2006)
8. Hausmann, J.H.: Dynamic Meta Modeling. PhD thesis, University of Paderborn (2005)

9. Meyer, B.: Applying design by contract. IEEE Computer 25(10), 40–51 (1992)
10. Rensink, A.: The GROOVE Simulator: A Tool for State Space Generation.. In: Pfaltz, J.L., Nagl, M., Böhlen, B. (eds.) AGTIVE 2003. LNCS, vol. 3062, pp. 479–485. Springer, Heidelberg (2004)
11. Corradini, A., Ehrig, H., Löwe, M., Montanari, U., Padberg, J.: The Category of Typed Graph Grammars and its Adjunctions with Categories. In: Cuny, J., Engels, G., Ehrig, H., Rozenberg, G. (eds.) Graph Grammars 1994. LNCS, vol. 1073, pp. 56–74. Springer, Heidelberg (1996)
12. van der Aalst, W., van Hee, K.: Workflow Management – Models, Methods, and Systems. MIT Press, Cambridge (2002)
13. van der Aalst, W.: Verification of Workflow Nets. In: ICATPN 1997: Proceedings of the 18th International Conference on Application and Theory of Petri Nets, London, UK, pp. 407–426. Springer, Heidelberg (1997)
14. Engels, G., Soltenborn, C., Wehrheim, H.: Analysis of UML Activities using Dynamic Meta Modeling. In: Bonsangue, M.M., Johnsen, E.B. (eds.) FMOODS 2007. LNCS, vol. 4468, pp. 76–90. Springer, Heidelberg (2007)
15. Chinnici, R., Moreau, J.J., Ryman, A., Weerawarana, S.: Web Services Description Language (WSDL) Version 2.0 Part 1: Core Language (2007), http://www.w3.org/TR/wsdl20/
16. Engels, G., Güldali, B., Lohmann, M., Juwig, O., Richter, J.P.: Industrielle Fallstudie: Einsatz visueller Kontrakte in serviceorientierten Architekturen. In: Biel, B., Book, M., Gruhn, V. (eds.) Software Engineering, GI. LNI, vol. 79, pp. 111–122 (2006)
17. Heckel, R., Ehrig, H., Wolter, U., Corradini, A.: Double-Pullback Transitions and Coalgebraic Loose Semantics for Graph Transformation Systems. APCS (Applied Categorical Structures) 9(1), 83–110 (2001)
18. Koehler, J., Gschwind, T., Küster, J., Pautasso, C., Ryndina, K., Vanhatalo, J., Völzer, H.: Combining Quality Assurance and Model Transformations in Business-Driven Development. In: Proceedings of third International Symposium AGTIVE 2007, pp. 1–16 (2007) (Selected and Invited Papers)
19. Eclipse Foundation: The Eclipse project, http://www.eclipse.org/
20. Lohmann, M., Engels, G., Sauer, S.: Model-driven Monitoring: Generating Assertions from Visual Contracts. In: 21st IEEE/ACM International Conference on Automated Software Engineering (ASE) 2006 Demonstration Session (September 2006)
21. Baresi, L., Denaro, G., Mainetti, L., Paolini, P.: Assertions to better specify the amazon bug. In: Proc. of the 14th international conference on Software engineering and knowledge engineering, SEKE 2002, pp. 585–592 (2002)
22. Baresi, L., Heckel, R., Thöne, S., Varró, D.: Modeling and validation of service-oriented architectures: application vs. style. In: Proc. of the 11th ACM SIGSOFT Symposium on Foundations of Software Engineering 2003 held jointly with 9th European Software Engineering Conference, ESEC / SIGSOFT FSE 2003, pp. 68–77 (2003)
23. Gönczy, L., Kovács, M., Varró, D.: Modeling and verification of reliable messaging by graph transformation systems. In: Proc. of the Workshop on Graph Transformation for Verification and Concurrency (ICGT 2006). Elsevier, Amsterdam (2006)
24. Koehler, J., Hauser, R., Sendall, S., Wahler, M.: Declarative techniques for model-driven business process integration. IBM Systems Journal 44(1), 47–66 (2005)

Transforming Scene Graphs Using Triple Graph Grammars – A Practice Report

Nina Aschenbrenner[1] and Leif Geiger[2]

[1] University of Kassel, Technische Informatik
[2] Software Engineering,
Department of Computer Science and Electrical Engineering,
Wilhelmshöher Allee 73,
34121 Kassel, Germany
n.aschenbrenner@inf.e-technik.uni-kassel.de, leif.geiger@uni-kassel.de
http://www.inf.e-technik.uni-kassel.de/,
http://www.se.eecs.uni-kassel.de/se/

Abstract. This paper shows the usage of Triple Graph Grammars for a project in the domain of computer graphics. This project aims to specify a conversion tool for two different computer graphic file formats: FBX and OSG. Our approach first builds a parse tree of the source file, then converts this tree into a parse tree of the target format using TGGs and then dumps the target file. Our approach relies on Java based technologies like JavaCC, the Fujaba Toolsuite and the MoTE TGG engine. The paper will show that those tools integrate very well. We will present our TGG-based approach for file conversion and demonstrate this with the FBX2OSG case study.

1 Introduction

"There exists more Triple Graph Grammar engines than case studies with TGGs." (Andy Schürr, April 2007).

The presented project is a research result of the Fachgebiet Technische Informatik at the University of Kassel. The research there focuses on virtual environments on two different platforms. On the one hand, there are ordinary desktop computers where the virtual environments should be able to be displayed, for example within e-learning applications. On the other hand, there is the so called CasCave. This is a 3-sided immersive projection environment, designed and built by the Fachgebiet Technische Informatik. To deploy virtual worlds for both systems, it is necessary to have a format that can be used in both cases. Unfortunately most computer graphics applications, which have to be used to build the scenes have no common file formats. The FBX[1] file format is commonly used to exchange scene data between different applications during the production process. But as mentioned before, sometimes there is the need to have the scene saved in another format after production. In contrast to most desktop applications the CasCave environment requires the scenes to be in OSG[2]

---

[1] FBX emerged as open file format from the older format FilmBoX.
[2] OpenSceneGraph.

A. Schürr, M. Nagl, and A. Zündorf (Eds.): AGTIVE 2007, LNCS 5088, pp. 32–43, 2008.

file format. Thus, the scene information needs to be converted from FBX to OSG for displaying them with CasCave.

For conversion of graphics scenes from one format to the other, one has to figure out how the objects and information are represented in the scene. Each format has its own way to store data like vertex information and textures, for example. Writing converters for these formats would traditionally lead to traversing the scene and adding conversion code for each visited nodes type. This does typically result in a not very modular piece of software that complicates making changes or adding new functionality. Additionally it would be nice to avoid manual coding of the whole conversion. Instead one would like to just specify the correct mapping for each format element and have the converter be generated. Thus, one would like to take advantage of model transformation techniques. Each file format using scene graphs can of course be described as a graph. So, graph transformations seems to be a "natural" way to convert scene graphs of different formats into each other. The graph transformation community offers Triple Graph Grammars to model bidirectional model mappings. With TGGs the developer just has to specify mappings for each node type in a graphical way. Thus, the conversion system is segmented to single rules, which can easily be changed. Additionally, it is easy to add new node types to this system by simply adding new rules.

2   Basics

To fully understand our application, we have to clarify some terms. First of all, we need to know what scene graphs are and what they are used for.

2.1   Scene Graphs

As scene graph we declare an object oriented data structure. This structure is often used in computer graphics to save two or three dimensional scene descriptions. The advantage of scene graphs is that the objects contained can be arranged both in logical and spatial order. There is no special way, in which scene graphs have to be implemented. Much more it is essential to take the basic ideas and create a data structure that best fits one's needs. This weak declaration leads to many different types of scene graphs within different software systems and thus to many different file formats. One example of building a scene graph and a discussion on the scene graph features can be found in [Ebe05].

Although scene graphs are graphs, many software systems use trees to represent them. There is one root node and depending on your file format one or more direct children of this root node. Normally the root node represents the scene and its children represent the objects of the scene, whereby these objects can also be constituted of one or more children. Each node has some transformation data, often represented as a transformation matrix, where translation, rotation and scale values relative to the ones in the parent node are saved. Therefore each change to the transformation values of one node affects each of its children in the same way. One can easily translate whole branches of a scene graph this way.

There is another advantage in using scene graphs which results from the hierarchical description of a scene. When rendering scenes, one can calculate the area of a scene that can be viewed by a virtual camera. Every object that is not within this area should not be rendered because this would just waste computing power. Using scene graphs one can easily exclude objects of the rendering process because when a parent node is not visible in the virtual camera all children are also not visible and you can simply exclude the whole branch without testing every child object for visibility. As you see, scene graphs built a simple and power saving data structure for scenes used in computer graphics. However, because of the loose definition of scene graphs, being a hierarchical data structure to store scenes, they may be represented in many different ways. This means that you have a dozen of different types of scene graphs in different computer graphic tools which might need to be translated into each other.

2.2   FBX

FBX is a platform independent 3D data format developed by a company called Alias. The format emerged from the need to transfer three dimensional data between different software systems and computer platforms. This transfer is widely needed within large computer game and cinematic productions. With FBX it is possible to transfer complex 3D structures like polygons, meshes or nurbs accomplished by animation data, audio- and video clips as well as cameras and lights. These extensive potentials of the FBX data format make it possible to translate whole 3D scenes across computer platforms and software systems within the production cycle. The ASCII-representation of this format allows the user to simply read and change settings within the scene file.

A FBX scene graph is a tree but a very flat one. The root node has many different children, which usually do not have many children themselves. FBX is not as much hierarchical as scene graphs normally are. Additionally information about the scene objects are spread in the whole FBX file, which means that there is not just one node being responsible for one special object. The information about an object is contained within more than one node in the tree. The nodes and information of the FBX scene graph are ordered by type not by scene object. This means, you have a separate branch containing information about animation data, for example. Besides the areas containing the specific information, you have a branch where the hierarchical information of the scene is handled and where the connections between animation, materials and geometry are stored.

2.3   OpenSceneGraph

OpenSceneGraph (OSG) [OSG07] is an OpenSource toolkit for the development of top quality graphics applications. OSG is built upon scene graphs and OpenGL (Open Graphics Library). OpenGL defines a graphics API for platform and programming language independent access of graphic card functionality. The application developer is shield from programming close to hardware. OSG itself defines a programming platform on top of OpenGL. It provides an object oriented way of graphics programming for the developer and includes scene graphs as data structure. OSG also has an ASCII-representation which can be read and changed easily. In contrast to FBX, OSG features a hierarchical scene graph structure. Every node has a transformation matrix containing object coordinates. OSG can be seen as a real tree structure, which can delve very deep down. The root node of an OSG scene graph is not the scene itself. Here you have a special root node, which forms a group containing the whole scene as children. Like FBX, OSG has many different kinds of nodes, representing the different types of scene objects and information. Every advantage listed in the scene graph section is an advantage of OSG.

3   FBX2OSG

The FBX2OSG project aims to build a conversion tool between the FBX and OSG file formats which should be bidirectional, easy to extend and to maintain. Using model-based technologies for this purpose seems to be the right decision for us. We decided to use Triple Graph Grammars because they offer bidirectional model transformations and their declarative nature makes them easy to extend.

3.1   Building the Parse Tree

Since TGG rules are specified on graphs, we needed to convert the file format to a graph representation. For both formats, there exist open APIs to access model information. But these APIs do not integrate well with existing TGG engines, are hard to extend or are even incomplete (e.g. the FBX API lacks the sound nodes). Therefore we created our own graph schema (meta model) for FBX and OSG. Our works on an enriched parse tree. Thus we first wrote a JavaCC [Ja07] grammar for both formats. In the following example, the FBX grammar is used. Of course, the same steps also need to be done for the OSG format. The following simplified rules (plus many more) are used to parse a FBX file (in EBNF):

```
FBXFile ::= ( Objects | Connections | Takes )+ <EOF>
Objects ::= "Objects:" "{" ( Model )+ "}"
Connections ::= "Connections:" "{" ( Connect )+ "}"
Takes ::= "Takes:" "{" ( Current | Take )+ "}"
Model ::= "Model:" <NAME> ( "," <NAME> )? "{" ( Type |
          Vertices | Edges | PolygonVertexIndex | Points )+ "}"
Connect ::= "Connect:" <NAME> "," <NAME> "," <NAME> (
          "," <NAME> )?
```

One FBXFile contains the components Objects, Connections and Takes and is always concluded by EOF. Within Objects there are the models our scene is built of. For this example, we suppose Model to be of such Type, that it contains the geometrical data of our scene (Vertices, Edges, PolygonVertexIndex,

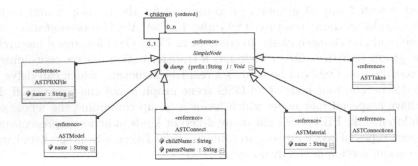

Fig. 1. Classes generated by JJTree from the JavaCC grammar shown above

Points). In more complicated FBX files, we can have models of different types, like cameras, lights etc. Within the Connections node, we have subnodes called Connect, which describe parent - child links between models in the scene. Takes nodes at last contain animation informations, they comprise of several Take nodes, which each contains several independent animation data.

From such a JavaCC grammar we use the JJTree Tool [JJT07] to generate a parser which is able to build a parse tree. The JJTree tool generates one Java class for every non-terminal in the grammar. These classes are structured as a tree using the composite pattern. Now we import these java classes with the Fujaba Tool Suite [FNT98, Fu07]. The resulting class diagram serves as an initial graph schema (cf. Figure 1).

The class SimpleNode acts as superclass for all parse tree nodes. It already implements the composite structure using the children edge. All node classes generated by JJTree start with the AST prefix. For the grammar above a class ASTFBXFile, a class ASTModel etc. is created.

To be able to really use the classes generated by JJTree with Fujaba, we had to make one little change to the SimpleNode class. We added two additional access methods for the children edge to make the code Fujaba compliant.

3.2   Enriching the Parse Tree

The parsing of a scene graph file results in a parse tree. Typically these trees represent graphs. Additional edges are modeled by references using an unique identifier of the referred node. We resolve those references and create real edges to better fit the graph paradigm of TGG rules. Therefore we use traditional graph transformations which work on the parse tree. For bidirectional mapping such transformations have to be specified for both parse trees, FBX and OSG. Figure 2 shows a transformation rule on the FBX parse tree.

As mentioned in Section 2.2, the FBX format has one container collecting all models and another one collecting the relations between those models. The node for storing the relation is of type ASTConnect and has two attributes childName and parentName storing the identifier of the referred model node. The graph transformation in the first activity

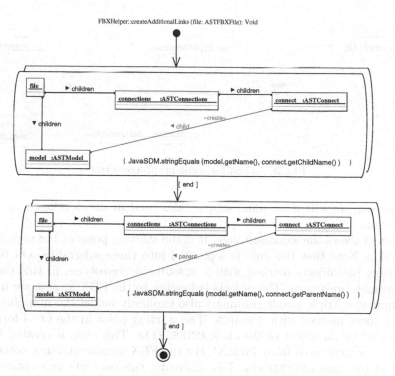

Fig. 2. Transformation rule for creating graph edges and needed objects in the parse tree

of Figure 2 now searches for all (denoted by the doubled border of the activity) pairs of nodes of type `ASTModel` and `ASTConnect` that fulfill the stated constraint. The constraint {JavaSDM.stringEquals (model.getName(), connect.getChildName())} ensures that the `name` attribute of the node `model` equals the `childName` attribute of the node `connect`. For each of those pairs a new `child` edge is created. Note, that we use Fujaba syntax here where left hand side and right hand side of a graph transformation rule are combined. The next activity does the same for the parent edge.

Note, that this step can result in new edges in the graph schema because we add edges which are not in the schema of the parse tree. The resulting "extended parse tree" is then the schema the TGG rules will depend on.

The Fujaba Tool can now generate Java code which performs this transformation on a parse tree generated by JJTree.

3.3 Triple Graph Rules

Next step is now to specify TGG rules which map the extended parse tree of the first file format onto the extended parse tree of the second one. We use the TGG Editor Fujaba plugin and the MoTE [GW06, TGG06] code generation since the generated code for the TGG rules can then directly be applied on the "extended parse tree".

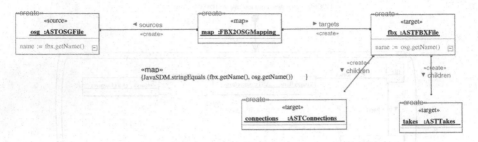

Fig. 3. Axiom for scene graph converter

Following, we will show some simple rules used in the developed converter application.

Figure 3 shows the axiomatic rule. It is the starting point of the scene graph conversion. Note that this rule is separated into three subgraphs. On the left hand side, the objects marked with a «source» stereotype, in this case the OSG format, are shown. The objects belonging to the FBX format are marked as «target». Triple graph grammars also explicitly model the mapping. This are the nodes marked with «map». The starting point in the OSG format is determined by an object of the class `ASTOSGFile`. This class is created by the OSG parser, generated from JavaCC. For the FBX format, starting point is an object of the class `ASTFBXFile`. The axiomatic rule converts an existing OSG file into an FBX file with the same name. For this purpose, the axiomatic rule defines a mapping node, which forms the mapping between the two file objects. To achieve equality of names, attribute assertions are added to each file node that assign the name of the partner file to the own name attribute.

The MoTE engine can generate three different transformations from one TGG rule. The forward rule which searches the pattern marked as source and creates the target side, the backward rule which does the same from target to source and the relational rule that searches for the source and the target pattern and just creates the mapping nodes where possible. For the last transformation

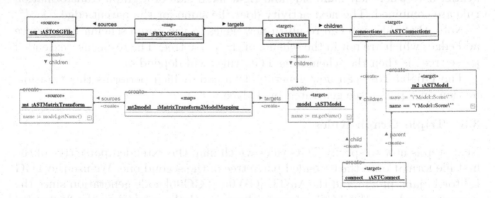

Fig. 4. Rule transforming first object within the scene graph

the mapping constraint {JavaSDM.stringEquals(fbx.getName(), osg.getName())} ensures that only files with the same name are related.

The ASTFBXFile class needs two children, which do not have a counterpart in OSG. These are Connections and Takes. Within these objects information about the scene configuration and about animation within the scene are stored. Because there are no counterparts in OSG, there is no special rule for these objects and they are created each time an ASTFBXFile is created.

Figure 4 shows the rule, which will mostly be executed after the axiomatic rule. As one can see, this rule shows not only objects displayed in green and marked with «create» stereotypes, indicating, that this object will be created. Additionally there are objects displayed in black, which indicates the precondition, that has to match before the rule will execute. The objects displayed in black exactly match the ones which where created within the axiomatic rule. Again, on the left hand side one can see the OSG classes and on the right hand side, the FBX classes are shown.

TGG rules specify parallel execution of graph grammar rules. If an ASTOSGFile is matched to an ASTFBXFile then the rule in Figure 4 can be applied. If an ASTMatrixTransform object is created, which will be connected to ASTOSGFile as child then the graph transformation for the target side has to be executed, too. On the target side, several objects within FBX have to be created. First of all, an ASTModel object is created and connected as child to the ASTFBXFile. Because in FBX every Model is connected to another model, there is one generic model called Model::Scene. This model also has to be created. These two objects are connected via one ASTConnect object, which has Model::Scene as parent and the other model as child. The ASTConnect object itself is connected to the ASTConnections object, that was created in the axiomatic rule. The model names again are transferred from one object to the other. Additionally, a mapping node is created.

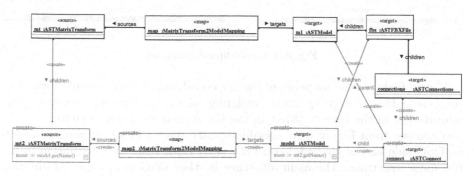

Fig. 5. Mapping ASTMatrixTransform to ASTModel

In OSG there can be more than one MatrixTransform in one scene. On the other hand, there is only one MatrixTransform acting as root object. This root object is the one created with the rule shown in Figure 4. The rule for the additional ASTMatrixTransform objects is shown in Figure 5. The rule specifies, that if a new `ASTMatrixTransform` object (`mt2`) is encountered that is assigned as child to another `ASTMatrixTransform` (`mt`), then a new `ASTModel` (`model`) has to be created in the target graph (FBX). This new model has to be connected to the corresponding parent object. This object can be found by simply searching the target, to which the `ASTMatrixTransform` parent is mapped. This `ASTModel` is exactly the one, which should be parent of our new ASTModel. As one can easily see, the rule is much the same, as the rule shown in Figure 4. But for our application, it is essential to divide this into two rules. On the one hand, we must only have one `ASTMatrixTransform` connected as child to our `ASTOSGFile`. On the other hand, we have only one `ASTModel` connected as child to our `Model::Scene` within FBX. And additionally, there has to be only one `Model::Scene` node in FBX.

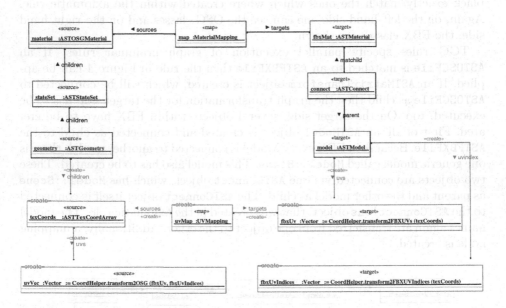

Fig. 6. UV coordinate mapping

Figure 6 shows the mapping of the uv coordinates[3] from one file format to the other. This is done by simply assigning the correct vectors containing uv information to the correct object in the file format we want to convert to. As you can see from Figure 6 uv coordinates are placed in `ASTGeometry` objects on OSG side and in `ASTModels` on FBX side. Both store uv information in list like data structures. The main difference is, that OSG stores this information

---

[3] Uv coordinates define the mapping of texture files to three-dimensional objects. This is done by "unrolling" the surface of the object. The surface is flatten this way and the two-dimensional representation can be marked with coordinates u and v for sideways and up. Every vertex contained within the three-dimensional object is connected to one uv coordinate this way. Since textures are two-dimensional too, they can easily be applied to objects this way.

as a list, where one uv coordinate is stored for each vertex of the associated geometry. FBX on the other hand saves this information divided into two lists, where the first one saves the different uv coordinates for the geometry object and the second one saves a list of indices, which associate uv coordinates with the geometry vertices. Thus, a coordinate transformation has to be done here. We do so by specifying constructor expression for the vectors uvVect, fbxUv and fbxUvIndices. This means, that if one of this objects is created the given expression is executed instead of the default object creation. We have written a helper class called CoordHelper which does all the needed coordinate transformations. Since this transformations are usually mathematical calculations they can hardly be specified using TGGs or graph transformations. Therefore we wrote those transformations by hand.

From such rules the MoTE Fujaba plugin is now able to generate Java code for the forward transformation, the backward transformation and the relational transformation. These transformations can be applied directly on the extended parse tree which results from the parsing process. MoTE includes a simple execution engine which does the rule execution at runtime (choosing the rules which might be applicable). To perform a conversion of a parse tree, we just have to include this engine, add the generated rules to it and trigger a forward or a backward transformation whether we want to convert OSG to FBX or other way round.

3.4   Dumping the Result Graph

At this point we are able to parse the source file format and map the resulting parse tree to a parse tree of the target format. Last thing to do is to dump the target parse tree to a file. Therefor we use a visitor which traverses the tree top down and prints the textual representation for every node. This visitor has to be implemented by hand. Since we support bidirectional transformation in our converter application, one visitor for each of the two formats has to be implemented.

4   Lessons Learned

We think that using TGGs for the OSG2FBX project was the right solution. Most of the rules were specified by the first author who had little experience with TGGs and graph transformation before. But after a short introduction adding new TGG rules was quite easy. Also, we found that it was quite easy for us explaining the triple rules to colleagues at the computer graphics department who did not have any background in graph transformations.

Choosing Fujaba and the MoTE TGG engine seems to be the right decision since the generated code could be easily used with the one generated by the JavaCC tool. Also, using Fujaba we were able to do the transformations for enriching the parse tree as described in Section 3.2 using graph transformations as well.

Fig. 7. The virtual factory used to test the converter

One thing we found that was needed for our approach and is usually not part of current TGG engines is the possibility to call external procedures. We need that to preform complex mathematical calculations like coordinate transformations as described in Section 3.3. The solution we came up with is to use constructor expressions as shown in Figure 6. This way the coordinate transformations can be done when constructing the corresponding node.

5   Conclusions

We have shown an approach how file format conversion can be done using triple graph grammars. We use a JavaCC grammar to build a parse tree, perform graph transformations with Fujaba on that tree to get a graph and use the MoTE TGG engine to do the mapping between the source graph and the target graph. Since the used tools all generate compatible Java code, they can be easily integrated. The only needed hand-written code are the visitors that dump the parse trees to a file and maybe complex calculations that can hardly be specified with TGGs have to be coded by hand. In our case study this complex calculations were the coordinate transformations mentioned above. These depend on mathematical algorithms can hardly be specified using graph transformations and therefore handled in helper classes. We have tested this approach in the OSG2FBX project where a converter between two scene graph file formats was developed. This converter has about 480 JavaCC rules and 15 TGG rules. It was tested with a FBX file of a virtual factory which has about 650 nodes. The conversion of this file takes a few seconds and the result can then be displayed using a standard OSG viewer, cf. Figure 7.

When thinking about text to text transformations, Pratt's pair grammars [Pra71] may be the first transformation technique that comes to mind. As mentioned above, the information stored in one node in OSG is spread over several nodes in FBX. Because of these different structures of the two formats, we think it would be very hard to model simultaneous text grammar rules like Pratt suggests. Using TGGs searching through graphs is very easy and thus the different structures are no problem. Another approach might be to write a visitor on the parse tree that does the transformation. But to get a bidirectional mapping one has to write two visitors, one for the forward direction and one for the reverse direction. That causes maintenance problems because when changing one visitor, one has to change the other correspondingly. We also think that our TGG approach is better to extend because of its declarative nature. When a new element has to be converted one can simply add a new rule. We also found that the TGG rules are relatively easy to understand and to specify even for novices. Thus, we think that TGGs were an excellent choice for our purpose and we would use them again for similar projects.

References

[Ebe05]   Eberly, D.H.: 3D Game Engine Architecture, Kapitel 3. Morgan Kaufmann, San Francisco (2005)

[FBX07]   FBX Whitepaper (2007), http://images.autodesk.com/emea_dach_main_germany/files/fbx_whitepaper.pdf

[FNT98]   Fischer, T., Niere, J., Torunski, L.: Konzeption und Realisierung einer integrierten Entwicklungsumgebung für UML, Java und Stroy-Driven-Modeling (german), Diploma thesis, Universität-Gesamthochschule Paderborn (1998)

[Fu07]   Fujaba Homepage, Universität Paderborn (2007), http://www.fujaba.de/

[GW06]   Giese, H., Wagner, R.: Incremental Model Synchronization with Triple Graph Grammars. In: Proc. of the 9th International Conference on Model Driven Engineering Languages and Systems (MoDELS), Genova, Italy (October 2006)

[Ja07]   Homepage of JavaCC (2007), https://javacc.dev.java.net/

[JJT07]   JJTree Reference Documentation (2007), https://javacc.dev.java.net/doc/JJTree.html

[Mer06]   Merz, A.: JavaCC, JJTree und das Visitor-Pattern (2006), http://www.alexander-merz.com/print_38.html

[OSG07]   OSG Homepage (2007), http://www.openscenegraph.com/

[Pra71]   Pratt, T.W.: Pair grammars, graph languages and string-to-graph translations. Journal of Computer and System Sciences 5, 560–595 (1971)

[Sch94]   Schürr, A.: Specification of graph translators with triple graph grammars. In: Mayr, E.W., Schmidt, G., Tinhofer, G. (eds.) WG 1994. LNCS, vol. 903, pp. 151–163. Springer, Heidelberg (1995)

[SQ07]   Scenegraphs: Past, Present and Future (2007), http://www.realityprime.com/articles/scenegraphs-past-present-and-future

[TGG06]   Incremental Model Transformation and Synchronization with Triple Graph Grammars (2006), http://wwwcs.uni-paderborn.de/cs/ag-schaefer/Lehre/PG/Fujaba/projects/tgg/index.html

Using Graph Transformation to Support Collaborative Ontology Evolution[*]

Pieter De Leenheer[1] and Tom Mens[2]

[1] Vrije Universiteit Brussel, STARLab, Belgium
pieter.de.leenheer@vub.ac.be
[2] University of Mons-Hainaut, Belgium
tom.mens@umh.ac.be

Abstract. In collaborative ontology engineering, contexts are key to manage the complexity of different dependency types between ontological artefacts. Instead of being frustrated by out-of-control evolution processes, proper context dependency management will allow human experts to focus on the meaning interpretation and negotiation processes. This requires support for the detection and resolution of meaning ambiguities and conflicts. In this article, we explore to which extent the theory of graph transformation can be used to support this activity. More specifically, we propose the use of critical pair analysis as a formal means to analyse conflicts between ontologies that are evolving in parallel. We illustrate this with an example from a realistic case study.

1 Introduction

The World Wide Web caused a shift in the way people collaborate and integrate within and between communities. A community constitutes a social system, where action and discourse is performed within more or less well-established goals, norms, and behaviour [6]. *Communication* is the primary basis for co-ordinated action, hence in order to collaborate and integrate between different and diverse communities, it is important to capture and agree on the semantics of the *concepts* being communicated, and reify them in so-called *ontologies*. Tools and methods for ontology engineering (e.g., [7,8,17]), are rapidly becoming a high priority for many organisations. Particularly, in a collaborative setting, mechanisms that support the detection and resolution of meaning ambiguities and conflicts are urgently needed [3].

In this article we explore to which extent the theory of *graph transformation* can be used to support this activity. More specifically, we propose the use of *critical pair analysis* [10] as a formal means to analyse conflicts between ontologies that are evolving in parallel. We will illustrate this by providing a proof-of-concept through a running example, the ideas of which are based on a realistic

---

[*] The research described in this paper was partially sponsored by the EU Leonardo da Vinci CODRIVE project (B/04/B/F/PP-144.339) and the EU FP6 IST PROLIX project.

A. Schürr, M. Nagl, and A. Zündorf (Eds.): AGTIVE 2007, LNCS 5088, pp. 44–58, 2008.

case study on competency-driven vocational education that forms part of the European CoDrive project[1].

2   Context Dependency Management

Contexts are key to explicate the relevant commonalities and differences during real-world, gradual ontology elicitation and application efforts. *Context dependencies* [15] are constructs that constrain the possible relations between the entity and its context. Many different types of context dependencies exist, within and between knowledge artefacts of various levels of granularity, ranging from individual concept definitions to full ontologies. These dependencies can be used to drive ontology engineering processes tailored to the specific requirements of collaborative communities.

Figure 1 shows an instance of a context dependency type: the interpretation of the terms that are *applied* in the template context (on the right-hand side) is dependent on their articulation (concept definition) and categorisation in the taxonomy on the left-hand side. Hence, this context dependency type is called an *application* (APP) context dependency.

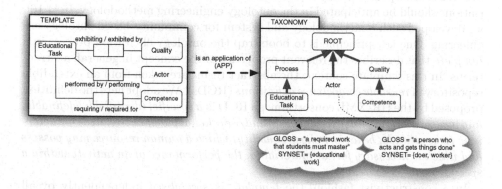

Fig. 1. An instance of an application context dependency

In [15], we showed that, when managed consistently and effectively, tracing context dependencies provides a better understanding of the whereabouts of ontological artefacts and their inter-dependencies, and consequently makes negotiation and application less vulnerable to ambiguity, hence more useful in practice. Instead of being frustrated by out-of-control change processes, proper context dependency management support will allow human experts to focus on the much more interesting meaning interpretation and negotiation processes. Automated support for detecting and resolving meaning ambiguities and conflicts within and between contexts plays a crucial role here.

---

[1] An EU Leonardo da Vinci Project: http://www.codrive.org

3   Running Example: Vocational Competency Ontology

Our running example is based on a realistic case study on *competency-driven vocational education* of the European CoDrive project. *Competencies* describe the skills and knowledge individuals should have in order to be fit for particular jobs. In the domain of vocational education, having a central shared and commonly used competency model is becoming crucial in order to achieve the necessary level of interoperability and exchange of information, and in order to integrate and align the existing information systems of competency stakeholders like schools, job providers, or public employment agencies. The CoDrive project contributes to this goal by using an ontology methodology and infrastructure in order to develop a conceptual, shared and formal knowledge representation of competence domains. Stakeholders include educational institutes and public employment organisations from various European countries. The resulting shared "Vocational Competency Ontology" (VCO) will be used by all partners to build interoperable competency models.

Constructing the VCO is not a sinecure: first, one has to determine what competency concepts are relevant for the VCO; and second, different stakeholders usually have overlapping or even contradicting opinions about the intended meaning and use (read: conceptualisation) of particular concepts. Hence, diverging conceptualisations should be anticipated in the ontology engineering methodology. In [4,16], we developed such a methodology and system for community-based ontology engineering. One key principle is to bootstrap the ontology elicitation process in a *template* that describes the relevant properties of the concept in general, abstract terms. In this template context, the abstract terms are taken from an extendible repository of *reusable competence definitions* (RCDs). We adopt here the definition proposed by the HR-XML consortium: an RCD is *a specific, identifiable, definable, and measurable knowledge, skill, ability and/or other deployment-related characteristic (e.g. attitude, behavior, physical ability) which a human resource may possess and which is necessary for, or material to, the performance of an activity within a specific business context*[2].

In a constructivist fashion, the *template* is *specialised* independently by all participating stakeholders, by replacing the general terms, by one or more concrete terms. Conflicts can easily arise when the template starts to evolve in a way that is incompatible with at least one of the specialisations.

Let us illustrate these ideas by means of an example fragment of the VCO. Fig. 2 shows an excerpt from the RCD taxonomy. It shows, among others, that *Deliver* is some kind of *Educational Task*, and that *Skill* is some kind of *Competence* which, in its turn, is considered to be some kind of *Quality*.

Figure 3 illustrates the process of using template contexts that can be specialised according to the needs of different stakeholders (only one such specialisation is shown, from an educational institute). The template explains how to define an *Educational Task*, the specialisation refines this to the subtask *Deliver*. The relations between terms in the template and the specialisation are

---

[2] See http://ns.hr-xml.org/2_5/HR-XML-2_5/CPO/Competencies.html

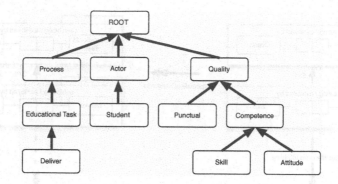

Fig. 2. Taxonomy of reusable competence definitions (RCD)

denoted by a *specialisation* (SPE) context dependency in Fig. 3. These context dependencies constrain the use of concepts, and definition of relations between concepts. In particular, *SPE*-dependencies are allowed only between terms that are in the correct (transitive) taxonomical relationship according to Fig. 2.

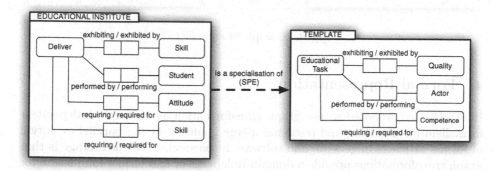

Fig. 3. Example of an ontology, constrained by the RCD taxonomy in Fig. 2. There is a specialisation context dependency between the template context and the educational institute context.

Now consider the scenario, depicted in Fig. 4, where two parallel evolutions occur between the template and (one of) its specialisation(s). Along the horizontal direction, the knowledge engineer administering the templates decides to specialise a relationship (differentia) in the template. This boils down to replacing *Quality* with one of its subconcepts *Competence* (according to the taxonomy of Fig. 2). In the vertical direction, the domain expert who created the specialisation decides to revise it: the task *Deliver* is no longer exhibiting a *Skill*, but rather another subtype of *Quality*, namely *Punctual*. These two parallel evolutions result in a conflict when trying to combine them: as depicted on the bottom-right of Fig. 4, *Punctual* is not a subtype of *Competence* (as is required by the *SPE*-dependency). In the next section, we argue how graph transformation theory can be used to detect and analyse such conflicts.

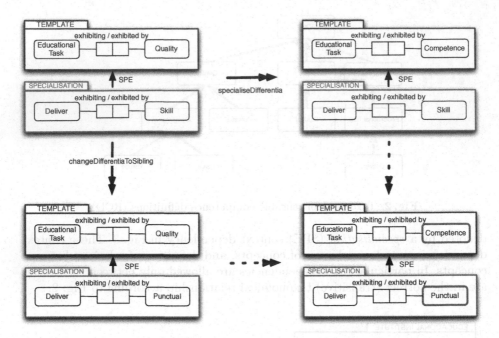

Fig. 4. Example of a conflict

4   Formal Representation

In [18,19], we proposed to use graph transformation as a domain-independent formalism for detecting and resolving merge conflicts during parallel evolution of formal artefacts in general, and software in particular. The advantage is that graph transformations provide a domain-independent and formal foundation for both *descriptive* and *operational* aspects. The formalism allows to describe a possibly infinite collection of graphs in a finite way: by stating a set of initial graphs and a set of graph transformation rules. Through repeated application of these rules, starting from one of the initial graphs, new graphs can be generated.

In this article, we apply this idea to the evolution of collaborative ontologies. Formalising ontology transformations in this way has several advantages: (i) the ontology engineer does not need to specify this sequence of rules explicitly: he only needs to specify what the new ontology should look like; (ii) we can rely on the concrete graphical syntax to which the users are accustomed to; (iii) we can provide a precise and unambiguous definition of complex context dependency operators; and (iv) we can formally analyse and reason about meaning conflicts between multiple parallel contextualisations of the same original ontology.

The main goal of this article is to explore points (iii) and (iv) above, the remaining claims will be explored in future work. For our experiments, we have used version 1.6.2 of *AGG*, a general-purpose graph transformation tool [27,28].

4.1 Representing Ontologies

The metamodel that we use for representing ontologies has been formalised by relying on the notion of a *type graph* [1]. It is given in Fig. 5. The ontologies themselves are then specified as *attributed graphs* that conform to this type graph. An example of such a graph is given in Fig. 7. It provides the abstract syntax representation of the ontology that we visualised in Fig. 3. The taxonomy of Fig. 2 is also formally represented as a graph, depicted in Fig. 6.

One can see that this abstract graph representation looks considerably more complex than the concrete syntax. In particular, we observe the use of *lexons*, an essential notion that is introduced in the *DOGMA* methodology and framework for ontology engineering [15]. Lexons are collected in a *lexon base*, a reusable pool of possible vocabularies. A lexon is a 5-tuple declaring *either* (in some *context C*):

1. a taxonomical relationship (*genus*), for example
   ⟨*C, punctual, is a, subsumes, quality*⟩
2. a non-taxonomical relationship (*differentia*), for example
   ⟨*C, educational task, exhibiting, exhibited by, quality*⟩

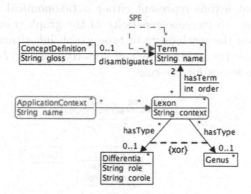

Fig. 5. Type graph representing the metamodel for ontologies

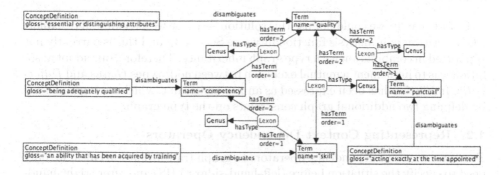

Fig. 6. Graph representing part of the taxonomy of Fig. 2

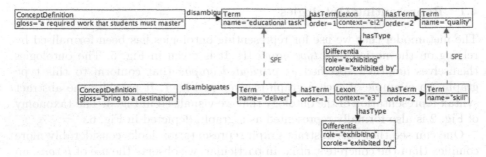

Fig. 7. Graph representing part of the ontology used as our running example

When trying to formalise this definition of lexon in AGG, we were confronted with several design choices. Rather than defining a lexon (5-tuple) as a node with 5 outgoing edges, we decided to use three edges only: two *hasTerm*-edges point to the *Term*s involved in the lexon, and a *hasType*-edge points to a node collecting the other relevant information (type of relationship, role, and co-role). To achieve this, we needed to introduce a node type *Genus* and *Differentia* in order to express the fact that lexons represent either a taxonomical relationship or a non-taxonomical one. To increase genericity of the graph transformation rules, we wanted to rely on the mechanism of type graph inheritance. As illustrated in Fig. 8, one can use the generic abstract supertype *LexonType* if the type of relationship is not relevant for the rule.

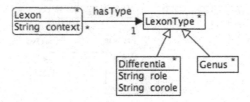

Fig. 8. Part of the type graph showing the use of inheritance for expressing the type of a lexon

Unfortunately, we could not use this solution, because we also wanted to exploit AGG's critical pair analysis functionality (see Sect. 4.3), and this is currently not supported in combination with type graph inheritance. Therefore, our adopted solution was to implement a mutual exclusion between node types *Genus* and *Differentia*. In Fig. 5 it has been expressed as an `xor` constraint, which we implemented by defining two additional graph constraints on the type graph.

4.2   Representing Context Dependency Operators

To express context dependency operators as graph transformation rules, we only need to specify the situation before (left-hand-side or LHS) and after (right-hand-side or RHS) applying the rule. Because AGG supports *conditional* graph transformation, we may additionally specify positive application conditions (PAC), or negative application conditions (NAC) [9]. A PAC indicates the obligatory *presence* of a given graph structure (i.e., a certain combination of nodes and edges) in order for the rule to be applicable. Similarly, a NAC indicates the required *absence* of a graph structure.

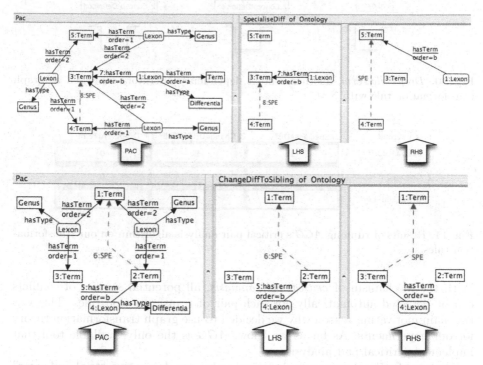

Fig. 9. Two context dependency operators for evolving ontologies, expressed as graph transformation rules with positive application condition (PAC)

Figure 9 provides the formal definition of the two operators used in our running example of Sec. 3. Both graph transformation rules, *specialiseDiff* and *changeDiffToSibling* have been expressed by using a PAC, because this avoids redundancy between the LHS and RHS, hence making the rules more readable and less complex. We also specified a third operator *dropChildTerm* (not mentioned in the running example) that can be used to remove terms that are not related to any other term in the taxonomy. This operator, shown in Fig. 10, requires the use of a NAC.

4.3 Detecting Conflicts

As explained in Sect. 3, in the context of collaborative ontology engineering we are confronted with a situation where a given ontology template is specialised and used by many different organisations. Both the template and the specialisations can evolve in parallel, which gives rise to many sources of meaning conflicts.

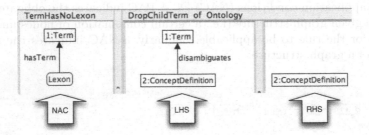

Fig. 10. *DropChildTerm*, another context dependency operator, expressed as graph transformation rule with NAC

first \ second	1: SpecialiseDiff	2: ChangeDiffToSibling	3: DropChildTerm
1: SpecialiseDiff	1	1	0
2: ChangeDiffToSibling	1	1	0
3: DropChildTerm	1	1	1

Fig. 11. Results of running *AGG*'s critical pair analysis algorithm on our transformation rules

With the mechanism of *critical pair analysis*, all potential sources of conflicts can be detected automatically, for each pair of transformation rules. This was the main motivating reason why we decided to use graph transformation theory for our experiments. As far as we know, *AGG* is the only available tool that implements critical pair analysis.

The use of critical pair analysis proved to be a real iterative "trial and error" process. The first time we ran the critical pair analysis algorithm on our transformation rules, we were confronted with severe performance problems. After a couple of hours the algorithm stopped with a sudden out of memory error. As a first improvement, we computed "essential" critical pairs only, an experimental feature of *AGG*. This allowed us to obtain some first results, but the computation still took a very long time, and there was a too large number of detected critical pairs, making the manual interpretation of the results nearly impossible. Therefore, as a second improvement we simplified the underlying graph representation, by replacing all lexons representing a genus (taxonomical relationship) by a directed *genus*-edge from the source term to the target term. This simplified the graph and the graph transformation rules considerably, since for each occurrence we replaced 2 nodes (Lexon and Genus) and 3 edges (all outgoing edges from Lexon) by a single *genus*-edge. We also avoided the use of PACs in our new version of the transformation rules, since they had a small negative impact on the computation time of critical pairs[3]. The number of detected critical pairs was now reduced to a manageable number, but manual analysis

---

[3] Note that all of these optimisations can be done in an automated way.

of the results still reveiled many unnecessary duplicates. Therefore, as another improvement, we added some additional graph constraints to express the absence of cyclic structures in the *genus* or *SPE* edges. This, finally, led us to the results summarised in Fig. 11. For every pair of transformation rules that was compared, at most one critical situation was reported, and all such critical pairs corresponded to what we intuitively expected.

As a first example, consider the critical pair between *ChangeDiffToSibling* (first rule) and *SpecialiseDiff* (second rule). The critical pair reported between both rules is displayed in Fig. 12[4]. The figure shows a *delete-use-conflict* for the *SPE*-edge with number 7. It arises because both graph transformations modify this *SPE*-edge in incompatible ways. *ChangeDiffToSibling* redirects its source edge, while *SpecialiseDiff* redirects its target edge. This potential conflict corresponds exactly to the conflict that we encountered in our running example. Indeed, if we ask AGG to check for actual conflicts in the host graph, it will report a match that corresponds to the situation of Fig. 4.

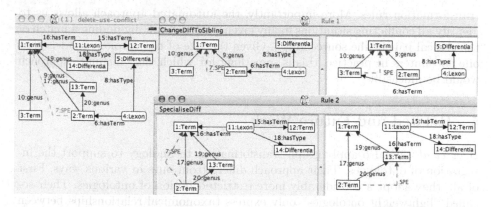

Fig. 12. Conflict between the rule *ChangeDiffToSibling* (first rule) and *SpecialiseDiff*. The critical situation is displayed on the left, and the green *SPE*-edge (number 7) indicates the source of the problem.

A second, and different, example of a critical pair occurs between rules *DropChildTerm* (first rule) and *SpecialiseDiff* (second rule). It is displayed in Fig. 13. This time, there is a *delete-use-conflict* for the *Term*-edge with number 1. It arises because *DropTerm* attempts to remove a *Term*-node, whereas *SpecialiseDiff* requires the presence of this node for its proper functioning. Although not explained in Sect. 3, it is another typical example of a conflicting situation that can arise when modifying a template ontology and one of its specialisations in parallel.

For our current "proof-of-concept" experiment, one could argue that the use of critical pair analysis is overkill since one could identify all potential conflict situations by hand. While this may be true, the point is that the automated analysis allows us to start using the approach on a much more elaborate set of

---

[4] Observe the use of *genus*-edges that significantly simplifies the representation of the graphs and graph transformations.

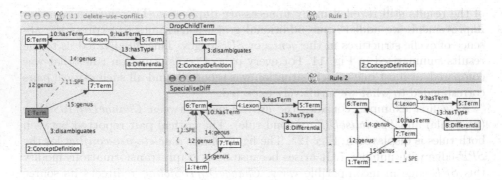

Fig. 13. Conflict between the rule *DropChildTerm* (first rule) and *SpecialiseDiff*. The critical situation is displayed on the left, and the green *Term*-node (number 1) indicates the source of the problem.

transformation rules. More importantly, the automated approach allows us to identify all conflicting situations in any given source graph, by finding a match of the critical pair in the source graph. Given the size of the ontology models that one encounters in practice, this is something for which the "manual" approach would be unfeasible.

5   Related and Future Work

Heer *et al.* [11] also apply graph transformation technology to support the integration of ontologies. Their approach differs from ours in various ways. First of all, they adopt a considerably more restricted notion of ontologies. Their so-called "lightweight ontologies" only express taxonomical relationships between concept labels, while ours can handle any other type of relationship[5]. Another, and more important, difference is that their approach seems to hard-code the conflicts that can arise during the ontology merging approach, whereas we rely on the generic technique of critical pair analysis. This makes our approach more generic and more tool-independent.

Another example of the use of graph transformation that can be reused for ontology engineering is [14], where graph transformation is applied for conducting quality assurance in business-driven development. For a comprehensive survey on ontology evolution state of the art and future directions, we refer to [3].

In [18,19], we claimed that graph transformation theory could be used as a domain-independent formalism for detecting and resolving merge conflicts during parallel evolution of formal artefacts. These claims seem to correct, since we have already been able to apply the ideas of critical pair analysis in various domains. In [21] we applied it to software refactoring, in [23] we applied it to

---

[5] In this article, we only showed the non-taxonomical relationship *differentia*, but our approach can be extended in a straightforward way to other types of relationships as well.

UML models, and in this article we applied it to ontologies. In [23,22] we even used the mechanism to detect *sequential dependencies* between transformations, and to provide semi-automated support for conflict resolution. The same results can also be achieved in the domain of ontology engineering. This is a topic of future work.

In order to make the proposed approach acceptable to our user community, we need to offer support using the representation that the users are familiar with. This means that our tools need to make use of the concrete syntax instead of an abstract graph-based syntax. More in particular, we want to be able to detect, report and manage conflicts using the concrete syntax of ontologies. We will work on this aspect in the future. It is worthwhile to note that a lot of progress in this direction has been made by the graph transformation community. Indeed, many different researchers have proposed solutions for trying to combine the virtues of a concrete domain-specific graphical syntax with the underlying mechanism of graph transformation. Examples of this are Tiger [29], DiaGen [25], DiaMeta [24], and ATOM^3 [2].

The second requirement to make the theory acceptable to our user community is by integrating it in a seamless manner into the ontology engineering tools that they are currently using. In particular, we envisage integration of the graph transformation approach into the DOGMA tool [4]. A natural way to achieve such integration is by relying on a common underlying development platform. Given that DOGMA is implemented as an Eclipse plug-in, Eclipse seems to be the platform of choice. Also for AGG, the graph transformation tool that we have used for our experiments, various Eclipse plug-ins exist. ROOTS [13] is an Eclipse plug-in that replaced the default GUI of AGG by an Eclipse-based one. The Tiger EMF transformation project [5] is another Eclipse plug-in for AGG that allows to generate domain-specific visual editors. By combining all of these plug-ins, we aim to develop a domain-specific tool whose underlying foundation of graph transformation is transparent to the user.

Our running example, although using only a few simple context dependency operators, already demonstrates the usefulness of graph rewriting for context dependency management emerging in a typical case of collaborative ontology engineering. When introducing additional context dependency operators and types, complexity only grows. Furthermore, we did not consider all primitive constructs of an ontology. For example, axioms constraining the possible use of concepts and relationships makes context dependency management even more difficult.

Finally, we also plan to consider other relevant applications of graph transformation. For example, in [22], we did a formal and static analysis of mutual exclusion relationships and causal dependencies between different alternative resolutions for model inconsistencies that can be expressed in a graph-based way. Currently, we are adopting these results for the DOGMA meta schema in particular. Doing so, this analysis can be exploited to further improve the conflict resolution process, e.g., by detecting possible cycles in the resolution process, by proposing a preferred order in which to apply certain resolution rules, and so on.

6 Conclusion

One of the goals of our work was to bring the research communities of software evolution [20] and ontology engineering [12] closer together. It turns out that both research domains can benefit from the same underlying foundation, in casu graph transformation theory. Graph transformation rules can be used to formally represent the evolution operators, and critical pair analysis can be used to automate the detection of merge conflicts between these operators.

In this article, we relied on graph transformation theory for supporting context dependency evolution processes, based on the DOGMA framework and methodology for scalable ontology engineering. Key notions are a set of transformation rules expressing context dependency operators, that can be combined to manage complex context dependencies like *SPE*-dependencies, which in turn can be used in context-driven ontology engineering processes tailored to the specific requirements of collaborative communities.

The detection of conflicts during ontology evolution was supported by the technique of critical pair analysis. A proof-of-concept experiment of this technique has been carried out with AGG, based on a running example of collaborative ontologies for vocational education taken from a European project. While the results are encouraging, further work is needed to integrate the approach in contemporary ontology engineering tools (such as DOGMA Studio WorkBench [26]), and to extend the idea to provide formally founded automated support for conflict resolution as well. We also need to validate the scalability of our approach on full-fledged industrial case studies.

References

1. Corradini, A., Montanari, U., Rossi, F.: Graph processes. Fundamenta Informaticae 26(3–4), 241–265 (1996)
2. de Lara, J., Vangheluwe, H.: ATOM³: A tool for multi-formalism and meta-modelling. In: Kutsche, R.-D., Weber, H. (eds.) FASE 2002. LNCS, vol. 2306, pp. 174–188. Springer, Heidelberg (2002)
3. De Leenheer, P., Mens, T.: Ontology Evolution: State of the Art and Future Directions. In: Ontology Management for the Semantic Web, Semantic Web Services, and Business Applications. Springer, Heidelberg (2008)
4. de Moor, A., De Leenheer, P., Meersman, R.: DOGMA-MESS: A meaning evolution support system for interorganizational ontology engineering. In: Schärfe, H., Hitzler, P., Øhrstrøm, P. (eds.) ICCS 2006. LNCS (LNAI), vol. 4068, pp. 189–203. Springer, Heidelberg (2006)
5. Ermel, C., Ehrig, K., Taentzer, G., Weiss, E.: Object-oriented and rule-based design of visual languages using tiger. In: Proc. workshop on Graph-Based Tools (GraBaTs). Electronic Communications of the EASST, vol. 1 (2006)
6. Falkenberg, E.D.: Frisco: A framework of information system concepts. Technical report, IFIP WG 8.1 Task Group (1998)
7. Gruber, T.: Cyc: a translation approach to portable ontologies. Knowledge Acquisition 5(2), 199–220 (1993)

8. Guarino, N.: Formal ontology and information systems. In: Proc. of FOIS 1998, pp. 3–15. IOS Press, Amsterdam (1998)
9. Heckel, R.: Algebraic graph transformations with application conditions. Master's thesis, Technische Universität Berlin (1995)
10. Heckel, R., Küster, J.M., Taentzer, G.: Confluence of typed attributed graph transformation systems. In: Corradini, A., Ehrig, H., Kreowski, H.-J., Rozenberg, G. (eds.) ICGT 2002. LNCS, vol. 2505, pp. 161–176. Springer, Heidelberg (2002)
11. Heer, T., Retkowitz, D., Kraft, B.: Algorithm and tool for ontology integration based on graph rewriting. In: Proc. Applications of Graph Transformations with Industrial Relevance (AGTIVE), Wilhelmshöhe, Kassel, Germany, pp. 484–490 (2007)
12. Hepp, M., De Leenheer, P., de Moor, A., Sure, Y. (eds.): Ontology Management for the Semantic Web, Semantic Web Services, and Business Applications. Springer, Heidelberg (2008)
13. Jurack, S., Taentzer, G.: ROOTS: An Eclipse plug-in for graph transformation systems based on AGG. In: Proc. Applications of Graph Transformations with Industrial Relevance (AGTIVE), pp. 491–496 (2007)
14. Koehler, J., Gschwind, T., Küster, J.: Combining quality assurance and model transformations in business-driven development. In: Proc.of Agtive 2007. Springer, Heidelberg (2007)
15. De Leenheer, P., de Moor, A., Meersman, R.: Context dependency management in ontology engineering: a formal approach. LNCS Journal on Data Semantics 8, 26–56 (2007)
16. De Leenheer, P., Meersman, R.: Towards community-based evolution of knowledge-intensive systems. In: Proc.of ODBASE 2007. Springer, Heidelberg (2007)
17. Meersman, R.: The use of lexicons and other computer-linguistic tools in semantics, design and cooperation of database systems. In: Proc.of CODAS 1999, pp. 1–14. Springer, Heidelberg (1999)
18. Mens, T.: A Formal Foundation for Object-Oriented Software Evolution. PhD thesis, Department of Computer Science, Vrije Universiteit Brussel, Belgium (September 1999)
19. Mens, T.: Conditional graph rewriting as a domain-independent formalism for software evolution. In: Münch, M., Nagl, M. (eds.) AGTIVE 1999. LNCS, vol. 1779, pp. 127–143. Springer, Heidelberg (2000)
20. Mens, T., Demeyer, S. (eds.): Software Evolution. Springer, Heidelberg (2008)
21. Mens, T., Taentzer, G., Runge, O.: Analyzing refactoring dependencies using graph transformation. Software and Systems Modeling (2007)
22. Mens, T., Van Der Straeten, R.: Incremental resolution of model inconsistencies. In: Fiadeiro, J.L., Schobbens, P.-Y. (eds.) WADT 2006. LNCS, vol. 4409, pp. 111–127. Springer, Heidelberg (2007)
23. Mens, T., Van Der Straeten, R., D'Hondt, M.: Detecting and resolving model inconsistencies using transformation dependency analysis. In: Nierstrasz, O., Whittle, J., Harel, D., Reggio, G. (eds.) MoDELS 2006. LNCS, vol. 4199, pp. 200–214. Springer, Heidelberg (2006)
24. Minas, M.: Generating meta-model-based freehand editors. In: Proc. Int'l Workshop Graph-Based Tools (GraBaTs), Natal, Brazil. Electronic Communications of the EASST (September 2006)
25. Minas, M., Viehstaedt, G.: DiaGen: A generator for diagram editors providing direct manipulation and execution of diagrams. In: Proc. IEEE Symp. Visual Languages, pp. 203–210 (1995)

26. Vrije Universiteit Brussel STAR.Lab. DOGMA Studio WorkBench (2007),
    http://www.starlab.vub.ac.be/website/dogmastudio
27. Taentzer, G.: AGG: A graph transformation environment for modeling and valida-
    tion of software. In: Pfaltz, J.L., Nagl, M., Böhlen, B. (eds.) AGTIVE 2003. LNCS,
    vol. 3062, pp. 446–453. Springer, Heidelberg (2004)
28. Taentzer, G.: AGG (November 2007), http://tfs.cs.tu-berlin.de/agg
29. Taentzer, G., Schmutzler, R., Ermel, C.: Generating domain-specific model editors
    with complex editing commands. In: Schürr, A., Nagl, M., Zündorf, A. (eds.) Pro-
    ceedings of AGTIVE 2007: Applications of Graph Transformations with Industrial
    Relevance, Wilhelmshöhe, Kassel, Germany (October 2007)

Modelling of Longitudinal Information Systems with Graph Grammars

Jens H. Weber-Jahnke

Department of Computer Science
University of Victoria, B.C., Canada
jens@acm.org

Abstract. Longitudinal information systems (LIS) manage and evolve data over extensive periods of time. Examples are "womb to tomb" electronic health records. How can we design such systems such that they are future-proof, i.e., evolvable in step with changing requirements? One approach that has been advocated is the "two-level modelling" approach, separating information and knowledge in terms of a small reference model and a larger archetype model. A textual archetype definition language has been proposed to define the mapping between these two models. In this paper, we explore an alternative way to define this mapping using triple graph grammars. The graph grammar based approach has several advantages over the textual approach, including better modularity and tool support.

Keywords: Triple graph grammars, data engineering, longitudinal health records, two-level modelling, archetypes.

1   Introduction

Longitudinal information systems (LIS) manage data about a population of subjects collected over a long period of time. An increasing number of LIS are being developed in public and private sectors such as health care, social security, law enforcement, and insurance. Canada is currently developing a pan-Canadian Electronic Health Record (EHR) to maintain "womb to tomb" health information for all citizens [6]. Similar systems are under development in other countries, e.g., the British NHS patient record and the French *Dossier medical personnel* [6]. A common challenge with the long-lived nature of LIS is on making them *future proof*. Data requirements change over time, particularly in knowledge-driven domains such as health care. In response to this challenge, Beale has proposed a *two-level modelling* approach to developing LIS [2]. He argues that the traditional single-level approach to coding domain concepts in database and software models is too rigid, since many concepts change over time. Two-level modelling addresses this issue by separating domain concepts into a small, stable *reference model* (RM) and a larger, more volatile *knowledge model* (KM). Only RM concepts are directly coded in the application. KM concepts are not hard-coded but defined as constraint-based views on (compositions of) RM concepts. These

A. Schürr, M. Nagl, and A. Zündorf (Eds.): AGTIVE 2007, LNCS 5088, pp. 59–65, 2008.

views are called *archetypes*. A textual *Archetype Definition Language* and a corresponding semantic object model have been developed for the purpose of formalizing archetypes [4]. Learning ADL and implementing ADL semantics is not a trivial task. As of version 2 of the language specification [4], ADL supports "pluggable" sub-languages that may replace the default language elements. This paper utilizes this concept and proposes an alternative, graph-grammar (GG) based approach to defining archetypes. We argue that the definition of GG based archetypes holds several advantages. The next section gives a brief introduction to the two-level modelling approach. Section 3 describes our new approach to defining archetypes using a GG based language. Section 4 provides a brief discussion of our results and related work.

2   Two-Level Modelling

The basic idea behind the Two-Level Modelling approach is not new. It is based on the idea of conceptual "views" applied in data engineering for many decades. Database languages feature mechanisms to construct virtual data types ("views") based on the logical data model defined in the database ("base tables"). The most important difference between typical database view mechanisms and the ADL as standardized by the OpenEHR foundation is that ADL has features specific to the health care domain and is not restricted to flat tables but rather assumes a nested, graph-oriented data model [4]. We illustrate the two-level modelling approach with the concept of a patient referral. Referral data may contain entries about the referring health care provider(s), the clinical issue, the envisioned treatment process, a maximal wait time etc. We show a simplified example of a referral data form in Fig. 1 and its data model in Fig. 2.

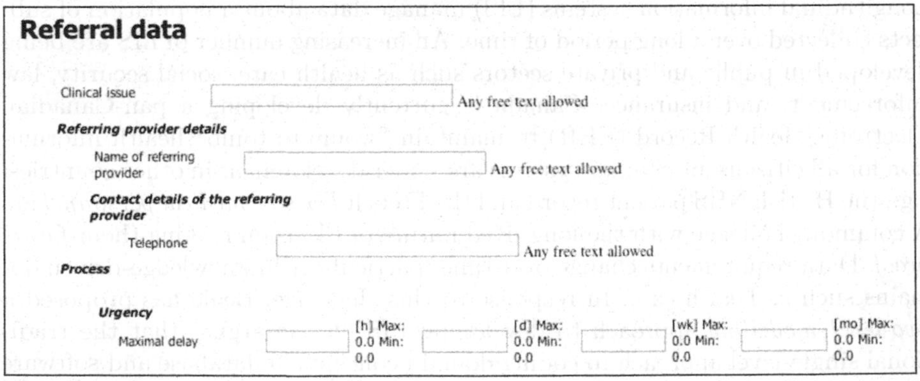

Fig. 1. Example user interface for referral form

Fig. 2. Data Model for the referral data example

2.1 Knowledge Model vs. Reference Model

The information associated with a referral is not standardized but is likely to evolve over time as knowledge develops. Consequently, the referral is an example for a concept that should not be "hard-wired" in the base schema (RM) of any LIS. In terms of the two-level modelling approach, the referral is a second level (*KM*) concept and should be defined as a view (*archetype*) based on the concepts defined in the RM. One of the challenges of two-level modelling is to decide which concepts are sufficiently stable to warrant their implementation in the RM. Considering our example data model from Fig. 2, we may decide that concepts *DATE_TIME* and *DELAY* are sufficiently stable. The OpenEHR foundation and other organizations (e.g., HL7) have published recommended RMs and guidelines for the health care domain. Fig. 3 shows an excerpt of a RM based on the OpenEHR recommendations. Th RM in Fig. 3 is sufficiently powerful to express all concepts shown in our referral example in Fig. 2. It implements a generic hierarchy of data *items*. Composite items are called *clusters* while the leaves of the hierarchy are called *elements*. Elements have a *value* according to one of several possible types. The only data type in Fig. 3 that may require further explanation is *CODED_TEXT*. It is used to represent values that are taken from a controlled terminology, e.g., the International Classification of Diseases (ICD), or a similar ontology. Any item carries a *meaning* attribute defining its semantics. In addition, clusters may be associated with coded values, defining their semantics in terms of a controlled vocabulary.

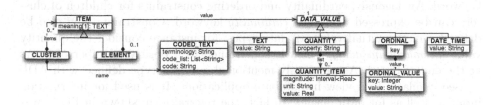

Fig. 3. Simplified RM

2.2 Archetype Definition Language

At this point the reader may have an intuitive idea on how KM concepts in our referral example (Fig. 2) can be represented in terms of concepts in our RM. Essentially, composite items (e.g., *REFERRAL_DATA* would be represented as clusters containing primitive elements (e.g., *clinical_issue*), as well as other composite clusters (e.g., *PROVIDER*). The two-level modelling approach advocated

```
CLUSTER[Referral_data] matches {
  items existence matches {0..1} cardinality matches {0..*; unordered} matches {
... CLUSTER[Referring provider details] occurrences matches {0..1} matches {
      items cardinality matches {1..1; unordered} matches {
        ELEMENT[Name of referring provider] occurrences matches {1..1} matches {
          value matches {TEXT matches {*}} } }
...   CLUSTER[Contact details] occurrences matches {0..1} matches {
        items cardinality matches {0..*; unordered} matches {
          ELEMENT[telephone] occurrences matches {0..*} matches {
            name matches {
              CODED_TEXT occurrences matches {0..1} matches {
                code_list matches {
                  [mobile,work,alternative work, direct work line, pager] } } }
            value matches {TEXT matches {*} } } } }
...   CLUSTER[Process] occurrences matches {0..1} matches {
        items cardinality matches {0..*; unordered} matches {
          CLUSTER[Urgency] occurrences matches {1..1} matches {
            items cardinality matches {0..*; unordered} matches {
...           ELEMENT[Maximal delay] occurrences matches {1..1} matches {
                value matches {
                  QUANTITY matches {
                    property matches "time"
                    units matches "h"
                    magnitude matches "|>0.0|" } } }
```

Fig. 4. Excerpt of a definition section for a referral archetype (simplified)

by the OpenEHR consortium uses a dedicated archetype definition language
(ADL) to formalize this mapping from KM concepts to RM. ADL uses a mixture of pattern matching, constraint-based queries, and path navigation. Its semantics is defined with UML [4]. Fig. 4 shows a simplified example for the
definition section of an archetype defining the KM concept *REFERRAL_DATA*
in our example. Since a detailed introduction to ADL is beyond the scope of
this paper, we will restrict ourselves to an informal explanation. Basically, the
example shows how the data structure for a referral is defined using a hierarchy
of items (clusters and elements) and data types. The semantics of each item is
defined in rectangular brackets ([]) and stored in the *meaning* attribute of class
ITEM. Each item can be defined mandatory or optional using the *occurrences*
keyword. Analogously, cardinality and ordering constraints for children of clusters can be expressed using the *cardinality* keyword. Constraints may also be
defined over the actual values of data types, for instance consider the quantity
value for *maximum delay*, which is constrained to a positive number of hours
at the end of Fig. 4. As previously mentioned, an archetype defined with ADL
is used similarly to a view in database applications. It is used for information
input as well as for data output. In fact, the referral form shown in Fig. 1 was
generated automatically from the archetype definition.

3   A Graph Grammar-Based Approach to Defining Archetypes

The OpenEHR's ADL actually consists of multiple sub-languages. The sub-
language used to define the mapping in Fig. 4 is called *cADL* (constraint ADL).
The sub-language used to compose new archetypes from existing archetypes
(not shown in this paper) is called *dADL* (definition ADL). The new version 2

of OpenEHR's ADL language specification accommodates language "plug-ins" to replace the default syntax of cADL or dADL with alternative languages. We argue that the default cADL shown earlier is difficult to read for more complex examples, which impedes implementation and maintenance. The textual syntax may be substituted by an alternative graph-grammar (GG) based cADL language plug-in. We believe that the GG-based cADL will be easier to understand, implement and maintain. Of course, this point of view is debatable and others may prefer textual languages. However, another, more objective benefit of a GG-based ADL is the closer connection to the archetype object model (AOM), which defines the semantics of ADL based on an abstract UML specification [4]. Currently, the textual syntax is "modelled after" the AOM and needs to be updated when the AOM changes, including all its tools, parsers, compilers etc. A GG-based ADL would greatly decrease this overhead.

Analogously to textual grammars, traditional GGs consist of a set of *production rules*, each with a left-hand side (LHS) and a right-hand side (RHS). Intuitively, production rules are applied to a graph G by matching the LHS to elements in G and replacing them with the RHS, while keep the elements that appear on both sides of the production. Application conditions can be added to productions to further constrain their application [5]. Special classes of GGs have been developed for the purpose of relating logically independent graph models. One such class is called *Triple Graph Grammar* TGG and has been invented in the early nineties by Schürr following Pratt's analogous concept for textual languages called *Pair Grammars* [1]. TGGs are very applicable in our problem context, since the goal of two-level modelling is basically to relate KM concepts to those concepts implemented in the RM.

A formal introduction to the TGGs is out of scope of this short-form paper and we refer the reader to [1]. Here, we use our referral application example to provide an intuitive understanding of the approach. TGG specifications are rule-based, i.e., a TGG consists of a collection of TGG rules. Therefore, TGG-based archetype definitions can provide a higher degree of modularity compared to the heavily nested textual ADL shown in Fig. fig:referralADL. Figure 5 shows four TGG rules for our example (R1-R4). The right side of each rule contains instances of the RM (e.g., cluster, element, etc.). The left side contains elements that belong to our archetype definition (e.g., referral data, provider, etc.). These concepts belong to our KM. Elements on both sides are related by special graph nodes labelled *MAP*. Intuitively, the first rule (R1: Map Referral) defines that the KM concept *Referral Data* is represented by a specific combination of RM concepts (*Cluster*, *Element* and *Text*). Note how the assertions in node 3 and 4 constrain the *meaning* attribute of these elements to represent the appropriate value. Further assertions demand that the value of attribute *clinical_issues* in node 1 be equal to the value of text node 5, i.e., the content of *clinical_issues* is represented by a corresponding text node in the generic RM. Rule R2 (Map Provider) extends the definition of the archetype by defining how the KM concept *Provider* is mapped to RM-level concepts. The bold graph elements at the top of R2 define the context in which such an extension is permissible, while the

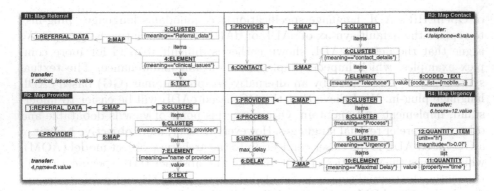

Fig. 5. TGG-based archetype definition

grey elements underneath specify the actual extension. Analogously R3 and R4 further extend the mapping defined by R2 and R3, respectively.

Since archetypes are seen as a way of defining database views, our discussion of their execution focusses on (1) data input (and validation) and (2) data output (and queries). The textual ADL as proposed by OpenEHR can be used for (1) only. The OpenEHR consortium is currently developing a further textual language for querying. In the following, we explain how TGG-based archetype specifications can be used for (1) *and* (2), adding a further advantage to our approach. The general TGG theory states that three traditional GG productions can be derived from every TGG rule: a left-right (LR) production, instantiating KM concepts from RM data, a right-left (RL) production, creating RM instances based on KM data, and a *mapping* production, instantiating a mapping between KM and RM data. We refer to [1] on details on how to derive these productions. We will only make one comment about the treatment of assertions, since they are not considered in [1]: Assertions on the right and left side of a TGG rule become assignments in the derived LR and RL productions, respectively. Let us now discuss how the generated productions can be used for data input and output in an LIS. Clearly, we could use the RL productions to generate KM view data for the entire database content (residing in the RM schema). However, in most cases we are interested in queries for targeted subsets of the data. We can provide this functionality by combining mapping productions with RL productions. For example, if we want to query for all referral data about a specific clinical issue, say Diabetes, the user may enter "Diabetes" under "Clinical issue" in the referral form (Fig. 1). As a result of this input, the software can instantiate an instance of KM node *Referral data* with attribute *clinical_issues* set to "Diabetes". We then apply the mapping production derived from R1 to associate this instance with an appropriate representation in the RM-based database schema. If such a representation is found, we can use the RL production of rules R2-R4 to output the details about the referral. We repeat this process starting with the creation of another instance of *Referral data* with clinical issue "Diabetes" to find further RM-level data that fits the pattern. Note that the TGG mapping production has to enforce that RM "referral" clusters is only mapped once. LR productions are used for data input, i.e., to generate the appropriate RM representation for the KM-level concepts entered.

4   Conclusions and Related Work

Two-level modelling is an important principle in the design of LIS in general, and EHRs in particular. Its implementation requires appropriate formalisms to describe the mappings between KM and RM. OpenEHR's ADL provides such a formalism, including a mechanism to replace part of it by other sub-languages. We have presented an approach to replace cADL with a TGG-based language. This approach has five main benefits: (1) The GG-based ADL is directly connected to the graph-based semantic model of OpenEHR archetypes (i.e., the AOM), (2) the GG-based ADL provides a higher degree of modularity (in terms of rules), (3) the GG-based ADL can be used to generate data input *as well as* output operations, (4) the GG-based ADL is easier to comprehend and maintain, (5) the GG-based ADL is supported by a rich set of tools developed in the GG community. We are currently evaluating TGG tool support for our application. Our notion of TGGs slightly deviates from existing tool implementations w.r.t. our treatment of assertions. We are also currently conducting a formal analysis about the expressiveness of TGG-ADL vs. the textual cADL. Certain aspects of cADL cannot be expressed in our current TGG formalism, e.g., cardinality and ordering constraints. Our approach is related to earlier work in the GG community on visual query languages [3].

References

1. Specification of Graph Translators with Triple Graph Grammars. In: 20th Intl. Workshop on Graph-Theoretic Concepts in Computer Science, London, UK. Springer, Heidelberg (1995)
2. Constraint-based Domain Models for Future-proof Information Systems. In: OOP-SLA Workshop on Behavioural Semantics (2002)
3. Andries, M., Engels, G.: Syntax and Semantics of Hybrid Database Languages. In: Proc. of Intl. Workshop on Graph Transformations in Computer Science. LNCS, p. 19. Springer, Heidelberg (1993)
4. Beale, T., Heard, S. (eds.): The openEHR Archetype Model - The Archetype Definition Language 2. openEHR Foundation (2007)
5. Rozenberg, G.: Handbook of graph grammars and computing by graph transformation, vol. I. foundations. World Scientific Publishing Co., Inc., River Edge (1997)
6. Weber-Jahnke, J.H.: Achieving interoperability among healthcare information systems. In: Encyclopedia of healthcare information systems, IGI Global (2007)

A Generic Layout Algorithm for Meta-model Based Editors

Sonja Maier and Mark Minas

Universität der Bundeswehr München, Germany

Abstract. The diagram editor generator framework DIAMETA utilizes meta-model based language specifications and supports free-hand as well as structured editing. This paper describes a generic layout algorithm that meets the demands of this kind of editors. The underlying concept of the algorithm is attribute evaluation. An attribute evaluator is best suited for an unambiguous layout, i.e. the diagram may not be represented in different ways. Especially in free-hand mode we want to give more freedom to the user when he edits a diagram, and thus a plain attribute evaluator is not sufficient. Therefore we combine this approach with a constraint satisfaction approach in the sense that constraints are used to activate particular attribute evaluation rules. This gives the layouter the flexibility it needs to deal with the situation in DIAMETA.

1 Introduction

Each visual editor implements a certain visual language. Several approaches and tools have been proposed to specify visual languages and to generate editors from such specifications. These attempts can be characterized by the way the diagram language is specified, and by the way the user interacts with the editor and creates respectively edits diagrams. Most visual languages have a model as (abstract) syntax specification. Models are essentially class diagrams of the data structures that are visualized by diagrams. When considering user interaction and the way how the user can create and edit diagrams, structured editing is usually distinguished from free-hand editing. Structured editors offer the user some operations that transform correct diagrams into (other) correct diagrams. Free-hand editors, on the other hand, allow to arrange diagram components from a language-specific set on the screen without any restrictions, thus giving the user more freedom. The editor has to check whether the drawing is correct and what its meaning is.

DIAMETA [1] follows the model-driven approach to specify diagram languages. From such a specification an editor, offering structured as well as free-hand editing, can be generated. In Fig. 1 we can see an editor that was generated with DIAMETA. We designed a generic layout algorithm that works for model-based visual languages. It meets the demands of structured as well as free-hand editing.

For structured editors, layout algorithms were studied in the past [2]. For free-hand editors, these layout algorithms cannot be adapted in a straightforward

A. Schürr, M. Nagl, and A. Zündorf (Eds.): AGTIVE 2007, LNCS 5088, pp. 66–81, 2008.

way. The layouter has to deal with the increase of flexibility and should only restrict the user in a moderate way. In the world of grammar-based editors, some layout algorithms have been established in the past. Our algorithm operates on a model instead. We will see how to define a layout algorithm that is specialized for a certain model, i.e. a certain visual language.

Chok et al. [3] distinguish between the two terms, *beautification* and *layout*: *Layout* is the general term, and covers the concept of *beautification*. *Beautification* (sometimes called layout refinement) starts with an initial layout and performs minor changes to improve it while still preserving the "feel" (or "mental map" [4]) of the original layout. Especially user interaction is considered in this context. *Layout* may also position components of the diagram from scratch without an initial layout. The layout algorithm presented in this paper focuses on *beautification*.

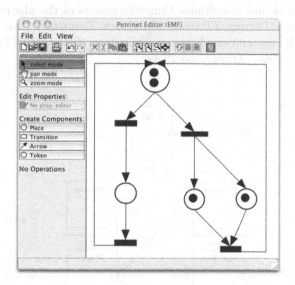

Fig. 1. Petri net Editor

One frequently used concept is attribute evaluation. An attribute evaluator is fast and best suited if the layout is unambiguous. This concept cannot deal with the situation that the same diagram may be represented in different ways. Especially in free-hand mode we want to leave more freedom to the user when he edits a diagram, and thus a conventional attribute evaluator is not sufficient.

Another concept that is frequently used for layout, is constraint satisfaction [1]. The disadvantages of this concept are that constraint satisfaction is (rather) slow and its behavior is unpredictable in some situations.

We combine the concepts constraints and attribute evaluation to an algorithm that is fast, flexible and behaves exactly the way we desire: Assertions ensure the characteristics of the layout. If they are not fulfilled, a set of attribute evaluation rules is switched on. These rules are evaluated, and the associated attributes are updated. In terms of constraint satisfaction, these rules act as a relaxation method.

Sect. 2 introduces the model of Petri nets, the visual language that is used as a running example. Sect. 3 explains the generic layout algorithm that we propose for meta-model based editors. Sect. 4 shows how this layout algorithm can be used for editors. Sect. 5 summarizes some implementation details, and gives an overview of DIAMETA, the environment in which the algorithm was tested. Sect. 6 contains related work, and Sect. 7 concludes the paper.

2   Petri Net Editor

Fig. 2 shows the (simplified) class diagram for Petri nets. It contains the class *Node* as an abstract base class of a Petri nets place or transition. *Node* has a member attribute *label*. *Edge* is the abstract base class of a Petri net's connection between places and transitions. Concrete classes of the abstract model are *Place*, *Transition*, *PTArrow*, *TPArrow* and *Token*. *Transition-Place* relations are represented by the associations between *Transition*, *TPArrow* (*TPArrow* stands for Transition-To-Place Arrow) and *Place*.

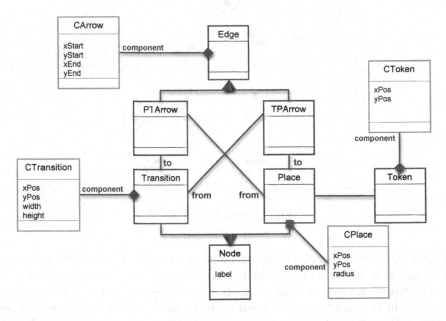

Fig. 2. Model of Petri nets

Place-Transition relations are represented by the associations between *Place*, *PTArrow* and *Token*. *Place-Token* relations are represented by the association between the classes *Place* and *Transition*. The classes *CPlace*, *CTransition*, *CArrow* and *CToken* represent aspects of the concrete syntax.

Each diagram consists of a finite set of diagram components. In Petri nets, these are places, transitions, tokens, and arrows between places and transitions. Each component is determined by its attributes.

A place is a circle whose top left corner (the corner of the bounding box) is determined by the attributes ($xPos$, $yPos$) and its radius by the attribute *radius*. A transition is a square whose top left corner is defined by the coordinate point ($xPos$, $yPos$) and its size by the attributes *width* and *height*. A token is a circle whose top left corner (of the bounding box) is again defined by ($xPos$, $yPos$). Its radius is a fixed value that cannot be modified by the user. *PTArrow* and *TPArrow* are arrows whose position is defined by its two end points, i.e. by the two coordinate pairs ($xStart$, $yStart$) and ($xEnd$, $yEnd$)[1].

Layouting means updating one or more of these attributes. For example, if an arrow should always be aligned vertically, then the layouter would give $xStart$ and $xEnd$ the same value.

3   Layout Algorithm

In this section, we give an overview of the layout algorithm. First, we describe the input parameters of the layouter. Then we summarize what components the layout specification consists of. As a last step, we describe the layout algorithm itself.

3.1   Input

The algorithm gets as input one or two sets of values - the *old values*, the *user desired values*, or both. Besides that, the layouter is aware of the current state. It knows, whether the user is in the process of modifying a component, e.g. is currently moving a place, or already finished modification. It also knows, which components the user changed. In addition, the layouter has access to the model of the visual language.

Attribute Values. The algorithm gets as input the *old values*, the *user desired values*, or both, depending on the kind of user interaction. We have to distinguish between three types of user interaction. The user has the possibility to add, modify or remove components. When the user adds a component at a desired position, the layouter gets one set of values as input - the *user desired values*. When the user modifies a component, e.g. moves a place from the position characterized by $xPos_{old}$ and $yPos_{old}$ to a new position $xPos_{user}$ and $yPos_{user}$, the layouter has two sets of values as input - the *old values* and the *user desired values*. In case of deletion, the layouter gets only the *old values* as input.

State. The layouter is automaton-based, and hence aware of the current state of user interaction. We distinguish between two states, the state *during modification* and the state *after modification*[2] that we treat in different ways. *During*

---

[1] They can be extended by a list of bends easily.
[2] *During modification* the model is not updated, *after modification* first the model is updated and then the layouter is called.

modification, some layouting constraints should be satisfied immediately. The satisfaction of other aspects may be postponed to the end of the user interaction, in order to allow for a fast editor response during interaction. Suppose we change the position of a place. While we move the component, we also want the arrows to be updated. As the layouter is responsible for the update of the attributes, it needs to be called several times *during modification* of the diagram via user input in order to update the arrows. For example the satisfaction of the constraint that arrows must have a minimal length may take place at the end of user interaction.

Another aspect we take care of is the information, what component, i.e., what attributes, the user changed. In our example we distinguish between moving arrows and moving places or transitions. When we move an arrow, we just want the arrow to be moved. Places and transitions remain unchanged. If we move a place or transition, we want arrows to stay connected to these components.

3.2   Layout Specification

The layouter uses this information to calculate *new values* that represent the updated diagram. To do that, it needs a layout specification. This specification consists of a set of constraints, each of them associated with classes like *Place* or *PTArrow*. For every constraint a list of attribute evaluation rules must be defined. Each of the constraints and attribute evaluation rules depend on the current state.

We may access attributes of the concrete classes. Suppose we have a constraint associated with the class *Place*. Then we may access the attribute *xPos* of the class *CPlace* via *component.xPos*. As usual, we may also access attributes of other objects. This can be done via the links between the objects given in the model (Fig. 2.). Suppose we have a rule associated with an object of the type *PTArrow*. Then we may access the *xPos* attribute of *CPlace* in the form *from.component.xPos*.[3] To keep it simple, we will omit the association *component* in expressions in the following. For example we will treat the classes *Place* and *CPlace* as one component and omit the association between them. Hence, *xPos* replaces *component.xPos* and *from.xPos* replaces *from.component.xPos*.

In contrast to the traditional usage of constraints and attribute evaluation rules, we do not only have one set of attributes, but three or more sets of values. We may access the *current values* of the attributes (the attributes in the current iteration of the layout algorithm), the *old values* or the *user desired values* at any time. We may also access intermediate results the layouter already has produced.

For example, we may access the (possibly) different values of *xPos* via

1. $xPos$: *current value*
2. $xPos_{old}$: *old value*
3. $xPos_{user}$: *user desired value*
4. $xPos_n$: intermediate results ($xPos_0$ is the *current value*, $xPos_1$ the value of the previous layout iteration and so on.)

---

[3] The syntax is similar to *OCL*, as specified in [5].

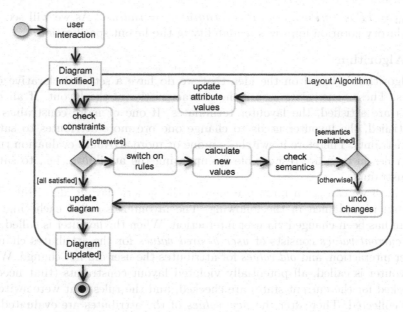

Fig. 3. Birds–eye view of the Generic Layout Algorithm

Only *current values* are changed during execution. All other attribute values remain unchanged. The algorithm presented uses an iterative approach. Intermediate results are created with each layout iteration.

Constraints are responsible for switching on and off attribute evaluation rules, attribute evaluation rules for calculating the set of *new values*. E.g., constraint (1) (that is associated with the class *Place*) switches on the rule (2) in case $xPos \leq yPos$. If this is not the case, $xPos$ remains unchanged by this rule[4].

$$[\text{after modification}]xPos > yPos \qquad (1)$$
$$xPos \leftarrow yPos + 5 \qquad (2)$$

As we explained in the last section, we also know the current state of user interaction. We may restrict constraints and attribute evaluation rules to be checked and executed only if we are in a special state (indicated by [state] in front of the constraint or rule). For example, if we add [after modification] in front of the constraint, this constraint is checked *after modification*. Otherwise, this constraint is checked each time the layouter is called.

We may also add [o1 changed] in front of the constraint. This means that the constraint is only executed if one of the attributes of the object o1 changed. Note that an object can be changed by user interaction or by the layouter in the previous layout iteration. [o1 changed] could be substituted by a constraint. The corresponding rule(s) is(are) used if the constraint is not satisfied. E.g. for an object *o1* of the class *Place*, [o1 changed] could be substituted by the constraint

---

[4] This is an example, not used for the layout specified later.

$xPos_{old} = xPos \wedge yPos_{old} = yPos \wedge radius_{old} = radius$.[5] As we will see, the abbreviatory notation improves readability of the layout specification.

3.3 Algorithm

The algorithm is based on the idea that we do have a set of declarative constraints. These constraints assure the characteristics of the layout. If all constraints are satisfied, the layouter terminates. If one or more constraints are not satisfied, the layouter needs to change one ore more attributes to satisfy the constraints. Therefore it switches on one or more attribute evaluation rules. These rules in turn are responsible for updating the attributes, i.e., to satisfy the constraints.

In Fig. 3 we can see a birds–eye view of the generic layout algorithm. This algorithm is explained in the following. The layouter is called each time the diagram has been changed via user interaction. When the layouter is called, the set of *current values* consists of *user desired values* for the attributes changed via user interaction, and *old values* for attributes the user did not change. When the layouter is called, all potentially violated layout constraints (that need to be checked for the current state) are checked, and the rules that were switched on are collected. Thereafter the *new values* of the attributes are evaluated via attribute evaluation.

The *current values* are substituted by the *new values* and the constraints are checked again. (New constraints may have become unsatisfied due to changes the layouter performed.) If all constraints are satisfied, the layouter has succeeded and may output the *new values*. If not, the layouter has to evaluate the rules again. If the layouter does not succeed after a certain number of iterations (this number may be user defined), the layouter stops and returns the *user values* as result. In this case, the layouter performs no changes.

Each time the layouter produces *new values*, it is checked whether the layout algorithm maintained the semantics of the diagram or not. If this is not the case, it undoes the changes and returns the last set of *new values* that were computed.

4   Layout Algorithm Used for Petri Nets

We now explore a concrete example, the layout algorithm used for Petri nets.

4.1   Constraints

Arrows, Places and Transitions. We demand that arrows start and end at the border of transitions and places. In addition, arrows must have a minimal length. The constraints associated with the classes *PTArrow* and *TPArrow*

$$[\text{from changed}] \quad xStart = from.xPos + \frac{from.width}{2} \qquad (\text{C01})$$

$$[\text{from changed}] \quad yStart = from.yPos + from.height \qquad (\text{C02})$$

$$[\text{to changed}] \quad xEnd = to.xPos + \frac{to.width}{2} \qquad (\text{C03})$$

$$[\text{to changed}] \quad yEnd = to.yPos \qquad (\text{C04})$$

---

[5] Here we check against the *current values*, not the *user desired values*. This includes the case, that the layouter has changed a component.

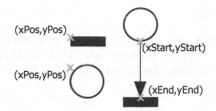

Fig. 4. Location of points

assure that arrows start and end at the top or bottom of a component[6]. The point $(xPos, yPos)$ is located in the top left corner of a component, as we can see in Fig. 4. The points $(xStart, yStart)$ and $(xEnd, yEnd)$ are located at the start and end of an arrow.

To assure that arrows have a minimal length, we introduce a constraint associated with the classes *PTArrow* and *TPArrow*.

$$[\text{after modification}] \quad (xEnd - xStart)^2 + (yEnd - yStart)^2 > 1000 \quad \text{(C05)}$$

Tokens. We claim that tokens are completely inside a place (completely inside the bounding box). To assure this, we add four constraints to the class *Token*.

$$[\text{in changed}] \qquad xPos \geq in.xPos \qquad \text{(C06)}$$
$$[\text{in changed}] \quad xPos + width \leq in.xPos + in.width \qquad \text{(C07)}$$
$$[\text{in changed}] \qquad yPos \geq in.yPos \qquad \text{(C08)}$$
$$[\text{in changed}] \quad yPos + height \leq in.yPos + in.height \qquad \text{(C09)}$$

4.2   Attribute Evaluation Rules

To satisfy constraints (C01-C04), we add the attribute evaluation rules (R01-R04). These rules update start and end point of the arrow. Rules (R05-R08) are introduced to satisfy constraint (C05). They update the location of the place or transition. Rules (R09-R12) are added to satisfy constraints (C06-C09). They update the position of tokens. We avoid cyclic dependencies as we use the *old values* of the attributes $xPos$ and $yPos$ on the right side of the equation.

$$xStart \leftarrow from.xPos + \frac{from.width}{2} \qquad \text{(R01)}$$
$$yStart \leftarrow from.yPos + from.height \qquad \text{(R02)}$$
$$xEnd \leftarrow to.xPos + \frac{to.width}{2} \qquad \text{(R03)}$$
$$yEnd \leftarrow to.yPos \qquad \text{(R04)}$$
$$[\text{from changed}] \quad to.xPos \leftarrow to.xPos_1 + \frac{to.xPos_1 - from.xPos}{|to.xPos_1 - from.xPos|} \qquad \text{(R05)}$$
$$[\text{from changed}] \quad to.yPos \leftarrow to.yPos_1 + \frac{to.yPos_1 - from.yPos}{|to.yPos_1 - from.yPos|} \qquad \text{(R06)}$$
$$[\text{to changed}] \quad from.xPos \leftarrow from.xPos_1 + \frac{from.xPos_1 - to.xPos}{|from.xPos_1 - to.xPos|} \qquad \text{(R07)}$$
$$[\text{to changed}] \quad from.yPos \leftarrow from.yPos_1 + \frac{from.yPos_1 - to.yPos}{|from.yPos_1 - to.yPos|} \qquad \text{(R08)}$$
$$xPos \leftarrow in.xPos \qquad \text{(R09)}$$
$$xPos \leftarrow in.xPos + in.width - width \qquad \text{(R10)}$$
$$yPos \leftarrow in.yPos \qquad \text{(R11)}$$
$$yPos \leftarrow in.yPos + in.height - height \qquad \text{(R12)}$$

---

[6] For places, *width* and *height* are internally mapped to 2·*radius*.

4.3   Sample Evaluation

In Fig. 5. we see a sample user interaction. The user moves the place from the top left (Pict. 1 of Fig. 5) to the bottom right (Pict. 2). He does not change the arrow. During user interaction, the layouter is called several times.

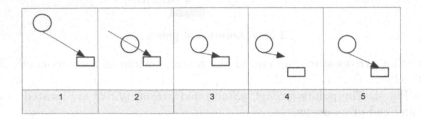

Fig. 5. Place movement

During movement, constraints (C01) and (C02) are not satisfied. Thus the attribute evaluation rules (R01) and (R02) are switched on. These rules update the attributes $xStart$ and $yStart$ of the arrow. The *new values* are calculated, and the constraints are checked again. All constraints are now fulfilled, and the layouter returns the *new values* (Pict. 3).

After movement the layouter is called again. A last time, constraints (C01) and (C02) are not satisfied and the attributes $xStart$ and $yStart$ of the arrow are updated ((R01) and (R02)).

The constraints are checked again, and this time constraint (C05) is not fulfilled. That means that the attribute evaluation rules (R05) and (R06) are switched on and all attributes are evaluated. These rules move the transition to the bottom right (Pict. 4).

The constraints are checked again. Now constraints (C03) and (C04) are not fulfilled and the values of the attributes $xEnd$ and $yEnd$ of the arrow ((R03) and (R04)) are updated. All constraints are now fulfilled and the layouter outputs the *new (final) values* (Pict. 5)[7].

5   Implementation

In this section, we will give an overview of DIAMETA [1], the environment the algorithm was implemented in and explain how the algorithm was integrated in the framework. We will then examine the algorithm in terms of usability and performance.

5.1   Integration of the Layout Algorithm in DIAMETA

DIAMETA provides an environment for rapidly developing diagram editors based on meta-modeling. Each DIAMETA editor is based on the same editor architecture

---

[7] These are the essential steps. Actually, the layouter needs a certain number of increments until constraint (C05) is satisfied.

which is adjusted to the specific diagram language. This architecture is described in the following. DIAMETAs tool support for specification and code generation, primarily the DIAMETA Designer are postponed to the next paragraph.

Architecture. Since DIAMETA is actually an extension of the diagram editor generator DIAGEN [6,7], DIAMETA [1] editors have a similar design like DIAGEN editors. Fig. 6 shows the structure which is common to all DIAMETA editors - editors generated and based on DIAMETA . Ovals are data structures, and rectangles represent functional components. The flow of information is indicated by arrows. If not labeled, the information flow means reading respectively creating the corresponding data structures.

The editor supports free-hand editing by means of the included drawing tool which is part of the editor framework, but which has been adjusted by the DI-AMETA Designer. With this drawing tool, the user is able to create, arrange and modify the diagram components of the particular diagram language. Editor specific program code, which has been specified by the editor developer and generated by the DIAMETA Designer, is responsible for the visual representation of these language specific components. The drawing tool creates the data structure of the diagram as a set of diagram components together with their attributes (position, size, etc.). The sequence of processing steps necessary for free-hand editing starts with the modeler and ends with the model checker; the modeler first transforms the diagram into an internal model, the graph model. The reducer then creates the diagrams instance graph that is analyzed by the model analyzer. This last processing step identifies the maximal subdiagram which is (syntactically) correct and provides visual feedback to the user by drawing those diagram components in a certain color; errors are indicated by another color. However, the model analyzer not only checks the diagrams abstract syntax, but also creates the object structure of the diagrams syntactically correct subdiagram. For further details on these steps, please refer to [1] and [6,7].

The layouter modifies attributes of diagram components and thus the diagram layout is based on the (syntactically correct subdiagram's) object structure. The layouter is optional for free-hand editing, but necessary for realizing structured editing. Structured editing operations modify the graph model by the means of the graph transformer and add or remove components to respectively from the diagram. The visual representation of the diagram and its layout is then computed by the layouter.

Framework. This paragraph completes the description of DIAMETA and outlines its environment supporting specification and code generation of diagram editors that are tailored to specific diagram languages. The DIAMETA environment shown in Fig. 7 consists of an editor framework, the DIAMETA Designer and the DIAMETA Layout Generator. The Layout Generator is the implementation of the Generic Layout Algorithm presented in this paper. The framework that is basically a collection of Java classes, provides the generic editor functionality, which is necessary for editing and analyzing diagrams. In order to create an editor for a specific diagram language, the editor developer has to provide

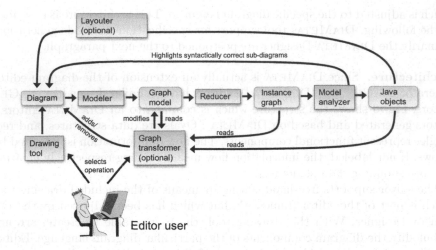

Fig. 6. Architecture of a diagram editor based on DIAMETA

two specifications: First, the abstract syntax of the diagram language in terms of its model, and second, the visual appearance of diagram components, the concrete syntax of the diagram language, the reducer rules and the interaction specification. Besides that, he may provide a layout specification, if he wants to define a specific layouter.

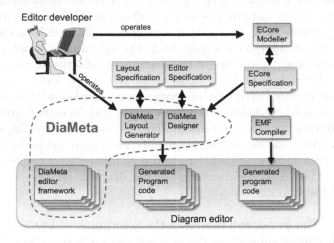

Fig. 7. Generating diagram editors with DIAMETA

DIAMETA can either use the Eclipse Modeling Framework [8] (DIAMETA *EMF* version [1]) or *MOFLON* [9,10] (DIAMETA */MOF* version [11]) for specifying language models and generating their implementations. Our algorithm implementation is based on the *EMF* version. But with minor changes, the algorithm may also work with the *MOF* version instead. A languages class diagram is specified as an *EMF* model that the editor developer creates by using the *EMF* modeller (e.g. the built-in *EMF* model editor of the *EMF* plugin for Eclipse). The *EMF* compiler, being part of the *EMF* plugin for Eclipse, is used to create Java code that represents the model. Fig. 2 shows the class diagram as an *EMF* model. The *EMF* compiler creates Java classes (respectively interfaces) for the specified classes. The editor developer uses the DIAMETA Designer for specifying the concrete syntax and the visual appearance of diagram components, e.g. places are drawn as circles, transitions as rectangles, and edges as arrows. The DIAMETA Designer generates Java code from this specification. In addition, he can provide a layout specification, e.g. he may indicate that arrows must have a minimal length. The DIAMETA Layout Generator generates Java code from this specification. This Java code, together with the Java code generated by the DIAMETA Designer, the Java code created by the *EMF* compiler, and the editor framework, implement an editor for the specified diagram language.

5.2   Usability and Performance

In the last section we described how the layout algorithm was integrated in DIAMETA. We now examine the algorithm in terms of usability and performance.

Usability. Creating an editor with DIAMETA is very simple. The only part the editor developer had to write by hand was the layouter. With the layout algorithm presented in this paper, the editor developer is no longer burdened with this task. He now only has to provide a layout specification.

We recognize that writing such a specification is still rather complicated and complex. Therefore, we are planning to encapsulate basic functionality, as it is done in [12], and give the user the opportunity to use these *patterns* (as they are called in [12]).

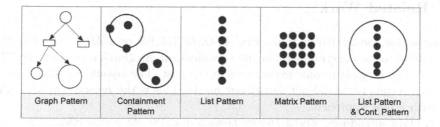

| Graph Pattern | Containment Pattern | List Pattern | Matrix Pattern | List Pattern & Cont. Pattern |

Fig. 8. Graph Pattern, Containment Pattern, List Pattern, Matrix Pattern

Actually, the first *patterns* have been implemented already, and it is possible to combine and extend these *patterns*. We can see four of these *patterns* in Fig. 8. The first one is the *Graph Pattern* that is responsible for layouting arrows, i.e., that they start and end exactly at the nodes, and that they have a minimal length. The second one is the *Containment Pattern*, that is responsible for moving components completely inside a surrounding component. The third and fourth picture show the *List Pattern* and the *Matrix Pattern*. They arrange components as a list or a matrix. The last picture shows the combined usage of *List Pattern* and *Containment Pattern*.

In all these cases, the user simply has to specify what *pattern* he wants to use on what part of the model. E.g., for the *Graph Pattern*, he has to specify what component plays the role node, and what component the role edge. Of course he has the opportunity to add some functionality or to adapt these *patterns* to his own needs.

If, for any reason, the editor developer wants to use another relaxation method, he could substitute a subset of the attribute evaluation rules by a traditional constraint solver, e.g. by the constraint solver *QOCA* [13]. He could also use a graph layouter like *yFiles* [14]. Due to the modularity of the algorithm implementation this functionality may be added in a straightforward way.

Performance. In [3], Chok et al. presented an algorithm that is based on constraint-satisfaction. The algorithm makes use of the constraint solver *QOCA* [13]. They mention that the weak point of the algorithm is performance.

Due to the incremental nature of the algorithm, we are calling the layouter several times during user interaction. This has the consequence that an algorithm solely based on constraint satisfaction would not be applicable. For this reason we introduced a new algorithm. In our algorithm we provide the constraints as well as the solution to these constraints (attribute evaluation rules), and hence layout computation is less time consuming. Nevertheless, we will have to investigate the applicability on a larger scale. Up to now, some implementation details result in a rather bad performance. E.g. constraints and attribute evaluation rules are parsed each time the layouter is called. The implementation of a "real" layout generator is up to future work.

6   Related Work

Comparable model-driven tools, like *ATOM3* [15,16] or *GMF* [17], offer the possibility to use constraints for layout specification. As *DiaGen* supports *QOCA* constraints, we gained some experiences in the past. The layout that was defined via constraints often did not satisfy our needs. This is the reason why we came up with a new approach.

ATOM3 introduced *Event-Driven Grammars* [18]. As a side effect, they can be used to specify the layout for a visual language. As in our approach, rules in these grammars are triggered by user actions. New values for attributes are then calculated via attribute evaluation. Advantage of this approach is the elegant specification via Triple Graph Grammar rules. Our algorithm is based on a combination of constraints and attribute evaluation rules, and hence is more expressive.

Besides the constraint-based approach, it is common to use a standard layout algorithm, such as *Hierarchical Layout* or *Flow Layout*. E.g. the tools *ATOM3*,

GMF and *Tiger* [19] offer this possibility. This is primarily useful for graph-based visual languages, such as statecharts or activity diagrams. For other visual languages, another concept is needed. Standard layout algorithms are best suited for static layout. Especially for a dynamic layout, which is needed in combination with structured editing or free-hand editing, this concept is not sufficient. Some recent work investigated dynamic graph layout. E.g. Castelló et al. presented an algorithm for the static and interactive visualization of statecharts [20]. Purchase et al. started to investigate the question of how important it is to preserve the "mental map" [4], which is also essential for our work.

7   Conclusions and Prospects

The diagram editor generator framework DIAMETA makes use of meta-model-based language specifications and supports free-hand as well as structured editing. This paper described a performant and modular layout algorithm that meets the demands of this kind of editors. The fundamental concept of the algorithm is attribute evaluation combined with constraint satisfaction in the sense that constraints are used to activate particular attribute evaluation rules. This combination gives the layouter a lot of flexibility - the flexibility it needs to support free-hand as well as structured editing. By means of the example we saw that it is possible to define a layout algorithm for diagrams that supports the user during user interaction, and meanwhile grants the user plenty of freedom. Furthermore, a layouted diagram is displayed at any time. The layouter starts with an initial layout and performs minor changes to improve it. Layouting the diagram from scratch without an initial layout is also possible, but has not been examined yet.

The next step will be to establish some case studies. Our algorithm is not restricted to graph-based visual languages. Hence we will examine the applicability of our algorithm to graph-based as well as other visual languages. In this context we will examine performance in more detail.

Up to now constraints are defined by a very simple syntax. The next step will be to use *OCL* constraints instead, as they are defined in [5]. This extension should be feasible without major changes. Then it will be possible to use the *OCL* implementation for *EMF* [21] and use *EMF* for both, the model definition and the layout specification.

For our algorithm, we specify models via *EMF*. We plan to use the algorithm for the *MOF* version [11]. The integration of the layout algorithm into the MOF version should be straightforward. But as the MOF version of DiaMeta is still in a rather experimental stage, it was not done yet. We want to benefit from the additional concepts this version offers, e.g. redefinement of associations [22]. We also plan to include the layout algorithm into other model-driven tools, for example into *GMF* [17].

Another challenge we are going to research is the idea that the layouter may *"learn"* how to change the diagram in order to fulfill the requests of the user. This would mean that the specification could be shortened, and the editor would take care of all remaining matters. But until now, this is just imagination.

References

1. Minas, M.: Generating Meta-Model-Based Freehand Editors. In: Electronic Communications of the EASST, Proc. of 3rd International Workshop on Graph Based Tools (GraBaTs 2006). Satellite event of the 3rd International Conference on Graph Transformation, Natal, Brazil (2006)
2. Jung, M.: Ein Generator zur Entwicklung visueller Sprachen. PhD thesis, Universität Paderborn, Germany (2006)
3. Chok, S.S., Marriott, K., Paton, T.: Constraint-Based Diagram Beautification. In: VL 1999: Proceedings of the IEEE Symposium on Visual Languages, Washington, DC, US. IEEE Computer Society, Los Alamitos (1999)
4. Purchase, H.C., Hoggan, E., Görg, C.: How Important is the "Mental Map"? – an Empirical Investigation of a Dynamic Graph Layout Algorithm. In: Kaufmann, M., Wagner, D. (eds.) Graph Drawing, Karlsruhe, Germany, pp. 184–195. Springer, Heidelberg (2007)
5. OMG: Object Constraint Language (OCL) Specification, Version 2.0 (2006)
6. Minas, M.: Concepts and Realization of a Diagram Editor Generator Based on Hypergraph Transformation. Science of Computer Programming 44(2), 157–180 (2002)
7. Minas, M.: VisualDiaGen – A Tool for Visually Specifying and Generating Visual Editors. In: Pfaltz, J.L., Nagl, M., Böhlen, B. (eds.) AGTIVE 2003. LNCS, vol. 3062, pp. 398–412. Springer, Heidelberg (2004)
8. Budinsky, F., Brodsky, S.A., Merks, E.: Eclipse Modeling Framework. Pearson Education, London (2003)
9. Amelunxen, C., Königs, A., Rötschke, T., Schürr, A.: MOFLON: A Standard-Compliant Metamodeling Framework with Graph Transformations. In: Rensink, A., Warmer, J. (eds.) ECMDA-FA 2006. LNCS, vol. 4066, pp. 361–375. Springer, Heidelberg (2006)
10. OMG: Meta Object Facility (MOF) Core Specification, Version 2.0 (2006)
11. Minas, M.: Generating Visual Editors Based on Fujaba/MOFLON and DiaMeta. In: Giese, H., Westfechtel, B. (eds.) Proc. Fujaba Days 2006, Bayreuth, Germany, pp. 35–42 (2006)
12. Schmidt, C.: Generierung von Struktureditoren für anspruchsvolle visuelle Sprachen. PhD thesis, Universität Paderborn, Germany (2006)
13. Marriott, K., Chok, S.S.: QOCA: A Constraint Solving Toolkit for Interactive Graphical Applications. Constraints 7(3-4), 229–254 (2002)
14. Wiese, R., Eiglsperger, M., Kaufmann, M.: yFiles: Visualization and Automatic Layout of Graphs. In: Mutzel, P., Jünger, M., Leipert, S. (eds.) Graph Drawing, Vienna, Austria, pp. 453–454. Springer, Heidelberg (2002)
15. de Lara, J., Vangheluwe, H.: AToM3: A Tool for Multi-formalism and Meta-modelling. In: FASE 2002: Proceedings of the 5th International Conference on Fundamental Approaches to Software Engineering, London, UK, pp. 174–188. Springer, Heidelberg (2002)
16. Dubé, D.: Graph Layout for Domain-Specific Modeling. Master's thesis, McGill University, Montréal, Canada (2006)
17. Eclipse Consortium: Eclipse Graphical Modeling Framework (GMF) (2007), http://www.eclipse.org/gmf/
18. Guerra, E., de Lara, J.: Event-Driven Grammars: Towards the Integration of Metamodelling and Graph Transformation. In: ICGT, pp. 54–69 (2004)

19. Ehrig, K., Ermel, C., Hänsgen, S., Taentzer, G.: Generation of Visual Editors as Eclipse Plug-Ins. In: ASE 2005: Proceedings of the 20th IEEE/ACM international Conference on Automated software engineering, pp. 134–143. ACM Press, New York (2005)
20. Castelló, R., Mili, R., Tollis, I.G.: A Framework for the Static and Interactive Visualization of Statecharts (2002)
21. Damus, C.W.: Implementing Model Integrity in EMF with OCL. Eclipse Corner Articles (2007)
22. Amelunxen, C., Bichler, L., Schürr, A.: Codegenerierung für Assoziationen in MOF 2.0. In: Proceedings Modellierung 2004, Bonn, Gesellschaft für Informatik. Lecture Notes in Informatics, vol. P-45, pp. 149–168 (2004)

Domain Specific Languages with Graphical and Textual Views

Francisco Pérez Andrés[1], Juan de Lara[1], and Esther Guerra[2]

[1] Polytechnic School, Univ. Autónoma de Madrid, Spain
{francisco.perez,jdelara}@uam.es
[2] Computer Science Department, Univ. Carlos III de Madrid, Spain
eguerra@inf.uc3m.es

Abstract. We show our approach for the definition of Domain Specific Languages integrating both graphical and textual views. The approach is based on the meta-modelling concepts provided by the AToM^3 tool. In this way, the language designer starts building the meta-model of the complete language. Then, he can select (possibly overlapping) submodels of the meta-model to define the different diagram types (i.e. language viewpoints). By default, the viewpoint is assigned a graphical concrete syntax, although a textual one can also be given. This is performed by selecting (or creating) triple graph grammar rules to translate from the viewpoint meta-model to a DSL called *Textual* that contains the most common elements of textual languages (such as expressions or operators). From a *Textual* model, a parser is automatically generated, where the semantic actions of the EBNF grammar are graph grammar rules, derived from the viewpoint meta-model. In this way, the parsing results in a model conformant to the viewpoint meta-model, which can be seamlessly integrated with other graphical and textual views.

1 Introduction

Domain Specific Languages (DSLs) are becoming increasingly popular in order to capture high-level, powerful abstractions of well-studied application domains. They are at the core of recent software engineering paradigms, like *Model Driven Development*. In this paradigm, models are the primary asset, from which code is generated, and DSLs are frequently used in order to configure the variable part of the final application. Specialized formalisms also proliferate in areas like modelling and simulation [7].

The increasing complexity of the systems to be described makes a common practice to split their specification into smaller, more comprehensible parts that use the most appropriate notation. We call *Multi-View* DSLs [8] to DSLs which are made of a family of graphical and/or textual notations each one of them used to describe the system under a different perspective or viewpoint. A prominent example of this kind of languages is the UML (but for a broader domain) [23].

In many cases, the multi-view language contains some portions that are more naturally expressed using text, while some others are inherently graphical. For

A. Schürr, M. Nagl, and A. Zündorf (Eds.): AGTIVE 2007, LNCS 5088, pp. 82–97, 2008.

example the UML meta-model contains parts that are graphical (e.g. the portions corresponding to state machines or sequence diagrams), while others are more suitable for a textual representation (e.g. the part dealing with action semantics). Moreover, UML diagrams are usually enriched with constraints expressed in the textual language OCL [23], also defined through a MOF compliant meta-model, which in fact can be thought as a part of the UML infrastructure meta-model.

The meta-modelling tool AToM^3 [4] allows the description of *Domain Specific Visual Languages* (DSVLs) by means of meta-modelling and their manipulation by means of graph transformation. It has been recently enhanced in order to enable the definition of multi-view DSVLs [10]. This is done by first defining the meta-model of the complete language, and then selecting submodels of it (i.e. defining projections), corresponding to different viewpoints. The concrete syntax of the viewpoints (i.e. the visualization) is given by assigning graphical icons to each element in the meta-model.

In this paper we present an improvement to this approach with the possibility of defining textual views. Following the meta-model centric approach of AToM^3, this is done by translating the meta-model of the viewpoint into a DSVL that we call *Textual* (by means of a Triple Graph Transformation System, TGTS). This language contains the main concepts for the specification of textual concrete syntax, such as expressions, operators or functions. From a *Textual* model, a parser is automatically derived that, given a textual specification, generates a model conformant to the original viewpoint meta-model. This is done by means of semantic actions which are indeed graph transformation rules derived from the meta-model. This is similar to the classical concept of pair grammars [20]. From these specifications, a customized environment is generated that allows the creation of instances of the different (graphical or textual) viewpoints. The tool creates a repository (an instance of the complete language meta-model) in the background that contains the gluing of all the views the user has created. In this way, both the textual and the graphical views can be seamlessly integrated for later manipulations.

Paper organization. Section 2 introduces TGTSs. Section 3 overviews our approach for the definition of multi-view DSVLs. It introduces an example that is used throughout the paper, a DSL for object-oriented simulation [7]. Section 4 shows our approach for adding textual concrete syntax to meta-models, and for adding textual views to multi-view languages. Section 5 enhances the previous example with textual views. Section 6 compares with related research and section 7 ends with the conclusions.

2 Triple Graph Transformation

Graph transformation [6] is being intensively used for in-place transformations, like model animation and refactoring. In model-to-model transformation, a source model conforming to a source meta-model is transformed into a target model conforming to a different meta-model. For this kind of transformation, it is usually preferred a means to cleanly separate source and target models (as well as the meta-models), which allows establishing mappings between both models.

Triple graph grammars (TGGs) [22] were invented by Andy Schürr as a means to translate and synchronize two different graphs (called *source* and *target* graphs) related by an intermediate graph (the *correspondence* graph). The nodes in the correspondence graph have morphisms to nodes in the source and target graphs. This structure is called *triple graph* and is represented as $G = (G_s \leftarrow G_c \rightarrow G_t)$. TGG rules allow rewriting triple graphs, and are useful for model-to-model transformation, allowing incrementality and a certain degree of bi-directionality. This is possible as, starting from high-level, *declarative* TGG rules (like a *creation* grammar for a triple graph language) it is possible to derive so called *operational* rules with different purposes: source-to-target or target-to-source translation, incremental updates or model synchronization [15].

In [9] we used the idea of TGGs with a more advanced graph concept, demonstrating that it forms an adhesive HLR category and thus can be used with the DPO approach to graph transformation [6]. In particular, we allow morphisms from nodes in the correspondence graph to reach nodes or edges in the other two graphs, or to be undefined. We also introduced the concept of meta-model triple, which allows typing a triple graph. We took advantage of the inheritance hierarchy (of nodes and edges) in the meta-model triple to define abstract rules, where an element in a rule can get instantiated with elements in the host triple graph having a concrete subtype of the original element's classifier.

In this paper, we use TGG rules, but we are not interested in bi-directionality, thus we work with operational rules. In order to avoid confusion we call these systems Triple Graph Transformation Systems (TGTSs). As an example, Fig. 1 shows a TGTS rule. The rule checks for a top-class (i.e. with no superclass, controlled by NAC$_1$) in one of the graphs of the triple graph. If it is not related to an *Abstract_Expression* instance in the other graph (NAC$_2$), it creates one with the same name related with the class through a node of type *Class2AbstractExpression* in the correspondence graph.

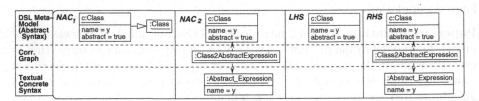

Fig. 1. Example TGTS Rule

3   Multi-view DSVLs in AToM^3

This section presents an overview of the AToM^3 approach for defining multi-view DSVLs. In the first step, the designer defines the complete language meta-model, and gives a graphical concrete syntax to its elements (i.e. icon-like appearance to classes and arrow-like to associations). Then, he defines the different viewpoints (diagram types) of the language. For each viewpoint, the multiplicity (i.e.

number of allowed diagrams of this type) as well as the meta-model should be specified. The latter must be a submodel of the complete meta-model. Thus, viewpoints are projections of the global meta-model containing a part of the classes, associations and attributes of classes and associations in it. A different concrete syntax (that overwrites the one given when defining the complete language meta-model) can be assigned to the elements in the viewpoint, and additional constraints can be given. Overlapping of different viewpoints is allowed, and consistency mechanisms based on TGTSs are provided by the tool [8]. A special viewpoint called "repository" contains the whole meta-model and is used for consistency checking purposes.

Fig. 2 shows the definition of a multi-view DSVL in the object-oriented continuous simulation domain (i.e. a continuous simulation language, CSL). This kind of languages is made of classes representing entities in the system under study. Classes in a CSL may have properties, whose time evolution is specified by some simulation formalism. Traditionally, this specification has been made with textual equations. In our example CSL, the evolution is specified by combining state automata and textual equations. Window 1 at the background in Fig. 2 shows its complete meta-model, which defines simulation classes (class *CSL_Class*) that can be connected through binary associations (association *CSL_association*) and may form inheritance hierarchies (through association *CSL_parent*). Associations in our CSL have role names and multiplicities for the endpoints. CSL_Classes may have properties (i.e. attributes, class *CSL_Property*) with a name, a type and an initial value.

The behaviour of classes (abstract class *CSL_Behaviour*) may be represented in the form of state machines (*CSL_StateAutomaton*) or equations (*CSL_Equation*). State automata contain states related through transitions that can be fired when one boolean property of the corresponding class becomes true. Equations are made of a left and a right hand side, both containing expressions (abstract class *CSL_Expression*) made of binary operators (*CSL_BinOperator*), functions with two (*CSL_Function2Parameters*) or three parameters (*CSL_Function3Parameters*), class properties and numeric values (*CSL_Value*). Operators and functions have an enumeration attribute *value* with the possible operators and functions. We have included common arithmetic binary operators like "+", "-", "*" and "/". For functions with two parameters, we have included as an example the "integral" function, which takes two expressions representing the initial value and the expression to be integrated. For functions with three parameters, we have included "instate", which returns one of two expressions depending if the class is in a certain state (defined by a state machine), given by the third parameter.

The tool shown in window 2 of Fig. 2 allows the declaration of the DSVL viewpoints. For the example, we have declared four viewpoints to describe the structure (classes, inheritance relations, associations and references to the behaviours they implement), the class properties, the state machines and the equations. Arrows from each viewpoint to the repository viewpoint contain automatically generated TGTS rules that will be used in order to build the latter from the viewpoint instances in the generated environment. Arrows from the repository to the

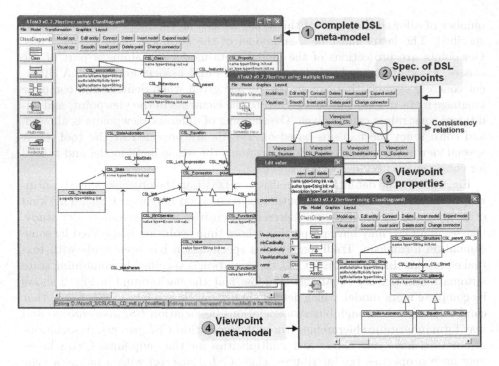

Fig. 2. Defining a Multi-View DSVL

viewpoints contain TGTS rules that propagate changes from the repository to the views when necessary. Thus, the working scheme of the final multi-view environment is similar to the model-view-controller pattern. Window 3 shows the attributes assigned to the structure viewpoint, such as its name and multiplicity (*minCardinality* and *maxCardinality*). One of the attributes is the viewpoint meta-model (shown in window 4), which is a submodel of the whole meta-model in window 1.

Fig. 3 shows (in window 1) the generated environment from the previous definition, which allows building instances of the defined viewpoints. For example, windows 3 and 4 show the editing of a state machine and an equation, respectively. Note that in the equation model we use class *CSL_Property* without attributes *pr_type* and *initial_value*, as these make sense when declaring the properties but not when using them. Moreover, the name of a property is keyword (i.e. unique value) in property diagrams but not in equation diagrams or in the repository. The reason is that the properties of a class are declared in property diagrams – the fact that only one class can be included is a constraint of the viewpoint – and names should be unique. On the contrary, in the repository, different classes may have equal names for attributes. Moreover, in one equation the name of a property can be referenced several times. Note also that in the equations viewpoint, we have changed the visualization of states and properties with respect to other viewpoints.

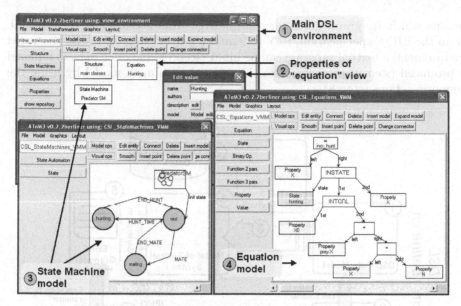

Fig. 3. Generated Multi-View Environment

Notice that in order to describe an equation a much more natural approach is to use a textual notation. Next section presents an improvement to the previous ideas in order to define multi-view DSLs supporting also textual viewpoints.

4   Specifying Viewpoints with Textual Concrete Syntax

This section presents our approach for providing a textual concrete syntax to meta-models. The overall architecture is shown in Fig. 4. The DSL designer starts by defining the language structure by means of a meta-model in step 1. If he wants to assign the DSL (or some of its viewpoints) a textual concrete syntax, he follows steps 2-9. With this purpose, we have defined a DSL called *Textual* with the most common concepts of textual languages (see section 4.1). In order to create a textual concrete syntax, a model conformant to the *Textual* meta-model should be provided (step 4 in the figure), together with a mapping to the DSL meta-model. This can be seen as annotations (expressed in *Textual*) for the DSL meta-model elements in order to produce the parser. This is similar to the concept of *model marking* proposed by the MDA [17]. The designer can either build the *Textual* model manually (together with mappings to the meta-model) or it can be automated with the help of predefined transformations (steps 2 and 3 in the figure) in the form of TGTSs (see section 4.2). In both cases, the target *Textual* model contains mappings to the DSL meta-model elements from which the textual elements are derived. For this we use the concept of TGTS explained before. Once the textual model is obtained, an EBNF grammar for PLY (a lex-yacc parsing tool for Python)[19] is generated (step 5) using a code generator we have built (see section 4.3). The grammar contains semantic actions which are graph grammar rules derived from the original meta-model. From the EBNF specification, PLY generates a parser (step 6). In the generated environment, a textual program can be input (step 7), and once parsed, a model is produced (step 9) conformant to the original DSL meta-model by using the semantic actions (step 8).

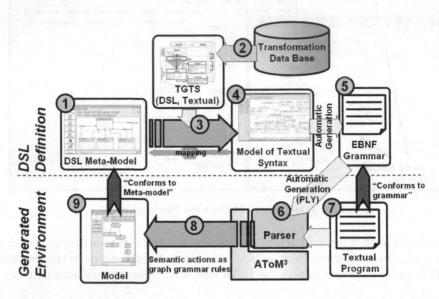

Fig. 4. Architecture for Assigning Textual Concrete Syntax to Meta-Models

Rationale of the Approach. The proposed process is very different from the one for textual languages, where the starting point is the definition of an EBNF grammar. On the contrary, we follow a meta-model centric approach, more in the style of the MDA paradigm [17], where the EBNF grammar is automatically generated from a higher-level model. According to [14], a number of arguments can be given to support this approach. First, in DSL engineering, one usually starts by working in the DSL abstract syntax, i.e., the meta-model. Later, it is decided whether a graphical or textual concrete syntax (or both) is appropriate. Starting with an EBNF from the beginning means starting from the concrete syntax. Second, the structure of the abstract syntax tree (AST) produced from parsing is not usually formally defined. This presents problems if such AST has to be integrated with a multi-view DSL, where other viewpoints are conformant to a meta-model. Certainly, we could leave the DSL designer to write the EBNF grammar (this in fact can be done in our approach by manually modifying the grammar produced in step 5). However, our aim is to provide higher-level mechanisms and automate the process, so that ideally, the DSL designer only has to "push a button" to obtain the textual concrete syntax (i.e. all steps in the definition of the DSL in Fig. 4 are automatic).

The remaining of this section explains these steps in detail. First, subsection 4.1 introduces our *Textual* DSL. Subsection 4.2 explains the automation of the transformation from a meta-model into a *Textual* model. Subsection 4.3 explains how the parser is generated. Finally, subsection 4.4 shows how these ideas have been integrated with our multi-view approach.

4.1   The "Textual" DSL

The main idea for providing a textual concrete syntax to a DSL is to associate a Textual model to the DSL meta-model. The *Textual* DSL contains the most common concepts of textual languages. Its meta-model is shown in Fig. **??** and also considers the requirements for building a parser, e.g. the need for a grammar axiom and the representation of the elements making a textual expression (tokens in the parser), which are instances of *Regular Expression* subclasses.

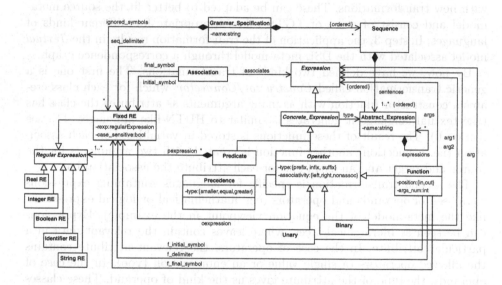

Fig. 5. Meta-Model of the *Textual* DSL

A valid *Textual* model consists of a unique instance of class *Grammar_Specification*, which specifies a name for the textual syntax, and represents the axiom in the textual parser; a set of symbols to be ignored in the parsing process such as spaces or tabs (*ignored_symbols* relation); and an ordered sequence of *Sequence* objects. These represent a sequence of expressions detached by a delimiter, given by a fixed regular expression (*Fixed RE*, through association *seq_delimiter*). Expressions can be concrete (*Concrete_Expression*, an abstract class) or abstract (*Abstract_Expression*). The latter can group different *Concrete_Expressions* under the same type. *Concrete_Expressions* can be *Predicates* or *Operators*, and are always represented by *Regular Expressions*, but *Operators* have always a fixed representation (*Fixed RE*). Depending on the number of arguments, an *Operator* can be *Unary*, *Binary* or *Function*. Moreover, it is possible to specify the operator's precedence, associativity (left, right and nonassoc), and its location with respect to operands (prefix, infix, suffix). Operands are instances of *Expression* or of its subclasses. *Predicates* are represented by one or more predefined *Regular Expressions* (i.e. concrete subtypes of it). Note that it is a parser requirement that there is only one instance of each type of *Regular Expression*, apart from *Fixed RE*. However, that does not mean that it is only possible to assign one different subtype of *Regular Expression* to each different *Predicate*.

4.2   Transformation into "Textual"

The process of generating the *Textual* model associated to the DSL is shown in steps 2 and 3 of Fig. 4. In step 2 the designer selects a *Textual transformation* among the ones predefined in the data-base. This data-base can be extended with new transformations. These can be adapted to better fit the source meta-model and consist of a set of TGTS rules, appropriate for different kinds of languages. In step 3, the application of the transformation results in the *Textual* model associated with the DSL meta-model through a correspondence graph.

By now, we have defined two kinds of transformations. The first one is a generic transformation called *Constructor/Connector*, which for each class creates a constructor function with as many arguments as attributes the class has (the textual language it generates is similar to HUTN-like languages [11], see section 6). The result of these functions is stored in variables. For each association (i.e. connection) another function is created with two arguments for the source and target and an extra one for each attribute the association has.

The second transformation is specific for languages containing expressions composed of operands and operators (e.g. mathematical or logical expressions, like the meta-model of the equation viewpoint in the example). Expressions can be seen as hierarchical trees, where leaves contain the relevant data in a particular attribute. In the case of operators, the relevant attribute contains the allowed operators (a single value or an enumeration type). In the case of operands, the type of the attribute gives us the kind of operand. These classes can also have connections with other classes (usually the root expression class), which determine whether they are considered predicates (zero connections) or operators (one or more connections).

This way, this second transformation creates *Abstract_Expressions* for each abstract class which is not a leaf of the hierarchical tree, and *Predicates*, *Unary Operators*, *Binary Operators* or *Functions*, depending on the number of output connections. These languages frequently associate expressions, so we have included a rule to generate an instance of *Association* over the main *Abstract_Expression*.

We now show some sample rules for this transformation. For clarity, we have used a simplified concrete syntax for the DSL meta-model and not the abstract syntax of the UML meta-model (e.g. we include inheritance relations, instead of meta-class "generalization" and so forth). The first rule was shown in Fig. 1 and creates an abstract expression in the *Textual* model for each abstract class in the DSL meta-model. The upper rule in Fig. 6 creates a unary operator for each class in the DSL meta-model which has a unique association (NAC$_1$) and which is the child of a class related to an abstract expression. The rule at the bottom creates a semantic action (i.e. a graph grammar rule) for each possible value of the unary operator (i.e. for each value of its x property). Each semantic action is associated to the mapping in the correspondence graph, and identified by attribute *order*. The rule implementing the action semantics has been depicted using a compact notation with its LHS and RHS together (the created elements are marked as "{add}"). It creates an instance of the class "y" (i.e. the class with role unary operator), and initializes the value of the attribute (named x). Moreover, the generated semantic action also connects the unary operator to the appropriate object (an instance of the class connected with class "y"). The semantic actions, stored in the correspondence graph nodes, will be used to build the parser. An example of generated semantic action is shown in Fig. 9(b). Note that in the correspondence graph, we may have nodes with attributes as well as relations between them. Therefore the implicit mappings of transformation language proposals like QVT [21] are not enough for us.

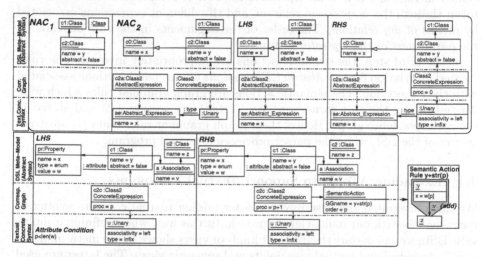

Fig. 6. Some TGTS Rules for Translating DSLs with Expressions

In general, it is not possible to ensure that the generated *Textual* model has all the necessary information to generate the parser. The transformation only guarantees that a valid instance of the *Textual* meta-model is created, with valid mappings to the DSL meta-model. It usually needs to be completed by hand with some details, e.g. to define the precedence between operators.

4.3 Generating the Parser

We generate a PLY parser specification [19] from the *Textual* model in three steps. The first one builds the lexer specification, which recognizes the elements of the language. It deals with the subclasses of *Regular Expression*. For each existing *Fixed RE*, a token with its regular expression is added to the lexer, except for the ones connected with an *ignored_symbols* association. Two new tokens with values

True and *False* are created if the *Boolean RE* class is instantiated. Finally, the instantiation of the remainder regular expressions generates specific functions to recognize every token of their respective data types.

The second step generates the EBNF rules for the parser specification. It starts processing the *Grammar_Specification* object, for which a rule dealing with the ordered sequence of expressions is produced. Afterwards, sequences are processed regarding the delimiter symbol between their expressions. These symbols are tokens previously generated in step one. Next, every *Abstract_Expression* is evaluated taking into account its different types of connections. If it has one *associates* relation, it means that the *Abstract_Expression* allows associativity, so a new rule with the association tokens surrounding the *Abstract_Expression* is created. If it has a *type* relation, there is at least one *Concrete_Expression* associated with this *Abstract_Expression*, and a rule is generated depending on the type of the *Concrete_Expression*. If it is a *Predicate*, the token associated with it (the *Regular Expression* connected through *pexpression* relation) is included in the rule. If it is an *Operator*, the rule is composed of the associated token through the *oexpression* relation, and the different expressions associated by means of *arg* relations. The order of the arguments in the rule depends on the parameters of the *Operator* instance.

In the third step, the semantic actions are appropriately invoked. The rules created for relation *type* on *Abstract_Expressions* take semantic actions associated with their execution. The semantic actions are graph grammar rules which were derived during the transformation into *Textual* (see section 4.2) and stored in the correspondence graph. Hence, these graph grammar rules build the abstract syntax of the DSL when the parser processes a textual program.

4.4 Extending AToM^3 to Support Textual Viewpoints

We have integrated the described ideas for adding textual concrete syntax to meta-models with our multi-view approach. In this way, when defining a multi-view DSL, we can declare the different kinds of views shown in the meta-model in Fig. 7: graphical and textual viewpoints and semantic views. The latter are used as a semantic domain for analysis by defining a TGTS and some analysis methods [8]. Viewpoints have consistency relations (*view_consistency* association), usually between each defined viewpoint and a special viewpoint called repository (see section 3). In the present work, we have extended the meta-model with class *TextualViewpoint*, which adds attributes *textualModel* and *transfGrammar*. The former is a triple graph that relates the viewpoint meta-model and the textual model. The latter is a TGTS that generates such triple graph.

The "Views" tool shown in window 1 of Fig. 8 has been generated from the previous meta-model by using the AToM^3 code generation capabilities (i.e., the model in this window conforms to the meta-model in Fig. 7). The generated tool was completed with hand-made code, and integrated into AToM^3 itself.

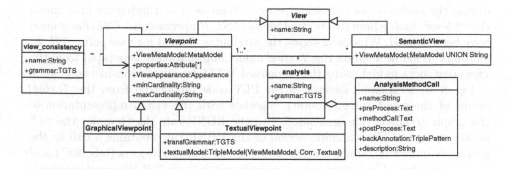

Fig. 7. Meta-Model with the Different kinds of Views of Multi-View DSLs

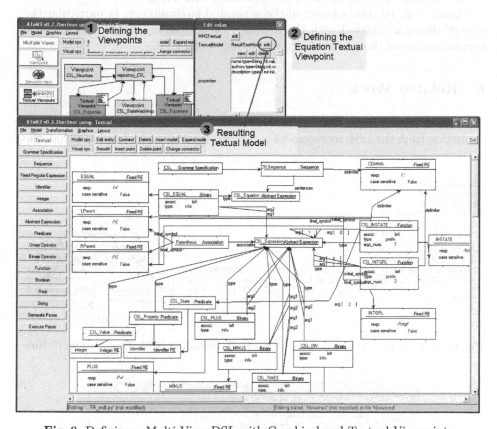

Fig. 8. Defining a Multi-View DSL with Graphical and Textual Viewpoints

5   Adding Textual Viewpoints to the Example

In this section, we improve the example of section 3 in order to consider textual views for the equations and the properties diagrams. Fig. 8 shows a screenshot during the environment definition process. Window 1 at the background shows the "Views" tool, where two textual views (*CSL_Properties* and *CSL_Equations*) have been defined. Window 2 shows the attributes defined for viewpoint *CSL_Equations*. Window 3 shows the *Textual* model automatically generated from the viewpoint meta-model, using the predefined TGTS for expression-like languages.

Fig. 9 shows a small excerpt of the PLY code (generated from the *Textual* model of the equations viewpoint), together with the visual representation of the graph grammar rule associated with the EBNF rule that handles the "+" binary operator. The semantic action of the EBNF rule contains a call to the graph grammar rule, which receives two *CSL_Expression* objects (labelled 1 and 2) as parameters. These parameters are assigned the two *CSL_Expression* objects from the RHS of the EBNF rule (p[1] and p[3]). The EBNF rule returns the created binary operator by the graph grammar rule (ret[3]).

Finally, Fig. 10 shows a part of the generated environment, in particular the control dialog associated with the textual view for the equations. It shows the textual syntax of the model shown in window 4 of Fig. 3.

6   Related Work

This paper greatly improves our previous work in [5], where we proposed a transformation from the DSL meta-model to a much lower-level meta-model than the

```
...
reserved_map = {}
tokens = ()
## INTGRL
tokens+=('INTGRL')
t_INTGRL = r'INTGRL'
reserved_map[r'Intgrl']='INTGRL'
...
## TX_type: TX_Binary
def p_CSL_Expression_3(p):
  'CSL_Expression: CSL_Expression PLUS CSL_Expression'
  ret=CSL_BinOperator1.exec(at3,at3.ASGroot,
                 [(1,p[1]), (2,p[3])])
  p[0]=ret[3]
...
```

(a)   (b)

Fig. 9. (a) Excerpt of the Generated PLY EBNF Rules (b) "CSL_BinOperator1" Rule

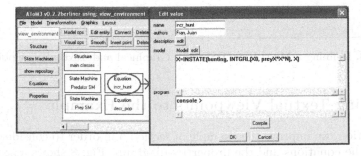

Fig. 10. Editing a Textual View in the Generated Environment

one shown in Fig. 5. In the present work, we have different predefined transformations depending on the source DSL. These transformations are expressed using TGTSs, and the semantic actions are graph grammar rules, automatically derived. Finally, the approach is integrated in a general framework for the definition of multi-view DSLs with graphical and textual views.

Many researchers have studied the problem of converting programs to models and vice versa. Note however that most of them are targeted to single-view DSLs. For example, in [1], an algorithm is given for converting in the two directions, but it is not adaptable to the source DSL. The work of [12] is similar to ours, as they define a textual DSL called TCS for defining the concrete syntax of meta-models. TCS is made of a number of templates, similar to the concepts in our Textual DSL. Whereas TCS specifications are written by hand, and may get complicated when the meta-model is not a tree, we provide TGTS rules for the partial automation of this task. Their approach is bidirectional, while this is up to future work in our case.

MontiCore [16] allows an integrated definition of abstract and textual concrete syntax by textual grammars enhanced with meta-modelling concepts like associations between nodes and inheritance. This approach does not use explicit meta-models and, as its target are textual DSLs, it could be difficult to integrate with languages combining graphics and text.

In [14], the DSL meta-model is transformed into a *Parse Model* (PM), a lower-level meta-model that contains auxiliary elements, e.g. to represent references. A transformation is given to derive EBNF rules from the PM. This transformation can be tuned by defining a property file. While the approach is similar, the intermediate model we use is conformant to the *Textual* DSL, which provides annotations on the roles the original meta-model elements have to play in the EBNF grammar. This is partially done in [14] by using the property file. Also, we provide different TGTSs to handle different kinds of meta-models, depending also on the intended style of the final textual concrete syntax.

Other approaches [18] are based on the UML Human-Usable Textual Notation (HUTN) [11]. HUTN was designed to provide a user-friendly textual syntax to MOF models, and can be configured in a limited way by creating instances of the *HutnConfig* meta-model. Our approach is more flexible, allowing a higher degree of customization to the source DSL by an explicit definition of a TGTS library from which the Textual models are generated. In fact, one of our TGTSs is able to generate HUTN-like textual notations. Finally, in [13] an EBNF approach was used to define both the textual and the graphical views.

A related issue is the consistency of code and models, which is treated using distributed graph transformation in [3]. In our case, issues regarding the updating of a textual view, and the subsequent modification of the underlying model (and the repository) are subject to further investigation.

According to [2], our approach can be seen as a bridge between the modelware and the grammarware technical spaces. This way, we can see our TGTSs as projectors at the M3 level, since the transformations are defined at the meta-metamodel level.

A hot topic in Model-Driven Development is the QVT language (Queries/ View/ Transformation) [21]. Instead, we have used TGTSs due to its formal nature, because it allows more control of the mappings (i.e. the correspondence graph is a real graph), and also as it allowed to reuse the transformation engine of AToM³.

7   Conclusions and Future Work

We have presented our approach to the definition of multi-view DSLs with graphical and textual views. A meta-model of the whole language has to be defined, and then submodels of it have to be selected for the different viewpoints. In the case of a textual view, the viewpoint meta-model is transformed into a *Textual* model, from which a parser is automatically derived and integrated with the generated multi-view DSL environment. The translation into *Textual* is automated using TGTS rules, and later completed by hand. We have illustrated these concepts with a language in the object-oriented simulation domain.

Our approach is original because: a) provides a library of transformations for different kinds of DSLs; b) we express the transformation to the textual syntax by means of TGTSs, which improves understanding and maintainability of the transformation; c) the semantic actions of the EBNF rules are graph grammar rules, which also makes them more understandable and maintainable; d) our approach is integrated in a framework for the definition of multi-view DSLs.

There are some open issues in this approach. For example, a viewpoint meta-model may include constraints. In this case, when the parser creates the model, these meta-model constraints should be evaluated, and appropriate errors should be given in the context of the textual program. This is also an open issue in [12]. We are also working in defining additional TGTSs, applicable to other kinds of DSLs. By now, our approach works in one direction, from text to models. It is up to future work to make it bidirectional. By now we obtain view consistency, but for textual views only at the level of the underlying models. Scalability issues that may arise with bigger DSLs are also under investigation.

Acknowledgements. Work supported by the Spanish Ministry of Education and Science, projects MOSAIC (TSI2005-08225-C07-06) and MODUWEB (TIN2006-09678). We would like to thank the referees for their very useful comments.

References

1. Alanen, M., Porres, I.: A Relation Between Context-Free Grammars and Meta Object Facility Metamodels. Tech. Rep. 606, TUCS, Turku, Finland (2004)
2. Bézivin, J., Devedzic, V., Djuric, D., Favreau, J.M., Gasevic, D., Jouault, F.: An M3-Neutral infrastructure for bridging model engineering and ontology engineering. In: Proc. INTEROP-ESA, pp. 159–171 (2005)
3. Bottoni, P., Parisi-Presicce, F., Pulcini, S., Taentzer, G.: Maintaining Coherence between Models with Distributed Rules: from Theory to Eclipse. In: Proc. GT-VMT 2006 (2006)

4. de Lara, J., Vangheluwe, H.: AToM³: A Tool for Multi-Formalism Modelling and Meta-Modelling. In: Kutsche, R.-D., Weber, H. (eds.) FASE 2002. LNCS, vol. 2306, pp. 174–188. Springer, Heidelberg (2002)

5. de Lara, J., Guerra, E.: Towards the Uniform Manipulation of Visual and Textual Languages in AToM³. In: Proc. PROLE 2003, pp. 45–58 (2003)

6. Ehrig, H., Ehrig, K., Prange, U., Taentzer, G.: Fundamentals of Algebraic Graph Transformation. Springer, Heidelberg (2006)

7. Fishwick, P.: Simulation Model Design and Execution: Building Digital Worlds. Prentice-Hall, Englewood Cliffs (1995)

8. Guerra, E., de Lara, J.: Model View Management with Triple Graph Transformation Systems. In: Corradini, A., Ehrig, H., Montanari, U., Ribeiro, L., Rozenberg, G. (eds.) ICGT 2006. LNCS, vol. 4178, pp. 351–366. Springer, Heidelberg (2006)

9. Guerra, E., de Lara, J.: Event-Driven Grammars: Relating Abstract and Concrete Levels of Visual Languages. Journal on Software and Systems Modelling 6(3), 317–347 (2007)

10. Guerra, E., de Lara, J.: Meta-Modelling and Graph Transformation for the Definition of Multi-View Visual Languages. In: Visual Languages for Interactive Computing: Definitions and Formalization. Idea Group Publishers (2007)

11. HUTN spec., http://www.omg.org/cgi-bin/doc?formal/2004-08-01

12. Jouault, F., Bézivin, J., Kurtev, I.: TCS: A DSL for the Specification of Textual Concrete Syntaxes in Model Engineering. In: Proc. GPCE 2006, pp. 249–254 (2006)

13. Klein, P., Schürr, A.: Constructing SDEs with the IPSEN Meta Environment. In: Proc. 8th IEEE Conf. on Software Engineering Environments, pp. 2–10 (1997)

14. Kleppe, A.: Towards the Generation of a Text-Based IDE from a Language Metamodel. In: Akehurst, D.H., Vogel, R., Paige, R.F. (eds.) ECMDA-FA. LNCS, vol. 4530, pp. 114–129. Springer, Heidelberg (2007)

15. Königs, A., Schürr, A.: Tool Integration with Triple Graph Grammars - A Survey. ENTCS 148, 113–150 (2006)

16. Krahm, H., Rumpe, B., Völkel, S.: Integrated Definition of Abstract and Concrete Syntax for Textual Languages. In: Engels, G., Opdyke, B., Schmidt, D.C., Weil, F. (eds.) MODELS 2007. LNCS, vol. 4735, pp. 286–300. Springer, Heidelberg (2007)

17. Mellor, S., Scott, K., Uhl, A., Weise, D.: MDA Distilled: Principles of Model-Driven Architecture. Addison Wesley, Reading (2004)

18. Muller, P.-A., Hassenforder, M.: HUTN as a Bridge between Modelware and Grammarware – An Experience Report. In: Proc. WiSME 2005 at MoDELS 2005 (2005)

19. Web page of PLY Lex-yacc, http://www.dabeaz.com/ply/

20. Pratt, T.W.: Pair grammars, graph languages, and string-to-graph translations. Journal of Computer and System Sciences 5, 560–595 (1971)

21. QVT specification, http://www.omg.org/docs/ptc/05-11-01.pdf

22. Schürr, A.: Specification of Graph Translators with Triple Graph Grammars. In: Mayr, E.W., Schmidt, G., Tinhofer, G. (eds.) WG 1994. LNCS, vol. 903, pp. 151–163. Springer, Heidelberg (1995)

23. UML spec., http://www.omg.org/technology/documents/formal/uml.htm

Generating Domain-Specific Model Editors with Complex Editing Commands

Gabriele Taentzer[1], André Crema[2], René Schmutzler[2], and Claudia Ermel[2]

[1] Philipps-Universität Marburg, Germany
taentzer@mathematik.uni-marburg.de
[2] Technische Universität Berlin, Germany
{crema,reneschm,lieske}@cs.tu-berlin.de

Abstract. Domain specific modeling languages are of increasing importance for the development of software and other systems. Meta tools are needed to support rapid development of domain-specific solutions. Using the Eclipse Graphical Modeling Framework (GMF), modeling languages are defined by providing a meta model using the MOF/EMF approach. Up to now, GMF provides basic editing commands only. It does not support the definition of complex editing commands which would allow e.g. to insert a complex structure into a diagram in one step. As practical tool support for the design and generation of visual editors with complex editing operations based on graph transformation, an extended version of GMF has been developed and is presented in this paper.

1 Introduction

In software system development, domain-specific visual notations are increasingly used and need a tool environment consisting of visual editors, simulators, model transformers, etc. Several ECLIPSE projects head for a meta technology to define domain-specific modeling languages. The ECLIPSE Modeling Framework (EMF) [5] can be used to define the underlying models of visual editors. Given an EMF model, a set of Java classes for manipulating the model and a basic, tree based editor for model instances are generated. The generated classes provide CRUD functionality for model elements, i.e. model elements can be created, read, updated, and deleted. To realize a graphical editor, the editor code may be hand-coded on the basis of GEF, the ECLIPSE Graphical Editor Framework [3], which offers basic and advanced editor functionalities.As another alternative, a visual editor may be generated using the *Graphical Modeling Framework (GMF)* [4] which started recently as Eclipse technology subproject aiming at providing an infrastructure for generating visual editors in ECLIPSE. In essence, GMF forms a bridge between EMF and GEF, whereby a diagram definition is linked to a domain model which serves as input to the generation of a visual editor.

GMF-generated editors offer basic editing commands to create, edit, move and delete single model elements (basic editing). Graph transformation-based editors (see e.g. TIGER [6]) show that the generation of editors with complex editing

A. Schürr, M. Nagl, and A. Zündorf (Eds.): AGTIVE 2007, LNCS 5088, pp. 98–103, 2008.
© Springer-Verlag Berlin Heidelberg 2008

commands is also possible. Editing e.g. control flow graphs, there might be editing commands available which insert or delete a complete decision structure in one step.

In the following, we present how meta model-based editor design and generation performed by GMF, can be extended by graph transformation concepts to define and generate complex editing commands to be used in GMF-generated visual editors.

2 Examples for Complex Editing Commands

Activity diagrams are used to describe the control flow within a system, based on activities. In the following, we consider the editor generation process for a simple variant of activity diagrams consisting of start, end, decision and simple activities.

The visual editor generated by pure GMF (without the extension for complex editing commands) is shown in Fig. 4 (a). It contains an example for an activity diagram with different kinds of activities mentioned above. We used the usual design process for visual editors offered by GMF. Considering the palette on the right of the generated editor, we notice that creation commands for each of the model elements are offered. Moreover, the context menus contain commands for editing and deleting model elements. Up to now, there is no way to design and generate more complex editing commands.

Complex editing commands for activity diagrams can help to easily edit the diagrams in mind. For example, a well-formed activity diagram contains at least one start and one end activity. Moreover, well-formed activity diagrams contain decision branches which are explicitly merged by a decision activity, only. An example for a well-formed activity diagram is shown in Fig. 4.

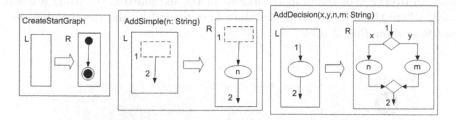

Fig. 1. Specification of complex editing commands

Fig. 1 shows the before and after patterns for sample complex editing commands. We define one editing command *CreateStartGraph* to generate the start diagram which consists of exactly one start and one end activity, connected by a next-relation. This command is executable in the empty editor panel only. Editing command *AddSimple* inserts a simple activity after another activity, where ⌐_⌐ is a symbol for an abstract figure which stands for one of the

following concrete figures   ● (start activity) or ⬭ (simple activity).
The name of the new activity is given by input parameter n. Please note that
the source activity of next-relation 2 changes after insertion. Editing command
AddDecision replaces a simple activity by a decision activity with two branches.
Each branch contains one simple activity. The branches are merged afterwards by
another decision activity. The *AddDecision* command has four input parameters:
two arc inscriptions x and y, and two names n and m for the new simple activities
in both branches.

3   Extending GMF by Complex Editing Commands

In this section, we discuss how GMF-based editor generation can be extended
by graph transformation concepts supporting the specification of complex editor
commands.

3.1   Extension of the GMF Development Environment

A language model is described in GMF by defining an EMF model, the so-called
domain model, while the layout is specified in the *graphical definition model*. Now,
an additional visual editor for defining complex editing commands is provided,
where EMF transformation rules for complex editing commands can be defined
as transformation rules based on the domain model. This step is optional. The
tooling definition model is used to define the commands for the editor palette.
After having defined all these models separately, the *mapping model* establishes
a connection between them and is the input for the generation process. Fig. 2
shows an overview of the design workflow in the extended GMF using a dashboard, where the original GMF workflow is extended by the specification of a
Transformation Rule Model.

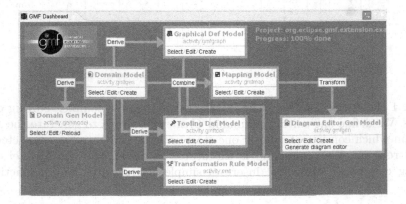

Fig. 2. GMF dashboard extended by transformation rule model for editing commands

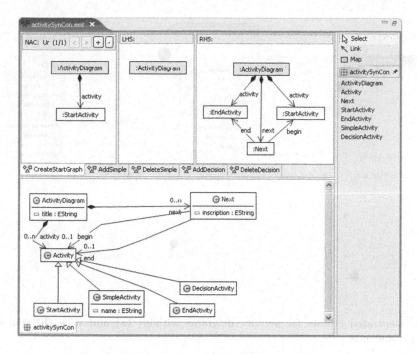

Fig. 3. Tool environment for EMF transformation

Before discussing the specification of concrete editing commands, we present the EMF model transformation approach [1] used to manipulate the underlying EMF models. The transformation concept is closely related to algebraic graph transformation. The main reason for this design decision is the basic opportunity to validate EMF model transformations on the basis of graph transformation. Basically, an EMF transformation is a rule-based modification of an EMF source model resulting in an EMF target model. Both, the EMF source and target models are typed over an EMF core model. All modifications are made in-place, i.e. the source model is not copied before modification. For efficient execution of model transformations, the rules can be translated to Java code to be integrated into generated EMF classes. Fig. 3 shows a designer for EMF transformations where the underlying meta model is depicted at the bottom and one of the transformation rules, i.e. a rule for inserting a start diagram, is shown at the top. A negative application condition ensures that this rule is applied only to the empty activity diagram. After having defined all editing commands needed analogously, all those which should show up in the palette have to be identified in the GMF tooling model, and the GMF mapping model is extended by the definition of the transformation model.

3.2   Extension of the GMF Runtime Environment

The editor generation process in the extended GMF version results in an editor as shown in Fig. 4 (b) where default editing operations as well as specifically

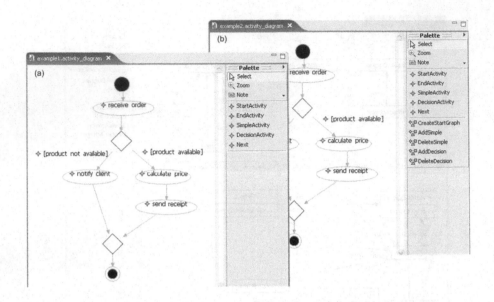

Fig. 4. Generated editors for activity diagrams without (a) and with (b) complex editing commands

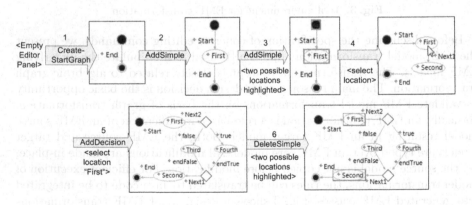

Fig. 5. Editing steps using complex editing operations in extended GMF

designed ones are provided by the palette. Please note that the editor designer selects those commands to be included in the palette.

We describe the usage of the generated editor in the extended GMF version along our running example. A sequence of steps to create our sample activity diagram is shown in Fig. 5. In step 1, we start with an empty editor panel and select command *CreateStartGraph* from the palette. Immediately, the start activity diagram appears in the editor panel. Step 2 selects command *AddSimple* to add a simple activity node. This node is added after the start activity, because the negative application condition of the rule forbids to insert an activity node after a final node. Since we have only one non-final activity node, the location to apply this command is unique in the current situation. In Step 3, we select command *AddSimple* again, but this time it can be applied at two locations: the new activity node can be inserted either after the start activity, again, or after the new simple activity node named "First". Thus, instead of applying the rule, the editor now highlights the two possible locations. In step 4, one of the highlighted nodes is selected per mouse click, and the command is applied accordingly. Step 5 combines two atomic steps: command *AddDecision* is selected, and the activity nodes "First" and "Second" are clicked on to specify between which two activity nodes the complete decision structure is to be inserted. Afterwards, in step 5, command DeleteSimple is selected in the palette. This leads to two activity nodes being highlighted, which may be deleted by the rule.

4 Conclusion

In this paper, we presented an approach generating visual editors by GMF extended by complex editing commands. Thus, using pure GMF, a visual editor can be generated which offers basic editor commands for each model element only. For the generation of complex editor commands an additional model is needed. We use EMF transformation rules to formulate commands based on the given domain model. To the best of our knowledge, no other meta CASE tool based on meta models offers the possibility to define complex editing commands.

Besides pure editing commands, also model optimizations such as model refactorings, may be realized with the proposed approach. Moreover, simulation of behaviour models can be defined by this approach. Thus, this work can be considered as a starting point for the generation of powerful and flexible domain-specific visual editors in Eclipse.

References

1. Biermann, E., Ehrig, K., Köhler, C., Kuhns, G., Taentzer, G., Weiss, E.: Graphical Definition of In-Place Transformations in the Eclipse Modeling Framework. In: Model Driven Engineering Languages and Systems, 9th International Conference, MoDELS 2006. LNCS. Springer, Heidelberg (2006), http://tfs.cs.tu-berlin.de/emftrans
2. Eclipse Consortium, Eclipse (2006), http://www.eclipse.org
3. Eclipse Consortium, Eclipse Graphical Editing Framework (GEF) (2006), http://www.eclipse.org/gef
4. Eclipse Consortium, Eclipse Graphical Modeling Framework (GMF) (2006), http://www.eclipse.org/gmf
5. Eclipse Consortium, Eclipse Modeling Framework (EMF) (2006), http://www.eclipse.org/emf
6. Ehrig, K., Ermel, C., Hänsgen, S., Taentzer, G.: Generation of Visual Editors as Eclipse-Plugins. In: Automated Software Engineering 2005. IEEE Computer Society, Los Alamitos (2005), http://tfs.cs.tu-berlin.de/~tigerprj

Specifying Domain-Specific Refactorings for AndroMDA Based on Graph Transformation

Gabriele Taentzer[1], Dirk Müller[1], and Tom Mens[2]

[1] Philipps-Universität Marburg, Germany
{taentzer,dmueller}@mathematik.uni-marburg.de
[2] University of Mons-Hainaut, Belgium
tom.mens@umh.ac.be

Abstract. Applying refactoring in a model-driven software engineering context raises many new challenges that need to be addressed. In this paper, we consider model-driven software development based on the code generation framework AndroMDA. Considering the UML profile for AndroMDA, we come up with a number of domain-specific model refactorings. In its most recent version, the AndroMDA code generation can be based on the Eclipse Modeling Framework (EMF) which has evolved towards the *de facto* standard technology to specify UML models. We show how domain-specific refactorings can be specified by EMF transformation incorporating graph transformation concepts. This opens up the possibility to reason about domain-specific refactorings in a formal way.

1 Introduction

In the realm of software engineering, we are witnessing an increasing momentum towards the use of models for developing software systems. This trend, commonly referred to as model-driven software engineering, emphasizes on models as the primary artifacts in all phases of software development, from requirements analysis over system design to implementation, deployment, verification and validation. This uniform use of models promises to cope with the intrinsic complexity of software-intensive systems by raising the level of abstraction, and by hiding the accidental complexity of the underlying technology as much as possible [6]. The use of models thus opens up new possibilities for creating, analyzing, manipulating and formally reasoning about systems at a high-level of abstraction.

To reap all the benefits of model-driven engineering, however, it is essential to install a sophisticated mechanism of model transformation, that enables a wide range of different automated activities such as translation of models (expressed in different modeling languages), generating code from models, model refinement, model synthesis or model extraction, model restructuring etc. To achieve this, languages, formalisms, techniques and tools that support model transformation are needed. Such tools and techniques are starting to emerge.

Model refactoring is a specific kind of model transformation that allows us to improve the structure of the model while preserving its semantics. In this

A. Schürr, M. Nagl, and A. Zündorf (Eds.): AGTIVE 2007, LNCS 5088, pp. 104–119, 2008.

paper, we consider refactoring in model-driven software development. In this context, two aspects of model refactoring are of special interest: (1) Domain-specific modeling languages or domain-specific extensions of existing modeling languages (such as UML profiles), are used and lead to new, domain-specific refactorings. (2) Models are used to generate code where especially the domain-specific extensions drive the code generation. By code generation, models get some kind of semantics. Thus, we consider the model semantics to be preserved, if the behavior of the generated application is preserved. Often, a substantial part of the source code can be generated automatically from the models, while other parts still need to be implemented manually. If a model is refactored, how should the associated hand-written source code be modified accordingly? Vice versa, if this source code is refactored, how will the models be affected?

In this paper, we concentrate on domain-specific refactorings and report on our experience with expressing such model refactorings for AndroMDA [2], a state-of-the-art tool for model-driven software development. The AndroMDA code generator is a generic code generation engine which can be adapted to certain domains by so-called cartridges. Pre-existing cartridges enable the generation of web applications based on open source libraries such as Spring, Hibernate, and J2EE. We use AndroMDA to generate a simple university calendar as web application from a UML model.

Since the Eclipse Modeling Framework (EMF) has become a key reference for UML model specification in the world of model-driven development, we propose to specify refactorings as EMF model transformations and use a rule-based approach to EMF transformation based on graph transformation concepts [4]. Although not shown in this paper, this opens up the possibility for formal analysis of EMF model refactorings. In [10], we consider the connection between EMF transformations and graph transformations in more detail. In [13], we show how conflicts and dependencies between refactorings can be analysed based on graph transformation.

This paper presents our recent work on refactoring of AndroMDA-generated applications on the model level. We present our ideas in a tutorial style, due to the complexity of the AndroMDA-approach and due to space limitations. In contrast to our previous work, this paper is therefore informal in nature. For a more comprehensive introduction to AndroMDA the reader is referred to [2].

This paper is structured as follows: In the next section, we give a short introduction to the main concepts of AndroMDA from the modeling point of view and discuss one concrete model refactoring. In Section 3, we present an overview on domain-specific refactorings in the AndroMDA context, before some of them are specified by EMF transformation rules in Section 4. We summarize our work and conclude with an outline of future work in Sections 5 and 6.

2   Model-Driven Development with AndroMDA

This section presents the model-driven development by AndroMDA, illustrated by developing a small web application for a simple university calendar. First the

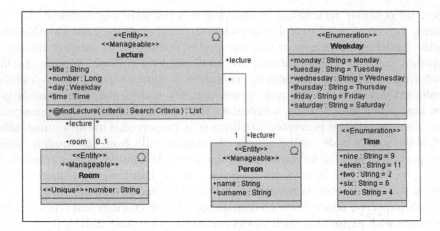

Fig. 1. Domain model for a simple university calendar

underlying data model is designed and thereafter, application-specific services and web presentation features are added in a model-driven way. This means that use cases are defined and refined by activity diagrams that can use controllers and services. The resulting application is not hundred percent generated, since service and controller bodies have to be coded by hand. After this tutorial introduction to AndroMDA, we discuss a refactoring step useful in this context.

2.1   Developing a Web Application with AndroMDA

AndroMDA is one of the main tools for model-driven software development. Its transformation engine is driven by so-called cartridges, structuring code generation. In the AndroMDA framework, a number of cartridges is already available realizing the generation of web applications based on UML models following a special profile. Both, the Java and the .NET platforms are supported by existing cartridges.

The model-driven development process of AndroMDA is based on use cases. A web application generated by AndroMDA has a three-tier architecture consisting of a service layer building up on a data base, controllers using the services defined, and a web presentation.

We illustrate the usage of AndroMDA by a simple university calendar application. The underlying data model for this application is shown in the class diagram in Figure 1, while its services and controllers are presented in the UML class diagram in Figure 2. The basic entities are Rooms that can be occupied for giving a Lecture or a Seminar. AndroMDA can generate a default web interface for managing lectures, seminars and rooms, just based on this class diagram. Users can add and delete instances, change attribute values and perform searches [2].

The AndroMDA-profile for UML can be considered to be a domain-specific modeling language, dependent on cartridges used, mainly dedicated to the generation of web applications. Stereotypes and tagged values especially guide the

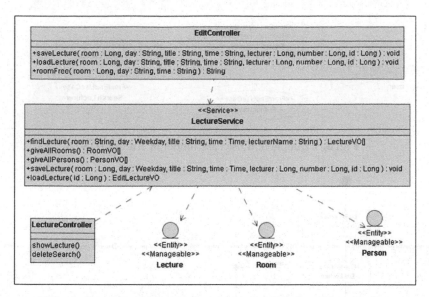

Fig. 2. Services and controllers for a simple university calendar

code generation process. We consider stereotypes and tagged values in the An-droMDA UML profile as far as they are needed to develop our example. For a complete overview of all available stereotypes and how to use them we refer to [2].

Stereotype ≪Entity≫ attached to a class is used to represent a data entity to be stored in a database. If, additionally, the ≪Manageable≫ stereotype is used, it causes AndroMDA to generate a default web presentation for manag-ing the corresponding entities. ≪Service≫ is a class stereotype used to specify application-specific services. These services typically use one or more entities that store the data used by the services. For example, LectureService imple-ments a service called findLecture() that relies on entities Lecture and Room for its proper functioning. Note that the implementation of this service needs to be hand-coded. Because of AndroMDA's naming conventions, the corresponding method should be called handleFindLecture().

For the model-driven development of a web presentation, we extend the model by use cases that are refined by activity diagrams. This model part describes the web presentation and its usage of controllers based on services. To illustrate the development of web applications, we develop a specific use case diagram for lectures (see Figure 3). Use case Search lectures has two stereotypes being ≪FrontEndUseCase≫, which determines the use case to be visible to the user in the form of a web page, and ≪FrontEndApplication≫, which defines this use case to be the starting one.

Use case Edit lectures is refined by an activity diagram in the following. It defines editing and storing of lectures (see Figure 4). Activity Load Lecture is an internal activity that calls controller method loadLecture() defined in class EditController. Again, this method needs to be hand-coded by relying on the service class LectureService.

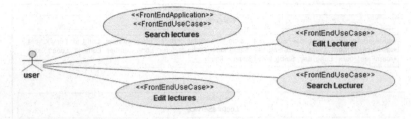

Fig. 3. Example of a use case model in AndroMDA

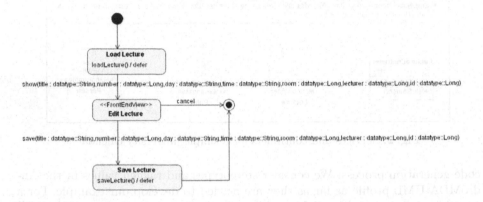

Fig. 4. Example of an activity diagram specifying use case Edit lectures

Activity Edit Lecture has stereotype ≪FrontEndView≫ implying that this activity models a web page. Both activities are connected by a transition which is equipped with signals being used to drive the generation process of web forms. Triggering signal save activity Save Lecture is performed which calls controller method saveLecture() using all signal parameters as input. Before saving, this method should also contain a consistency check for room usage. Thereafter, the control flow leads back the use case Search lectures. This is also the case if signal cancel is triggered after having edited a lecture. Both transitions head to an end activity which is connected to use case Search Lectures and its refining activity diagram. A connection to another use case is realized by naming the end activity alike. However, names of end activities are not shown in the diagram view.

The class model in Figure 1 only shows the data model, but there are also value object classes for web presentation. To show lectures, a special value object class for lectures has to be used which is specified by stereotype ≪ValueObject≫. This makes sense in terms of encapsulation (think of security, extensibility, etc.) and corresponds to the layered model-view-controller approach. Necessary information of the business layer is wrapped into so-called "value objects" which are used for the transfer to the presentation layer. Passing real entity objects to the client may pose a security risk. Do you want the client application to have access to the salary information inside a potentially extended Person

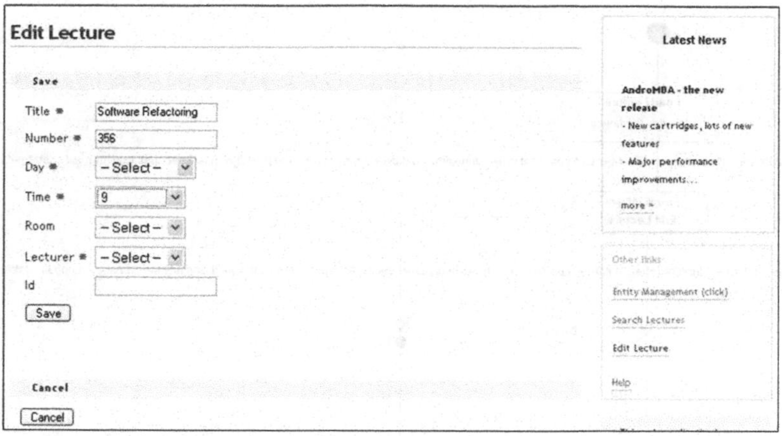

Fig. 5. Generated web page for editing lectures

entity? Since value objects are used at the presentation layer, the types used are primitive ones; entity types are not used in that layer.

The model which is shown in the previous figures (except of details and manually written code parts), is used to generate a web application that contains, among others, the web page shown in Figure 5. Please note that the names used as page title, in the edit form and for the buttons are specified as class and attribute names as well as signal names and parameters in the model. As a result, a renaming in the class model will have a direct effect in the web page.

2.2   A Refactoring Example

As an example for domain-specific model refactoring, we discuss the insertion of a decision structure into an activity diagram. Consider Figure 6 for the refactored activity diagram in Figure 4. The consistency check which used to be included in method `saveLecture` so far, has now been made explicit into the diagram. The restructuring is useful for further diagram extensions allowing an overview on available rooms. For explication of the consistency check, a decision structure is inserted after activity `Edit Lecture` which calls a new controller method, called `roomFree`, and dependent on its result stores the lecture. We assumed that this consistency check has been included in the controller method before. Now, this check is made explicit.

Beside model modifications, also hand-written code is affected. Controller method `roomFree` is new and has to be implemented. Checking code formerly integrated in controller method `saveLecture` has to be extracted and adapted, as well as method `saveLecture` itself. After having performed this refactoring, the web page for editing lectures has not changed, since this modification is completely internal.

Based on a first analysis of domain-specific model refactorings carried out, we can derive the following preliminary conclusions:

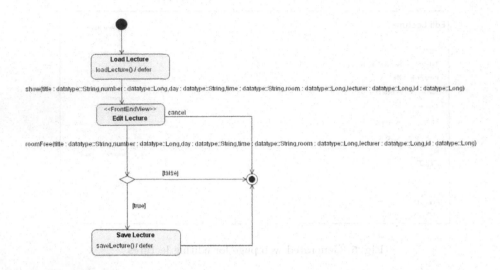

Fig. 6. Activity diagram specifying use case `Edit Lecture` after renaming

- Generic model refactorings need to be adapted and refined in presence of domain-specific models.
- Model refactoring may also affect, and require changes to, the hand-written source code, in order to keep it synchronized with the generated code. This may require the need to perform code-level refactorings.

3   Domain-Specific Refactoring

In Section 2, a concrete model refactoring has been applied to a sample AndroMDA model: the insertion of a decision structure in activity diagrams. In this section, we explore further examples of domain-specific refactorings for AndroMDA models. Often domain-specific refactorings are deduced from "standard" model refactorings. As it turns out, most of these refactorings have observable effects on the generated application, due to the AndoMDA code generator. It has to be discussed how far these modifications shall be considered as refactorings. For more information on this topic, see [12]. Next to these "standard" refactorings, we also require dedicated "domain-specific" refactorings for AndroMDA models, as shown in the concrete example above. In the following, we discuss three categories of transformations and classify them as follows:

1. transformations that do not affect the user interface at all;
2. transformations that do affect the user interface with respect to the usability, but that do not affect the functionality of the application; and
3. transformations that also affect the actual behaviour of the application.

The latter category does not contain real refactorings in the strict sense of the word, but it is nevertheless useful and necessary to specify such model modifications. As pointed out above, transformations which are perceived as normal refactorings at the model level, can actually extend the behavior, due to the code generation process.

Pull up Entity Property. When pulling up an entity property to a superclass, the code generator will automatically generate a new web page corresponding to this superclass, with search functionality for each manageable entity. Thus, this transformation belongs to category (3).

Create Value Object. A domain-specific refactoring for AndroMDA models is the creation of value objects for entities. Given a class with stereotype ≪Entity≫ (for example, class Lecture), a new class with stereotype ≪Value Object≫ is created and the entity class becomes dependent on this new class. The value object class is named after its entity class followed by suffix "VO" (for example, value object class LectureVO). The entity properties are copied to the value object class, keeping names and types, by default. If internal information needs to be kept hidden from the client, the corresponding property is not copied. This refactoring belongs to category (1) and does not affect any other part of the model, since the value object class is only created without being used yet.

Rename Entity. Renaming a manageable entity class is reflected by a change in the title of the corresponding web page for manageable entities. In case that the renamed entity class comes along with a value object class whose name is derived from the entity class name (e.g. "LectureVO" is derived from "Lecture" by suffixing "VO"), renaming has to be accompanied by a renaming of its corresponding value object class. Furthermore, the renaming has to be propagated to the hand-written code. This refactoring belongs to category (2). Renaming an entity property can be handled in a similar way, as shown by an example in [12]. This renaming concerns not only with entity properties, but also with the properties of derived value objects.

Rename Use Case. Similar to entities, use cases can be renamed as well. This might have an effect on activity diagrams, since AndroMDA supports the connection of several activity diagrams via use case names. For example, an end activity of one activity diagram may be named as a use case, which means that the control flow would continue at the start activity of the corresponding activity diagram. (For an example see Figure 4.) In the generated web applications, use cases are listed on the right-hand side of each web page. Again, a renamed use case would change the usability of the web application, but not its functionality, so the refactoring belongs to category (2).

Further domain-specific refactorings for AndroMDA models are e.g., *Merge Services* where two ≪Service≫ classes are merged into one and all their incoming and outgoing dependencies are adapted, *Split Activities* where one activity is split into two consecutive ones, linked by a transition, and *Extract Method* which originates from the standard refactoring set, but shows new effects in the context of model-driven development. Starting with refactoring at source code

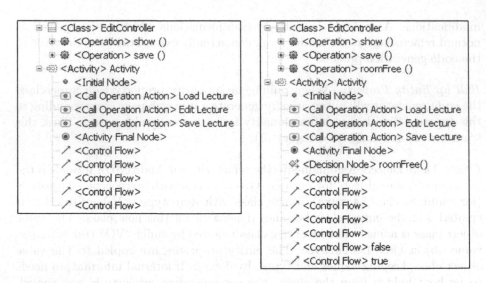

Fig. 7. Activity diagrams from Figures 4 and 6 as UML2 EMF instance models

level, it may require synchronization of the corresponding model which, after regenerating the code may involve another modification to the hand-written part of the code.

4 Specifying Domain-Specific Model Refactorings

To realize tool support for domain-specific model refactoring in the context of AndroMDA, we propose to consider standard technologies. Since the Eclipse Modeling Framework (EMF) [1] has become a key reference for model specification in the world of model-driven development, we rely our approach to model refactoring on EMF model transformation.

4.1 AndroMDA Models as EMF Models

As a prerequisite, a specification of the underlying modeling language is needed which is the UML2 EMF model extended by AndroMDA profiles. The activity diagrams in Figures 4 and 6 are shown as UML2 EMF model instances in Figure 7.

4.2 Refactoring as EMF Transformation

EMF model refactoring can be expressed by EMF model transformation as shown in [4]. This kind of model transformation is based on the algebraic graph transformation approach [7] and is performed in-place, i.e., the current model is directly changed and not copied. Each transformation rule consists of a left-hand side (LHS), indicating the preconditions of the transformation, a right-hand side

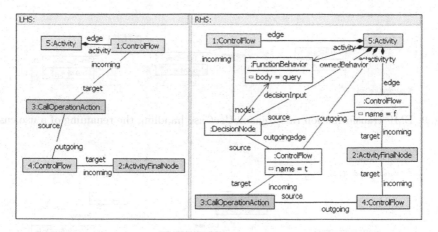

Fig. 8. EMF model transformation rule InsertDecision for inserting a new decision structure into an activity diagram

(RHS), formulating the post conditions of the transformations, and optional negative application conditions (NAC), defining forbidden structures that prevent application of the transformation rule. Objects that are checked as precondition preserved during a transformation are indicated by colors. Object nodes of the same color (and having the same number) present one and the same object in different parts of a rule. While attributes in the LHS may have constant values or rule variables only, they are allowed to carry Java expressions in the RHS, too. If the same variable name occurs at different places in a rule, it has the same value at all these places.

Simple model refactorings can be specified by just a single rule. In the following, we show one refactoring of this kind which specifies the refactoring dicussed in Section 2.2. Thereafter, we concentrate on refactorings which are described by one trigger rule applied exactly once in the beginning, and another rule which is applied afterwards as long as possible, keeping the same parameter setting. This control flow is directly expressed in Java. It is obvious that also other kinds of control flow can be specified in this way.

Insert Decision Structure. In Section 2.2, we considered a refactoring of activity diagrams where a decision structure has been inserted. Figure 8 shows a transformation rule which specifies this kind of structure modification. Here, a special case is considered where a decision structure is inserted before an action which is followed by a final node. This model refactoring has to be accompanied by a refactoring of the corresponding controller method not shown here, due to space limitations.

Rename Use Case. Figure 9 shows a transformation rule that renames a use case. Use case names may be used as names of final activities to connect several activity diagrams. Rule RenameFinalActivity in Figure 10 handles the case where the use case name is used in some final activity. Thus, its name has

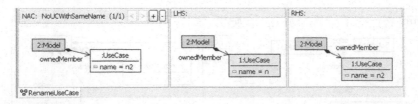

Fig. 9. EMF transformation rule RenameUseCase handling the renaming of a use case

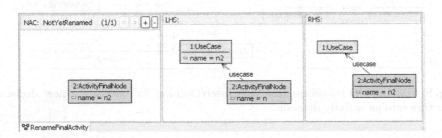

Fig. 10. EMF transformation rule RenameFinalActivity handling the renaming of a final activity

to be updated. This rule has to be applied to all final activities which refer to the renamed use case. As regular expression, the control flow can be formulated as follows:

```
RenameUseCase(n,n2) (RenameFinalActivity(n,n2))*
```

A graphical way for control flow modeling such as story diagrams in Fujaba [8], would also be suitable. Directly based on the EMF transformation framework, the following code snippet specifies this control flow in a new method `renameUC()`. After automatically generating Java code from transformation rules, this method is defined manually in plain Java.

```
public void renameUC(Model model, String useCaseName, String newUCName) {
    Boolean triggered = false;
    Parameter parameter = new Parameter();
    parameter.addParameter("n", useCaseName, "String");
    parameter.addParameter("n2", newUCName, "String");
    triggered = interpreter.applyRule(model, "RenameUseCase",
                                      null, parameter);
    while (triggered)
        triggered = interpreter.applyRule(model,"RenameFinalActivity",
                                      null,parameter));
}
```

Create Value Object. In Figures 11 and 12, two model transformation rules are shown, which both are needed to perform refactoring *Create Value Object*

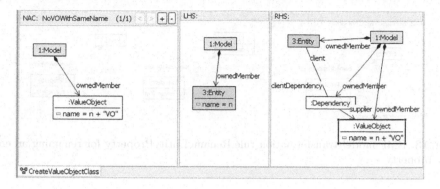

Fig. 11. EMF model transformation rule CreateValueObjectClass for creating a value object

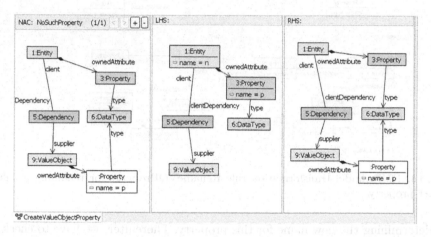

Fig. 12. EMF model transformation rule CreateValueObjectProperty for refactoring Create Value Object

explained in Section 3. Rule CreateValueObjectClass is applied once, creating a new value object class and a dependency of the entity class on this new class. A model with an entity class is needed to create a value object class and a dependency in between. The name of this new value object class is constructed by taking the entity class name n and adding suffix "VO". This rule is applied only if a value object class of this name has not been created yet.

Thereafter, rule CreateValueObjectProperty is applied for each of the properties of the entity class that should occur also in the value object class. Each time it is applied, it copies a property that has not yet been copied into the value object. This rule execution is summarized in method `createVO()` which can be defined similarly to method `renameUC()` above.

Rename Entity Property. The renaming of an entity property is specified in Figure 13 by giving the names of the entity and its property to be renamed and

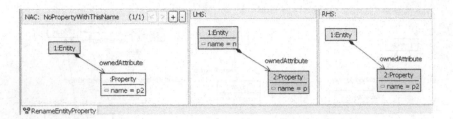

Fig. 13. EMF model transformation rule RenameEntityProperty for renaming an entity property

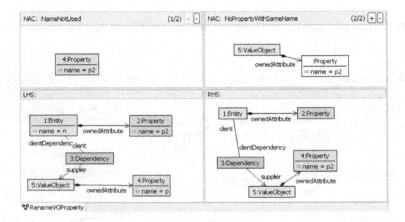

Fig. 14. EMF model transformation rule RenameVOProperty for renaming a value object property

by determining the new name for this property. Thereafter, we have to check if this entity has a value object containing a property with the old name. For these value objects, the rule in Figure 14 is the appropriate one.

The whole control flow is specified similarly to the refactorings above. Note that renamed properties might be used in hand-written code implementing controller and service methods. That means EMF model refactoring has to be combined with source code refactoring (here renaming). The development of corresponding tool support is left for future work.

4.3   Analysis of Refactorings

To open up the possibility for analyzing EMF model refactorings, we translate EMF transformations to graph transformations. In this way, the formal analysis for graph transformation becomes available for EMF model refactoring. To give a flavor of what can be achieved, we refer to [13]. A formal specification of refactorings as graph transformation rules allows us to reason about dependencies between different types of refactorings. Such a static analysis of potential conflicts and dependencies between refactorings can be helpful for the user during the interactive process of trying to improve the software quality by means of disciplined model transformations.

Although EMF models show a graph-like structure and can be transformed similarly to graphs, there is an important difference between both. In contrast to graphs, EMF models have a distinguished tree structure that is defined by the containment relation between their classes. Each class can be contained in at most one other class. Since an EMF model may have non-containment references in addition, the following question arises: What if a class, which is transitively contained in a root class, has non-containment references to other classes not transitively contained in some root class? In this case, we consider the EMF model to be inconsistent. A transformation can invalidate an EMF model, if its rule deletes one or more objects. To ensure consistent transformations only, rules that delete objects or containment links or redirect them, have to be equipped with additional NACs. The rules we have shown in this section, do not delete any object, thus can be easily translated to graph transformation rules.

5   Related Work

Sunyé et al. [17] were the first to apply the idea of refactoring at the level of UML models. Others like Astels [3] and Markovic and Baar [11] followed. They considered mainly class models and ported refactoring known from object-oriented programming to UML class models. With respect to refactoring of behavioral models, not much work is available. We are only aware of a few approaches that address the problem of refactoring state diagrams, as presented in [15,16,20]. In our approach, we consider also the refactoring of use case and activity diagrams.

Various researchers have proposed to use some kind of rule-based approach to specify model refactorings, so it appears to be a natural choice: Graph transformation-based approaches are used in [5,9,13]. Porres [15] presents the transformation language SMW to specify model refactorings. This script language is also rule-based and resembles the Object Constraint Language (OCL). Van Der Straeten and D'Hondt [18] use a rule-based approach to apply model refactorings, based on description logics. We decided for a specification of UML model refactoring based on EMF model transformation to be compatible with upcoming UML CASE tools based on EMF.

6   Conclusion and Open Problems

Model-driven software engineering offers automated code generation techniques which can be used to deal with complex software in a systematic way. The level of abstraction is raised from code to models. Software refactoring is a proven technique to improve software in a structured, semi-automated manner. By integrating the process of refactoring into model-driven software development, we arrive at what we call model-driven software refactoring. We have chosen AndroMDA as concrete approach to model-driven development and illustrated it by developing a simple web application. On this base, we discussed a number of domain-specific model refactorings. Larger applications will certainly lead to further kinds of domain-specific model refactorings. A catalog of domain-specific model refactorings for AndroMDA-generated web applications is left to future work.

We have expressed AndroMDA model refactorings as EMF model transformations. This approach has the advantage of defining refactorings in a generic way, while still being able to provide tool support with commonly used modeling frameworks such as EMF. Since the EMF transformation approach we use is very close to algebraic graph transformation, it provides a basis for a translation of model refactorings to graph transformations and thus to formally specify and analyse model refactorings.

The code generation of AndroMDA is organized in cartridges. Different UML profiles, also combinations of those, are assigned to cartridges. They are used for modeling the application and for driving the code generation process. The model semantics are dependent on the code generation cartridges used. Considering model refactoring in this context means to take domain-specific model elements into account and to come up with so-called domain-specific refactoring. Since code generation is not hundred percent, it might happen that model refactorings require code modifications to keep model and code synchronized. The other way around, refactoring of manually written code might lead to model adaptation, and after another code generation might cause a further adaptation of the just refactored code. In future work, the formal specification and analysis of synchronized model and code refactoring needs to be further investigated. (For more information on source code-consistent UML refactorings see [19].)

Although the chosen EMF transformation approach is powerful enough to specify EMF model refactorings, features such as multi-nodes representing sets of model elements, and optional nodes that do not have to exist, are useful to allow a more compact notation of refactorings. These features are offered by graph transformation approaches as used in Fujaba [8] and Moflon [14]. To further reason about refactorings, the translation of such features to algebraic graph transformation has to be considered and analysis techniques have to be extended to cover these features.

We have seen that refactorings in model-driven development may have a high impact. Due to the fact that the code generator automatically produces new types of elements based on existing elements, a seemingly simple change might already propagate to many different places. A tool that implements such model refactorings will therefore need to take these issues into account to ensure that the refactoring does not lead to inconsistent models and code. A precise specification of such refactorings having effect on several model parts is an important first step.

References

1. Eclipse model development tools (2007), http://www.eclipse.org/modeling/mdt
2. AndroMDA (2007), http://www.andromda.org
3. Astels, D.: Refactoring with UML. In: Proceedings of 3rd International Conference eXtreme Programming and Flexible Processes in Software Engineering, pp. 159–174 (2002)

4. Biermann, E., Ehrig, K., Köhler, C., Kuhns, G., Taentzer, G., Weiss, E.: Graphical definition of rule-based transformation in the Eclipse Modeling Framework. In: Nierstrasz, O., Whittle, J., Harel, D., Reggio, G. (eds.) MoDELS 2006. LNCS, vol. 4199, pp. 425–439. Springer, Heidelberg (2006)
5. Bottoni, P., Parisi-Presicce, F., Taentzer, G.: Specifying Coherent Refactoring of Software Artefacts with Distributed Graph Transformations. In: van Bommel, P. (ed.) Handbook on Transformation of Knowledge, Information, and Data: Theory and Applications, pp. 95–125. Idea Group Publishing (2005)
6. Brooks, F.P.: No silver bullet: Essence and accidents of software engineering. In: The Mythical Man-Month: Essays on Software Engineering, 20th Anniversary Edn. Addison-Wesley, Reading (1995)
7. Ehrig, H., Ehrig, K., Prange, U., Taentzer, G.: Fundamentals of Algebraic Graph Transformation. In: EATCS Monographs in Theoretical Computer Science. Springer, Heidelberg (2006)
8. Fujaba (2007), http://www.fujaba.de
9. Grunske, L., Geiger, L., Zündorf, A., Van Eetvelde, N., Van Gorp, P., Varro, D.: Using graph transformation for practical model driven software engineering. In: Beydeda, S., Book, M., Gruhn, V. (eds.) Model-driven Software Development, pp. 91–118. Springer, Heidelberg (2005)
10. Köhler, C., Lewin, H., Taentzer, G.: Ensuring containment constraints in graph-based model transformation approaches. In: Ehrig, K., Giese, H. (eds.) 6. Int. Workshop on Graph Transformation and Visual Modeling Techniques. Electronic Communication of the EASST, vol. 6 (2007)
11. Markovic, S., Baar, T.: Refactoring OCL annotated UML class diagrams. In: MoDELS, pp. 280–294 (2005)
12. Mens, T., Taentzer, G., Müller, D.: Model-driven software refactoring. In: Rech, J., Bunse, C. (eds.) Model-Driven Software Development: Integrating Quality Assurance. Idea Group Publishing (to appear, 2008)
13. Mens, T., Taentzer, G., Runge, O.: Analysing refactoring dependencies using graph transformation. Software and System Modeling 6(3), 269–285 (2007)
14. Moflon (2007), http://www.moflon.org
15. Porres, I.: Model Refactorings as Rule-Based Update Transformations. In: Stevens, P., Whittle, J., Booch, G. (eds.) UML 2003. LNCS, vol. 2863, pp. 159–174. Springer, Heidelberg (2003)
16. Pretschner, A., Prenninger, A.: Computing refactorings of state machines. Journal on Software and Systems Modeling (January 2007)
17. Sunyé, G., Pollet, D., Le Traon, Y., Jezequel, J.M.: Refactoring UML models. In: The Unified Modeling Language, pp. 134–148 (2001)
18. Van Der Straeten, R., D'Hondt, M.: Model refactorings through rule-based inconsistency resolution. In: Proceedings Symposium on Applied Computing, pp. 1210–1217. ACM Press, New York (2006)
19. Van Gorp, P., Stenten, H., Mens, T., Demeyer, S.: Towards automating source-consistent UML refactorings. In: Stevens, P., Whittle, J., Booch, G. (eds.) UML 2003. LNCS, vol. 2863, pp. 144–158. Springer, Heidelberg (2003)
20. Van Kempen, M., Chaudron, M., Koudrie, D., Boake, A.: Towards proving preservation of behaviour of refactoring of UML models. In: Proceedings SAICSIT 2005, pp. 111–118 (2005)

Defining Abstract Graph Views
as Module Interfaces

Ulrike Ranger[1], Katja Gruber[1], and Marc Holze[2]

[1] RWTH Aachen University
Department of Computer Science 3 (Software Engineering)
Ahornstraße 55, 52074 Aachen, Germany
{ranger,grubi}@i3.informatik.rwth-aachen.de
[2] University of Hamburg
Distributed Systems and Information Systems
Vogt-Kölln-Straße 30, 22527 Hamburg, Germany
holze@informatik.uni-hamburg.de

Abstract. Graph transformation languages offer the ability to model the structure and behavior of a software system visually. While providing extensive language constructs for specifying in the small, they lack sophisticated concepts for specifying in the large. In particular, a mature module concept is still missing. In our project, we develop appropriate concepts and extend the graph transformation languages PROGRES and Fujaba for these concepts. By now, we have already included a mechanism for exporting and importing module interfaces consisting of a subset of specification elements.

In this paper, we extend our module concept for supporting updateable abstract graph views as module interfaces. These views may abstract from specification details allowing a convenient usage of modules. For this purpose, a unique mapping between view elements and specification elements has to be defined. Exported view elements may be used by other modules in the same way as locally-defined specification elements.

1   Introduction

Graph transformation languages (GTL), like PROGRES [1] and Fujaba [2], can be used for specifying complex software systems. Their main advantages are the mathematical foundation and the possibility to model both the structure and the behavior of a software system in a visual way. GTLs have been successfully applied in several software projects, e.g. E-CARES, ConDes, and Fujaba Real-Time Tool Suite. Although GTLs offer expressive language constructs, they lack concepts for *specifying in the large*, including a mature module concept. Additionally, concepts for specifying distributed systems are missing.

Our project aims at developing concepts for modularization and for modeling distributed systems. We do not start the development of the concepts from scratch, but analyze existing approaches and adopt some aspects. We regard modules as self-contained software components which are based on separated

A. Schürr, M. Nagl, and A. Zündorf (Eds.): AGTIVE 2007, LNCS 5088, pp. 120–135, 2008.

specifications consisting of data types and graph transformations. For using modules' functionality from the outside, *module interfaces* are used. These interfaces abstract from the modules' internal specifications and define the publicly available elements. A module can use elements of imported interfaces in the same way as locally-defined elements, e.g. within visual language constructs.

Our module concept does not only provide a *static semantics* in terms of separated module specifications, but also offers a *runtime semantics* for the modules. That is, the division in several software modules is preserved at runtime by using separated runtime graph for each module. These runtime graphs store the individual states of the modules. Thus, both the specification and the runtime graph of a software system are divided into smaller parts, which improves the maintainability and scalability of a complex software system. The runtime semantics of our module concept also enables the development of distributed systems: The applications of a distributed system are modeled in the same way as modules of a local system. Due to their separated runtime graphs, the applications participating in the distributed system can be executed on different computers. The coupling of the applications is defined on top of their interfaces.

We integrate the described concepts into the GTLs PROGRES and Fujaba with focus on practical usage, so that the concepts can be easily applied in software projects. E. g. we test and evaluate our concepts using the project management system AHEAD, which is based on a PROGRES-specification consisting of more than 200 pages. We have divided the complex specification of AHEAD into several modules with separated responsibilities. These modules are executed on different computers as independent software applications.

Currently, the module interfaces of our concept reflect either the complete graph specification or a subset of it. That is, there is always a unique mapping between the elements of the interface and the elements of the internal specification. We refer to these interfaces as *simple interfaces*. Experiences have shown that exposing the internal specification details at the interface is often not suitable. Instead, the interfaces should hide internal complexity and provide interface robustness against implementation changes.

In this paper, we extend simple interfaces for offering updateable *abstract graph views* as module interfaces. Thus, a module consists of a specification covering its implementation and an abstract graph view which serves as interface. Between these two parts, a *n-to-m mapping* is defined which maps elements of the view to elements of the internal specification. E. g., a view may export one combined node type for two node types of the internal specification. For lack of space, we concentrate on a local software system throughout the paper, although the concepts can also be used for distributed systems (see Section 7).

The paper is structured as follows: Section 2 introduces a module providing a list structure, which serves as running example throughout the paper. Section 3 sketches our module concept without the extension for abstract graph views. The concept of abstract graph views is described in Section 4. Section 5 shows the realization of abstract views in GTL. In Section 6 we compare our module concept to related approaches. We conclude with a summary in Section 7.

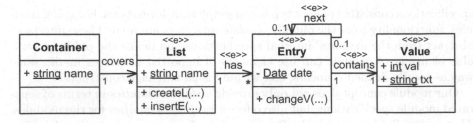

Fig. 1. Graph schema of module Data Storage

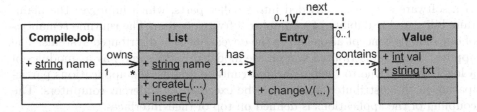

Fig. 2. Graph schema of module IDE using a simple interface of Data Storage

2   Example

To illustrate our concepts, we use the simple module Data Storage. It constitutes an abstract data type (ADT) for managing linear lists, which store entries consisting of integer and string values. Figure 1 depicts the schema of Data Storage, showing the main attributes and signatures of graph transformations.

Every linear list is represented by an instance of node type List, which offers a name attribute and graph transformations for creating lists and inserting entries. Linear lists are managed by instances of type Container. For storing data in a linear list, node types Entry and Value are applied. Instances of node type Entry represent the elements of a list and store the date of creation. Entries are used for managing the list structure by referencing their successors by next edges. To simplify the example, the list is unordered and new entries are always inserted at the end. Every entry is associated with an instance of type Value which stores an integer (val) and a string (txt) for the entry. Due to this separation, the ADT may be easily extended to store arbitrary data without changing the list management. For this purpose, only node type Value has to be modified or substituted.

To show the usage of module Data Storage, we introduce a second module IDE which constitutes a simplified integrated development environment. The main purpose of IDE is to compile the source code of a software system. If compilation fails, the module stores all detected errors within failure lists. An error consists of an error message and the line number, in which the error occurs.

Figure 2 shows the graph schema of IDE. The schema defines the node type CompileJob, which can be instantiated for compile processes. For storing compile errors, IDE uses the functionality of Data Storage. Thus, IDE must import the interface of Data Storage. In Figure 2, a simple interface is used for this purpose,

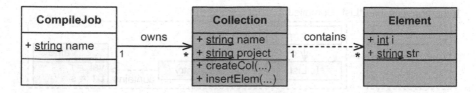

Fig. 3. Graph schema of module IDE using an abstract graph view of Data Storage

which consists of the necessary node and edge types of Data Storage (depicted as gray rectangles and dotted edges). Simple interfaces are introduced in Section 3.

Simple interfaces cannot abstract from specification details. Hence, IDE has to regard the separation between node types Entry and Value. To provide a convenient usage of Data Storage, a graph schema as depicted in Figure 3 is desirable. In this case, the imported interface abstracts from the separation of Entry and Value by offering the abstract node type Element. Additionally, node type Collection abstracts from Container and List. We show how our approach of abstract graph views can be used to achieve this goal in Sections 4 and 5.

3   Module Concept with Simple Module Interfaces

In this section, we shortly introduce our existing module concept supporting updateable simple interfaces for modules. These interfaces consist of specification elements that are explicitly marked as to be included in the interface. For marking, the ≪e≫-stereotype is used within specifications (abbreviation for *export*). An interface may cover node types (including public attributes and transformations), edge types, and type-independent graph transformations. For transformations, only their signatures are listed in the interface. A valid interface must contain the source and target node types for every included edge type.

Example. For using module Data Storage in other modules, the main elements for storing data have to be exported. As shown in Figure 1, the interface consists of the node types List with the name-attribute and its transformations, Entry with its transformation, and Value with its attributes. Additionally, edge types has, next, and contains are exported.

Interfaces may be imported by other modules. We offer *use*-relations for import-export relationships between modules. This way, a module imports all elements contained in a used interface. A module may use imported elements in the same way as locally-defined elements, but the definition of imported elements must not be changed, e.g. by adding new attributes. In particular, imported node types can be related to local node types by defining new edge types between them. In case of importing several interfaces, name clashes between imported elements are internally solved by renaming the corresponding elements.

Example. IDE imports the simple interface of Data Storage, which is shown in Figure 2. IDE defines an edge type owns relating the local type CompileJob and the imported interface.

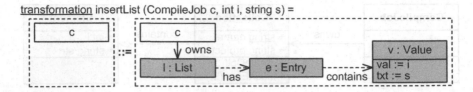

Fig. 4. Graph transformation insertList of module IDE

Imported elements may be used within graph transformations leading to *distributed graph transformations*, whose execution affects several modules in parallel. Regarding procedural GTLs, a module may call imported transformations by using their signatures within textual statements. This possibility resembles (remote) procedure calls of conventional programming languages. Additionally, imported node and edge types may be used within visual graph transformations, in which they are depicted as gray rectangles resp. dotted edges.

Example. Figure 4 shows the visual graph transformation insertList, which is defined in IDE. The transformation creates a new list storing the compile error of a compile job. The compile job c, the line number i, and the error message s are given as input parameters. The left-hand side consists of the given compile job c. The right-hand side of the transformation defines that for c a list l and an entry e with a corresponding value v have to be created. Additionally, edges are created which connect the created objects and the compile job.

Due to the runtime semantics, every module stores its own runtime graph. For accessing data of other modules, a module uses *reference objects* in its runtime graph. These objects do not store any data but only the location of the objects they are pointing to. Thus, for accessing an attribute of a reference node, a query to the module storing the original node has to be performed. The advantage of using references is that relations between data of different modules may be managed within the modules' runtime graphs. Additionally, the data has not to be replicated in every module, because this would complicate the consistency maintenance between all existing copies [3]. In [4], we describe the runtime semantics and the definition of distributed graph transformations in detail.

Example. Revisiting the graph transformation insertList of Figure 4, the effects of executing the transformation are shown in Figure 5. The figure depicts the runtime graphs of Data Storage and IDE before and after the application of insertList. As IDE uses Data Storage, the runtime graph of IDE consists of both local and reference graph objects. Reference objects are depicted as gray circles resp. dotted edges. The depicted ids of reference nodes are equal to the ids of the original nodes. Before applying insertList, IDE holds a list l2 for a compile job cj1 whose actual data l2, e2 and v2 are stored in Data Storage. Besides these objects, Data Storage stores the objects c1, l1, e1, and v1 which are only used internally by the module. When executing the transformation, a list, an entry, and a value are created which affects both runtime graphs: In Data Storage the objects l3, e3, v3, and edges are created and in IDE appropriate reference objects are inserted.

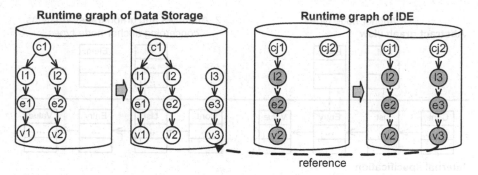

Fig. 5. Executing graph transformation insertList

Integrating modularization in GTLs introduces a significant problem which is called *graph rewriting dilemma* [5]. A module's interface abstracts from the internal specification by hiding some specification elements. If another module applies imported schema types within visual graph transformations, this may cause inconsistencies in the runtime graph of the module providing the interface. For example, the execution of transformation insertList in Figure 5 leads to an inconsistency in Data Storage, because the new list l3 is not related to a container although this is required by the internal graph schema of Data Storage (see Figure 1). For avoiding the graph rewriting dilemma, we provide a runtime mechanism which adapts a graph transformation (using interface elements) into module-specific consistent transformations [6]. These adapted transformations consider all internally imposed constraints of the modules and keep the runtime graphs consistent. In the example of Figure 5, the adapted transformation would additionally create an edge of type covers from a container to the list l3.

4   Concept of Abstract Graph Views

Our concept of abstract graph views extends the concept of simple interfaces. The new concept allows the definition of a view on the graph specification as the module interface. This view supports the declaration of new types and transformations in the interface, by defining a mapping between the view and the internal specification. For the mapping between view node types and internal node types, a n-to-m relationship may be defined. That is, a node type of the view may be mapped to several node types in the internal specification and vice versa. At runtime, view types are not instantiated, but *objects of view types* are mapped to *objects of internal types*. Therefore, we call these views *abstract*.

Like simple interfaces, the definition of a view may not be changed by other modules. Other modules may only use imported view types in the graph schema definition and within graph transformations. If such a transformation is executed, all operations concerning view objects are translated to operations on objects of internal types. This translation process is automatically derived from the mapping definition. Similar to simple interfaces, every module currently may offer only one view, i.e. every module using the interface gets the same view.

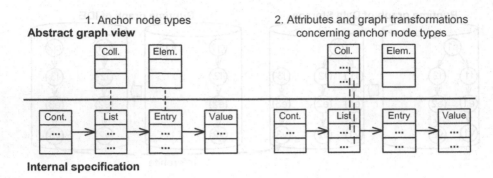

Fig. 6. Concept of anchor node types considering the example of Data Storage

The advantage of graph views is the possibility to completely decouple a module's internal specification from its interface. Thus, a module's internal specification can be modified without adapting the modules using its interface. The decoupling is realized by offering only an indirect access on the internal specification and on the internal runtime graph from the outside. The mapping of view elements to the internal specification is completely transparent to module users. To handle the complexity of views and to support updateable views, we define the following constraints on the mapping definition[1]:

Anchor Nodes. For every node type of a view, one node type of the internal specification has to be determined as *anchor node type*. This anchor type serves as main point of reference for the view type. The view type may provide a subset of the attributes and transformations specified in its anchor type.

As defined above, view types are not instantiated themselves, but are always mapped to objects of internal types. Thus, reference objects in the runtime graphs of module users actually point to objects of the anchor type in the module's runtime graph. If an anchor object is deleted in the module's runtime graph, all reference objects pointing to it in module users are deleted, too.

The usage of anchor types allows the seamless integration of abstract graph views into our module concept. We can keep the runtime semantics based on the reference approach. The usage of concrete objects for view objects as entry points for the view mapping leads to deterministic results when dealing with view objects. It must be pointed out that every node type of the internal specification may serve at most once as anchor node type in the view. Otherwise, modules would have several reference objects of different view types in their runtime graph pointing to the same node object. This would lead to confusing and inaccurate results when using view objects of different view types.

Figure 6 shows the schematic definition of an abstract view considering the sample Data Storage. The view is modeled according to the aspired view in Figure 3 consisting of the view node types Coll. and Elem.. In the figure, dots

---

[1] Due to lack of space, a formal description is omitted in this paper, but can be found in [7].

are used as placeholders for attributes and graph transformations. The left part of the figure illustrates the definition of anchor node types for view node types by dashed lines. The right part of the figure depicts the relation between attributes and graph transformations of abstract node types and their anchor node types.

Context Nodes. In addition to its anchor type, several *context node types* may be defined for a view node type. In this manner, one view node type may be mapped on multiple node types of the internal specification. For example, one view node type may cover attributes and graph transformations defined in several node types of the internal specification. To relate the context node types with their corresponding anchor node type, it is required that each context node type is directly connected to the anchor node type by at least one edge type of the internal specification. For node types in the view definition, it is then required to choose exactly one of the edge types for every context node type as *context edge type*. Thus, the context objects of a view object can be found by traversing context edges incident to the anchor object. In contrast to anchor objects, the deletion of context objects in the module providing the graph view does not affect the view objects in module users.

Depending on the cardinality of the context edge type, two cases have to be distinguished: First, the context edge type is of cardinality to-1, i.e. the anchor object is connected to (at most) one object of the context type. In this case, the context object of a view object can be easily determined by traversing the context edge incident to the anchor object of the view object. Thus, the attributes of view objects which are mapped to attributes of a to-1 context object can be directly changed from outside. Second, the context edge type is of cardinality to-n, i.e. the anchor object is connected to several objects of the context type. In this case, all objects of the context type incident to the anchor object have to be considered. If the view node type covers an attribute of a context node type, the value of the attribute is a set consisting of the attribute values of all context objects. This value set must not be changed by modules using the view object due to the following reason: Graph transformation systems use a strategy that searches for objects non-deterministically. Thus, the order of the value set is also non-deterministic. Therefore, modifications on the set may not be mapped back on the context objects unambiguously.

The concept of context node types is illustrated on the left of Figure 7. For the view node types, the context node types and their context edges are defined by dotted lines. Relations between attributes and graph transformations of view node types and internal node types are shown as dashed lines.

Aggregated Attributes. We also support the definition of *aggregated attributes*. These attributes are based on an aggregation function and on an attribute of a context type which is related to the anchor type by a to-n-edge type. E. g. if the values of the context objects are added up by the aggregation function, then the sum of these values constitutes the attribute value of the view object. Values of aggregated attributes must not be changed by module users as the modification can not be mapped uniquely back to the individual context objects.

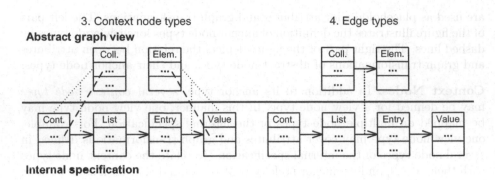

Fig. 7. Concept of context node types and edge types considering the example of Data Storage

Edges. Besides node types, edge types may be defined in graph views relating view node types. Every view edge type is mapped to exactly one edge type (anchor edge type) of the internal specification. This internal edge type has to relate the anchor node types of the corresponding view node types. In this way, a unique mapping of view edges is guaranteed. On the right of Figure 7, an edge type is defined, which connects the two view node types by an anchor edge type.

Our project focuses on and extends the GTLs PROGRES and Fujaba which do not support *attributed edge types*. However, our concepts for abstract graph views allow to define attributed edge types. These may be imported and used by modules specified in a GTL providing attributed edge types, like AGG [8].

In the above paragraphs, we have defined constraints that apply to the definition of abstract graph views. These constraints serve as a basis for up-dateable graph views, thus allowing the module users to modify their view by modeling graph transformations on imported types. However, for mapping these view-operations on the internal objects, there are different possibilities shown in Table 1. There are four possibilities to handle the creation of a view node object: The creation could not be mapped to internal node objects at all (Nothing), or internal node objects could be created (Create), or the runtime graph could be searched for existing node objects that match the properties of the newly created view node object. If matching node objects were found, they could be used as the internal node objects for the view node object. Otherwise, the transformation might fail (Search–Fail), an internal node objects might be created (Search–Create) or nothing is done (Search–Nothing). For deleting view node objects, there are only two mapping strategies: the corresponding internal node objects may either be deleted (Delete) or not (Nothing). It is important to note that different strategies can be chosen for every internal anchor and context node object. Besides view node objects, also view edge objects may be created or deleted by module users. As for view nodes, the semantics of creating a view edge object may be Noth-ing, Search–Nothing, Search–Create, or Create, and for deleting an view edge object Nothing or Delete. The change of a view attribute value may be mapped on the corresponding internal attribute (read/write) or ignored (read_only).

Table 1. Possible semantics for modifying view objects

	Internal node object		Internal edge object	Internal attribute
	Anchor object	Context object		
Create view object	Nothing Search–Fail Search–Nothing Search–Create **Create**	Nothing Search–Fail Search–Nothing Search–Create Create	Nothing Search–Fail Search–Nothing Search–Create **Create**	—
Delete view obj.	Nothing **Delete**	Nothing Delete	Nothing **Delete**	—
Modify view attr.	—	—	—	Read_only Read/Write

For the concept of abstract graph views, on the one hand we explicitly require the views to be updateable by the module user. Hence, choosing the Nothing strategy in general (including Search–Nothing) for all node types is not applicable, because then create/delete operations would have no semantics in the module providing the view. On the other hand, we want to preserve the flexibility of the view concept as far as possible. Thus, we have chosen to use the following combination of the above strategies, which we refer to as the *minimal semantics* (depicted by the bold strategies in Table 1): If a view node or edge object is created, a corresponding anchor object is created internally (Create, but Search–Create would also be possible). For both nodes and edges, a reference object is then created in the module user's runtime graph. Likewise, if the deletion of a view object is triggered, the reference object and the corresponding anchor object are deleted (Delete). In contrast to operations concerning anchor objects, the minimal semantics does not apply to context objects. That is, for every context node type of a view node type the strategy, which is applied when modifying the view object, can be specified explicitly. Furthermore, the modification semantics (read/write or read_only) for attributes may also be specified.

5   Realization of Abstract Graph Views

This section describes the realization of abstract graph views in GTLs. For defining a view, we introduce the *view diagram* as new diagram type. Based on the view definition, the implementation of the presented concepts is able to translate transformations using view types into transformations using internal types.

View Diagram. The abstract graph view is defined in a view diagram which declares the abstract schema types and graph transformations. For every view type, its mapping to an anchor and context types of the internal specification is defined. Additionally, attributes and graph transformations in the graph view are mapped to the internal specification.

Example. Figure 8 shows the view diagram defining the abstract graph view on Data Storage. The view consists of the two node types Collection and Element,

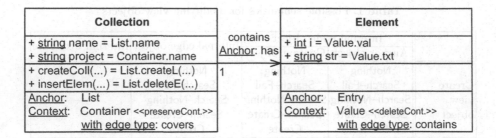

Fig. 8. Definition of an abstract graph view for module Data Storage

and an edge type has (renamed from contains) connecting both view node types. For Collection, the internal node type List is chosen as anchor node type and Container as context node type. The name attributes of List and of Container are adopted by Collection, where the name attribute of Container is changed to project. Furthermore, Collection covers the transformations of List which are named to createColl and insertElem. Module IDE may use node type Collection for managing the files of software systems. Thus, the name of a software system may be stored as project attribute and the file may be stored as name attribute of Collection. Figure 9 depicts the realization of abstract graph views for this example. For the view object cl2 in IDE, l2 of Data Storage constitutes the anchor object, and by traversing the covers-edge c1 is obtained as context object. Although view objects cl1 and cl2 point to different anchor objects in Data Storage (l1 and l2), their context object c1 is the same. Besides Collection, the view of Data Storage defines the node type Element, with node type Entry as anchor type and Value as context type. Thus, Element abstracts from the internal decoupling of a list entry and its value. In our example, Element is used by IDE to store a compile error for a certain file. Figure 9 illustrates how the object el2 references the anchor object e2 in Data Storage with context object v2. This figure also shows that edges of view type contains have an explicit representation in the runtime graph of IDE.

Stereotypes. For defining the behavioral semantics of context objects, we introduce *stereotypes* in the view diagram. They determine the strategies from Table 1 that have to be applied on creating or deleting view objects. For each context node type, one stereotype for its creation and one for its deletion has to be set. Currently, we support the creation stereotypes newContext for the Create strategy, useExistingOrFail for the Search–Fail strategy, useExistingContext for the Search–Nothing strategy, and searchExistingOrNewContext for the Search–Create strategy. The stereotype newContext creates a new context object and automatically connects it to its anchor object by an edge of the context edge type. In contrast, useExistingOrFail searches the runtime graph nondeterministically for an appropriate context object. When a match is found, an edge object of the context edge type is created which connects the found object and the new anchor object. If such an object is not found, the creation of the view object fails. To avoid this failure, the searchExisting stereotype just ignores the failure and the searchExistingOrNewContext stereotype creates a new context object. The deletion

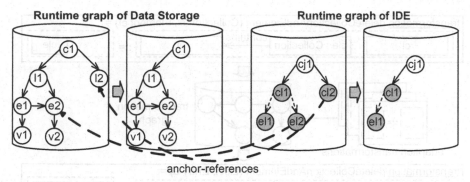

Fig. 9. Effects of deleting collection cl2 and element el2 in module IDE

of a context object can be controlled by the deleteContext for the Delete strategy from Table 1, and the preserveContext stereotype for the Nothing strategy. In our concept, the deletion of context objects is the only operation that may be defined to use the Nothing strategy, because – as the following example shows – it may be important to preserve certain context information for other anchor objects.

Example. Due to lack of space, only the delete stereotypes depicted in Figure 8 are presented here. Two different stereotypes for deletion have been chosen in the example. preserveContext has been chosen for the context of node type Collection, leading to the preservation of the context object of type Container when a view object of type Collection is deleted. The deletion of the context object of view type Element is specified as deleteContext. Thus, the deletion of a view object of type Element leads to the deletion of the corresponding list entry and its value. The top of Figure 10 shows the graph transformation deleteCollectionAndElement, which deletes a Collection cl and an Element el. Figure 9 shows the effects of executing this transformation for Data Storage and IDE. Considering the case of deleting cl2 in IDE: cl2 references l2 in Data Storage. According to preserveContext, cl2 in IDE and l2 in Data Storage are deleted, but the context c1 in Data Storage is kept. Considering the case of deleting el2 in IDE: el2 references e2 in Data Storage. According to deleteContext, el2 in IDE and e2 and v2 in Data Storage are deleted.

Translation. To execute a transformation using view types, it is translated into a transformation operating on internal types. For the translation, we re-use our runtime mechanism [6] for solving the graph rewriting dilemma. The runtime mechanism consists of the following three steps. First, the transformation is translated into a graph representing the elements and operations of the transformation. Second, the graph is transformed using *adaption transformations* leading to a graph storing appropriate elements and operations of internal types. [6] describes the adaption transformation approach in general. The adaption transformations are automatically generated from the view definition according to the minimal semantics and the stereotypes for context types. Because of the mapping definition of the view, the generation algorithm for the adaption

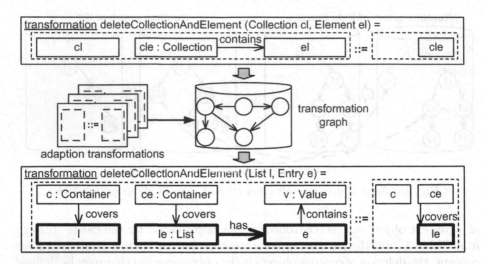

Fig. 10. Translation of graph transformations via adaption transformations

transformation is straight-forward and thus omitted in this paper. In the third step, the graph is re-translated into a graph transformation which can then be executed in the runtime graph of the module providing the view.

Example. Figure 10 illustrates the approach by considering the transformation deleteCollectionAndElement defined in module IDE. The top of the figure shows the transformation using view types of Data Storage. Then, this transformation is translated into a graph representation and modified by adaption transformations. Afterwards, at the bottom of Figure 10, a new transformation is derived from the modified graph which shows the transformation deleteCollectionAndElement only using internal specification types of Data Storage. The minimal semantics of deleteCollectionAndElement is denoted by the bold modeling elements which affect the corresponding anchor objects of the view objects. By executing this adapted transformation, l2, e2 and v2 are deleted as shown in Figure 9.

6   Related Work

[9] introduces *views in database management systems* (DBMS), where every view is defined as a query over several database tables. Although a view is perceived as a single database table from the outside, the view columns may actually be derived from several relations. In general, a database view is read-only for database users. However, some DBMS offer *updateable views* [10]. For realizing these views, the DBMS must be able to determine a unique mapping between the modifiable columns of the view and the corresponding columns of the affected database tables. The database approach is comparable to abstract graph views as proposed in this paper: A database view and its columns correspond to a graph view type and its attributes. Similar to the unique anchor node type of our approach, a unique key-element must be defined for each column of a database

view. In analogy to aggregated attributes in graph views, aggregated columns of a database view must not be changed by database users. [10] forbids the union of tables in updateable views. This restriction is softened in our approach as we allow to change attribute values of context objects which are obtained by traversing context edges of cardinality to-1 from the anchor object.

In [11], an approach is presented which offers abstract views on graph specifications. The approach extends triple graph grammars (TGG) for *virtual triple graph grammars* (VGTT), such that the abstract view and the correspondence graph are not materialized. The mapping of the abstract view to the internal specification is defined by modeling *declarative rules*. These rules define how operations concerning view objects are mapped to internal objects. Thus, the mapping of view operations is explicitly defined by declarative rules. In contrast, our approach enables the mapping definition on a more abstract level in the graph schema. From this mapping definition, the transformations are automatically derived. As views in [11] can not be materialized, the approach can not be applied for modeling distributed systems.

[5] introduces a package concept for PROGRES which resembles the UML package concept. As package interfaces are restricted to simple interfaces, the concept does not provide means for defining abstract graph views. [5] only offers a static semantics for packages, so that the concept can not be reused for modeling distributed systems. In contrast to our module concept, [5] supports package inheritance and tags for restricting the access on interface elements.

[12] presents another module concept for the GTL GRACE. As GRACE modules are defined over a common graph schema, interfaces only contain transformation signatures. These transformations may be called within transformation units of importing modules. Similar to the PROGRES package concept, GRACE modules do not provide abstract graph views or a runtime semantics.

DIEGO [13] combines the approaches of hierarchically distributed graph transformations and of encapsulated graph objects. Similar to GRACE modules, DIEGO modules are based on one common graph schema. Thus, module interfaces cover only transformation signatures and not abstract graph views. DIEGO offers a runtime semantics for modules which is based on the synchronous execution of transformations with same names in all modules. In this way, modules are coupled by a common subset of graph transformations instead of defining visual graph transformations by applying imported types.

Another approach for coupling modules is presented in [14] in which interfaces correspond to simple interfaces. [14] provides a runtime semantics for modules based on *rule refinements*, so that modules may refine imported graph transformations. Similar to DIEGO, the modules are synchronized by executing the (possible refined) transformations in parallel. Thus, the coupling of modules is based on a predefined set of graph transformations.

In [15], another module concept is introduced which offers means for module inheritance and import-export relationships between modules. This concept provides a runtime semantics for modules, but module interfaces are restricted to simple interfaces and do not support abstract graph views.

[16] describes *open graph transformation systems* (OGTS) which enable the modeling of interaction between design views using a common reference model. Comparing [16] to our approach, design views correspond to simple interfaces, but allow a renaming of view elements. In OGTS, schema types may be declared as *open types*. Open types provide a *loose semantics* for creating and deleting appropriate instances and for manipulating attribute values. In our approach, interface types are automatically open for both creation and deletion. It is future work to extend our concepts for providing open types similar to [16] which distinguish between a loose semantics for creating and deleting instances of interface types. Similar to schema types, [16] offers a loose semantics for graph transformations based on subrule relations. The loose semantics of graph transformations can be compared to the minimal semantics of our distributed graph transformations. The advantage of our approach is the ability to specify new graph transformations visually instead of having a predefined set of common transformations as in the reference model of [16].

7 Summary

The introduction of abstract graph views decouples a module's specification from its interface. The view declares new schema types and transformations which are defined by a n-to-m mapping to elements of the internal specification. To preserve the visual modeling of GTLs, our concepts offer updateable graph views. For realizing updateable views, the view has to fulfill some constraints, which allow the unique translation between view objects and internal objects. For performing an update, we have introduced minimal semantics: All operations that are performed on view objects are performed on their corresponding anchor objects. For context objects, the specifier may configure the behavior by using predefined stereotypes leading to a flexible view concept. According to the view definition, our implementation translates graph transformations concerning view objects into transformations concerning internal objects.

The presented approach for abstract graph views can also be applied in distributed systems, because the runtime semantics of our module concept is preserved. Thus, the coupling of different distributed applications can be specified by using their interfaces constituting abstract graph views. Our approach for abstract graph views is currently tested within a distributed process management system (resembling AHEAD). The approach has proven to be promising and well suited, so that we will apply the approach in further projects.

References

1. Schürr, A.: Operationales Spezifizieren mit programmierten Graphersetzungssystemen. Deutscher Universitäts-Verlag, Wiesbaden (1991)
2. Fischer, T., Niere, J., Torunski, L., Zündorf, A.: Story diagrams: A new graph rewrite language based on the Unified Modelling Language and Java. In: [17], pp. 296–309

3. Tanenbaum, A., Steen, M.V.: Distributed Systems – Pinciples and Paradigms, 2nd edn. Prentice Hall PTR, Upper Saddle River (2006)
4. Ranger, U., Schultchen, E., Mosler, C.: Specifying distributed graph transformation systems. In: Zündorf, A., Varró, D. (eds.) GraBaTs 2006. ECEASST, vol. 1 (2006)
5. Winter, A.: Visuelles Programmieren mit Graphtransformationen. Aachener Beiträge zur Informatik, vol. 27. Wissenschaftsverlag, Mainz (2000)
6. Ranger, U., Hermes, T.: Ensuring consistency in distributed graph transformation systems. In: Dwyer, M.B., Lopes, A. (eds.) FASE 2007. LNCS, vol. 4422, pp. 368–382. Springer, Heidelberg (2007)
7. Ranger, U.: Visuelle Modellierung von verteilten Systemen mit Graphersetzungssprachen (to appear, 2008)
8. Ermel, C., Rudolf, M., Taentzer, G.: The AGG approach: Language and environment. In: [18], pp. 551–603
9. Date, C.J., Darwen, H.: A Guide to the SQL Standard, 3rd edn. Addison Wesley, Boston (1993)
10. Gottlob, G., Paolini, P., Zicari, R.: Properties and update semantics of consistent views. ACM Transactions on Database Systems 13(4), 486–524 (1988)
11. Jakob, J., Königs, A., Schürr, A.: Non-materialized model view specification with triple graph grammars. In: Corradini, A., Ehrig, H., Montanari, U., Ribeiro, L., Rozenberg, G. (eds.) ICGT 2006. LNCS, vol. 4178, pp. 321–335. Springer, Heidelberg (2006)
12. Heckel, R., Hoffmann, B., Knirsch, P., Kuske, S.: Simple modules for GRACE. In: [17], pp. 383–395
13. Taentzer, G., Schürr, A.: DIEGO, Another step towards a module concept for graph transformation systems. In: Corradini, A., Montanari, U. (eds.) SEGRAGRA 1995. ENTCS, vol. 2. Elsevier Science Publishers, Amsterdam (1995)
14. Große-Rhode, M., Parisi-Presicce, F., Simeoni, M., Taentzer, G.: Modeling distributed systems by modular graph transformation based on refinement via rule expressions. In: Münch, M., Nagl, M. (eds.) AGTIVE 1999. LNCS, vol. 1779, pp. 31–45. Springer, Heidelberg (2000)
15. Ehrig, H., Engels, G.: Pragmatic and semantic aspects of a module concept for graph transformation systems. In: Cuny, J., Engels, G., Ehrig, H., Rozenberg, G. (eds.) Graph Grammars 1994. LNCS, vol. 1073, pp. 137–154. Springer, Heidelberg (1996)
16. Heckel, R., Ehrig, H., Engels, G., Taentzer, G.: A view-based approach to system modeling based on open graph transformation systems. In: [18], pp. 639–668
17. Ehrig, H., Engels, G., Kreowski, H.J., Rozenberg, G. (eds.): TAGT 1998. LNCS, vol. 1764. Springer, Heidelberg (2000)
18. Ehrig, H., Engels, G., Kreowski, H.J., Rozenberg, G. (eds.): Handbook on Graph Grammars and Computing by Graph Transformation: Applications, Languages, and Tools, 1st edn., vol. 2. World Scientific, Singapore (1999)

Programmed Graph Rewriting with DEVS

Eugene Syriani and Hans Vangheluwe

School of Computer Science
McGill University, Montréal, Québec, Canada

Abstract. In this article, we propose to use the Discrete EVent system Specification (DEVS) formalism to describe and execute graph transformation control structures. We provide a short review of existing programmed graph rewriting systems, listing the control structures they provide. As DEVS is a timed, highly modular, hierarchical formalism for the description of reactive systems, control structures such as sequence, choice, and iteration are easily modelled. Non-determinism and parallel composition also follow from DEVS' semantics. The proposed approach is illustrated through the modelling of a simple PacMan game, first in AToM³ and then using DEVS. We show how the use of DEVS allows for modular modification of control structure.

1 Introduction

In 1996, Blostein et al.[1] described some issues regarding the, at that time very sporadic, practical use of graph rewriting. Graphs are a versatile and expressive data representation, and there are many advantages to the explicit representation (as opposed to encoding in the form of programs) of graph transformations. Issues such as expressiveness, scale-ability and re-use of models of graph transformation as well as the ability to integrate such models with traditional software components were considered critical enablers for wide-spread use of graph transformations. During the last decade, several of these issues have been addressed and tools have been developed. In particular, tools such as FUJABA [2] allow for *programmed graph rewriting*. The purpose of programmed graph rewriting is to be able to model the control structure of (graph) transformation. This is done in terms of control flow primitives such as *sequence*, *branching* (choice), and *looping* (iteration). *Hierarchical encapsulation* allows for *modular construction* (and re-use) of control flow structures. Some tools add expressiveness through *non-determinism* and *parallel composition*. In general, it is also desirable for a control structure language to be target (programming) language *neutral*. The explicit incorporation of *time* is rare in current tools. The above requirements were summarized recently in [3].

In our quest for the most appropriate formalism (*i.e.*, which optimally satisfies the above requirements) to describe programmed graph transformation, we now briefly present the features of tools with programmed graph transformation capabilities, based on [4]. Note that our own AToM³ [5,6], "A Tool for Multiformalism and Meta-Modelling" which has very limited (priority-based) control structuring, will be introduced in section 3.

A. Schürr, M. Nagl, and A. Zündorf (Eds.): AGTIVE 2007, LNCS 5088, pp. 136–151, 2008.
© Springer-Verlag Berlin Heidelberg 2008

Graph Rewriting and Transformation (GReAT). [7,8,9] treats the source model, the target model and the temporary objects created during the transformation as a single graph using a unified metamodel.

The GReAT graph transformation language uses the Single Pushout algebraic approach for subgraph matching. Rules consist of a pattern graph described using UML Class Diagram notation where the elements can be marked to match a pattern (**Bind role**), to remove elements (**Delete role**) or to create elements (**CreateNew role**). A guard is associated with each production; this is an OCL expression that operates on vertex and edge attributes. An attribute mapping can also be defined to generate values of vertex and edge attributes with arithmetic and string expressions.

GReAT's control flow language uses a control flow diagram notation where a production is represented by a block. Sequencing is enabled by the use of input and output interfaces (**Inports** and **Outports**) of a block. Packets (the graph model) are fed to productions via these ports. The **Inport** also provides an optimization in the sense that it specifies an initial binding for the start of the pattern matcher. Two types of hierarchical rules are supported. A **block** pushes all its incoming packets to the first internal rule, whereas a **forblock** pushes one packet through all its internal rules. Branching is achieved using test case rules, consisting of a left-hand side (LHS) and a guard only. If a match is found, the packet will be sent to the output interface. Parallel execution is possible when the **Outports** of a production are connected to different **Inports**. There is no notion of time.

Visual Modelling and Transformation System (VMTS). In VMTS [3,10], the LHS and right-hand side (RHS) of a graph transformation rule are represented as two separate graphs. They can be linked (internal causality) by XSL scripts. These scripts allow attribute operations and represent the **create** and **modify** operation of the transformation step. Also, parameters and pivot nodes can be passed to a step for optimization.

The programmed graph rewriting system of VMTS is the VMTS Control Flow Language (VCFL), a stereotyped Activity Diagram. This abstract statemachine handles pre- and post-conditions of rules. Sequencing is achieved by linking transformation steps; loops are allowed. Branching in VCFL is conditioned by an OCL expression. In case of multiple branching (step connected to more than one step), only the first successfully evaluated branch will apply its transformation step. Iteration is controlled by loops in a sequence of steps. A branch can also be added to provide conditional loops. Hierarchical steps are composed of a sequence of primitive steps. A primitive step ends with success if the terminating state is reached and ends with failure when a match fails. However, in hierarchical steps, when a decision cannot be found at the level of primitive steps, the control flow is sent to the parent state or else the transformation fails. Parallelism is not yet implemented in VCFL. VMTS is language-oriented towards the .NET framework. There is no notion of time.

PROGReS, FUJABA and MOFLON. The PROgrammed Graph REwriting System (PROGReS) [11,12] was the first fully implemented environment to allow programming through graph transformations. It has very advanced features not found in other tools such as back-tracking. Insights gained through the development of PROGReS have led to FUJABA (From UML to Java and Back Again) [2,13], a completely redesigned graph transformation environment based on Java and UML. FUJABA's programmed graph rewriting system is based on Story Charts, a combination of Story Diagrams [13] and Statecharts. An activity in such a diagram contains either graph rewrite rules, which adopt Collaboration Diagram-like representation, or pure Java code. The graph schemes for graph rewriting rules exploit UML class diagrams. With the expressiveness of Story Charts, graph transformation rules can be sequenced (using success and failure guards on the linking edges) along with activities containing code. Branching is ensured by the condition blocks which act like an if-else construct. An activity can be a for-all story pattern, which acts like a while loop on a transformation rule.

FUJABA's approach is implementation-oriented. Classes define method signatures and method content is described by Story Chart diagrams. All models are compiled to Java code. There is no notion of time.

The MOFLON [14] toolset uses the FUJABA engine for graph transformation, since the latter already features UML-like graph schemata. It provides an environment where transformations are defined by Triple Graph Grammars (TGGs) [15]. These TGGs are subsequently compiled to Story Diagrams [13]. This adds declarative power to FUJABA similar to that of the OMG's QVT (Query/View/Transformation – www.omg.org).

In the sequel, we propose the Discrete EVent system Specification (DEVS) formalism [16] to describe transformation control structures. Using DEVS gives us sufficient expressiveness to match that of the tools described above, thus satisfying the requirements for transformation control structure description languages listed before. Furthermore, as with the adaptation of known formalisms such as Activity Diagrams in tools such as FUJABA, using DEVS means that no new formalism needs to be invented (and its properties investigated). Also, existing tools for analysis, simulation, and code synthesis may thus be re-used for the control structure part of a graph transformation model.

The remainder of this paper is structured as follows. Section 2 describes the DEVS formalism. Section 3 describes PacMan, a small case study, and how it is modelled in AToM^3. Section 4 describes how the priority-based graph rewriting semantics of AToM^3 can be modelled using DEVS. The combination of DEVS with Graph Rewriting rules is very elegant and orthogonal. It is shown how the modularity of DEVS allows for easy modification of the transformation control structure. This modification includes the specification of real-time user interaction. Section 5 describes the advantages of using DEVS for programmed graph transformation and section 6 summarizes and concludes.

2   Discrete Event System Specification (DEVS)

This section introduces the *Discrete EVent system Specification* (DEVS) formalism. In the rest of the paper, it will be shown how the modularity and expressiveness of DEVS are well suited to encapsulate graph rewriting building blocks.

The DEVS formalism was introduced in the late seventies by Bernard Zeigler to develop a rigorous basis for the compositional modelling and simulation of discrete event systems [16]. The DEVS formalism has been successfully applied to the design, performance analysis and implementation of a plethora of complex systems.

A DEVS model is either *atomic* or *coupled*. An atomic model describes the behaviour of a reactive system. A coupled model is the composition of several DEVS sub-models which can be either atomic or coupled. Submodels have *ports*, which are connected by channels. Ports are either *input* or *output*. Ports and channels allow a model to receive and send signals (events) from and to other models. A channel must go from an output port of some model to an input port of a different model, from an input port of a coupled model to an input port of one of its sub-models, or from an output port of a sub-model to an output port of its parent model.

An **atomic DEVS**[1] model is a tuple $(S, X, Y, \delta^{int}, \delta^{ext}, \lambda, \tau)$ where S is a set of sequential **states**, one of which is the *initial* state. X is a set of allowed **input events**. Y is a set of allowed **output events**. There are two types of transitions between states: $\delta^{int} : S \to S$ is the **internal transition function**, $\delta^{ext} : Q \times X \to S$ is the **external transition function**, Associated with each state are $\tau : S \to \mathbb{R}_0^+$, the **time-advance** function and $\lambda : S \to Y$, the **output function**. In this definition, $Q = \{(s, e) \in S \times \mathbb{R}^+ \mid 0 \le e \le \tau(s)\}$ is called the **total state space**. For each $(s, e) \in Q$, e is called the **elapsed time**. $\mathbb{R}_0^+$ denotes the positive reals with zero included.

Informally, the operational semantics of an atomic model is as follows: the model starts in its initial state. It will remain in any given state for as long as the time-advance of that state specifies or until input is received on some port. If no input is received, after the time-advance of the state expires, the model first (before changing state) sends output as specified by λ, and then instantaneously jumps to a new state specified by δ^{int}. If input is received however before the time for the next internal transition, then it is δ^{ext} which is applied. The external transition depends on the current state, the time elapsed since the last transition and the inputs from the input ports.

The following definition formalizes the concept of coupled DEVS models. A **coupled DEVS**[1] model named D is a tuple $(X, Y, N, M, I, Z, select)$ where X is a set of allowed **input events** and Y is a set of allowed **output events**. N is a set of **component names** (or labels) such that $D \notin N$. $M = \{M_n \mid n \in N, M_n$ is a DEVS model (atomic or coupled) with input set X_n and output set $Y_n\}$ is a set of DEVS **sub-models**. $I = \{I_n \mid n \in N, I_n \subseteq N \cup \{D\}\}$ is a set of **influencer** sets for each component named n. I encodes the connection topology of sub-models. $Z = \{Z_{i,n} \mid \forall n \in N, i \in I_n.Z_{i,n} : Y_i \to X_n$ or $Z_{D,n} : X \to X_n$ or $Z_{i,D} : Y_i \to Y\}$ is a set of **transfer functions** from each component i to some component n. $select : 2^N \to N$ is the **select** or tie-breaking function. 2^N denotes the powerset of N (the set of all sub-sets of N).

---

[1] For simplicity, we do not present a formalization of the concept of "ports".

The connection topology of sub-models is expressed by the influencer set of each component. Note that for a given model n, this set includes not only the external models that provide inputs to n, but also its own internal sub-models that produce its output (if n is a coupled model.) Transfer functions represent output-to-input translations between components, and can be thought of as channels that make the appropriate type translations. For example, a "departure" event output of one sub-model is translated to an "arrival" event on a connected sub-model's input. The *select* function takes care of conflicts as explained below.

The semantics for a coupled model is, informally, the parallel composition of all the sub-models. A priori, each sub-model in a coupled model is assumed to be an independent process, concurrent to the rest. There is no explicit method of synchronization between processes. Blocking does not occur except if it is explicitly modelled by the output function of a sender, and the external transition function of a receiver. There is however a *serialization* whenever there are multiple sub-models that have an internal transition scheduled to be performed at the same time. The modeller controls which of the conflicting sub-models undergoes its transition first by means of the *select* function.

We have developed our own DEVS simulator called `pythonDEVS` [17], grafted onto the object-oriented scripting language Python. In a recent M.Sc. thesis [18], a compiler for Modelica (`www.modelica.org`) textual representations of DEVS models as well as a visual modelling environment were developed.

3   A Small Case Study: PacMan in AToM³

In this section, we describe the simple priority-based graph rewriting in our meta-modelling and model transformation tool AToM³ [5,6]. In the next section, this hard-coded control structure will be modelled explicitly using DEVS. As an example, we use a simplified version of the PacMan video game used in Heckel's tutorial introduction of graph transformation [19].

3.1   The PacMan Language (Abstract and Concrete Syntax)

The PacMan language has five distinct elements: PacMan, Ghost, Food, GridNode and ScoreBoard. Fig. 1 shows the meta-model (model of the abstract syntax) of this modelling language in AToM³. PacMan, Ghost and Food objects can be linked to GridNode objects; note the use of associations. This depicts that these objects can be "on" a gridNode. The self-association between GridNode objects represents the geometric organization of the game area, similar to the classical PacMan video game. At a semantic level, this will also denote that PacMan and Ghost "may move" to a connected gridNode. A Scoreboard object holds an integer valued attribute score. The reason for having different associations from the classes to the GridNode class is for concrete visual syntax purposes. AToM³ allows one to associate a visual representation to each class and association. Associations can be concretely represented visually by means of arrows or by a geometric/topological constraint relation, such as a PacMan being centered over a GridNode. Note how in this example there are no restrictions on the number of instances of each element, nor on the number of links to a GridNode instance.

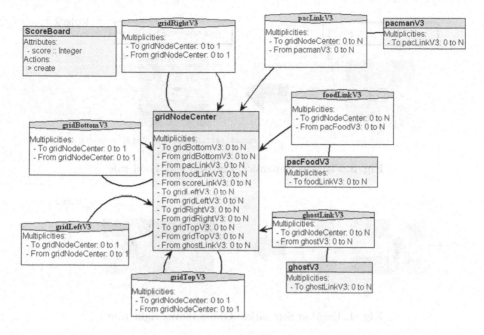

Fig. 1. The PacMan Meta-Model

3.2   The PacMan Semantics (Graph Grammar)

The operational semantics of the PacMan formalism is defined in a Graph Grammar model which consists of a number of rules. In the rules in the following figures, concrete syntax is used. this is a useful feature for domain-specific modelling unique to AToM[3]. Dashed lines were added to explicitly show the "on" links. Rule 1 in Fig. 2 shows killing: when a Ghost object is on a GridNode which has a PacMan object, the PacMan is removed. Rule 2 in Fig. 3 shows eating: when a PacMan object is on a GridNode which has a Food object, Food is removed and the score gets updated (using an attribute update expression). Rule 3 in Fig. 4 expresses the movement of a Ghost object to the right and rule

Fig. 2. PacMan Semantics: Ghost kills PacMan rule

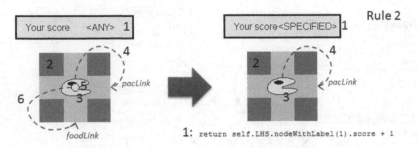

Fig. 3. PacMan Semantics: PacMan eats Food rule

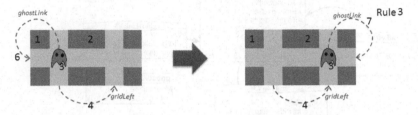

Fig. 4. PacMan Semantics: Ghost moves right rule

8 in Fig. 5 the movement of a PacMan object to the left. Similar rules to move Ghosts and PacMan objects up, down, left and right are part of the grammar but are not shown. Rules 1 and 2 have priorities 1 and 2 respectively. All remaining rules have the same priority 3.

3.3   AToM³'s Graph Grammar Semantics

AToM³'s graph rewriting engine supports priority-based execution of rewrite rules. Rules are grouped based on their priority. Rewriting starts with the highest-priority group of rules. If for at least one of the rules in the group, a match if found in the host graph, one of those rules is chosen non-deterministically. Subsequently, the re-write is performed on the host graph and control goes back to the group of rules with the highest priority. If none of the rules in the group

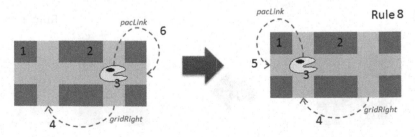

Fig. 5. PacMan Semantics: PacMan moves left rule

match, control goes to the group of rules with the next lower priority, and so on. If no groups of rules are left (even the lowest-priority rules do not yield a match), the transformation terminates. In AToM³, execution can be done step-by-step (for simulation purposes) or in continuous mode (useful for terminating model-to-model transformations). Note that AToM³ allows the specification of (real-)time taken by each rule-rewrite. The time may be extracted from model attributes. This allows for meaningful simulation animation.

4   Programmed Graph Rewriting Using DEVS

The purpose of programmed graph rewriting is to explicitly model the control flow of (graph) transformation. This is done in terms of control flow primitives such as sequence, choice, and looping. Hierarchical encapsulation allows modular construction (and reuse) of control flow structures. Some tools increase expressiveness through constructs such as non-determinism and parallelism. Rather than inventing a new language for control structure description, we propose to use the DEVS formalism, with its precisely defined syntax and semantics, presented above.

As an illustration of how this approach satisfies the requirements stated earlier, we explicitly model AToM³'s Graph Transformation execution engine described above. The starting point of our approach is to

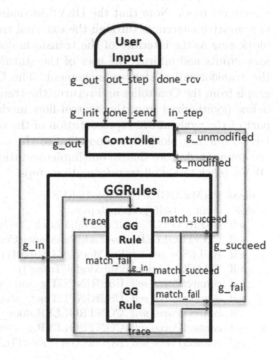

Fig. 6. The overall coupled DEVS model

encapsulate to-be-transformed graphs in DEVS events. These events will be sent between the DEVS building blocks encoding graph transformation rules. Additionally, events may encode control signals which can be sent to designated ports of DEVS building blocks. Only atomic DEVS models perform actual transformations. Coupled DEVS models allow one to hierarchically construct complex transformation models. Atomic DEVS models are highly encapsulated (they can only communicate via their input- and output-ports) and can be used to represent a variety of models in different formalisms, ranging from code (in the target language of the DEVS simulator used – Python in our case) to Statecharts. The only constraint is that building blocks need to accept graphs on their input port and, after transformation, produce graphs on their output port. The topology of the coupled DEVS models encodes the control structure. As a result of the DEVS semantics, the flow of events (graphs) through a DEVS coupled model resembles data flow more than control flow. In the construction which follows, we will only allow one model to flow through the network at any time. This effectively makes data flow and control flow identical. In the future, we will however exploit the data flow nature of DEVS networks, in particular for parallel implementations.

Fig. 6 shows the overall structure of the DEVS model for AToM^3-style graph transformation. Each block is shown with its ports along with the connections. Execution (transformation) is triggered by some user control. User intervention (such as a possible interruption of a running simulation) is modelled in the UserInput block. Note that the DEVS formalism allows one to specify external pre-emptive interrupts through the external transition function. The Controller block acts as the interface of the transformation system to the user: it receives user inputs and informs the user of the status of the execution. It also models the transformation steps management. The GGRules block receives the host graph from the Controller and returns the transformed graph. The Python code below (synthesized from the control flow model given in Fig. 6) shows a small part of the **pythonDEVS** representation of the overall model. Instances of atomic DEVS building blocks corresponding to the control flow model building blocks are **connected**. Note that in our implementation, we have added a Trace atomic DEVS block to log all transformation steps.

```
1  class PacManGGExec(CoupledDEVS):
2  def __init__(self, graph, steps):
3      self.USERINPUT = self.addSubModel(UserInput(graph=graph, steps=steps))
4      self.CONTROLLER = self.addSubModel(Controller())
5      self.RULES = self.addSubModel(GGRules())
6      self.TRACE = self.addSubModel(Trace())
7      self.connectPorts(self.USERINPUT.g_out, self.CONTROLLER.g_init)
8      self.connectPorts(self.USERINPUT.out_step, self.CONTROLLER.in_step)
9      self.connectPorts(self.CONTROLLER.done_send, self.USERINPUT.done_rcv)
10     self.connectPorts(self.CONTROLLER.g_out, self.RULES.g_in)
11     self.connectPorts(self.RULES.trace, self.TRACE.in_rule)
```

4.1   The User Input Block

UserInput is an atomic DEVS block that sends graphs and "steps" control signals and receives termination events. The graphs are Abstract Syntax Graphs (ASGs), AToM^3's basic internal data structure, of models in the PacMan language. Steps represent the number of steps the user requests the simulator to perform in a row. 0 ends the simulation. ∞ runs the simulation in continuous mode, executing till termination (or until interrupted by an external signal). The reception of a Termination event means that either the requested number of steps have been performed or that the execution has reached its end. In the latter case, no more transformations can be applied to the graph. The inports and outports of the UserInput block are connected to the Controller block.

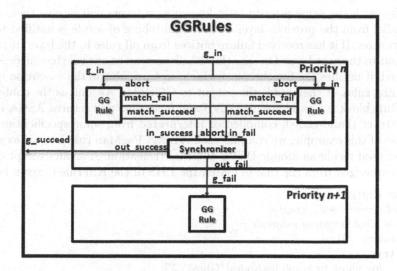

Fig. 7. Managing priorities

4.2   The Controller Block

The Controller atomic DEVS block encodes the coordination logic between the external input and the transformation model. It is the control that receives the graph to transform and the number of steps to be applied. It also notifies the user about termination. The Controller sends the graph to the transformation model and waits for a graph in return. The returned graph may or may not be modified. This is repeated depending on the "steps" requests received. Note that the system could in principle receive multiple graphs at any time (thanks to the data flow nature of DEVS). Also, the user could request more "steps" even when there are some steps left in the running transformation.

4.3   The Graph Grammar Rule Blocks and Priority

The graph rewriting rules presented in section 3.2 including the semantics of prioritized rewriting, are encoded in the transformation block GGRules. GGRules is a coupled DEVS model which receives a graph and outputs a graph. GGRules is composed of one or more GGRule blocks. Each GGRule satisfies certain properties. There is at most one rule that is applied per step. If a rule fails, the graph is sent to the next rule until the last rule is reached. If the last rule also fails, then no rules have been applied in this step, hence GGRules sends back its input graph. Otherwise it is the newly transformed graph that is sent back, directly from the rule where the match occurred.

The AToM[3] graph rewriting system allows assigning priorities to rules to order their execution. If multiple rules happen to have the same priority, AToM[3] non-deterministically chooses one of those yielding a match. A Synchronizer block is introduced to model this situation in our DEVS model. This is depiced in Fig. 7.

All rules with the same priority (also known as a layer) will receive their input in parallel from the previous layer. A failed matching of a rule is notified to the Synchronizer. If it has received failure notices from all rules in the layer, it passes the input to the next layer. On the other hand, as soon as one rule has successfully executed, it notifies the Synchronizer which, in turn, aborts the execution of the remaining rules. It then sends the output to GGRules. As long as the content of a GGRule block is a valid atomic DEVS and it accepts and returns ASGs, it can be arbitrary (hand-coded, compiled or interpreted from some specification). In the case of this example, we compile each AToM³ PacMan rule into an **execute** method used inside an atomic DEVS external transition. A small excerpt of the code synthesized from the rule to match the LHS of the Kill rule is given below:

```
1    class Kill(Rule):
2      def execute(self, graph):
3        # Find matching subgraph #
4        match = 0
5        try:
6          for ghost in graph.listNodes['GhostV3']:
7            for ghostLink in ghost.out_connections_:
8              if ghostLink.__class__.__name__ == 'GhostLinkV3':
9                for pacman in contains.out_connections_:
10                 if pacman.__class__.__name__ == 'PacmanV3':
11                   for pacLink in contains.out_connections_:
12                     if pacLink.__class__.__name__ == 'PacLinkV3':
13                       match = 1 # First occurence of the subgraph
14                       break
15                 if match: break
16              if match: break
17            if match: break
18        except:
19          return None
20        if not match:
21          return None
22        # Transform subgraph #
23        ....
24        return graph
```

4.4   Extending the Model

To illustrate the power of this formalism to describe control flow of graph rewrinting systems, we now *extend* the previous model. Consider the PacMan formalism described in section 3 and the graph grammar that described its behaviour. Suppose we would like more interaction with the user. In the model used before, the simulation could be triggered by the user specifying the numbers of steps to be performed or continuous execution (till termination). We will now allow user control of PacMan movement to more closely mimic the behaviour of the classic PacMan video game. Fig. 8 shows the extended model. The UserInput block remains unchanged, with an outport added. The user can now send a pressed Key code to the Controller block. This enables us to simulate the user interrupts to move the PacMan up, down, left or right. The behaviour of the Controller block is the same as long as no Key is recieved. If this event occurs however, the Controller waits for the reception of a graph from the transformation block(s) and then sends the Key and the Graph to the UserControlledRules block. Otherwise, graphs are always sent to the AutonomousRules block. The AutonomousRules encapsulates all the rules that do not need user intervention: PacMan eating, Ghost killing PacMan and Ghost moving. The structure of this block is exactly the same as the original GGRules block.

The UserControlledRules model consists of the remaining rules, those resposible for PacMan movement (left, right, up, down). This coupled DEVS block recieves a Key and an input graph and outputs a graph that has undergone the requested transformation. Fig. 9 presents the content of this block. The received Key goes through a Dispatch block. This block choses where to send the graph depending on the key pressed. The graph is sent to at most one of the Up, Down, Left and Right blocks. These blocks have the exact same structure as their counterpart in the original GGRule model. Note that event-based selec-

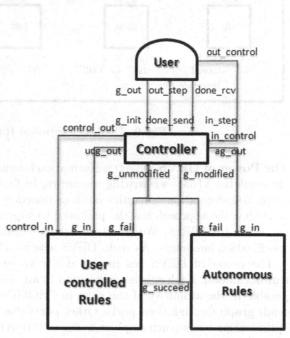

Fig. 8. The Extended DEVS model

tion of rules has previously been called "Event-driven Graph Rewriting".

With the first model, we showed how to model a simulator for graph grammar execution to mimic the AToM³ behaviour. Then, we showed how to extend continuous execution with user control over the execution. Note how the extension of the former model needed very little effort thanks to the modularity of DEVS blocks and the ability of DEVS to represent interrupts. Only adding blocks and connections but no modification of any original blocks was needed.

5   Advantages of Using DEVS

The approach described above elegantly satisfies all the requirements enumerated at the beginning of this paper.

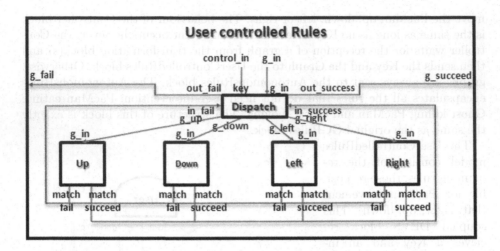

Fig. 9. The User-controlled Rules block

The Power of DEVS. The transformation language used in the PacMan example emulates AToM^3's rewriting semantics. In fact, we could have used another graph transformation semantics (such as unordered or layered graph rewriting). Note that the approach has the potential to support features such as backtracking as in PROGReS. We could even have combined different transformation specification languages. As such, DEVS acts as a "glue" language.

The power of DEVS lies in the ability to express the control flow of the transformation. Each rule is represented in an atomic-DEVS block (this is comparable to the atomicity of the rules in PROGReS). Blocks receive graphs and sends graph through their ports. Other ports can be added to for example send optimization hints (such as pivot nodes in GReAT and VMTS) or to pass some information on the flow of the rule set (like the Key in the extended PacMan model). DEVS allows modularity. Indeed, coupled DEVS blocks can be treated as black boxes. The use of DEVS allows for multi-level hierarchies in models. Sequencing is treated as in GReAT by simply connecting block ports. Iteration and loops can thus be modelled. A given block can be a test block for branching if we give it such a semantics (*i.e.,* no transformation occurs). This is what the Dispatch block in the PacMan example depicts. Parallel execution is provided by the DEVS formalism when an output port is connected to many input ports. If execution (not simulated) parallelism is needed, the parallel DEVS [20] formalism can be used.

Using the DEVS formalism as a control flow language for graph rewriting enabled us to not only model the AToM^3 simulator for graph grammar execution but also to provide an improved version of it which combined continuous execution and user interaction. Note that we are thus modelling control structures supporting step by step simulation, continuous simulation and user controlled simulation which are not in the system under study, but rather in the execution environment.

Scalability and Multi-Formalism Modelling. The beauty of DEVS models lies in the modularity of its building blocks. In fact, each block performs an action given some input and can produce outputs. This modularity trivially supports the combination of building blocks specified using *multiple formalisms*. Hence, we may combine graph grammars with for example Statecharts and code. This is the key to scaling up (graph) transformation modelling to arbitrarily more complex models, far beyond the limits of pure graph grammar systems.

Modelling Time. Timed Graph Transformation, as proposed by Gyapay, Heckel and Varró [21] integrates time in the double push-out approach. They extend the definition of a production by introducing, in the model and rules, a chronos element that stores the notion of time. Rules can monotonically increase the time. DEVS is inherently a timed formalism, as explained in section 2. In contrast with [21], it is the execution of a rule that can increase time and not the rule itself. Hence, the control flow (of the graph transformation) has full access to it. As pointed out in [21], time can be used as a metric to express how many time units are consumed to execute a rule. Having time at the level of the block containing a rule rather that in the rule itself does not lose this expressiveness. Also, providing time to the control flow structure can enhance the semantics of the transformation. AToM^3 for example provides control over execution time delay for animation (see section 3). In the PacMan example, when modelling the user we can give meaning to the time delay between the execution of different rules. As an example, the autonomous rules may take more time than the user controlled rules moving PacMan. This gives more time for the user to "interrupt". But if, for instance, the ghost-moving rules take less time, then the user needs to interrupt faster to move PacMan. This becomes closer to a game especially if a real-time simulator such as RT-DEVS [22] is used.

6   Conclusions and Future Work

In this article, we have introduced the Discrete Event system Specification (DEVS) formalism to describe and execute graph transformation control structures. We provided a short review of existing programmed graph rewriting systems, listing the control structures they provide. As DEVS is a timed, highly modular, hierarchical formalism for the description of reactive systems, control structures such as sequence, choice, and iteration are easily modelled. Non-determinism and parallel composition also follow from DEVS' semantics. The proposed approach was illustrated through the modelling of a simple PacMan game, first in AToM^3 and then with DEVS. We showed how the use of DEVS ultimately allows real-time simulation/execution.

We plan to further investigate the use of DEVS. This will include various types of code synthesis from rules on the one hand and visual control structure specifications on the other hand, beyond our current non-optimized prototype. We also consider mapping our control flow formalism onto formalisms other than DEVS, more suited for real (as opposed to simulated) parallel execution.

We plan to completely model our AToM^3 environment in DEVS. We will then be able to explicitly model users interacting with a transformation environment. This will allow for automated testing of interactive transformations as well as for optimization of transformation models for different types of users.

As consistency is a very important issue in modelling, we plan to integrate Triple Graph Grammars [15] in our DEVS framework. This will allow model synchronization and bi-directional transformations.

Acknowledgments

The authors thank the participants of the 2007 Bellairs CaMPAM workshop for stimulating discussions on programmed graph rewriting as well as the AGTIVE conference attendees for insightful comments. The Natural Sciences and Engineering Research Council (NSERC) of Canada is gratefully acknowledged for partial support of this work.

References

1. Blostein, D., Fahmy, H., Grbavec, A.: Issues in the practical use of graph rewriting. In: Selected papers from the 5th International Workshop on Graph Grammars and Their Application to Computer Science, pp. 38–55. Springer, Heidelberg (1996)
2. Nickel, U., Niere, J., Zündorf, A.: Tool demonstration: The FUJABA environment. In: ICSE 2000: Proceedings of the 22nd International Conference on Software Engineering, pp. 742–745. ACM Press, New York (2000)
3. Lengyel, L., Levendovszky, T., Mezei, G., Charaf, H.: Control flow support in metamodel-based model transformation frameworks. In: EUROCON 2005 International Conference on "Computer as a tool", pp. 595–598. IEEE, Los Alamitos (2005)
4. Ehrig, K., Guerra, E., de Lara, J., Lengyel, L., Levendovszky, T., Prange, U., Taentzer, G., Varró, D., Varró-Gyapay, S.: Model transformation by graph transformation: A comparative study. In: MTiP 2005, International Workshop on Model Transformations in Practice (Satellite Event of MoDELS 2005), Montego Bay, Jamaica (2005)
5. de Lara, J., Vangheluwe, H.: AToM^3: A tool for multi-formalism and meta-modelling. In: Kutsche, R.-D., Weber, H. (eds.) ETAPS 2002 and FASE 2002. LNCS, vol. 2306, pp. 174–188. Springer, Heidelberg (2002)
6. de Lara, J., Vangheluwe, H., Alfonseca, M.: Meta-modelling and graph grammars for multi-paradigm modelling in AToM^3. Software and Systems Modeling (SoSyM) 3, 194–209 (2004)
7. Vizhanyo, A., Agrawal, A., Shi, F.: Towards generation of high-performance transformations. In: Karsai, G., Visser, E. (eds.) GPCE 2004. LNCS, vol. 3286, pp. 298–316. Springer, Heidelberg (2004)
8. Agrawal, A.: Metamodel based model transformation language. In: OOPSLA 2003: Companion of the 18th annual ACM SIGPLAN Conference on Object Oriented Programming Systems Languages and Applications, pp. 386–387. ACM Press, New York (2003)

9. Agrawal, A., Karsai, G., Kalmar, Z., Neema, S., Shi, F., Vizhanyo, A.: The design of a language for model transformations. Software and Systems Modeling (SoSyM) 5, 261–288 (2005)
10. Lengyel, L., Levendovszky, T., Mezei, G., Charaf, H.: Model transformation with a visual control flow language. International Journal of Computer Science (IJCS) 1, 45–53 (2006)
11. Blostein, D., Schürr, A.: Computing with graphs and graph rewriting. Proceedings in Informatics, 1–21 (1999)
12. Schürr, A., Winter, A.J., Zündorf, A.: Graph grammar engineering with progres. In: Botella, P., Schäfer, W. (eds.) ESEC 1995. LNCS, vol. 989, pp. 219–234. Springer, Heidelberg (1995)
13. Fischer, T., Niere, J., Turunski, L., Zündorf, A.: Story diagrams: A new graph grammar language based on the Unified Modelling Language and Java. In: Ehrig, H., Engels, G., Kreowski, H.-J., Rozenberg, G. (eds.) TAGT 1998. LNCS, vol. 1764, pp. 296–309. Springer, Heidelberg (2000)
14. Amelunxen, C., Königs, A., Rötschke, T., Schürr, A.: Moflon: A standardcompliant metamodeling framework with graph transformations. In: Rensink, A., Warmer, J. (eds.) ECMDA-FA 2006. LNCS, vol. 4066, pp. 361–375. Springer, Heidelberg (2006)
15. Schürr, A.: Specification of Graph Translators with Triple Graph Grammars. In: Mayr, E.W., Schmidt, G., Tinhofer, G. (eds.) WG 1994. LNCS, vol. 903, pp. 151–163. Springer, Heidelberg (1995)
16. Zeigler, B.P.: Multifacetted Modelling and Discrete Event Simulation. Academic Press, London (1984)
17. Bolduc, J.S., Vangheluwe, H.: The modelling and simulation package Python-DEVS for classical hierarchical DEVS. MSDL Technical report MSDL-TR-2001-01, McGill University (2001)
18. Song, H.: Infrastructure for DEVS modelling and experimentation. MSc dissertation, McGill University (2006)
19. Heckel, R.: Graph transformation in a nutshell. In: Proceedings of the School on Foundations of Visual Modelling Techniques (FoVMT 2004) of the SegraVis Research Training Network. Electronic Notes in Theoretical Computer Science (ENTCS), vol. 148, pp. 187–198. Elsevier, Amsterdam (2006)
20. Chow, A.C.H.: Parallel devs: a parallel, hierarchical, modular modeling formalism and its distributed simulator. Transactions of the Society for Computer Simulation International 13, 55–67 (1996)
21. Gyapay, S., Heckel, R., Varró, D.: Graph transformation with time: Causality and logical clocks. In: Corradini, A., Ehrig, H., Kreowski, H.-J., Rozenberg, G. (eds.) ICGT 2002. LNCS, vol. 2505, pp. 120–134. Springer, Heidelberg (2002)
22. Hong, J.S., Song, H.S., Kim, T.G., Park, K.H.: A real-time discrete event system specification formalism for seamless real-time software development. Discrete Event Dynamic Systems 7, 355–375 (1997)

Relational Growth Grammars – A Parallel Graph Transformation Approach with Applications in Biology and Architecture

Ole Kniemeyer[1], Günter Barczik[2], Reinhard Hemmerling[1], and Winfried Kurth[1]

[1] Brandenburgische Technische Universität Cottbus, Department of Computer Science, Chair for Practical Computer Science/Graphics Systems, Ewald-Haase-Straße 12/13, 03044 Cottbus, Germany
[2] Brandenburgische Technische Universität Cottbus, Department of Architecture, Chair for Contextual Building, Design and Construction, Konrad-Wachsmann-Allee 8, 03046 Cottbus, Germany

Abstract. We present the formalism of relational growth grammars. They are a variant of graph grammars with a principal application for plant modelling, where they extend the well-established, but limited formalism of L-systems. The main property is the application of rules in parallel, motivated by the fact that life is fundamentally parallel. A further speciality is the dynamic creation of right-hand sides on rule application. Relational growth grammars have been successfully used not only for plant modelling, but also to model general 3D structures or systems of Artificial Life. We illustrate these applications at several examples, all being implemented using our programming language XL which extends Java and provides an implementation of relational growth grammars.

1 Introduction

The field of applications where graph transformations today are most often used is the construction of models for software systems [1]. In this paper we will introduce a variant of parallel graph grammars which was designed with another sort of applications in mind, namely, the short and unobscured specification of multiscaled functional-structural models of growing organisms, particularly plants [2]. There is evidence that this class of rewriting systems, which we have called *relational growth grammars* in view of the intended principal application, is well-suited to model the dynamics of complex arrangements of three-dimensional components. These 3D structures can be living (e. g., plant organs) or artificial (e. g., buildings, in this case the dynamics corresponds to the design process and the final result is the actual blueprint). In computer science as well as in bioinformatics and systems biology there is significant interest in models describing dynamical systems with a dynamical structure [3], and relational growth grammars seem to be a good candidate for a formalism capable to express such models in a quite intuitive way [4].

A. Schürr, M. Nagl, and A. Zündorf (Eds.): AGTIVE 2007, LNCS 5088, pp. 152–167, 2008.

Until now, true graph grammars were seldom applied for dynamical simulations of the 3D structure of plants. Instead, other concepts were used for this purpose: L-systems (string grammars with parallel replacement) [5,6], finite automata [7], Markov chains [8,9], cellular automata [10], or the paradigm of object-oriented programming (OOP) [11,12,13]. The latter is especially useful when a linkage between structures and processes (implemented as methods) is intended, and the combination of L-systems and an object-oriented language (C++) led to the language L+C [14]. In fact, the automata-based approaches from the above list can principally be translated into grammars of L-system type (see, e. g., [15]), and the same holds for Markov chains if stochastic grammars are allowed – hence, all can be roughly subsumed under L-systems and OOP.

However, in their nearly 40 years of use in plant modelling, L-systems have shown some deficiencies (see also [16]):

- Structures have to be serialized into strings of symbols in order to make them representable by an L-system. This is acceptable for tree-like structures, but it hinders the modelling of more complex topologies.
- The strings produced by an L-system have to be interpreted geometrically, usually by *turtle geometry* [17], which implies a sort of semantic gap and an extra step of processing between the rewriting formalism and the 3D structures, in contrast to modern data structures for 3D worlds (e. g., scene graphs) where information is more directly represented.
- L-systems give no support for calculations involving the whole created structure (e. g., determination of total available carbon in a plant).
- In a structure generated by an L-system with turtle interpretation, basically only two relations can be modelled: 'direct successor' and 'branch'. In many applications, particularly for multiscaled models, it is desirable to have more relations at hand, like in semantic networks.

It is somewhat astonishing that true graph transformations were so rarely used in plant modelling (with some exceptions in the wake of the evolution of L-systems, see, e. g., [18]), given the fact that graphs appear in prominent roles throughout biology: graphs can, e. g., represent biochemical and regulatory networks, phylogenetic descent, structures of macromolecules, the architecture of cell layers and tissues, transportation networks in cells and in organisms, neural networks, and the arrangement of components of an organism at different levels of resolution (multiple-scaled tree graphs, [19]). Furthermore, system dynamics, which is a paradigmatic notion for a host of biological phenomena, is often modelled in graphical form (e. g., [20]). Hence it seems that graph rewriting has a great future in biological applications. However, in our work not all of these potential applications of graphs are already taken into account.

We will first present the theoretical background of relational growth grammars, then the programming language XL for which this formalism was implemented, and finally its application. Plant models obtained with our software GroIMP (Growth grammar related Interactive Modelling Platform) will be shown. We will also show some first results of a students' course where GroIMP was employed for architectural design, and we will discuss future perspectives.

2 Relational Growth Grammars

In this section, we define the formalism of *relational growth grammars* (RGG for short) as a special kind of graph grammars based on the algebraic single-pushout approach [21]. Section 3 presents the XL programming language, a concrete programming language for which the RGG formalism can be implemented easily. The intent of the following discussion is to clarify the formal basis of relational growth grammars, although we cannot present every detail.

2.1 Graph Model

A seamless integration of an imperative object-oriented programming language requires a typing system for graphs which reflects the principles of inheritance and polymorphism. In order to generalize parameterized symbols of parametric L-systems and to represent properties of objects, attributed graphs are the natural choice. Both inheritance and attribution can be combined, resulting in *typed attributed graphs with inheritance* [22]. Our definition of graphs is that of [22] with the restriction to acyclic inheritance graphs (so that the induced inheritance relation is a partial order) and with an exception regarding the treatment of edges: since the semantics of edges within the RGG formalism is to stand for plain relationships between their incident nodes, we exclude the possibility of edge attributes, and parallel edges of the same type are not allowed. The latter means that the edges of a graph G are simply represented as a subset of $G_V \times \Lambda_E \times G_V$, where G_V denotes the nodes of G and Λ_E is the set of edge types.

In order to instantiate the single-pushout (SPO) approach for RGG graphs, we have to define a corresponding category of graphs and their homomorphisms [21]. The single-pushout approach works with *partial homomorphisms*, i.e., graph homomorphisms $G \to H$ which are defined on some subgraph of their domain G. In order to integrate the inheritance relation in the notion of a graph homomorphism, we use a technique based on [23] instead of the approach of [22]. This means that a graph homomorphism $f : G \to H$ is a structure-preserving mapping such that for every object (node or edge) $x \in G$ the type of its image $f(x)$ is a subtype of the type of x (with the convention that a type is a subtype of itself). Having specified graphs and their homomorphisms, we can define the category of relational growth grammars:

Definition 1 (category RGGGraph). *Let type graph and inheritance relation be fixed. The set of RGG graphs together with their partial homomorphisms defines the category* **RGGGraph***.*

We do not give the complete definitions of the graph model here since they are quite technical and not new in themselves, they can be found in [24]. But from the previous remarks and the cited literature, the main features should be sufficiently clear for the sequel.

2.2 Rules

The *rules* are the central part of the RGG formalism, since they define how graphs are transformed. The application of a rule shall remove the match of its left-hand side (LHS, the *predecessor*) from the *host graph* and insert its right-hand side (RHS, the *successor*) at the same place. The exact definition is based on an SPO production [21]. However, a rule is not an SPO production, it rather generates such a production dynamically on the basis of a match. This is very useful in practice: think of a growth rule of a plant where the number of generated plant segments (i. e., nodes of the graph) within a fixed time step depends on the local vitality of the plant. If we were constrained to conventional static productions, we would have to either specify several productions (one for each possible number of generated segments) or to use several derivation steps (with the complicating possibility of different numbers of steps at different locations of the plant). Both solutions are not feasible from a practical point of view. The dynamic generation of a production provides a solution to this problem of a dynamic RHS and formally captures the introduction of the repetition operator in growth grammars [6], the dynamic generation of the successor in L+C [14] and the theoretical approach in [25] which defines the successor of an L-system production to be given by a mapping of the predecessor and its parameters. In practice, the mapping from a match to the RHS can be conveniently specified by imperative control structures enclosing parts of the RHS (see Sect. 3).

As part of the dynamic generation of a production, we may also extend the match by further objects of the host graph. This is used if one wants to establish an edge to some distinguished, previously existing node n (e. g., the closest node to some other node in 3D space), but n is not yet part of the original match. There are cases where such a situation cannot be handled by the inclusion of n in the original match together with a suitable application condition, e. g., if n is needed only conditionally on the right-hand side. Since the intent of additional objects in the match is exactly to be able to reference them on right-hand sides for edge creation purposes, we demand their appearance on right-hand sides. As a consequence within the SPO approach, they may not be deleted.

Let $\mathrm{Hom}(L, \cdot)$ denote the set of all total graph homomorphisms with domain L and $\mathrm{Mon}_P(\cdot, \cdot)$ the set of all partial, injective homomorphisms, then we define a simple RGG rule as follows:

Definition 2 (simple RGG rule). *A simple RGG rule $r = (L, c, p)$ is given by a graph L, an application condition c (i. e., a predicate on the set $\mathrm{Hom}(L, \cdot)$), and a mapping $p : \mathrm{Hom}(L, \cdot) \to \mathrm{Mon}_P(\cdot, \cdot)$, such that the image of $m : L \to G \in \mathrm{Hom}(L, \cdot)$ is an SPO production $M(m) \xrightarrow{p(m)} R(m)$ whose domain (in the categorical sense) $M(m)$ is a subgraph of G and a supergraph of $m(L)$, and which is defined (as a function) for objects (i. e., nodes, edges) not in $m(L)$.*

Definition 3 (RGG match). *A match for a simple rule $r = (L, c, p)$ in a host graph G is a total graph homomorphism $m : L \to G$ such that the application condition c is fulfilled.*

Definition 4 (simple RGG derivation). *Let* $m : L \to G$ *be a match for a simple rule* $r = (L, c, p)$. *A direct derivation* *using* r *via* m, *denoted as* $G \overset{r,m}{\Longrightarrow} H$, *is given by a direct SPO derivation using* $M(m) \overset{p(m)}{\longrightarrow} R(m)$ *via the inclusion* $M(m) \hookrightarrow G$, *i. e., by the following commutative diagram in the category* **RGG-Graph**, *where the square is a pushout:*

$$L \dashrightarrow m(L) \hookrightarrow M(m) \overset{p(m)}{\longrightarrow} R(m)$$
$$m \searrow \qquad \downarrow \qquad \downarrow$$
$$G \longrightarrow H$$

The following is an example for a simple RGG rule which moves some sort of animal (A-typed node) along a path of X-typed nodes if its energy is above the threshold 1 and creates some children at the left location, the number depending on the energy. (The reduction of energy on movement and the initial energy of children are omitted for the sake of simplicity.)

$$L = \boxed{\begin{array}{c} {}^{a}\boxed{A} \\ \uparrow \\ {}^{x}\boxed{X} \overset{y}{\longmapsto} \boxed{X} \end{array}} , \; c = (a.\text{energy} > 1), \; p(m) = m(L) \to R_{\lfloor a.\text{energy}-1 \rfloor}$$

with $R_0 = \boxed{\begin{array}{c} {}^{a}\boxed{A} \\ \uparrow \\ {}^{x}\boxed{X} \overset{y}{\longmapsto} \boxed{X} \end{array}}$, $R_1 = \boxed{\begin{array}{c} \boxed{A} \quad {}^{a}\boxed{A} \\ \uparrow \qquad \uparrow \\ {}^{x}\boxed{X} \overset{y}{\longmapsto} \boxed{X} \end{array}}$, $R_2 = \boxed{\begin{array}{c} \boxed{A} \quad \boxed{A} \quad {}^{a}\boxed{A} \\ \nwarrow \quad \uparrow \qquad \uparrow \\ {}^{x}\boxed{X} \overset{y}{\longmapsto} \boxed{X} \end{array}}$, $\ldots$

Here, nodes are represented as oval boxes around their type, node identifiers are placed in front of the upper left corner. $a.\text{energy}$ refers to the value of the energy attribute of the A-typed node a, and $\lfloor x \rfloor$ denotes the integral part of x (floor function). The mapping $p(m)$ is indicated by the reuse of node identifiers of the LHS within the RHS.

Motivated by the fact that a living system is parallel, it has to be possible to apply RGG rules in parallel. While a parallel mode of rewriting can be easily defined for strings – in this case we obtain L-systems –, the situation is intricate for general graphs. Relatively simple cases like the independent (parallel) movement of animals on a grid can be solved by *parallel derivations* of the generated SPO productions [21] since the grid plays the role of a fixed context for gluing.

Definition 5 (simple parallel RGG derivation). *Let* G *be a graph,* I *a finite index set,* $r = (r_i)_{i \in I}$ *a family of simple rules with* $r_i = (L_i, c_i, p_i)$, *and* $m = (m_i)_{i \in I}$ *a family of finite sets of corresponding matches, i. e., every* $f \in m_i$ *is a match for* r_i *in* G. *A direct parallel derivation* *using* r *via* m *is given by a direct parallel SPO derivation using* $\sum_{i \in I, f \in m_i} p_i(m)$ *via the match* $\sum_{i \in I, f \in m_i} (\text{dom} \, p_i(f) \hookrightarrow G)$.

The following shows the parallel RGG derivation using the single example rule from above as singleton family via the two obvious matches, if we assume that the energy of node a is 1.5 and that of b is 4.1.

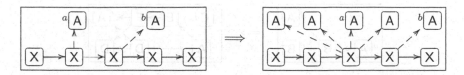

Unfortunately, this straightforward parallelism fails if successors of neighbouring parts shall be connected by edges, which is a very important case and needed by the embedding of L-systems in the RGG formalism. Several *connection mechanisms* were studied in [18] to address this problem, of which the *operator approach* [26,27] turns out to be a suitable technique for relational growth grammars. In our variation of the operator approach as an addition to the SPO approach, the application of a rule to a match also establishes *connection transformations* which can be imagined as special temporary edges from nodes of the old host graph to nodes of the derived graph, attributed by an *operator*, a direction flag ("in" or "out") and an edge type. An operator A yields for every node n of the host graph G a set $A_G(n)$ of related nodes of G (e. g., its neighbours).

Definition 6 (RGG rule, match). *An RGG rule $r = (L, c, p, z)$ is a simple RGG rule (L, c, p) together with a mapping z which assigns to each match $m :$ $L \to G$ for the simple rule a set of connection transformation edges $(s, (A, d, \gamma), t)$ with $s \in M(m)$ (domain of $p(m)$), $t \in R(m)$ (codomain of $p(m)$), an operator A, a direction $d \in \{\text{in}, \text{out}\}$ and a concrete edge type γ. A match for an RGG rule is given by a match for the corresponding simple rule.*

If a node t of the derived graph H is the target of a connection transformation edge with source s, operator A, direction d and edge type γ, an additional γ-typed edge between t and all those nodes $t' \in H$ is created which either are targets of connection transformation edges $(A', d', \gamma), d' \neq d$ with source s' such that the old nodes are mutually contained in the sets yielded by the operators, i. e., $s' \in A_G(s)$ and $s \in A'_G(s')$, or which have already existed as s' in the host graph, have no connection transformation edge $(A', d', \gamma), d' \neq d$ and fulfil $s' \in A_G(s)$. t is the source of the new edge if $d = \text{out}$, otherwise t is the target.

Definition 7 (parallel RGG derivation). *Let G be a graph, I a finite index set, $r = (r_i)_{i \in I}$ a family of rules with $r_i = (L_i, c_i, p_i, z_i)$, and $m = (m_i)_{i \in I}$ a family of finite sets of corresponding matches. A direct parallel derivation using r via m is given by the graph which results from the parallel derivation of the corresponding simple rules and which contains additional edges as prescribed by the connection transformations (see above, a complete definition is given in [24]).*

As an example, consider the rules (in a simplified notation)

$$r_1 = {}^\alpha\boxed{A} \to {}^\alpha\boxed{A}\!\!\to\!\boxed{C}, \quad r_2 = {}^\beta\boxed{B} \to {}^\lambda\boxed{D}, \quad r_3 = {}^\gamma\boxed{B} \to {}^\mu\boxed{E}\!\!\to\!\!{}^\nu\boxed{F}$$

where r_2, r_3 are additionally equipped with orientation-preserving connection transformations of depth 1 (i. e., their operators yield adjacent nodes; see [26]): r_2 has transformations in both directions from β to λ, r_3 has a transformation with $d = \text{in}$ from γ to μ and with $d = \text{out}$ from γ to ν. Then the derivation is a

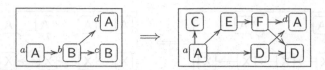

parallel RGG derivation where r_1 has been applied to a, r_2 to b and c, and r_3 to b. Note that r_1 is a pure SPO production, while r_2 and r_3 can be seen as representatives of L-system productions, translated to graph grammars by the additional connection transformations.

Sequential derivations are a special case of RGG derivations if the family m contains only a single match. On the other hand, the simulation of an L-system is obtained if every rule is applied via every possible match within a single parallel derivation and suitable operators establish the connections [24]. Generalizations like table L-systems [28] divide the set of productions into subsets such that, depending on the current state, only productions from one subset are active within a derivation. Similar regulations of active productions have also been defined for graph grammars, a review is contained in [29]. All these mechanisms can be captured by a *control flow* which selects rules and sets of matches for them based on the current state which is taken here to be the host graph.

Definition 8 (control flow). *Let r be a family of rules as before. A control flow φ for r is a mapping which assigns to each graph G a family of finite sets of matches for r in G, $\varphi : G \mapsto (m_i)_{i \in I}$ with $m_i \subseteq \mathrm{Hom}(L_i, G)$. The derivation $G \overset{\varphi}{\Rightarrow} H$ according to φ is the parallel RGG derivation using r via $\varphi(G)$.*

Definition 9 (relational growth grammar). *A relational growth grammar is given by a family r of rules with a control flow φ and a start graph α. The sequence of generated graphs G_n is given by $\alpha \left(\overset{\varphi}{\Rightarrow} \right)^n G_n$. The language generated by the grammar is the set of all generated graphs, $\bigcup_{n \in \mathbb{N}_0} G_n$.*

As a simple example for a relational growth grammar, consider the Sierpinski grammar [30]. If we use a node type V for vertices and three edge types e_0, e_{120}, e_{240} which stand for edges at $0°$, $120°$, $240°$, respectively, in the usual 2D representation of a Sierpinski triangle and which are drawn as solid, dashed, or dotted arrows, the single RGG rule is

$$r = \left(L = \boxed{} , \mathrm{true}, m \mapsto \left(m(L) \to \boxed{} \right), m \mapsto \emptyset \right).$$

The complete grammar has r as a singleton family of rules. The start graph has the same structure as the left-hand side of r, and the control flow has to apply r in parallel at every possible location:

$$\alpha = L, \quad \varphi : G \mapsto (\mathrm{Hom}(L, G)).$$

Then the language of this relational growth grammar consists of all finite approximations of the Sierpinski graph.

3   The XL Programming Language

Relational growth grammars are a theoretic formalism, not a concrete programming language. The *XL programming language* is a concrete textual (non-visual) programming language which extends Java in such a way that an RGG-compliant system for use within XL can be easily implemented. We cannot give a complete specification of XL here, but some examples should illustrate syntax and semantics (see also Sect. 4). The following rules implement the examples of Sect. 2:

```
x:X [a:A] y:X, (a.energy > 1) ==>>
    x for(int i = 2; i <= a.energy; i++) ( [A] ) y [a];

a:V -e0-> b:V -e120-> c:V -e240-> a ==>>
  a -e0-> ab:V -e0-> b -e120-> bc:V -e120-> c -e240-> ca:V -e240-> a,
  ca -e0-> bc -e240-> ab -e120-> ca;

a:A ==>> a C; B ==> D; B ==> E F;
```

The LHS of the first rule is a graph of three nodes of Java classes X, A with identifiers x, a and y, together with an application condition separated by a comma. From x to a there is an edge of the standard type 'branch', from x to y there is an edge of the standard type 'successor' which is the implicit edge type if nodes are separated by whitespace and complete bracketed sequences only. The treatment of square brackets follows the convention of L-systems which use them to enclose branches. The RHS changes the edges according to the example of Sect. 2. Namely, if for example a.energy is 4.1, the RHS is expanded to x [A] [A] [A] y [a]. Since A is no node identifier, it is interpreted as the Java expression **new** A(), and three new A-typed nodes are added as branches to x. The edge from x to y is reproduced, and finally a 'branch'-edge from y to a is established. Like **for**, every control-flow statement of Java can be used, blocks of conventional Java-code can be included in braces. Thus, the graph of the RHS and the whole SPO production $p(m)$ dynamically depend on the match m.

The second rule for the Sierpinski grammar shows how model-specific edge types can be used. A comma between node expressions serves to separate the nodes, i.e., no implicit edge is created between comma-separated nodes.

Besides the rule arrow ==>>, also ==> can be used. Then the RGG implementation automatically adds connection transformations to the otherwise simple RGG rule so that the effect of its application corresponds to that of an L-system production, i.e., there are direction-preserving connection transformations of depth 1 from the textually leftmost (rightmost) node of the LHS to the first (last) produced node of the RHS. This is used for the last list of three rules.

The left-hand sides of the presented rules are examples for *queries*. Queries may also use complex path patterns as in x:A (-(branch|successor)->)* y:B which represents a pattern of two nodes of types A and B, respectively, together with the application condition that the node y can be reached from x by traversing an arbitrary number of edges of type 'branch' or 'successor' (i.e., the transitive and reflexive closure of the relation "there exists a 'branch'- or 'successor'-edge").

In order to implement these rule-based features for XL, two main parts are necessary: the query syntax has to be completed by the implementation of the corresponding semantics which actually finds matches in the host graph, and given a match m for a rule, the RHS syntax has to be translated into the construction of the production $p(m)$. Queries locate all matches in the host graph; the underlying pattern matching algorithm is implemented in a depth-first manner as part of a run-time library, including, e. g., the computation of transitive closures. The algorithm heuristically chooses a search plan for matching using a cost model similar to [31]. Then it accesses the graph via a general *data model interface* so that it can operate on basically any structured data, e. g., XML DOM trees, component trees of GUI frameworks, scene graphs of 3D frameworks.

The way how the semantics of RHS of XL rules is defined is very general and not in itself related to relational growth grammars: it is solely defined by *operator overloading*. The mere adoption of C++-like overloading to XL (operator overloading is not defined for Java) would not result in a convenient syntax for RHS, so we designed a special syntax and translation scheme for this purpose. For example, the RHS `x y -branch-> a` becomes translated to the Java expression

`producer.operator$space(x).operator$space(y).operator$arrow(a, branch)`

where `producer` is an instance provided by the used implementation of the data model interface. Its methods like `operator$space` and `operator$arrow` have to be suitably implemented. Their RGG implementation precisely does what is specified by the definitions of the RGG formalism in Sect. 2 [24], but the general approach via operator overloading also allows to implement other rule-based formalisms like, e. g., a rule-based variant of vertex-vertex algebras for the specification of surface subdivision algorithms [32,24].

For every sort of modification in parallel, the run-time system of XL manages a set of *queues*: as an extension of Java, XL in itself executes statements sequentially. So if modifications shall take place as if they were executed in parallel, their actual execution has to be deferred by means of a corresponding queue entry until all modifications which shall be executed in parallel have been collected this way. For the RGG implementation, the content of the queues represents the current result of the sum of the applied SPO productions ($\sum_{i \in I, f \in m_i} p_i(m)$ in Def. 5) together with all connection transformations, namely a set of queue entries of the form "create/delete an edge of type γ from s to t" and "use connection transformation $(s, (A, d, \gamma), t)$". So the application of an RGG rule within XL does not directly modify the graph but only creates a number of queue entries which can be applied afterwards by draining the queues.

The current RGG implementation for XL leads to a control flow according to Def. 8 which is governed by the control flow of XL as an extension of Java. When a rule is encountered, either a single sequential RGG derivation (with a pseudorandomly chosen match) or a parallel RGG derivation via *all* matches is performed, depending on the current choice of derivation mode. Strictly speaking, the derivations are not directly performed, just the queues are filled with modification entries whose later execution completes the parallel derivation of all collected rule/match pairs. This execution is triggered by a special method.

4   Applications

In this section, we will present applications of (the XL implementation of) the RGG formalism. The main part describes applications within our open-source modelling platform GroIMP which includes a subset of the following and some further examples [33]. GroIMP provides a rich set of geometric objects such as cylinders, boxes, spline surfaces and transformations which can be used directly as nodes in the graphs. Visible nodes are equipped with attributes controlling their appearance (e. g., colours, texture images). Thus, there is no semantic gap between the graph and its three-dimensional representation.

4.1   Artificial Life

Conway's famous Game of Life [34] as a representative of cellular automata can be implemented easily within XL. The following source code is complete except for the initialization of the universe. The universe consists of a number of Cell nodes connected by edges of type **neighbour**, the latter representing the Moore neighbourhood (eight neighbours) of a cell.

```
import de.grogra.rgg.*; // for classes RGG, Cell (provided by GroIMP)
import static de.grogra.xl.lang.Operators.sum; // for aggregate method sum

public class GameOfLife extends RGG { // RGG is base class for RGG models
    ... // initialization of (finite) universe
    public void run() [
        x:Cell, (x[state] == 1), // living cells
                (!(sum((* x -neighbour-> Cell *)[state]) in (2 : 3)))
          ==>> x {x[state] := 0;}; // death due to loneliness/overcrowding
        x:Cell, (x[state] == 0), // dead cells
                (sum((* x -neighbour-> Cell *)[state]) == 3)
          ==>> x {x[state] := 1;}; // cell comes to life
    ]
}
```

As can be seen, blocks of rules are enclosed in brackets. Here, the complete method **run** has a single such block as body which contains the two transition rules of the Game of Life. Both rules utilize queries within their application condition: (* x -neighbour-> Cell *) is a query which finds all Cell nodes which are connected with x by an edge of type **neighbour**. The method **sum** is an *aggregate method* which computes the sum of a sequence of values, in this case of the states of neighbours. The states are represented as *properties* of Cell nodes. For the access of properties, XL uses a bracket syntax as in x[state]. The main advantage of properties over Java fields is that they can be used with *parallel assignments* :=. These are deferred by means of a queue and actually performed together with graph modifications at the end of a parallel derivation.

XL has been used for the implementation of a number of additional models of Artificial Life, among them virtual ants [35] and biomorphs [36,37]. In the latter model, genetic operations like crossing-over and mutation were easily specified as graph productions, while growth was implemented in an L-system style.

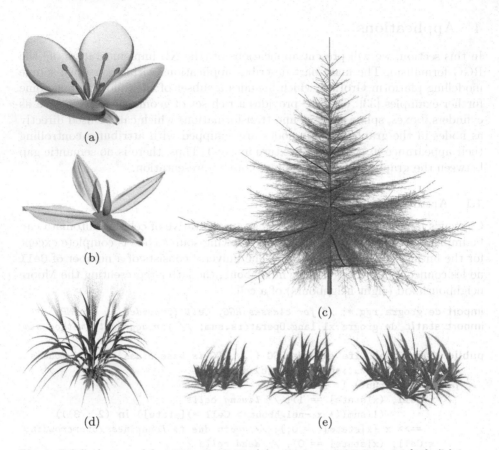

Fig. 1. RGG plant models within GroIMP: **(a)** wild type of ABC model [35]; **(b)** loss-of-B mutant of ABC model; **(c)** young spruce tree [38]; **(d)** a barley individual; **(e)** barley individuals competing for light, increased spacing from left to right [39]

4.2 Biology

This section outlines some biological applications in the field of plant modelling. They have been published previously, so we do not go into the details. Figure 1(a) and (b) show the outcome of the ABC model of flower morphogenesis [35], based on [40]. A gene regulatory network was implemented as a graph, its dynamics of transcription factor concentrations governs flower growth. The wild type (a) shows the usual final shape, the mutant (b) results from a modified network: due to the differing dynamics of concentrations, not all flower organs were created.

Figure 1(c) shows a model of a young spruce tree which is a translation of an L-system model presented in [38] to XL. Figure 1(d) shows an individual barley, (e) three sets of nine competing individuals [39]. The L-system like growth is controlled by metabolic networks, implemented by RGG rules, which in turn are regulated by the local light quality. The quality decreases with increasing plant density, this leads to a reduced growth for dense spacings as shown in the figure.

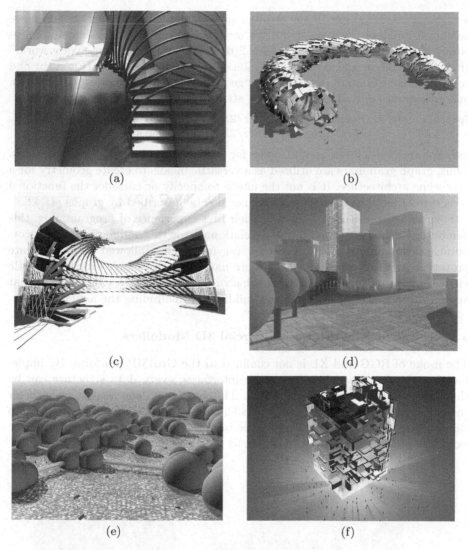

Fig. 2. Application of relational growth grammars to architecture

4.3 Architecture

Compared to many structures found in nature, especially living structures like plants and animals, buildings, indeed most objects and structures conceived and built by men, appear somewhat primitive. One reason for this might lie in the fact that plants and animals grow, and grow quite differently than anything man-made. Designing and educating architects are interested in what might be learnt from such growth processes in nature for architectural design. For this purpose, relational growth grammars, embedded in GroIMP, might be helpful.

In a seminar "Artificial Growth Processes", students of architecture created RGGs to grow buildings by rules. The first task assigned to them was to create a staircase. An example of the results can be seen in Fig. 2(a). Later on more advanced buildings were created like a meeting centre (Fig. 2(f), human figures added afterwards) or a city centre (Fig. 2(d)). Further results were "Waterworld" (Fig. 2(e), balloon and boats added afterwards) and showrooms (Fig. 2(b) and (c)). All these examples represent their geometry directly by nodes of the graph, and appearance is controlled by visual attributes. E. g., the "Waterworld" rule

```
Sphere(r) ==> RL(random(-90,90)) [M(r/2) Sphere(r/2+random(-0.5,0.5))]
                                 [M(r/2) RL(90) Sphere(r/2)];
```

uses Sphere nodes for houses, RL nodes for rotations and M nodes for translations. Thus, graph grammars are utilized as a versatile means to create geometry for a prototype architecture. It is not the intent to specify or consider the functional structure of buildings. This can of course also be described by graphs [41,42].

For most of the students this was their first experience of programming, this demonstrates how easy and intuitive relational growth grammars can be. Incorporating randomness (for instance by varying angles) allowed them to create prototype architecture that looked more natural than before. From an artistic view, these prototypes conserve enough structure to enable a viewer to feel that an algorithm was used to create the buildings, while hiding the actual rules.

4.4   Usage of XL within Commercial 3D Modellers

The usage of RGG and XL is not confined to the GroIMP platform. By implementing the data model and run-time interfaces, every data structure can be the target of rules specified within XL. This has been done as part of bachelor theses for the commercial 3D modellers Cinema 4D (René Herzog), Maya (Udo Bischof) and 3ds Max (Uwe Mannl), the target being their 3D scene graph. The examples of Fig. 3 have been modelled by Udo Bischof using his Maya plugin.

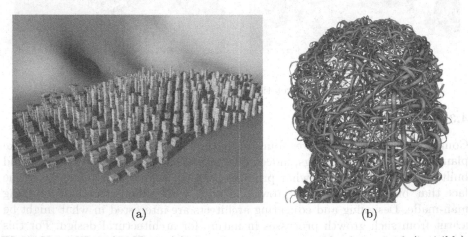

(a)   (b)

Fig. 3. Using XL within Maya: **(a)** city generator on a curved landscape with (invisible) bounding object; **(b)** creeping 'plants' on a head-shaped surface

5 Discussion

As an extension of L-systems and graph grammars, relational growth grammars and their implementation for the language XL generalize the notion of rule application. The programmer can combine rule-based with imperative programming, making use of the best of both worlds. Nevertheless, the language is easy to learn and to apply to specific problems, as was shown, e.g., by the architects.

The parallelism of relational growth grammars makes them very suitable for the modelling of living systems. We have started investigation in this direction with the implementation of paradigmatic models of Artificial Life, and with the implementation of plant models whose growth is modelled in an L-system style from a macroscopic point of view, but with internal processes at a microscopic point of view which could not have been modelled as easily using L-systems alone. Research in this field of application is ongoing, inspired by the increasing biological knowledge. Of particular interest is to refine spatial resolution by the modelling of cellular structures and their geometric shape.

Acknowledgements. We thank Udo Bischof and the students of architecture Manuela Fritzsche, Christopher Jarchow, Jennifer Koch, Liang Liang and Simon Winterhalder for their examples. This research was funded by the DFG under grant Ku 847/5-1 and Ku 847/6-1. All support is gratefully acknowledged.

References

1. Baresi, L., Heckel, R.: Tutorial introduction to graph transformation: A software engineering perspective. In: [43], pp. 431–433
2. Buck-Sorlin, G., Kniemeyer, O., Kurth, W.: Barley morphology, genetics and hormonal regulation of internode elongation modelled by a relational growth grammar. New Phytologist 166(3), 859–867 (2005)
3. Giavitto, J.L., Michel, O.: MGS: a rule-based programming language for complex objects and collections. Electronic Notes in Theoretical Computer Science 59(4) (2001)
4. Kurth, W., Kniemeyer, O., Buck-Sorlin, G.: Relational growth grammars – a graph rewriting approach to dynamical systems with a dynamical structure. In: Banâtre, J.-P., Fradet, P., Giavitto, J.-L., Michel, O. (eds.) UPP 2004. LNCS, vol. 3566, pp. 56–72. Springer, Heidelberg (2005)
5. Prusinkiewicz, P., Lindenmayer, A.: The Algorithmic Beauty of Plants. Springer, New York (1990)
6. Kurth, W.: Growth grammar interpreter GROGRA 2.4 – a software tool for the 3-dimensional interpretation of stochastic, sensitive growth grammars in the context of plant modelling. Introduction and reference manual. Berichte des Forschungszentrums Waldökosysteme, B 38, Göttingen (1994)
7. Barczi, J.F., de Reffye, P., Caraglio, Y.: Essai sur l'identification et la mise en oeuvre des paramètres nécessaires à la simulation d'une architecture végétale. Le logiciel AMAPSIM. In: Bouchon, J., de Reffye, P., Barthélémy, D. (eds.) Modélisation et Simulation de l'Architecture des Végétaux, pp. 205–254. Science Update, INRA, Paris (1997)

8. Maillette, L.: The value of meristem states, as estimated by a discrete-time Markov chain. Oikos 59, 235–240 (1990)
9. Renton, M., Guédon, Y., Godin, C., Costes, E.: Similarities and gradients in growth-unit branching patterns during ontogeny in fuji apple trees: A stochastic approach. Journal of Experimental Botany 57(12), 3131–3143 (2006)
10. Sonntag, M.: Effect of morphological plasticity on leaf area distribution, single tree, and forest stand dynamics. Bayreuther Forum Ökologie 52, 205–222 (1998)
11. Breckling, B.: An individual based model for the study of pattern and process in plant ecology: An application of object oriented programming. EcoSys. 4, 241–254 (1996)
12. Perttunen, J., Sievänen, R., Nikinmaa, E., Salminen, H., Saarenmaa, H., Väkevä, J.: Lignum: A tree model based on simple structural units. Annals of Botany 77, 87–98 (1996)
13. Eschenbach, C.: Emergent properties modelled with the functional structural tree growth model ALMIS: Computer experiments on resource gain and use. Ecological Modelling 186, 470–488 (2005)
14. Prusinkiewicz, P., Karwowski, R., Lane, B.: The L+C plant modelling language. In: [47], 27–42
15. Françon, J.: Sur la modélisation informatique de l'architecture et du développement des végétaux. Document R90/12, Université Louis Pasteur, Strasbourg, Département d'Informatique (1990)
16. Kniemeyer, O., Buck-Sorlin, G., Kurth, W.: GroIMP as a platform for functional-structural modelling of plants. In: [47], 43–52
17. Abelson, H., diSessa, A.: Turtle Geometry. MIT Press, Cambridge (1982)
18. Lindenmayer, A., Rozenberg, G. (eds.): Automata, Languages, Development. North Holland, Amsterdam (1976)
19. Godin, C., Caraglio, Y.: A multiscale model of plant topological structures. Journal of Theoretical Biology 191, 1–46 (1998)
20. Renton, M., Thornby, D., Hanan, J.: Canonical modelling. In: [47], 151–164
21. Ehrig, H., Heckel, R., Korff, M., Löwe, M., Ribeiro, L., Wagner, A., Corradini, A.: Algebraic approaches to graph transformation II: Single pushout approach and comparison with double pushout approach. In: [46], ch. 4, pp. 247–312
22. Ehrig, H., Ehrig, K., Prange, U., Taentzer, G.: Fundamentals of Algebraic Graph Transformation. Springer, New York (2006)
23. Parisi-Presicce, F., Ehrig, H., Montanari, U.: Graph rewriting with unification and composition. In: Ehrig, H., Nagl, M., Rosenfeld, A., Rozenberg, G. (eds.) Graph Grammars 1986. LNCS, vol. 291, pp. 496–514. Springer, Heidelberg (1987)
24. Kniemeyer, O.: Design and Implementation of a Graph Grammar Based Language for Functional-Structural Plant Modelling. PhD thesis, BTU Cottbus (forthcoming, 2008)
25. Chien, T.W., Jürgensen, H.: Parameterized L systems for modelling: Potential and limitations. In: Rozenberg, G., Salomaa, A. (eds.) Lindenmayer Systems, pp. 213–229. Springer, Berlin (1992)
26. Nagl, M.: On a generalization of Lindenmayer-systems to labelled graphs. In: [18], pp. 487–508
27. Nagl, M.: Graph-Grammatiken: Theorie, Anwendungen, Implementierungen. Vieweg, Braunschweig (1979)
28. Rozenberg, G.: T0L systems and languages. Information and Control 23(4), 357–381 (1973)
29. Schürr, A.: Programmed graph replacement systems. In: [46], ch. 7, pp. 479–546

30. Taentzer, G., Biermann, E., Bisztray, D., Bohnet, B., Boneva, I., Boronat, A., Geiger, L., Geiß, R., Horvath, Á., Kniemeyer, O., Mens, T., Ness, B., Plump, D., Vajk, T.: Generation of Sierpinski triangles: A case study for graph transformation tools. In: Schürr, A., Nagl, M., Zündorf, Λ. (eds.) AGTIVE 2007. LNCS, vol. 5088. Springer, Heidelberg (2008)
31. Batz, G.V., Kroll, M., Geiß, R.: A first experimental evaluation of search plan driven graph pattern matching. In: [45], pp. 468–483
32. Smith, C., Prusinkiewicz, P., Samavati, F.F.: Local specification of surface subdivision algorithms. In: [48], pp. 313–327
33. Kniemeyer, O., Kurth, W.: The modelling platform GroIMP and the programming language XL. In: Schürr, A., Nagl, M., Zündorf, A. (eds.) AGTIVE 2007. LNCS, vol. 5088. Springer, Heidelberg (2008)
34. Gardner, M.: Mathematical Games: The fantastic combinations of John Conway's new solitaire game Life. Scientific American 223(4), 120–123 (1970)
35. Kniemeyer, O.: Rule-based modelling with the XL/GroIMP software. In: Schaub, H., Detje, F., Brüggemann, U. (eds.) GWAL-6, pp. 56–65. Akademische Verlagsgesellschaft, Berlin (2004)
36. Kniemeyer, O., Buck-Sorlin, G., Kurth, W.: Representation of genotype and phenotype in a coherent framework based on extended L-systems. In: Banzhaf, W., Ziegler, J., Christaller, T., Dittrich, P., Kim, J.T. (eds.) ECAL 2003. LNCS (LNAI), vol. 2801, pp. 625–634. Springer, Heidelberg (2003)
37. Kniemeyer, O., Buck-Sorlin, G., Kurth, W.: A graph-grammar approach to artificial life. Artificial Life 10, 413–431 (2004)
38. Kurth, W.: Die Simulation der Baumarchitektur mit Wachstumsgrammatiken. Wissenschaftlicher Verlag, Berlin (1999)
39. Buck-Sorlin, G., Hemmerling, R., Kniemeyer, O., Burema, B., Kurth, W.: A rule-based model of barley morphogenesis, with special respect to shading and gibberellic acid signal transduction. Annals of Botany (in press, 2008)
40. Kim, J.T.: transsys: A generic formalism for modelling regulatory networks in morphogenesis. In: Kelemen, J., Sosík, P. (eds.) ECAL 2001. LNCS (LNAI), vol. 2159, pp. 242–251. Springer, Heidelberg (2001)
41. Szuba, J., Ozimek, A., Schürr, A.: On graphs in conceptual engineering design. In: [48], pp. 75–89
42. Heer, T., Retkowitz, D., Kraft, B.: Algorithm and tool for ontology integration based on graph rewriting. In: [45], pp. 484–490
43. Ehrig, H., Engels, G., Parisi-Presicce, F., Rozenberg, G. (eds.): ICGT 2004. LNCS, vol. 3256. Springer, Heidelberg (2004)
44. Schürr, A., Nagl, M., Zündorf, A. (eds.): AGTIVE 2007. LNCS, vol. 5088. Springer, Heidelberg (2008)
45. Schürr, A., Nagl, M., Zündorf, A. (eds.): Proceedings of the International Workshop on Applications of Graph Transformations with Industrial Relevance, October 10-12, 2007. University of Kassel, Kassel (2007)
46. Rozenberg, G. (ed.): Handbook on Graph Grammars and Computing by Graph Transformation. Foundations, vol. I. World Scientific, Singapore (1997)
47. Vos, J., Marcelis, L.F.M., de Visser, P.H.B., Struik, P.C., Evers, J.B. (eds.): Functional-Structural Plant Modelling in Crop Production, International Workshop. Wageningen UR Frontis Series, vol. 22. Springer, Heidelberg (2007)
48. Pfaltz, J.L., Nagl, M., Böhlen, B. (eds.): AGTIVE 2003. LNCS, vol. 3062. Springer, Heidelberg (2004)

Applications and Rewriting of Omnigraphs – Exemplified in the Domain of MDD

Oliver Denninger, Tom Gelhausen, and Rubino Geiß

Institute for Program Structures and Data Organization (IPD)
University of Karlsruhe (TH), Germany
http://www.ipd.uni-karlsruhe.de/

Abstract. Graph rewrite systems provide only elementary primitives – many applications require more complex structures though. We present a rewrite system for omnigraphs, a formal extension of hypergraphs with the ability to connect multiple nodes *and edges* with a single edge. We exemplify the adequacy of this approach in the domain of Model Driven Development (MDD): Using our system trivializes the representation and transformation of advanced UML structures that are awkward to handle with common approaches.

Keywords: Graph rewriting, hypergraph, omnigraph, supergraph.

1 Introduction

Graph rewrite systems elegantly handle various tasks; they have sound and concise fundamentals and their computational power is Turing equivalent. But the operational primitives of current graph rewrite systems are quite elementary, quite assembler-language-like. Several application domains demand more powerful primitives. One example for such a domain is the representation and transformation of UML within MDD.

UML class diagrams allow n-ary associations which are de facto hyperedges [1] (cf. Fig. 2 for example). Furthermore, they allow relations between associations (cf. Fig. 3). In order to express these relations directly, we would need to additionally allow *edges* to be end points of edges – and that is precisely what omnigraphs[1] are about.

In 1998, Minas showed the advantage of hypergraphs over traditional graphs for representing various kinds of diagrams [9], but no available graph rewrite system has support for hypergraphs so far, not to mention omnigraphs. Therefore, we developed languages for model definition, graph definition and rewrite specifications for omnigraphs. Compilers [18] translate these languages into semantically equivalent definitions for a traditional graph rewrite system. In this paper, we present these languages (Section 2), their theoretical fundamentals (Section 3), and the functionality of the compilers (Section 4).

---

[1] In previous work [5,7], we referred to 'omnigraphs' as 'supergraphs', but we changed the name in order to avoid further confusion with the antonym of 'subgraphs'.

A. Schürr, M. Nagl, and A. Zündorf (Eds.): AGTIVE 2007, LNCS 5088, pp. 168–183, 2008.

2   Omnigraphs in Use – A Problem-Oriented Introduction

Before giving a formal definition of omnigraphs in the next section, we will introduce omnigraphs by means of their application to a specific problem: representation and transformation of UML. We thereby demonstrate how the concepts of omnigraphs ease the handling of advanced UML structures.

2.1   UML Models as Omnigraphs

We show how to represent UML class diagrams using the syntax of our custommade graph rewrite system Ogre (OmniGraph REwriting[2]). For the complete syntax of Ogre, please refer to [18]. We have taken all examples from the "UML Superstructure Specification" version 2.1.1 [12].

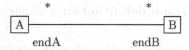

Fig. 1. Simple association, Fig. 7.19 from the UML Superstructure Specification

Defining a Model. Figure 1 shows a simple association between two classes A and B with multiplicities and the roles endA and endB. Listing 1 shows the definition of an accordant model for omnigraphs: Ogre provides nodes, omniedges, and roles as graph primitives. A definition starts with the type of the primitive, so line 1 defines a type for nodes named Class. Line 4 defines a type for omniedges named Association. Constraints for omniedges (in parentheses) specify the allowed types of roles. The constraint in line 4 states that the omniedges need a least one (+) end point of role type AssociationEnd. In line 5, this class of roles is defined with the constraint that it is only applicable on nodes of the type Class. An AssociationEnd has two attributes: name and multiplicity. Please note that already managing these two attributes is cumbersome in graph rewrite systems that do not support attributed endpoints on edges.

```
1  node Class {
2      name : string;
3  }
4  omniedge Association (AssociationEnd+);
5  role AssociationEnd (Class) {
6      name : string;
7      multiplicity : string;
8  }
```

Listing 1. Model for UML classes and associations

---

[2] Previous name: SUGR – SUperGraph Rewriting [5].

Instantiation. Having defined the model, we will now set up an instance of this model – an omnigraph representing the UML class diagram depicted in Figure 1. Let's begin with the one line statement depicted in Listing 2: The graph definition starts with an omniedge of the type Association. Inside the body of the omniedge we define two new nodes of type Class. Their corresponding roles (AssociationEnd in both cases) follow, separated by vertical bars. The two nodes with their roles form the end points of the surrounding omniedge. In general, nodes and omniedges are declared by an optional identifier (before) and a type (after the colon). The declaration of an omniedge additionally has a body (in square brackets) defining its end points. As we will not refer to any of the declared graph elements again in the code snippet in Listing 2, we omit the identifiers here. But what we effectively lack in this declaration are attributes!

```
1   : Association [ : Class | AssociationEnd   : Class | AssociationEnd ]
```

Listing 2. Graph definition for a simple association

Now we define a new graph *with* attributes (cf. Listing 3). This time we also show how to declare identifiers and how to reference graph elements. In line 1 and 2, the required Class nodes are defined. They have identifiers (a and b) and attributes to hold the names "A" and "B". In line 4 and 5, a and b are referenced (indicated by the @ character). By this means, they are defining end points. The nodes take the role AssociationEnd as above, but this time we additionally define attributes for the end points: "endA" respectively "endB" as value for the name attribute, and "*" as value for the multiplicity attribute of the respective ends of the association. Now we have completely represented the association from Figure 1.

```
1   a : Class (%name="A" )
2   b : Class (%name="B" )
3   : Association [
4       @a | AssociationEnd (%{name="endA" ,  multiplicity="*"})
5       @b | AssociationEnd (%{name="endB" ,  multiplicity="*"})
6   ]
```

Listing 3. Graph definition for a simple association (with attributes)

Ternary Associations. UML enables the declaration of n-ary associations which are not directly expressible by simple binary associations. The ternary association in Figure 2 is an example.

Binary as well as ternary edges are only special cases of omniedges; we do not need to extend the previous model from Listing 1: It already accepts an arbitrary number of AssociationEnds for each Association. So we can immediately denote the example as an omnigraph definition as shown in Listing 4. We simply define a third end point inside the Association omniedge. The Class nodes are defined within the omniedge body.

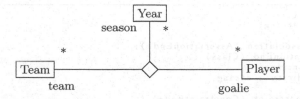

Fig. 2. Ternary association, Fig. 7.21 from the UML Superstructure Specification

```
1    : Association [
2      : Class (%{name="Team" } ) | AssociationEnd (%{name="team" ,  multiplicity="*"})
3      : Class (%{name="Year" } ) | AssociationEnd (%{name="season" ,  multiplicity="*"})
4      : Class (%{name=" Player" } ) | AssociationEnd (%{name=" goalie" ,  multiplicity="*"})
5    ]
```

Listing 4. Graph definition for the ternary association

Higher Order Predicates. Figure 3 shows an example for a second order predicate in UML class diagrams: The {xor} constraint is a predicate over two associations which are predicates over (Class-) nodes themselves. Omnigraphs remove the restriction of hypergraphs by allowing higher order predicates. To express this UML constraint, our model needs an extension: a new type of omniedge named Constraint and a new role ConstraintEnd. We only want omniedges of the type Association to take this role, so we restrict the role to this type. The complete model definition is shown in Listing 5. The graph definition in Listing 6 consists of two associations (line 1 and 4). The constraint is an additional omniedge with the two associations as end points (line 7). The two associations share a common node, so this node is identified by a (line 2) and referenced (line 5).

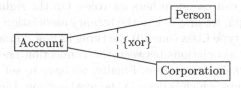

Fig. 3. {xor} constraint, Fig. 7.34 from the UML Superstructure Specification

2.2   Transforming UML with Ogre

After having shown how to represent a UML class diagram as omnigraph, we will show how to define an elementary transformation: We want to transform the ternary association form the preceding example (cf. Figure 2 and Listing 4) into adequate binary associations. This transformation is an inevitable step in every model driven process; we repeat it every time we decompose our model to obtain executable code. The rule according to this transformation demonstrates the pragmatical simplification of writing rules the omnigraph approach has been designed for: no need to think about any extra nodes and edges, their names, types, and directions – simply because we have omniedges with attributed end points.

```
1  node Class {
2      name : string;
3  }
4  omniedge Association (AssociationEnd+);
5  role AssociationEnd (Class) {
6      name : string;
7      multiplicity : string;
8  }
9  omniedge Constraint (ConstraintEnd+) {
10     type : string;
11 }
12 role ConstraintEnd (Association);
```

Listing 5. Model for UML classes, associations, and constraints

```
1  a1: Association [
2      a : Class (%name="Account") | AssociationEnd
3      : Class (%name="Person") | AssociationEnd ]
4  a2: Association [
5      @a | AssociationEnd
6      : Class (%name="Corporation") | AssociationEnd ]
7  : Constraint [@a1 | ConstraintEnd  @a2 | ConstraintEnd ] (%type="xor")
```

Listing 6. Graph definition for the {xor} constraint

Transforming Ternary Associations. The rewriting rule in Listing 7 decomposes ternary associations into adequate binary associations. The left-hand side, the **pattern** graph, matches an omniedge a of type Association with three end points c1, c2, and c3 of type Class and with roles ae1, ae2, and ae3 of type AssociationEnd. The syntax is similar to graph definitions: we use an identifier followed by a colon and a type. The role type is separated by a vertical bar; in contrast to graph definitions we can use identifiers for roles. On the right-hand side of the rule, the **modify** graph, we first delete the ternary association a (line 9) and create a new node c4 of type Class (line 10) – serving as new connection node. Then we create three new associations between the connection node and the former end points of the ternary association. Finally, we have to set the attributes for the new graph elements, which is done in the **eval** section. Line 15, for example, sets the name for the newly created class c4: It consist of the names of the classes c1, c2, c3 and the suffix "Triple".

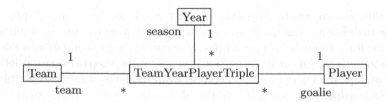

Fig. 4. Ternary Association after the transformation by the rule

```
 1      pattern {
 2          a: Association [
 3              c1: Class | ae1: AssociationEnd
 4              c2: Class | ae2: AssociationEnd
 5              c3: Class | ae3: AssociationEnd
 6          ];
 7      }
 8      modify {
 9          delete(a);
10          c4: Class;
11          : Association [c4 | ae11: AssociationEnd  c1 | ae21: AssociationEnd ];
12          : Association [c4 | ae12: AssociationEnd  c2 | ae22: AssociationEnd ];
13          : Association [c4 | ae13: AssociationEnd  c3 | ae23: AssociationEnd ];
14          eval {
15              c4.name = c1.name+c2.name+c3.name+"Triple";
16              ae11.multiplicity = ae1.multiplicity;
17              ae21.multiplicity = "1";  ae21.name = ae1.name;
18              ae12.multiplicity = ae2.multiplicity;
19              ae22.multiplicity = "1";  ae22.name = ae2.name;
20              ae13.multiplicity = ae3.multiplicity;
21              ae23.multiplicity = "1";  ae23.name = ae3.name;
22          }
23      }
```

Listing 7. Rule for processing ternary associations

Figure 4 shows the ternary association after transforming it into an extra class and appropriate binary associations. The rule also changed all multiplicities as necessary for a correct transformation.

The Rewriting Semantics of Ogre. In Ogre, rules consist of a `pattern` graph and a `replace` or a `modify` graph. Each element of these graphs has a name, either user defined or internally defined. Consider a graph element defined in the `pattern` part: If its name is used in the `replace` graph, the denoted graph element will be kept during the execution of the rule. Otherwise the graph element will be deleted from the host graph. A graph element is created in the host graph by defining a name in the `replace` graph. Anonymous graph elements in a `replace` graph always create new elements in the host graph. Using a name multiple times has the same effect as a single occurrence.

The `modify` variant is syntactic sugar for copying the `pattern` graph to the `replace` graph – in this case deletions from this replacement graph are triggered by the `delete` keyword; additions work the usual way. In case of a conflict between deletion and preservation, deletion is prioritized. It is convenient to use the `modify` variant for modifying only small parts of a large pattern graph.

For a proper graph rewriting system, we need a sound approach on how incident objects are treated when other objects are deleted. Traditional graph rewrite systems can be classified according to SPO or DPO, but both approaches are obviously not applicable for omnigraphs. Our definition of omnigraphs (cf. Section 3.2) allows edges to have an arbitrary number of end points, including zero. Deletion of an incident node of an omniedge just reduces the number of end points of that omniedge. Deletion of an omniedge always requires an explicit statement, and removing it does not bother the objects it connected any further. Thus deletion can never lead to a data structure that is not an omnigraph.

2.3   Advanced UML Structures in Practice

The UML structures we are referring to in this publication are surprisingly uncommon and many software engineers are unfamiliar with these features of UML.
Nevertheless, one may have a hard time trying to encode their semantics *without* these structures. In our opinion, this already justifies their existence and
their use – leading to the necessity for their support in modelling tools. Some
more structures of UML that lend themselves to be realized via omniedges are
attributed associations, qualified associations, fork-, join, merge- and decision
nodes, or duration constraints.

3   Formal Definition of Omnigraphs

Before we present the formalism we discuss some issues regarding our approach
of generalizing "direction". This discussion should explain our perspective on
hypergraphs and demonstrate that the given definition is adequate.

3.1   Roles

In a traditional (directed) graph, each edge has a direction, a point of origin and an
aiming point. But how can we specify something comparable for omnigraphs with
arbitrary numbers of end points? The following paragraphs present an approach
that renders the ordinary directed edge a special case of a more general concept.

Every formalism – every way of representing information – provides certain
primitives to store pieces of information and other primitives to relate these
fragments. The available primitives determine the semantics that can be encoded
directly with this formalism. Graphs, too, are just a special way of representing
information. Their primitives are usually nodes and edges with labels. We use the
labels to store pieces of information. Contiguity relates the information stored
in a graph.

On closer inspection, one can see that there is a third primitive in graphs
that allows information storage: the direction of edges. Direction enables us to
store several extra bits per edge – one extra bit if only unidirectional edges are
permitted, two extra bits if multidirectional edges are permitted, and no extra
bits if only undirected edges are permitted in the graph. Initially, these bits
encode the direction of an edge. Additional information, for example "who loves
whom" or "which code block precedes another", is an interpretation that has
been agreed on. This agreement constitutes which bit-value represents which role
in the relation. Thus, we are effectively interested in the *roles* an edge assigns
and *not* in its direction.

Taking into account that we are interested in roles rather than directions, we
could as well provide roles immediately in our way of representing information.
Instead of storing one direction per edge, each end of an edge is assigned a role.
The advantage of this approach is that it scales a lot better: Now, it is irrelevant
how many ends (these "ends" are called "tentacles" in hypergraphs) an edge
has, including the special cases "one" and "zero".

Another conclusion we can draw from the above consideration is, that the roles we are effectively interested in are seldom "source" and "target". We would rather allow arbitrary roles. Accordingly, the number of available roles does not need to be limited to two.

For these reasons, our omniedges do not have a direction and no inherent order or numerical limitations of their tentacles. Instead, each tentacle is assigned a role out of an arbitrary, finite set of roles. Initially, the combinations of roles within one omniedge are unrestricted. One might want to impose constraints about the legal role sets per omniedge, though.

A classic approach to assign meaning to the tentacles of a hyperedge (or the components of a tuple) is position: Any term-based syntax for the declaration of hyperedges imposes a sequence of tentacle declarations, and the position within this sequence assigns its meaning to a tentacle. The downside of this approach is that the sequence always needs to be specified completely and in order, and that no meaning can be assigned to additional tentacles. In programming languages like Eiffel or Visual Basic, some of these drawbacks can be resolved by *named* function arguments. The role-based approach is a generalization thereof.

For illustration, we show that an ordinary (directed, two-ended) edge can be expressed immediately in terms of this approach: It is an omniedge with two tentacles of which one has the role "source" and the other has the role "target". A traditional graph is thus completely representable as omnigraph. As also omnigraphs are representable via traditional graphs (cf. Section 4) both formalisms are *theoretically* equally expressive. Yet the *practical* expressiveness of omnigraphs is more suitable for certain applications as we show in this publication.

3.2   Definition

Definition 1 (Omnigraph). *Let N, O, T, R be arbitrary finite pairwise disjoint[3] sets, $C := N \cup O$, and src, tgt, and rol total but not necessarily injective or surjective functions with*

$$src : T \longrightarrow O$$
$$tgt : T \longrightarrow C$$
$$rol : T \longrightarrow R$$

then the 7-tuple $G = (N, O, T, src, tgt, R, rol)$ is an omnigraph.

Explanation and Implications. We call N the nodes, O the omniedges, T the tentacles, and R the roles of an omnigraph. $C = N \cup O$ is the set of all connectable objects. The tentacles link the elements of C to their connections $o \in O$; these links are denoted by the *src* and *tgt* functions assigning the obvious direction[4] to the tentacle. It is specific to omnigraphs that the tentacles can

---

[3] For clearness we require N, O, T, R to be pairwise disjoint. Formally it is only necessary that $N \cap O = \emptyset$ holds.

[4] Please note that only the tentacles but not the omniedges themselves are directed.

only start at omniedges but end at omniedges and nodes. So by definition, no node can have an outgoing tentacle whereas incoming tentacles are allowed. Each tentacle linking a connectable object $c \in C$ to an omniedge $o \in O$ also specifies a role $r \in R$ that c takes in o. This is denoted by the *rol* function.

As omniedges may connect other omniedges, the tentacles are directed to make clear which omniedge establishes the connection between the other ones. It is only usual to utilize the concept of 'direction' here – but it is not necessary: It is sufficient to *somehow* distinguish which tentacles belong to which omniedge. Accordingly, it is irrelevant which direction the tentacles exactly have, as long as it is consistent for all omniedges.

Multigraphs are defined by their allowance for multiple edges between two distinct nodes. For omnigraphs this property is obtained by our function-based definition instead of the commonly used tuple-based definition. Thus an arbitrary number of omniedges can occur between every set $C' \subseteq C$. Furthermore, this property allows multiple tentacles of the same or different roles between an omniedge and one connected object $c \in C$. Moreover, if not every node or omniedge has an incident tentacle, *src* and *tgt* are not surjective. We require *src* and *tgt* to be *total* such that no dangling tentacles can occur.

Omnigraphs as defined here have two properties that may appear strange, but are harmless consequences of the generality of the concept: (a) Omniedges may have one or zero tentacles and (b) omniedges may connect to themselves.

Discussion. Our definition is rather close to the function-based definition of ordinary hypergraphs. One *could* picture the set T as "edges" and C as "vertices". But this picture is only half true, because the set C has an internal structure: The "edges" can only start at elements $o \in O \subseteq C$ and end at *any* element $c \in C = O \cup N$. This way, the property of being representable as bipartite graphs (like ordinary hypergraphs) is lost. Clearly, every omnigraph G can be turned into an omnigraph G' without nodes by turning every node into an omniedge not having any outgoing tentacles ("virtual nodes"). Yet in this case, certain runtime checks and validation procedures on the graph and its model must be put into place if we want to distinguish omniedges and (virtual) nodes in a typesave way. We chose the intuitive and computationally cheaper alternative, namely to enforce this distinction by the formalism and in the Ogre language.

Formally speaking, our definition is a direct extension of hypergraphs. But we define names and interpretations of the sets C, O, N, and T to suit our need for a vocabulary of concepts on a higher level of abstraction.

3.3 Examples

We will present two of the examples from Section 2 as formal omnigraph definitions. The first example is the formal definition of the hyperedge depicted in Figure 2. The second example is the formal definition of the constraint edge between two association edges depicted in Figure 3.

The ternary association from Figure 2 has three nodes: Team, Year, and Player. They respectively take the roles team, season, and goalie in the omniedge Association.

$N = \{\text{Team}, \text{Year}, \text{Player}\}$ $O = \{\text{Association}\}$
$T = \{t_0, t_1, t_2\}$ $R = \{\text{team}, \text{season}, \text{goalie}\}$
$src(t_0) = \text{Association}$ $tgt(t_0) = \text{Team}$ $rol(t_0) = \text{team}$
$src(t_1) = \text{Association}$ $tgt(t_1) = \text{Year}$ $rol(t_1) = \text{season}$
$src(t_2) = \text{Association}$ $tgt(t_2) = \text{Player}$ $rol(t_2) = \text{goalie}$

The formal definition of the $\{\text{xor}\}$ constraint has three nodes: Account, Person, and Corporation, and three omniedges: Association_0, Association_1, and Constraint. Each omniedge has two tentacles, so that we have in total six tentacles, but only two different roles associationEnd and constraintEnd. An illustration of the formal definition is shown in Figure 5.

$N = \{\text{Account}, \text{Person}, \text{Corporation}\}$
$O = \{\text{Association}_0, \text{Association}_1, \text{Constraint}\}$
$T = \{t_{a0}, t_{a1}, t_{a2}, t_{a3}, t_{c0}, t_{c1}\}$ $R = \{\text{associationEnd}, \text{constraintEnd}\}$
$src(t_{a0}) = \text{Association}_0$ $tgt(t_{a0}) = \text{Account}$ $rol(t_{a0}) = \text{associationEnd}$
$src(t_{a1}) = \text{Association}_0$ $tgt(t_{a1}) = \text{Person}$ $rol(t_{a1}) = \text{associationEnd}$
$src(t_{a2}) = \text{Association}_1$ $tgt(t_{a2}) = \text{Account}$ $rol(t_{a2}) = \text{associationEnd}$
$src(t_{a3}) = \text{Association}_1$ $tgt(t_{a3}) = \text{Corporation}$ $rol(t_{a3}) = \text{associationEnd}$
$src(t_{c0}) = \text{Constraint}$ $tgt(t_{c0}) = \text{Association}_0$ $rol(t_{c0}) = \text{constraintEnd}$
$src(t_{c1}) = \text{Constraint}$ $tgt(t_{c1}) = \text{Association}_1$ $rol(t_{c1}) = \text{constraintEnd}$

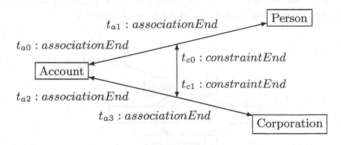

Fig. 5. Formal graph for the $\{\text{xor}\}$ constraint (names of omniedges omitted)

3.4   Extensions

For an efficient use of a graph rewriting *tool* we need (a) labels on nodes, edges, and roles, and want (b) these labels to obey certain constraints, i.e. typing. Furthermore, (c) inheritance relations among these types are needed for an easier declaration of rules. Accordant extensions to the formal basis of omnigraphs can be defined the usual way without difficulty.

Ogre implements these features. It seamlessly incorporates them from the underlying graph rewrite system (cf. Section 4). In contrast to some formalizations of hypergraphs, we assign the type of an omniedge directly to it and do not derive it from the number or types of tentacles. In particular, omniedges of a certain type may have arbitrary numbers of tentacles. However, Ogre supports constraints about the legal role types for each omniedge type.

4 Implementation

To avoid developing a graph rewrite system from scratch, we chose to decompose omnigraph model-, rule-, and graph-definitions to model-, rule-, and graph-definitions for the traditional graph rewrite system GrGen.NET [6]. Ogre provides three compilers for this task. As the space in this paper is limited, we only give a rough outline of these transformations. Details can be found in [5], the compilers including source code are available from [18].

4.1 Mapping Ogre Definitions to GrGen.NET Definitions

As GrGen.NET has no support for omniedges and roles, we need a mapping to translate omniedges and roles into nodes and edges, the primitives provided by GrGen.NET. We map omniedges by introducing an additional interconnection node. As a consequence, each tentacle becomes an independent edge between the interconnection node and the node connected by the tentacle; the role of the tentacle is mapped to the type of the according edge. This approach is quite obvious and well-known from treating hyperedges as bipartite graphs. But in the context of omniedges we have to pay special attention to the direction of decomposed edges: their tentacles are directed, as discussed in Section 3.2. Correspondingly, we realize tentacles with directed edges. Figure 6 shows the mapping for the {xor} constraint example from Figure 3.

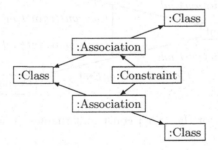

Fig. 6. Mapping of the {xor} constraint

Mapping Models. Listing 8 shows the result of mapping our model from Listing 1 to GrGen.NET syntax. We can see that the omniedge type Association has become a node type (line 9) and the role type AssociationEnd has become an edge type (line 4). Line 5 shows a GrGen.NET constraint defining the allowed source and target types for this edge type.

Figure 7 shows the visualization of the mapped model for the ternary association. We can clearly see the interconnection node with the omniedge type and the edges with the role types.

```
1  node class Class extends NODE {
2      name : string;
3  }
4  edge class AssociationEnd extends ROLE
5      connect Association[1:*] -> Class[*] {
6      name: string;
7      multiplicity: string;
8  }
9  node class Association extends OMNIEDGE;
```

Listing 8. Model from Listing 1 after translation *in GrGen.NET syntax*

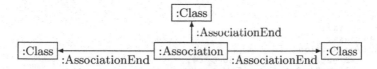

Fig. 7. Mapping of the **model** for the ternary association

Mapping Graphs. Listing 9 shows the ternary association from Listing 4 after the mapping to GrGen.NET syntax. The omniedge Association is decomposed into an interconnection node (line 1) and edges representing the tentacles (line 3, 5, and 7). In GrGen.NET edges are denoted by an arrow from the source to the target node. Identifier, type and attributes of the edge are stated between beginning and end of that arrow. The dollar sign is a build-in attribute of GrGen.NET keeping the identifier of the graph primitive for debugging purposes. The Class nodes and their declared attributes are preserved during the mapping.

```
1  new s_3:Association($="s_3")
2  new n_0:Class($="n_0", name="Team")
3  new s_3 -:AssociationEnd(name="team", multiplicity="*")-> n_0
4  new n_1:Class($="n_1", name="Year")
5  new s_3 -:AssociationEnd(name="season", multiplicity="*")-> n_1
6  new n_2:Class($="n_2", name="Player")
7  new s_3 -:AssociationEnd(name="goalie", multiplicity="*")-> n_2
```

Listing 9. Graph from Listing 4 after translation *in GrGen.NET syntax*

This listing shows how the concept of omnigraphs disburdens the user from the necessity to fragment his or her thoughts for the input into a traditional graph rewrite system. Besides this semantic advantage, the Ogre syntax eliminates the need to constantly repeat identifiers for miscellaneous nodes and edges. This is not so much a quantitative but a qualitative alleviation, as repeating numerous – only technically induced – identifiers is an error prone work. However, an IDE or a graphical notation could alleviate this work, while the model and its instances will still be polluted with artificial entities.

Mapping Rules. Basically, rules are processed by treating the left-hand and right-hand side patterns individually as graph definitions and mapping them separately. As the syntax for patterns is quite similar to graph definitions we reuse the mappings for graph definitions with some minor changes. Listing 10 shows the rule from Listing 7 after mapping to GrGen.NET syntax. The content of the **eval** section can just be copied as it is, because it does not need to be changed by the mapping.

```
1   pattern {
2       a: Association;
3           a —ae1: AssociationEnd—> c1: Class;
4           a —ae2: AssociationEnd—> c2: Class;
5           a —ae3: AssociationEnd—> c3: Class;
6   }
7   modify {
8       delete(a);
9       c4: Class;
10      x2: Association;
11          x2 —ae11: AssociationEnd—> c4;
12          x2 —ae21: AssociationEnd—> c1;
13      x5: Association;
14          x5 —ae12: AssociationEnd—> c4;
15          x5 —ae22: AssociationEnd—> c2;
16      x8: Association;
17          x8 —ae13: AssociationEnd—> c4;
18          x8 —ae23: AssociationEnd—> c3;
19      eval {
20          c4.name = c1.name+c2.name+c3.name+"Triple";
21          ae11.multiplicity = ae1.multiplicity;
22          ae21.multiplicity = "1";   ae21.name = ae1.name;
23          ae12.multiplicity = ae2.multiplicity;
24          ae22.multiplicity = "1";   ae22.name = ae2.name;
25          ae13.multiplicity = ae3.multiplicity;
26          ae23.multiplicity = "1";   ae23.name = ae3.name;
27      }
28  }
```

Listing 10. Rule from Listing 7 after translation *in GrGen.NET syntax*

Obviously, the semantics of our rules are derived directly from the semantics of GrGen.NET rules [2]. GrGen.NET implements closely the SPO semantics, so deleting an incident node of an edge will also delete that edge. This behaviour is well suited for our needs: If we want to delete an omniedge, we can just delete the interconnection node. The SPO semantics will lead to the deletion of edges representing its tentacles. As we allow omniedges to have an arbitrary number of tentacles (including zero), deleting an incident connectable object (and thus 'losing' a tentacle) cannot lead to an invalid omnigraph (cf. Section 2.2).

5   Related Work

Graph rewrite systems have been under research for several decades. Research in Model Driven Development has lead to a strong demand for model transformation technology. This has brought graph rewriting – as one possible solution for model transformation – to industrial relevance.

In this paper, we discuss omnigraph rewriting. To the best of our knowledge, no system with this capability has been published, yet. In Ogre, omniedges– and

Table 1. Overview Graph Rewriting Tools

	Fujaba	GReAT	VIATRA	GrGen.NET	Ogre
Typed Domain	yes	yes	yes	yes	yes
Type Inheritance	single	multi	multi	multi	multi
Node Attributes	Java types	simple types, enumerations	simple and complex types	simple types, enumerations	simple types
Edge Attributes	same as nodes	no	same as nodes	same as nodes	same as nodes
Role Attributes	no	no	no	no	yes
NACs	yes	yes	yes	yes	yes
Hyperedges	no	no	no	no	yes
Omniedges	no	see text	see text	no	yes
Rule Definition	programmed	programmed	declarative	declarative	declarative
Rule Notation	graphical	graphical	textual	textual	textual
Parameterization	all types	no	all types	graph entities	no
Rule Scheduling	story diagrams	sequence diagrams	state machine	similar regular expressions	similar regular expressions
Rule Iteration	loop	loop, recursion	loop, recursion, fix point iteration	loop, fix point iteration, transaction	loop, fix point iteration, transaction

thus also hyperedges – are first-class citizens among the graph primitives: They are quasi materialized in the graph and can seamlessly be used in search and replacement patterns. Thus Ogre is also a hypergraph rewriting system. But even for hypergraph rewriting[5], there is no comparable system available. A property-besides allowing edges to be endpoints of edges– that distinguishes our notion of omnigraph rewriting from the usual *theoretical* notion of hypergraph rewriting is that omniedges have no fixed number of tentacles defining their type. Furthermore, the tentacles of omniedges have no inherent order. Both properties are by design, as we discuss in Section 3.

The Graph eXchange Language (GXL) supports omnigraphs using `rel`- and `relend`-elements. But as already suggested by its name, GXL is not a rewrite system but an exchange format and only serves to store graphs – it can neither store rules nor rewrite sequences. For solely exchanging omnigraphs, GXL would suit very well, but we could not find a tool to exchange omnigraphs graphs with: Holt [8] gives an overview of GXL capable tools, namely GRAS [15], DiaGen [10], Fujaba [13], GenSet [14] and PROGRES [19]. Except DiaGen[6], all these systems ignore `rel` tags, they have no support for hyper- or omniedges. The same holds for GROOVE [17].

AGG-graphs [3], a variant of ALR-graphs and the formal basis of AGG, explicitly enable edges between edges. But these edges are only binary, hyperedges are not first-class citizens in AGG-graphs. Instead, AGG-graphs come with a direct support for 'abstractions' which in turn are not first-class citizens in omn-

---

[5] Please note that 'hypergraph rewriting' and 'hyperedge replacement' [11] are different things: In hyperedge replacement, hyperedges are only special left-hand side patterns of replacement rules. Our concept of hypergraph rewriting is much broader.

[6] DiaGen is a tool for generating diagram editors based on hypergraphs. We aim to develop a general purpose graph rewrite system.

igraphs. So AGG-graphs and omnigraphs are skew to each other. However, AGG
(the tool) has no support for edges between edges.

GReAT [16] and VIATRA [20] partially support edges between edges: GReAT
can define edges between edges in models, but has no possibility to use them in
graphs or rules. VIATRA can use edges between edges in graphs and rules, but
cannot define them in models. In both systems, edges are always binary.

Apart from the support for omniedges, we regard Ogre as ordinary general
purpose graph rewrite system. Table 1 compares the features of Ogre with those
of Fujaba, GReAT, VIATRA and GrGen.NET [6], some of the most popular general purpose graph rewriting tools today. The criteria are adopted from Czarnecki
and Helsen [4].

6   Conclusion

We presented omnigraphs together with an appropriate rewrite system called
Ogre. Omnigraphs are an extension of the well known hypergraphs, enabling the
attachment of multiple nodes *and edges* to edges. In this paper, UML structures
like *n*-ary associations and constraints between associations served as examples
for the usefulness of omnigraphs. Besides model transformations, we use omnigraphs for the representation of natural language [7]. In this domain, hyper- and
omniedges are essential as natural language includes complex sentence structures with higher order relations. Bond angles are an example from the domain
of chemistry where one would like to declare edges between edges.

The rewrite system Ogre provides custom-made languages for the definition
(i. e. typing) and instantiation of omnigraphs as well as the declaration of rules
for their transformation. As the implementation of Ogre is based on a traditional
graph rewrite system, we provide compilers [18] and can thus incorporate many
features from our underlying system.

The reduction to normal graph rewrite systems is straight forward, but the
provided abstraction eases the task of specifying transformations and graphs.
The automatic transformation unburdens the user from consistently and continuously regarding auxiliary nodes and edges. Instead, the user can directly express
his intention. This makes omnigraphs and Ogre *practically* more expressive than
common approaches – and thus well suited to simplify model transformation for
advanced UML structures.

References

1. Berge, C.: Graphs and Hypergraphs. Elsevier Science Ltd., Amsterdam (1985)
2. Blomer, J., Geiß, R.: The GrGen.NET User Manual. University of Karlsruhe, Technical report, ISSN 1432-7864 (2007)
3. Conrad, M., Gajewsky, M., Holl-Biniasz, R., Rudolf, M., Demuth, J., Weber, S.,
   Heckel, R., Müller, J., Taentzer, G., Wagner, A.: Graphische Spezifikation aus-
   gewählter Teile von AGG – einem algebraischen Graphgrammatiksystem, Technical report, no. 95-07, TU Berlin (1995)

4. Czarnecki, K., Helsen, S.: Feature-based survey of model transformation approaches. IBM Systems Journal 45(3) (2006)
5. Denninger, O.: Erweiterung des Kantenkonzepts deklarativer Graphersetzungssysteme von Einfachkanten über Hyperkanten zu, Superkanten. Diplomarbeit, Universität Karlsruhe (2007)
6. Geiß, R., Batz, G.V., Grund, D., Hack, S., Szalkowski, A.M.: A Fast SPO-Based Graph Rewriting Tool. In: Corradini, A., Ehrig, H., Montanari, U., Ribeiro, L., Rozenberg, G. (eds.) ICGT 2006. LNCS, vol. 4178, pp. 383–397. Springer, Heidelberg (2006)
7. Gelhausen, T., Tichy, W.F.: Thematic Role based Generation of UML Models from Real World Requirements. In: First IEEE International Conference on Semantic Computing (ICSC), pp. 282–289 (2007)
8. Holt, R., Schürr, A., Elliott, S., Winter, A.: GXL: A graph-based standard exchange format for reengineering. Science of Computer Programming (2005)
9. Minas, M.: Hypergraphs as a Uniform Diagram Representation Model, TAGT. In: Ehrig, H., Engels, G., Kreowski, H.-J., Rozenberg, G. (eds.) TAGT 1998. LNCS, vol. 1764, pp. 281–295. Springer, Heidelberg (2000)
10. Minas, M.: Concepts and realization of a diagram editor generator based on hypergraph transformation. Science of Computer Programming 44, 157–180 (2002)
11. Rozenberg, G. (ed.): Handbook of Graph Grammars and Computing by Graph Transformation. Foundations, vol. 1. World Scientific, Singapore (1997)
12. OMG: Unified Modeling Language: Superstructure, version 2.1.1 (2007)
13. Fujaba Tool Suite. University of Paderborn Software Engineering Group
14. GenSet: Design Information Fusion. University of Oregon
15. GRAS – A graph oriented database system for (software) engineering environments. Lehrstuhl für Informatik 3, University of Technology Aachen (RWTH)
16. GReAT – Graph Rewrite and Transform System. Institute for Software Integrated Systems, Vanderbilt University, Nashville
17. GROOVE – GRaphs for Object-Oriented VErification. University of Twente
18. OGRE – OmniGraphREwriting System. Institute for Program Structures and Data Organization (IPD), University of Karlsruhe (2007)
    http://sf.net/projects/ogre-system/
19. PROGRES – A Graph Grammar Programming Environment. Lehrstuhl für Informatik 3, University of Technology Aachen (RWTH)
20. VIATRA – Visual Automated model Transformations. Dept. of Measurement and Information Systems, Budapest University of Technology and Economics

A Single-Step Term-Graph Reduction System for Proof Assistants

Maarten de Mol, Marko van Eekelen, and Rinus Plasmeijer

Department of Software Technology, Nijmegen University, The Netherlands
maartenm@cs.ru.nl, marko@cs.ru.nl, rinus@cs.ru.nl

Abstract. In this paper, we will define a custom term-graph reduction system for a simplified lazy functional language. Our custom system is geared towards *flexibility*, which is accomplished by leaving the choice of redex free and by making use of single-step reduction. It is therefore more suited for formal reasoning than the well-established standard reduction systems, which usually fix a single redex and realize multi-step reduction only. We will show that our custom system is correct with respect to the standard systems, by proving that it is *confluent* and allows standard lazy functional evaluation as a possible reduction path.

Our reduction system is used in the foundation of SPARKLE. SPARKLE is the dedicated proof assistant for CLEAN, a lazy functional programming language based on term-graph rewriting. An important reasoning step in SPARKLE is the replacement of an expression with one of its reducts. The *flexibility* of our underlying reduction mechanism ensures that as many reduction options as possible are available for this reasoning step, which improves the ease of reasoning.

Because our reduction system is based on a simplified lazy functional language, our results can be applied to any other functional language based on term-graph rewriting as well.

1 Introduction

CLEAN[1] and HASKELL[2] are lazy functional programming languages that have a semantics based on term-graph rewriting. Due to their mathematical nature, functional programming languages are well suited for formal methods. Industry is beginning to acknowledge the importance of formal methods for verifying safety-critical components of both hardware and software (for instance, see [3]). Consequently, functional languages are being used increasingly often in industrial practice (for instance, see [4]).

The distribution of CLEAN was extended with the dedicated proof assistant SPARKLE[5,6] in 2001. A proof assistant is a tool that supports formal reasoning about programs. Since its introduction, SPARKLE has been used in practice for various purposes. It has been used for proving properties of I/O-programs by Dowse[7] and Butterfield[8]. An extension for dealing with temporal properties has been proposed for it by Tejfel, Horváth and Koszik[9,10]. It has been used in education at the Radboud University of Nijmegen. Furthermore, support for class-generic properties has been added to it by van Kesteren[11].

A. Schürr, M. Nagl, and A. Zündorf (Eds.): AGTIVE 2007, LNCS 5088, pp. 184–200, 2008.

A very important reasoning step in the library of SPARKLE is 'Reduce', which makes use of the operational semantics of CLEAN to replace an expression with one of its reducts. The usefulness of 'Reduce' depends on the reduction options that are made available by the underlying formal reduction system, which must therefore be sufficiently *flexible*. Of course, it also has to support lazy evaluation, graphs and sharing. Normally, the natural choice would be the well-established system of Launchbury[12]. This system, however, is geared towards evaluation: it uses multi-step reduction and fixes a single redex. Therefore, both *partial* and *inner* reductions are not elements of its reduction relation and are not provided as reduction options, which is undesirable for formal reasoning.

In this paper, we will define a custom and flexible reduction system for a lazy functional language. Our system is based on Launchbury's, but uses single-step reduction and leaves the choice of redex free. The formalized reduction relation therefore contains partial and inner reducts as well, which makes our system suited for formal reasoning. We will show that our system is confluent and that the standard lazy functional reduction path is allowed by it. This ensures that our system behaves correctly with respect to Launchbury's system.

An extended version of our reduction system is used in the full mathematical foundation of SPARKLE, which is described in [13]. There are two main differences between this paper and the extended version. Firstly, this paper uses a simplified generic expression language, which makes our reduction system applicable to other functional languages as well. Secondly, this paper improves on the handling of sharing, by explicitly enforcing it for function arguments beforehand and by not making use of external environments. This makes unsharing in our system much easier, and allows for *local* confluence as well.

This paper is structured as follows. In Section 2, we examine the desired level of flexibility. We introduce our expression language in Section 3, and describe our reduction system in Section 4. We show how to express standard reduction paths in our system in Section 5, and we prove confluence of our system in Section 6. Finally, we discuss related work in Section 7 and draw conclusions in Section 8.

2   Desired Level of Flexibility

Replacing expressions with reducts is a very natural and intuitive reasoning step. The flexibility of the underlying reduction system determines the number of reduction options that are available for this step. In principle, having more reduction options increases the power of reasoning. This reasoning power is only useful, however, if the options can intuitively be recognized as reducts.

In the introduction, two factors were mentioned that influence flexibility: the granularity of the reduction relation (single-step vs multi-step), and the freedom of choice of redex (fixed redex vs free redex). In the following sections, we will examine the precise effect of these factors on formal reasoning more closely.

2.1 Granularity of Reduction Steps

On the intuitive level, reduction is mainly considered to be defined by means of
the reduction steps, and only secondary by means of the overarching reduction
relation. On the reasoning level, the reduction options that are offered to the
proof builder should therefore include the results of partial reductions as well. To
formalize this, a single-step reduction system is needed, in which the reduction
relation is defined in terms of single applications of individual reduction steps.

Example: *(proof that requires intermediate reducts)*
    Assume that the following property has been proved:
        '$\forall_b[\text{not } (\text{not } b) = b]$'.
Using this property, assume that we now want to prove the following:
        '$\text{not } (\text{id } (\text{not } X)) = X$' (where X is some complex computation)
On the intuitive level, this is a trivial proof: simply replace '$\text{id } (\text{not } X)$'
with '$\text{not } X$', and then apply the assumed property. QED.
This intuitive proof, however, relies on single-step inner reduction. If no inner
reduction is available, then '$\text{id } (\text{not } X))$' cannot be selected as redex; if no
single-step reduction is available, then the reduction of '$\text{id } (\text{not } X))$' cannot
be stopped after the first step and 'X' will be evaluated unnecessarily.

2.2 Choice of Redex

Because lazy functional languages are referentially transparent, it is always safe
to apply reduction to an inner redex. Formally, however, referential transparency
has to be proved too. This proof can be constructed in two different ways:

1. Start with a reduction system that allows leftmost-outermost reduction only.
   Define semantic equality on top, and prove that it is referentially transparent.
2. Start with a reduction system that allows arbitrary redexes to be reduced.
   Prove that this system is confluent, define a semantic equality on top of it,
   and let referential transparency follow from the already shown confluence.

Because semantic equality needs to cope with infinite reductions (bisimulation),
the second approach is much easier to carry out. Therefore, in this paper we will
allow the redex to be chosen freely, and we will explicitly prove confluence.

3 The Expression Language

Our expression language models the core of an arbitrary lazy functional language.
The basic components of our language are variables, functions, applications and
let expressions. Without loss of generality, we assume that each function symbol
has a fixed arity, and we abstract from constructors and cases, which can be
added without difficulties. We represent function definitions in a constant external environment, and do not use lambda expressions. We consider sharing to be
a basic component of any lazy functional language.

Notations: *(variables, function symbols and lists)*
Let $\mathcal{V}$ denote the set of variable names, $\mathcal{F}$ the set of function symbols, and *Arity* $: \mathcal{F} \rightarrow \mathbb{N}$ the function that obtains the arity of a function symbol. Let *Vars* and *Bound* denote the functions that obtain the free and bound variables of an expression respectively. Let '$\langle$' and '$\rangle$' denote lists, $\#xs$ the length of a list xs, and $xs!i$ the i-th element of xs, if it exists. Let $Unq(xs)$ denote that all elements in xs occur only once.

Notation: *(construction of sets)*
In this paper, sets will be denoted by means of $\{O(x_i) \mid x_i \in X_i \mid P(x_i)\}$, in which $O(x_i)$ describes the syntactical shape of the set elements, $x_i \in X_i$ describes the domains of the variable placeholders, and $P(x_i)$ describes the condition that all elements of the set must adhere to.

Definition 3.1: *(set of expressions)*
The set $\mathcal{E}$ of expressions is defined recursively by:
$$\begin{aligned}
\mathcal{E} = \;&\{\text{var } x && \mid x \in \mathcal{V}\} \\
\cup\;&\{\text{fun } f \text{ on } xs && \mid f \in \mathcal{F}, xs \in \langle \mathcal{V} \rangle \mid Arity(f) \geq \#xs\} \\
\cup\;&\{\text{app } e \text{ to } x && \mid e \in \mathcal{E}, x \in \mathcal{V}\} \\
\cup\;&\{\text{let } xs = es \text{ in } e \mid xs \in \langle \mathcal{V} \rangle, es \in \langle \mathcal{E} \rangle, e \in \mathcal{E} \mid \#xs = \#es \wedge Unq(xs)\}
\end{aligned}$$

Example: *(term-graph expression with cycles)*
Our representation of expressions allows cycles to be represented by means of recursive lets. For instance, assuming the availability of a function symbol F (arity 2) and a variable x, and assuming that the leftmost occurrence of F is the root, the following graph and expression are equivalent:

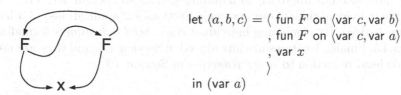

$$\begin{aligned}
\text{let } \langle a, b, c \rangle = \langle\; &\text{fun } F \text{ on } \langle \text{var } c, \text{var } b \rangle \\
,\; &\text{fun } F \text{ on } \langle \text{var } c, \text{var } a \rangle \\
,\; &\text{var } x \\
&\rangle \\
\text{in } (\text{var } a)&
\end{aligned}$$

Assumption 3.2: *(programs)*
Assume the function *Body* $: \langle \mathcal{V} \rangle \times \langle \mathcal{V} \rangle \times \mathcal{F} \rightarrow \mathcal{E}$, which models the program context and binds function symbols to fresh copies of their function bodies. Assume that $Body(xs, ys, f)$ denotes the body of f in which the arguments have been replaced by xs and the bound variables have been replaced by ys.

Example: *(use of the program function)*
Assume that the function f is defined as follows:
```
f x = let y = x+x in y+y
```
Formalized by means of the *Body*-function, this becomes:
$$Body(E, z, f) = (\texttt{let } z \texttt{ = E+E in } z\texttt{+}z)$$
The *Body*-function therefore expands a function on given arguments, using the argument variables to create a fresh instantiation of the function body.

Note that there are two different alternatives for application in our language. The 'fun'-alternative is used for lifting function symbols to the expression level, and for gradually collecting function arguments. The 'app'-alternative is used for applications of expressions that still have to be reduced to function symbols.

Note further that the arguments of both kinds of applications must always be variables. Because of this convention (which we borrow from [12]), expressions need to be converted before they can be represented in our language. Each application that occurs in the expression has to be transformed as follows:

$$Transform(\text{fun } f \text{ on } es) = \text{let } xs = es \text{ in } (\text{fun } f \text{ on } xs)$$
$$Transform(\text{app } e_1 \text{ to } e_2) = \text{let } \langle x \rangle = \langle e_2 \rangle \text{ in } (\text{app } c_1 \text{ to } x)$$

This transformation has to be carried out recursively, and the variables that are created must be fresh. We do not lose expressiveness, because each expression can be transformed this way. The advantage of this convention is that function arguments can be duplicated without loss of sharing. This makes our function expansion rule much easier, as it is no longer necessary to create fresh variables (for sharing function arguments) within the rule itself.

Note that the transformation can never be reversed, because the result would be an expression that cannot be represented in our system. This is not a problem, because reduction never requires the transformation to be reversed.

4   Reduction System

In the following sections, we will introduce our reduction system step-by-step. First, we introduce our approach to handling sharing in Section 4.1. Then, we describe the individual rules of our system in Sections 4.2(applications), 4.3(lets) and 4.4(unsharing). By combining individual rules, *head reduction* is formalized in Section 4.5. Finally, locations are introduced in Section 4.6, and they are used to upgrade head reduction to *inner reduction* in Section 4.7.

4.1   Graphs as Self-contained Expressions

Sharing is handled in our reduction system in a way that is not standard. We do not use an external environment for storing graph nodes, and we do not have a reduction rule that removes let bindings from an expression and transfers them to an external environment. Instead, we store graph nodes *within* the expression by means of lets and use a *let-lifting* mechanism.

The goal of our method is get rid of external environments completely, which normally have to be dragged along continuously. By maintaining graph nodes internally, expressions become self-contained; they can be reduced and given a meaning without pairing them to an external object. This makes handling expressions more transparent, and makes subsequent definitions and proofs easier.

The disadvantage of our method is that additional functionality is needed for maintaining let definitions internally. Two tasks have to be performed:

- *If reduction requires a subexpression at a specific location to be in a certain form, then it must be possible to remove a leading let from that location.*

Example: 'app (let $\langle x \rangle = \langle e \rangle$ in (fun f on $\langle x \rangle$)) to y'.   *(arity of f is 2)*

Reduction should first join the outer app and the inner fun, adding y to the argument list $\langle x \rangle$. Then, reduction should expand f.

Unfortunately, the let expression in the middle prevents the contraction rule from matching immediately. Normally, this would not be a problem, because reduction would be able to move the inner let to an external environment. In our case, the inner let cannot be removed, and another solution is needed.

- *If reduction requires a variable to be unshared, then an explicit link has to be created to the corresponding let binding.*

Example: 'let $\langle x \rangle = \langle e \rangle$ in (app (var x) to y)'.   *(assume that e is in nf)*

Reduction should now replace the inner 'var x' with e. This requires the inner reduction of 'var x' to know about the external binding of x to e.

Normally, reduction of the expression as a whole would introduce $x = e$ into the external environment, by means of which the information would be made available. Because we do not use external environments, we have to find another way of passing down this information.

Fortunately, solutions to the issues above can be realized easily, see Sections 4.3 and 4.4 respectively. Overall, our reduction system remains very simple.

4.2   The Reduction Rules for Applications

In our system, applications are contracted from initial sequences of app-nodes into fun-nodes. When sufficient arguments have been collected, the function is expanded. This process can be realized by the following two reduction rules:

- The collect-rule accumulates function arguments into a central fun-node by removing them from surrounding app-nodes. This process is repeated until the fun-node is filled and contains as many arguments as its arity describes.
- The expand-rule replaces a filled fun-node with (a fresh copy) of the body of the function (obtained with *Body*, see Assumption 3.2). Additional context information is required in the form of a list of fresh variables, which are used as instantiation for the bound variables of the body.

In this paper, we will formalize reduction by means of deterministic functions, because this makes proving confluence much easier. If additional information is required to accomplish deterministic behavior, then it is assumed to be available by means of input arguments. In the later stages of the formalization of reduction, it will be described how this information is obtained.

The reduction rules collect and expand are formalized as follows:

Definition 4.2.1: *(the realization of the* collect*-rule)*
The function $Collect : \mathcal{E} \rightarrow \mathcal{E}$ is defined by:

$$Collect(e) = \begin{cases} \text{fun } f \text{ on } \langle xs:x \rangle & \text{if } e = (\text{app (fun } f \text{ on } xs) \text{ to } x) \\ & \wedge \; Arity(f) > \#xs \\ e & \textbf{otherwise} \end{cases}$$

Definition 4.2.2: *(the realization of the* expand*-rule)*
The function $Expand : \langle \mathcal{V} \rangle \times \mathcal{E} \rightarrow \mathcal{E}$ is defined by:

$$Expand(ys, e) = \begin{cases} Body(xs, ys, f) & \text{if } e = (\text{fun } f \text{ on } xs) \wedge Arity(f) = \#xs \\ e & \textbf{otherwise} \end{cases}$$

Note that, as a consequence of allowing only variables at argument positions, the reduction rules for function application do not have to take sharing into account in any way. Instead, sharing is preserved automatically.

4.3   The Reduction Rules for Let Lifting

For the administration of sharing, our reduction system maintains lets within expressions, instead of moving them into an external environment. This means that lets may get in the way of reduction: when a subexpression has to be brought into a certain form, it is possible that a let is created on its outer level. For reduction to continue, it must be possible to remove this hindering let.

Our basic idea is to move lets upwards until they are no longer in the way. This approach works, because: (1) lets at the outermost level can never be in the way; and (2) upward moves can be achieved easily at all relevant locations. We will call the upward move of a let a let lift; our alternative for external environments is therefore the process of *let lifting*.

In our system, there are two places where a let must be lifted upwards:

– *On the left-hand-side of an application.*
  The expression on the left-hand-side of an app-node must be reduced to a fun-node in order for reduction to continue by means of an application of the collect-rule. If a let expression appears at the outermost level of the left-hand-side of an application, it therefore has to be moved out of the way.
– *On the right-hand-side of a let binding.*
  An important step in the functional reduction strategy is the unsharing of a stored let binding. This is only allowed if the binding is in a certain form; in particular, it may not be a let expression. If a let expression appears at the outermost level of the right-hand-side of a let binding, it therefore has to be moved out of the way.

The two reduction rules that perform let lifting are lift app and lift let. They are formalized by means of the functions *LiftApp* and *LiftLet*. The function *LiftApp* does not require additional context information, but *LiftLet* requires the index of the let binding to be lifted for reasons of disambiguation.

Definition 4.3.3: *(the realization of the* lift-app-*rule)*
The function $LiftApp : \mathcal{E} \to \mathcal{E}$ is defined by:

$$LiftApp(e) = \begin{cases} \text{let } xs = es \text{ in (app } e'' \text{ to } x) & \text{if } e = (\text{app } e' \text{ to } x) \\ & \wedge \ e' = (\text{let } xs = es \text{ in } e'') \\ e & \textbf{otherwise} \end{cases}$$

Definition 4.3.4: *(the realization of the* lift-let-*rule)*
The function $LiftLet : \mathbb{N} \times \mathcal{E} \to \mathcal{E}$ is defined by:

$$LiftLet(i, e) = \begin{cases} \text{let } \langle xs_1 : ys : x_i : xs_2 \rangle & \text{if } e = (\text{let } \langle xs_1 : x_i : xs_2 \rangle = \\ = \langle as_1 : bs : b : as_2 \rangle & \qquad \langle as_1 : a_i : as_2 \rangle \text{ in } a \\ \text{in } a & \qquad \wedge \ \#xs_1 = \#as_1 = i - 1 \\ & \qquad \wedge \ a_i = (\text{let } ys = bs \text{ in } b) \\ e & \textbf{otherwise} \end{cases}$$

Note that *LiftLet* joins two let expressions into a single new one. The argument i determines which inner let should be lifted. It is required, because multiple inner bindings may be a let itself. The bindings of the inner let are inserted in the outer let just before the original binding. This ensures that the order in which inner lets are lifted does not matter; the result will always be the same.

Example: *(example of the* lift-app-*rule)*
In Section 4.1, the following example of a hindering let was given:
'app (let $\langle x \rangle = \langle e \rangle$ in (fun f on $\langle x \rangle$)) to y'.   *(arity of f is 2)*
By applying *LiftApp*, this expression can now be transformed to:
'let $\langle x \rangle = \langle e \rangle$ in (app (fun f on $\langle x \rangle$) to y)'.
Reduction can now continue on the inner let by means of a collect.

Example: *(example of the* lift-let-*rule)*
In the following expression, both the inner lets can be lifted:
'let $\langle x : y \rangle = \langle \text{let } xs = as \text{ in } a : \text{let } ys = bs \text{ in } b \rangle$ in e'.
Lifting the second inner let (using *LiftLet* on index 2) leads to:
'let $\langle x : ys : y \rangle = \langle \text{let } xs = as \text{ in } a : bs : b \rangle$ in e'.
Lifting the remaining inner let (using *LiftLet* on index 1) leads to:
'let $\langle xs : x : ys : y \rangle = \langle as : a : bs : b \rangle$ in e'.
First lifting index 1 and then index 2 would have given the same result.

4.4   The Reduction Rule for Unsharing

The last remaining task for which a reduction rule has to be defined is the task of *unsharing*. This is the process of replacing variables with the expressions that they are associated with by means of a let binding. We will model one single unshare at a time. Note that cyclic let definitions are allowed; therefore, the process of repeated unsharing does not always terminate. A single unshare, however, always terminates.

Because efficiency is important even when building proofs, we do not allow duplication of unfinished computations. Therefore, an expression may only be unshared if it can statically be determined that it does not contain any redexes. In our language, this is only the case for *partial applications*. Chains of variables $(x = y, y = \ldots)$ cannot be unshared immediately. Instead, the final binding has to be reduced to a partial application first, after which the chain can be collapsed.

The rule for unsharing is called unshare, and its function is *Unshare*. The function can only be applied to a variable, and takes the binding as additional input. It is assumed that the binding occurs in the context of the redex.

Definition 4.4.5: *(the realization of the* unshare-*rule)*

The function $Unshare : \mathcal{E} \times \mathcal{E} \to \mathcal{E}$ is defined by:

$$Unshare(x, u, e) = \begin{cases} u & \textbf{if } e = (\textsf{var } x) \wedge u = (\textsf{fun } f \textsf{ on } xs) \\ & \wedge \, Arity(f) < \#xs \\ e & \textbf{otherwise} \end{cases}$$

Note that this unshare can replace a variable x with any expression u that it is given as additional argument. On this level, there is no verification that $x = u$ actually appears in the context of the redex. This verification is performed later, on the level of inner reduction (see Section 4.7).

4.5   Head Reduction

Head reduction is the combination of the five reduction functions defined in the previous sections. It operates on a *rule selector* and an expression. Based on the rule selector, one of the five reduction functions is selected, which is then applied to the expression. A *rule selector* is an artificial identifier that denotes one of the five reduction rules. For simplicity, we incorporate the additional input arguments of the individual rules into the rule selectors defined below:

Definition 4.5.6: *(set of rule selectors)*

The set $\mathcal{R}$ of rule selectors is defined by:

$$\mathcal{R} = \{\textsf{collect}, \textsf{lift app}\}$$
$$\cup \, \{\textsf{expand } xs \quad | \; xs \in \langle \mathcal{V} \rangle\}$$
$$\cup \, \{\textsf{lift bind } i \quad | \; i \in \mathbb{N}\}$$
$$\cup \, \{\textsf{unshare } x \textsf{ to } u \mid x \in \mathcal{V}, u \in \mathcal{E}\}$$

The head reduction function is simply a case distinction on the rule selector:

Definition 4.5.7: *(head reduction)*

The function $HeadReduce : \mathcal{R} \times \mathcal{E} \to \mathcal{E}$ is defined by:

$$\begin{aligned} HeadReduce(\textsf{collect}, & \quad e) &= Collect(e) \\ HeadReduce(\textsf{expand } xs, & \quad e) &= Expand(xs, e) \\ HeadReduce(\textsf{lift app}, & \quad e) &= LiftApp(e) \\ HeadReduce(\textsf{lift bind } i, & \quad e) &= LiftLet(i, e) \\ HeadReduce(\textsf{unshare } x \textsf{ to } u, & \quad e) &= Unshare(x, u, e) \end{aligned}$$

A summary of the total system of reduction rules is given in Table 1.

Table 1. The reduction system as a whole

name	rule	conditions
collect	$$\dfrac{\text{app (fun } f \text{ on } xs) \text{ to } x}{\text{fun } f \text{ on } \langle xs : x \rangle}$$	$Arity(f) > \#xs$
expand ys	$$\dfrac{\text{fun } f \text{ on } xs}{Body(xs, ys, f)}$$	$Arity(f) = \#xs$
lift app	$$\dfrac{\text{app (let } xs = es \text{ in } e) \text{ to } x}{\text{let } xs = es \text{ in (app } e \text{ to } x)}$$	—
lift bind i	$$\dfrac{\text{let } \langle x_1 \ldots x_n \rangle = \langle e_1 \ldots e_n \rangle \text{ in } e}{\begin{array}{l}\text{let } \langle x_1 \ldots x_{i-1} : ys : x_i : x_{i+1} \ldots x_n \rangle \\ = \langle e_1 \ldots e_{i-1} : as : a : a_{i\,|\,1} \ldots a_n \rangle \text{ in e}\end{array}}$$	$\begin{array}{l}1 \le i \le n, \\ e_i = (\text{let } ys = as \text{ in } a)\end{array}$
unshare x to u	$$\dfrac{\text{var } x}{u}$$	$\begin{array}{l}u = (\text{fun } f \text{ on } xs), \\ Arity(f) < \#xs\end{array}$

4.6   Locations

All the reduction functions that have been defined so far can only be applied to the head of an expression. In order to lift these function to inner reduction, we will use the concept of *locations*. A location is an artificial identifier that points to a specific subexpression within a compound expression. The basic operations on locations are *Get* and *Set*. For a full formalization of locations we refer to the technical report [14]. Here, we introduce locations informally only:

Notation 4.6.8: *(locations and operations on locations)*
Let $\mathcal{L}$ denote the set of available locations, $Get : \mathcal{L} \times \mathcal{E} \hookrightarrow \mathcal{E}$ the function that gets the subexpression from an indicated location, and $Set : \mathcal{L} \times \mathcal{E} \times \mathcal{E} \hookrightarrow \mathcal{E}$ the function that sets the subexpression at an indicated location.

Note that both *Get* and *Set* are partial functions; they fail when the location is not valid within the indicated expression.

4.7   Inner Reduction

The final step in defining our custom reduction system is the upgrade of head reduction to *inner* reduction, which allows reduction to take place on an arbitrary redex. Inner reduction is represented by a function that operates on a location, a rule selector and an expression. It selects the redex at the indicated location, and applies head reduction to it using the given rule selector as argument.

Inner reduction performs partial verification of the incoming rule selector as well. It checks two conditions, namely: (1) whether the variables of an expand are indeed fresh with respect to the expression that is reduced; and (2) whether the binding of an unshare is indeed available in the context of the redex. These conditions are checked using a combination of the redex location and the expression as a whole. The other reduction functions operate on the redex alone, and can therefore not perform these verifications themselves.

The verification of the freshness of an expand-rule is formalized by means of the relation *Fresh*. It simply extracts the variables from the rule and checks whether there is an overlap with the bound variables of the expression.

Definition 4.7÷9: *(verification of an* expand-*rule)*
The relation *Fresh* $\subseteq \mathcal{R} \times \mathcal{E}$ is defined by:
$$Fresh(r, e) \Leftrightarrow \forall_{xs \in \langle \mathcal{V} \rangle}[r = (\text{expand } xs) \Rightarrow \neg \exists_{x \in \mathcal{V}}[x \in xs \wedge x \in Bound(e)]]$$

The verification of an unshare-rule is formalized in two steps. First, an auxiliary function *Defs* is defined which collects *all* let bindings within an expression. Then, the relation *Occurs* extracts the binding from an unshare-rule and checks whether it is an element of *Defs*. Because reduction is only allowed on wellformed expressions (i.e. they must be closed and they must have unique variables), being an element of *Defs* automatically ensures the validity of a let binding.

Definition 4.7÷10: *(let bindings within an expression)*
The function *Defs* : $\mathcal{E} \to \wp(\mathcal{V} \times \mathcal{E})$ is defined recursively by:
$$
\begin{aligned}
Defs(\text{var } x) &= \emptyset \\
Defs(\text{fun } f \text{ on } xs) &= \emptyset \\
Defs(\text{app } e \text{ to } x) &= Defs(e) \\
Defs(\text{let}\langle x_1 \ldots x_n \rangle = \langle e_1 \ldots e_n \rangle \text{ in } e) &= \cup_{i=1}^{n}[\{(x_i, e_i)\} \cup Defs(e_i)] \cup Defs(e)
\end{aligned}
$$

Definition 4.7÷11: *(verification of an* unshare-*rule)*
The relation *Occurs* $\subseteq \mathcal{R} \times \mathcal{E}$ is defined by:
$$Occurs(r, e) \Leftrightarrow \forall_{x \in \mathcal{V}} \forall_{u \in \mathcal{E}}[r = (\text{unshare } x \text{ to } u) \Rightarrow (x, u) \in Defs(e)]$$

The verification of a rule selector can now be formalized by means of the relation *Valid*, which is simply a conjunction of *Fresh* and *Occurs*:

Definition 4.7÷12: *(verification of a rule selector)*
The relation *Valid* $\subseteq \mathcal{R} \times \mathcal{E}$ is defined by:
$$Valid(r, e) \Leftrightarrow Fresh(r, e) \wedge Occurs(r, e)$$

Inner reduction is formalized by means of the total function *InnerReduce*. This function acts as the identity if the input arguments are not wellformed, or the reduction rule cannot be applied successfully. The input is wellformed if: (1) the location is valid; (2) the rule selector is valid; (3) the expression is closed; and (4) the bound variables within the expression are unique. The explicit conditions (3) and (4) restrict reduction to wellformed expressions only.

Definition 4.7÷13: *(inner reduction)*
The function *InnerReduce* : $\mathcal{L} \times \mathcal{R} \times \mathcal{E} \to \mathcal{E}$ is defined by:
$$
InnerReduce(l, r, e) = \begin{cases} Set(l, HeadReduce(r, e'), e) \\ \quad \text{if } Get(l, e) = e' \wedge Valid(r, e) \\ \quad \wedge Vars(e) = \emptyset \wedge Unq(Bound(e)) \\ e \quad \textbf{otherwise} \end{cases}
$$

Note that the result of reduction is always a wellformed expression itself. This property can be verified easily; therefore, its proof is omitted here.

5 Correctness of Let Lifting

Our system is non-standard only in the handling of sharing. Other than that, it can be regarded as a simplification of a single-step version of [12]. It is easy to see, however, that our approach with let lifting is equivalent to the standard approach which makes use of external environments:

– Suppose that R is our reduction system, and that R' is obtained out of R by replacing the let-lifting mechanism with a usual external environment mechanism. That is, R' is obtained out of R by:
  - leaving out the rules lift app and lift let;
  - introducing external environments $\Gamma \subseteq \mathcal{V} \times \mathcal{E}$;
  - changing the signature of reduction from $\mathcal{E} \to \mathcal{E}$ to $\Gamma \times \mathcal{E} \to \Gamma \times \mathcal{E}$;
  - adding a rule introduce let that removes a let expression and moves the let bindings in the external environment; and
  - altering the rule unshare to use the external environment.
– Then, all reduction paths of R' can be transformed to R by:
  - leaving out external environments and all applications of introduce let;
  - inserting as many lift app's before each application of collect as there are inner lets in the application node;
  - inserting as many lift let's before each application of unshare as there are inner lets in the binding to be unshared; and
  - augmenting each unshare with the let binding used.

This simple algorithm maps any traditional reduction path into an equivalent reduction path in our system. Because R' can be considered as an extension of Launchbury's system, this means that all reduction paths of Launchbury have an equivalent in our system. The reverse does not hold, however, because our paths do not always choose the left-most outer-most redex, and do not always end with a normal form. Due to confluence (see next section), however, the paths in our system that cannot be converted to Launchbury's system are equivalent to the paths that can be converted.

6 Confluence

Confluence is a well-known property of rewrite systems. It is important for our system, because it ensures that all possible reductions preserve the meaning of an expression, and can therefore safely be applied in the context of reasoning.

In our reduction system, confluence only holds *modulo α-conversion*, because no explicit α-conversion rule is available. Therefore, if two expands are carried out on the same redex, or two expands are carried out on different redexes but there is an overlap in the variables that they introduce, then the reduction results cannot be brought together. This precondition of confluence is formalized by the relation *Joinable*. Furthermore, *Joinable* also excludes the irrelevant and trivial case that the two reductions are identical.

Definition 6.1: *(precondition of confluence)*
The relation $Joinable \subseteq \mathcal{L} \times \mathcal{R} \times \mathcal{L} \times \mathcal{R}$ is defined by:
$$Joinable(l_1, r_1, l_2, r_2) \Leftrightarrow \neg(l_1 = l_2 \wedge r_1 = r_2)$$
$$\wedge\ \forall_{xs, ys \in \langle \mathcal{V} \rangle}[(r_1 = \mathsf{expand}\ xs \wedge r_2 = \mathsf{expand}\ ys) \Rightarrow$$
$$(l_1 \neq l_2 \wedge \neg \exists_{x \in \mathcal{V}}[x \in xs \wedge x \in ys])]$$

Below we present the proofs of confluence, which are built incrementally. First, we prove confluence for two single head steps, then for one head step and one inner step, and then finally for two inner steps. Without loss of generality, we present simplified proofs and abstract from wellformedness altogether.

Lemma 6.2: *(confluence - head/head version)*
$$\forall_{e \in \mathcal{E}} \forall_{r_1, r_2 \in \mathcal{R}}[Joinable(\langle \rangle, r_1, \langle \rangle, r_2)$$
$$\Rightarrow \exists_{r_3, r_4 \in \mathcal{R}}[HeadReduce(r_3, HeadReduce(r_1, e)) =$$
$$HeadReduce(r_4, HeadReduce(r_2, e))]]$$

Proof

Assume $e \in \mathcal{E}$, $r_1, r_2 \in \mathcal{R}$ and $[1]Joinable(\langle \rangle, r_1, \langle \rangle, r_2)$.
As can be seen in Table 1, on each kind of expression there is only one kind of reduction rule available. Therefore, r_1 and r_2 must be of the same kind.

Due to assumption [1], r_1 and r_2 cannot be the same and cannot be expand's. Therefore, r_1 and r_2 can only be different applications of lift bind:
Assume $[2]r_1 = (\mathsf{lift\ bind}\ i)$, $[3]r_2 = (\mathsf{lift\ bind}\ j)$, $[4]i \neq j$.
$[5]e = (\mathsf{let}\ xs = bs\ \mathsf{in}\ e_1)$,
$[6]1 \leq i < j$ (if $i > j$ then simply swap them),
$[7]xs = \langle xs_1 : x_i : xs_2 : x_j : xs_3 \rangle$ (with $\#xs_1 = i\text{-}1$ and $\#xs_2 = j\text{-}i\text{-}1$),
$[8]bs = \langle bs_1 : b_i : bs_2 : b_j : bs_3 \rangle$ (with $\#bs_1 = i\text{-}1$ and $\#bs_2 = j\text{-}i\text{-}1$),
$[9]b_i = (\mathsf{let}\ ys = gs\ \mathsf{in}\ g)$ and $[10]b_j = (\mathsf{let}\ zs = hs\ \mathsf{in}\ h)$.
The basic idea is that the let lifts can simply be swapped. However, the index of the binding in r_3 has to be increased, because the let lift performed by r_1 has pushed additional bindings upwards. This is not necessary in the reverse case, because the lift of j takes place behind the lift of i.
Choose $[11]r_3 = (\mathsf{lift\ bind}\ j + \#ys)$ and $[12]r_4 = (\mathsf{lift\ bind}\ i)$.
Now, using HR as abbreviation for $HeadReduce$, the following holds:

$HR(r_3, HR(r_1, e))$ {2,5}
$= HR(r_3, HR(\mathsf{lift\ bind}\ i, \mathsf{let}\ xs = bs\ \mathsf{in}\ e_1))$ {11,HR,7,8,9}
$= HR(\mathsf{lift\ bind}\ j + \#ys, \mathsf{let}\ \langle xs_1 : ys : x_i : xs_2 : x_j : xs_3 \rangle$ {12,HR}
$\qquad = \langle bs_1 : gs : g : bs_2 : b_j : bs_3 \rangle \mathsf{in}\ e_1)$
$= (\mathsf{let}\ \langle xs_1 : ys : x_i : xs_2 : zs : x_j : xs_3 \rangle = \langle bs_1 : gs : g : bs_2 : hs : h : bs_3 \rangle\ \mathsf{in}\ e_1)$.

Again using HR as abbreviation for $HeadReduce$, the following also holds:

$HR(r_4, HR(r_2, e))$ {3,6}
$= HR(r_4, HR(\mathsf{lift\ bind}\ j, \mathsf{let}\ xs = bs\ \mathsf{in}\ e_1))$ {12,HR,7,8,10}
$= HR(\mathsf{lift\ bind}\ i, \mathsf{let}\ \langle xs_1 : x_i : xs_2 : zs : x_j : xs_3 \rangle$ {11,HR}
$\qquad = \langle bs_1 : b_i : bs_2 : hs : h : bs_3 \rangle\ \mathsf{in}\ e_1)$
$= (\mathsf{let}\ \langle xs_1 : ys : x_i : xs_2 : zs : x_j : xs_3 \rangle = \langle bs_1 : gs : g : bs_2 : hs : h : bs_3 \rangle\ \mathsf{in}\ e_1)$.

Therefore, $HR(r_3, HR(r_1, e)) = HR(r_4, HR(r_2, e))$. **QED.**

Lemma 6:3: *(confluence - head/inner version)*
$$\forall_{e \in \mathcal{E}} \forall_{r_1, r_2 \in \mathcal{R}} \forall_{l \in \mathcal{L}} [Joinable(\langle \rangle, r_1, l, r_2)$$
$$\Rightarrow \exists_{r_3, r_4 \in \mathcal{R}} \exists_{l' \in \mathcal{L}} [InnerReduce(l', r_3, HeadReduce(r_1, e)) =$$
$$HeadReduce(r_4, InnerReduce(l, r_2, e))]]$$

Proof

Assume $e \in \mathcal{E}$, $r_1, r_2 \in \mathcal{R}$, $l \in \mathcal{L}$ and $Joinable(\langle \rangle, r_1, l, r_2)$.

If $l = \langle \rangle$, then the previous Lemma can simply be applied.

If l occurs within a free expression variable of the left-hand-side pattern of r_1 (i.e. no overlap with r_1), then the following arguments hold:

- *Rule r_2 on a modified l_2' is applicable on $HeadReduce(r_1, e)$.*
  All expression variables that are used in the left-hand-side of a reduction rule occur unchanged in the right-hand-side. In other words: r_1 moves the redex of r_2 around, but does not change it.
- *Rule r_1 is applicable at the head of e_2.*
  The reduction r_2 only changes the contents of an expression variable in the left-hand-side pattern of r_1. If r_1 matches on e, it therefore also syntactically matches (at the head) on e_2. Furthermore, note that it is not possible that the conditions of r_1 are falsified by r_2, or vice versa.
- *The reductions r_1 and r_2 can be swapped, without changing the result.*
  This follows from the two arguments above.

This only leaves a partial overlap between r_1 and r_2 to be considered. An inspection of Table 1 reveals that there are two such cases: either r_1 is a 'lift app' and r_2 is a 'lift bind'; or r_1 is a 'lift bind' and r_2 is an inner 'lift bind'.

In both cases, r_1 and r_2 can be swapped, similarly to Lemma 6:2. The full proof is omitted here, but it can be found in [14].   **QED.**

Theorem 6:4: *(confluence)*
$$\forall_{e \in \mathcal{E}} \forall_{r_1, r_2 \in \mathcal{R}} \forall_{l_1, l_2 \in \mathcal{L}} [Joinable(l_1, r_1, l_2, r_2) \Rightarrow$$
$$\exists_{r_3, r_4 \in \mathcal{R}} \exists_{l_1', l_2' \in \mathcal{L}} [InnerReduce(l_1', r_3, InnerReduce(l_1, r_1, e)) =$$
$$InnerReduce(l_2', r_4, InnerReduce(l_2, r_2, e))]]$$

Proof

Assume $e \in \mathcal{E}$, $r_1, r_2 \in \mathcal{R}$, $l_1, l_2 \in \mathcal{L}$ and $Joinable(l_1, r_1, l_2, r_2)$.

Assume that l_1 is at least as close to the root of e as l_2. If otherwise, then simply swap l_1 and l_2. We distinguish two cases:

- CASE 1: l_2 *is a sublocation of* l_1. Now, r_1 is a head reduction of $Get(l_1, e)$, and r_2 is an inner reduction of $Get(l_1, e)$. By applying Lemma 6:3, r_1 and r_2 can be brought together in the context of $Get(l_1, e)$. Because a reduction of a subexpression is always also a reduction of the expression as a whole, r_1 and r_2 can be brought together in the context of e as well.
- CASE 2: l_2 *is not a sublocation of* l_1. In this case, r_1 and r_2 are completely disjoint. Their redex transformations therefore do not interfere with each other at all, and can be swapped leading to the same single result. **QED.**

7 Related Work

Our reduction system is based on reduction as proposed by Launchbury in [12], which has since 1993 been used as the de facto standard for evaluating lazy functional programs. Several systems have been derived from Launchbury's, but none that we know of leaves the choice of redex free. Derived systems of interest are [15], which defines an operational semantics specifically for CLEAN, and [16], which defines a *single-step* reduction system for parallel evaluation. Both systems fix a single redex, however, and are therefore less suited for formal reasoning.

In [17] the authors describe a single-step reduction system based on a call-by-need extension of the lambda calculus, which fully supports lazy evaluation and sharing. It is both single-step and leaves the choice of redex free. The disadvantage of this system, however, is the syntactical distance between the lambda calculus and (the core of) a lazy functional programming language. This distance is most apparent in the representation of functions and applications. Due to this distance, the system of [17] is not suited for *dedicated* formal reasoning on the level of the program, which is one of the trademark features of SPARKLE.

Related more generally is the ρ_g-Calculus[18], which integrates term-rewriting with lambda-calculus, expressing sharing and cycles. It uses both unification and matching constraints, leading to a term-graph representation in an equational style. This calculus is more general than classical term graph rewriting[19,20], which can be simulated in it. We feel that our work can serve as a first basis for creating a reduction system for a proof assistant based on the ρ_g-calculus.

Another future issue concerns the addition of tactical support for equivalency of cyclic graphs. This may be based upon the work of [21], which establishes the bisimilarity of different proof systems for equational cyclic graph specifications.

8   Conclusions

We have defined a term-graph reduction system for a simplified lazy functional language. Our system uses single-step reduction and leaves the choice of redex free. This offers a degree of flexibility that is not available in the commonly used reduction systems for functional languages. Due to this degree of flexibility, our system is much better suited for the foundation of formal reasoning. Our reduction system is used in the foundation of SPARKLE, CLEAN's proof assistant.

Our system maintains sharing within expressions and does not use external environments. This offers the advantage of orthogonality: expressions can be given a meaning as they are, whereas in the common reduction systems they have to be combined with an environment first. The internal maintenance of sharing does not make the reduction system more complicated; it suffices to add two additional rules for let-lifting . All in all, our system consists of five reduction rules only, and is very simple.

All common reduction paths can be expressed in our system. Furthermore, we have proved that our system is confluent. This implies that our system is equivalent to the standard systems: there is at least one reduction path that corresponds to normal reduction, and all other paths can be converged to it.

References

1. van Eekelen, M., Plasmeijer, R.: Concurrent CLEAN language report (version 1.3). Technical Report CSI–R9816, Radboud University Nijmegen (1998)
2. Hudak, P., Jones, S.L.P., Wadler, P., Boutel, B., Fairbairn, J., Fasel, J.H., Guzmán, M.M., Hammond, K., Hughes, J., Johnsson, T., Kieburtz, R.B., Nikhil, R.S., Partain, W., Peterson, J.: Report on the Programming Language Haskell, A Non-strict, Purely Functional Language. SIGPLAN Notices 27(5), R1–R164(1992)
3. Brim, L., Haverkort, B.R., Leucker, M., van de Pol, J. (eds.): FMICS 2006 and PDMC 2006. LNCS, vol. 4346. Springer, Heidelberg (2007)
4. Moran, A.: Report on the First Commercial Users of Functional Programming Workshop. SIGPLAN Notices 39(12) (2004)
5. de Mol, M., van Eekelen, M., Plasmeijer, R.: Proving properties of lazy functional programs with SPARKLE. In: Horváth, Z. (ed.) 2nd Central-European Functional Programming School, CEFP 2007, Cluj-Napoca, Romania. LNCS Tutorial Series. Springer, Heidelberg (to appear, 2008)
6. de Mol, M., van Eekelen, M., Plasmeijer, R.: Theorem proving for functional programmers - SPARKLE: A functional theorem prover. In: Arts, T., Mohnen, M. (eds.) IFL 2002. LNCS, vol. 2312, pp. 55–72. Springer, Heidelberg (2002)
7. Dowse, M., Butterfield, A., van Eekelen, M.C.J.D.: Reasoning About Deterministic Concurrent Functional I/O. In: Grelck, C., Huch, F., Michaelson, G.J., Trinder, P. (eds.) IFL 2004. LNCS, vol. 3474, pp. 177–194. Springer, Heidelberg (2005)
8. Butterfield, A., Strong, G.: Proving Correctness of Programs with I/O - a paradigm comparison. In: Arts, T., Mohnen, M. (eds.) IFL 2002. LNCS, vol. 2312, pp. 72–88. Springer, Heidelberg (2002)
9. Tejfel, M., Horváth, Z., Kozsik, T.: Extending the sparkle core language with object abstraction. Acta Cybern. 17(2) (2006)
10. Horváth, Z., Kozsik, T., Tejfel, M.: Proving invariants of functional programs. In: Kilpeläinen, P., Päivinen, N. (eds.) SPLST, University of Kuopio, Department of Computer Science, pp. 115–126 (2003)
11. van Kesteren, R., van Eekelen, M., de Mol, M.: Proof support for general type classes. In: Loidl, H.W. (ed.) Trends in Functional Programming 5: Selected papers from the 5th Int. Symposium on Trends in Functional Programming, TFP 2004, München, Germany, Intellect, pp. 1–16 (2004)
12. Launchbury, J.: A natural semantics for lazy evaluation. In: Conference Record of the Twentieth Annual ACM SIGPLAN-SIGACT Symposium on Principles of Programming Languages, Charleston, South Carolina, pp. 144–154 (1993)
13. de Mol, M., van Eekelen, M., Plasmeijer, R.: The mathematical foundation of the proof assistant sparkle. Technical Report ICIS–R07025, Radboud University Nijmegen (2007)
14. de Mol, M., van Eekelen, M., Plasmeijer, R.: Proving confluence of term-graph reduction for sparkle. Technical Report ICIS–R07012, Radboud University Nijmegen (2007)
15. Barendsen, E., Smetsers, S.: Graph rewriting aspects of functional programming. In: Handbook of Graph Grammars and Computing by Graph Transformation, pp. 63–102. World Scientific, Singapore (1999)
16. Hall, J.G., Baker-Finch, C.A., Trinder, P.W., King, D.J.: Towards an operational semantics for a parallel non-strict functional language. In: Hammond, K., Davie, T., Clack, C. (eds.) IFL 1998. LNCS, vol. 1595, pp. 54–71. Springer, Heidelberg (1999)

17. Ariola, Z.M., Maraist, J., Odersky, M., Felleisen, M., Wadler, P.: A call-by-need lambda calculus. In: POPL 1995: Proceedings of the 22nd ACM SIGPLAN-SIGACT symposium on Principles of programming languages, pp. 233–246. ACM Press, New York (1995)
18. Baldan, P., Bertolissi, C., Cirstea, H., Kirchner, C.: A rewriting calculus for cyclic higher-order term graphs. Mathematical Structures in Computer Science 17(3), 363–406 (2007)
19. Sleep, M.R., Plasmeijer, M.J., van Eekelen, M.C.J.D. (eds.): Term graph rewriting: theory and practice. John Wiley and Sons Ltd., Chichester (1993)
20. Barendregt, H.P., van Eekelen, M.C.J.D., Glauert, J.R.W., Kennaway, R., Plasmeijer, M.J., Sleep, M.R.: Term graph rewriting. In: de Bakker, J.W., Nijman, A.J., Treleaven, P.C. (eds.) PARLE 1987. LNCS, vol. 259, pp. 141–158. Springer, Heidelberg (1987)
21. Grabmayer, C.: A duality between proof systems for cyclic term graphs. Mathematical Structures in Computer Science 17(3), 439–484 (2007)

Shaped Generic Graph Transformation

Frank Drewes[1], Berthold Hoffmann[2], Dirk Janssens[3],
Mark Minas[4], and Niels Van Eetvelde[3]

[1] Umeå universitet, Sweden
[2] Universität Bremen, Germany
[3] Universiteit Antwerpen, Belgium
[4] Universität der Bundeswehr München, Germany

Abstract. Since the systematic evolution of graph-like program models has become important in software engineering, graph transformation has gained much attention in this area. For specifying model evolution concisely, graph transformation rules should be as expressive as possible. The generic rules proposed in this paper may contain placeholders for graphs of varying number and shape. Expansion of these placeholders by graphs yields the actual transformation rules to be applied. Even rather complex transformations occurring in real-life applications, such as the *Pull-Up-Method* refactoring operation, can be specified by a single generic rule.

1 Introduction

The systematic transformation of models and programs has become an important issue in the world of software engineering. On the one hand, the general idea of model-driven engineering has attracted a lot of attention from both the academic and the industrial communities, and on the other hand the need for better support of software evolution has become clear. In the model-driven approach, a software system is seen as a cluster of models, on various levels of abstraction and with various characteristics. Each of these models captures certain features or aspects of the systems, allows its own kind of analysis, and has its own tools available. In this way one may apply the many sophisticated tools and theories that have been developed for particular models by the research community. It is clear, however, that this will not work unless one develops powerful tools for integrating the various models, transforming them into one another, generating code from them, and keeping them consistent. Thus model transformation is a key issue here. In the area of software evolution, a lot of attention has been devoted to refactoring: the stepwise modification of programs, aimed at improving their internal organization, but preserving their behavior. The list of refactoring operations published by Fowler [12] is a well-known example. In order to get to a precise and manageable definition of what constitutes a model (or program) transformation, it is quite natural to view a model or program as a graph, and to describe large transformation processes as being compositions of "small" transformations – and thus, to describe model transformations by graph transformation systems.

A. Schürr, M. Nagl, and A. Zündorf (Eds.): AGTIVE 2007, LNCS 5088, pp. 201–216, 2008.
© Springer-Verlag Berlin Heidelberg 2008

Unfortunately, the rules of classical graph transformation formalisms are rather restricted. E.g., double pushout (DPO) rules [10] just allow to remove a constant subgraph from a host graph, and insert another constant graph for it. For describing the behavior of complex real-life systems, one needs a large number of such rules, and may have to program their application using control structures. In this paper, which continues [17], we pursue another idea: we make rules *generic* by introducing *(i)* multiple nodes that represent sets of nodes and *(ii)* placeholders for subgraphs of various shapes. A *shape* is a set of graphs that may be assigned to a given placeholder. A generic transformation rule abstracts from a (possibly infinite) set of ordinary graph transformation rules, one for every assignment of node sets and subgraphs to its multiple nodes and placeholders, respectively. Thus graph transformation is a two-level process: it first instantiates a generic rule, and then applies the resulting ordinary rule to the host graph afterwards.

To define the shapes that may replace the placeholders in generic rules, we use *adaptive star grammars*. These have been introduced in [9], partly motivated by earlier research on modeling and refactoring of object-oriented programs [21]. A first issue to be addressed was the specification of the set of graphs representing programs. Being context-free devices with nice computational properties, hyperedge and node replacement grammars [14,8,11] have proven particularly useful for defining graph languages. Unfortunately, these types of graph grammars turned out to be too weak to generate program graphs in a reasonable way. Therefore, we have proposed the adaptive star grammar as an extension which is able to generate languages of this type. The rules of an adaptive star grammar have a context-free flavor: each of them replaces a so-called star (a nonterminal node and its incident edges) with another graph.

The remainder of this paper is structured as follows. In the next section, we recall basic notions regarding graphs and graph transformation, and discuss how refactoring can be modeled. It turns out that we need a grammatical mechanism to specify the shape of graph models, and generic rules to specify their transformation in a concise way. In Section 3, we define adaptive star grammars and show as an example how they can be used to define the shape of method bodies, a part of program graphs. Section 4 constitutes the main part of this paper. Here we introduce generic rules, and define how placeholders are expanded by shaped graphs, before the resulting rule is applied. We also sketch how expansion and cloning can be done by incrementally matching of a generic rule to a host graph. Section 5 discusses related work. Finally, we summarize our results, and indicate future work in Section 6.

2   Graph Transformation

In this section, we recall standard notions of graphs and graph transformation, and check how useful they are for model transformation, by discussing a case study on refactoring.

Graphs. Graph-like diagrams have become very popular for representing arte-facts that describe software in all its development phases, especially after the Unified Modeling Language (UML) emerged. We recall a general notion of graphs, and show how it is used for a language-independent representation of object-oriented programs, called *program graphs*.

Throughout the paper, we let **S** be our universe of symbols to be used as *labels*. It is the union of two disjoint infinite sets $\dot{\mathbf{S}}$ and $\bar{\mathbf{S}}$ of node and edge labels, resp. For $S \subseteq \mathbf{S}$, we let $\dot{S} = S \cap \dot{\mathbf{S}}$ and $\bar{S} = S \cap \bar{\mathbf{S}}$.

Definition (Graph). A *graph* $G = \langle \dot{G}, \bar{G}, s_G, t_G, \dot{\ell}_G, \bar{\ell}_G \rangle$ consists of disjoint finite sets $\dot{G}$ of *nodes* and $\bar{G}$ of *edges*, of two functions $s_G, t_G \colon \bar{G} \to \dot{G}$ defining the *source* and *target* nodes of its edges, and of two functions $\dot{\ell}_G \colon \dot{G} \to \dot{\mathbf{S}}$ and $\bar{\ell}_G \colon \bar{G} \to \bar{\mathbf{S}}$ that assign labels to its nodes and edges.

If all labels of nodes and edges in G are in $S \subseteq \mathbf{S}$, then G is a *graph over S*. Let $\mathcal{G}_S$ denote the set of all graphs over S.

We use common terminology regarding graphs. For instance, an edge is said to be incident with its source and target nodes, and makes these nodes adjacent to each other. $G \subseteq H$ denotes that G is a subgraph of H, and $G \uplus H$ is the disjoint union of G and H. If a graph G contains a node y, the subgraph $G(y)$ consisting of y, all its incident edges, and all its adjacent nodes is called the neighborhood of y. Finally, $G \setminus \{y\}$ denotes G without the node y, and without the edges of $G(y)$. A pair $g = \langle \dot{g}, \bar{g} \rangle$ of bijective functions $\dot{g} \colon \dot{G} \to \dot{H}$ and $\bar{g} \colon \bar{G} \to \bar{H}$ that preserve sources, targets and labels is called an isomorphism; it makes the graphs G and H isomorphic, written $G \cong_g H$.

Example 1 (Program Graphs). In the case study [21] of refactoring, *program graphs* have been proposed as a language-independent representation of object-oriented programs. Fig. 1 shows two subgraphs of a class of program graphs.

The labels $\{\mathsf{B}, \mathsf{C}, \mathsf{E}, \mathsf{M}, \mathsf{V}\}$ classify nodes as program entities: *bodies* of methods, *classes*, *expressions*, *method signatures*, and *variables*, respectively. The labels $\{\mathsf{a}, \mathsf{ap}, \mathsf{c}, \mathsf{e}, \mathsf{fp}, \mathsf{i}, \mathsf{l}, \mathsf{m}, \mathsf{u}, \mathsf{val}\}$ represent relations between entities: *access*, *actual parameter*, *call*, *element*, *formal parameter*, *inheritance*, *lookup*, *membership*, *update*, and *value*.

A graph must satisfy certain constraints in order to be a valid program graph. The following are typical examples of constraints:

- *Incidence*: An i-edge (modeling inheritance) must be incident with C-nodes (representing classes) only.
- *Cardinality*: An E-node (representing an expression) may have at most one outgoing edge labeled a or u (modeling access resp. update).
- *Structure*: The i-edges must induce a partial order on classes.
- *Context*: An E-node may access a variable (via an a-edge) only if that variable is visible in the context to which the E-node belongs.

In Section 3, we propose graph grammars for specifying the *shape* of graphs, which comprises structural and contextual constraints, e.g., of program graphs, in an intuitive way. Incidence or cardinality constraints can be inferred automatically from the definition of such a grammar. Note also that such constraints can be specified by meta-models (like UML class diagrams or type graphs [4]) along with certain well-formedness constraints (expressed, e.g., by OCL formulas), too. However, we prefer graph grammars for the following reasons:

- Using graph grammars is not only elegant, but also provides a sound foundation for parsing and analysis, as witnessed by the well-developed theory of graph transformation.
- We aim at graph languages like the language of program graphs. Graph grammars are particularly well suited for specifying such recursive (graph) languages which are not that easily specified by meta-models with constraints.

Graph transformation. Since software models can be represented as graphs, graph transformation is a natural candidate for specifying the evolution of models. We use a simple form of DPO graph transformation with injective occurrences. [10].

Definition (Graph Transformation). A *(graph transformation) rule* $r = L/R$ consists of two graphs L and R so that the nodes $\dot{I} = \dot{L} \cap \dot{R}$ define a discrete *interface graph* $L \supseteq I \subseteq R$.

Consider a graph G and a rule $r = L/R$. A subgraph $O \subseteq G$ is an *occurrence* of r in G if $O \cong_g L$ for some isomorphism g so that no node in $\dot{O} \setminus g(\dot{I})$ is incident with an edge in $\bar{G} \setminus \bar{O}$. Then r *transforms* G (via the isomorphism g) to a graph that is denoted as $G[L /_g R]$ and is obtained from the disjoint union $G \uplus R$ by *(i)* removing $\bar{O}$ and $\dot{O} \setminus g(\dot{I})$ from G, and *(ii)* identifying every interface node $x \in \dot{I}$ with $\dot{g}(x) \in \dot{G}$.

Example 2 (Pull-Up-Method). *Pull-Up-Method* is a refactoring used when each subclass of a class A defines a method with the same signature and behavior. These methods are then removed from each subclass of A and replaced by a single, equivalent method in A. In the following, we assume that equivalence of different methods has been checked before *Pull-Up-Method* is applied.

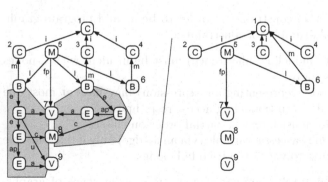

```
void m5(v7) {
    v9 := v7;
    m8(v9);
}


void m5(v7) {
    m8(v7);
}
```

Fig. 2. Pseudo code for the method bodies in Fig. 1

Fig. 1. A concrete rule for *Pull-Up-Method*

Fig. 1 shows a rule implementing a specific case of a *Pull-Up-Method* refactoring for program graphs. The interface nodes of the rule are specified by annotating them with the same number in *L* and *R*.

The C-nodes represent a class (4) with its superclass (1) and two sibling classes (2, 3). A method signature (5) with one parameter (7) has overloaded bodies (B-nodes) in the sibling classes (2, 3); both implementations make a call to another method (8). The one of class (3) uses the formal parameter (7) as its actual parameter, whereas the other assigns this parameter to a variable (9) first, and calls method (8) with this variable afterward (cf. Fig. 2). Obviously, these implementations have the same semantics but differ syntactically.

The implementations of method (5) in the sibling classes (2, 3), which are emphasized in gray, are removed on the right-hand side of the rule, and its body (6) is moved to the superclass (1). The expressions defining the body (6) need not be mentioned in the rule as they are not changed by the refactoring.

This rule does not define *Pull-Up-Method* in general, however, as it only applies to particular situations:

- Here the class (4) has two sibling classes (2, 3); the method (5) has one parameter, and its bodies in the sibling classes use two and three visible names, respectively. In general, there can be any number of sibling classes, parameters, and names.
- The syntactic structure of the method bodies in this example is fixed, but a general rule should be applicable to bodies of different forms. However, the graph of a method body is not just an arbitrary graph, but must have the shape of a method body.

Note that several transformation rules would be needed in order to express the general *Pull-Up-Method* refactoring in the usual graph transformation systems: some for checking that the method is implemented in all sibling classes, others for removing all but one of its implementations, and finally a rule pulling up the remaining implementation. The applications of these rules would have to be controlled in a non-trivial way, and it might not be easy to see that they do what they should, let alone to prove it. As an alternative, we propose to define this refactoring by a single generic rule that is expanded w.r.t. the form of certain subgraphs. Section 4 describes this generic graph transformation approach.

Example 3. As a running example – besides *Pull-Up-Method* in Example 2 – let us consider a graph transformation as shown in Fig. 3: An S-node is connected to several M-nodes that point to linear lists of Q-nodes being connected by next-edges. Each Q-node is connected to each V-node by a var-edge. The transformation removes one of the M-nodes and its list of Q-nodes, and "bends" the m-edge to the remaining M-node. Fig. 3 shows the case where a list of two Q-nodes is removed. The following sections introduce the concepts of shaped graphs and generic rules which allow to specify this transformation for Q-node lists of arbitrary length.

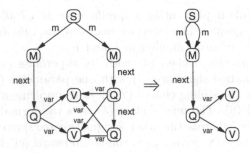

Fig. 3. A sample transformation

3 Shapes

The shape of (a class of) graphs, i.e., their structural and contextual constraints can be specified by graph grammars, like Chomsky grammars specify languages of strings. For describing software models like the program graphs of Example 1, we propose adaptive star grammars [9], which combine star replacement, a very simple way of graph transformation, with an operation called cloning.

Star Replacement. A star replacement replaces a node with its incident edges and adjacent nodes by a graph. Later on, the replaced nodes will be considered to be nonterminals.

A *star* X is a graph that consists of a *center node* y, $n \geqslant 0$ *border nodes*, and n edges making y adjacent to all border nodes.

A rule X/P is a *star rule* if X is a star and the interface graph I consists of the border nodes of X; star rules are denoted as $X ::= P$ to emphasize that they are used to generate languages, like context-free Chomsky rules.

According to the definition of graph transformation, a star $\tilde{X} \subseteq G$ is an *occurrence* of a star rule $X ::= P$ if $\tilde{X} \cong_g X$ and $\tilde{X}$ is the neighborhood of its center node in G. Then star replacement via g yields the graph $G[X /_g P]$.

Cloning. Star replacement is closely related to hyperedge replacement [14,8]. For grammars based on star replacement, this implies certain limitations. For instance, the maximal number of border nodes in the left-hand sides of a grammar restricts the connectivity of the generated graphs, so that star replacement cannot generate the class of all graphs, or the class of all complete graphs, over any set S of labels (provided that $\dot{S} \neq \emptyset \neq \bar{S}$).

To overcome these limitations, we introduce *multiple nodes* that are placeholders for any number of nodes. The latter are called *clones* because each of them has the same incident edges, and is adjacent to the same nodes as the multiple node.[1]

---

[1] Note that cloning is not "deep copying" of subgraphs; it just copies a single node with its incident edges. Deep copying can be achieved by cloning placeholders of subgraphs (see Section 4).

We designate multiple nodes by a special set of *multiple node labels* $\ddot{S} \subset \dot{S}$. The remaining node labels $\dot{S} \setminus \ddot{S}$ are called *singular*. We further assume that there is a bijection ˙˙: $\dot{S} \setminus \ddot{S} \to \ddot{S}$ that maps every singular label s to its multiple counterpart $\ddot{s}$. A node is called singular or multiple depending on its label. The set of multiple nodes in a graph G is denoted by $\ddot{G}$. In figures, we draw multiple nodes as circles or boxes with a "shadow", e.g., the V-nodes in Fig. 4.

The cloning operation turns a multiple node into any number of singular and multiple clones: we define $G\frac{x}{(m,k)}$ to be obtained from G by replacing the multiple node x with $m + k$ clones whereof m are multiple, and k are singular.

Formally, for a graph G with a multiple node $x \in \ddot{G}$, and $m, k \geq 0$, the graph $G\frac{x}{(m,k)}$ is constructed as follows. Let $G'(x)$ be obtained from the neighborhood $G(x)$ by replacing the label $\ddot{s}$ of x by the singular label s. Then take the disjoint union of the graph $G \setminus \{x\}$ with m copies of $G(x)$ and k copies of $G'(x)$. Finally, identify the $m + k + 1$ copies of each node in $\dot{G}(x) \setminus \{x\}$ with each other.

As an example, consider Fig. 10 with its multiple V-node in the left-hand side G. The left-hand side of the rule shown in Fig. 11 is $G\frac{3}{(0,2)}$, i.e., the multiple node 3 is turned into two singular nodes and no multiple node.

Obviously, $G\frac{x}{(m,k)}$ is defined only up to isomorphism. Note that cloning is closely related to node replacement. It cannot be specified by finitely many graph transformation rules in the sense of Definition 2, because a multiple node x may have a neighborhood $G(x)$ of arbitrary size.

Although distinct multiple nodes may be adjacent to each other, cloning is commutative: For a graph with distinct multiple nodes x, x', and numbers $m, k, m', k' \geqslant 0$, $\left(G\frac{x}{(m,k)}\right)\frac{x'}{(m',k')} \cong \left(G\frac{x'}{(m',k')}\right)\frac{x}{(m,k)}$. We can thus define an operation that clones all multiple nodes in a graph G. The number of desired clones is indicated by a so-called *multiplicity function* $\mu: \ddot{G} \to \mathbb{N}^2$. If $\ddot{G}$ contains n multiple nodes $x_1, \ldots, x_k$, the μ-*clone of* G is defined as $G^\mu = \left(\cdots \left(G\frac{x_1}{\mu(x_1)}\right) \cdots \frac{x_k}{\mu(x_k)}\right)$.

Adaptive Star Replacement. Star replacement is made adaptive by cloning the star rule and the graph to be transformed before performing the replacement. Let G be a graph containing a star $\tilde{X}$, and consider a star rule $X ::= P$. We assume without loss of generality that the nodes of G and P are disjoint.

A multiplicity function $\mu: \ddot{G} \cup \ddot{P} \to \mathbb{N}^2$ is an *adapter of* X/P and $\tilde{X}$ if $X^\mu \cong_g \tilde{X}^\mu$ for some isomorphism g. Then, the *adaptive replacement* of $\tilde{X}$ by P using μ is defined as $G[X\,{}^\mu/_g\,P] = G^\mu[X^\mu\,/_g\,P^\mu]$.

It is straightforward to show that adaptive star replacement is commutative and associative. We note this result, but leave out the proof:

Lemma 1 (Commutativity and Associativity). *If* $H = G[X\,{}^\mu/_g\,P][\tilde{X}\,{}^{\tilde{\mu}}/_{\tilde{g}}\,\tilde{P}]$ *for some graph* G, *star rules* X/P, $\tilde{X}/\tilde{P}$, *adapters* μ, $\tilde{\mu}$, *and isomorphisms* g, $\tilde{g}$, *then, for suitable adapters* μ', $\tilde{\mu}'$ *and isomorphisms* g', $\tilde{g}'$,

1. $H = G[\tilde{X}\,{}^{\tilde{\mu}'}/_{\tilde{g}'}\,\tilde{P}][X\,{}^{\mu'}/_{g'}\,P]$ *if the center of the occurrence* $\tilde{g}(\tilde{X}^{\tilde{\mu}})$ *is in* G *(commutativity), and*

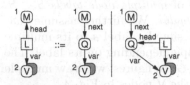
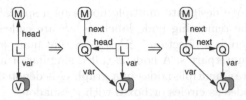

Fig. 4. Adaptive star rules generating linear Q-node lists of arbitrary length

Fig. 5. A derivation of a list of two Q nodes using the adaptive star rules in Fig. 4

2. $H = G[X \, ^{\tilde{\mu}}\!/_{\tilde{g}'} \, P[\tilde{X} \, ^{\mu}\!/_{g'} \, \tilde{P}]]$ *if the center of the occurrence* $\tilde{g}(\tilde{X}^{\tilde{\mu}})$ *is in* P *(associativity).*

We can now define adaptive star grammars and the graph languages they generate. We write $G \Rightarrow_P H$ if $H \cong G[X \, ^{\mu}\!/_g \, P]$ for some adapter μ, isomorphism g, and rule $p = X ::= P$ from a set $\mathcal{P}$ of star rules, and $G \Rightarrow_P^* H$ if $G \cong G_0 \Rightarrow_P \cdots \Rightarrow_P G_n \cong H$ for $n \geqslant 0$; thus $\Rightarrow_P^*$ is the transitive-reflexive closure of $\Rightarrow_P$.

Definition. An *adaptive star grammar* is a tuple $\Gamma = \langle S, N, \mathcal{P}, Z \rangle$ consisting of a finite set $S \subseteq \mathbf{S}$ of *terminal labels*, a finite $N \subseteq \dot{\mathbf{S}} \setminus \dot{S}$ of singular *nonterminal labels*, a finite set $\mathcal{P}$ of star rules $X ::= P$, where X and P are graphs over $S \cup N$, and an *initial star* Z over $S \cup N$.

For Z as well as the left- and right-hand sides of rules in $\mathcal{P}$, we require that the neighborhoods of all nonterminal nodes are stars with terminal border nodes (where a node is called terminal or nonterminal according to its label). Moreover, the center nodes of Z and all left-hand sides are required to be nonterminal. Stars of this kind are called N-stars.

The *language generated by* Γ is defined as

$$\mathcal{L}(\Gamma) = \{G \in \mathcal{G}_{S \backslash \ddot{s}} \mid Z \underset{\mathcal{P}}{\overset{*}{\Rightarrow}} G\}.$$

Note that, in an adaptive star grammar (and in the graphs they generate), nonterminal nodes cannot be adjacent to each other.

As an example, consider the language introduced in Example 3. Fig. 4 shows the adaptive star rules of the adaptive star grammar that generates this language. L is the only nonterminal label (note that nonterminal nodes are drawn as rectangles whereas terminal nodes are drawn with round corners). The common left-hand side of both rules is the initial star Z. Fig. 5 shows a derivation of a graph consisting of a Q-node list of length two. Note that the derived graph does not belong to the generated language, because it still contains a multiple V-node that has to be turned into an arbitrary number of singular V-nodes.

Adaptive star grammars generate languages that cannot be generated by node replacement [11], like the class of all graphs, or classes of graphs defined by contextual constraints such as the program graphs from Example 1.

It should be mentioned that the variant of adaptive star grammars originally introduced in [9] is more general than the one considered here, because stars with parallel edges (being incident with the same border node) and rule application using non-injective occurrences are considered. In [9], the resulting type of adaptive star grammar is shown to generate all recursively enumerable string languages (represented as chain graphs), whereas the one considered in the present paper is shown to have a decidable membership problem.

Example 4 (Adaptive Star Rules for Method Bodies). The rules in Fig. 6 generate simple method bodies for the program graphs discussed in Example 1 if the left-hand side of the rule for the nonterminal ST* is the initial star. A method body has a root labeled B pointing to E-nodes representing the assignments and calls in the body; the right-hand sides of assignments, and the actual parameters of calls may again be calls. All stars in these rules have a def-edge to a singular node representing the subgraph generated by the star, and vis-edges to multiple or singular nodes representing the methods (labeled M) and variables (labeled V) that are visible in these subgraphs. A call to a method, or an access or update of a variable within an expression is represented as an edge to one of these nodes. The rules for ASS, CALL, and ACC introducing these edges apply only if corresponding nodes are visible. Thus every entity used in the body is a clone of the multiple border nodes of the initial star. This expresses the contextual constraint that every used entity should have a declaration. In the complete program graph grammar given in [27], these entities are generated as members of the class hierarchy that are visible in the context of the method body. There, method bodies may also contain control structures and local declarations.

In the rules for ST* and CALL, we introduce a useful shorthand for star rules, somewhat similar to the use of the Kleene star in the right-hand side of a context-free Chomsky rule. The shaded subgraphs on the right-hand sides of these rules are called *iterated subgraphs*. As this name suggests, an iterated subgraph may be copied any number of times, the copies sharing the nodes on its border. To emphasize this, we draw the nodes to be copied similarly to multiple nodes and annotate their "shades" with a common index (k and n, resp.). Iteration can

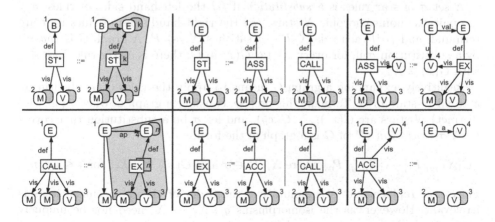

Fig. 6. Adaptive star rules defining the structure of method bodies

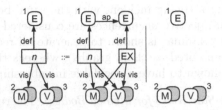

Fig. 7. Adaptive rules for Subgraph Iteration

obviously be implemented by adding a star rule that differs from the given one in that its right-hand side contains an additional star, isomorphic to the left-hand side and connected to the nodes on the border of the shaded part. The star rules generating the iterated subgraph in the rule for CALL in Fig. 6 is shown in Fig. 7.

4   Generic Transformation Rules

This section contains the main contribution of the paper. We extend the transformation rules of Section 2 so that they become generic: their graphs may contain multiple nodes and nonterminal nodes. Multiple nodes are cloned, as in adaptive star grammars, and nonterminal nodes are expanded to graphs before a generic rule is applied.

Shaped Expansion. Shaped expansion allows for graphs (in transformation rules) that contain N-stars as placeholders. These can be expanded to graphs generated by an adaptive star grammar, where isomorphic stars are expanded to isomorphic graphs. For this, and throughout the rest of this paper, let $\Gamma = \langle S, N, \mathcal{P}, Z \rangle$ be an adaptive star grammar. In the following, we will only consider graphs over $S \cup N$.

A set σ of star rules is a *substitution* if *(i)* the left-hand sides of rules in σ are pairwise nonisomorphic N-stars, *(ii)* the right-hand sides of rules in σ are terminal, and *(iii)* each rule $X/P \in \sigma$ satisfies $X \Rightarrow_{\mathcal{P}}^* P$. A graph G is *covered* by a substitution σ if, for every N-star $G(x)$ in G, there is a star rule $X/R \in \sigma$ with $G(x) \cong X$.

Intuitively, expanding a graph G means to apply the rules of a substitution σ to all N-stars in G. To make this precise, consider a graph G whose (pairwise distinct) N-stars are $G(x_1), \ldots, G(x_n)$, and let σ be a substitution that covers G. A *σ-expansion* G^σ of G is a graph of the form

$$G[X_1 /_{g_1} P_1] \cdots [X_n /_{g_n} P_n] \text{ where } X_i/P_i \in \sigma \text{ and } G(x_i) \cong_{g_i} X_i, \text{ for } 1 \leqslant i \leqslant n.$$

Since star replacement is commutative, the order of the replacement steps is irrelevant. However, as the isomorphisms $g_i \colon X_i \to \tilde{X}_i$ need not be uniquely determined, there may be several σ-expansions of G.

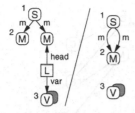

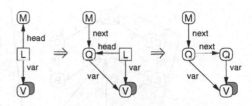

Fig. 8. The generic rule r used for the transformation in Fig. 3

Fig. 9. The derivation of Fig. 5, using the adaptive star rules in Fig. 4 for specifying a substitution σ

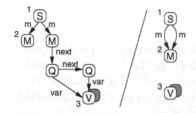

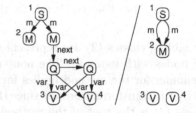

Fig. 10. σ-expansion L^σ/R^σ of r in Fig. 8 using substitution σ in Fig. 9

Fig. 11. The ordinary transformation rule $(L^\sigma)^\mu/_g(R^\sigma)^\mu$ obtained from L^σ/R^σ in Fig. 10 by multiplicity function $\mu : 3 \mapsto (0,2)$

Generic Transformation. Generic graph transformation is plain transformation with transformation rules that have been expanded and cloned. More precisely, let us call a transformation rule $r = L/R$ *generic* if its interface nodes are terminal. A multiplicity function $\mu: \ddot{G} \to \mathbb{N}^2$ is *singular* if $\mu(x) = (0,k)$ with $k \geqslant 0$ for every $x \in \ddot{G}$.

Now, let G, H be graphs, $r = L/R$ a generic rule, and σ a substitution covering $L \cup R$. Consider a σ-expansion L^σ/R^σ of r, consisting of σ-expansions L^σ and R^σ of L and R, resp. Then r *transforms* G into H, written $G \Longrightarrow_{r,\sigma,\mu} H$, if $H = G[(L^\sigma)^\mu/_g(R^\sigma)^\mu]$ for some singular multiplicity function $\mu: \ddot{L}^\sigma \cup \ddot{R}^\sigma \to \mathbb{N}^2$, and an isomorphism g.

Fig. 8 shows the generic rule $r = L/R$ that is used for the transformation shown in Fig. 3, i.e., that removes an M-node together with its list of Q-nodes. The contained L-star is the placeholder for an arbitrary list of Q-nodes pointing to all V-nodes. This graph language is specified by the adaptive star rules in Fig. 4. The transformation shown in Fig. 3 uses the ordinary transformation rule shown in Fig. 11 that is generated by first substituting the L-node by substitution σ specified in Fig. 9, yielding L^σ/R^σ (Fig. 10), and then choosing a multiplicity function $\mu : 3 \mapsto (0,2)$ for turning the multiple V-node into two singular V-nodes, yielding $(L^\sigma)^\mu/_g(R^\sigma)^\mu$ (Fig. 11).

Example 5 (A Generic Rule for Refactoring). The general *Pull-Up-Method* rule is specified in Figure 12. The rule applies to a class (3) with its superclass (1), and a set of other subclasses (2); the method signature (5) has parameters (6), and is implemented by bodies that may refer to variables (7) and methods (8).

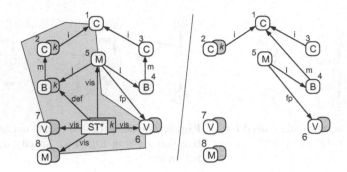

Fig. 12. The generic rule for the *Pull-Up-Method* refactoring

The sibling classes (2) are represented by an iterated subgraph (designated by the nodes with index k). The nonterminal ST* in the iterated subgraph is a placeholder for the method bodies for the signature (5). These bodies are removed by the transformation rule since they do not appear on its right-hand side. The node (4) is the root of the method body that will be moved to its superclass (1). No variable is needed for the body itself, because only its membership (the m-edge) is changed.

The ST*-star is a placeholder for method bodies. Thus, the expansions of these stars are shaped according to the method body grammar. Recall that the iterated subgraph is a shorthand for a star which can be turned into any number of copies of the given subgraph, using iteration rules added to Γ, as described in Example 4. Here, a minor technical complication is caused by the fact that one of the nodes (2) of the iterated subgraph is an interface node. The (intuitively obvious) meaning of this is that all copies of this node are intended to belong to the interface as well.

In a generic rule, all occurrences of a nonterminal n are expanded to isomorphic subgraphs; having several occurrences of n on the left-hand side thus allows to check equality of subgraphs of the host graph, whereas having several occurrences of n on the right-hand side allows one to make so-called deep copies of the expansions.

Goal-Oriented Matching. The definition of generic transformation is not operational: In order to transform a graph with a generic rule, we cannot generate all its expansions, and choose one of them for application, because generic rules usually have infinitely many expansions.

However, the instantiation of a rule (i.e. expansion and cloning) can be done in a more *goal-oriented fashion*. In order to apply a generic rule $r = L/R$ to a graph G, one may proceed as follows:

- *Find* a *kernel occurrence* $\underline{O}$ of the constant subgraph $\underline{L}$ of L in G.
- *Match* the stars and multiple nodes in r one after another, by expanding and cloning them, respectively, so that $\underline{O}$ is gradually extended to a complete occurrence O of the instantiated left-hand side L.

- *Instantiate* the right-hand side R according to the substitution and multiplicity function found in the matching process, and *insert* the instantiated right-hand side for O. If, for every star X in R, there is an isomorphic star X' in L, the instantiation is uniquely determined.

Moreover, the matching of a star can be done *incrementally*, applying one of the star rules defining the shape of a star at a time.

Since adaptive star grammars are parseable, it is decidable whether an expansion exists. Parsing may be complex in general. However, for grammars occurring in practice, like those for method bodies, and for program graphs as a whole, we expect parsing to be reasonably efficient. Experiments with an implementation of a star grammar parser suggest the parsing time for such grammars is polynomial [22].

For the intended application area of software refactoring (and certainly many other application areas as well), it must be pointed out that the matching process sketched above should be coupled with user interaction to resolve the inherent nondeterminism. Obviously, there may be many generic rules that can be applied, at many different places in the host graph, and with many different expansions. Thus, a reasonable implementation must present the different possibilities to the user, and let her choose the one that reflects her refactoring intentions.

5 Related Work

Generic rules have been proposed quite early for string languages, e.g., *Van Wijngaarden grammars* [28]. A precursor of the generic graph transformation rules described in this paper has been investigated in [23], where the placeholders are stars with a fixed number of adjacent nodes (called hyperedges). Substitutions shaped according to hyperedge replacement grammars have been proposed in [16]. Path expressions specifying implicit edges, as known in programmed graph transformation [26], can be considered as a special case of substitutions shaped according to the path expression. The set nodes in that work have been the model for our multiple nodes. In fact, cloning concepts have become quite popular. Apparently, sesqui-pushout rewriting [6] and Kahl's approach [18] support cloning as well. In a recent paper, Lindqvist *et al.* have proposed the *star operator* that is motivated by the *Kleene star* [20]. Patterns are generated from generic patterns by deep copying and chaining of so-called star regions. The graph transformation language GREAT used for model transformation also allows to specify patterns containing multiple objects that can be single nodes or compound patterns containing subgraphs [1]. Several graph transformation tools have been further extended by "set" operators: VIATRA2 allows to match graph patterns recursively, which allows for dealing with set-valued patterns [29]. A *grouping operator* has been introduced to GREAT [2]. This operator allows to simultaneously operate on the set of all isomorphic matches of a single pattern. And PROGRES has been extended by two such operators: A new language construct has been introduced to specify and operate on *successively connected repetitive subgraphs* [19], and the extension for *set-valued transformations* [13] is very similar to [17].

Finally, amalgamated graph transformations (e.g., [3]) are related to set nodes. This approach does not introduce multiple objects, but it provides a formalism to generate ordinary transformation rules from rule templates by applying these templates in parallel. This allows to specify the cloning of set nodes presented in this paper or in previous papers [9,17].

However, apart from our previous work [17], we are not aware of any kind of graph transformation that combines cloning with expansion, i.e., with the instantiation of placeholders by subgraphs that are shaped according to graph grammars.

6   Conclusions

Being a formalism that allows a direct manipulation of the diagrammatic representations of programs, graph transformation is a natural candidate to be used as the formal foundation for tools supporting program transformations. Such transformations are at the heart of the model-driven approach to software development, and also of so-called refactoring techniques, where the structure of existing software is improved through the application of certain precisely specified operations. Modeling such operations by graph transformation rules requires, however, that these rules are sufficiently expressive, so that they can be considered to be at the same level of abstraction as the operations one wants to model. If the rules lack expressive power, one is forced to govern their application by more complicated control programs, and the result may be that much of the inherent complexity of the operations to be modeled is reflected in this control structure rather than in the graph rewriting.

In order to improve the expressive power of graph rewriting rules so that the complexity of control programs is reduced, we have proposed generic graph transformation rules wherein placeholders are expanded to graphs, and multiple nodes are cloned as often as necessary. Expansions of placeholders are shaped, i.e., the placeholders are nonterminal stars whose possible expansions are defined by an adaptive star grammar. This allows for structural and contextual constraints on graphs to be described. The concept makes it possible to specify complex transformations, e.g., the *Pull-Up-Method* refactoring [12], by a single generic rule in an intuitive manner. The parsing algorithm for adaptive star grammars opens the door to a goal-oriented matching algorithm that will be an essential part of a forthcoming implementation of generic rules.

The work on shaped generic graph transformation rules and their properties is not finished. As a first step toward extending the results for DPO graph transformation to generic rules, a *parallel independence theorem* has been shown in [15], for generic rules wherein stars have a fixed rank, unshaped substitutions, and are not cloned. This work shall be extended to the study of critical pairs, for the generic rules defined here.

For practical use, we need graphs with attribute values, and rules that specify attribute evaluation. For instance, signature nodes in program graphs could have an attribute counting its parameters, and transformation rules would update this value when necessary. In [24], attribute values are (additional) labels, and rules are labeled with expressions specifying computations on these values. This fits well with the variable concept in generic rules. The values and expressions could be taken from some host language, but they could also be defined by (nested) graphs and transformations, as in [16].

Adaptive star grammars fail to describe some contextual constraints of program graphs, like the correspondence of formal to actual parameters of a method. However, these properties can be specified with pre- or post-conditions of the star rules, sacrificing neither commutativity nor associativity. For practical applications, like the definition of software models, one should focus on grammars generating connected, or tree-like graphs with "cross-links" (like the program graphs). This will not only make parsing more efficient, but is also supposed to be useful in order to establish a static type discipline as in [16]: If the rules, and the contexts of their application are "shaped" like the substitutions, it can be shown that transformations preserve the shape of the graphs being transformed. In other words: such transformation rules can be guaranteed to preserve the integrity of a model.

References

1. Agrawal, A., Karsai, G., Neema, S., Shi, F., Vizhanyo, A.: The design of a language for model transformations. J. Software and System Modeling 5(3), 261–288 (2006)
2. Balasubramanian, D., Narayanan, A., Neema, S., Ness, B., Shi, F., Thibodeaux, R., Karsai, G.: Applying a grouping operator in model transformations. In: Schürr, A., Nagl, M., Zündorf, A. (eds.) AGTIVE 2007. LNCS, vol. 5088. Springer, Heidelberg (2008)
3. Boehm, P., Fonio, H.-R., Habel, A.: Amalgamation of graph transformations: A synchronization mechanism. J. Computer and System Sciences 34, 377–408 (1987)
4. Corradini, A., Ehrig, H., Montanari, U., Padberg, J.: The category of typed graph grammars and its adjunction with categories of derivations. In: [7], pp. 56–74
5. Corradini, A., Ehrig, H., Montanari, U., Ribeiro, L., Rozenberg, G. (eds.): 3rd Int. Conf. on Graph Transformation (ICGT 2006). LNCS, vol. 4178. Springer, Heidelberg (2006)
6. Corradini, A., Heindel, T., Hermann, F., König, B.: Sesqui-pushout rewriting. In: [5], pp. 30–45
7. Cuny, J.E., Ehrig, H., Engels, G., Rozenberg, G. (eds.): Graph Grammars 1994. LNCS, vol. 1073. Springer, Heidelberg (1996)
8. Drewes, F., Habel, A., Kreowski, H.-J.: Hyperedge replacement graph grammars. In: [25], pp. 95–162
9. Drewes, F., Hoffmann, B., Janssens, D., Minas, M., Van Eetvelde, N.: Adaptive star grammars. In: [5], pp. 77–91
10. Ehrig, H., Ehrig, K., Prange, U., Taentzer, G.: Fundamentals of Algebraic Graph Transformation. In: EATCS Monographs on Theoretical Computer Science. Springer, Heidelberg (2006)
11. Engelfriet, J., Rozenberg, G.: Node replacement graph grammars. In: [25], ch. 1, pp. 1–94
12. Fowler, M.: Refactoring—Improving the Design of Existing Code. Object Technology Series. Addison-Wesley, Reading (1999)

13. Fuss, C., Tuttlies, V.E.: Simulating set-valued transformations with algorithmic graph transformation languages. In: Schürr, A., Nagl, M., Zündorf, A. (eds.) AGTIVE 2007. LNCS, vol. 5088. Springer, Heidelberg (2008)
14. Habel, A.: Hyperedge Replacement: Grammars and Languages. LNCS, vol. 643. Springer, Heidelberg (1992)
15. Habel, A., Hoffmann, B.: Parallel independence in hierarchical graph transformation. In: Ehrig, H., Engels, G., Parisi-Presicce, F., Rozenberg, G. (eds.) ICGT 2004. LNCS, vol. 3256, pp. 178–193. Springer, Heidelberg (2004)
16. Hoffmann, B.: Shapely hierarchical graph transformation. In: Proc. IEEE Symposia on Human-Centric Computing Languages and Environments, pp. 30–37 (2001)
17. Hoffmann, B., Janssens, D., Van Eetvelde, N.: Cloning and expanding graph transformation rules for refactoring. Electronic Notes in Theoretical Computer Science 152(4), 53–67 (2006); Proc. GraMoT 2005
18. Kahl, W.: A relation-algebraic approach to graph structure transformation, 2001. Habil. Thesis, Fak.für Informatik, Univ. der Bundeswehr München, TR 2002-03
19. Körtgen, A.-T.: Modeling successively connected repetitive subgraphs. In: Schürr, A., Nagl, M., Zündorf, A. (eds.) AGTIVE 2007. LNCS, vol. 5088. Springer, Heidelberg (2008)
20. Lindqvist, J., Lundkvist, T., Porres, I.: A query language with the star operator. In: Proc. 6th Int. Workshop on Graph Transformation and Visual Modeling Techniques (GT-VMT 2007). Electronic Comm. of the EASST, vol. 6 (2007)
21. Mens, T., Demeyer, S., Janssens, D.: Formalising behaviour-preserving transformation. In: Corradini, A., Ehrig, H., Kreowski, H.-J., Rozenberg, G. (eds.) ICGT 2002. LNCS, vol. 2505, pp. 286–301. Springer, Heidelberg (2002)
22. Minas, M.: Parsing of adaptive star grammars. In: Proc. GraMoT 2006. Electronic Comm. of the EASST, vol. 4 (2006)
23. Plump, D., Habel, A.: Graph unification and matching. In: [7], pp. 75–89
24. Plump, D., Steinert, S.: Towards graph programs for graph algorithms. In: Ehrig, H., Engels, G., Parisi-Presicce, F., Rozenberg, G. (eds.) ICGT 2004. LNCS, vol. 3256, pp. 128–143. Springer, Heidelberg (2004)
25. Rozenberg, G. (ed.): Handbook of Graph Grammars and Computing by Graph Transformation. Foundations, vol. I. World Scientific, Singapore (1997)
26. Schürr, A.: Introduction to the specification language PROGRES. In: Nagl, M. (ed.) IPSEN 1996. LNCS, vol. 1170, pp. 248–279. Springer, Heidelberg (1996)
27. Van Eetvelde, N.: A Graph Transformation Approach to Refactoring. Doctoral thesis, Universiteit Antwerpen (May 2007)
28. van Wijngaarden, A., Mailloux, B.J., Peck, J.E.L., Koster, C.H.A., Sintzoff, M., Lindsey, C.H., Meertens, L.G.L.T., Fisker, R.G.: Revised report on the algorithmic language ALGOL 68. Acta Informatica 5, 1–236 (1975)
29. Varró, G., Horváth, A., Varró, D.: Recursive graph pattern matching with magic sets and global search plans. In: Schürr, A., Nagl, M., Zündorf, A. (eds.) AGTIVE 2007. LNCS, vol. 5088. Springer, Heidelberg (2008)

Code Graph Transformations for Verifiable Generation of SIMD-Parallel Assembly Code[⋆]

Christopher Kumar Anand and Wolfram Kahl

Software Quality Research Laboratory
Department of Computing and Software, McMaster University
{anandc,kahl}@mcmaster.ca

Abstract. The Coconut code generator produces highly efficient assembly code, targeting signal processing applications such as Magnetic Resonance Imaging. It takes advantage of SIMD-parallelism, and captures as patterns assembly language "tricks" that produce very efficient, but highly convoluted code — the motivation is to beat the expert assembly tuner, while producing reliable output and maintainable input. On a growing set of benchmarks, it produces code with peak or near-peak efficiency.

To facilitate formal verification of the resulting code, the intermediate languages used in compilation are all variations on term hypergraphs (jungles) that we call "code graphs". To verify the results of compilation, schedulable code graphs containing hyperedges labelled by instructions operating on vectors of components are transformed by replacing SIMD instructions with non-vector instructions, applying simplification rules, and comparing the result to specifications.

1 Introduction

Many medical imaging applications, *e.g*, Magnetic Resonance Imaging (MRI), rely on highly efficient signal processing software, and with the invention of new algorithms and new clinical applications, some applications are growing faster than the growth of conventional microprocessors. Successful treatment often depends on timely diagnoses, which puts performance requirements on image reconstruction and processing. The state of the art in the development of such software is that a scientist co-develops a mathematical model and signal processing algorithm; this algorithm is translated into a prototype program (often in a "matrix manipulation" environment), with reasonable confidence in its correctness, but not its completeness. This is then checked for completeness and augmented by informal specifications by a software engineer. In performance-critical cases, the prototype and specification are then turned over to a "digital signal processing guru" who applies — manually! — different kinds of code transformations and optimisations, including (1) translation between languages, (2) parallelisation, (3) implementation of non-garbage collected memory management, and (4) hand-tuned assembly language, with the extent of optimisation indicated by a performance analysis or benchmarking.

[⋆] The authors thank CFI, OIT, NSERC and IBM Canada for financial support.

A. Schürr, M. Nagl, and A. Zündorf (Eds.): AGTIVE 2007, LNCS 5088, pp. 217–232, 2008.
© Springer-Verlag Berlin Heidelberg 2008

Such a process is prone to error, given that it is often necessary for performance experts to modify small parts of larger software systems whose complete specification is outside their area of expertise. Given the safety issues, considerable care is taken in testing, but defects can still go undetected. It is easy for low-level optimisations to interact with high-level specifications in complicated ways, resulting in mis-sequenced images, images with incorrect orientation, or scale, or locally distorted to be unusable. Some of these errors will prevent a diagnosis from being made in a timely manner. Others, if used for surgical planning, could be fatal. It is the experience of the first author that defects arising from such incorrect "optimisations" can persist in commercial software through several lifecycles including extensive black-box testing by professional testers.

The COCONUT project aims to produce a system that provides a coherent and consistent path from a mathematical specification of signal processing problems to verified *and* highly optimised machine code. Our targets are vectorised and pipelined CPUs that are commonly used in signal processing applications; currently we are targeting, in particular, the Cell Broadband Engine.

To encapsulate low-level assembly language patterns, we produced a domain-specific language (DSL) embedded into the purely functional programming language Haskell. This provides a convenient language for domain experts to specify both efficient code fragments and generators, and increases reliability by making specifications smaller, but it does not make complicated instruction sequences any easier to understand [1]. Therefore transformation from SIMD to scalar code graphs first of all helps the designer understand code which does not work, and also provides support for formal verification against scalar specifications, which is vital for high-reliability applications.

To this end, we have developed a transformation framework which makes it easy to specify simple transformations, and possible to express more complicated transformations. Correctness of individual rules is often easy to establish (although depending on the correctness of the hardware); some can even be verified by exhaustive testing.

Decades of work on compilers have resulted in large sets of code transformations incorporated into different optimisation phases. Users can turn them on or off, but usually cannot contribute new transformations. The interaction of these transformations can make it difficult to diagnose compiler defects, and some transformations change the semantics in unacceptable ways. This is a particular problem for floating-point computations in which even moving a variable from memory to a register (to eliminate loads and stores) can change the accuracy of the result.

In some application domains with high performance requirements, such generic code optimisation is not sufficient, and developers will either transform compiler-produced assembly code by hand, or will write assembly coded functions from specifications. As hardware has evolved to include features not reflected in the semantics of C (notably SIMD parallelisation in a register), ways of including small sections of assembly code in C source files have evolved, but there is, as yet, no safe way of modifying control flow in this way. Loops in imperative languages and higher-order functions like map in functional languages must be translated into assembly language, and the resulting code can usually be made much more efficient if the context of the control flow, or the special hardware features of the processor, are taken into account when making the transformation.

In addition to control flow, array structures in source languages do not exist in machine languages. In Sect. 4, we show that even in the very simple case of a loop mapping a function over an array, modern hardware features enable complicated performance-enhancing code graph transformations.

2   Overview of SIMD and the SPU ISA

Single Instruction Multiple Data (SIMD) instructions operate on more than one data element in parallel. Current implementations, which were developed to support multi-media applications, are much more flexible than the first generation designed for fast linear algebra. Efficient code is often difficult to develop, and also hard to follow.

The instruction set architecture (ISA) of the "synergistic processing units" (SPUs) of the Cell Broadband Engine [9] uses 128-bit operands. It contains a rich set of operations formed by dividing the 128-bit operands into 8-, 16-, 32- or 64-bit quantities and performing the usual scalar operations independently on each. See Fig. 1 for an example 32-bit add instruction operating on four elements.

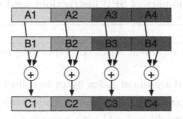

Fig. 1. fma, a 32-bit add operating on two 128-bit wide operands

This results in a useful level of parallelism, but introduces alignment issues in data. To be able to handle arbitrarily-structured data (necessary if you want to be able to insert SIMD-optimised functions into existing applications) all SIMD instructions have some instructions to rearrange data. Two approaches are possible, a large set of instructions with specific functions (e.g. unpacking pixel data into vectors by component), or a small set of software-controllable instructions. All ISAs follow a middle path, with VMX/SPU ISA being the more generic. The instructions of most use in synthesising loop overhead are the byte permute instruction **shufb** (analogous to VMX's *vperm*), shown in Fig. 2, and quadword rotate instructions, including **rotqby** shown in Fig. 3. As shown in the figures, SPU byte permutation can be used to move 32-bit components from one slot to another one (useful for transposing single-precision floating point matrices, for example), or duplicate bytes.

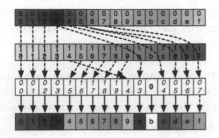
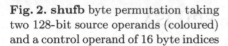

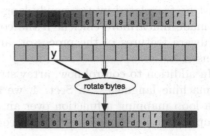

Fig. 2. shufb byte permutation taking two 128-bit source operands (coloured) and a control operand of 16 byte indices

Fig. 3. rotqby, a 16-byte register byte rotate, using a run-time value from a second operand

It can rotate bytes through cycles, which can be used to count through loop induction variables when the loop sizes are known at compile time. Unlike the *vperm* instruction of VMX, **shufb** can also insert three special byte values (zero, minus one, and high-bit set) if it encounters special byte values in the index quadword, see byte b in the figure. Byte and bit rotate instructions (like **rotqby** in Fig. 3) take both immediate counts and counts from operand registers.

To make the paper self-contained, we include in Table 1 a description of the most important machine instructions we use in the paper.

Table 1. Summary of SPU instructions used in this paper

Instruction	Description
selb	bits in third argument select corresponding bits in first or second argument
shufb	bytes in third argument index bytes to collect from first two arguments
fma, fm, fa	32-bit floating point fused multiply-add, multiply and add
a, ai	32-bit integer add and add with immediate
rotqbii	rotate whole quadword up to 7 bits left, number given by immediate
rotqbyi	rotate whole quadword left in byte increments, number given by immediate
shli	shift each 32-bit word left by an immediate constant number of bits

3   Code Graphs

Term graphs are usually represented by graphs where nodes are labelled with function symbols and edges connect function calls with their arguments [15]. We use the dual approach of *code graphs* which are directed hypergraphs where nodes are only labelled with type information, function names are hyperedge labels, and each hyperedge has a sequence of input tentacles and a sequence of output tentacles (each incident with a node):

Definition 3.1. A *hypergraph* $H = (\mathcal{N}, \mathcal{E}, \mathsf{src}, \mathsf{trg}, \mathsf{nLab}, \mathsf{eLab})$ over a node label set NLab and an edge label set ELab consists of
- a set $\mathcal{N}$ of *nodes* and a set $\mathcal{E}$ of *hyperedges* (or *edges*),
- two functions $\mathsf{src}, \mathsf{trg} : \mathcal{E} \to \mathcal{N}^*$ assigning each hyperedge the sequence of its *source nodes* and *target nodes* respectively, and
- two functions $\mathsf{nLab} : \mathcal{N} \to \mathsf{NLab}$ and $\mathsf{eLab} : \mathcal{E} \to \mathsf{ELab}$ assigning labels to nodes and hyperedges. □

We use the naturally arising definition of hypergraph homomorphisms, i.e., pairs consisting of a total node mapping and a total edge mapping, preserving src, trg, nLab, and eLab, and thus obtain a category of hypergraphs.

Definition 3.2. A *primitive hypergraph* has only one edge, and all nodes are connected to that edge.

A *hypergraph alphabet* is a hypergraph where the labelling functions nLab and eLab are the identities on the respective label sets.

A *typed hypergraph* is a hypergraph together with a homomorphism into a hypergraph alphabet. □

We will restrict our attention to typed hypergraphs with an implicitly given alphabet; this guarantees that hyperedges with the same label have the same numbers of input and output nodes, and the same type sequences on their input and output nodes.

The category of hypergraphs is essentially the common substrate on top of which all the other necessary concepts can be defined, but we rarely deal directly with hypergraphs. Instead, we deal with hypergraphs that represent programs in a certain sense, with an input/output interface:

Definition 3.3. A *code graph* $G = (H, \mathsf{In}, \mathsf{Out})$ over a node label set NLab and an edge label set ELab consists of
- a hypergraph $H = (\mathcal{N}, \mathcal{E}, \mathsf{src}, \mathsf{trg}, \mathsf{nLab}, \mathsf{eLab})$ over NLab and ELab, and
- two node sequences $\mathsf{In}, \mathsf{Out} : \mathcal{N}^*$ containing the *input nodes* and *output nodes* of the code graph. □

Code graph homomorphisms are hypergraph homomorphisms that also preserve input and output sequences — since this makes the code graph category $\mathcal{CG}$ of limited use for code graph transformation, we will normally use the hypergraph category $\mathcal{HG}$.

In COCONUT, node labels are *types*. We occasionally draw nodes with type information omitted; output tentacles are arrows from hyper-edges to nodes, and input tentacles are arrows from nodes to hyperedges — the ordering relation between in- resp. output tentacles incident with the same hyperedge is not always made explicit in drawings, but is part of the graph structure.

Since some operations produce more than one result, our hyperedges can have multiple output tentacles. For example, in the PowerPC ISA, most arithmetic instructions can produce both a value and a condition code placed into a named condition register; on all architectures, load, store and synchronisation instructions produce and/or consume state, which we represent by separate nodes; on most architectures, floating-point exceptions are generated without having named outputs in the machine language instructions. We treat all these side-effects uniformly using explicit nodes.

4 Code Graph Generators

The declarative patterns we have abstracted as generators (up to now), fall into three classes: synthetic control flow, support for actual control flow (*e.g.* loop overhead), and support for linear algebra.

In this section we present, as a "simple" example, the loop overhead for mapping a function over an array. The complexity of this example also serves to motivate the particular need for verification based on code graph transformations for code which exercises the more powerful SIMD features available in current processors. To specify correct iterator code, it is necessary to understand loop software pipelining and keep track of several details. To hide these intricacies at the application site, the loop overhead is turned into a code generator wrapping an arbitrary data-flow function. This also simplifies the verification process, since the generator can be verified using a dummy body, and any errors will be easy to detect.

Since execution of branch instructions is expensive, and getting more expensive as processor clock rates increase, and pipeline depth lengthens, avoiding branches is a key step in performance tuning on all recent microprocessors. Synthetic control flow is the use of architecture-specific support for predicates and value selection, or the generic transformation of nested if-then-else patterns into integer and logical machine instructions.

For example, $z := max\,(x, y)$ can be implemented as $z = \mathbf{selb}\ x\ y\ (\mathbf{fcgt}\ y\ x)$, in which **fcgt** compares the four float values in x pairwise to the four float values in y and produces a vector of four logical values, each either $0\ x00000000$ or $0\ xFFFFFFFF$ according to the result of the individual comparison. This is used as the third argument of **selb** to have each bit from the comparison result select the corresponding bit of either x or y. Therefore, these two instructions implement the calculation of four independent *max* results without a single branch instruction. Although synthetic control flow can dramatically improve performance, it can obfuscate underlying semantics by "reusing" the same code paths for multiple types of data. Code transformation normalizes these implementation differences so that they can be verified against generic code graph representations.

Control flow, per se, is outside of the scope of this paper, but in our approach, already the declarative code graphs contain significant complexity.

A recurring pattern in signal processing is the *map* of a function over a list of values stored in an array, with the output written to the same array or a different array. An optimized library of procedures which map standard math functions (addition, complex multiplication, sine, *etc.*) over arrays is called a *vector library*, and the importance of this mapping pattern is underlined by the fact that hardware manufacturers still provide such libraries *written in assembly language*. Because this pattern is so common, small performance increases justify complicated code transformations, especially in the loop overhead (the assembly instructions implementing the counting and pointer moving common to all instances of the pattern).

This is our smallest non-trivial example. It contains a small code fragment which is difficult to verify by inspection. We will go through all of the loop overhead, in which a single arithmetic instruction is sufficient to move two pointers, update a counter and calculate the branch address for the loop. This implementation is difficult to understand, because it uses a range of instructions in uncommon ways. It underlines both the need for automatic verification and the need for a pattern interface, so that such complicated patterns need only be understood by the original developer.

We will show it for the case of mapping a function, *body* :: *REG* → *REG*, with one input and one output. There is one unused word in our control quadword, so this approach works just as well for three-pointer maps (one input and two outputs, or two inputs and one output)[1].

To understand this example, consider a C version

```
for (i = 0; i < N; i ++) { out[i] = body(in[i]); }
```

which applies a function body, *e.g.*, cosine, to the elements of an array. Note that even at the C level, array indexing is only syntactic sugar for pointer calculations, so the above turns into:

```
for (i = 0; i < N; i ++) { *(out + i) = body( *(in + i) ); }
```

A compiler must translate this into assembly code. Assuming a RISC-like processor, like the Cell BE, this involves loads to registers and saves from registers, assigning the index variable i to a register, including a register addition or increment instruction, a compare and a branch when the condition i < N is no longer true. A typical implementation requires three registers assigned to the input and output pointers and the index variable, assuming that the compiler recognizes the continuous array access pattern and replaces the array index calculations with fixed pointer increments. Another common optimization applied by compilers is to unroll the loop, for example, unrolling by a factor of two:

```
for (i = 0; i < N; i += 2)
    {   *(out + i    ) = body( *(in + i    ) );
        *(out + i + 1) = body( *(in + i + 1) );    }
```

In addition, the compiler must insert instructions to appropriately initialize the registers used in the loop body, and, for unrolled or more complex loops, instructions to handle exceptional cases and store state. These instructions form the loop prologue and epilogue — in the above example, the following epilogue would be sufficient to deal with the possibility of N being odd:

```
if (i < N) { *(out + i) = body( *(in + i) ); }
```

---

[1] Less obvious is that the same idea works for up to seven-pointer cases, if the pointer arithmetic is performed using 16-bit integers. If the ranges permit, the 16-bit integers can be used as-is, but in general it is necessary to put addresses modulo 16 in the control quadword, and shift the result by four bits before extracting pointers.

Looking at the last C loop again, it is obvious that some additions can be shared, but in every iteration, at least three additions still have to be done: one for the iteration count N, and one each for the input and output pointers in and out. Using further transformations, this can be reduced to two additions, but it is in general not obvious how to reduce this further.

On the SPU, additions are executed in the arithmetic pipeline, which is the bottleneck for most mathematical functions. The loop overhead we present in the following moves the three additions into a single SIMD instruction **a**, and uses instructions executing in the non-arithmetic pipeline to move the individual vector components around so they can be used as addresses for load and store instructions, and trigger loop termination. An additional complication arises when N is not divisible by the unroll factor; we deal with this by having the second iteration repeat some of the work of the first iteration, without introducing any (expensive) branches for this (further explanation below).

In Fig. 4, we (schematically) show the four instructions of loop overhead for such loops (this is not a code graph); we explain this now in detail. The control quadword (1) contains the input and output pointer and the counter (and one unused 32-bit word), saving two registers over a non-SIMD version. A single SIMD add instruction (2) updates the two pointers and the counter by the increments in the register constant (3), again saving additional register constants. Single-word add is an arithmetic instruction and slants to the right. All other instructions are non-arithmetic and slant to the left.

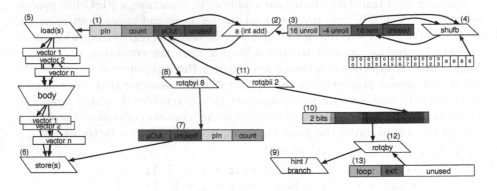

Fig. 4. Overhead for a map loop

If the loop *count* is 0 modulo *unroll* (which is always the case if no unrolling is done), the increments (3) are constant, and the **shufb** (4) can be ignored. Otherwise, the first increment of the output pointer is by the remainder, *rem =* *count* mod *unroll*, after which the **shufb** (4) copies the increment used for the input pointer to the output pointer. To handle the case that *count* < *unroll* requires changes to the prologue and epilogue.

All non-immediate load/store instructions take the first word in a register quadword as their address, so the loads (5) use the control word as an argument. The stores (6) need their argument (7) rotated (8) by two words, *i.e.*, 8 bytes.

The branch address (9) used by the branch and the hint instructions is calculated via a byte rotation count (10) which is calculated by shifting (11) the two high-order bits from the count word into the low-order bits of the first word. Since loads and stores are 16-byte aligned, the four low-order bits of *pOut* will always be zero, so the only significant bits of the rotation count (10) are the two bits shifted in from the count word. If the count is initialized to the number of elements to be mapped, then the first count times through the loop, those two bits are zero, but on iteration (count + 1), the count becomes negative and the high bits are set. So the rotation count is either zero (initially) or three (on the ultimate iteration). The count is used to rotate (12) a quadword (13) composed of the addresses of the top of the loop and the loop exit. If the function ends with the loop doing the mapping, and no non-volatile registers are used in the body, then the exit address for the loop can be the address in the link register. In this case the function return is hinted and the total number of branches is equal to the number of values mapped divided by the unroll factor.

Developers of high-performance numerical software are conservative, and require strong reasons to change design methods and tools. Before making arguments about productivity, safety and maintainability, performance questions have to be answered, which we do by comparing measured performance with the lower bound given by dividing the number of instructions of each type by the number of instructions of that type which can be executed, and (to verify that the graph model faithfully reflects the machine architecture) with the estimated number of cycles per iteration calculated by the scheduler, see Fig. 5.

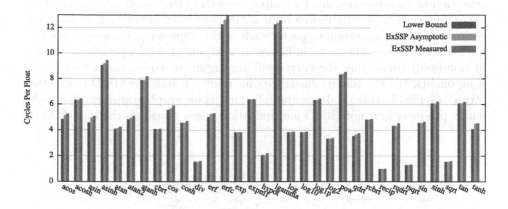

Fig. 5. Timing for the same code scheduled with Coconut near optimal

The code graphs tested calculate the elementary functions listed in the figure mapped over arrays of 32-bit floating point numbers, and are benchmarked using standard methodology [4]. Coconut functions are in-lined by the higher-order DSL function *mapTicker* presented above, and scheduled using Explicitly Staged Software Pipelining [17].

A compiler using a conventional loop overhead and scheduling it equally efficiently would still require an extra cycle per loop. On all the loops in this benchmark, this one cycle still means a speed-up of between 1% and 2.5%.

5   Code Graph Transformation

The code graphs produced by our generators for Cell SPU code contain SIMD instructions as their hyperedge labels, connecting nodes labelled with either the type "*REG*" for SPU registers, or a state type (displayed as "<>").

For verification, we need to extract the action of the generated code on individual vector components; we represent this as code graphs with nodes labelled with component types, like *FLOAT, INT32, UINT8*, etc., and with edge labels representing primitive operations on these types. (For convenience, we largely use the same labels as for the vector instructions; for example, we will use "**fm**" as the display form of the edge labels both for multiplication of *REG*s considered as four-element vectors of *FLOAT* values, and "fm" for multiplication of *FLOAT* values.) For moving between the two worlds, we use *mixed type* code graphs that can be labelled with both kinds of types and instructions, and include also additional "adaptation" edge labels representing, for example, the composition of a *REG* from four *FLOAT*s, and the corresponding decomposition. Semantically, these adaptations represent natural isomorphisms between different interpretations of bit-vectors of the same length.

The first step of mapping an assembly graph to a more direct symbolic representation of its semantics involves, after converting the graph into mixed type, expanding each hyperedge representing a SIMD-parallel instruction into a graph consisting of decomposition edges for each of the arguments, composition edges for each of the results, and, in-between, component-level operations (drawn in non-bold) connecting the corresponding argument components with result components. For the ternary floating-point multiply-and-add SIMD instruction "**fma**" of Fig. 1, this produces the following code graph transformation rule, which produces four non-SIMD multiplication edges "fma" on the type *FLOAT*:

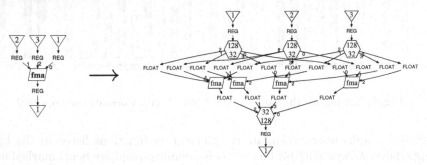

The so-called "quadword rotations" are not typical SIMD instructions since they move data across all vector component boundaries; since they involve only vector-internal data movement, they can be represented in terms of decomposition and composition alone, with appropriate permutation of the intermediate

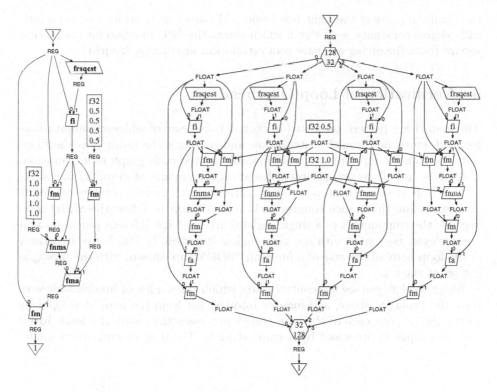

Fig. 6. Square root calculation: SIMD instructions (left), component expansion (right)

tentacles. In cases where, for example, the arguments of one floating point operation have been produced by another, the adjacent composition and decomposition edges can be eliminated.

Formally, these transformations are morphism equations in the monoidal code graph category $\mathcal{CGM}$; their application as graph transformation is easily understood as applying double-pushout rules in the hypergraph category $\mathcal{HG}$, where the rule is a span in $\mathcal{HG}$ underlying a span in the code graph category $\mathcal{CG}$, typically with a discrete gluing graph with disjoint input and output nodes.

For the implementation, the replacement mechanism is not a problem, but, among other reasons since rule schemas involving vector constants have on the order of 2^{128} instances, sometimes with significantly different right-hand sides, matching and rule identification are best performed by a programmed solution instead of a generic matching mechanism. Code graphs also have a natural concept of "garbage", which is slightly complicated by the fact that hyperedges can have multiple result nodes; we are able to perform full transforming graph traversals with limited rule sets between garbage collections without the danger of performing unnecessary work. We also implement maximal unification; this is particularly useful for some rules involving partial interaction between composition and decomposition edges, since it allows us to formulate these situations as rules with a single sink edge (i.e., without successor edges), and automatically share the common parts of the right-hand sides. Maximal unification also automatically shares constants, as in Fig. 6 which shows the SPU function for calculating square roots (involving a square root estimation instruction **frsqest**).

6 Verification of Loop Overhead

The map ticker pattern presented in Sect. 4 takes care of address computations for load, store, and branch instructions, and packages the result plus the function body and load/store into a schedulable nested code graph representation. Constants and offsets are generated based on the amount of unrolling and staging, and all of these constants and operations on them mix pointers for loads and stores and the branch counter. It is very difficult to follow the SIMD code because the components of a single register are used for different purposes, and are not even associated with the same logical iteration. In Fig. 7, five iterations of the loop body of the *map* of a function "BODY" are shown, with the prologue cut off at the top.

Along the left you see the control state, which takes a list of branch addresses from the prologue above, and indexes into the list from the main development to the right. Then each of the loop bodies processes the result of a load, **lqd** 0 and its output is processed by a store **stqd** 0. The 0 is an immediate index,

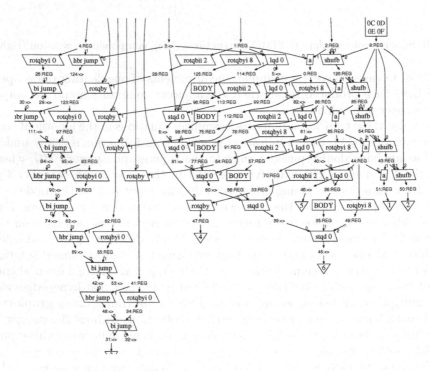

Fig. 7. Map ticker loop developed over five iterations

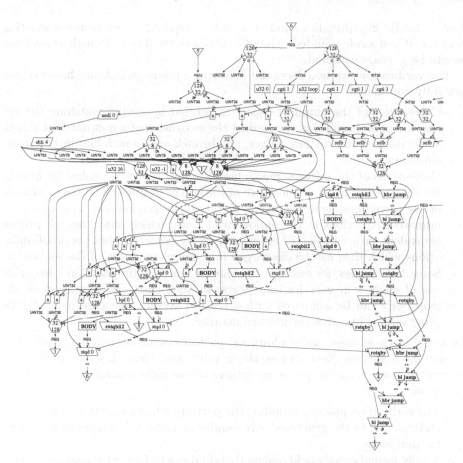

Fig. 8. Map ticker loop developed over five iterations, SIMD expanded

and takes nonzero values in unrolled cases of the loop body. The base addresses
for the loads and stores come from the string of **as** (four-way, 32-bit integer
add) near the right of the code graph. This single register value is consumed
by the loads and indirectly by the stores and the branch logic. The increments
are not constant but updated by the **shufb** instructions along the right of the
code graph. For determining whether the graph is consistent with the normal
understanding of the loop, it is necessary to track individual vector components
within register values.

The expanded graph, Fig. 8, makes the role of these component 32-bit integers clear by expanding SIMD operations into their constituents and recognising
applications of **shufb** and **rotqbyi** which can be reduced to graph operations
statically — this turns an essentially opaque instruction (**shufb**) into transparent structure in the code graph. The chain of "add" instructions at the heart
of the loop is now shown as four separate chains of component "add"s, which
makes clear which component is used for the load and which for the store. The
component used for the branch calculation is not resolved, because it does not

have a SIMD interpretation, and so is not recognised by rules in the existing schema. When a rule is added to handle this case, the $32 \to 128$ node conversion would be garbage collected.

For verification, we now have the following options, which are however not yet fully automated:

- Correctness of the unrolling aspect is verified by simply matching the expansion of an unrolled graph against the expansion of a non-unrolled graph, with "decided control flow" edges, i.e., branch and branch hint instructions, eliminated.
- Correctness of the software pipelining (staging) aspect is verified by matching the expansion of a development of the staged graph against the expansion of the corresponding development of the non-staged version. This will leave unmatched portions in the prologues of both, which must then be proven equivalent, either by partial evaluation, or by exporting them as proof obligations which then can be discharged in a complete theory of the semantics.
- Some loop bodies, for example the one for matrix multiplication, also make use of shuffles in very intricate ways; in such cases the expansion of the loop body can be compared with a trusted version that can frequently be programmed in a straight-forward manner.

In many of these cases, some additional partial evaluation may be required to enable the matching. Nevertheless, the graph transformation approach still has advantages over trying to prove correctness of the code generator using a proof assistant:

- The verification process, including the partial evaluations, can be automated, and changes to the generator only require incremental changes to the "verification script".
- A fully formal proof would frequently boil down to large case analyses, where some of the cases may never be needed in practise.
  The verification will be run only on the instances which meet performance and code size requirements.
- The graph transformation approach affords much better traceability than direct generation of proof obligations in theorem provers. This significantly aids development and debugging, and also has advantages for possible certification.

7   Related Work

Pnueli et al. introduced in 1998 the approach of "translation validation" which adds, for example, to a compiler, an a posteriori "validation" pass that automatically verifies that input and output are semantically equivalent [12]. Necula applied this approach to several optimisation passes of the GNU C compiler [10]. Leviathan and Pnueli apply the translation validation approach to software pipelining optimisations [8] in the context of an architecture with a rotating register file, but without specific use of SIMD instructions, and using symbolic evaluation of machine state transitions. Tristan and Leroy report an application of the translation validation approach to instruction scheduling optimisations [19].

The way we target the translation validation approach differs from all these in performing the semantic equivalence proof at a higher level of abstraction, significantly simplifying the modeling of machine state by incorporating it into a syntactic framework based on data flow graphs. Our code graphs are a generalisation of Hoffmann and Plump's jungles [5,11], corresponding to Ştefănescu's "flow graphs" [16], and use a functorial semantics, described in [7], which follows the approach of Corradini and Gadducci [3].

However, this happens to be dual to the conventional view of intermediate representations in compilers where operations are node labels. For that dual view of SIMD instructions, Schösser and Geiss use graph transformation with exhaustive search of SIMD-ification rule applicability for remarkably successful automatic vectorisation [14]. This is in some sense the converse to the SIMD expansion presented in Sect. 5; our approach of Sect. 6 is aimed at the verification of transformations that an automated pass would be unlikely to identify, but is equally applicable to the verification of automated transformations.

The SPIRAL project [13] of Moura and Püschel uses the computer algebra system GAP [18] to verify rules and formulae used in its search-based approach to generation of efficient SIMD implementations of signal processing transformations. SPIRAL apparently generates very simple SIMD code which, by construction, implements a linear function, such that testing on a basis of the relevant vector space would be sufficient to prove correctness (numerical concerns aside); the SPIRAL system currently only provides for automated systematic and random testing. This apparent restriction to strict SIMD instructions insulates the SPIRAL project from the complexities of the more complex vector manipulations that are the key to the efficiency of the loop overhead of Sect. 4 and of many other code generators we have developed [1].

8 Conclusion

We have demonstrated the feasibility of using code graph transformations to verify the correctness of complicated SIMD assembly code, and equally importantly, to understand developmental versions (before they are correct).

These graph transformation capabilities are a key feature enabling us to produce special-purpose code generators from which we obtain assembly code running at or near the theoretical peak performance of the hardware. Previously this would have only been possible for experienced assembly code tuners, at great expense in terms of implementation effort, necessarily expensive testing and prohibitively expensive maintenance. Our approach is more flexible, not limited by human understanding, and in addition affords high confidence in correctness.

The simple DPO graph transformations discussed in this paper are sufficient for SIMD expansion and partial evaluation; for larger-scale transformation like the transformations that enable software pipelining [2,17], we employ higher-level graph transformations in the context of nested code graphs; for full formalisation of this we will need an approach like that of [6] to deal with graph variables that can be duplicated.

References

1. Anand, C.K., Kahl, W.: A Domain-Specific Language for the Generation of Optimized SIMD-Parallel Assembly Code. SQRL Report 43, McMaster University (2007), http://sqrl.mcmaster.ca/sqrl_reports.html
2. Anand, C.K., Kahl, W.: MultiLoop: Efficient Software Pipelining for Modern Hardware. In: CASCON 2007: Proc. 2007 Conference of the Center for Advanced Studies on Collaborative Research, pp. 260–263. ACM, New York (2007)
3. Corradini, A., Gadducci, F.: An Algebraic Presentation of Term Graphs, via GS-Monoidal Categories. Applied Categorical Structures 7(4), 299–331 (1999)
4. Enenkel, R.: A Comprehensive Test Environment for Mathematical Functions. IBM Technical Report TR-74.200, IBM Corp. (2004)
5. Hoffmann, B., Plump, D.: Jungle Evaluation for Efficient Term Rewriting. In: Gabrowski, J., Lescanne, P., Wechler, W. (eds.) ALP 1988. Mathematical Research, vol. 49, pp. 191–203. Akademie-Verlag (1988)
6. Kahl, W.: A Relation-Algebraic Approach to Graph Structure Transformation. Habil. Thesis, Informatik, UniBw München, Techn. Ber. 2002-03 (2001)
7. Kahl, W., Anand, C.K., Carette, J.: Control-Flow Semantics for Assembly-Level Data-Flow Graphs. In: MacCaull, W., Winter, M., Düntsch, I. (eds.) RelMiCS 2005. LNCS, vol. 3929, pp. 147–160. Springer, Heidelberg (2006)
8. Leviathan, R., Pnueli, A.: Validating Software Pipelining Optimizations. In: Compilers, Architecture, and Synthesis for Embedded Systems, CASES 2002, pp. 280–287. ACM, New York (2002)
9. IBM Corp. Synergistic Processor Unit Instruction Set Architecture. IBM Systems and Technology Group, Hopewell Junction, NY (2006)
10. Necula, G.C.: Translation validation for an optimizing compiler. In: Programming Language Design and Implementation (PLDI 2000), pp. 83–95. ACM, New York (2000)
11. Plump, D.: Term Graph Rewriting. In: Ehrig, H., Engels, G., Kreowski, H.J., Rozenberg, G. (eds.) Handbook of Graph Grammars and Computing by Graph Transformation. Applications, Languages and Tools, ch. 1, vol. 2, pp. 3–61. World Scientific, Singapore (1999)
12. Pnueli, A., Siegel, M., Singerman, E.: Translation Validation. In: Steffen, B. (ed.) TACAS 1998. LNCS, vol. 1384, pp. 151–166. Springer, Heidelberg (1998)
13. Püschel, M., Moura, J.M.F., et al.: SPIRAL: Code Generation for DSP Transforms. Proc. IEEE, Program Generation, Optimization, and Adaptation 93(2), 232–275 (2005) (special issue)
14. Schösser, A., Geiss, R.: Graph Rewriting for Hardware Dependent Program Optimisations. In: Schürr, A., Nagl, M., Zündorf, A. (eds.) AGTIVE 2007. LNCS, vol. 5088. Springer, Heidelberg (2007)
15. Sleep, M., Plasmeijer, M., van Eekelen, M. (eds.): Term Graph Rewriting: Theory and Practice. Wiley, Chichester (1993)
16. Ştefănescu, G.: Network Algebra. Springer, London (2000)
17. Thaller, W.: Explicitly Staged Software Pipelining. Master's thesis, McMaster University, Department of Computing and Software (2006), http://sqrl.mcmaster.ca/~anand/papers/ThallerMScExSSP.pdf
18. The GAP Group. GAP – Groups, Algorithms, and Programming, Version 4.4.10 (2007), http://www.gap-system.org/
19. Tristan, J.B., Leroy, X.: Formal Verification of Translation Validators, A Case Study on Instruction Scheduling Optimizations. In: Principles of Programming Languages, POPL 2008, pp. 17–27. ACM, New York (2008)

Graph Rewriting for Hardware Dependent
Program Optimizations

Andreas Schösser and Rubino Geiß

Universität Karlsruhe (TH), 76131 Karlsruhe, Germany
{andi,rubino}@ipd.info.uni-karlsruhe.de

Abstract. We present a compiler internal program optimization that uses graph rewriting. This optimization enables the compiler to automatically use rich instructions (such as SIMD instructions) provided by modern CPUs and is transparent to the user of the compiler. New instructions can be introduced easily by specifying their behaviour in a high-level programming language. The optimization is integrated into an existing compiler, gaining high speedup.

1   Introduction

Current programming languages don't pay much attention to *rich instructions* provided by recent CPUs. By *rich instruction* we mean a small program implemented in hardware, consisting of several conventional instructions and capable of operating on multiple data in parallel. For example, SIMD[1] instructions fall in this category. Rich instructions are applied to benefit from shorter execution time compared to executing conventional instructions. Programmers have different options to take advantage of rich instructions:

Using assembly language. This option can quickly lead to a huge programming effort and maintenance overhead.

Using compiler specific intrinsics. Requires adaptation of a program when changing the target architecture or the compiler. Moreover, existing programs can only be optimized if their source code is rewritten manually.

Using a compiler internal optimization. Transparent to the programmer; the compiler decides automatically when to use a rich instruction instead of several basic instructions, depending on the target architecture.

Assembly language and intrinsics are not applicable since we want to keep the source code portable. Most compilers currently available don't fully support optimizations mentioned above. Some compilers use a so-called *Vectorizer* to vectorize loops but don't optimize programs outside loops and fail for rich instructions which are more complex than pure vector instructions.

To overcome these limitations we present a new approach to implement such an optimization. Optimizations are usually done on a compiler internal intermediate program representation (IR). Modern IRs are graph based, consisting

---

[1] Single Instruction Multiple Data.

A. Schürr, M. Nagl, and A. Zündorf (Eds.): AGTIVE 2007, LNCS 5088, pp. 233–248, 2008.

of nodes representing operations and edges representing data and control flow. Since an IR needs to be hardware independent, it does not initially contain node types for hardware specific rich instructions. Instead, we can find rich instructions as *subgraphs* of an IR graph. These subgraphs are composed of several basic instructions. To perform an optimization, we transform the original graph by replacing these subgraphs by a single corresponding, hardware specific node[2].

Figure 1 shows a small example of how such an optimizing transformation looks like. The graph shown on the left—executing two *Load* operations on consecutive storage locations starting at a base address *Base*—is replaced by the graph shown on the right, which executes both *Load* operations at once by using a rich instruction named *VectorLoad*. *VectorLoad* delivers the same results as the graph we replaced. To distinguish the two partial results of the *VectorLoad* instruction, we use edge types *Result 1* and *Result 2*. Note that data dependency edges instead of data flow edges were used in this example. That is, to get the execution order of the statements you have to read the dependency edges backwards.

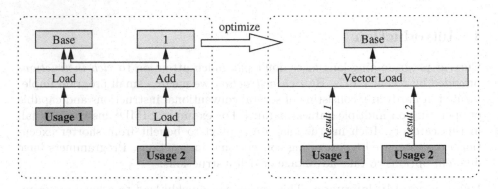

Fig. 1. Optimizing transformation of an IR graph

This paper presents new techniques to perform such a transformation:

- In the field of compiler construction it's common to do graph transformations manually. Though, finding a *pattern graph* in a host graph and replacing it by a *replacement graph* are tasks that can be delegated to a *graph rewrite system* (GRS) (Section 2). Doing this allows us to specify graph transformations in an abstract way.
- Up to now, *pattern graphs* had to be specified manually. This method is very time consuming and error-prone (Section 2). Our idea is to *generate* the pattern graphs from a specification that describes the *behaviour* of a rich instruction in a standard programming language (Section 3).
- We show how to automatically generate and apply graph rewrite rules to perform program optimization (Section 4).

---

[2] Therefore, we require that the IR is extendable and especially enables the introduction of hardware specific nodes after high level optimizations are completed.

– We provide benchmark results to show the benefit gained by our optimization
  and that it is performed by the GRS in admissible time (Section 6).

2   The Problem

Our first problem to solve is choosing a graph rewrite system suitable for our
needs. We use *GrGen* [1,2] which is a well-known and fast graph rewrite tool.
It features an extensive specification language and can operate directly on our
compiler's IR [3]. We don't want to search and replace patterns manually because
pattern graphs can grow huge in our case. This is because of the complexity of
rich instructions on the one hand and the complexity of the IR on the other
hand.

2.1   The Complexity of Rich Instructions

We already presented a rather simple *VectorLoad* instruction, but also more
complex instructions, e.g. incorporating forked control flow, are possible. For
example, the following C code calculates the *Sum of Absolute Differences (SAD)*
of two vectors and could be replaced by a rich instruction named *psadbw* taken
from the *Intel SSE2* instruction set [4].

```
unsigned char a[16], b[16];
int result = 0, i;
...
for(i = 0; i < 16; i++) {
    if(a[i] > b[i])
        result += a[i] - b[i];
    else
        result += b[i] - a[i];
}
```

When applying rich instructions, we have to take into account that they often
handle *vectors* instead of *scalar values* and can operate on special *vector register*
sets.

2.2   The Complexity of an IR

The complexity of rich instructions together with the complexity of an IR makes
it very difficult to integrate new rich instructions manually, even for experts. For
example, one of the main problems when creating pattern graphs is program
variation, i.e. pattern graph and host graph may differ even though both have
equivalent semantics. Since the problem of proofing the equivalence of two programs is undecidable in general, it's not possible to find *every* subgraph having
the same semantics as the pattern graph. Yet, we can try to find as many subgraphs as possible by applying special techniques like *normalization* and *creating
variants*. Figure 2(a) shows an example pattern graph for a *VectorLoad* instruction which differs significantly from the host graph given in figure Figure 2(b).
Both graphs are variants of the code fragment

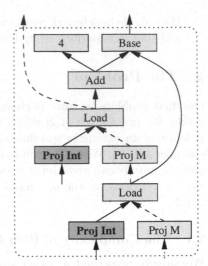

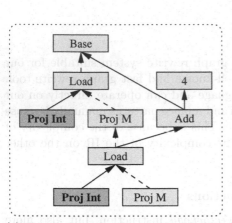

(a) Pattern graph of a *VectorLoad* instruction

(b) Host graph containing a *VectorLoad* subgraph

Fig. 2. Difference between pattern graph and host graph

```
int a, b, c[2];
...
a = c[0];
b = c[1];
...
```

transformed to our IR called FIRM [5]. To help you understand this example, we have to provide you with some technical details about FIRM:

FIRM is a graph based IR which satisfies the SSA[3] property [6,7]. Most operations in FIRM are self-explanatory, yet there are some node types to be explained more closely. Nodes of type *Proj* are used to simulate *edge types*, a concept with doesn't exist in FIRM. Hence, they won't produce any assembler code. Edges of type *memory* (denoted as *memory edge* in the following) are used to serialize memory operations in order of appearance in the source code. They are marked with a *Proj M* node and drawn as a dotted line for clarity. Edges of type *integer*, marked with a *Proj Int* node, represent an integer result. In FIRM, *Proj* nodes are omitted if the edge type is non-ambiguous, that is, if the edge type is implicitly given by the result type of the edge's target node.

The difference between the pattern graph in Figure 2(a) and the host graph in Figure 2(b) is that the *Load* operations are serialized in a different order by memory edges. Other differences not shown here may occur in arithmetic expressions, which is important especially in the context of address calculation. For example, the simple expression $a + b + c$ can be scheduled as $(a + b) + c$ or $a + (b + c)$. Note that it depends on the programming language whether re-ordering of arithmetic expressions is allowed.

---

[3] Single Static Assignment.

In general, the patterns are much more complex, including several basic blocks and forked control flow (not modelled here for conciseness). By creating pattern graphs manually, it's easy to make mistakes due to the complexity of the IR, even for experts. Therefore, introducing new rich instructions to the compiler is very time consuming this way. Moreover, changes made to the IR require the patterns to be rewritten. We're heading for a solution to generate graph rewrite rules automatically.

2.3 Inserting Rich Instructions

Further questions arise when it comes to create the replacement graph which is used to insert the new rich instruction. At first, we have to decide where to schedule the rich instruction. Secondly, it's important to connect the new instruction to the right operands. Moreover, we have to investigate a way to make the result of the rich instruction public so that up-following instructions are able to use it. This is not trivial because rich instructions may save their results in vector registers, which conventional instructions cannot access. We therefore have to find a way to transport data to those vector registers and back.

After graph rewrite rules have been created, we need a method to decide which rules we shall apply. This is especially interesting when different subgraphs to be replaced overlap. In some cases, we're not allowed to replace a subgraph due to constraints of the IR in order to keep the semantics of the rewritten program exactly as it was before the rewrite. Hence, we have to analyze the host graph carefully before replacing.

A solution to these problems is presented in the following sections.

3 Using GrGen for Program Optimization

As described in Section 2, creating pattern graphs by hand is an arduous task, especially for complex rich instructions. Our solution is to specify *the behaviour* of rich instructions in a standard programming language and generate the graph rewrite rules *automatically*. In the following, we present an instruction specification language based on the programming language C and show how to integrate such an optimization into an existing compiler. The optimization is divided into two steps described in the following sections.

3.1 Generating Graph Rewrite Rules

The first step is to generate graph rewrite rules to be used for optimization. The pattern and replacement graphs are derived from specifications of the behaviour of a rich instruction stated in the programming language C. Thus, the instruction specifications can easily be drawn from pseudo code descriptions of CPU instructions used in reference manuals (cf. [4,8]).

Listing 1. Example specification of a rich instruction

```
1  void VectorAdd(void)
2  {
3      /* Definition part */
4      double *a = Operand_0("vector", "memory",   "gp");
5      double *b = Operand_1("vector", "register", "xmm");
6      double *res =  Result("vector", "register", "in_r1");
7      Emit("addpd %S0, %S1");
8
9      /* Behaviour of the instruction */
10     res[0] = a[0] + b[0];
11     res[1] = a[1] + b[1];
12 }
```

Instruction Specification. Listing 1 gives an example of how such a specification looks like: It consists of one or more functions, each function describing the behaviour of a rich instruction. In this example, the instruction `VectorAdd` is specified. Each function consists of a *definition part* and a *behaviour part*.

In the definition part, a call of the function `Operand_n` or `Result` defines a variable the rich instruction operates on. `Operand_n` means that the variable represents the nth operand of the instruction, `Result` means that the variable represents it's result. Each variable has additional attributes, which are set by passing parameters to those functions. These attributes specify the kind of data the variable represents (`vector` or `scalar`), the location of the data (`register` or `memory`) and the name of the register class in which the data is passed. Beyond variable definition, the assembler code to emit has to be specified here, using the function `Emit(char *assembler_template)`. Our example uses the *Intel SSE3* instruction set and emits the instruction `addpd` which adds two vectors of two double precision floating point components. The wildcards `%S0` and `%S1` stand for source register 0 and 1, in which the operands 0 and 1 are passed. The compiler backend replaces these wildcards by the actual registers it allocated.

The behaviour part describes the exact behaviour of the rich instruction in plain C, using the variables defined in the definition part. The instruction presented in this example performs a vector addition of two vectors given by the variables `a` and `b`, and writes the result to the location represented by the variable `res`.

Note that the specification uses plain C syntax for the definition and behaviour part. We just added some extra semantics. The elements used in this example can be used to specify a wide range of rich instructions. Yet, the specification language can be enhanced easily (see sections 4.4 and 4.7).

Integration. Figure 3 shows how we integrate the rule creation step into an existing compiler (marked dark and light grey): We use the unmodified *compiler frontend* to transform the *instruction specification* to an *IR* graph (called *initial pattern*). This is possible because the specification consists of plain C code. The

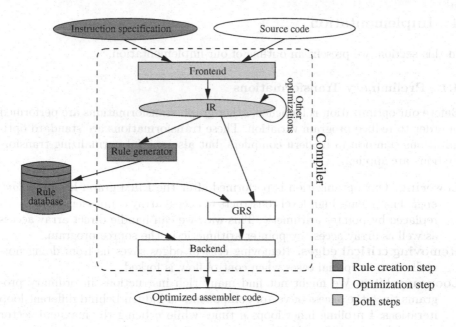

Fig. 3. Compiler integration

initial pattern is analyzed and then transformed to the pattern and replacement graph by the *rule generator*. The generated graph rewrite rules are saved in an appropriate format in a *rule database* to be used by the *GRS* in the optimization step. In addition, we need to tell the compiler backend about the newly introduced instruction. Therefore, we also generate annotations for the backend in order to be able to produce the right assembler code. All information needed is found in the initial pattern.

This rule creation step has to be performed only once when new rich instructions are introduced. After the *rule database* has been filled, it can be used to perform the optimization step.

3.2   Performing the Optimization

In the second step, we use the rules saved during the first step to perform the actual optimization (marked white and light grey in Figure 3). First we use the compiler frontend to transform the *source code* to an *IR* graph, on which we can perform pattern matching using the *GRS*. A subgraph found, representing a rich instruction, is called a *match*. Beyond pattern matching and replacement, there are further tasks to perform during the optimization step. Because we generate the pattern graph as general as possible to avoid being too restrictive, we have to test whether we're really allowed to replace a match before actually replacing it. During the rewrite, a new node representing the rich instruction is introduced. We have to schedule this node correctly, e.g. put it in the right basic block and serialize it correctly with regard to its memory dependency. We will discuss this more closely in Section 4.

4   Implementation

In this section, we present an outline of our implementation.

4.1   Preliminary Transformations

Before our optimization is launched, other graph transformations are performed in order to reduce program variation. These transformations are standard optimizations common in modern compilers, but also special normalizing transformations are applied:

Lowering. Our optimization is performed after the FIRM graph has been *lowered*. That means high-level constructs to access array components have been replaced by pointer arithmetic. This way, we can handle direct array access as well as array access by pointer arithmetic in the source program.

Removing critical edges. Removing critical edges saves us from doing normalization in special cases when control flow is forked.

Loop unrolling. We might not find many rich instructions in ordinary programs since the access of vector components is hidden behind different loop iterations. Unrolling inner loops n times while n being the maximal vector size might reveal those hidden instructions.

Load-Store optimization. An optimization which uses information returned by an alias analysis to eliminate unnecessary *Load* operations and deserializes memory accessing operations if possible. Therefore, a good alias analysis is essential for our needs. We use a so-called *memory disambiguator* built into our compiler [9].

Special normalizations. For example, arithmetic expressions used for address calculation are brought to a consistent form. Hofmann presented a way to normalize generic arithmetic expressions [10].

4.2   Matching

In this paragraph, we describe the pattern creation and pattern matching process more closely. We start with the initial pattern delivered by the compiler frontend. The initial pattern contains the operations of the specification's definition and behaviour part, whereas, for the pattern graph only the behaviour part is needed. We designed the instruction specification language in the way that all information the user specified can be regained from the initial pattern. To generate the pattern graph, we first extract all important information the user specified in the definition part and then clip the initial pattern by the nodes not needed any more.

The pattern graph now consists of the nodes representing the behaviour part. The names of the variables defined in the instruction specification are not important any more, because FIRM graphs satisfy the SSA property. That means each data flow edge represents a *value* and by matching the dataflow edges exactly we make sure that matches found in the host graph have identical behaviour as the pattern graph.

Matching the exact dataflow must not be confused with matching the statement-level control flow. We do not match the statement-level control flow because only the control flow between basic blocks is represented in FIRM. All possible control flows inside a basic block are implicitly given by the dataflow. This makes the pattern graph more general with regard to the source program to be optimized.

In section 2 we stated that we want to deal with program variation shown in Figure 2. The problem is the serialization of memory operations by memory edges. Our solution is not to match the memory dependency at all. Instead, we check the memory dependencies for consistency after finding a match. To do so, we take advantage of a feature of *GrGen* to be able to insert processing between matching and rewrite.

The initial pattern may contain *Load* and *Store* operations which represent an access to a vector register instead to a memory location, depending on the user specification. To insert this information explicitly into the graph, we introduce a new node type *VProj* representing a specific component of a vector register. The component number is given by a node attribute.

In general, *edge positions* are important in FIRM. That's because nodes represent operations and the operand order is very important for example for a *Sub* operation. Hence, we check edge position numbers exactly except for commutative operations like *Add* or *Mul* of integer type.

4.3 Replacement

At first glance, it seems obvious that inserting a new rich instruction after finding a match allows us to delete all the basic operations contained in that match. On closer examination we recognize that executing the basic operations might produce intermediate results not produced by the rich instruction. If operations outside the match use those intermediate results, the code that calculates them must not be deleted. Therefore, the nodes contained in the pattern graph are also included in the replacement graph, except for the end results also produced by the rich operation. Unnecessary basic instructions are deleted in a later step, when it turns out that their result is not used. This is done by standard compiler optimizations like the *Dead Node Elimination*, the *Control Flow Optimization* and *Load-Store Optimization* [11].

Figure 4 shows how the replacement works in general. The left hand side represents a match we found. It uses n operands—*Op 1* to *Op n*—and a set of basic *operations* to calculate a result vector of m components—*Res 1* to *Res m*. Now we want this match to be rewritten so that the corresponding new rich instruction is inserted and the program uses the result of the rich instruction.

This is shown on the right hand side which corresponds to the host graph after the rewrite. The rewrite step inserts a new node representing the rich instruction. The operands of the new instruction are already contained in the found match, so the rewrite step also connects the rich instructions to it's operands. The number of usages is not known at pattern creation time. In order to connect the results of the rich instruction, we would have to reroute an unknown number of edges,

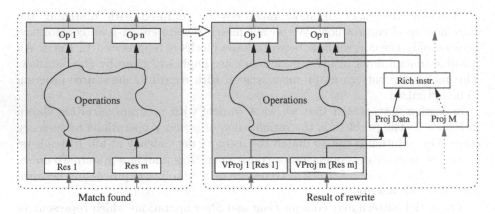

Fig. 4. Match found (left) and result graph (right)

which is hard to express with one single graph rewrite rule. To avoid this problem, we *retype* the previous result nodes to *VProj k* nodes, which indicate that this node represents the $k'th$ component of the result vector. Also, the retyped nodes are disconnected from their previous operands and connected with the result of the rich instruction. This way each node that previously used an end result calculated by basic instructions now uses an end result calculated by the rich instruction. A *VProj* node indicates, that the result of the rich instruction is passed in a vector register and if basic instructions want to use the result, some kind of code which transfers the results to general purpose registers has to be inserted.

After rewriting is finished, we have to perform further transformations which can not be expressed through the graph rewrite rule. At first, the new rich instruction has to be inserted into a certain basic block. We insert the rich instruction in the basic block which dominates all other basic blocks contained in the match because we want to make the results of the rich instruction available as soon as possible. This can not be done by the GRS since we can't know the exact basic block layout of the host graph at pattern creation time. It's important that the operands of the rich instruction are available *before* the rich instruction is scheduled. Otherwise a *deadlock* occurs which means that an operation was scheduled without its operands being available. We prevent deadlocks by analysing the host graph before rewriting and only apply a rule if it's safe to rewrite.

Secondly, we have to insert the rich instruction into the memory dependency chain. Again, to make the results of the rich instruction available early, we place it before any memory operation contained in the match. Please note, that this method prevents deadlocks but also introduces further issues: If the rich operation writes to a memory location it has already read by a *Load* node, then this *Load* is not allowed to have usages outside the match. The node that uses the *Load*'s result would receive an invalid value. To recognize this and similar cases, detailed analysis is necessary.

4.4 Priorities

Introducing *VProj* nodes makes graph rewrite rules dependent on each other. Consider, for example, rules for a *VectorLoad* and a *VectorStore* instruction. We assume that the *VectorStore* expects data located in a vector register, represented by several *VProj* nodes in the FIRM graph. The *VProj* nodes are not initially in the FIRM graph, they are produced by the *VectorLoad* graph rewrite rule. That's why the *VectorLoad* rule has to be applied before the *VectorStore* rule. To specify that, we introduce *priorities*. The user can assign a priority class to each rule and put rules depending on each other into ascending priority classes. Rules not depending on each other may remain in the same priority class. The syntax to assign an instruction to a priority class—e.g. 5—is

`Priority(5);`

4.5 Variants

As a result of loop unrolling, the values of vector components are often dependent on one or more induction variables which do not occur in the specification of the rich instruction. In this case, one or more additional summands have to be added to all parts of the pattern which calculate a memory address. We create variants for each additional summand. This way, we can even handle access to vector components which are located in multi-dimensional arrays.

4.6 Replacement Strategies

Having several graph rewrite rules at stock, the optimization has to apply these rules automatically. We want to apply the rules resulting in the maximal saving of costs according to a cost model. The saving of costs for each replacement can be pre-calculated by taking the costs of the operations to replace and the costs of the rich instruction into account. Dynamic costs occur when matched nodes can not be deleted because they deliver an intermediate result (see Section 4.3). The most problematic situation we have to deal with is overlapping matches.

Unfortunately, we can not locally decide which match to choose for replacement because we don't know which subsequent matches will follow and in which saving of costs this will result. One approach would be to replace one of the overlapping patterns and determine its cumulative costs and then use a *roll-back* function to re-establish the graph to try out the second pattern. Seeing how subsequent matches depend on *VProj* nodes, our approach is not to replace overlapping matches at first but only insert all the corresponding *VProj* nodes into the graph in parallel. Thus, subsequent matches can also be found in parallel, making a cost intensive rollback function unnecessary. This approach completely separates the pattern matching step from the rewrite step. All matches that can be found in an IR graph and their savings of costs are represented in a so-called *search tree*. A walk over the search tree selects all matches to be rewritten, thus resulting in an optimal solution according to our cost model. One problem when applying this explorative approach is that search trees can grow big. To reduce the size of the search tree, it's possible to build a search tree for each priority class only (see Section 4.4). This works fine for all our test programs and covers most, but not all, dependencies between rich instructions. Therefore, our current research is to use a heuristic PBQP[4]-solver for rule selection [12,13].

4.7 Clean-Up Operations

It might occur that there are still *VProj* nodes in the graph but no subsequent match can be found. The compiler backend however, cannot select code for *VProj* nodes. A solution to the problem is to perform an undo-operation which rolls back the last replacement(s) until no *VProj* nodes are present in the graph any more.

The other possibility is to convert the *VProj* nodes. This is not trivial because the value represented by a *VProj* node has to be extracted from a vector register and copied to a general purpose (GP) register. Some processor architectures (like SSE2) don't have dedicated instructions to do so[5].

This means that two instructions have to be performed: shifting and copying. This can easily be done using our specification language by declaring both instructions in the *Emit* statement separated by a line break. This way, a *virtual instruction node* is created representing both operations:

```
Emit(".⊔psrldq⊔$8,⊔%S0\n.⊔movq⊔%S0,⊔%D0");
```

This virtual instruction not only destroys the value contained in the destination register, but also the one contained in the source register. Therefore, the user can specify

```
Destroys(Operand);
```

to indicate that an operation also destroys the register which contains Operand besides the register where the result is stored.

5 Related Work

5.1 Algorithm Recognition

Metzger and Wen extensively present an approach to recognize algorithms in the so-called *computational kernel* of a program and replace them by a call to an optimized library function, thus saving execution time [14]. The optimization is carried out on an IR that has tree shape and which was used in the *Convex Application Compiler* [15]. Data structures used are the *control tree* containing the statements and the control flow. *Expression trees* are used to represent expressions and the *i-val tree* representing the dependencies of induction values of loops. Also the statement-level data flow graph is computed. To speed up

---

[4] Partitioned Binary Quadratic Problem.
[5] Only extracting single-word integer values is possible with SSE2 by using the pextrw instruction. A pextrd instruction is planned to be introduced with SSE4.

```
1  unsigned int sad(int test_blockx, int test_blocky, int *best_block_x,
2                   int *best_block_y, unsigned char frame[256][256])
3  {
4      int i, x, y, blocky, blockx;
5      unsigned tmp_diff, min_diff = 0xFFFFFFFF;
6
7      // Iterate over whole frame; x,y=coords of current block
8      for(x = 1; x < 256 - 16; x++)
9          for(y = 0; y < 256 - 16; y++) {
10             tmp_diff = 0;
11             // Compare current block with reference block
12             for(blocky = 0; blocky < 16; blocky++) {
13                 for(blockx = 0; blockx < 16; blockx++)
14                     if(frame[blocky][blockx] > frame[blocky + y][blockx])
15                         tmp_diff += (frame[blocky][blockx] - frame[blocky + y][blockx]);
16                     else
17                         tmp_diff += (frame[blocky + y][blockx] - frame[blocky][blockx]);
18             }
19
20             // Check if the current block is least different
21             if(min_diff > tmp_diff) {
22                 min_diff = tmp_diff;
23                 *best_block_x = x;
24                 *best_block_y = y;
25             }
26         }
27     }
28     return(min_diff);
29 }
```

pattern matching the control tree, expression trees and the i-val tree are converted into a *canonical form*. This is especially useful for handling commutative operators. The reordering of the tree is based on an encoding of nodes of the control tree. Metzger and Wen also explain how to extract subprograms from the computational kernel and select the best *feasible replacement* to gain maximal benefit.

We share the same idea that a database of pre-created patterns has to be maintained and even that these patterns should be created by specifying an algorithm in a high-level language. This makes it easy for the end-user to add new patterns and optimizations can be performed without modifying the source code. Reducing program variation to keep the number of patterns to maintain small using standard compiler optimizations amongst others is an idea found in both approaches. We also seek a (good or even the best) selection of replacements for the patterns we found in order to accelerate the program.

We differ in the form of IR we use: A graph-based IR with integrated data and control flow, instead of a tree based IR. Metzger and Wen claim to find and replace complete algorithms including loops while we want to find DAGs (direct acyclic graphs) representing the behaviour of rich instructions. They have to extract subprograms for comparison by reordering the statements in the control flow tree as allowed by the dataflow. We don't have this problem, because we don't consider the statement-level control flow. Our optimization is more back-end oriented since we don't replace patterns by function calls but by hardware dependent assembler instructions. Hence we have to deal with hardware specific features like register classes when specifying new patterns. We use a modern GRS to match patterns instead of transforming IR programs to a canonical form and comparing patterns node by node. Finally, Metzger and Wen only implemented the normalization process and did not implement the pattern matching process.

5.2 Previous Implementations

Hofmann implemented an early version of the optimization presented in this article [10], which was mainly a proof of concept of how automatic pattern creation works. This first implementation wasn't able to optimize realistic programs automatically, and hence no serious run-time tests were possible.

6 Benchmarks

We have tested our implementation on a Pentium 4 (Prescott), 3.2 GHz, which features the *Intel SSE3* instruction set. The system has 2 GB main memory and runs Suse Linux 9.3.

Our test program implements a *block-matching* algorithm to perform *motion estimation* used for MPEG compression in video codecs [16]. The block-matching algorithm operates on a frame of 256x256 bytes size and is performed 100 times.

The changes made to the host graph during optimization are presented in Table 1(a). The patterns found, and the assembler instructions applied, are shown

Table 1. Benchmark results

(a) Execution time and graph statistics

	standard opt.	rich instructions opt.	factor
# nodes	2392	680	3.52
# edges	5324	1480	3.60
running time	13.55 s	420 ms	Speedup: 32.26

(b) Rich instructions applied

pattern	applied	instructions	# nodes	# edges
VectorLoad_16b_v1	1x	lddqu	82	96
VectorLoad_16b_v3	1x	lddqu	84	128
SAD_16b	1x	psadbw pshudf paddd	289	461
Component_0Iu	1x	movd	3	2

in Table 1(b). Compared to compiling the program with conventional optimizations, we gain a maximal speedup of 32.26. Compared to programs compiled by the Intel C compiler, which also does hardware-specific optimizations, we still gain a speedup of 9.52. The whole optimization process took 1.2 seconds. *GrGen* spent only 40ms for matching 4480 nodes and 17853 edges and rewriting 4 matches. The rest of the time was spent for additional analysis and node elimination.

7   Conclusion

We have presented a novel optimization framework to speed up programs by using rich instructions. Our optimization works on the compiler internal IR and uses a GRS to find patterns representing rich instructions and automatically replaces them by a corresponding rich assembler instruction. The rules for the GRS are created automatically using a specification of the rich instruction's behaviour, based on the programming language C. Rules are selected automatically to receive the most efficient program according to a cost model. The optimization is integrated into an existing compiler.

The advantage is that source programs can be optimized without modification. Therefore, a source program stays portable and changing the compiler or the target architecture is still possible. In addition, the user can easily introduce new patterns for rich instructions without being a compiler engineer, because he can specify graph rewrite rules indirectly in a familiar language.

Validating our implementation with different test programs covering the fields video processing, sound processing and numerical calculations, showed that it outperforms traditional compilers, gaining speedup ranging from 1.05 to 32. Therefore, there is potential to optimize programs using rich instructions. The pattern matching core of the optimization, performed by the graph rewrite system *GrGen*, takes only milliseconds.

We haven't addressed rich instructions which require data to be specially aligned in memory, so far. When using such instructions, we have to test whether the data they access is aligned [17]. Additionally, we also need a good alias analysis. There are ways to support the alias analysis manually. E.g. the programmer could use the C qualifier `restrict` (C99) to indicate that a pointer has no alias. We're using an explorative algorithm to control rule application but are also researching on how a PBQP-solver could solve the problem more efficiently.

Acknowledgments. We thank all co-workers and students at the *IPD, Universität Karlsruhe* for their support and proof-reading, especially Christian Würdig, Christoph Hermann Mallon, Edgar Jakumeit, Gernot Veit Batz, Matthias Braun, Michael Beck, Moritz Kroll, and the anonymous reviewers. Also we thank Prof. Dr. Gerhard Goos for the generous support he provides at his chair.

References

1. Geiß, R., Kroll, M.: GrGen.NET: A Fast, Expressive, and General Purpose Graph Rewrite Tool. In: Schürr, A., Nagl, M., Zündorf, A. (eds.) AGTIVE 2007. LNCS, vol. 5088. Springer, Heidelberg (2008)
2. Geiß, R., Batz, G.V., Grund, D., Hack, S., Szalkowski, A.: GrGen: A Fast SPO-Based Graph Rewriting Tool. In: Corradini, A., Ehrig, H., Montanari, U., Ribeiro, L., Rozenberg, G. (eds.) ICGT 2006. LNCS, vol. 4178, pp. 383–397. Springer, Heidelberg (2006)
3. Batz, G.V.: Graphersetzung für eine Zwischendarstellung im Übersetzerbau. Master's thesis, Universität Karlsruhe (2005)
4. Intel Corporation, O. Box 5937, Denver, CO 80217-9808: Intel 64 and IA-32 Architectures Software Developer's Manual – Instruction Set Reference (2007)
5. Trapp, M., Lindenmaier, G., Boesler, B.: Documentation of the Intermediate Representation FIRM. Technical Report 1999-14, Universität Karlsruhe, Fakultät für Informatik (1999)
6. Cytron, R., Ferrante, J., Rosen, B.K., Wegman, M.N., Zadeck, F.K.: Efficiently Computing Static Single Assignment Form and the Control Dependence Graph. ACM Trans. Program. Lang. Syst. 13(4), 451–490 (1991)
7. Cooper, K.D., Torczon, L.: Engineering a Compiler. Morgan Kaufmann Publishers Inc., San Francisco (2004)
8. Motorola Phoenix, AZ, USA: AltiVec Technology Programming Environments Manual (1998)
9. Ghiya, R., Lavery, D., Sehr, D.: On the Importance of Points-To Analysis and Other Memory Disambiguation Methods for C Programs. In: Proceedings of the ACM SIGPLAN 2001 PLDI, pp. 47–58 (2001)
10. Hofmann, E.: Regelerzeugung zur maschinenabhängigen Codeoptimierung. Master's thesis, Universität Karlsruhe (2004)
11. Aho, A.V., Sethi, R., Ullman, J.D.: Compilers: Principles, Techniques, and Tools. Addison-Wesley, Reading (1986)
12. Eckstein, E., König, O., Scholz, B.: Code Instruction Selection Based on SSA-Graphs. In: Krall, A. (ed.) SCOPES 2003. LNCS, vol. 2826, pp. 49–65. Springer, Heidelberg (2003)
13. Jakschitsch, H.: Befehlsauswahl auf SSA-Graphen. Master's thesis, Universität Karlsruhe (2004)
14. Metzger, R., Wen, Z.: Automatic Algorithm Recognition and Replacement: A new Approach to Program Optimization. MIT Press, Cambridge (2000)
15. CONVEX Computer Corp. O. Box 5937, Denver, CO 80217-9808: CONVEX Application Compiler User's Guide, 2nd ed. (1992)
16. Intel Corporation: Block-Matching In Motion Estimation Algorithms Using Streaming SIMD Extensions 3. Technical report, Intel Corporation, O. Box 5937, Denver, CO 80217-9808 (2003)
17. Pryanishnikov, I., Krall, A., Horspool, N.: Pointer Alignment Analysis for Processors with SIMD Instructions. In: 5th Workshop on Media and Streaming Processors (2003)

Transforming Timeline Specifications into Automata for Runtime Monitoring*

Eric Bodden and Hans Vangheluwe

School of Computer Science
McGill University, Montréal, Québec, Canada

Abstract. In runtime monitoring, a programmer specifies code to execute whenever a sequence of events occurs during program execution. Previous and related work has shown that runtime monitoring techniques can be useful in order to validate or guarantee the safety and security of running programs. Those techniques have however not been incorporated in everyday software development processes. One problem that hinders industry adoption is that the required specifications use a cumbersome, textual notation. As a consequence, only verification experts, not programmers, can understand what a given specification means and in particular, whether it is correct. In 2001, researchers at Bell Labs proposed the Timeline formalism. This formalism was designed with ease of use in mind, for the purpose of static verification (and not, as in our work, for runtime monitoring).

In this article, we describe how software safety specifications can be described visually in the Timeline formalism and subsequently transformed into finite automata suitable for runtime monitoring, using our meta-modelling and model transformation tool AToM³. The synthesized automata are subsequently fed into an existing monitoring back-end that generates efficient runtime monitors for them. Those monitors can then automatically be applied to Java programs.

Our work shows that the transformation of Timeline models to automata is not only feasible in an efficient and sound way but also helps programmers identify correspondences between the original specification and the generated monitors. We argue that visual specification of safety criteria and subsequent automatic synthesis of runtime monitors will help users reason about the correctness of their specifications on the one hand and effectively deploy them in industrial settings on the other hand.

1 Introduction

Static program verification in the form of model checking and theorem proving has in the past been very successful, however mostly when applied to small embedded systems. The intrinsic exponential complexity of the involved algorithms makes it hard to apply them to large-scale applications. Runtime monitoring or runtime verification tries to find new ways to support automated verification

---

* An extended technical report version [1] of this paper is available at http://www.
sable.mcgill.ca/

A. Schürr, M. Nagl, and A. Zündorf (Eds.): AGTIVE 2007, LNCS 5088, pp. 249–264, 2008.

of such applications. This is done by combining declarative safety specifications with automated tools that allow verification of these properties, not statically but dynamically, when the program under test is executed. Research has produced a variety of such tools over the last years, many of which have helped find real errors in large-scale applications. Yet, those techniques have not yet been able to make the transition to everyday use in regular software development processes. This is due to two reasons. Firstly, many of the existing runtime monitoring tools cause a significant runtime overhead, lengthening test runs unduly. Secondly, the kind of specifications that can be verified by such tools often use a quite cumbersome notation. This leads to the fact that only verification experts, not programmers, can understand what a given specification means and in particular, whether it is correct.

The first problem of generating efficient runtime monitors has been addressed extensively in previous [3,4,5] and related [6,7] work. In particular, our research group maintains an efficient implementation of *tracematches* [8], an implementation of runtime monitoring that allows specifications to match on the dynamic execution trace, using regular expressions with free variables than can bind objects. For instance, a pattern of the form `File f: open(f) dispose(f)` over the alphabet $\Sigma = \{$`open,dispose`$\}$ could denote disposing a file that is currently open. Such a specification might seem easy to read, but sometimes subtle problems can arise. For example, the aforementioned pattern would also match the event sequence `open(f1) close(f1) dispose(f1)`, where a file `f1` is properly closed before it is disposed. In order to fix the pattern, one would have to change the alphabet of the regular expression to $\Sigma = \{$`open,close,dispose`$\}$. We strongly believe that such subtle difficulties with existing specification formalisms are among the main reasons why formal verification techniques such as runtime monitoring have, despite their effectiveness and efficiency, not yet found widespread industry adoption.

In 2001, Smith et al. from Bell Labs proposed the *Timeline* formalism as a way to ease the specification of temporal properties [9]. They presented a visual tool to design Timeline specifications. The tool converts those specifications into Büchi automata, suitable for static verification. However, this translation is done in code, and hence it is hidden from the user. We believe that the Timeline formalism is indeed much more comprehensible than many other temporal specification formalisms. However, we also believe that a tool can and should benefit from explicit visual graph rewriting techniques. Implementing formalism (such as Timeline) semantics via visual graph transformations allows (1) to easily experiment with different semantics by altering transformation rules and (2) once the semantics is fixed, to easily reason about its correctness. Hence, in the following, we propose an explicit visual graph transformation using the AToM^3 tool [10], that rewrites specifications in the Timeline formalism to corresponding finite state machines suitable for runtime monitoring. Those state machines can then be fed into our tracematch-based back-end, which generates an equivalent and efficient runtime monitor. This monitor can be applied to arbitrary Java programs through compilation.

It is also noted that Smith et al. did not take into account per-object specifications such as the per-file specification mentioned above. In this work we show how the Timeline formalism can be used for such specifications as well. The generated Java monitors automatically take into account the necessary object bindings, exploiting our performance optimizations from previous work.

The remainder of this paper is organized as follows. In Section 2 we introduce the Timeline formalism, its visual concrete syntax, and its semantics. The visual specification of transformation into finite automata is described in Section 3. In Section 4, we sketch how the resulting automata can be used in our runtime monitoring back-end. Finally, we conclude and state future work in Section 6.

2   The Timeline Formalism

Each Timeline specification consists of a single time line, which is independent of all the others. This is important, as it enabled modular reasoning. A time line makes sense in its own right and its truth value does not depend on the presence of other time lines.

Each time line represents an ordered sequence of events. The first event is a distinguished start event, representing the time of start-up of the application. All events but this start event are associated with a label and one of the following three event types.

regular event. Such an event may or may not occur. It imposes no requirement and is only used to build up context for a complete pattern match. Regular events are denoted with the letter **e**.

required event. A required event *must* occur, whenever its left-context on the time line was matched. Required events are denoted with the letter **r**.

fail events. A fail event *must not* occur after its left context has matched. Such an event is denoted with the letter **X**.

Along with those events, a time line can be augmented with constraints, restricting the matching process. A constraint holds a Boolean combination of propositions and may include or exclude the start and/or end event it is attached to.

While Smith et al. used a motivating example [9] specifying a dial-tone feature used at Bell labs, we here use a running example motivated by our own work. Fig. 1 shows an extension of the aforementioned file/dispose example. We wish to specify that a file must not be disposed as long as it is open. Furthermore, we would like to make sure that any open file is closed at some point in time, before the program exits. The Timeline specification directly states *both requirements together*: After seeing a *regular* event **open**, we *require* an event **close** (in the end of the time line) and in between we state that no **dispose** event may occur (excluded event, marked with an **X**). A constraint between the **open** and **dispose** events is used to state that those requirements only apply if the file has not been closed already prior to disposal. A second constraint on the left states that we are only interested in the last **open** event, as our translation will assure that former

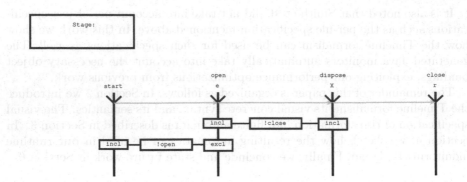

Fig. 1. Timeline specification stating that any opened file should be closed and should not be disposed before closing it

events were already handled once we get to this stage of evaluation. Fig. 1 shows the Timeline specification as it is denoted in a modelling environment built using AToM³ [10]. This environment uses the following abstract syntax in order to represent such specifications.

2.1   Timeline Abstract Syntax in AToM³

We model an event as an object with a string label and one of five types: *start*, *regular*, *required*, *fail* and *end*. The "end" event is artificial. It cannot be specified by the user and is only used within the translation to finite automata.

A time line consists of a sequence of events. The sequence is established via an ordering relation. A further relation between events describes the constraints among them. Each constraint is modelled as an edge between two events. It can include or exclude the event at its start and/or end. Furthermore it is labelled with a string label, stating the actual constraint expression.

Fig. 2 shows the class diagram for the abstract syntax of Timeline in AToM³. In addition to the aforementioned entities, it shows a *Stage* class. As we will explain in Section 3, we use a singleton object of this class for each Timeline specification to be able to implement its translation in a stateful way. This is a workaround because the version of AToM³ used did not yet support programmed graph rewriting.

The static semantics of the Timeline formalism imposes the following type checks on correct Timeline specifications. (see [9] for details)

1. Each time line must be fully connected by the Order relationship. In particular, this order is anti-symmetric, transitive and total.
2. In each time line, the smallest event in this relationship must be of type "start".
3. Each event must have at most one immediate predecessor and successor in this relationship.

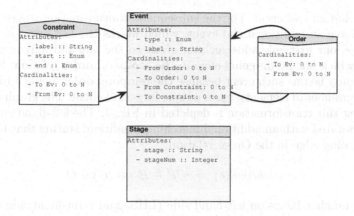

Fig. 2. Abstract syntax of the Timeline formalism in AToM³

4. When a constraint relation starts at an event e_1 and ends at e_2, then e_1 must be smaller than e_2 in the Order.
5. There must not exist any two subsequent fail events.
6. A constraint may not begin or end at a fail event, unless the fail event is the first event or last event of the time line.

The translation we give in Section 3 is based on the above assumptions. They can relatively easily be verified in the AToM³ modelling tool, at design time.

2.2 Timeline Concrete Syntax in AToM³

Each abstract syntax entity is given a concrete visual representation. Events are represented by vertical lines, while the temporal order relation between them is drawn as a directed edge. Constraints are undirected edges with labels. As Fig. 1 shows, AToM³ has built-in support for displaying attribute values of entities in a text box as of its visual representation.

3 Transformation into Finite Automata

We assume a given time line t which fulfils the constraints mentioned in Section 2.1. Further, we formally denote t by $t = (E, O, C)$ with:

- E, a finite set of events;
- $O \subset E \times E$, a total order, the temporal order relationship;
- C, a finite set of constraints.

Each event $e \in E$ is of the form $e = (l_e, t_e)$ with l_e a string label and

$$t_e \in \{start,\ regular,\ required,\ fail,\ end\}.$$

We then transform each Timeline specification into a finite state machine, using eight transformation stages that are executed in sequential order. In our model-driven approach, each of those stages is explicitly modelled by one or more graph grammar rules. In the following, we explain each stage in detail.

Stage 1 - Add an end event. For the subsequent transformation stages it will be useful to have an additional end event, which marks the last event in the time line. Hence, our first rule adds such an event to the one and only event of the time line which has no outgoing edge in the temporal order relation. Note that there can only be one such event because the temporal order, being a total order on a finite number of elements, has a unique largest element. The graph rewriting rule stating this transformation is depicted in Fig. 3. The left-hand side of this rule is annotated with an additional matching condition, stating that there may be no outgoing edge in the Order relation:

$$matchcond(e) := \neg\exists e' \in E . (e, e') \in O$$

Note how number labels on left-hand side (LHS) and right-hand side (RHS) of rules allow one to relate nodes on both sides. Labels present on both sides denote retained nodes, labels present only on the LHS denote deleted nodes, and labels present only on the RHS denote created nodes. On the LHS, <ANY> matches any attribute value. On the RHS, the notation <COPIED> denotes attribute copying from the LHS, <SPECIFIED> denotes an explicitly computed attribute.

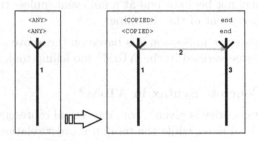

Fig. 3. Adding the artificial end event

Stage 2 - Add states. For each event we then generate a state which reflects the point in time immediately before the associated event occurs. We do so by using four different transformation rules, one each for regular, required and fail events plus one for the end event. We use multiple rules here, because the kind of state we generate depends on the event type.

The rules are shown in Fig. 4. For a regular event (marked with an **e**), we simply generate a non-final state. We add a generic edge between the event and the state to be able to relate them to each other in later transformation stages. AToM³ allows generic edges to connect any kind of nodes. Other connections are constrained by the formalism's meta-model. For a required event we generate a final state accordingly. This is because the generated state machine is meant to accept an input stream of events if and only if it *violates* the specification. Hence, in case the monitor has not seen a required event yet, it has to be in an accepting state. Similarly, for a fail event we actually add two states. The first one is non-final and reflects the point in time before the event occurs. The second

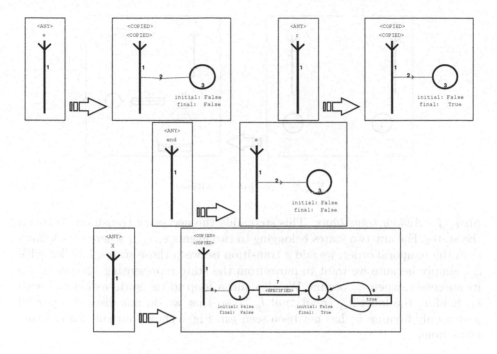

Fig. 4. Adding states

one is final and contains a *true* loop. This "sink" state has special semantics in the sense that it allows for early error detection: once it is visited, we know that the property is violated no matter what suffix of the trace will follow. The incoming transition to this state is labelled with l_e, the label of the matched event. We copy the value from the event label. Finally, the end event is treated as a regular event.

Stage 3 - Marking the initial state. In order to construct a valid finite automaton, we have to mark its initial state as initial. We identify this initial state as the unique state that is associated with the unique successor of the start event in the temporal order relation. The corresponding rule is shown in Fig. 5.

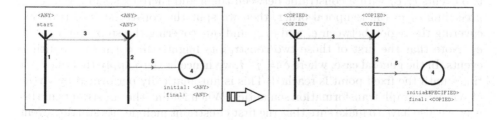

Fig. 5. Marking the initial state

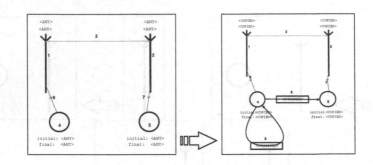

Fig. 6. Creating transitions

Stage 4 - Adding transitions. This step adds the necessary transitions between the states. For any two states belonging to two events e_i, e_{i+1} where e_{i+1} follows e_i in the temporal order, we add a transition between those states, labelled with l_{e_i}, simply because we want to move from the state representing "before e_i" to its successor, when l_{e_i} occurs. We also add a loop to the state associated with e_i, holding the label $!l_{e_i}$ (read "*not* l_{e_i}"), so that we do not discard a partial match only because l_{e_i} has not been seen *yet*. Fig. 6 shows our rule for creating transitions.

Stage 5 - Folding constraints. The automaton we now have associated with the original time line is already a valid finite automaton, equivalent to the time line, not taking constraints into account. Hence, the constraints are handled next. The idea is to copy constraints over from the time line onto the transitions of the resulting automaton. However, one problem still exists: a constraint may be linked to two states which are *not* immediate successors in the temporal order, i.e., between events e_i, e_j with $j - i > 1$. In such a case, the constraint also takes effect at all events $e_{i+1}, \ldots, e_{j-1}$, *even though* those are not directly connected to the constraint. In [9], Smith et al. propose a tableau based approach in order to calculate the constraints which apply to each single transition. We rather opted for a visual approach, which we find easier to understand and implement.

The rule we describe here resolves the transitive notion of a constraint by connecting all the intermediate events *explicitly* to an equivalent constraint. This is depicted in Fig. 7 and makes the above observation explicit: whenever we see two events e_i, e_j with a constraint between them and there exists an event e_{j-1} preceding e_j in the temporal order, then we split the constraint into two, one covering the region between e_i and e_{j-1} and one covering the step from e_{j-1} to e_j. Note that the first of those two constraints might still reach over multiple events. In the general case, where $\delta := j - i$, we hence have to apply this rule $\delta - 1$ times until the fixed point is reached. This is automatically performed by virtue of AToM^3's graph transformation semantics. When folding the constraints in this way, we also have to make sure that the first constraint includes its starting event only when the original constraint did so. Similarly, the second constraint must include its end event only if the original constraint did so. We hence copy over

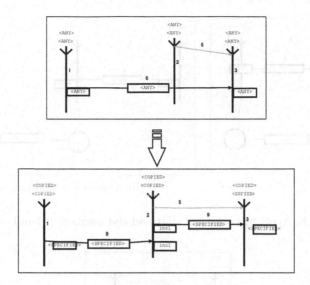

Fig. 7. Folding constraints

those properties. Fig. 7 reflects this by showing `<SPECIFIED>` at the appropriate labels. For the intermediate events it is clear that those have to be included. Hence, we set this property explicitly to that value.

Stage 6 - Applying the constraints. After having folded the constraints, we can safely assume that constraints only exist between immediate successor events e_i, e_{i+1}. This assumption provides us with a direct and local mapping between any two events, their associated constraints and states. In the following, we explain three different rules which are used to propagate the constraints onto the related transitions of the finite automaton.

Applying a constraint at its start point. The first rule is shown in Fig. 8(a) (we only show the left-hand side here, as the right-hand side has the same structure). Its purpose is to propagate a constraint from an included start event of a constraint to the corresponding transition. If a starting event e is included in a constraint c this means that we only accept this event (i.e., make progress in the automaton) if c holds when e occurs. Consequently, we propagate c from the left event onto the transition connecting the two associated states — the label of that transition changes from l to (l *and* c). We remind the reader that the left state of the two reflects the point in time before e was read and the right one the point in time after e was read. Also, we should mention that we made the rule match only if the constraint does not already exist at the target transition. This prevents AToM³ from applying the same rule repeatedly.

Applying a constraint at its end point. Similarly, we have to handle cases where the end point of a constraint is included. The rule in Fig. 8(b) shows how we

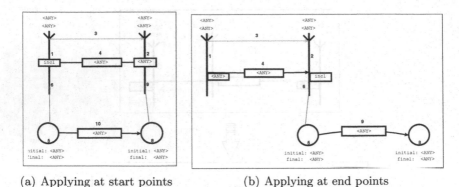

(a) Applying at start points   (b) Applying at end points

Fig. 8. Applying constraint start and end points (left-hand sides)

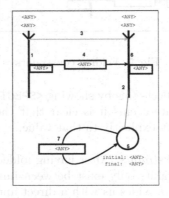

Fig. 9. Applying constraint bodies to the loops (left-hand side)

propagate the constraint label onto any transition moving out of the end state of the constraint, in case the right event is included in the constraint.

Applying a constraint to an interval. The "body" of the constraint, i.e., the part between its start point and end point finally has to be applied to the corresponding loop, since the loop — as is the case with the constraint — describes what behaviour is allowed *before* the next event occurs. The left-hand side of the equivalent transformation rule is shown in Fig. 9. For each such match we add the negation of the label of the constraint onto the label of the loop, which means that whenever the constraint is violated, we may *not* return to this state, i.e., in the absence of other matching transitions, the partial match is discarded.

Stage 7 - Implement semantics of fail events. The way we generated states for fail events does not yet exactly reflect the semantics given in [9]. In the current state machine, the scope of a fail event would extend until the end of the input instead of only until the event following the fail event. This means that we would falsely detect a violation if the fail event occurs *anywhere* on the remaining path.

However the semantics state that it only must not occur until the next regular (or required) event occurs. The rule shown in Fig. 10 depicts the appropriate change to implement the correct fail event semantics.

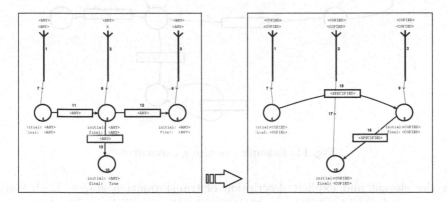

Fig. 10. Correcting the semantics of fail events

Assume that e is a fail event. We eliminate the state q_e, changing its incoming transition to have q_{e+1} as target state. The transition from q_e to the failure state q'_e is changed to start at q_{e+1}.

We wish to remind the reader that each state q_e in the automaton models the point in time right *before* event e was seen. Taking this into account, we can now see that after the transformation, the semantics are implemented correctly: when reading the event preceding e, we move to the state associated with the event following e directly, because this is the next event on our "progress path". Should in the meantime however, the fail event occur, then we move to the failure state.

Stage 8 - Removing the events. After all the previous steps we now have a finite automaton model which encodes the semantics of the original Timeline model. Hence, we can remove all event information. Here, it suffices to remove the events alone, because AToM³ automatically removes all (dangling) associated relations automatically. Consequently, we can simply implement this step by means of a rule with an unspecified event on the left-hand side and an empty right-hand side. Fig. 11 shows the result of the complete translation (steps 1 through 8) of our example from Fig. 1.

Stateful transformations, termination and correctness. In order to prevent unwanted recursive application of the different transformations, we had to make parts of the graph transformation model stateful, which means that we carry around an explicit state, giving information about what rule was last applied. This prevents for instance the rule for "adding transitions" being applied again after transitions have been removed by the correction step for the fail event semantics. We store the state in a visual label called "stage" as shown in Fig. 11. Future versions of AToM³ will support programmed graph rewriting, allowing

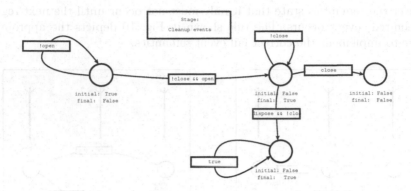

Fig. 11. Example - resulting automaton

for the elegant and explicit description of transformation stages. Each stage terminates due to implicit or explicit termination conditions. The folding of constraints, for instance, automatically reaches a fixed point when there is no constraint any more that spans more than two events. The propagation of constraint values, however, uses a hand-coded check as described above. With respect to correctness it is noted that a formal proof of transformation properties such as termination is out of the scope of this paper. Nevertheless, such a proof by structural induction over the different Timeline language constructs is quite straightforward.

4   Applicability to Runtime Monitoring

As mentioned earlier, the generated finite state machines can be used for the purpose of runtime verification. While Büchi automata, which are used for static verification, read an input of infinite length, the automata we use here accept a finite input. This is because in runtime verification a program is indeed executed and hence, every event sequence is terminated as the program shuts down.

As described in [8], our current implementation of *tracematches* generates finite-state monitors from regular expressions with free variables, where each variable is bound to matching objects at runtime. Hence, it is relatively easy to modify the back-end in such a way that it does not generate the finite state monitor from a given regular expression but instead reads it in directly. In tracematches, abstract events are mapped onto concrete events in the code via *pointcuts* in the aspect-oriented programming language AspectJ [11]. A pointcut in this setting is a predicate over runtime events.

Fig. 12 shows what such a state-based tracematch syntax could look like for our *file* example (automatic generation of this textual representation is future work). In its header in line 1, the tracematch declares to reason about a single file f. Lines 2-4 hold two user-defined symbols based on AspectJ pointcuts. The transition table for the tracematch automaton follows in lines 6-7. This part of the specification can be directly generated from the visual state machine model.

```
1  tracematch(File f) {
2      sym close after returning: call(* File.close ()) && target(f);
3      sym write before: call(* File.write (..))  && target(f);
4      sym dispose before: call(* File.delete ()) && target(f);
5
6      initial state 0; final state 1; final state 2;   //define  states
7      (0,open,1);  (1,dispose ,2);                     //define  transitions
8      { System.err.println ("State violation on file  "+f+"."); }
9  }
```

Fig. 12. Automaton-based tracematch checking for writes to closed files

Note that unreachable states do not show up. This is because we remove unproductive states from the automaton, still in the visual model. We refer to our technical report [1] for further details. Also, certain negated labels on transitions do not need to be copied due to the event-based semantics of tracematch automata. Line 8 finally holds the body of code that is to be executed on each single match. Note that this body has access to the bound variable of f, an important feature of tracematches.

5 User Experience with AToM³ Suggested Improvements of the Tool

In this section we briefly summarize our experience with using AToM³ as a tool for visual specification of modelling languages and model transformations. We highlight what worked for us but also needs for further improvements.

5.1 What Worked Well

The following worked very well.

Modelling with concrete syntax. The ability to describe both models and transformations, in concrete syntax is useful for domain experts. Indeed, we identified this as the number one reason for using visual graph transformations opposed to hand written code. With concrete syntax, the transformation becomes visually explicit to the modeller. It is straightforward to picture the effects of a transformation in one's mind, because this transformation can directly be *seen* already in the transformation rules themselves.

Large productivity increase. In [9] the original creators of the Timeline formalism reported that they spent about one month on implementing a modelling environment for Timeline. Using AToM³ we were able to achieve the same task in less than three days. A more experienced user of AToM³ would probably have been able to finish the implementation in an even smaller amount of time. Furthermore, because in AToM³ the semantics are implemented via visual graph transformation rules, this implementation will easily allow us to experiment with different semantics, by just modifying the rewrite rules accordingly.

5.2   Suggestions for Improvements

We believe that although our overall user experience with AToM^3 was highly satisfying, the following issues remain.

Negative application conditions. In many instances *negative application conditions* (NACs) would have been very useful to prevent a rule from applying in certain situations. The Montréal version of AToM^3 we used allowed such conditions only in hand coded form, via inserting Python code. Note that the Madrid version of AToM^3 does have support for NACs.

Programmed graph rewriting was lacking. In addition, we had to insert the aforementioned "Stage" label into each of our visual specifications. This label was then used to keep track of the current rewriting phase in order to schedule the rewriting correctly. The actual scheduling was again written in Python code. *Programmed graph rewriting* is a solution to this problem as put forward by the PROGRES [12] model transformation tool. Recent AToM^3 developments [13] presented at AGTIVE do support programmed graph rewriting.

Copying/computation of labels not visually explicit. We further found that the way in which labels are copied from one model object to another should be more visually explicit. As our figures show, AToM^3 currently only shows <SPECIFIED> at labels where values are explicitly specified. In our opinion it would help if the labels that are specified to be copied there were displayed. A color-coding scheme could enhance user experience further.

Static semantics were hard to specify. Often the programmer of a graph transformation might wish to specify rules that check the static semantics of a given visual model. For instance in our case we wanted to make sure that the "Order" relationship is a total ordering, without cycles. In AToM^3 we had to program this check manually in Python code. However for future versions we envision a more explicit mechanism in the form of negative application conditions that are evaluated not at transformation time but rather when the model is saved. In our particular case, the user could draw a circular dependency with the "Order" relation. The semantics would then demand that this pattern may not match when the validity of a given model is evaluated. Note that PROGRES [12] has some limited support for static checks of that kind.

Layouting not yet optimal. We found the layout algorithms in AToM^3 to be suboptimal. Although in general best effort is made by the AToM^3 modelling environment, it still happens that nodes or edges overlap. Even in cases where no overlapping occurs, objects might be arranged in a way that to the tool user hardly makes sense. For instance in the case of Timeline, the time line should really be a line, with arrows starting on the left and ending to the right. There should be layout algorithms available which take such constraints into account. Maier and Minas have devised a generic layout algorithm for meta-model based editors [14] which promises to mitigate some of those problems.

6 Conclusion and Future Work

In this work we have shown that it is feasible to visually specify the transformation from the Timeline temporal specification formalism to finite automata suitable for runtime monitoring. The resulting automata can directly be used to generate efficient finite-state monitors for Java programs using an existing back-end for tracematches [8].

We believe that this explicit way of transforming specifications to monitors facilitates reasoning about and debugging of specifications. In particular, our translation is completely visual and provides a one-to-one mapping between entities in the Timeline specification and the resulting finite automaton. We plan to express this bi-directional relationship (i.e., backward trace-ability) between Timeline and finite automata in the form of Triple Graph Grammars [15]. These allow for the declarative specification of consistency relationships between graphs. This will enable us to easily relate errors at execution level to constraints in the original Timeline specification. We believe that our approach is yet another stepping stone on our path to bringing temporal specifications and runtime monitoring closer to widespread industry adoption.

In future work, we also plan to give a formal description of the actual tracematch code and how it is generated from the obtained finite state machines. We also wish to study the scalability of temporal specification formalisms with respect to the size of the pattern that needs to be specified. Last but not least, we want to apply our approach to real-world applications, for instance parts of the DaCapo benchmark suite [16].

Acknowledgements. We wish to thank the anonymous reviewers for their pertinent comments. Further we thank the organizers of AGTIVE for making this symposium an unforgettable event. Last but not least, the first author wished to express his gratitude towards the Deutsche Forschungsgemeinschaft (DFG) and the AGTIVE steering committee for the awarded travel grant. The second author acknowledges partial support of this work by the Canadian National Sciences and Engineering Research Council.

References

1. Bodden, E., Vangheluwe, H.: Transforming Timeline specifications into automata for runtime monitoring (extended version). Technical Report SABLE-TR-2008-1, Sable Research Group, School of Computer Science, McGill University, Montréal, Québec, Canada (February 2008)
2. 1st to 7th Workshop on Runtime Verification (RV 2001 - RV 2007) (2001-2007), http://www.runtime-verification.org/
3. Avgustinov, P., Tibble, J., Bodden, E., Lhoták, O., Hendren, L., de Moor, O., Ongkingco, N., Sittampalam, G.: Efficient trace monitoring. Technical Report abc-2006-1 (March 2006), http://www.aspectbench.org/
4. Avgustinov, P., Tibble, J., de Moor, O.: Making trace monitors feasible. SIGPLAN Not. 42(10), 589–608 (2007)

5. Bodden, E., Hendren, L.J., Lhoták, O.: A staged static program analysis to improve the performance of runtime monitoring. In: Ernst, E. (ed.) ECOOP 2007. LNCS, vol. 4609, pp. 525–549. Springer, Heidelberg (2007)
6. Martin, M., Livshits, B., Lam, M.S.: Finding application errors using PQL: a program query language. In: Proceedings of the 20th Annual ACM SIGPLAN Conference on Object-Oriented Programming, Systems, Languages and Applications, pp. 365–383 (2005)
7. Fink, S., Yahav, E., Dor, N., Ramalingam, G., Geay, E.: Effective typestate verification in the presence of aliasing. In: ISSTA 2006: Proceedings of the 2006 international symposium on Software testing and analysis, pp. 133–144. ACM Press, New York (2006)
8. Allan, C., Avgustinov, P., Christensen, A.S., Hendren, L., Kuzins, S., Lhoták, O., de Moor, O., Sereni, D., Sittampalam, G., Tibble, J.: Adding Trace Matching with Free Variables to AspectJ. In: Object-Oriented Programming, Systems, Languages and Applications, pp. 345–364. ACM Press, New York (2005)
9. Smith, M.H., Holzmann, G.J., Etessami, K.: Events and Constraints: A Graphical Editor for Capturing Logic Requirements of Programs. In: Proceedings of the 5th IEEE International Symposium on Requirements Engineering, pp. 14–22 (2001)
10. de Lara, J., Vangheluwe, H.: AToM^3: A tool for multi-formalism and meta-modelling. In: Kutsche, R.-D., Weber, H. (eds.) FASE 2002. LNCS, vol. 2306, pp. 174–188. Springer, Heidelberg (2002)
11. Kiczales, G., Hilsdale, E., Hugunin, J., Kersten, M., Palm, J., Griswold, W.G.: An overview of AspectJ. In: Knudsen, J.L. (ed.) ECOOP 2001. LNCS, vol. 2072, pp. 327–353. Springer, Heidelberg (2001)
12. Schürr, A.: Developing Graphical (Software Engineering) Tools with PROGRES. In: International Conference of Software Engineering, pp. 618–619 (1997)
13. Syriani, E., Vangheluwe, H.: Programmed Graph Rewriting with DEvS. In: Schürr, A., Nagl, M., Zündorf, A. (eds.) AGTIVE 2007. LNCS, vol. 5088. Springer, Heidelberg (2008)
14. Maier, S., Minas, M.: A Generic Layout Algorithm for Meta-model based Editors. In: Schürr, A., Nagl, M., Zündorf, A. (eds.) AGTIVE 2007. LNCS, vol. 5088. Springer, Heidelberg (2008)
15. Schürr, A.: Specification of Graph Translators with Triple Graph Grammars. In: Mayr, E.W., Schmidt, G., Tinhofer, G. (eds.) WG 1994. LNCS, vol. 903, pp. 151–163. Springer, Heidelberg (1995)
16. Blackburn, S.M., Garner, R., Hoffman, C., Khan, A.M., McKinley, K.S., Bentzur, R., Diwan, A., Feinberg, D., Frampton, D., Guyer, S.Z., Hirzel, M., Hosking, A., Jump, M., Lee, H., Moss, J.E.B., Phansalkar, A., Stefanović, D., VanDrunen, T., von Dincklage, D., Wiedermann, B.: The DaCapo benchmarks: Java benchmarking development and analysis. In: OOPSLA 2006: Proceedings of the 21st annual ACM SIGPLAN conference on Object-Oriented Programing, Systems, Languages, and Applications, pp. 169–190. ACM Press, New York (2006)
17. Schürr, A., Nagl, M., Zündorf, A. (eds.): AGTIVE 2007. LNCS, vol. 5088. Springer, Heidelberg (2008)

Visualization, Simulation and Analysis of Reconfigurable Systems*

Claudia Ermel[1] and Karsten Ehrig[2]

[1] Institut für Softwaretechnik und Theoretische Informatik
Technische Universität Berlin, Germany
claudia.ermel@tu-berlin.de
[2] Department of Computer Science
University of Leicester, UK
karsten@mcs.le.ac.uk

Abstract. Meta-modeling is well known to define the basic concepts of domain-specific languages in an object-oriented way. Based on graph transformation, an abstract meta-model may be enhanced with information on concrete visualization of objects and relations, and the language syntax is defined by a graph grammar. Moreover, graph transformation can also formalize the semantic aspects of models, thus providing a basis for model validation by simulation.

Apart from editing and simulating the behavior of a system, there may be necessary reconfiguration operations which change the underlying system structure at runtime. In this paper, we focus on the interrelation of simulation and reconfiguration operations using formal verification techniques based on graph transformation. Our approach is demonstrated by the definition of a domain-specific language for building, simulating and reconfiguring small railway systems, using the TIGER tool environment. For further verification, we define a model transformation from the railway domain to Petri nets.

Keywords: Graph transformation, model transformation, reconfigurable system, visualization, simulation, analysis.

1 Introduction

Domain-specific modeling (DSM) aims to model a system at the same level of abstraction with the domain itself. This reduces mental mapping by moving the modeling language closer to the domain as perceived by designers, and improves the model quality compared to using generic modeling languages. The disadvantage of DSM is that for each domain a different visual modeling tool is needed. Here, meta CASE tools can help (like e.g. *MetaEdit+* [1]), which generate e.g. a visual editor on the basis of a definition of the visual domain-specific language.

---

* This work has been partially sponsored by the IST-2005-16004 Integrated Project SENSORIA (Software Engineering for Service-Oriented Overlay Computers).

A. Schürr, M. Nagl, and A. Zündorf (Eds.): AGTIVE 2007, LNCS 5088, pp. 265–280, 2008.

Two main approaches to visual language definition can be distinguished: grammar-based approaches or meta-modeling. Using graph grammars [4], multi-dimensional representations are described by graphs. This allows not only a visual notation of the concrete syntax, but also a visualization of the abstract syntax. While the concrete syntax contains the concrete layout of a visual notation, the abstract syntax abstracts from the layout and provides a condensed representation to be used for further processing, e.g. behavior simulation or system reconfiguration. Graph rules are used to manipulate the graph representation of a language element. Meta-modeling (see e.g. [2]) is also graph-based, but uses constraints instead of a grammar to define a visual language. While visual language definition by graph grammars can borrow a number of concepts from classical textual language definition, this is not true for meta-modeling.

Graph transformation can also formalize the semantic aspects of models. There are numerous formal graph-transformation-based semantics definitions [3]. In this paper, we use graph transformation not only to construct and visualize domain-specific visual models, but also to simulate dynamic model behavior. Apart from operations for editing, there may be necessary operations to change the underlying system structure at runtime (i. e. during simulation). Systems allowing to be changed have become an important topic in recent years since the adaption of a system to a changing environment plays a significant role e. g. in computer supported cooperative work, multi agent systems or mobile networks. In our approach, such reconfiguration operations are modeled by *reconfiguration rules*, and the corresponding systems are called *reconfigurable systems*.

As running example, we model a toy railway system. The visualization shows different kinds of tracks and switches which can be glued at connection points. Simulation rules allow to move a train to an adjacent track, respecting the switch modes. Reconfiguration rules allow to toggle between two modes of a switch. Graph transformation as a formally defined calculus [4] offers well-founded theoretical results that support the formal reasoning about graph-based models at all levels. We apply formal graph transformation techniques to reason about the independence of simulation and reconfiguration steps. For further verification, we define a model transformation from the railway system language to Petri nets. We apply the TIGER environment [5] for generating visual editor plug-ins in ECLIPSE [6] from graph grammars. TIGER is based on the graph transformation engine and analysis tool AGG [7].

The paper is structured as follows: Section 2 reviews the concepts for the graph-grammar based definition of visual languages, demonstrated by a domain-specific language to model small railway systems. In Section 3, concepts for simulation and reconfiguration of discrete-event systems by graph transformation are discussed, and the railway system is coming to life by operations for moving trains and changing switch modes. Section 4 applies verification techniques to analyze the interrelation of reconfiguration and simulation steps. Furthermore, a model transformation to Petri nets is defined, which allows to verify further dynamic system properties.

2   Defining Visual Domain-Specific Languages

Meta-modeling uses UML class diagrams to model a visual languages abstract syntax (see e.g. the MOF approach by the OMG [2]). While class diagrams appear to be more intuitive than graph grammars, they are also less expressive. Therefore, meta-modeling additionally uses context conditions to overcome the weaker expressive power. In the MOF approach, for instance, the Object Constraint Language (OCL) is used for this purpose. The advantage of meta-modeling is that UML users, who probably have basic UML knowledge, do not need to learn a new external notation to be able to deal with syntax definitions. Graph grammars are more constructive, i.e. closer to the implementation, and provide a formal basis for visualizing, validating and verifying model behavior. Hence, in our TIGER approach, we combine the visual definition of domain-specific languages by meta-modeling, and the definition of editing operations by graph transformation rules.

2.1   Graph Transformation

The main idea of graph grammars and graph transformation is the rule-based modification of graphs where each application of a graph transformation rule leads to a graph transformation step. Graph grammars can be used on the one hand to generate graph languages, and on the other hand to model state changes (operational behavior). Meanwhile, graph transformation has been investigated as a fundamental concept for programming, specification, concurrency, distribution, visual modeling and model transformation [4,8].

The core of a graph transformation rule $(LHS \xrightarrow{p} RHS)$ is a pair of graphs (LHS, RHS), called left-hand side and right-hand side, and an injective (partial) graph morphism $p : LHS \to RHS$. Applying the rule $(LHS \xrightarrow{p} RHS)$ means to find a match of LHS in the source graph and to replace this matched part in the source graph by the corresponding RHS, thus transforming the source graph into the target graph of the graph transformation.

Especially for the application of graph transformation techniques to visual language (VL) modeling, *typed attributed graph transformation systems* [4] have proven to be an adequate formalism. A VL is modeled by a type graph capturing the definition of the underlying visual alphabet, i.e. the symbols and relations which are available. Sentences or diagrams of the VL are given by graphs typed over (i.e. conforming to) the type graph. Such a VL type graph corresponds closely to a meta model. In order to restrict the visual sentences to valid visual models, a syntax graph grammar is defined, consisting of a set of language-generating graph transformation rules, typed over the abstract syntax part of the VL type graph. The rules describe editing operations which lead to the construction of valid visual models only.

Intuitively, the application of rule p to graph G via a match m from LHS to G deletes the image $m(LHS)$ from G and replaces it by a copy of the right-hand side $m^*(RHS)$. Note that a rule may only be applied if the so-called *gluing condition* is satisfied, i.e. the deletion step must not leave *dangling edges*, and for two objects which are identified by the match, the rule must not preserve one of them and delete the other one.

Definition 1 (Graph Transformation). *Let* $(LHS \xrightarrow{p} RHS)$ *be a typed graph transformation rule and* G *a typed graph with a typed graph morphism* $LHS \xrightarrow{m} G$, *called match. A graph transformation step* $G \xRightarrow{p,m} H$ *from* G *to a typed graph* H *via rule* p, *match* m, *and co-match* m^* *is shown in the diagram to the right.*
The rule r *may be extended by a set of negative application conditions (NACs) [9,4]. A match* $LHS \xrightarrow{m} G$ *satisfies a NAC with the injective NAC morphism* $n : LHS \rightarrow NAC$, *if there is no injective graph morphism* $NAC \xrightarrow{q} G$.

$$NAC \xleftarrow{n} LHS \xrightarrow{r} RHS$$

A sequence $G_0 \Rightarrow G_1 \Rightarrow ... \Rightarrow G_n$ *of graph transformation steps is called* graph transformation *and denoted as* $G_0 \xRightarrow{*} G_n$.

The language of a graph grammar consists of the graphs that can be derived from the start graph by applying the transformation rules.

Although we do not define the attribution concept for graphs formally in this paper (see [4] for a complete definition of the theory), we use node attributes in our examples, e.g. text for the names of nodes, or integers for their positions. This allows us to perform computations on attributes in our rules and offers a powerful modeling approach.

2.2   Type Graph and Syntax Rules for a Railway System

Using graph transformation, a *type graph* defines the visual alphabet, i.e. the symbols and symbol relations of a visual language. Layout information is integrated in the type graph by special shape types connected to symbol nodes, and by constraints on the relations of visual representations. The shape types include information about the symbol's shape (any kind of graphical figure or line), and the constraints establish certain visual relations (like "The shape for this symbol type is always glued to the shape for another symbol type," or "The shape for this symbol type has always a minimal size of ...").

Fig. 1 shows the definition of the type graph of our domain-specific language for building railway systems (without trains so far) in TIGER *(Transformation-based Generation of Environments)* [5,10], a visual editor generation tool. In the upper editor, we see the abstract syntax type graph with symbol types like Track, End and Buffer. For each type variant, a child inheriting from the corresponding abstract type is added to the type graph (e.g. StraightH for a horizontal straight track, Bend1 for a bend which is curved up-left/right-down, and HL for a track End which is the gluing point gluing two tracks at the first track's horizontal-left side). Note that the nodes in the abstract syntax type graph contain layout positions (x, y: int) allowing the editing rules to set the position of the corresponding figures in the editor accordingly. In the lower part of Fig. 1, editors for shape types are shown, depicting the visualization of different track types and the Buffer type.

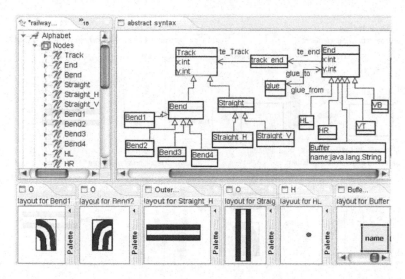

Fig. 1. Type Graph for the Domain-Specific Railway Language

A type graph together with a syntax graph grammar is used as high-level visual specification mechanism for VLs. The grammar restricts the allowed visual sentences conforming to the type graph to the meaningful ones. Grammar rules define syntactical editing operations. Such an operation is modeled as a graph rule typed over the VL type graph being applied to the syntax graph of the current diagram. Thus, only such syntactical changes are allowed which are described by a syntax rule and which result again in a valid VL diagram. An editing operation (i.e. the application of a syntax rule) results in a corresponding change of the internal abstract syntax graph of the diagram and the layout positions of the corresponding symbols.

Fig. 2 shows four of the syntax rules for the railway VL. Rule newStraightH produces an unconnected track, the other rules add tracks, switches and buffers by gluing them to tracks which already exist in the model. Numbers $(m = ..)$ at objects indicate mappings from a rule's LHS to its RHS. Input parameters (objects to be identified for the match by mouse click) are indicated by numbers $(in = ..)$ in a rue's LHS. NACs (not depicted) forbid gluing tracks to tracks at endpoints where already other tracks are glued. Positions relating objects to each other are defined in each rule's properties view.

A visual language (VL) definition based on a type graph and a set of syntax rules is used in TIGER to generate a corresponding visual editor. TIGER combines constructive VL specification using graph transformation with sophisticated graphical editor development features offered by the ECLIPSE Graphical Editing Framework (GEF) [11]. The execution of editor commands available in the generated editor correspond to the application of syntax rules to the underlying abstract syntax graph of a diagram. The rule application is performed by the graph transformation engine AGG [7]. TIGER extends AGG by a concrete visual syntax definition for flexible means for visual model representation. From

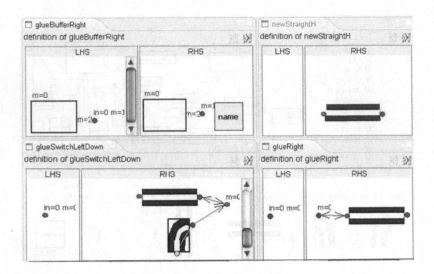

Fig. 2. Syntax Rules for the Railway Language

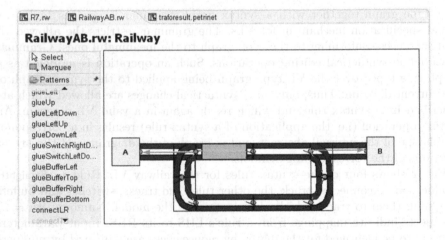

Fig. 3. TIGER-generated Visual Editor for the Railway Language

the definition of the VL, the TIGER *Generator* generates Java source code. The generated Java code implements an ECLIPSE visual editor plug-in based on GEF which makes use of a variety of GEF's predefined editor functionalities. Layout information (e.g. color, shape, and size, ..) are coded in the corresponding GEF editor classes. Fig. 3 shows the graphical user interface of the railway editor generated by TIGER from the VL specification consisting of the railway type graph similar to the one in Fig. 1, but now also allowing to edit train symbols (light-blue rectangles), and a railway syntax grammar. Basic editor operations are available in the tool palette on the left-hand side, or by the context menu which offers a list of operations depending on the selected symbol type.

3   Validation by Simulation

If a visual language models dynamic aspects of systems, visual simulation is inter-esting. Usually, a prerequisite for simulation is a (slight) extension of the visual language such that different execution states can be distinguished. In the case of our railway system, this is the addition of trains. Simulation then is specified by a set of *simulation rules*, typed over the extended VL type graph. The simulation rules specify the possible simulation steps (e.g. train movements) which do not change the underlying system structure. A sequence of simulation steps is called *simulation run* or *simulation scenario*. In general, we have non-determinism in simulation in the sense that there are more than one rules applicable at more than one possible matches. Up to now, TIGER supports stepwise simulation only, i.e. the user selects an applicable rule from the rule palette, and defines the match by clicking on relevant objects in the editor panel.

Fig. 4 shows the abstract syntax of the railway simulation rules. The first rule allows to add a train to a track, thus determining how many trains are distributed initially on which tracks in the railway system. The NAC (drawn as crossed-out part in the LHS) specifies that there must not be another train on this track. The second rule has to be applied after the first one, and models the movement of a train to the next track. Note that using the abstract nodes of type Track and Train, we only need one abstract rule for moving trains. Again, the NAC makes sure that the rule is only applied if there is not yet another train on the target track.

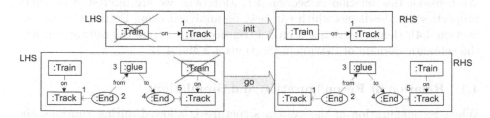

Fig. 4. Simulation Rules for Initial Train Distribution and for Train Movements

In railway simulation not only the position of trains is changing, but also the underlying net topology is adapted when a switch is changing its mode. In our approach, such reconfiguration operations are modeled by *reconfiguration rules*. Simulation and reconfiguration rules may be applicable to the same system states. In our railway system, changing the modes of switches is realized by applying a reconfiguration rule. A switch consists of two tracks (one bend and one straight track) and may be crossed by a train in only one way. The directions a train is allowed to go are modeled by the glue edges connecting track end points. The reconfiguration rule switch is shown in the top row of Fig. 5, and the effect of its application (a transformation step changing the mode of a sample switch) is shown in the bottom row of Fig. 5, where the match mapping of the track end points is indicated by corresponding numbers. In the concrete syntax, a green arrow indicates the current switch mode.

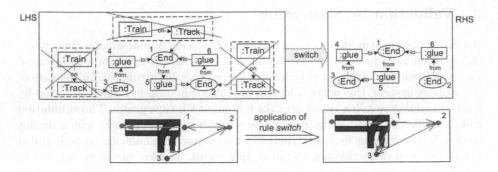

Fig. 5. Reconfiguration Rule realizing Switch Modes

4   Analysis

The aim of analyzing the railway specification is to avoid unsafe states in the simulation. For example, we would like to be sure that

(i) there are never more than one trains on a track,
(ii) a switch can only change its mode when there is no train on it.

In order to check condition (ii), we have to relate a reconfiguration operation (changing the switch mode) and a simulation operation (moving a train). We consider this relation in Section 4.1. Moreover, we are interested in safety properties like deadlocks which can best be analyzed using Petri net tools (see Section 4.4). Hence, we define a model transformation from the railway VL into the semantic domain of Petri nets (Sections 4.2 and 4.3).

4.1   Relation of Reconfiguration and Simulation

When reconfiguration of the system structure is allowed during runtime, the question arises under which conditions a simulation step is independent of a reconfiguration step, i.e. can the two transformations starting from the same system state be applied in any order, leading to the same result. The Local Church-Rosser Theorem for graph transformation systems [4] states that, for two parallel independent graph transformations $G \overset{p_1,m_1}{\Longrightarrow} H_1$ and $G \overset{p_2,m_2}{\Longrightarrow} H_2$, there is a graph G' together with graph transformations $H_1 \overset{p_2,m_2'}{\Longrightarrow} G'$ and $H_2 \overset{p_1,m_1'}{\Longrightarrow} G'$. In our case, we need to analyze the parallel independence of rules belonging to two different rule sets (simulation and reconfiguration rules). To this end, we use the automatic *critical pair analysis* offered by AGG, where rule pairs are analyzed to find out critical pairs of rule matches. Each parallel dependent transformation is an extension of a critical pair. The result of the critical pair analysis applied to the reconfiguration rule switch and the simulation rule go yields e.g. the critical pair shown in Fig. 6.

Analyzing this pair, we see that reconfiguration rule switch cannot be applied if simulation rule go has been applied before and has been moving a train onto

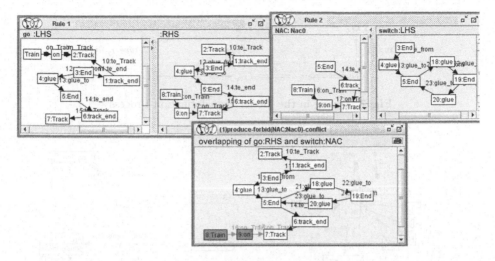

Fig. 6. Critical Pair Analysis of Railway Simulation and Reconfiguration

a track which is part of the switch, because the NAC of rule switch forbids to reconfigure switches with trains on it. Here, we have a so-called *produce-forbid* conflict, where one rule produces an object which is forbidden in the match of the other rule. Applying critical pair analysis to the reconfiguration rule switch and the other simulation rule init yields a similar conflict. Both conflicts together confirm that condition (ii) is valid for all possible railway models. Here, conflict detection is used to analyze safety conditions. Analogously, critical pair analysis of both simulation rules can be performed to check condition (i).

4.2   Model Transformation from Railway Models to Petri Nets

In this section we present a model transformation from the railway system to Petri nets with the aim to use Petri net analysis and verification techniques to analyze the railway behavior. Surely, only a limited class of simulation problems is sufficiently "Petri net like" to allow transformation of the more powerful graph rewriting model into Petri nets. Here, the distinction of simulation rules and reconfiguration rules helps to find the part of the system which behaves "Petri net like" (e.g. the trains moving along the tracks), and which can be analyzed using Petri net techniques.   The other parts describe reconfiguration operations (e.g. adding tracks or changing switches) and rather correspond to changes of the Petri net structure, but not to Petri net firing behavior.

Model transformations between visual languages is defined in our approach by graph transformation rules, as well. We transform the abstract syntax graph of a source model (e.g. a railway system state) by applying transformation rules resulting in the abstract syntax graph of the target model (e.g. a state of a Petri net). The abstract syntax of source and target models are specified by the type graphs TG_S and TG_T. A model transformation is defined by a graph transformation system $GTS = (TG, P)$ consisting of type graph TG and a set

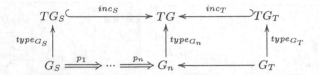

Fig. 7. Typing in the Model Transformation Process

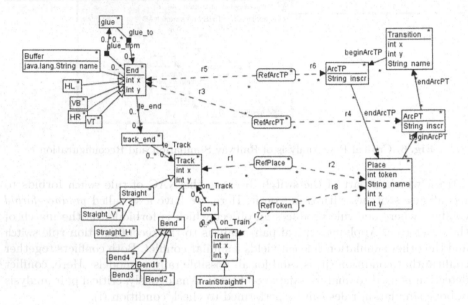

Fig. 8. Type Graph for the Model Transformation *Railway2Petri*

of TG-typed model transformation rules P, where both type graphs TG_S and TG_T have to be subgraphs of TG (see Fig. 7). The model transformation starts with the abstract syntax graph G_S of the source model. As TG_S is a subgraph of TG, G_S is also typed over TG. Please note that TG may contain not only TG_S and TG_T, but also additional types and relations which are needed for the transformation process.

After application of all model transformation rules P as long as possible, the resulting graph G_n is typed over TG, but not yet over the type graph TG_T of the target language. In order to delete all items in G_n which are not typed over TG_T we apply a restriction construction, which restricts G_n to those objects typed over TG_T. The model transformation process is visualized in Fig. 7.

Fig. 8 shows the type graph TG for the model transformation from railway systems to Petri nets. TG relates elements of the source type graph for railway systems (see Fig. 1) to elements of the target type graph for Petri nets, consisting of symbol types for Places, Transitions and Arcs in two directions. Tokens are modeled by an integer attribute of the Place type.

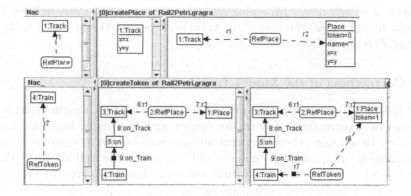

Fig. 9. Two Rules for the Model Transformation *Railway2Petri*

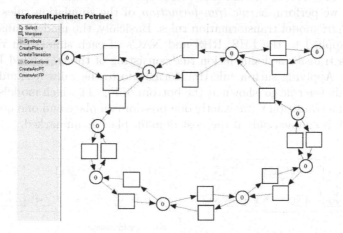

Fig. 10. Petri Net Obtained by Model Transformation of the Railway System in Fig. 3

Two of the model transformation rules are shown in Fig. 9. Obviously, tracks are mapped to places (see rule *createPlace*), and trains to tokens (see rule *createToken*). Here, the possibility to use abstract types like Track or End in the rules proves to be very useful, since we do not have to relate e.g. all different types of tracks to places. When mapping connections between tracks to arcs and transitions in the Petri net, the gluing of ends must be considered to determine the direction of Petri net arcs. (Rule *createTransition* is not shown explicitly.)

Model transformations based on graph transformation have been investigated e.g. in [12], where also techniques are presented to show that a model transformation has functional behavior, and is syntactically correct, i.e. for each diagram in the source language we obtain in a finite number of steps in a unique well-defined diagram in the target language. To execute model transformation rules and to check functional properties of model transformations (termination and confluence), the graph transformation engine AGG [7,13] can be used. Furthermore, TIGER [10] also offers tool support for model transformation by graph transformation between two generated ECLIPSE editor plug-ins. Fig. 10 shows the Petri net resulting from the model transformation of the train system depicted in Fig. 3 using the *Railway2Petri* model transformation rules.

4.3   Correctness of the Model Transformation

Apart from syntactical properties of a model transformation, we can argue about its semantical correctness if both the source and the target language have a semantics. In our case, the behavioral semantics of railway systems is given by the simulation rules, and the semantics of Petri nets is the well-known Petri net firing behavior. We have to show that for each simulation step in the source railway model, there is a corresponding simulation step in the target model, i. e. a firing step in the corresponding Petri net. Using formal properties of model-and-rule-transformation based on graph transformation [14,15], we argue as follows: we perform a *rule transformation* of the simulation rules using the *Railway2Petri* model transformation rules. Basically, the model transformation rules are applied to the LHS, RHS and NACs of each simulation rule. This results in a transformed simulation rule consisting of the translated LHS, RHS and NACs. Applying such a rule transformation to the railway simulation rule go, we obtain the rule go' shown at the bottom of Fig. 11 which models the firing behavior of a transition with exactly one pre-domain place and one post-domain place which is enabled only if the post-domain place is unmarked.

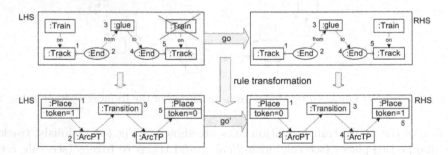

Fig. 11. Rule Transformation of the Railway simulation rule go in Fig. 3

All Petri nets which are results of a railway model transformation, have only transitions of that type. So, the firing rule go' in Fig. 11 describes the firing behavior for all possible resulting railway nets, provided that we assume elementary Petri nets (or *condition-event (C/E) nets* [16]) as underlying semantic domain, a restricted kind of place/transition nets where place capacity and arc weights are always one. The semantics of general place/transition nets would *not* correspond to the firing rule in Fig. 11, since in place/transition nets more than one token may be put to a post-domain place. In the case of C/E nets, each simulation step in the railway model (a train movement from one track to the next) corresponds to a transition firing step of the transition between the places corresponding to the two tracks, and we have the situation depicted in the following commuting correspondence diagram:

$$G_1 \xrightarrow{\;model\ trafo\;*\;} N_1$$

$Railway\ simulation\ step$ $\Big\downarrow$ $\qquad\qquad$ $\Big\downarrow$ $C/E\ net\ simulation\ step$

$$G_2 \xRightarrow{\;model\ trafo\;*\;} N_2$$

In this diagram, we start with a graph G_1 of the railway domain, such that the model transformation $G \xRightarrow{*} N_1$ yields the Petri net N_1, where a transition can be fired, leading to the Petri net N_2 with a different marking. Then, there exists a simulation step in the railway domain $G_1 \to G_2$ such that the model transformation of G_2 yields the same Petri net N_2. In fact, we have that the source railway simulation model and the target Petri net are always bisimilar. The model transformation establishes one equivalence relation relating railway graphs and marked C/E nets, and another one relating railway simulation rules and Petri net transitions. Then, given a railway graph G_1 and a corresponding Petri net N_1 resulting from the model transformation of G_1, i.e. $G_1 \sim N_1$, the equivalence is a bisimulation since for rule r used in the transformation step $G_1 \xrightarrow{r} G_2$ there exists a transition t with $r \sim t$ and $N_1 \xrightarrow{[t\rangle} N_2$ and $N_2 \sim G_2$.

4.4   Analysis in the Petri Net Domain

Now the resulting Petri net can be analyzed using Petri net techniques, e.g. for liveness (any transition can fire eventually), for place invariants (sets of places where the sum of tokens remains constant), transition invariants (sets of transitions the firing of which does not change the marking), deadlocks (sets of places that will never be marked again, once they are empty) or traps (sets of places that will never loose their tokens). An example is the trap in the net in Fig. 10, consisting of the places corresponding to the horizontal tracks from A to B in Fig. 3, since in the current switch mode, the train will never leave those tracks.

An interesting aspect in model transformation for analysis is the back-annotation of analysis results to the source model. In our case, places can be traced back to the corresponding tracks easily, as we have a one-to-one correspondence between them (see Fig. 8 and rule createPlace in Fig. 9). Thus it is possible to visualize e. g. deadlocks in the railway system by highlighting the corresponding tracks in a certain color. Other interesting properties concern path finding (the shortest connection from point A to point B), and collision detection.

All these properties of reconfigurable systems should be analyzed having in mind the possible reconfiguration operations. For instance, more interesting than knowing whether there is a deadlock considering a fixed switch mode is it to know whether there are deadlocks independent of all possible switch modes. In order to obtain all possible switch configurations, we can apply the *Railway2Petri* model transformation not only to the simulation rules but also to the reconfiguration rule. This results in a Petri net transformation rule which allows the modeler to change the Petri net structure corresponding to a change of a switch mode in the railway system. Thus, Petri nets for different switch modes can be obtained and analyzed without performing the complete model transformation all over again for each different switch mode. In [17,18], an ECLIPSE plug-in is described for modeling, simulating and analyzing such reconfigurable Petri nets [19].

5   Related Work

While Petri net modeling and analysis tools like Netlab [20] and CPNTools [21], are well known and frequently used, domain specific modeling languages as supported by TIGER may be generated using meta CASE tools like DiaGen [22] and AtoM³ [23]. Those tools have no direct support for model driven analysis techniques and do not support reconfiguration of systems during runtime. Petri net transformations that aim at changing the net in arbitrary ways have been described in [24], and runtime system reconfiguration has been investigated in [25], but a user friendly, graphical environment for the design and analysis of reconfigurable systems is still missing.

Model transformations are supported from various tools like VIATRA2 [26], GrEAT [27], and tools from the ECLIPSE Generative Modeling Tools (GMT) project [28]. In most cases these transformations have to be described textually, and user friendly support for visual analysis and testing is generally missing.

6   Conclusion

This paper gives an example for using the unifying approach of graph transformation to define the syntax and semantics of a domain-specific visual modeling language. The language models a small railway system, and from the graph-transformation based language definition, a visual editor is generated as ECLIPSE plug-in. The type hierarchy used for syntax definition provides a good basis also for describing the semantics of the system in terms of simulation rules, and for a model transformation from the domain-specific language into Petri nets. Since many systems have to be reconfigurable during runtime, we have investigated the relation of reconfiguration operations (e.g. changing the mode of a switch) and simulation operations (e.g. move the train to the next track) by analyzing rule dependencies. Tool support for language definition, visualization and visual editor generation is available by the TIGER tool environment and the graph transformation engine AGG, providing support to analyze termination, conflicts and dependencies in graph transformation systems.

Using graph transformation for modeling and analyzing reconfigurable systems has shown to be a solid basis to reason about system properties in different reconfiguration modes. In this context, interactions between simulation states and structure should be investigated in more detail, since reconfiguration is often triggered by certain system state changes [29].

As future we envisage an extension of TIGER 's editing and simulation features. We intend to provide basic syntax-oriented operations automatically instead of requiring the language designer to specify them manually for each VL element. For simulation, we aim at structuring simulation rules into units using control structures. Abstract rules and rule structuring techniques are the basis of a scalable approach usable for modeling and analyzing also larger case studies.

Acknowledgements

The authors would like to thank Szilvia Varró-Gyapay and the anonymous referees for their useful comments.

References

1. Tolvanen, J., Rossi, M.: MetaEdit+: Defining and Using Domain-Specific Modeling Languages and Code Generators. In: Proc. Conf. on Object-oriented programming, systems, languages, and applications (OOPSLA 2003), pp. 92–93. ACM Press, New York (2003)
2. Object Management Group: Meta-Object Facility (MOF), Version 1.4 (2005), http://www.omg.org/technology/documents/formal/mof.htm
3. Kreowski, H.J., Hölscher, K., Knirsch, P.: Semantics of visual models in a rule-based setting. Electr. Notes Theor. Comput. Sci. 148(1), 75–88 (2006)
4. Ehrig, H., Ehrig, K., Prange, U., Taentzer, G.: Fundamentals of Algebraic Graph Transformation. In: EATCS Monographs in Theor. Comp. Science. Springer, Heidelberg (2006)
5. Ermel, C., Ehrig, K., Taentzer, G., Weiss, E.: Object Oriented and Rule-based Design of Visual Languages using TIGER. In: Proc. Workshop on Graph-Based Tools (GraBaTs 2006), Electronic Communications of the EASST, vol. 1 (2006)
6. Eclipse Consortium: Eclipse – Version 3.2.1 (2007), http://www.eclipse.org
7. Taentzer, G.: AGG: A Graph Transformation Environment for Modeling and Validation of Software. In: Pfaltz, J.L., Nagl, M., Böhlen, B. (eds.) AGTIVE 2003. LNCS, vol. 3062, pp. 446–456. Springer, Heidelberg (2004)
8. Ehrig, H., Engels, G., Kreowski, H.J., Rozenberg, G. (eds.): Handbook of Graph Grammars and Computing by Graph Transformation. Applications, Languages and Tools, vol. 2. World Scientific, Singapore (1999)
9. Habel, A., Heckel, R., Taentzer, G.: Graph Grammars with Negative Application Conditions. Fundamenta Informaticae 26(3-4), 287–313 (1996) (special issue)
10. Tiger Project Team, Technical University of Berlin: Tiger: Generating Visual Environments in Eclipse (2005), http://www.tfs.cs.tu-berlin.de/tigerprj
11. Eclipse Consortium: Eclipse Graphical Editing Framework (GEF) – Version 3.2 (2006), http://www.eclipse.org/gef
12. Ehrig, H., Ehrig, K.: Overview of Formal Concepts for Model Transformations based on Typed Attributed Graph Transformation. In: Proc. Workshop on Graph and Model Transformation (GraMoT 2005). ENTCS, vol. 152. Elsevier, Amsterdam (2005)
13. AGG Homepage, http://tfs.cs.tu-berlin.de/agg
14. Ermel, C., Ehrig, H., Ehrig, K.: Semantical Correctness of Simulation-to-Animation Model and Rule Transformation. In: Proc. Workshop on Graph and Model Transformation (GraMoT 2006). EC-EASST, vol. 4 (2006)

15. Ermel, C., Ehrig, H.: Behavior-preserving simulation-to-animation model and rule transformation. In: Proc. of Workshop on Graph Transformation for Verification and Concurrency (GT-VC 2007). ENTCS (to appear, 2008)
16. Reisig, W.: Systementwurf mit Netzen. Springer, Heidelberg (1985)
17. Biermann, E., Ermel, C., Hermann, F., Modica, T.: A Visual Editor for Reconfigurable Object Nets based on the Eclipse Graphical Editor Framework. In: Proc. Workshop on Algorithms and Tools for Petri Nets (2007)
18. Biermann, E., Modica, T.: Independence Analysis of Firing and Rule-based Net Transformations in Reconfigurable Object Nets. In: Proc. 7th Workshop on Graph Transformation and Visual Modeling Techniques. EC-EASST (to appear, 2008), http://tfs.cs.tu-berlin.de/gtvmt08/GTVMT-program.htm
19. Ehrig, H., Hoffmann, K., Padberg, J., Prange, U., Ermel, C.: Independence of net transformations and token firing in reconfigurable place/transition systems. In: Kleijn, J., Yakovlev, A. (eds.) ICATPN 2007. LNCS, vol. 4546, pp. 104–123. Springer, Heidelberg (2007)
20. RWTH Aachen: Petrinetz-Tool Netlab (Windows) (2007), http://www.irt.rwth-aachen.de/typo3/index.php?id=101\&L=0
21. CPN Group, University of Aarhus, Denmark: CPN Tools: Computer Tool for Coloured Petri Nets (2005), http://wiki.daimi.au.dk/cpntools/cpntools.wiki
22. Minas, M., Viehstaedt, G.: DiaGen: A Generator for Diagram Editors Providing Direct Manipulation and Execution of Diagrams. In: Proc. IEEE Symp. on Visual Languages, pp. 203–210 (1995)
23. de Lara, J., Vangheluwe, H., Alfonseca, M.: Meta-Modelling and Graph Grammars for Multi-Paradigm Modelling in AToM^3. Software and System Modeling 3(3), 194–209 (2004)
24. Padberg, J., Urbášek, M.: Rule-Based Refinement of Petri Nets: A Survey. In: Ehrig, H., Reisig, W., Rozenberg, G., Weber, H. (eds.) Petri Net Technology for Communication-Based Systems. LNCS, vol. 2472, pp. 161–196. Springer, Heidelberg (2003)
25. Matevska-Meyer, J., Hasselbring, W., Reussner, R.: Software architecture description supporting component deployment and system runtime reconfiguration. In: Proc. Workshop on Component-Oriented Programming (WCOP 2004) (2004)
26. Csertán, G., Huszerl, G., Majzik, I., Pap, Z., Pataricza, A., Varró, D.: VIATRA: Visual automated transformations for formal verification and validation of UML models. In: Proc. Automated Software Engineering, pp. 267–270. IEEE Press, Los Alamitos (2002)
27. Narayanan, A., Karsai, G.: Towards Verifying Model Transformations. In: Proc. Graph Transformation and Visual Modeling Techniques. ENTCS. Elsevier, Amsterdam (2006)
28. Eclipse Generative Modeling Tools (GMT) (2007), http://www.eclipse.org/gmt
29. Wikipedia: Reconfigurable computing (accessed 28-August-2007) (2007)

Communities of Autonomous Units for Pickup and Delivery Vehicle Routing*

Hans-Jörg Kreowski and Sabine Kuske

University of Bremen, Department of Computer Science
P.O. Box 330440, D-28334 Bremen, Germany
{kreo,kuske}@informatik.uni-bremen.de

Abstract. Communities of autonomous units are being developed for formal specification and semantic analysis of systems of interacting and mobile components. The autonomous units of a community are rule-based, self-controlled, goal-driven, and operate and move in a common environment. We employ communities of autonomous units to model the dynamic pickup and delivery problem with the general idea to demonstrate their suitability for a range of logistic tasks.

1 Introduction

Many recent approaches in computer science like, communication networks, multi-agent systems, swarm intelligence, ubiquitous, wearable, and mobile computing involve widely spread autonomous components that interact and communicate with each other, move around or connect themselves to other components to form networks. To cover such new programming and modeling paradigms in a formally well-founded and visually well-describable way we proposed autonomous units, as a rule-based, self-controlled, and goal-driven concept (see, e.g., [1]).

A system of autonomous units forms a community provided with a common environment where the units interact and may have an overall goal. The autonomous units of a community apply transformation rules to the common environment in a self-controlled and goal-driven manner. A transformation rule application may modify the environment, send messages to other autonomous units, react to received messages or to environment modifications performed by other units, connect and disconnect the unit to and from other units, or move the unit around the environment.

For this purpose an autonomous unit is composed of a set of transformation rules, a control component to regulate its rule application process and a goal that the unit tries to achieve. Moreover, a unit has a private state in which the unit can store private data and which can only be transformed by the unit itself. A transformation rule r may simultaneously transform the common environment

---

* Research partially supported by the Collaborative Research Centre 637 (Autonomous Cooperating Logistic Processes: A Paradigm Shift and Its Limitations) funded by the German Research Foundation (DFG).

A. Schürr, M. Nagl, and A. Zündorf (Eds.): AGTIVE 2007, LNCS 5088, pp. 281–296, 2008.

and the private state of the unit. This means that r is a product rule consisting of two transformation rules: one for the common environment and the other for the private state (cf. [2]).

In order to keep the rule set of an autonomous unit readable and small, it can be structured hierarchically into transformation units each of which consists of a set of transformation rules and a control condition. These reusable transformation units perform actions that require the controlled application of several rules (cf. for example [3] and [4]).

In general, autonomous units can work in parallel. The operational semantics of a community consists of (perhaps never-ending) sequences of states such that every state is composed of the current common environment plus all current private states. A transformation from one state to the next happens if some or all units of the community apply one or more rules in parallel. Hence, state transformation consists of the parallel application of a set product rules.

Since environments can often be modeled and visualized as graphs, since graphs can be modified in a straightforward way by graph transformation rules, and since graph transformation has a precisely defined semantics [5] it seems to be natural to specify the actions of autonomous units with graph transformation rules. However, the concept of autonomous units is not restricted to the graph transformational approach.

The aim of this paper is to illustrate and demonstrate the potential of autonomous units to model logistic applications by presenting a case study that models the basic operations of the dynamic pickup and delivery problem (see e.g. [6,7,8]) by a community of autonomous units. To keep the paper technically simple, we introduce autonomous units in a rather informal way. Formal descriptions can be found in [4,9]. Nevertheless, it is worth noting that autonomous units as presented in the following are more sophisticated than those of previous papers because private states have not been considered before.

The development of autonomous units has its origin within the Collaborative Research Centre *Autonomous Cooperating Logistic Processes: A Paradigm Shift and Its Limitations* in which we investigate in an interdisciplinary way how self-controlled units can be successfully employed for logistic applications with the aim to get better results concerning time, costs and robustness (see also [10]). The central idea of autonomous units is to introduce self-control explicitly into the modeling of (logistic) processes in order to create a semantically well-founded framework in which different self-control-based mechanisms become comparable (cf. [1]).

The paper is organized as follows. Section 2 briefly recalls basic concepts, like graphs, graph transformation rules, graph class expressions and control conditions. Section 3 is dedicated to the private states and common environments of communities. In Sections 4 it is shown how the behavior of autonomous units can be modeled with product rules. Section 5 illustrates how the actions and interactions occuring in the dynamic pickup and delivery problem can be modeled with a community. Section 6 presents the semantics of autonomous units based on which some correctness results concerning the case study are formulated. Section 7 discusses related work. The paper ends with the conclusion.

2 Basic Concepts

The basic components of autonomous units, namely graphs, graph transformation rules, graph class expressions, and control conditions are taken from an underlying graph transformation approach. In this section we present an instance of a graph transformation approach that will be used throughout this paper. Further examples and formal definitions can be found in e.g. [5,3].

Graphs. A graph consists of a set of labeled or unlabeled nodes and a set of labeled or unlabeled edges such that every edge connects two nodes. An edge can be directed or undirected. Nodes may be depicted in different shapes illustrating in this way the entities they represent. Fig. 5 shows an example of a graph where the houses, trucks, and rectangles are the nodes and the arrows are the directed edges. The houses are labeled with letters, the rectangles and the edges between houses with natural numbers whereas the trucks and the edges from rectangles to houses are unlabeled.

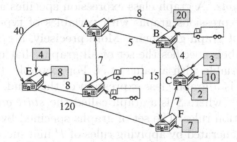

Fig. 1. Example of a graph

Graph transformation rules. A graph transformation rule consists of three graphs: a left-hand side, a right-hand side and a common part. An example of a rule is depicted in Fig. 2. The left-hand side is a house and the right-hand side consists of the same house, a rectangle labeled with m and an edge pointing from the rectangle to the house. The common part is the house, because it has the same number in the left- and the right-hand side of the rule. Often, the numbers of common nodes are not depicted. In this case the common items of a rule consist of the nodes and edges that occur in the left- as well as in right-hand side in the same relative positions. Please note that if the label m of the right-hand side is a variable of type $\mathbb{N}$ the rule represents a set of rules: one for each value in $\mathbb{N}$. These so-called parameterized rules will be often used in the following.

The application of a rule to a graph comprises the following steps: (1) Choose an image of the left-hand side in the graph. (2) Delete everything of this image that does not belong to the common part. (3) Glue the right-hand side into

Fig. 2. Example of a rule

Fig. 3. A rule application

the graph such that the items of the common parts are identified with their images. Fig. 3 shows the application of the above rule after having substituted the variable m with the number 5. The rule is applied to a graph consisting of two houses that are connected by a directed edge labelled with 20, and a truck that is connected to the right house. The application of the rule adds a rectangle labeled with 5 to the right house. Clearly, the rule could also be applied such that the rectangle would be connected to the left house.

Graph class expressions. A graph class expression specifies a set of graphs. We use as graph class expressions graphs with variables of type $\mathbb{N}$ as node labels and a special form of graph grammars. More precisely, a graph with variables of type $\mathbb{N}$ as node labels specifies the set of all graphs that can be obtained by substituting each variable with a value of $\mathbb{N}$. For example, the right-hand side of the rule in Fig. 2 is a graph class expression of this kind. A graph grammar is a pair $GG = (S, P)$ where S is a graph called the *start graph* and P is a set of graph transformation rules. The set of graphs specified by GG consists of all graphs that can be generated by applying rules of P in a successive way starting from the start graph S.

Control conditions. A control condition is any expression that specifies a set of sequences of graphs. In this paper we use priorities and the special condition *free*. Given a set P of rules, a priority is a partial order $\leq$ on P and it specifies all sequences s of graphs such that for $i = 1, \ldots, n$ if $s = (G_1, \ldots, G_n)$ and for $i \in \mathbb{N}$ if s is infinite, G_i is obtained from G_{i-1} by applying a rule $p \in P$ and there is no rule $p' \in P$ with $p' > p$ that is applicable to G_{i-1}. In other words, this control condition allows to apply a rule to the current graph whenever there is no rule of a higher priority applicable. The condition *free* is the special case where all rules have the same priority.

3   Common Environments and Private States

Autonomous units act and interact within a common environment. In many cases an environment can be modeled as a graph in which certain nodes represent instances of autonomous units. In our case study of the pickup and delivery problem the environment contains nodes representing trucks, customers and packages and the behavior of each of these nodes is specified by an instance of an autonomous unit.

Every community starts to work in an initial environment specified by a graph class expression. If one takes houses as customers and rectangles as packages, the graph in Fig. 1 is an initial environment of our case study. The set of all initial environments of the case study can be visually specified in a rule-based form by the graph grammar consisting of the rule set in Fig. 4 plus the empty graph (containing neither nodes nor edges) as start graph. The first rule generates customers. It contains a negative application condition [11] in its left-hand side which means that an A-labeled customer can only be generated if there doesn't exist one with the same label. In this way we make sure that all generated customers have different labels. The second rule connects different customers by edges labeled with a distance d of type N. The application condition $A \neq B$ below the arrow requires that d-labeled edges be inserted between different customers, i.e. it avoids the insertion of loops at customers. The label d represents the time it lasts to move from the source customer to the target customer. If one wants to generate environments without parallel edges between customers, a convenient negative application condition could also be added to the second rule. The third rule inserts trucks and the fourth packages so that every truck is in the location of some customer and every package is offered by some customer. The label m is some natural number representing the weight of a package.

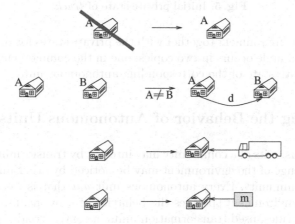

Fig. 4. Specification of the initial common environments

Obviously, trucks, customers and packages behave differently. Trucks, for example, can move, transport packages, plan their tours, etc. Packages select trucks for their transport, enter trucks and get out of them. Customers may offer or demand packages. As mentioned before, the behavior of these components is modeled with autonomous transformation units. Hence, after generating an initial environment, every truck node, every package node and every customer node is associated with (an instance of) the autonomous unit that specifies its behavior. Technically, this can be achieved by adding a loop to every node v that is associated with a unit $type(v)$ and labeling this loop with $type(v)$. In the following every environment node v that is associated with an autonomous unit $type(v)$ is called the *local node* of $type(v)$.

Additionally to the common environment which can be transformed by all autonomous units of the community, every unit may have its own private state that can only be modified and seen by the unit itself. In this first approach, this private state contains the local node of the unit plus some additional information. For example, the private state of the autonomous unit *truck* stores its capacity, the weight of its current load and the weight of all packages which it has accepted to pickup later. Initially the latter two values are set to zero. The specification of the initial private states of the unit *truck* is depicted in Fig. 5 where the *max*-edge points to the capacity of the truck, the *w*-edge to the weight of the current load and the *r*- edge to the weight reserved for accepted packages. The reserved weight means the following. When a package asks a truck for being picked up the truck can accept this. In this case it reserves some weight (or place) in it for the package until the package enters the truck or until the truck starts to move.

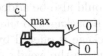

Fig. 5. Initial private state of *truck*

The common environment together with the private states form a set of graphs where each local node occurs in two copies: one in the common environment and one in the private state of the corresponding autonomous unit.

4   Modeling the Behavior of Autonomous Units

The autonomous units of a community may interact by transforming the environment, i.e. a change of the environment may be noticed by other units (re-)acting in the same community. Every autonomous unit *aut* that is associated with a node v in the environment specifies the behavior of v by means of some graph transformation rules, used transformation units, a control condition, a goal, and a private initial state containing the local node v plus some further private data. The rules of *aut* are split into common and private ones for transforming the common environment and the private state, respectively. Every rule r of *aut* that contains the node v in its left- and right-hand side should be applied in such a way that v is matched to the local node in the environment if r is a common rule and to the local node in the private state if r is private. In the following, every occurrence of v in a rule of *aut* is drawn with thick lines. In the rest of this section we show how autonomous units may communicate and change the common environment and private states with the use of graph transformation rules.

4.1   Interaction of Autonomous Units

A special form of interaction frequently used is *message sending*. This is modeled by the insertion of an edge labeled with the message content and going from the sender to the receiver. For example, if a package wants to enter into a truck it sends the message *enter?* to the truck. This can be modeled with the rule in Fig. 6 which belongs to the *package*-unit. It inserts an edge labeled with *enter?* from the local package to some truck that is at the same location and that will pass through the destination of the package. (Further details of the rule will be explained below.)

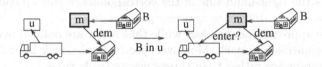

Fig. 6. Message sending

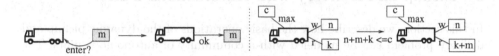

Fig. 7. Accepting a package

After receiving the *enter?*-message the truck can accept or reject to pickup the package. In case of acceptance the truck sends an *ok*-message to the package. This reaction is modeled with the left rule in Fig. 7. As one will see in Section 5, the truck changes its private state, simultaneously.

4.2   Modeling Behavior by Product Rules

Every autonomous unit can modify the environment by applying a graph transformation rule to it. Simultaneously, it can transform its private state to modify private data. This is achieved with the concept of product rules [2,12]. For our purpose we use a special form of product rules consisting of a pair $(com, priv)$ of rules which are applied simultaneously so that *com* modifies the common environment and *priv* the private state. In more detail, the application of $(com, priv)$ of a unit *aut* to a pair $(env, prist)$ consisting of a common environment *env* and a private state *prist* yields a pair $(env', prist')$ if *env'* can be obtained from *env* by applying *com*, and if the application of *priv* to *prist* yields *prist'*. As explained above, the rules must be applied in such a way that the local nodes be matched to the nodes associated with *aut*. This can be achieved with particular loops at the local nodes in rules, private states, and the common environment.

For example, if a truck accepts a package p, it reserves some of its capacity for this package. Hence, it applies the rule in Fig. 7 to the common environment and simultaneously, it adds the weight of the package to its reserved weight by applying the right rule in Fig. 7. This rule (and hence the whole product rule) can only be applied if the transport of the package can be realized without exceeding the maximal capacity i.e. if $n + m + k \leq c$ where n is the current load of the truck, k is the reserved load, m is the weight of the package that is going to be accepted, and c is the maximal capacity of the truck. This application condition is denoted below the arrow of the private rule. Please note that c, n and k are variables that should be substituted with values when applying the rule.

It is worth noting that every product rule $(com, priv)$ of this special kind can be regarded as a triple graph transformation rule $(com, cp, priv)$ [13] where the left- as well as the right-hand side of the correspondence rule cp consists of the local node. One main difference between product rules and triple rules is that the former are approach independent while that latter are defined over a specific graph transformation approach. Moreover, product rules may have an arbitrary number of components rather than three ones as triple rules.

5   Pickup and Delivery with Autonomous Units

In this section, we describe how the basic operations of the dynamic pickup and delivery problem can be modeled with a community of autonomous units. The pickup and delivery problem consists of a set of customers, a set of vehicles (here trucks) and a set of packages. Basically, trucks move around in an environment to pickup and deliver packages thereby satisfying transport requests. Packages select trucks which they ask for being picked up and in case of acceptance they may enter into a truck and get out at their destination. Customers may offer or demand packages. In order to model the pickup and delivery problem conveniently, certain contraints must be satisfied such as time contraints or simply the requirement that the capacity of trucks should never be exceeded. The goal of every component (i.e. of every truck, customer, and package) is some objective function, like minimization of route length, costs, time, etc (cf. [6]).

The aim of this first approach towards modeling the pickup and delivery problem with autonomous units is to show how the basic operations of the dynamic pickup and delivery problem can be modeled based on graph transformation, so that trucks, packages and customers behave as autonomous entities in a common transport network where central control is dropped. A case study where the pickup and delivery problem is modeled with a single hierarchically structured transformation unit is presented in [14].

We assume in this stage of the case study that the goal of every autonomous unit is some objective function but we do not yet consider how it can be formulated in a graph transformational way and how control conditions can become goal driven. This will be studied in future work.

The basic behavior of the autonomous unit truck is specified in Fig. 8 where the parts com and $priv$ of every product rule $(com, priv)$ are drawn side by side and with a dashed vertical line between them. As mentioned before the bold

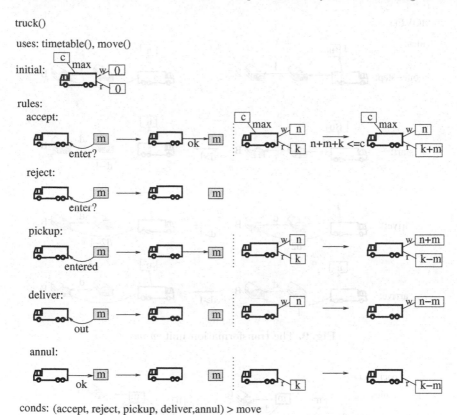

Fig. 8. The unit *truck*

nodes in the rules represent the local nodes of the unit. When applying a rule, these nodes must always be matched to the node associated with the unit which contains the rule.

The rules of the unit *truck* model interaction between trucks and packages from the point of view of the truck. As already explained in the previous section, the product rule *accept* can be applied if the truck has got a message *enter?* from some package. The application of the rule *accept* sends a message *ok* to the package and adds the weight of the package to the reserved load of the truck represented in the private state. Alternatively, the truck may reject the package by applying the second rule that deletes the *enter?*-edge. This rule does not modify the private state of the truck, i.e. the private part of the product rule is the empty rule and hence not depicted. The third product rule *pickup* can be applied when the truck receives an *entered*-message from a package. The edge from the truck to the package in the right-hand side models the fact that the package is in the truck. In the private rule of *pickup* the current weight of the truck is updated. The forth rule *deliver* can be applied if the truck has got an *out*-message from some package. When applying this rule, the truck deletes the *out*-egde and updates its current load. With the rule *annul* the truck can cancel

MOVE()

rules:

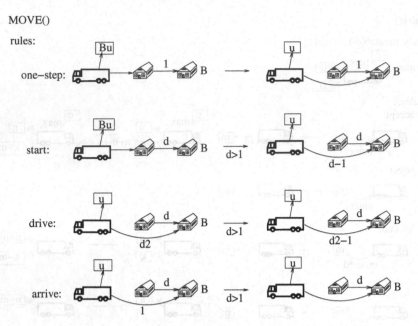

Fig. 9. The transformation unit *move*

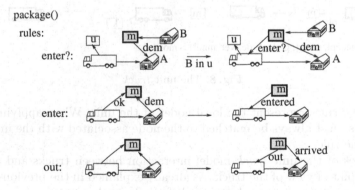

Fig. 10. The unit *package*

reservations. The imported unit *timetable* is not presented in detail. It links a node to the truck that is lableled with a string of customer names and which represents the tour the truck is going to move along. More precisely, a *tour* is a word $x_0 \cdots x_n$ of customer names such that for $i = 1, \ldots, n$ the customer x_{i-1} is connected to x_i through an edge.

The autonomous unit *truck* uses the transformation unit *move* depicted in Fig. 9. It models the movement of a truck from one customer to the next in the tour of the truck. The movement lasts exactly d steps (i.e. rule applications) if the edge has distance d.

The unit *package* is shown in Fig. 10. It contains three rules that modify the common environments. In the first rule the package wants to enter into a truck which is at the same location as the package's owner A, provided that the package is demanded (denoted by the label *dem* at the edge from the package to A), and that the customer B who demands the package occurs in the route u of the truck. If the package gets an *ok*-message from a truck the former can decide with the second rule to enter the truck provided that the latter has not yet moved away. The application of the rule deletes the *dem*-edge from the package's owner. Hence, this rule can only be applied if the package is not on another truck. With the last rule a package can send an *out*-message to the truck provided that the package is in the truck and arrived at the customer who demanded it.

Please note that in this simplified case study the unit *package* has no private state. But in a further step we plan to include also a private state for packages that stores relevant information to choose a *good* truck (a cheap and fast one that transports the package safely within certain prescribed time windows) and not an arbitrary one.

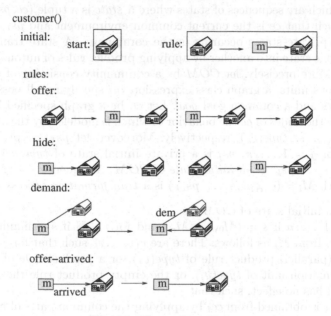

Fig. 11. The unit *customer*

The autonomous unit *customer* is depicted in Fig 11. It may offer and demand packages and in its private state it stores private packages that are not offered to the community. If a customer wants to offer a private package, it applies the product rule *offer* that inserts it into the common environment. On the other hand, it can hide offered packages with the rule *hide*. With the rule *demand* the customer demands a package p that is offered by another customer A. This is modeled by inserting a new edge from the customer to p and labeling the edge from A to p with *dem* representing in this way the fact that p cannot be demanded anymore. Finally, with the rule *offer-arrived*, the customer can convert a recently obtained package into an offered one.

The community for the basic operations of the pickup and delivery problem can now be defined as $pdp = (ini, \{truck, package, customer\}, goal)$ where ini is the grammar of Fig. 4, and the goal could be specified in this first approach such that all environments are accepted.

6 Semantics

In this section we describe the semantics of communities. In [4] a sequential semantics is given, but it is not fully adequate for the pickup and delivery problem because several trucks may move simultaneously and several packages may be loaded and reloaded at the same time. Hence, we adopt the parallel semantics introduced in [9]. But since private states and used transformation units were not considered in [9], we have to generalize the parallel semantics.

The operational semantics of communities consists of a set of transformation processes which are sequences of states where a *state* is a tuple $(ce, ps_1, \ldots, ps_k)$ of graphs such that ce is the current common environment and $ps_1 \ldots, ps_k$ are the current private states occuring in the community. A state transformation transforms one state into another by applying product rules of autonomous units in parallel. More precisely, let COM be a community consisting of a set AUT of autonomous units, a graph class expression ini specifying all possible initial environments and a common goal $goal$. Let ce be a graph specified by ini. Let $v_1, \ldots, v_k$ be the nodes of ce the behavior of which is modeled by the autonomous units $type(v_1), \ldots, type(v_k)$, respectively. Moreover, let $ps_1, \ldots, ps_k$ be graphs such that for $j = 1, \ldots, k$, ps_j is a private initial state of $type(v_j)$. Then the tuple $(ce, ps_1, \ldots, ps_k)$ is an *initial state* of COM. A sequence $s = (M_0, M_1, \ldots)$ of states with $M_i = (ce_i, ps_{i,1}, \ldots, ps_{i,k})$ is a *transformation process* of COM if

1. M_0 is an initial state of COM,
2. for $i = 1, \ldots, n$ if $s = (M_0, \ldots, M_n)$ and for $i \in \mathbb{N}$ if s is infinite, M_{i+1} is obtained from M_i as follows: There are $r_1, \ldots, r_k$ such that for $j = 1, \ldots, k$, r_j is a (parallel) product rule of $type(v_j)$, or a product rule of some used transformation unit of $type(v_j)$, or the empty product rule the application of which has no effect, such that
   - ce_{i+1} is obtained from ce_i by applying the common parts of $r_1, \ldots, r_k$ in parallel so that the local nodes are matched as required (see Section 4);[1]
   - for $j = 1, \ldots, k$ the graph $ps_{i+1,j}$ is obtained from $ps_{i,j}$ by applying the private part of r_j so that the local nodes are matched as required;
3. for $j = 1, \ldots, k$ the sequence $((ce_0, ps_{0,j}), (ce_1, ps_{1,j}), \ldots)$ is allowed by the *flattened*[2] control condition of $type(v_j)$.

Please note that the semantics of control conditions introduced in Section 2 must be generalized here to product rules, i.e. every control condition specifies

---

[1] In general, for applying rules in parallel, certain independence criteria must be satisfied (see e.g. [9]).

[2] We require that every autonomous unit can be flattened without changing its semantics (see also [3]).

sequences of pairs of graphs. This generalization can be done for the considered control conditions in a straightforward way. Moreover, the priority control conditions as used in this paper can be flattened as follows. Let aut be a unit with $(N, \leq_{aut})$ as control condition, i.e. N is composed of rules and used units of aut. Clearly, if N consists of rules only, its flattened condition $(flat(aut), flat(\leq_{aut}))$ is equal to $(N, \leq_{aut})$. Otherwise, for every used unit $t \in N$ with control condition $(N_t, \leq_t)$ let its flattened condition $(flat(t), flat(\leq_t))$ be already defined; and for every rule r in N, let $flat(r) = \{r\}$ and $flat(\leq_r) = \emptyset$. Then the flattened control condition of aut is equal to $(flat(aut), flat(\leq_{aut}))$ where $flat(aut) = \uplus_{n \in N} flat(n)^3$ and $flat(\leq_{aut})$ is the reflexive and transitive closure of

$$\bigcup_{n \in N} flat(\leq_n) \cup \{r_1 \leq r_2 \mid r_1 \in flat(i), r_2 \in flat(j),\ i \leq_{aut} j,\ i, j \in N\}.$$

This means that the rule set $flat(aut)$ of the flattened condition of aut consists of all rules occurring in N and in the flattened conditions of the used units in N. The priority relation consists of the priority relation between the rules in the flattened conditions of the used units. Additionally, for two rules r_1 and r_2 in $flat(aut)$ we have that r_1 is of a higher priority than r_2, if $t_1 >_{aut} t_2$ in the control condition of aut where for $i \in \{1, 2\}$, t_i is either equal to the rule r_i or t_i is a used unit and r_i is a rule of the flattened condition of t_i.

Every finite transformation process is *successful* if its last state is specified by the goal of the community. Every infinite transformation process is *successful* if it contains infinitely many states that satisfy the goal (see [9] for more details).

The formal framework of communities of autonomous units based on graph transformation does not only allow one to model interacting logistic processes, but provides also means for their analysis.

One important aspect is the possibility of correctness proofs which are usually done by induction on the lengths of derivation sequences. With respect to our case study, many properties which one would expect of a solution of the pickup and delivery problem can be verified. The following observation lists a few explicit examples of such properties.

Observation 1. For every state in the operational semantics of the community pdp the following holds.

- The current load of every truck is equal to the sum of the weights of all packages in the truck.
- The maximal capacity of every truck is not smaller than its current load.
- A truck only moves (i.e. the move unit is only applicable) if there are no incoming messages left.
- A package can only enter into a truck if both are at the same location.
- A package is never in two trucks.
- A package can only get out of a truck if the truck has reached the customer who demanded the package.

---

[3] $\uplus$ denotes the disjoint union.

- Every package cannot be demanded by more than one customer at the same time.

The proof is omitted because it is beyond the scope of this paper.

Another matter is the parallelism analysis. There is some machinery available in the area of graph transformation (see e.g. [5,15]) to find out which rules can be applied in parallel. This is very helpful with respect to any case study, because our semantics embodies parallelism explicitly. Unfortunately, there is not enough space for a more detailed consideration.

7   Related Work

In the literature there are some approaches that focus on modeling multi-agent or agent-oriented systems based on graph transformation. These approaches are closely related to our approach because of the special features inherent to agents such as autonomy or reactivity (cf. [16] where autonomous units are related to the VSK model of multi-agent systems, see e.g., [17]).

In [18] an approach for modeling agent-oriented systems is proposed that is based on UML and typed graph transformation. It concerns mainly the modeling process which consists of three stages (requirement specification, analysis, and design) where the second and the last stages are refinements of their predecessors. The relations between the distinct stages are formalized using typed graph transformation systems and graph processes. In the last stage, every agent corresponds to an active class where operations are modeled as graph transformation rules and the control component as a state chart.

In [19] an approach to model and verify multi-agent systems is given that is also based on typed graph transformation and UML. A complete system is composed of communities that can be entered or left by agents. A community is obtained by associating a culture specification with an environment specification where the former specifies social components such as roles and intentions and the latter specifies (physical) entities, agents as well as sensors and effectors. The whole system can be formalized as a graph transformation system.

Communities of autonomous units are also closely related to [20] where distributed systems are modeled by graph grammars that modify distributed graphs via distributed graph productions. Distributed graphs are network graphs with local graphs as node labels and graph morphisms as edge labels.

All three approaches are based on particular graph transformation approaches (single- and double-pushout) while our framework is independent of a particular graph transformation approach. Similarly, we employ a quite generic concept of control conditions while the other three approaches use particular control concepts or none at all. Moreover, in [18] and [19] certain types of multi-agent systems are formalized by graph transformation while autonomous units can be considered as an operational model of an axiomatic notion of multi-agent systems.

8 Conclusion

In this paper we have demonstrated that the basic operations of the pickup and delivery problem can be visually modeled in a rule-based way by means of a community so that central control is omitted, but spread over a set of autonomous units each of which specifies the behavior of a component occurring in the pickup and delivery problem, such as trucks, customers, and packages. The autonomous units communicate and interact in a common environment consisting of roads, customers, trucks, and packages and the actions of a unit comprise the controlled application of parallel product rules which modify the common environment of the community and the private state of the unit simultaneously and in a controlled way. Moreover, in order to keep large rule sets manageable, they can be divided into smaller transformation units. Semantically, a community specifies possibly infinite sequences of states consisting of the current common environment and the current private states of the units.

The presented case study points out that the private states and the use of product rules constitute an adequate and useful generalization of the hitherto defined autonomous units with parallel semantics [9]. Moreover, the case-study stresses that operations of logistic processes can be visually and easily modeled by graph transformation-based autonomous units, i.e. these operations which include message sending, moving around the environment, entering or leaving other units can be visually represented by means of small graph transformation rules.

In order to be able to present this case study within the scope of this paper we have simplified it w.r.t. various aspects. In an extended study we will investigate how the following aspects can be solved in a graph-transformational way. (1) A more detailed communication concerning prices, tours, etc. between the different units; (2) routing algorithms for the truck units; (3) capability of packages to change trucks; and (4) different behaviors of units of the same type.

Acknowledgement. We are very grateful to the anomymous reviewers of this paper for their helpful comments.

References

1. Hölscher, K., Klempien-Hinrichs, R., Knirsch, P., Kreowski, H.J., Kuske, S.: Autonomous units: Basic concepts and semantic foundation. In: [10], pp. 103–120
2. Klempien-Hinrichs, R., Kreowski, H.J., Kuske, S.: Typing of graph transformation units. In: Ehrig, H., Engels, G., Parisi-Presicce, F., Rozenberg, G. (eds.) ICGT 2004. LNCS, vol. 3256, pp. 112–127. Springer, Heidelberg (2004)
3. Kreowski, H.J., Kuske, S.: Graph transformation units with interleaving semantics. Formal Aspects of Computing 11(6), 690–723 (1999)
4. Hölscher, K., Kreowski, H.J., Kuske, S.: Autonomous units and their semantics—the sequential case. In: Corradini, A., Ehrig, H., Montanari, U., Ribeiro, L., Rozenberg, G. (eds.) ICGT 2006. LNCS, vol. 4178, pp. 245–259. Springer, Heidelberg (2006)

5. Rozenberg, G. (ed.): Handbook of Graph Grammars and Computing by Graph Transformation. Foundations, vol. 1. World Scientific, Singapore (1997)
6. Savelsbergh, M., Sol, M.: The general pickup and delivery problem. Transportation Science 29(1), 17–29 (1995)
7. Nagy, G., Salhi, S.: Heuristic algorithms for single and multiple depot vehicle routing problems with pickup and deliveries. European Journal of Operational Research 162(1), 126–141 (2005)
8. Fabri, A., Recht, P.: On dynamic pickup and delivery vehicle routing with several time windows and waiting times. Transportation Research Part B: Methodological 40(4), 335–350 (2006)
9. Kreowski, H.J., Kuske, S.: Autonomous units and their semantics - the parallel case. In: Fiadeiro, J., Schobbens, P. (eds.) Recent Trends in Algebraic Development Techniques, 18th International Workshop, WADT 2006. LNCS, vol. 4408, pp. 56–73. Springer, Heidelberg (2007)
10. Hülsmann, M., Windt, K. (eds.): Understanding Autonomous Cooperation & Control in Logistics The Impact on Management, Information and Communication and Material Flow. Springer, Heidelberg (2007)
11. Habel, A., Heckel, R., Taentzer, G.: Graph grammars with negative application conditions. Fundamenta Informaticae 26(3,4), 287–313 (1996)
12. Klempien-Hinrichs, R., Kreowski, H.J., Kuske, S.: Rule-based transformation of graphs and the product type. In: van Bommel, P. (ed.) Transformation of Knowledge, Information, and Data: Theory and Applications, pp. 29–51. Idea Group Publishing, Hershey (2005)
13. Schürr, A.: Specification of graph translators with triple graph grammars. In: Mayr, E.W., Schmidt, G., Tinhofer, G. (eds.) WG 1994. LNCS, vol. 903, pp. 151–163. Springer, Heidelberg (1995)
14. Klempien-Hinrichs, R., Knirsch, P., Kuske, S.: Modeling the pickup-and-delivery problem with structured graph transformation. In: Proc. APPLIGRAPH Workshop on Applied Graph Transformation, pp. 119–130 (2002)
15. Ehrig, H., Kreowski, H.J., Montanari, U., Rozenberg, G. (eds.): Handbook of Graph Grammars and Computing by Graph Transformation. Concurrency, Parallelism, and Distribution, vol. 3. World Scientific, Singapore (1999)
16. Timm, I.J., Knirsch, P., Kreowski, H.J., Timm-Giel, A.: Autonomy in software systems. In: [10], pp. 255–273
17. Wooldridge, M., Lomuscio, A.: A logic of visibility, perception, and knowledge: Completeness and correspondence results. In: Proc. Third International Conference on Pure and Applied Practical Reasoning, London, UK (2000)
18. Depke, R., Heckel, R., Küster, J.M.: Formal agent-oriented modeling with UML and graph transformation. Science of Computer Programming 44, 229–252 (2002)
19. Giese, H., Klein, F.: Systematic verification of multi-agent systems based on rigorous executable specifications. International Journal on Agent-Oriented Software Engineering (IJAOSE) 1(1), 28–62 (2007)
20. Taentzer, G.: Parallel and Distributed Graph Transformation: Formal Description and Application to Communication-Based Systems. PhD thesis, TU Berlin. Shaker Verlag (1996)

Efficient Graph Matching with Application to Cognitive Automation

Alexander Matzner[1], Mark Minas[2], and Axel Schulte[1]

[1] Institute for Flight Dynamics & Flight Guidance
[2] Institute for Software Technology
Universität der Bundeswehr München, Germany
{alexander.matzner,mark.minas,axel.schulte}@unibw.de

Abstract. Cognitive automation has proven to be an applicable approach to handle increasing complexity in automation. Although fielded prototypes have already been demonstrated, the real time performance of the underlying software framework COSA is currently a limiting factor with respect to a further increase of the application complexity. In this paper we describe a cognitive framework with increased performance for the use in cognitive systems for vehicle guidance automation tasks. It uses a combination of several existing graph transformation algorithms and techniques. We show, that for our approach, the incremental rule matching that we propose yields a performance gain over the non-incremental algorithm and a large increase over the existing generic cognitive framework COSA for a typical application.

1 Introduction

The demand for tasks to become automated in vehicle guidance and process control tasks, e.g., in the domain of uninhabited aerial vehicles (UAVs) is continuously increasing. The performance provided by conventionally automated systems has its advantages, but the associated increase in complexity becomes a challenge for system designers and the human operator as well (see e.g., [21], [1]). The approach of *Cognitive Automation* is a contribution to cope with this complexity. Core features of this approach are machine capabilities such as a comprehensive situation understanding and decision making based upon explicit goals for acting. The dynamic knowledge about the situation is kept in a central situation representation and modified either by external events or by the application of stored behavior rules, the so called a-priori knowledge. In our implementation of the so called *Cognitive Process* we use a host graph to represent the current situation representation and a knowledge base consisting of two types of rules that are applied to this host graph. The two types are (i) *inference rules* that cause a reversible modification of the host graph which is retracted, once the rules left hand side does not match anymore and (ii) *graph transformation rules* that cause persistent modifications of the host graph, i.e. used to mimic long term memory. Independent of its type an efficient graph pattern matching

A. Schürr, M. Nagl, and A. Zündorf (Eds.): AGTIVE 2007, LNCS 5088, pp. 297–312, 2008.

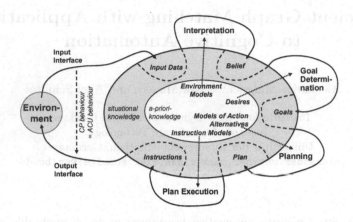

Fig. 1. Model of the *Cognitive Process* by Onken [15]

for the left hand side of the rule is the key to performance of such an implementation. To achieve this, we developed an incremental pattern matching approach that is the focus of this paper.

In chapter 2 we describe our specific application domain and how graphs and graph transformations are used to implement the *Cognitive Process*. Chapter 3 gives a very brief overview of related work, from which the algorithms and techniques in our approach were derived. Chapter 4 describes the two related approaches that we developed and evaluated. The benchmarking scenario and the results of this evaluation are described in chapter 5. Finally we conclude the paper with chapter 6 and give an outlook on our future work.

2   Problem Representation

Over the last decade the increasing challenge for human operators to handle complexity in automation led to several approaches to apply methods and techniques of Artificial Intelligence to automation problems to overcome the limitations of conventional automation. Our work is based on the *Cognitive Process* (CP) by Onken [15] that proposes a generic model of information processing, based upon findings on human behavior and cognition. The Cognitive Process shall be and has already been used as central knowledge-processing entity within so called artificial cognitive units (ACU), performing co-operative guidance of multiple uninhabited aerial vehicles and within so called assistant systems. A main feature of such an ACU is to solve complex automation tasks while generating *transparent* behavior that is consistent with the overarching *goals*. It has been implemented in the framework COSA (Cognitive System Architecture) [19] that is based on SOAR [11]. COSA has already been widely used for application development in the UAV guidance domain and proven its productivity (see e.g., [14][15]).

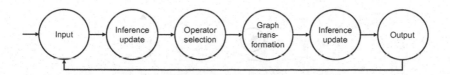

Fig. 2. Implemented automaton controlling the application of inference and graph transformation rules to implement the *Cognitive Process*

Figure 1 shows the *Cognitive Process* as proposed by Onken. Information that entered the system via the input interface (sensors) is interpreted using environment models to derive an internal situation representation of the environment (*Beliefs*). Effective *Goals* for further action are determined using this representation and the overarching hypothetical goals, here called desires. Based on models of action alternatives, sequences of actions are assembled to *Plans* that are expected to achieve the determined goals, and the generated plans are executed by translating them into specific *Instructions* that are sent to the systems output interface (actuators). All these processes run simultaneously.

To implement this model a rule based approach was chosen in the architecture COSA using a simple automaton as depicted in Figure 2 that operates on the working memory representing the systems state. The knowledge required to apply the modifications in the *Cognitive Process* is encoded in inference and graph transformation rules and the working memory is implemented as a state graph representing the current internal situation representation.

After reading the input the automaton updates the inference rules by firing the newly applicable ones and retracting the invalidated ones. In this phase all firings occur in parallel until no inference rule is applicable. This state is referred to as *quiescence*. Inference rules can propose the creation operator nodes that enable graph transformation rules by generating operator proposal nodes in working memory. During *operator selection* the automaton selects one of the operator proposal nodes and creates an operator node from it (the selection algorithm is beyond the scope of this paper). This operator serves as a pre-condition for the graph transformation rules that are then applied. In the next step the inference rules are again updated to incorporate the modifications of the graph transformation rules and the operator node created during operator selection is deleted. Finally the automaton generates the output and starts over again.

This way the automaton provides the flow control required by the *Cognitive Process* that (i) separates the parallel execution of the inference rules from the sequential execution of the graph transformation rules and (ii) allows priority based decisions on the order of the application sequence of the latter (see [11] for an in depth description of this concept).

COSA, as an operational framework, implements this model using the rule based architecture SOAR [11] as its processing kernel. The *Cognitive Process* itself is implemented using a the *Cognitive Programming Language (CPL)* that is an enhanced version of the SOAR language enabling basic object oriented principles

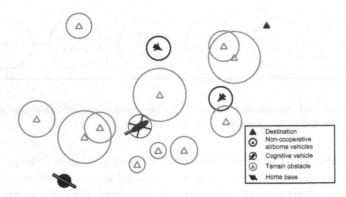

Fig. 3. Typical Situation from the scenario of the benchmark application: The cognitive vehicle is on its way from its home base to the destination and encounters a terrain obstacle

like instantiation, inheritance, and structuring the situational knowledge using namespaces. It is implemented using a library of SOAR rules that among other tasks prioritize the knowledge rules or create and maintain the model of the *Cognitive Process* in the working memory.

The COSA implementation approach has been extensively used in a complex application in the field of multiple co-operating semi-autonomous aerial vehicles [14]. A respective prototype has been demonstrated in a collaborative simulation environment with great success [18]. With respect to forthcoming field experiments including the use of COSA on embedded platforms the observed runtime performance of the existing system is not sufficient. We are therefore reimplementing the system – customized to the structure of the *Cognitive Process* – to achieve the mandatory significant performance enhancement in terms of processing speed an memory demands. While there are many relevant performance issues to be addressed in our re-implementation, in this paper we will only focus on our approach to the graph matching problem that builds the foundation for the cognitive behavior and consumes most of the systems resources.

To validate the aspired performance increase and the adequate behavior, we compare the performance of our new approach to the existing system in a typical benchmark application. As mentioned, cognitive automation and COSA are currently used in the domain of knowledge based assistant systems and semi-autonomous flight [15], the much simplified but typical benchmarking application has therefore been chosen from this area: An uninhabited helicopter is tasked to take off at its home base with a payload of supplies, fly to a predefined destination while avoiding terrain obstacles and non-cooperative airborne vehicles, deliver the supplies and return home safely. As it implements basic cognitive behavior we refer to the protagonist of our application as *cognitive vehicle*.

The base on which the considerations and actions of a cognitive system are founded, is a comprehensive internal representation of the relevant parts of its external world. We use directed graphs consisting of typed nodes with attributes and typed edges for this representation – the so called instance graph.

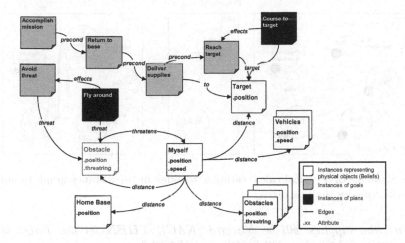

Fig. 4. Simplified snapshot of the instance graph representing the situation depicted in Figure 3

The instance graph can store sensor data generated by real or simulated sensors like the position information of a terrain obstacle, but also abstract instances like the goal to deliver supplies to a target destination. Abstract instances are generated in the *Cognitive Process* using the knowledge the application developer defined at design time.

A typical situation of the benchmark is illustrated in Figure 3. The cognitive vehicle started at its home base and was tasked to deliver the supplies to the destination. En route it encounters an obstacle that initiates the cognitive problem solving by firing inference and graph transformation rules. In this process it will choose one of the available action options – in this case to fly around the obstacle. Figure 4 shows the simplified instance graph of this situation. The boxes are nodes in the instance graph representing the current situation as perceived by the ACU. The white boxes represent physical objects, gray boxes the current goals and the black boxes the plans, the ACU chose to execute, in order to achieve its goals.

The edges in this graph specify the relations between the objects. The ACU *believes* that the left *"Obstacle"* instance *"threatens"* the *"MySelf"* instance. The goal *"Avoid threat"* was therefore instantiated and the plan *"Fly around"* was instantiated to achieve this goal.

The knowledge used for the manipulation of the instance graph is stored in inference and graph transformation rules consisting of a left hand side (LHS) with preconditions for the rule, negative application conditions (NAC) [8] that can eliminate matches and a right hand side (RHS) with the transformations, that are applied to the instance graph after the rule was activated (fired). Figure 5 depicts a typical rule stating the following:

*"**IF** there is an instance of type MySelf that is at the home base and has the goal to deliver supplies AND there is an instance of type Target that requires more than 5 units of supplies (LHS) **AND** the Target is **NOT** already the destination*

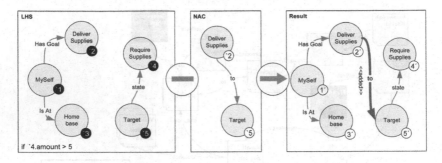

Fig. 5. Example of a typical rule creating a 'to'-edge in the instance graph to indicate where the supplies shall be delivered to

to which the supplies will be delivered (NAC), **THEN** *let the Target be the destination to which they will be delivered (RHS)."*

Every pattern node of the LHS has a unique identifier (indicated by the numbers in Figure 5). The NACs and the RHS use these identifiers to determine which of the LHS nodes their nodes refer to.

Our experimental results show, the graph transformation, currently done by the SOAR-kernel, is the bottleneck in the COSA implementation of the *Cognitive Process* - more than 90% of the runtime is spent in this phase. Therefore we especially focus on using findings from research in the field of graph transformation to increase performance.

Additionally to the complex graph matching problem itself the performance of COSA is influenced by a couple of architectural performance issues. The main ones are the required emulation of object oriented features on top of a non-object-oriented SOAR-kernel, many expensive string operations within SOAR and translation of data from one representation to another at the interface between the surrounding framework and the SOAR-kernel. While all these issues are relevant to our re-implementation, in this paper we will only focus on our approach to the graph matching problem.

3   Related Work

As mentioned, each graph transformation rule consists of an LHS represented by a model graph (pattern) that has to be matched by the instance graph for the rule to be fired. A pattern is represented by several typed *nodes* and *edges*. The pattern matching algorithm tries to find all nodes from the instance graph that have the required type and are linked with the required edges as defined by the pattern.

This pattern matching is generally done either by a graph pattern matching algorithm that is based on constraint satisfaction ([12], application e.g., in AGG [5]), local searches (e.g., FUJABA [6] or [4]) or a combination of both (e.g., PROGRES [22]). An overview of pattern matching methods is given in [16].

Conventional pattern matching algorithms however share the same handicap: they omit their results after the graph transformation cycle has been finished. In our application, we have many consecutive decision cycles. Within every cycle, a part of the graph is changed by the application of inference and graph transformation rules and after every decision cycle the instance graph is updated to reflect changes in the environment. Even though these changes to the instance graph can be significant, it would be more efficient to store and re-use at least some of the results in order to avoid recalculating them again from scratch in every cycle.

There are several approaches to this problem and some incremental approaches have already been successfully applied in various graph transformation engines such as the RETE algorithm ([2], [7]) used in SOAR [11] or attribute updates [9] in PROGRES.

The RETE algorithm is the incremental approach used in SOAR, being part of COSA. In the initialization phase it stores intermediate matching results in its alpha-network and updates the contents of this network incrementally with the occurring changes in the consecutive cycles. It is therefore well suited for problems with large instance graphs that are only affected by minor changes in every transformation cycle and for rules which patterns do not overlap. A lot of research has been done on optimizations of the RETE algorithm (i.e. [2], [3]). One of the most important optimizations is Doorenbos proposal of *left and right unlinking* [3] by which the propagation of a change through the RETE network is stopped when it becomes obvious, that no further changes will occur.

As the algorithm stores all the intermediate results, it carries the burden of a large administrative overhead, especially in environments with an ever changing instance graph. Additionally it does not support attributes, instantiation and inheritance, which are core features of the COSA framework and that must be emulated by COSA using additional graph transformation rules.

The TREAT algorithm [17] is an adaption of the RETE algorithm to reduce the administrative overhead in cases with many changes to the graph. To achieve this, it trades reduced administrative overhead in the update phase with reduced efficiency in the matching phase by only storing the intermediate results and omitting the final results. Like the RETE algorithm it does not support attributes, instantiation and inheritance.

Lately, Varró, Varró and Schürr proposed an incremental approach that supports attributes [20] and uses cached *queries* to store intermediate results similar to the RETE algorithm. It also introduces new ideas like *notification arrays* to speed up updates.

4   Approach

In our approach we use three techniques to improve the performance of the algorithm: (i) Host graph nodes are cached in *filtered type caches* for each unique pattern node, (ii) the LHS of each rule is split in its independent sub patterns (the maximally connected sub-graphs) that are then shared between rules and (iii) a tree-formed match-cache is maintained for each sub pattern and each rule to incrementally generate and maintain the matches.

To do so, we separate the rule matching process in three subsequent stages: (1) *domain reduction:* reduction of the number of host graph nodes (instances) that are potential candidates for a pattern node using the filtered type caches, (2) *incremental sub pattern matching:* incremental creation of the valid sub-pattern matches using the mentioned incrementally updated sub pattern match-caches, (3) *rule matching:* creation of the rule matches and validation of the NAC using incrementally updated rule match-caches. The actions commanded by the firing of the activated rules are collected and applied as a batch after the matching has finished.

(1) Domain reduction. The time required for a pattern matching largely depends on the size of the search space. We reduce the size of the search space for each pattern by two relational consistency algorithms for domain reduction that were proposed by McGregor and others [13]:

First we filter out single instances by requiring them to be of a certain type and their attribute values to be in a specified range.

Secondly we use the edges that are linked to a node in the pattern representation (see Figure 5) as a means for forcing 'weak' arc consistency. A pattern node can filter out single host graph nodes from its domain by requiring the existence of directed edges of a certain type and with a specified direction (inbound or outbound). In contrast to true arc-consistency at this point we do not make sure that the host graph node at the end of this edge is part of the linked pattern nodes domain.

To store these results, we maintain a cache, called *filtered type cache* for every unique node v in the host graph. This cache stores the references to the host graph nodes that compose the domain D of v, i.e., that satisfy all of the pattern nodes requirements regarding the existence of defined edges and the allowable range for defined attributes. If a node is deleted from the host graph, it has to be removed from the caches that contain its reference. If it is updated by changing the value of an attribute or linking with a new edge, the caches that contain a reference are notified to test if the instance still meets their requirements. Additionally and for all new instances all the caches that allow instances of the respective type are asked to test if the instance meets their requirements. If it does, the instance is added to the cache. Every cache provides information on its added and changed references which is used to update the match-cache in the incremental pattern matching in the next stage.

Caching allows for faster access to potential candidates for the pattern nodes and sharing them between patterns. In return we incur a little administrative overhead for updating the caches after adding and deleting instances, changing values of node attributes or adding and removing edges.

If the content of a cache and therefore the list of candidates for a pattern node was changed, the node notifies all patterns that use it and the notified patterns request to be recalculated. (Similar to the notification arrays proposed in [20]).

(2) Incremental sub pattern matching. A sub pattern consists of a set of n connected pattern nodes v_i that each have their domain D_i of host graph nodes (instances), and a set of edges that specify required relations between them. To obtain the set of valid matches for a pattern we initially build a tree of the depth n with one level for each pattern node v_i. The tree nodes on each level i represent the host graph nodes that are valid candidates for the respective pattern node after a host graph node was selected for every pattern node $v_1 \ldots v_{i-1}$ (Figure 6). Starting with the host graph nodes in the domain of the first pattern node in the search path[1] we extend each branch with only those instances in the domain of the next pattern node that satisfy all relations imposed by the instances previously bound in this branch. This extension is repeated until the last pattern node in the search order is reached or no matching instances for a pattern node are found. In the latter case the algorithm tracks back to the previous pattern node and tries to extend with the next instance in the nodes domain. The sub pattern matches can easily be generated from this tree by traversing from the leaves to the root.

The tree itself is stored for each pattern and maintained incrementally. If an instance is added to the domain of a pattern node, a new sub tree and potentially a new match is extended. If an instance is deleted from the domain, the corresponding sub tree with the corresponding match is removed. If the attribute of an instance in the tree is changed, the algorithm tests whether the instance and the related matches still satisfy the patterns conditions and removes the respective sub tree if required. Information on added and deleted matches for the pattern are provided by each pattern for use in the incremental rule matching in the next stage

If the new set of matches differs from the old set, the pattern notifies all rules that use it either as a LHS condition or as a NAC and the notified rules request to be recalculated.

(3) Rule matching. A rule consists of a LHS pattern which consists of a set of n independent LHS sub-patterns p_i that each have to have at least one valid match M_i in their set of matches, and a (possibly empty) set of NAC sub-patterns N_j none of which may have a valid match for the rule to fire and apply the RHS. To obtain the valid rule matches we calculate the set of valid matches $M_{pot} = M_1 \times \ldots \times M_n$ excluding those matches that would be a valid match for at least one of the NAC and store the results in a tree. Similar to the pattern matching, the matching tree is updated whenever at least one of the rules sub-patterns matches changed. In this case not only the new ones but also all existing rule matches are checked against the NAC to ensure that they are still valid.

The rule is then fired meaning the actions in its RHS are collected for every rule match. Only for inference rules a simple control structure ensures, that each rule is only fired once for the same match and that productions are retracted in case the match that caused the productions is no longer valid. Finally the collected actions are applied in a batch.

---

[1] Currently the search path is defined by the knowledge engineer at design time. The use of more elaborate search plans is part of our future work.

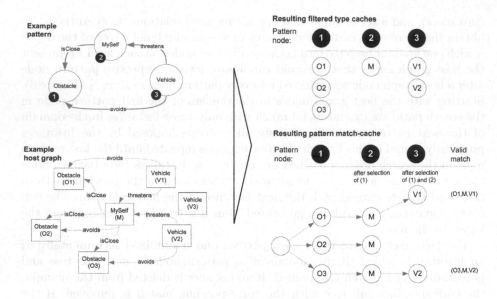

Fig. 6. Example pattern and example host graph to illustrate the filtered type caches and the pattern match tree

The matches on each stage – patterns or rules – are not recalculated from scratch every time, but are updated using the old set of matches and information on changes from the previous stage (the patterns use changes to their nodes domains, the rules use changes to their patterns matches). We therefore refer to this approach as the *incremental* approach.

To examine the effect of the incremental approach we implemented a second system without using the match-caches for sub patterns and rules. In this approach, the pattern and rule matching is done from scratch when triggered. We refer to this as the *non-incremental* approach. No additional administrative overhead for the update of pattern matches is required.

5   Experimental Evaluation

To validate the effect of the incremental optimization on performance, we specified a relevant benchmarking task that was solved by the three frameworks: Our newly developed framework with (i) the non-incremental algorithm, (ii) the incremental algorithm and (iii) to compare overall system performance, the existing COSA using SOAR.

5.1   Benchmarking Application

In our scenario, the cognitive vehicle, i.e. the rescue helicopter, is controlled by one of the three competing frameworks, while the environment, including the non-cooperative vehicles and the cognitive vehicles movement, are simulated separately. The resulting status updates to the instance graph, containing the situation representation, are performed after each decision cycle.

The simulated scenario, depicted in Figure 3, consists of 20 physical objects, including the home base, the destination, the cognitive vehicle itself, two non-cooperative airborne vehicles, and 15 terrain obstacles that are represented through their center location and a ring indicating the safe distance. In addition to that there are up to 50 abstract objects, like distance relations, goals, and plans that are generated by rule application. In total up to 70 instances are considered during reasoning. Figure 4 illustrates the simplified internal representation of the situation.

The cognitive vehicle encounters several typical situations for which we require a defined, very simple behavior. In total there are 37 rules defined, consisting of 79 sub patterns. Some examples of these rules[2] are:

- IF *supplies not yet delivered* THEN activate goal to deliver supplies (implies setting target as current destination)
- IF *supplies are delivered* THEN activate goal to return home (implies setting the home base as current destination)
- IF *not threatened and destination exists* THEN set heading to fly directly to the destination
- IF *collision with terrain impending* THEN change heading to fly around the encountered obstacle in the shorter direction to the current destination until a safe distance is reached
- IF *collision with non-cooperative airborne vehicle impending* THEN change heading to fly away from the vehicle while leaning toward the current destination and accelerate until a safe distance is reached
- IF *collision with terrain impending while avoiding a vehicle and vice versa* THEN change heading to fly away from the vehicle and the obstacle until a safe distance is reached

External state changes caused by the simulation or the environment have to be interpreted all the time. However, actions are required in the specified situations only. In our case 19 of the 37 rules fire in every decision cycle. They update e.g., the distance-relations after position changes or evaluate whether the cognitive vehicle is within a threat-ring of an obstacle.

The duration of the decision cycle from sensory input at t_i to output via the actuators at t_{i+1} is called the *decision cycle time* $t_{c_i} = t_{i+1} - t_i$ and is a key performance indicator for the cognitive system. It is a measure for the speed, the system can react on external state changes. Its reciprocal is the *decision frequency*. In real world application the system will generally receive data at a certain sampling frequency f_s, meaning a new sample needs to be processed every $t_s = 1/f_s$. Therefore the minimum time between data samples at which the system can process every sample without delay is $t_{s_{min}} = t_{c_{max}}$. Its reciprocal is the maximum sampling frequency $f_{s_{max}}$.

---

[2] The depicted rules were implemented as graph transformation rules in the benchmark application.

The systems behavior can be affected if t_s is smaller than $t_{c_{max}}$, meaning, the system can not react on every state change. This would cause that the decision cycle times at the same decision cycle would not be comparable anymore between systems with differing performance. The faster system would have reacted in an earlier cycle, this might lead to subsequent changes in flightpath and therefore different situations. In order to ensure comparable behavior in the benchmarking application, therefore we eliminate the effect of the system reaction time by selecting the simulation sample time t_s much longer than the longest decision cycle time $t_{c_{max}}$, in our case 1 second. With this adaption the systems using the different approaches show the same behavior and require the same amount of decision cycles for completing the task. This does not preclude the designer of a real world application from running the cycles without this artificial delay, but in our comparison this ensures the same behavior and therefore comparable measurements for every decision cycle.

All measurements were conducted on a 1.6 MHz Intel Centrino processor with 1GB RAM.

5.2 Results

Figure 7 illustrates the situations encountered in the benchmark in a typical simulation run. The dashed line indicates the trajectory of the cognitive vehicle (i.e., the rescue helicopter), the solid line indicates the trajectory of a non-cooperative airborne vehicle.

At the start of the simulation the cognitive vehicle recognizes the target, takes off and sets course to the destination. At point (1) it encounters a terrain obstacle that it avoids (avoiding the obstacle is controlled by firing the corresponding rules which causes the peaks in decision cycle time that can be seen in Figure 8 between decision cycles 128-180). It then finds itself too close to an airborne vehicle at (2) and changes its course to avoid it (cycles 221-321). Shortly after the initial heading change it encounters another obstacle while flying away from the

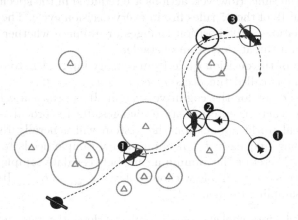

Fig. 7. Typical simulation run of the benchmark application

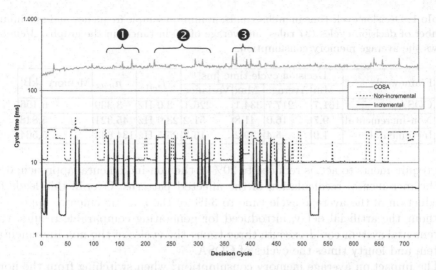

Fig. 8. Decision frequency of decision cycle for COSA, non-incremental and incremental algorithm (logarithmic scale)

vehicle which leads to an additional heading change (cycle 238). At point (3) it reaches the destination and delivers its payload (cycle 366). Now it re-determines its goals, sets the home base as the new destination and returns home. The peaks between cycle 406-475 are due to a last terrain avoiding maneuver, not depicted in Figure 7. From here the cognitive vehicle does not encounter another obstacle until reaching its home base. This is clearly illustrated by the short cycle time of the incremental algorithm in Figure 8. The non-incremental algorithm however shows some fluctuations in cycle time because of recalculations of pattern matchings.

The duration of the simulation t_{sim} is 727 cycles at 1 second simulated time each summing up to 12 minutes and 7 seconds. The average of the decision cycle times $t_{c_{avg}}$ is used to approximate the maximum number n_{max} of decision cycles, $n_{max} = t_{sim}/t_{c_{avg}}$, that would have been possible within the simulated time, if run continuously and not limited to the simulation sample frequency.

Table 1 shows a significant decrease in decision cycle time from COSA to the newly developed frameworks. These results do not necessarily show an advantage of our matching algorithm over the RETE algorithm but depict the performance increase of the complete new framework compared to the existing one. This is mainly due to two reasons: (i) the support for the object oriented features is now part of the pattern matching algorithm which reduces the number of rules to be handled as the administrative rules are not needed anymore, (ii) the data representation was optimized, largely reducing the number of string operations and data translations.

Table 1 shows that resulting peak times of the non-incremental and the incremental approach are nearly the same. The incremental approach looses its advantage in situations with many affected rules. At the same time, the minimum time spent per cycle, i.e., the time used for state interpretation without

Table 1. Decision cycle time in milliseconds, minimum sample frequency and maximum number of decision cycles (37 rules, an average of 60 instances in the graph). *Memory* shows the average memory consumption.

Framework	Decision cycle time [ms]				$f_{s_{min}}$	n_{max}	Memory [kB]
	Min	Average	Max	Variance			
COSA	161.7	217.7	334.1	226.1	3.0 Hz	3,339	6,196
Non-incremental	9.7	16.0	41.8	51.2	23.9 Hz	45,321	5,848
Incremental	1.9	5.4	39.2	16.3	25.5 Hz	134,643	5,564

any requirements to act, is reduced to 20% of the non-incremental approach, due to the incremental recalculation of the affected patterns. Overall this leads to a reduction of the average cycle time to 34% of the non-incremental approach. Without the artificial delay, introduced for generating comparable results, the incremental system could execute three times the cycles of the non-incremental system and fourty times the cycles of COSA.

The impact on average memory consumption[3] when switching from the non-incremental to the incremental approach is determined by two counteracting effects. In the later additional memory is required for storing current, added and deleted matches of every pattern. However, less memory is required because of less pattern matches and less subsequent rule matches. Overall the memory consumption therefore slightly decreases from the non-incremental to the incremental approach as Table 1 depicts. The memory consumption of COSA is added for completeness and is not directly comparable to the other results as it uses different libraries.

6   Conclusion

The performance of the examined system does not depend on the domain it is used in, but on the way the knowledge is encoded, i.e. size of the LHS and the amount of rules that fire each cycle, and the amount of knowledge in the knowledge base (the amount of rules). The rules used in the benchmark application used to compare COSA and our implementations are very similar to those in the previously developed COSA applications but the number of rules in the simple benchmark application is significantly lower. Therefore a next step will be to examine the results for significantly larger knowledge bases.

For the selected benchmark our experimental results show that performance is improved by our incremental rule matching approach compared to the non-incremental approach. The small additional overhead incurred through maintaining the filtered type caches and generating the notification arrays, is more than compensated by the gain due to less pattern matchings. The magnitude of this effect depends on the amount of changes to the instance graph per decision cycle, the amount of common nodes, the sub patterns share, and the number of rules fired every decision cycle.

---

[3] Average memory consumption was measured with the UNIX standard tool *top* for COSA and *ProcessExplorer* for the new implementations.

In our benchmarking application, despite the fact that about 50% of the rules are fired in each decision cycle for situation interpretation, a significant reduction in average cycle time could be observed. We expect this effect to be even larger with a larger knowledge base and a resulting lower share of rules that are fired in each decision cycle.

Compared to the existing framework COSA, the same behavior could be achieved at an average decision cycle time that was reduced by 97.5%. As mentioned, this is mainly due to the implementation being customized for the cognitive model used and the more efficient data representation.

In our future work we will examine the effect of the complexity of the environment and the number of rules in the rule base on performance. Also the use of search plans as applied e.g., in PROGRES and further optimization of the rule matching algorithm could further improve performance.

With a reliable implementation of the optimized framework we will prove the concept in a real world application using a real, uninhabited helicopter platform under development [10].

References

1. Billings, C.E.: Human centered automation: A concept and guidelines (1991)
2. Bunke, H., Glauser, T., Tran, T.-H.: An efficient implementation of graph grammar based on the RETE-matching algorithm. In: Ehrig, H., Kreowski, H.-J., Rozenberg, G. (eds.) Graph Grammars 1990. LNCS, vol. 532. Springer, Heidelberg (1991)
3. Doorenbos, R.B.: Combining Left and Right Unlinking for Matching a Large Number of Learned Rules. School of Computer Science, Carnegie Mellon University, Pittsburgh, PA (1994)
4. Dörr, H.: Efficient Graph Rewriting and Its Implementation. LNCS, vol. 922. Springer, Heidelberg (1995)
5. Ermel, C., Rudolf, M., Taentzer, G.: The AGG-approach: Language and tool environment. In: Ehrig, H., Engels, G., Kreowski, H.-J., Rozenberg, G. (eds.) Handbook on Graph Grammars and Computing by Graph Transformation, vol. 2. World Scientific, Singapore (1999)
6. Fischer, T., Niere, J., Torunski, L.: Story diagrams: A new graph rewrite language based on the unified modeling language. In: Ehrig, H., Engels, G., Kreowski, H.-J., Rozenberg, G. (eds.) TAGT 1998. LNCS, vol. 1764, pp. 296–309. Springer, Heidelberg (2000)
7. Forgy, C.L.: RETE: A fast algorithm for the many pattern/many object match problem. Arificial Intelligence (1982)
8. Habel, A., Heckel, H., Taentzer, G.: Graph grammars with negative application conditions. Fundamenta Informaticae 26(3/4), 287–313 (1996)
9. Hudson, S.E.: Incremental attribute evaluation: an algorithm for lazy evaluation in graphs. Technical Report, 87-20, University of Arizona (1987)
10. Kriegel, M., Meitinger, C., Schulte, A.: Operator assistance and semi-autonomous functions as key elements of future systems for multiple UAV guidance. In: 7th Conference on Engineering Psychology and Cognitive Ergonomics, in conjunction with HCI International, Beijing, China (2007)
11. Laird, J.E., Newell, A., Rosenbloom, P.S.: Soar: An architecture for general intelligence. Arificial Intelligence 33, 1–64 (1987)

12. Larrosa, J., Valiente, G.: Graph pattern matching using constraint satisfaction. In: International Workshop on Graph Transformation, Berlin, pp. 189–196 (2000)
13. McGregor, J.J.: Relational consistency algorithms and their application in finding subgraph and graph isomorphisms. Information Sciences 19, 229–250 (1979)
14. Meitinger, C., Schulte, A.: Cognitive machine co-operation as basis for guidance of multiple UAVs. In: NATO RTO HFM Symposium on Human Factors of Uninhabited Military Vehicles as Force Multipliers, Biarritz, France (2006)
15. Meitinger, C., Schulte, A.: Human-centered automation for UAV guidance: Oxymoron of tautology? The potential of cognitive and co-operative systems. In: 1st Moving Autonomy Forward Conference, Grantham, UK (2006)
16. Messmer, B.T.: Efficient Graph Matching Algorithms for Preprocessed Model Graphs. PhD thesis, Universität Bern (1995)
17. Miranker, D.P.: TREAT: A better match algorithm for AI production systems. In: AAAI 1987 Sixth National Conference on Artificial Intelligence, Los Altos, CA, vol. 1, pp. 42–47 (1987)
18. Platts, J.T.: Final report of the GARTEUR flight mechanics (FM) AG-14. Autonomy in UAVs (in press, 2007)
19. Putzer, H., Onken, R.: COSA - a generic cognitive system architecture based on a cognitive model of human behavior. In: 8th European Conference on Cognitive Science Approaches to Process Control CSAPC 2001, Universität der Bundeswehr, München (2001)
20. Varró, G., Varró, D., Schürr, A.: Incremental graph pattern matching. Electronic Communications of the EASST: Graph and Model Transformation 2006 4 (2006)
21. Wiener, E.L.: Human Factors in Aviation. Academic Press, San Diego (1993)
22. Zündorf, A.: Graph pattern matching in PROGRES. In: Cuny, J., Engels, G., Ehrig, H., Rozenberg, G. (eds.) Graph Grammars 1994. LNCS, vol. 1073, pp. 454–468. Springer, Heidelberg (1996)

Checking and Enforcement of Modeling Guidelines with Graph Transformations

Carsten Amelunxen[1], Elodie Legros[1], Andy Schürr[1], and Ingo Stürmer[2]

[1] Darmstadt University of Technology, Real-Time Systems Lab
{amelunxen,legros,schuerr}@es.tu-darmstadt.de
http://www.es.tu-darmstadt.de
[2] Model Engineering Solutions, Berlin
stuermer@model-engineers.com
http://www.model-engineers.com

Abstract. In the automotive industry, the model driven development of software for embedded controller units evolves to become the standard paradigm. In this domain, the development is based on executable block diagrams and StateCharts which are provided by the commonly used tool MATLAB Simulink/Stateflow. Huge catalogues with hundreds of modeling guidelines have already been developed to increase the quality of models and ensure the safety and reliability of the generated code. Checking these guidelines and eliminating detected violations manually during audits is a tremendous amount of boring work. In this paper, we show how graph transformations can be used to automate the process of guideline checking and the execution of repair actions. Based on our experiences in an industrial context, we discuss the pros and cons of graph transformations compared to other specification approaches and we finally present a proposal how to combine graph transformations with other modeling paradigms as the most promising approach.

1 Introduction

Nowadays, model-driven development is common practice within a wide range of automotive embedded software development projects. In this domain, the standard modeling language UML still plays a neglectible role and the *MathWorks MATLAB Simulink/Stateflow (MATLAB SL/SF)* [MAT] environment is used as a de facto standard. Simulink supports a block-oriented style of modeling that combines the data-flow programming paradigm with differential equation solvers; Stateflow adds a discrete event and state-oriented style of modeling based on Harel's concepts of hierarchical automata (StateCharts).

Embedded controller software is either manually developed by programmers using Matlab SL/SF models as executable requirements specifications or generated automatically by code generators which translate Matlab SL/SF models into rather efficient C code. In both cases the reliability, robustness, and efficiency of the developed code heavily depends on the quality of the specified models.

A. Schürr, M. Nagl, and A. Zündorf (Eds.): AGTIVE 2007, LNCS 5088, pp. 313–328, 2008.

Therefore, generally accepted modeling guidelines – such as the MathWorks Automotive Advisory Board (MAAB) guidelines – are usually adopted. These modeling guidelines are either manually or automatically checked during audits using tools like the Mathworks Model Advisor. However, for huge models, this can add up to a few hundreds or even thousands of violations that must be corrected manually by the modeler.

A recent in-house study at DaimlerChrysler showed us that automated and partly interactive model corrections can reduce the effort of model refactoring activities up to 70 percent. Nevertheless, we are not aware of any tool support in this direction except of our *Matlab SL/SF Model Analysis and Transformation Environment MATE*. MATE has been developed in a joint effort of four universities and two companies [SDG+07]. The main motivation for starting the MATE project was our observation that the implementation of modeling guidelines today takes place on a very low level of abstraction using imperative programming languages. Therefore, the realization of really complex checks is almost infeasible as well as the development of even more complex model transformations that eliminate identified guideline violations automatically. It is our impression and the intention of this paper to show that, in general, graph transformations offer significantly better support for the specification and implementation of modeling guidelines and refactorings. Furthermore, we will discuss the pros and cons of graph transformations compared to a limited number of other specification paradigms. We will conclude the paper with a proposal how to extend graph transformations to overcome some limits that still impact their usefulness in this application domain.

The rest of this paper is, therefore, organized as follows: section 2 discusses the motivations for this work and the MATE project in general, whereas section 3 compares the MATE environment with other MATLAB SL/SF guideline checking frameworks and points out the highlights of a graph transformation based approach. Section 4 then introduces a representative set of guidelines as running example and explains the overall structure of MATLAB Simulink models. Afterwards, section 5 discusses the specification of some guidelines using a mixture of regular expressions and 1st order logic expressions, whereas section 6 then presents some graph transformations that specify the selected guidelines and appropriate repair actions where possible. Finally, section 7 summarizes the results of the comparison of different specification paradigms and discusses our plans for future work concerning the design and implementation of a more powerful graph transformation environment.

2   The MATE Project

The MATE project [SDG+07] provides support for semi-automatic checking and enforcement of modeling guidelines as well as for version management, design pattern instantiation, and interactive model refactoring and beautifying operations. It is a joint project of two companies (DaimlerChrysler, Model Engineering Solution) and four universities (Technical University of Darmstadt, University of Kassel, University of Paderborn, University of Siegen). This project was born out of an urgent need of the automotive industry for more sophisticated tool support in this area. Automotive software developers using MATLAB SL/SF are confronted with the same well-known and ordinary maintenance and quality assurance problems of everyday life programming. Due to the fact, that the main application domain of MATLAB SL/SF models is the simulation and code generation for safety-critical embedded systems, the importance of quality assurance becomes even more significant. A MATLAB SL/SF code generator may only produce high quality C code if its input models are of high quality, too.

Therefore, rigorous model audits (review processes) play an important role for a model-driven automative software development process. The significance of model reviewing is supported by a case study [SCFD06] which presents 146 critical model changes due to findings from a multi-iterative reviewing process on a model of 9308 blocks. All in all, the reviewing took a netto time of 1600 minutes, nearly 27 hours. Since, reviewing is a time-consuming and thus cost-intensive process, it is a highly desirable task to ensure the quality of a model already during its creation and, thereby, reduce the efforts of reviewing. This can be done by formulating a set of modeling guidelines that are checked continuously and automatically earlier on during the model development process.

Therefore, modeling guidelines for MATLAB SL/SF are very popular in the automotive industry. There are e.g. modeling guidelines provided by the Math-Works Automotive Advisory Board (MAAB) [MAA]. These guidelines focus on several aspects like naming and graphical layout conventions, tool and model configurations, logical errors, forbidden design anti-patterns and recommended design pattern, and so on. In fact, most of these guidelines imply one or more repair actions, which often can be executed automatically or semi-automatically with some degree of user feedback. We expect, based on practical experiences, that from all captured guideline violations approximately

- 45% can be eliminated automatically
- 43% can be fixed with additional user input
- 4% can only be removed manually
- 8% are not classified yet

Analysis as well as refactoring of MATLAB SL/SF models demands full access to MATLAB's model repository. Such an access is provided by an API written in M-Script, a proprietary script language. Both the used C-like scripting language and the tool's API evolved over many years. As a consequence, it takes quite some time and efforts to learn how to program reliable model checks and transformations using this approach. The MATE project overcomes these problems by providing a layer of uniform API adapters on top of which visual graph queries and transformations can be developed on a considerably higher level of abstraction. First experiences indicate that encoding new guidelines on this new level of abstraction reduces the needed efforts up to a factor of four and results in definitely more readable code as you will see later on.

The MATE project right now uses the Fujaba graph transformation tool [Fuj] and its meta-modeling plug-in MOFLON [MOF] to specify the needed graph queries and transformations. Generated Java code either directly manipulates MATLAB SL/SF models via the tool's API or works on an offline model repository. Both solutions have their specific pros and cons: working directly on the tool's API is the preferred solution, when interactive model refactoring and beautifying operations have to be implemented. Working with an offline repository with special indexes has some advantages, when complex analysis operations have to be executed. A more detailed description of the MATE system's architecture and its functionality as well as its integration with the MathWorks tool suite is out-of-scope of this paper.

3   Related Work

Well-known examples of other MATLAB SL/SF analysis tools are MathWork's own Model Advisor [MAT] and MINT [Min]. Both tools rely on the execution of MATLAB M-Scripts to identify modeling rule violations within Simulink and Stateflow models. As already mentioned, this approach requires intimate knowledge of a tool API that has been developed over a period of many years always having backward compatibility in mind. Furthermore, a concise description of the abstract syntax and (static) semantics of manipulated modeling language instances does not exist and has to be inferred step by step by testing the functionality of one API operation after the other. Furthermore, M-Script developers have to use imperative programming constructs for data flow analysis, pattern matching and rewriting activities – a very error-prone and time-consuming task.

Therefore, the MESA project [FR07] started to develop an own meta model for the modeling languages Simulink and Stateflow that captures the abstract syntax and part of the static semantics of these two languages. This meta model is used to generate an offline model repository for guideline checking purposes (as we do in the MATE project). Guidelines are specified in the logic-based Object Constraint Language OCL of the OMG. The specification of refactoring operations is still out-of-scope due to the fact that OCL does not offer any support for modifying models. Similarly, the GME/GReAT team developed a MATLAB SL/SF meta model with the intention to specify model/graph transformations that either create or translate MATLAB SL/SF models [NKS+05]. As far as we know, guideline checking and repair actions have not yet been addressed. Furthermore, the experiment reported in [MSD06] describes a successful use of graph transformations for the detection and resolution of UML model inconsistencies.

Despite of the obvious deficiency of OCL compared to graph transformation languages, it is not clear whether a logic-based textual language like OCL or a visual rule-based approach as offered by Fujaba/MOFLON or GReAT is more appropriate for the specification of modeling guidelines. It is the main purpose of this paper to start a systematic comparison of both specification paradigms. We will see later on that both approaches have their pros and cons and should be combined with other concepts to obtain a more powerful (meta) modeling and specification language.

4 Modeling Guidelines for MATLAB Simulink

This section introduces our running example, four different guidelines for MAT-LAB Simulink models. These examples constitute a representative set and are well-suited for the comparison of different specification paradigms. Furthermore, we present a considerably simplified meta model of MATLAB Simulink.

4.1 Guidelines

In the following, we discuss guidelines that involve string pattern matching, calculation of complex arithmetic expressions as well as local and global pattern matching operations. Aspects concerning a proper model layout are out of scope of this paper, but can be handled in similar ways.

Guideline 1: Naming of Subsystems. Usually modeling guideline catalogues list quite a number of naming conventions that impose certain restrictions on the name/identifier of a single modeling element. Often these restrictions are intended to increase the readability of a model or to forbid the usage of identifiers that are known to cause troubles during code generation. We have selected a typical naming convention for Simulink subsystems. The name of a subsystem may consist of lower and upper case alphabetic characters, including numeric characters and underscore. There must neither be more than one consecutive underscore nor an underscore at the beginning or the end of a subsystem's name. Number are also forbidden as first character of a subsystem's name.

Guideline 2: Naming of Enable Port block. The second modeling guideline concerns the naming of **Enable Port** blocks. An enable block of a subsystem permits or blocks its execution depending on the signal that is processed by this block. In order to be able to identify enable port blocks immediately, a guideline demands that the **Enable** block's name matches the name of the corresponding enable signal of the regarded subsystem (cf. Fig. 1).

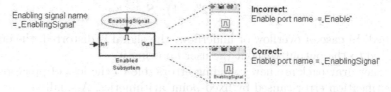

Fig. 1. Naming restrictions for Enable Port block

Guideline 3: Unconnected signals. This guideline ensures that every element of a Simulink model is connected. Unconnected subsystems, basic block inputs, outputs or unconnected signal lines are not allowed. Thus, this rule is rather important for the structural correctness of a model. A violation of this rule inevitably leads to an erroneous model (cf. Fig. 2). Nevertheless, a violation of this guideline is quite easy to fix by connecting the unconnected inputs to ground blocks and the unconnected outputs to terminator blocks (if affected inputs and outputs are not needed during model execution).

Unconnected input:

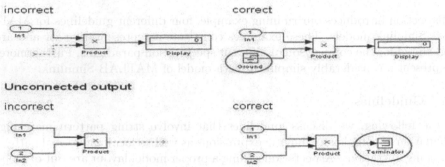

Fig. 2. Restrictions concerning unconnected signals

Guideline 4: Numerical and Dataflow Analysis. It is possible to design control and signal processing systems that will be implemented using fixed-point arithmetic. Two drawbacks must be considered, when using fixed-point arithmetic [Soh06]. The first one is the risk to introduce new sources of over-flow/underflow (compared to a floating point arithmetic execution of the same model). An overflow/underflow occurs, when a calculation produces a result greater/smaller than the number that can be stored in the specified fixed-point format. The fixed-point representation is defined by the number of bits used and the scale factor which corresponds to the least significant bit in base 2. A number x in fixed-point arithmetic with n bits and a scale factor S_x must be a value in the range of

$$-2^{n-1} \cdot S_x \leq x \leq (2^{n-1} - 1) \cdot S_x \qquad (1)$$

if signed or in the range of

$$0 \leq x \leq (2^n - 1) \cdot S_x \qquad (2)$$

if unsigned. In case of overflow or underflow, the signal is distorted, the error is propagated to the output without the user knowing it.

The other drawback are new rounding errors due to the loss of precision and the quantification error caused by fixed-point arithmetics. A small output error usually can be ignored, but further processing and propagation of numerical errors often leads to problems. That is why we need analysis rules that compute lower and upper bounds for computed fixed-point arithmetic values as well as conservative estimates for rounding errors using interval arithmetic. In some cases precision problems can be easily fixed automatically by increasing the scale factors of affected blocks. In other cases, complete subsystems have to be restructured manually. Furthermore, it is possible to automatically rewrite Simulink models such that they are able to handle overflows and underflows either by simply truncating output values using `SaturateBlocks` or creating signals that trigger later on manually added error-handling computations.

4.2   MATLAB Simulink Metamodel

In the past quite a number of meta models for MATLAB Simulink have already been developed. Most of them are quite simple and introduce a rather generic abstract syntax model with a small number of concepts. A Simulink model is a `System` that may contain a hierarchy of `Subsystems` with `Blocks` as leafs. `Blocks` are the atomic processing units. They are connected to each other by connecting their `Outports` and `Inports` via `Lines`. Furthermore, blocks have attributes in the form of `PropertyName` pairs that are either atomic or consist of properties in turn.

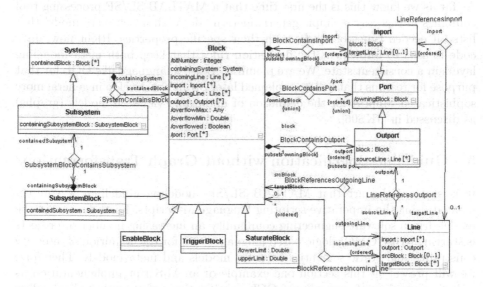

Fig. 3. Simplified metamodel of Matlab Simulink

Such a meta model does not contain any information about required or optional properties of certain types of blocks. It simplifies the development of import and export functions for a model repository or the implementation of an API considerably, but it is not very useful for the specification of guideline checks and repair actions for the following reasons: accessing specific property values of blocks of specific types is very awkward and error-prone. To solve this problem a meta model must be introduced, where each block type is defined as a separate meta class with its properties listed as (meta) attributes of this meta class. Furthermore, we often have to navigate from one `Block` to another one identifying first the right `Inport` or `Outport`, following then a list of `Lines` to the opposite `Outport` or `Inport`, and finally traversing the link from this element to its own `Block`. Last but not least, when writing analysis rules, we often have to identify patterns, where a block has a certain combination of property values or a certain number of outgoing or incoming connections.

For these purposes we have added another meta model layer on top of the generic Simulink meta model, where we introduce specific block types like

SaturateBlock with specific properties like lower/upperLimit (cf. Figure 3). These model elements represent *derived data* that is automatically computed using the generic meta model elements as input. In fact they are a kind of *updatable view* that can be used to specify rather compact and readable model queries and transformations. A transformation that creates e.g. a single virtually existing SaturateBlock object with appropriate property values in reality creates a generic Block object with two associated Property objects for its two attributes lower/upperLimit.

Furthermore, we are using derived attributes and associations that are needed for data flow analysis purposes or simplify navigation between connected blocks. As far as we know this is the first time that a MATLAB SL/SF processing tool combines in this way a simple generic meta model with a rich meta model that lists all needed types of blocks with their specific properties. Right now, Java code is used to implement the derivation rules that keep both meta modeling layers in a consistent state. We are planning to use a language like OCL for that purpose for reasons that will be explained later on and to develop in general more sophisticated support for the definition of updatable views on models (graphs) as discussed in [JKS06].

5   Guideline Specification without Graph Transformations

It is state of the art that MATLAB SL/SF modeling guidelines are implemented using the imperative scripting language M-Scripts. Furthermore, in the model-driven software engineering community an increasing number of projects is starting to use OMG's logic-based language OCL for the definition of integrity constraints and static semantics rules for models and meta models. Therefore, we will present in this section one example of an M-Script implementation as well as a number of examples of OCL specifications of the selected modeling guidelines. In the following section we will then present graph transformation specifications of the same set of guidelines for comparison purposes.

5.1   M-Script

Today almost all modeling guideline checks are implemented using the programming language M-Script that is part of the MATLAB SL/SF tool suite – on a very low level of abstraction. In the following we present the M-Script implementation of the analysis of guideline 2 as an example. We skip the detailed explanation since the example is serving its purpose of giving an impression of what M-Script checks are suffering from.

In fact, the implementation of model guidelines with M-Script is nothing else than traversing graph structures and implementing graph pattern matching operations with an imperative language. Thus, implementing guidelines with M-Script is rather a task of programming skills and detailed API knowledge than a task of a conceptual and well structured conversion of an informal description into a formal one.

```
function f_block_h = guideline_2(system, cmd_s)
  top_h = get_param(bdroot,'Handle');
  f_block_h = [];
  subsys = get_param(get_param(find_system(top_h, 'BlockType',
                     'EnablePort'), 'Parent'), 'Handle');
  for k=1:length(subsys)
    subsys_handle = get_param(subsys{k},'Handle');
    porth = get_param(subsys{k},'PortHandles');
    enable_port_name = get_param(porth.Enable,'Name');
    enableh = find_system(subsys{k},'SearchDepth',1,
                     'BlockType','EnablePort');
    enable_block_name = get_param(enableh,'Name');
    if ~(strcmp(enable_port_name, enable_block_name))
        f_block_h = [f_block_h;subsys_handle];
    end
  end % for
end % function
```

5.2   Regular Expressions

Since consistent naming is a very important feature of high quality MATLAB
SL/SF models, an approach replacing M-Script as first choice approach has to
provide regular expressions for the description of string restrictions. Regular
expressions provide a technique to describe legal sets/languages of strings based
on syntactical rules only. Thus, regular expressions cannot act as a substitution
of M-Script. They rather provide a powerful addition to an existing guideline
implementation approach. In the following, we demonstrate the usefulness of
regular expressions by the implementation of guideline 1.

The pattern which is intended by guideline 1 is formulated in the syntax of
regular expressions. Then, the negation of this pattern is used to detect guideline
violations. Since the name of a subsystem can neither start with an underscore
nor a number, the name must start with an alphabetic character, which is represented by the term **[A-Z a-z]**. Furthermore, the rest of a subsystems's name
consists of an arbitrary number of alphabetical characters and numbers which
must not be separated by more than one consecutive underscore and must not
end with an underscore. Thus, the following regular expression matches a correct
subsystem name:

```
[A-Z a-z](([A-Z a-z 0-9]*)(\_?)([A-Z a-z 0-9]+))*
```

5.3   The Object Constraint Language

The application of the Object Constraint Language (OCL) provides an approach
which could in general act as a basis for the formalization of all kinds modeling
guidelines. OCL is a precise logic-based language which provides constraint and
object query expressions on MOF/UML compliant models or meta models. Since
modeling guidelines represent constraints on model elements or relations between
model elements which have to be respected, OCL can be used for a formal

description of such rules. In the following, we demonstrate the application of OCL by the implementation of guideline 2 and 3. In case of guideline 2, the two different cases of unconnected lines and unconnected ports have to be considered. Both can be covered by OCL invariants in different contexts. First of all, the following invariant applies in the context of a line, stating that a line must have one source and one target block.

```
context Line
inv: (srcBlock != null) and (targetBlock != null)
```

Furthermore, a port has to be connected to a line. Since the classes `Inport` and `Outport` are connected to the class `Line` by different associations, we have to write two different constraints for the two regarded classes. Both invariants are listed in the following.

```
context Inport                   context Outport
inv: targetLine != null          inv: sourceLine != null
```

As a consequence guideline 3 is formalized by a set of three OCL invariants. In fact, all three invariants are quite trivial and a tremendous improvement compared to the corresponding M-Script implementation presented above. The presented OCL specification has only one drawback: a single modeling guideline is translated into three different constraints instead of being a single piece of code. If a one-to-one correspondence of guidelines and constraints is an issue (e.g. for reasons of maintainability of guideline implementations) then we can resort to the following solution, where a single more complex OCL constraint enforces the same guideline.

```
context Block
inv: incomingLine->forAll( srcBlock != null ) and
     outgoingLine->forAll ( targetBlock != null ) and
     inport->forAll(targetLine != null) and
     outport -> forAll(sourceLine != null)
```

The OCL expressions presented above probably give the reader the impression that it is straight-forward to produce and to understand logic-based specifications of modeling guidelines. But this is no longer true, when more complex patterns have to be specified. Let us consider our modeling guideline 2. This guideline requires that the enable block name matches the name of the signal enabling the subsystem. The class `SubsystemBlock` that contains both the regarded block and its corresponding signal is an obvious choice as context for the to be defined OCL expression.

First of all, we have to check that the regarded subsystem contains an `EnableBlock`. Then two elements of the subsystem must be determined and compared: the name of the enabling signal and the name of the corresponding enable block. To compute the name of the enabling signal, we must match that instance of the class `Line`, whose value of `PropertyName` "DstPort" is equal to "enable" and return its name (cf. subexpression starting at label (1) below). To find the name of the enable block, we must select the block instance of the class *EnableBlock* contained in the subsystem and return its name (cf. subexpression starting at label (2) below).

Please note that a subsystem neither may contain more than one enable block or more than one enabling signal. That means that the intersection of the computed sets of signal and block names is either the single common name (the guideline is respected) or empty (a violation of the guideline).

```
if self.containedBlock
     ->exists(b:Block | b.oclIsTypeOf(EnableBlock) )
then
(1) self.containingSubsystemBlock.incomingLine
     ->select( line | line.dstPort = "enable" )
     ->collect(qualifiedName)
   -> intersection (self.containedBlock
(2)   ->select(b:Block | b.oclIsTypeOf(EnableBlock))
     ->collect(qualifiedName) )
   -> notEmpty()
endif
```

This example clearly shows that OCL is not very well-suited for the specification of complex patterns, where we have to navigate along different paths through a model and to compare their results. Even worse, it is almost unfeasible to encode guideline 1 or guideline 4 using OCL. In the first case the pattern matching facilities of regular expressions are missing, in the second case we are running into problems, when we have to compute intervals of possible value ranges as well as upper bounds for rounding errors. OCL offers some basic operators on integers and reals for that purpose, but does not directly support more complex arithmetic operations like the calculation of two to the power of a negative value. It is, therefore, necessary to delegate these computations to a host programming language via method calls embedded in OCL expressions. As a consequence, we will not present a specification of guideline 4 here.

6 Analysis and Refactoring with Graph Transformations

In this section we finally present graph transformation specifications of our guidelines. For this purpose the visual SDM (story driven modeling) diagram syntax is used [Fuj] that is supported by the graph transformation tool Fujaba and our plug-in MOFLON [MOF]. Each of these specifications relies on the existence of a context/parameter object (as the OCL expressions presented before) and it is evaluated for all objects of the regarded context class.

The first specification presented in Fig. 4 consists of four different SDM activity diagram nodes: a start node follwed by a pattern node containing a single object with a complex attribute condition, followed by an action node with a piece of Java code and a terminate node. The presented graph pattern checks the qualifiedName attribute of a given SubsystemBlock using a regular expression. The check either succeeds and the execution of the small SDM activity diagram terminates or it fails. In the latter case an external Java method is called that logs the detected modeling guideline violation. Please note that SDM diagrams

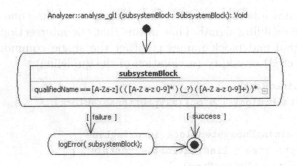

Fig. 4. Graph query for the analysis of guideline 1

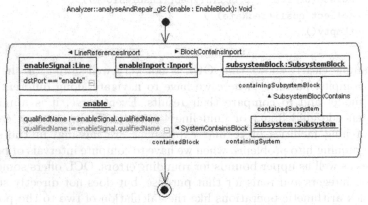

Fig. 5. Transformation that checks and fixes violations of guideline 2

right now do not directly support regular expression checking as suggested in Fig. 4. The actual specification uses a work-around based on regular expression-handling mechanisms that are available in the Java programming language. Fortunately, SDM diagram nodes may contain an arbitrary piece of Java code such as the logging method `logError` used in the regarded diagram.

Fig. 5 simultaneously checks and fixes violations of guideline 2. It matches any occurrence of a pattern, where an `EnableBlock` and an `EnableSignal` object, which belong to the same `Subsystem`, do not have the same `qualifiedName` attribute. The grey/green line inside the `enable` object rectangle assigns the name of the matched `enableSignal` to the regarded `enable` object.

Please compare this specification of the guideline check with an incorporated repair action and the M-Script implementation and the OCL specification presented beforehand. It clearly shows the advantage of graph transformations, when more complex object/link patterns have to be found and modified – at least when we use derived elements to hide certain details of the "real" object structure. In our example, both `qualifiedName` and `dstPort` are derived but nevertheless updatable attributes that are internally represented as separate `PropertyName` objects with a `name` and a `value` attribute. The pretty straight-forward code needed for the construction of these updatable views is still hand-coded in Java. We are

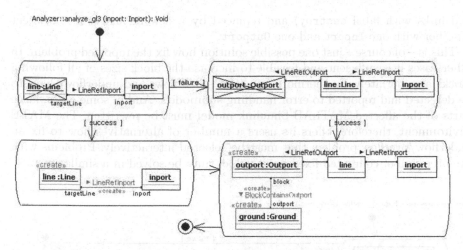

Fig. 6. Transformation that checks and fixes violations of guideline 3

working on a new specification approach for updatable views that relies on a special variant of triple graph grammars [JKS06].

The specification of the third guideline is also rather straighforward. It first checks whether the given **inport** object does *not* have an associated **Line** object. If this check fails (and a **Line** object does exist) it then goes ahead and checks for the non-existence of an **Outport** object of the **line** associated with the regarded **inport**. Finally, the programmed graph transformation rule creates the missing objects and links (depicted as grey/green objects and links with stereotype **create**).

The specification of this guideline is more complex than its OCL counterpart presented beforehand for the following reasons: if we want to create missing objects, which is outside the scope of the OCL expression, then we have to distinguish whether just a **Ground** object or a **Ground** object together with an associated **Line** object is missing.

Finally, we have to translate guideline 4 into an SDM diagram specification, which is the most complex of the selected guidelines. Standard data flow analysis is used to compute lower and upper bounds for block outputs as well as upper bounds for numerical errors. For this purpose derived attributes are used, whose evaluation functions are implemented in Java and not in OCL as originally planned for reasons discussed beforehand. The Java code is a straightforward translation of the directed equations presented in [Soh06] and will be omitted due to lack of space here. The graph transformation program presented in Fig. 7 accesses the derived attribute **overflowed** that signals a potential overflow of the output of the regarded block. It then eliminates the detected numerical problem as follows: first of all the bit size of the directly affected block output is increased and then a so-called **SaturationBlock** is introduced that simply restricts the upper and lower boundaries of the computed value range such that we don't have to modify those blocks that process the regarded output as input. For that purpose the direct connection between **aOutport** and **aInport** is deleted (objects and links with label `destroy`) and replaced by a new `SaturateBlock` object together with one `Inport` and one `Outport`.

This is – of course – just one possible solution how fix the reported problem. In other cases it is sufficient and feasible to increase the block sizes of all following blocks appropriately. Furthermore, sometimes overflows and underflows have to be detected and reported to error handling submodels. And in some cases, large parts of the affected MATLAB Simulink model must be rewritten. The MATE environment, therefore, offers its users a number of alternatives how to fix an underflow/overflow problem that must be selected interactively. Problems with the precision of computed fixed-point values may be solved in a similar way.

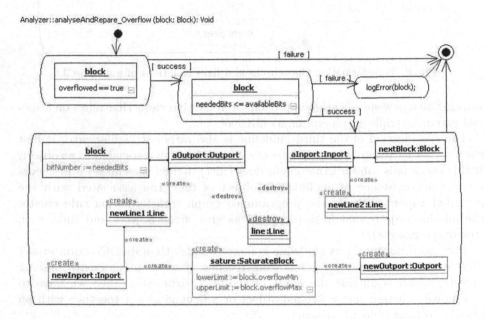

Fig. 7. Graph query for the analysis and reparation of overflows

7   Conclusion

In this paper we have presented specifications of model guideline checking and refactoring operations using a variety of different approaches. In the related discussions we pointed out that neither the logic-based language OCL nor the graph transformation rules of Fujaba/MOFLON are well equipped for handling *all sorts* of modeling guidelines. In principle, SDM diagrams together with their option to insert arbitrary pieces of Java code where needed are an excellent choice for the specification of model analysis and refactoring operations as discussed in this paper.

But, our daily work with the specification of a comprehensive set of model analysis and transformation operations in an industrial setting revealed some important still existing deficiencies of the MOFLON/FUJABA model transformation language and environment.

First of all some of us are not convinced that the usage of a visual notation has significant advantages compared to a textual notation as supported by other declarative model transformation languages. A textual notation is more compact, simplifies all kinds of version and configuration management tasks and does not force its users to spend hours beautifying the layout of huge diagrams. Therefore, we are planning to develop an alternative concrete textual syntax for MOF 2.0 class diagrams and SDM graph transformation diagrams as a new front-end for Fujaba/MOFLON.

Furthermore, we have made the experience again and again that graph transformation rules are very useful for the specification of structural model properties and transformations, but shouldn't or even can't be used for purposes such as regular expression checking, complex mathematical computations, or navigation along complex paths through a network of linked objects. As a consequence, Fujaba/MOFLON already offers means to combine SDM diagrams with pure Java code, OCL expressions, and a small proprietary path expression language. All these three extensions have serious draw-backs: OCL and path expressions are not expressive enough, whereas programming in Java requires intimite knowledge of the environment's code generator backend. Therefore, we are just designing a Java-like action language for Fujaba that extends the Java programming language conservatively with a small number of urgently needed constructs and hides any details concerning e.g. the design of the API of our model repository.

Finally, we are still looking for more appropriate solutions how to write reusable pieces of graph queries and transformations. Right now concepts are missing for the definition of generic queries or transformations that are parametrizable with names of attributes, associations (association ends), and classes. Furthermore, support for the definition of user-defined constructors and destructors is missing that are automatically called when graph transformation rules create or destroy objects. In this way, it would be possible to encapsulate handling of auxilary objects and object properties at well-defined places in a graph transformation specification.

There are further issues that cannot be explained here due to lack of space which may be summarized as follows: declarative graph/model transformation languages support — compared to standard imperative programming or scripting languages — the specification of model analysis and transformation operations on a considerably higher level of abstraction. But all graph transformation languages we are aware of have quite a number of deficiencies as explained above. They still need careful fine-tuning of their design (but not the development of yet another completely new transformation language). Otherwise, industry will still continue to use existing imperative (object-oriented) languages to solve their model analysis and transformation problems in the future.

References

[FR07]   Farkas, T., Röbig, H.: Automatisierte, werkzeugübergreifende Richtlin-
            ienprüfung zur Unterstützung des Automotive-Entwicklungsprozesses. In:
            Rumpe, B., Conrad, M., Giese, H., Schätz, B. (eds.) Dagstuhl-Workshop
            MBEES: Modellbasierte Entwicklung eingebetteter Systeme III, Infor-
            matik Bericht TU Braunschweig, vol. 2007-01. Institut für Software Sys-
            tems Engineering, Technische Universität Braunschweig, Germany (2007)
            (in German)
[Fuj]   Fujaba Homepage, http://www.fujaba.de
[JKS06]   Jakob, J., Königs, A., Schürr, A.: Non-materialized Model View Specifi-
            cation with Triple Graph Grammars. In: Corradini, A., Ehrig, H., Monta-
            nari, U., Ribeiro, L., Rozenberg, G. (eds.) ICGT 2006. LNCS, vol. 4178,
            pp. 321–335. Springer, Heidelberg (2006)
[MAA]   MAAB Homepage,
            http://www.mathworks.com/industries/auto/maab.html
[MAT]   MATLAB Homepage, http://www.mathworks.com/products/
[Min]   Mint Homepage, http://www.ricardo.com/engineeringservices/
            controlelectronics.aspx?page=mint
[MOF]   MOFLON Homepage, http://www.moflon.org
[MSD06]   Mens, T., Van Der Straeten, R., D'Hondt, M.: Detecting and resolving
            model inconsistencies using transformation dependency analysis. In: Nier-
            strasz, O., Whittle, J., Harel, D., Reggio, G. (eds.) MoDELS 2006. LNCS,
            vol. 4199, pp. 200–214. Springer, Heidelberg (2006)
[NKS⁺05]   Neema, S., Kalmar, Z., Shi, F., Vizhanyo, A., Karsai, G.: A visually-
            specified code generator for simulink/stateflow. In: VLHCC 2005: Pro-
            ceedings of the 2005 IEEE Symposium on Visual Languages and Human-
            Centric Computing (VL/HCC 2005), Washington, DC, USA, pp. 275–277.
            IEEE Computer Society, Los Alamitos (2005)
[SCFD06]   Stürmer, I., Conrad, M., Fey, I., Dörr, H.: Experiences with Model and
            Autocode Reviews in Model-based Software Development. In: Salzmann,
            C., Rappl, M., Pretschner, A., Stauner, T. (eds.) Proc. of 3rd Intl. ICSE
            Workshop on Software Engineering for Automotive Systems (SEAS 2006).
            ACM Press, New York (2006)
[SDG⁺07]   Stürmer, I., Dörr, H., Giese, H., Kelter, U., Schürr, A., Zündorf, A.: Das
            MATE Projekt-visuelle Spezifikation von MATLAB Simulink/Stateflow
            Analysen und Transformationen. In: Rumpe, B., Conrad, M., Giese, H.,
            Schätz, B. (eds.) Dagstuhl-Workshop MBEES: Modellbasierte Entwick-
            lung eingebetteter Systeme III, number, 2007-01 in Informatik Bericht
            TU Braunschweig, Institut für Software Systems Engineering, Technische
            Universität Braunschweig, Germany (2007) (in German)
[Soh06]   Sohn, M.: Korrektheitsbegriffe für modellbasierte Codegeneratoren. Mas-
            ter's thesis, Martin Luther University of Halle-Wittenberg (June 2006)

Aspect Diagrams for UML Activity Models

Roy Grønmo[1,2] and Birger Møller-Pedersen[1]

[1] Department of Informatics, University of Oslo, Norway
[2] SINTEF Information and Communication Technology, Oslo, Norway
{roygr,birger}@ifi.uio.no

Abstract. Aspect-orientation has gained increasing popularity, especially within the programming domain, with textual-based approaches
such as AspectJ. Aspect-orientation provides an approach to the organization and management of code that cross-cut elements of the base
program or library. Cross-cutting aspects is also an issue within the
modeling domain, and it is therefore likely that modeling languages can
benefit from the aspect-oriented approach. This paper proposes activity
aspect diagrams for UML 2 activity models. Activity aspect diagrams
are defined directly in the concrete syntax of activity models in order to
enable a user-friendly way of specifying aspects. The activity aspect diagrams and base activity models are transformed into the abstract syntax
of algebraic graph transformation systems, where the model weaving is
carried out using the well-established AGG tool. The approach is demonstrated by two examples and a proof-of-concept aspect diagram editor
has been implemented.

1 Introduction

Activity models [12] is a popular tool to model workflow systems, service-oriented
models and business processes. An activity model consists of activities that are
connected/linked by means of control -and data flows in a graph-layout. An activity may range from a human step such as contact-the-boss to an automated
service such as a call to a Web service. Control flow includes support for sequential, choice, parallel and events. Activities may be grouped in subactivities and
can be nested at arbitrary levels.

In aspect-oriented programming the *base program* is the main program upon
which one or more aspects may define some cross-cutting code as additions or
changes. An aspect is defined by a pair (pointcut and advice), where the *pointcut*
defines where to affect the base program and the corresponding *advice* defines
what to do in the places identified by the pointcut. Analogously we term our
main activity diagrams as the *base models*, and we define an aspect diagram
to consist of a pointcut diagram and an advice diagram, both based upon the
concrete syntax of activity models. From the base model and an aspect, an aspect
weaver can produce a woven result in the form of a new model.

We have chosen to use the aspect terminology instead of the more general
model transformation terminology. This is because our aspects, the source models and the target models are all based upon the same language (activity models),
and because we define a transformation as a pair of pointcut and advice.

A. Schürr, M. Nagl, and A. Zündorf (Eds.): AGTIVE 2007, LNCS 5088, pp. 329–344, 2008.

The need to transform activity models include model refactoring, model checking, quality-of-service aggregation [5] etc. Another important application of aspects at the model level is to achieve good separation-of-concern. A base model may for instance model the functional parts, while a set of aspect models may define non-functional aspects such as exception handling, security and quality-of-service properties. In many situations the updated model or aggregated result shall be viewed by the modeler. In other cases the transformation may only simplify or restructure the model so that the model can be interpreted by other processing tools that require a specific structure. Assume there is a transformation script that can produce BPEL code [14] for execution, but it requires that subactivities are not used. In such a case, we may define a first transformation which removes all subactivities to a collapsed structure, and which preserves the execution semantics.

Traditional model transformation approaches suffer from being either textual and/or working at the abstract syntax also known as the metamodel level. With our proposed activity aspect diagrams, the modeler can define the model-to-model transformation rules directly upon the already familiar environment of the graphical, concrete syntax of activity models. The hypothesis is that defining graph-based transformation rules operating directly on concrete syntax would provide the transformation modeler with a better tool for defining model transformations.

The base models upon which aspects can be applied, cannot in general predict the aspects that one wants to apply. Thus, the base model specification should be independent of the aspect model specification. This is called *obliviousness* and is one of the key factors behind the success of AOP. We want to apply the same principle to our activity aspect diagrams. Furthermore, the aspect models should be easy to specify and understand, so that many typical cross-cutting properties are expressible in a simple manner. We propose to introduce high-level operators to be able to express transformation needs using a single rule, where multiple rules otherwise needs to be defined within traditional graph transformation approaches.

2   Examples

We will demonstrate our approach by two examples. In **the first example** we assume that the base activity model has been used to model a Web service composition [16]. In a service composition there are several calls to distributed services, in general provided by external parties. In such a scenario it is a typical problem that individual services become temporarily (or permanently) unavailable due to network problems, server problems etc. A service composition will fail if any of its individual services fail.

We propose an exception handler aspect, based on timeouts, to improve the reliability of the service composition. It is assumed that it is more reliable to terminate with a proper timeout message instead of being a non-responding service which only hangs. For all the services we specify a timeout value indicating

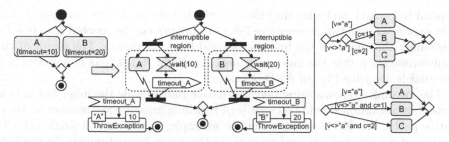

Fig. 1. *Examples:* Exception handler (left) Redundant `DecisionNode` (right)

unreasonable long time to process the service. If no timeout value is defined we may use a default value such as 20 seconds. The timeout value is specified by a `tagged value` (`tagged value` is a name-value pair which is used to extend the UML metamodel to make user-defined UML profiles). Notice that by omitting all the timeout annotation and applying default timeouts to all the services, we will achieve full obliviousness if desired.

An activity model uses rounded rectangles to represent activities, diamond symbols to represent DecisionNodes (or-split) and MergeNodes (or-join), bars to represent parallel flow (and-split/and-join), a filled circle represents InitialNode, a circle with a smaller filled circle inside represents FinalNode, and directed edges represent control flow.

The left part of Figure 1 shows the proposed transformation to be applied on the base model which consists of two activities. Each time an activity is executed (call to a Web service in this case) a timer (displayed as hourglass) is started in parallel, with the timeout value taken from the activity. There is now a racing condition between these two actions, where the first one to terminate should enforce the termination of the other. This is achieved by placing an `InterruptibleRegion` (dashed rounded rectangle) around these two parallel activities. An interrupt control flow leaves the ordinary activity and will by definition terminate all other flows inside the `InterruptibleRegion`. The timer activity is immediately followed by a send timeout signal.

The timeout signal is received by a global `acceptEventAction`. One `accept-EventAction` is produced for each activity. This is to make the exception message specific to the activity which had the timeout. Thus, the `acceptEventAction` can be immediately followed by `ThrowException` activity which reports back the name of the activity and associated timeout value that caused the exception. The `ThrowException` activity is followed by a `FinalNode` which will terminate all other flows within the entire activity model.

In this example the resulting model will be very cluttered and hard to read if the timeout exception is included. In this case, the new model should not be used for viewing, only as an intermediate step prior to execution.

The second example is a model refactoring example taken from Eder et al. [6] who present a number of model refactoring rules for workflow models. We have adopted his `WFT-JC1` example as our second example for activity models. The right part of Figure 1 shows an example base model before the rule is applied (top part), and after the rule has updated the model (bottom part). The rule expresses that two consecutive DecisionNodes can be merged into one by combining the guards of the first and second DecisionNodes. The result of the transformation is that the inner pair DecisionNode/MergeNode is removed and the guards are joined by an AND-operator.

The example is shown using two alternative paths inside the inner Decision-Node, but a solution should be capable of handling an arbitrary number of alternative paths. We do however restrict the example, so that only a single activity is allowed within each alternative path of the inner DecisionNode/MergeNode pair.

3   Architecture of the Approach

Figure 2 shows the architecture of our approach. The base model is specified within an existing UML 2 activity modeling tool. Our proposed graphical language, called activity aspect diagrams, define aspects to be applied on activity models. To support the approach we need to develop a new editor for the activity aspect diagrams. One or more activity aspect diagrams may apply to the same base model. An activity aspect diagram uses the concrete syntax, in this case activity models, and it is based upon algebraic graph transformation.

Since both the base model and the transformation rules are defined using a concrete syntax, one cannot directly use existing graph transformation tools, as these are based upon transformations on abstract syntax. So, in order to perform rule analysis (correctness, termination, confluence) and the actual weaving, we must either implement all this from scratch, or provide a mapping between the concrete and abstract syntax. We choose the latter to benefit from existing well-established graph transformation tools.

We need to transform UML 2 activity models into graph representation and back again. The graph representation will be a typed attributed graph, where nodes and edges are assigned to types, and the nodes and edges can have associated attributes. Similarly the aspect diagrams need to be transformed into graph transformation rules. The transformations from the concrete syntax of base models and aspect model should be fully automatic, and the modeler should not need to see or worry about the graph transformation tool operating on the abstract syntax.

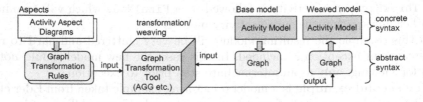

Fig. 2. Approach: From aspect diagrams to graph transformation rules

The graph transformation tool performs the weaving by applying the generated transformation rules on the generated abstract syntax representation of the base model. The result is an abstract syntax representation of the new activity model. The new model will be translated back to concrete syntax and presented to the user in a UML modeling tool.

4 Activity Aspect Diagrams

The activity aspect diagram consists of two parts: **pointcut diagram** and **advice diagram**. The pointcut diagram is shown on the left hand side and the advice digram is shown on the right hand side. The weaving semantics of the aspect diagram follows the basic principles of a traditional graph transformation system, where the pointcut diagram models an activity fragment for which we are looking for potential matches (often referred to as a *morphism* within graph theory) within the base model. The advice diagram instructs how a base model shall be changed relative to the match. We require that matches of the pointcut are injective, meaning that every separate element defined in the pointcut needs to be mapped to separate elements in the match.

Elements appearing in the pointcut and not in the advice, are to be deleted, while elements appearing only in the advice, are to be added. Elements appearing in both the pointcut and advice are to be unchanged or they may change their properties or relationships to other elements. Furthermore we adopt the double-pushout approach which excludes application of rules deleting nodes that are attached via edges to nodes in the remaining graph. The precise meaning of this depends on the mapping from concrete syntax to abstract syntax (section 6).

Elements will only be matched if they have the exact same context in the base model as within the pointcut diagram. Thus all relations need to be present also in the base model. Assume that the pointcut diagram defines an activity with an attached note and a single outgoing control flow reaching the finalNode. In such a case both these relations need to be associated with the matching activity within the base model. The base model element may however have additional relations and still be a match, such as incoming control flow (most likely) and data flow leading into its input pins.

Both the pointcut and advice modeling languages build upon activity models. In the sequel of this paper we will use the shorter term 'aspect diagram' for 'activity aspect diagram' as the context is given to be activity models.

In the simplest form a pointcut diagram is an ordinary activity model fragment. A pointcut diagram extends activity models with **property matching** expressions. The property matching expression goes into the exact same place as the corresponding property of an ordinary activity model. Properties in an activity model include names, stereotypes, tagged values, guard expressions etc. Each property matching can use any legal Java string expression combined with the two wildcards (*,?). The star matches an arbitrary sequence of characters and the question mark matches any single character.

Identifiers are defined with a question mark prefix and may be used to identify both elements and properties. The identifiers and property matching are combined in a syntactic pair such as `?actId <*Service>` placed in the name property of an activity. `actId` will be the identifier of a matching activity that has a name ending with `Service`. Identifiers in the name position is by default an element identifier.

Property assignment is available to update the property values in the advice. A property assignment is defined directly at the value place of the the property, and it can be any legal Java expression that evaluates to a string. The Java expression can use the identifiers as variables holding the value of properties matched by the pointcut. An identifier will be bound to the matched property value (the name in case of an element identifier).

We extend the pointcut modeling language with **boolean operators** (not applicable to the advice diagram). All selection elements in the pointcut model are implicitly joined by and-operators. In addition there are or-, xor- and not-operators available to use in other cases. These are displayed as `{operator}` and are attached to its operands via dotted lines. The not-operator has one or more operands, while the others have two or more operands. One element can only be an operand of one operator.

The boolean operators may also be used as part of the property matching expression. *Example*: We want to match all Activities with stereotype Service or Webservice. This can be expressed as `«Service» {or} «Webservice»`.

In order to make the aspect diagrams better suited to specify transformation rules in a simple manner, we propose to introduce a few, but powerful **high-level operators**. We will see in the transformation section that the use of high-level operators typically needs to be translated into a set of basic graph transformation rules. This also motivates the use of such high-level operators, because the rule modeler can define a single rule using a powerful, but intuitive high-level operator instead of defining several basic transformation rules. Due to limited space, we will only present one high-level operator, the `collection` operator, in this paper.

An aspect model consists of a set of aspect diagrams which can be non-deterministically applied or they may be applied according to some **rule control structure**. To define the control structure of the rules, one alternative is to use activity models.

5   Aspect Diagram Examples

After having introduced the aspect diagram language, we will now show how aspect diagrams can solve the two examples from section 2. Before solving the **timeout exception handler** case, we assume for simplicity that an activity can have at most one incoming control flow and at most one outgoing control flow. This is without loss of generality, since many incoming control flows represent an implicit join node, while many outgoing control flows represent an implicit fork node. Thus, any activity model can be translated into a semantically equivalent

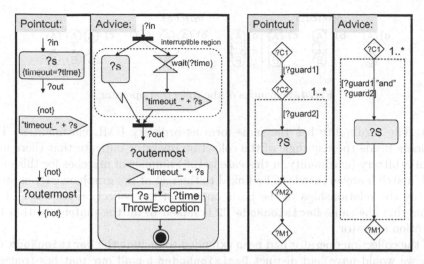

Fig. 3. *Aspect diagrams:* Exception handler (left) Redundant `DecisionNode` (right)

activity model with our proposed restriction. In fact, the modeler may quite easily use aspect diagrams to define such a translation.

We also assume that each activity has an associated tagged value, `timeout`, indicating the timeout of the service it invokes. Again, an aspect diagram could easily introduce this tagged value with a default value for all activities without such annotation.

The left-most aspect diagram in Figure 3 shows the proposed solution. For each activity with incoming and outgoing control flow and a timeout value (shown at the top of the pointcut), we add all the structure necessary to introduce the exception handling. The pointcut definition includes the usage of two not-operators attached to control flows of the activity identified as `?outermost`, which ensure that no incoming and no outgoing control flow is associated with the outermost activity. This condition will only hold for the outermost activity. By placing all the exception handlers in the outermost activity we will terminate all flows within the entire activity model when we go to the finalNode.

We need to ensure the aspect is only applied once for each activity. The throw event signal named `timeout_+?S` (`?S` is bound to activityName) is added by the advice. The same signal is therefore added to the pointcut with a not-operator attached to it, meaning that it cannot be present for the aspect to be applied. The aspect should only apply to activities that are leaf activities and not subactivities. For simplicity we assume that only leaf activities have the timeout values. If this condition does not hold, we could strengthen the aspect diagram by inserting an initialNode connected to a not-operator inside the `?s`-activity.

In the second example we introduce the high-level collection operator. Remember that in the example there is an inner, **redundant decisionNode**, which can have an arbitrary number of alternative paths. The right-most aspect diagram in Figure 3 shows usage of the collection operator, where the dotted rectangle surrounds the collection elements and a cardinality is provided next

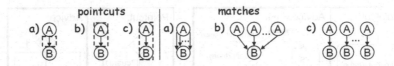

Fig. 4. Semantics of the collection operator

to it. The cardinality has the same form as ordinary UML cardinalities. The elements inside the rectangle of the collection operator indicate that there may be an arbitrary (cardinality in this case is 1..*) number of matches for this part. Each match however, needs to be linked to the rest of the graph exactly as specified by the relationships to the parts outside of the collection rectangle. This means that the same `DecisionNode` C2 is linked to all the matches within the collection operator.

If the collection operator had been extended to include the `DecisionNode` C2, then we would have had distinct `DecisionNodes` for all our matches (remember that the matches are injective, which also applies to the collection operator matches). Identifiers inside the collection pattern denote different elements or properties for each match, such as the guard in the example. The collection operator is normally used also in the advice to indicate the changes to the matches in the collection. If the collection operator is absent in the advice, it implies a request to delete all the collection elements. No boolean operators are allowed inside the collection operator. Within this paper we also assume that only a single collection operator is used within the same aspect diagram. By this we avoid a lot of complexity which we do not have space to cover here.

Figure 4 shows the relationship between the collection operator in the pointcut and possible matches. For the illustration only we use a circle to denote some element A and B (eg. InitialNode, DecisionNode, JoinNode) that can be the source or target of a control flow edge. In case a) only the edge is inside the collection while the source and target elements are outside the collection operator. This means that possible matches will have a set of edges between the same A and B elements. In case b) the source A is also inside the collection which means that a match will contain a set of distinct A elements with edges leading to the same B target element. In case c), both the source and target is inside the collection, which means that a match will contain a set of distinct A and B elements each having their own control flow. We require that a collection match shall be *maximal*, meaning that the largest set of elements, limited by the upper bound cardinality, must be gathered before the advice is applied to the match.

6   Transformation between Concrete and Abstract Syntax

The AGG tool [18] is chosen as the graph transformation tool, and parts of the mapping is tailored for this purpose. We need to transform both ways between the concrete syntax of **activity models** and the abstract syntax of graphs. For this purpose we define a one-to-one correspondence, which is quite straightforward for activity models since they are very close in nature with graph representation.

`Activity`, `InitialNode`, `FinalNode`, `DecisionNode`, `MergeNode`, `ForkNode`, `JoinNode` and data objects appear as nodes in the activity model and we choose to represent these as nodes (with different types) also in the graph representation. The control and data flow edges of activity models are also represented as nodes (with different types), in the graph representation, with two directed outgoing edges labelled `src` and `trg`. By this circumstantial mapping of the activity model edges, missing edge sources or targets, at the concrete syntax, will be translated into rules where the source and target of an edge are always present at the abstract syntax. We discuss this further in section 7 after all the transformation rules are presented.

Properties of the different UML types are mapped to node attributes of the corresponding graph node. An activity name is mapped to a name attribute belonging to the activity graph node, while a control flow guard is mapped to a guard attribute of the control flow graph node. The definition below provides the one-to-one relation between Activity model and graph representation.

The operator $\leftrightarrow$ defines the one-to-one relation between Activity model elements and graph elements. It uses an overloaded mapping function ϕ which is either $\phi : Id \rightarrow Id$ or $\phi : Attrs \rightarrow Attrs$, to map from activity element ids/properties to graph ids/attributes. To the left we show the Activity elements and on the right we show the corresponding graph elements. Nodes are given by a triple $(Id, Type, Attrs)$ and edges are given by a quintuple $(Id, Type, src, trg, Attrs)$:

$$Activity(aId, attrs) \leftrightarrow node(\phi(aId), "Activity", \phi(attrs))$$

$$cFlow(cId, \underbrace{AId}_{srcId}, \underbrace{BId}_{trgId}, attrs) \leftrightarrow \left\{ \begin{array}{l} node(\phi(cId), "cFlow", \phi(attrs)) \\ edge(genId(), "src", \phi(cId), \phi(AId), \epsilon) \\ edge(genId(), "trg", \phi(cId), \phi(BId), \epsilon) \end{array} \right.$$

The mapping of `InitialNode`, `MergeNode`, `ForkNode`, `JoinNode`, `DecisionNode` and `FinalNode` is similar to the `Activity` mapping, and the mapping of `dFlow` is similar to the `cFlow` mapping. ϵ denotes an empty set of attributes, Ids are suffixed by Id, and $genId()$ makes a new id. Due to limited space, we do not present a full mapping of the activity models as graph representation within this paper.

We define a one-way transformation from the aspect diagrams to graph transformation rules in the abstract syntax. Often a single aspect diagram will be mapped to several graph transformation rules. Since the aspect diagrams are designed as extended activity models, the mapping concerning the activity models can follow the mapping defined by $\leftrightarrow$. In an aspect diagram without high level operators, the pointcut diagram will be mapped to the left part(s) of one or more graph transformation rule(s), and the advice diagram will be mapped to the right part(s).

For the **property matching and assignment**, the identifiers are mapped to AGG identifiers and variables, while Java string expressions can be read directly by AGG. We omit wildcard expressions (*,?) since it is not supported by AGG.

We need to map the **boolean operators** of the pointcut language. All elements not explicitly defined as an operand, will implicitly belong to the global and-operator. This is directly supported by normal graph transformation rules, and no additional mapping is needed.

Each *not-operator* will be mapped to a Negative Application Condition (NAC) associated with the corresponding mapped rule of the aspect diagram. The occurrence of a matching negative application condition in combination with left part matches of the rule, prevents the application of the rule. Algorithm 6.1 shows pseudocode on how to map a single not-operator into a NAC. The not-operands will be removed from the pointcut and inserted into a NAC rule instead. If the not-operand is an edge, then its source and target nodes (retrieved by the *directAssoc* method) will be copied into the NAC rule (and not moved from the pointcut). The rules *left*, *right* and *NAC* definitions are finalised by translating to abstract syntax with the *toAbsSyntax* method.

Algorithm 6.1: TRANSFORMNOTOPER($AD : aspectDiagram$)

$notExpr = AD.getNotExpr;$ $NAC =$ **new** $NACRule$
for $i \leftarrow 1$ **to** $notExpr.numOperands$
$$\textbf{do} \begin{cases} notElem = notExpr.operand(i) \\ AD.pointcut.remove(notElem) \\ NAC.add(notElem + notElem.directAssoc) \end{cases}$$
$NewRule =$ **new** $Rule;$ $NewRule.left = AD.pointcut.toAbsSyntax$
$NewRule.right = AD.advice.toAbstSyntax$
$NewRule.addNAC(NAC.toAbsSyntax)$

The three not-operators in the exception handler aspect diagram of Figure 3 will be mapped to three different NAC rules associated with a single graph transformation rule. The first NAC will ensure that the rule is only applied once (timeout signal as not-operand), and the latter two not-operands ensure that the outermost activity will not have incoming nor outgoing control flow.

The *or-operator* leads to several copies of the rule, one for each operand of the or-operator. Algorithm 6.2 shows pseudocode for an aspect diagram with a single or-operator. *outsideOrExpr* retrieves all elements that are not part of the or-expression.

An *xor-operator* will be mapped in the same way as an or-operator with a special metanode to be produced by each rule generated by the xor-expression. The metanode acts as a flag to indicate that one of the rules has been applied. The metanode is added as a NAC rule associated with each of the rules generated for the xor-expression, which ensures that at most one of the xor-rules will be performed.

Algorithm 6.2: TRANSFORMOROPER(AD : $aspectDiagram$)

$orExpr = AD.pointcut.getOrExpr$
for $i \leftarrow 1$ **to** $orExpr.numOperands$
$\qquad \begin{cases} NewRule = \textbf{new } Rule \\ NewRule.left = orExpr.operand(i).toAbsSyntax + \\ \qquad\qquad\qquad AD.pointcut.outsideOrExpr.toAbsSyntax \\ NewRule.right = AD.advice.toAbsSyntax \\ AllRules.addRule(NewRule) \end{cases}$
do

Now we map the **high-level collection operator**. For simplicity we assume that only two cardinalities are available for the collection operator: $0..*$ or $1..*$. The collection operator can be represented by an ITER-rule and a FINAL-rule.

ITER-rule. *Intention:* The iteration rule shall be applied to a single match in a collection of matches and it shall be applied for as long as possible. That means that it shall be applied the same number of times as there are individual matches of the collection pattern. *Mapping:* Simply remove the collection operator marking (the rectangle and cardinality) in the pointcut. Construct the advice by combining the outside of the collection operator from the original pointcut with the inside of the collection operator of the original advice. This will ensure that the necessary changes are applied to each match of the collection. At the same time we preserve the elements outside the collection rectangle, so that all individual collection matches get an equal chance to be matched. To preserve the intended semantics at the end, we let the FINAL-rule sort this out.

FINAL-rule. *Intention:* The final rule shall be applied only once after all matches in the collection have been applied with the ITER-rule. *Mapping:* Both the pointcut and advice is constructed by removing both the collection operator (the rectangle and cardinality) including its inside content. This will result in a rule that finally does all the adding and deletion of elements outside of the collection part. These changes cannot take place before all possible applications of the ITER-rule.

The transformation of the collection operator can be summarized by the pseudocode of algorithm 6.3. The algorithm assumes there is exactly one collection operator in the input. The *toAbstractSyntax* method will transform from concrete to abstract syntax. In this step the inside of the collection operator will contain all node elements resulting from any elements inside the collection of the concrete syntax. The *removeCollOper* method will remove the Collection operator but keep all the elements inside and outside of the collection. The *outsideCollection* and *insideCollection* will keep only elements outside or inside the collection operator. The $+$ operator produces a new graph where the node/edge set is the union of the nodes/edges of the operands.

Algorithm 6.3: TRANSFORMCOLLOPER(*AD : aspectDiagram*)

$AD = AD.ToAbsSyntax$; $Iter = $ **new** $Rule$; $Final = $ **new** $Rule$
$Iter.left = AD.pointcut.removeCollOper$
$Iter.right = AD.pointcut.outsideCollection + $
$\qquad\qquad AD.advice.insideCollection$
$Final.left = AD.pointcut.outsideCollection$
$Final.right = AD.advice.outsideCollection$

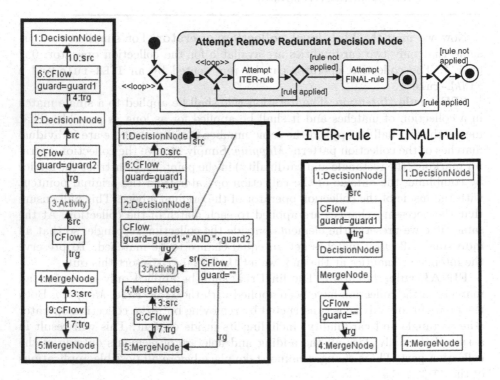

Fig. 5. Aspect diagram of redundant `decisionNode` example mapped to AGG rules

Figure 5 shows the result of transforming the redundant `DecisionNode` aspect diagram into AGG graph transformation rules. An aspect diagram may have an arbitrary number of potential matches in the base model. We need to ensure that all these matches are found by forcing the `ITER-rule` and `FINAL-rule` to be repeated as long as possible. By doing so we will achieve the desired behavior as if the pointcut had a maximal matching (section 5) upon which the advice was applied. The top of Figure 5 shows how the **rule control structure** can be defined using activity models. AGG does not support all the control structure power of activity models, so in general we need a scheduler component on top of AGG. The AGG layered approach will however support the two paper examples. Notice that the gluing condition (double-pushout) ensures that the example `FINAL-rule` is applied after all corresponding `ITER-rule` applications are finished, but this is not the general case.

7 Discussion

An activity model looks quite like an abstract syntax graph representation with nodes and directed edges, and one could question if the abstract syntax could directly represent the concrete syntax. However, since activity models have elements that contain other elements (e.g. `subactivity`, `expansionRegion` and `interruptibleRegion`), this is not possible. In addition, activity `inputPins` and `outputPins` pose a problem as they have a specialized notation in that they are displayed on the border of the owning activity.

Representing control flows as edges also in the abstract syntax would make things much more difficult. It would not be possible to define a rule without the source or target of a control flow edge. In the aspect diagram, however, we use explicitly that a missing source or target expresses a wildcard node. Without this possibility in the exception handler example, we would have to explicitly express all the different node options to be source of the `?in`-labeled edge, and similarly for the target of the `?out`-labeled edge. We could at least have the options of `IntialNode`/`FinalNode` (`?in`/`?out`), `activity`, `subactivity`, `ForkNode`/`JoinNode` (`?out`/`?in`) and `DecisionNode`/`MergeNode` (`?out`/`?in`). To cope with all combinations we would have to make 25 (5x5) different graph transformation rules.

An interesting question is to what extent our approach can be generalized: *Is the approach also appropriate for other kinds of models than activity models, so that we could introduce the same kind of aspect diagrams for UML sequence diagrams, class diagrams etc.?* This remains to be investigated, but an observation is that the closer the modeling language concrete syntax is to a typed attributed labelled graph, the easier it will be to follow the graph transformation approach. Class diagrams are close to such graphs, while sequence diagrams are different kinds of graphs. In a mapping from the concrete syntax of a sequence diagram into an abstract syntax as graphs, we get an explosion in the number of elements. This means that it is highly questionable if the approach, presented in this paper, is suitable for sequence diagrams.

The property matching, property assignment, boolean operators and rule control structure are general mechanisms and should be applicable to other kinds of models. The generality of high-level operators, and which high-level operators are needed, may vary with the kind of model. To achieve an intuitive and easy to comprehend aspect diagram language, we believe it should be tailored to the actual source and target modeling language.

We have developed a proof-of-concept Eclipse GMF-based [3] editor for the aspect diagrams. It currently supports Activity, DecisionNode and MergeNode of Activity models, in addition to the use of single collection operator, which was enough to successfully demonstrate the redundant DecisionNode example.

The transformation from aspect diagrams to AGG rules has been implemented using the MOFScript language ([11]). For other examples, including the second paper example, we have manually followed the mapping definitions described between abstract and concrete syntax, and tested the graph transformations in AGG upon several base activity models with successful results.

8 Related Work

Several approaches (QVT [13], Zhang et al. [20], graph transformation approaches such as AGG [18], Ehrig et al. [4] and PROGRESS [15]) provide model transformation languages and tools that can define transformations between general source and target modeling languages, and where one transformation may operate on different source and target modeling languages. In cases where the source and target languages are both activity models, they suffer from using abstract syntax instead of the more intuitive concrete syntax on which our aspect diagrams are defined.

Lindqvist et al. [9] propose the star operator which can be used in a pointcut language to find repetitive occurrences of a specific modeling pattern and is complementary to our collection operator. The star operator is limited to repetitive occurrences that constitute a sequential path, and is thus not strong enough to model the collection operator. It is only proposed within a pure query part (like our pointcut), and has no associated advice part as we have defined. Furthermore, the star operator is presented on abstract syntax only. However, the authors share our opinion with respect to concrete syntax: *In a tool environment, however, creating the queries using the concrete syntax of the modeling language can be beneficial.*

Aspect-oriented behavior modeling approaches so far have been dominated by UML sequence diagram attempts [19] [1] [2] [17]. Solberg et al. [8] and Whittle and Araújo [19] perform weaving at the model level as in our approach. Deubler et al. [2] and Stein et al. [17] use sequence diagrams to model the aspects at a conceptual level to be mapped to some aspect programming language such as AspectJ [7]. Stein et al. [17] focus only on the conceptual modeling of the pointcut, and do not cover advice modeling.

Klein et al. [8] propose semantic-based weaving of Hierarchical Message Sequence Charts (close to UML sequence diagrams). Their approach focuses on the weaving algorithm that takes the execution semantics into account in the weaving process. This is a benefit compared to our approach since the aspect diagrams and the graph transformation system performs pure syntax-based weaving. To illustrate the aspect definition, they provide an example of a pointcut and advice which is similar to the graph transformation principle aspect diagrams are built upon. However, the aspect definition given only explains the example, and no further attempt to define an aspect-oriented modeling specification language is given.

Mehner et al. [10] analyzes if a set of aspects may be properly woven with the base model by considering possible conflicts and dependencies. Pre- and post-conditions expresses the effects of each activity in the AGG tool where automated analysis is carried out. The aspect definitions proposed in their paper are limited to inserting an entire new use case before, after or as a replacement of some previous activity. None of our two example aspects are expressible with this definition.

9   Conclusions and Future Work

We have proposed activity aspect diagrams as a way to define aspects upon activity models. The approach is built upon transformation of both activity - and activity aspect diagrams in concrete syntax to an abstract syntax of a graph transformation tool, which then performs the weaving. A major benefit is that the aspect modeler can operate directly within the familiar syntax of activity models instead of the more general graph transformation rules of traditional graph transformation approaches. At the same time we can benefit from analysis of confluence and termination in the graph transformation tool.

Transformation approaches have been dominated by textual languages, even though the source and target languages may be graphical languages. One reason is that textual programming languages have been widely used for decades with lots of practical experience and improvements. While the earlier attempts used low-level, non-comprehensible constructs, todays textual programming languages use several high-level constructs (eg. while-loops, inheritance, recursion) to allow for user-friendly programming. By introducing high-level operators also for graphical transformation languages, we believe that the graphical languages can learn from the history of textual programming language development. One such high-level operator, the collection operator, has been introduced in this paper to demonstrate the principle.

As future work we may look into nested collection operators, and investigate more practical examples to see if we need additional high-level operators. We would also like to explore the relationship between termination and confluence criteria at the concrete vs. the abstract representation of the transformation rules.

Acknowledgment. The work reported in this paper has been funded by The Research Council of Norway, grant no. 167172/V30 (the SWAT project).

References

1. Clarke, S., Walker, R.J.: Composition Patterns: An Approach to Designing Reusable Aspects. In: Proceedings of the 23rd International Conference on Software Engineering (ICSE), Toronto, Ontario, Canada (2001)
2. Deubler, M., Meisinger, M., Rittmann, S., Krüger, I.: Modeling Crosscutting Services with UML Sequence Diagrams. In: Briand, L.C., Williams, C. (eds.) MoDELS 2005. LNCS, vol. 3713, pp. 522–536. Springer, Heidelberg (2005)
3. Eclipse Consortium. Eclipse Graphical Modeling Framework (GMF) (2007), http://www.eclipse.org/gmf

4. Ehrig, K., Ermel, C., Hänsgen, S.: Towards Model Transformation in Generated Eclipse Editor Plug-Ins. Electr. Notes Theor. Comput. Sci. 152, 39–52 (2006)
5. Grønmo, R., Jaeger, M.C.: Model-Driven Methodology for Building QoS-Optimised Web Service Compositions. In: Kutvonen, L., Alonistioti, N. (eds.) DAIS 2005. LNCS, vol. 3543, pp. 68–82. Springer, Heidelberg (2005)
6. Eder, J., Gruber, W., Pichler, H.: Transforming Workflow Graphs. In: Proceedings of the First International Conference on Interoperability of Enterprise Software and Applications (INTEROP-ESA 2005), Geneva, Switzerland (February 2005)
7. Kiczales, G., Hilsdale, E., Hugunin, J., Kersten, M., Palm, J., Griswold, W.G.: An Overview of AspectJ. In: Knudsen, J.L. (ed.) ECOOP 2001. LNCS, vol. 2072. Springer, Heidelberg (2001)
8. Klein, J., Hélouët, L., Jézéquel, J.-M.: Semantic-based weaving of scenarios. In: Proceedings of the 5th International Conference on Aspect-Oriented Software Development, Bonn, Germany (2006)
9. Lindqvist, J., Lundkvist, T., Porres, I.: A Query Language With the Star Operator. In: Proceedings of the 6th International Workshop on Graph Transformation and Visual Modeling Techniques, Braga, Portugal (April 2007)
10. Mehner, K., Monga, M., Taentzer, G.: Interaction Analysis in Aspect-Oriented Models. In: 14th IEEE International Conference on Requirements Engineering (RE 2006), Minneapolis/St.Paul, Minnesota, USA (2006)
11. Oldevik, J., Neple, T., Grønmo, R., Aagedal, J.Ø., Berre, A.-J.: Toward standardised model to text transformations. In: Hartman, A., Kreische, D. (eds.) ECMDA-FA 2005. LNCS, vol. 3748, pp. 239–253. Springer, Heidelberg (2005)
12. OMG. UML 2.0 OCL Specification, OMG Adopted Specification ptc/03-10-14 (October 2003)
13. OMG. MOF QVT Final Adopted Specification, OMG Document: ptc/05-11-01 (November 2005)
14. Tatte, S. (ed.): Business Process Execution Language for Web Services Version 1.1 (February 2005)
15. Schürr, A.: Introduction to PROGRESS, an Attribute Graph Grammar Based Specification Language. In: Nagl, M. (ed.) WG 1989. LNCS, vol. 411. Springer, Heidelberg (1989)
16. Skogan, D., Grønmo, R., Solheim, I.: Web Service Composition in UML. In: Proceedings of the 8th IEEE Intl Enterprise Distributed Object Computing Conf (EDOC 2004), Monterey, California (September 2004)
17. Stein, D., Hanenberg, S., Unland, R.: Join Point Designation Diagrams: a Graphical Representation of Join Point Selections. International Journal of Software Engineering and Knowledge Engineering 16(3), 317–346 (2006)
18. Taentzer, G.: AGG: A Graph Transformation Environment for Modeling and Validation of Software. In: Pfaltz, J.L., Nagl, M., Böhlen, B. (eds.) AGTIVE 2003. LNCS, vol. 3062, pp. 446–453. Springer, Heidelberg (2004)
19. Whittle, J., Araújo, J.: Scenario modelling with aspects. IEE Proceedings - Software 151(4), 157–172 (2004)
20. Zhang, J., Lin, Y., Gray, J.: Generic and Domain-Specific Model Refactoring using a Model Transformation Engine. In: Model-driven Software Development, ch. 9, pp. 199–218 (2005)

Model-Driven Software Development with Graph Transformations: A Comparative Case Study

Thomas Buchmann, Alexander Dotor, Sabrina Uhrig, and Bernhard Westfechtel

Lehrstuhl Angewandte Informatik 1, University of Bayreuth
D-95440 Bayreuth
firstname.lastname@uni-bayreuth.de

Abstract. Significant achievements have been made in the design and implementation of languages and tools for graph transformation systems. However, many other competing approaches have been developed for model-driven software development. We present a case study in which we applied different modeling approaches in the construction of a tool for software process management. We compare these approaches with respect to the respective levels of abstraction on which models are defined, the language concepts offered, and the resulting modeling effort. The case study identifies the benefits and shortcomings of the selected modeling approaches, and suggests areas of future improvement.

1 Introduction

Model-driven software development promises to increase the productivity of software developers significantly with the help of high-level, executable models. In many application areas, the data maintained by the system to be developed may be represented as graphs in a natural way. Furthermore, graph modifications may be described declaratively by graph transformation rules. Thus, model-driven software development can be supported by generating executable code from graph transformation rules.

To date, several languages and tools for developing *graph transformation systems* are available and have been applied in diverse application domains (e.g., PROGRES [1], Fujaba [2], MOFLON [3], AGG [4], GenGed [5], DiaGen [6], VIATRA [7], and GReAT [8]). Significant advances have been achieved in language and tool development. Moreover, graph transformations have been applied successfully in various domains [9,10]. On the other hand, dispersal of the graph transformation approach outside the graph transformation community seems to have taken place only to a limited extent.

This paper presents a *case study* for the application of graph transformations. The subject of our study is a software process management system based on dynamic task nets (Sect. 2). We have realized this application with the help of three systems (Sect. 3): (1) GMF/EMF, i.e., a combination of the Graphical Modeling Framework for graphical editors and the Eclipse Modeling Framework, which both are not based on graph transformations; (2) PROGRES, a system for specifying programmed graph transformation systems; and (3) Fujaba, an object-oriented system where graph transformation rules have been incorporated into the UML. These solutions are evaluated and compared against each other in Sect. 4.

A. Schürr, M. Nagl, and A. Zündorf (Eds.): AGTIVE 2007, LNCS 5088, pp. 345–360, 2008.

Speaking in terms of the well-known model-view-controller design pattern, we focus exclusively on the *model*, i.e., the application logic. Furthermore, we study model-driven software development from the perspective of the *user* of the respective *modeling language*. Thus, we are interested in the language concepts, the levels of abstraction at which models are defined, expressiveness of the modeling languages, model size, readability, modeling effort, and efficiency of the code generated from the model.

An important issue addressed by our case study is the significance and role of graph transformations: We consider GMF/EMF to be a framework of industrial relevance which does not make use of graph transformations. Thus, it is fair to ask for the added value of graph transformations. We hope that this case study contributes to answering this question and thus to the mission of this workshop (applications of graph transformations with industrial relevance).

2 Dynamic Task Nets

Dynamic task nets represent software processes which evolve during execution. They were described earlier, e.g. in [11]. For this case study, we considered a "light" version of dynamic task nets which comprises only some of the core concepts. The case study goes beyond previous work only inasmuch as inconsistencies with respect to the underlying process meta model can be tolerated.

Figure 1, a screenshot taken from one of the prototypes which we constructed for this case study, shows an example of a task net. Each task is represented by a box containing its name (A . . . G) and its state of execution. States and transitions are defined

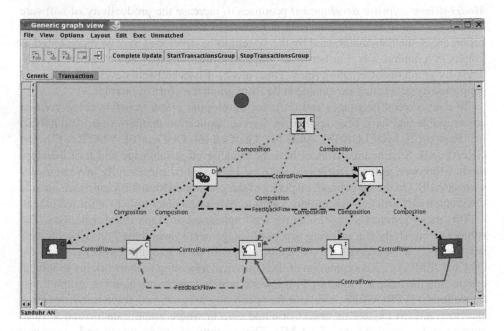

Fig. 1. Dynamic task net

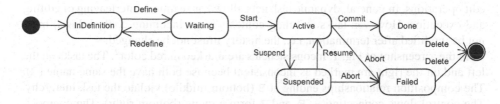

Fig. 2. State diagram

by the state diagram in Fig. 2. In Fig. 1, states are shown as icons (paper and pencil: InDefinition, sand-glass: Waiting, gearwheels: Active, tick: Done). Tasks are arranged in a hierarchy via composition relationships (dotted lines). Control flows (solid lines), which resemble precedence relationships in project plans, constrain the order of task execution. Finally, feedback flows (dashed lines) represent feedback to earlier steps in the process. Further concepts of dynamic task nets, e.g., data flows and task versions, are not covered here to keep the case study small.

The process meta model defines *constraints* for dynamic task nets which may be classified in two orthogonal dimensions: (1) Static constraints are defined as invariants which have to hold for each task net. Dynamic constraints are pre- and postconditions of operations which cannot be expressed as invariants. (2) Structural constraints define the rules which have to be followed when constructing task nets via edit operations. In contrast, behavioral constraints are concerned with state restrictions which have to be obeyed for the execution of tasks.

The following *static structural constraints* have to be satisfied[1]: (1) Each task must have a globally unique name. (2) Composition relationships must be free of cycles (likewise for control flows and feedback flows). (3) Each task may be contained in at most one parent task. (4) Each control flow must be either local, i.e., source and target must have the same parent, or balanced, i.e., the parents of source and target are different and are connected by a control flow (likewise for feedback flows). (5) Each feedback flow must be oriented in the opposite direction of a control flow, i.e., there must be a path of control flows from the target of the feedback flow back to the source.

All *static behavioral constraints* can be expressed via compatibilities of states of adjacent tasks. For each type of task relationship, a corresponding compatibility matrix is defined (see [12], pp. 91). Here, we discuss only compatibilities of states of tasks connected via a control flow. There are three types of control flows: If a control flow is sequential, the successor may start only after termination of the predecessor. A standard control flow is used to express that the successor can be terminated only after its predecessor. In the case of a simultaneous control flow, the successor may be activated only after its predecessor, and it may also be terminated only after its predecessor. These rules can be translated into legal and illegal state combinations. For example, the combination Active → Done is illegal for all types of control flows.

The state diagram of Fig. 2 defines *dynamic behavioral constraints* for state transitions: Each transition may be performed only in its source state and moves the task to which it is applied into its target state. In addition, there are some state constraints on

---

[1] There are no dynamic structural constraints.

edit operations. In general, dynamic task nets allow for seamless interleaving of editing and execution. However, tasks and their contexts (e.g., incoming control flows) must not be modified after termination, i.e., the history must not be changed.

In the screenshot of Fig. 1, inconsistencies are marked in red color[2]. The tasks on the left and on the right are marked as inconsistent because both have the same name (G). The composition relationships ending at B (bottom middle) violate the task hierarchy. The control flows connecting B, F, and G form a cycle (bottom right). The composition relationship from E (top) to D is behaviorally inconsistent: a child task must not be activated before its parent. Similarly, the control flow from G to C (bottom left) is inconsistent because the states of source and target are not compatible (C cannot terminate before G). Finally, the feedback flow from B to C is structurally consistent (e.g., it is balanced by the feedback flow from A to D), but behaviorally inconsistent: B cannot raise feedback even before it has started execution[3].

The following requirements have to be met by the process management tool to be constructed: The user is supplied with a graphical view of the task net which signals all inconsistencies. *Edit operations* are offered to build up and modify task nets by creating/deleting tasks and relationships and by changing task names. *Execution operations* are used to perform state transitions (Start, Suspend, etc.). With respect to constraint checking, the tool has to provide two working modes: In *enforcing mode*, the task net must not contain any inconsistency, and each command violating a static or dynamic constraint is rejected. In *permissive mode*, constraint violations are tolerated and marked (as shown in the screenshot above). The markings are updated after each command to provide immediate feedback to the user. Dynamic constraints are simply ignored in this mode.

In this case study, the commands for editing and execution perform rather simple transformations (insertion/deletion of tasks and relationships, changes of attribute values). The main challenge lies in the validation of constraints, which can be realized in different ways: In the case of *global validation*, constraints are checked on the whole graph (representing a task net). Since the user has to be provided with feedback on each command, global validation causes performance problems in the case of large graphs. In contrast, *incremental validation* checks only those parts of the graph which are affected by a change. The requirements of our case study call for incremental rather than global validation.

3   Models

In this section, we present alternative models used for the development of a process management tool based on dynamic task nets. Please recall that we are concerned with the model only and ignore the view and controller part of the application. The models are evaluated and compared against each other in Sect. 4.

---

[2] In gray-scale reproduction, dark boxes indicate inconsistent tasks, but inconsistent relationships are hard to identify.

[3] Feedback flows are inserted only on demand.

3.1 GMF/EMF

The Eclipse *Graphical Modeling Framework* (GMF [13]) supports the generation of a graphical editor for a custom model. The model is defined with the help of the *Eclipse Modeling Framework (EMF)*. This way each model is based on the *Ecore* (EMOF) meta model (a UML dialect and a variant of the OMG proposal for *Essential Meta Object Facility*[14]). Various ways exist to define an Ecore model: UML class diagrams, Java interfaces or directly via Ecore-XML (analogous to XMI). Please note that this paper deals only with the semantic model and not with the notational model, which is also required for building a graphical tool with GMF.

Figure 3 shows a UML diagram of the dynamic task net model. Each instance of DTNDynamicTaskNet consist both of DTNConnection and DTNTask objects. Each DTNConnection has one source and one target DTNTask object. DTNConnection is specialized to distinguish between the three types of connections in our dynamic task net case study: DTNSubtaskFlow, DTNFeedbackFlow and DTNControlFlow.

To deal with constraints, GMF supports *audit rules* which are based on OCL 2.0 [15]. Each *static constraint* of a task net (see Sect. 2) is defined by a corresponding audit rule. Figure 4 shows the OCL statement of the audit rule for detecting control flow cycles. First we select the targetTask of the connection for which the constraint is evaluated (self). Then we select the set that is reached via transitive closure of all tasks that can be reached via a connection (outgoingEdges) of type control flow (oclIsTypeOf(DTNControlFlow)). This set must not contain the source task of the connection (excludes(self.sourceTask)) – or the connection is part of a cycle. The closure operator, which is not included in the OCL standard and has been added in EMF as an extension, is indispensable for declaratively specifying some of the constraints defined for dynamic task nets. Note that the rule is declared as invariant, i.e. it is true iff the task net is cycle free.

In addition, GMF partially supports the specification of *dynamic constraints*. OCL constraints may be defined as preconditions of commands for creating relationships; thus, they are called *link constraints* in GMF. For example, there is a link constraint which forbids the insertion of an incoming control flow of a terminated task. For other

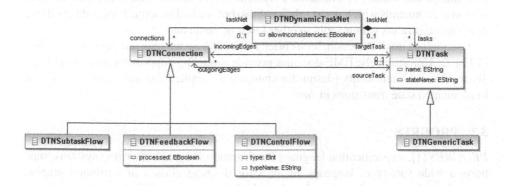

Fig. 3. EMF class diagram of the DTN-Model

```
self.targetTask
  ->closure(t|t.outgoingEdges
  ->select(e|e.oclIsTypeOf(DTNControlFlow)).targetTask)
  ->excludes(self.sourceTask)
```

Fig. 4. OCL expression for checking control flow cycles

types of commands, we wrote Java code for checking dynamic constraints (e.g., in order to preserve the history of task executions, a terminated task must not be deleted).

GMF supports the following mechanisms for validation: Audit rules for static constraints may be declared for *batch validation*, which has to be invoked explicitly by the user. All of these rules are checked on the complete model instance, and model elements are marked with constraint violations. In between two batch validations, rules declared for batch validation are not checked, and the markings are not updated.

Audit rules for static constraints may also be declared for *live validation*. These rules are checked immediately <u>after</u> each command execution; when some constraint violation is detected, the command is rolled back. Please note that live validation operates incrementally. Finally, link constraints are checked as preconditions <u>before</u> a command is executed. When a link constraint is violated, the respective command cannot be executed.

It is important to note that the validation mechanisms offered by GMF do not adequately support the validation modes required for our case study (see end of Sect. 2). We used batch validation for partially realizing the *permissive mode*. However, batch validation does not provide immediate feedback, and if it did, it would not provide fast responses when working on large model instances (due to global rather than incremental validation). Furthermore, live validation and link constraints cannot be used because constraint violations are not tolerated.

Likewise, we realized the *enforcing mode* only partially with live validation and link constraints. The audit rules for live validation were created by copying and modifying the rules for batch validation (the modifications are necessary to ensure that the rules are evaluated only when the enforcing mode is active). Unfortunately, live validation works incrementally, but not correctly: We would have had to customize the live validation by hand (by writing Java code) to make sure that all constraints on model elements affected by a change are actually re-evaluated. Furthermore, we defined link constraints in OCL for those commands which insert relationships, but we had to write Java code for those dynamic constraints which apply to other kinds of commands.

To conclude this subsection, let us briefly discuss how we realized the state machine of Fig. 2. Unfortunately, EMF does not provide modeling support for state machines. To improve maintainability (design for change), we applied the *state pattern* [16] and implemented state transitions in *Java*.

3.2 PROGRES

PROGRES [1], a specification language for programmed graph rewriting systems, supports a wide variety of language features for defining classes of attributed graphs, consisting of typed and attributed nodes which are connected by directed, binary relationships (edges) without attributes. Language features include multiple inheritance

```
node class + CONTROL_FLOW is a TASK_RELATIONSHIP
  ...
  derived
    BalancedControlFlow : boolean
      = card ( self.(        (    -ToSource->
                          &  <=Contains=
                          &  <-ToSource-
                          &  instance of CONTROL_FLOW )
                    and  (    -ToTarget->
                          &  <=Contains=
                          &  <-ToTarget-
                          &  instance of CONTROL_FLOW ) ) ) >= 1;
  ...
end;
```

Fig. 5. Textual specification of node class CONTROL_FLOW

on node classes, a stratified type system (nodes are instances of node types which are in turn instances of node classes), definition of derived attributes and relationships (the latter of which are called paths), graph transformation rules with flexible graph patterns, and control structures supporting non-determinism and transactional behavior. Some specification elements such as derived attributes and relationships may be specified both textually and graphically.

In our case study, constraint checking plays a crucial role. In the specifications we prepared for the case study, constraint checking is realized with the help of *derived attributes*. The user of the PROGRES language may define constraints in a declarative way with the help of equations. The underlying runtime system, including the database management system GRAS [17], provides for incremental evaluation of derived attributes. Thus, the user of the PROGRES language does not have to take care of the maintenance of the values of derived attributes.

The textual definition of derived attributes is illustrated in Fig. 5, which shows an excerpt of the declaration of the node class CONTROL_FLOW. The derived attribute BalancedControlFlow is used to check whether a control flow is balanced, and is defined by a textual expression in a similar way as an OCL constraint. Starting from the current flow, a navigation is performed to the source, the parent, and to its adjacent control flows on the next layer upward the task hierarchy; likewise for the target. The resulting sets of control flows are intersected. The control flow is balanced if the cardinality of the intersection is greater than 0, i.e., the intersection set is not empty.

Alternatively, constraints may be defined graphically rather than textually. In particular, a rule for a derived attribute may refer to a graphical *restriction*, i.e., a unary relation on nodes of a certain class. A node meets the restriction if it is part of a graph pattern defined in the body of the restriction. Figure 6 shows a graphical restriction for the balancing of control flows. We consider the graphical restriction easier to read than the corresponding textual expression shown in Fig. 5. Since textual and graphical notations are both offered by PROGRES, the user may select the notation which is more appropriate for the problem at hand.

In the specifications of the case study, we separated graph transformations from constraint checking. An example is given in Fig. 7. Tasks and their relationships form an overall process which is represented by a node of class PROCESS. All elements of some process are connected to the process node by Has edges (declared outside the

```
restriction + BalancedControlFlowRestriction : CONTROL_FLOW =
   `1 in
```

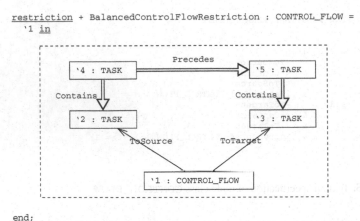

```
end;
```

Fig. 6. Graphical specification of control flow balancing

```
node class + PROCESS is a NODE
   intrinsic
      InconsistenciesAllowed : boolean := true;
   redef derived
      Consistent = for all element := self.Has ::
                      element.Consistent
                end                          ;
   methods
      ...
      transformation + EditCreateControlFlow
         ( sourceTask, targetTask : TASK ;
           controlFlowType : type in CONTROL_FLOW ;
           out taskRelationship : controlFlowType)
      =
           self.CheckPreconditionOfEditOperation ( targetTask )
         & self.AuxCreateTaskRelationship
               ( sourceTask, targetTask, controlFlowType,
                 out taskRelationship )
         & (self.InconsistenciesAllowed or self.Consistent)
      end
      ...
end
```

Fig. 7. Creation of a control flow

class PROCESS). The process node carries an intrinsic attribute for controlling whether inconsistencies are allowed, and a derived attribute which evaluates to true when all elements are consistent. The derived attributes attached to the process elements refer to other derived attributes such as e.g. BalancedControlFlow (Fig. 5).

All operations for creating or deleting process elements are attached as methods to the node class PROCESS. For example, when a control flow is created, the graph transformation rule which actually inserts the control flow is embraced by actions dedicated to checking constraints. The transformation EditCreateControlFlow is an atomic transaction, i.e., either all of its steps succeed, or it fails and leaves the host graph unchanged. CheckPreConditionOfEditOperation checks a dynamic precondition: The target task of the control flow would be affected by this edit operation. If inconsistencies are not allowed and the target task has already terminated, the check fails, and the transaction is rolled back. Please note that this check cannot be postponed: It cannot be recognized after the fact that the in-context of a terminated task was modified after termination. In the next step, the control flow is created by a graph transformation rule which simply creates the control flow node and its adjacent edges without performing any further constraint checking. Finally, after the control flow has been inserted, it is checked whether inconsistencies are allowed. If this is not the case, it has to be checked whether any inconsistencies have been introduced into the process. Please note that access to the derived attribute triggers all necessary re-evaluations at runtime. If the overall process is no longer consistent, the check fails, and the transaction is rolled back.

The PROGRES specification meets all of the requirements imposed by the case study. In particular, it realizes both the permissive and the enforcing mode with incremental validation. From the specification, executable code is generated which is hooked into the UPGRADE framework [18] to produce a graphical tool for software process management. The screen shot of Fig. 1 was taken from this tool.

So far, we have not discussed how we realized the state machine of Fig. 2. Unfortunately, PROGRES does not provide modeling support for state machines. We simply added a state attribute to the TASK and wrote methods for the state transitions which check their preconditions (legal source state) and invariants (compatibility with states of neighbor tasks).

3.3 Fujaba

Fujaba [19] is an environment for developing executable models with the help of class, story, and state diagrams. It is being developed jointly at multiple sites and has been used in numerous research projects. Fujaba strongly supports graphical modeling, while PROGRES offers a mix of graphical and textual modeling elements. Fujaba's most distinctive feature are the so called story diagrams, a combination of activity and communication diagrams, from which Fujaba is able to generate executable code. We used the CASE tool Fujaba in our case study to design and implement the application logic of our process management tool. Fujaba has been integrated into various user interface tool kits such as GEF, GMF, and UPGRADE, but user interface issues go beyond the scope of this paper.

While Fujaba does not support OCL constraints, constraints may be expressed graphically by *story patterns* with embedded path expressions. With the help of story patterns, constraints may be written in an intuitive way; in some cases, they are much easier to understand than OCL constraints. An important difference to the OCL constraints as supported in GMF/EMF consists in the use of story patterns: In Fujaba, story patterns are embedded in story diagrams and thus belong to the dynamic rather than the static model.

In the case of Fujaba, we fully realized both the permissive and the enforcing mode of operation required for the process management tool. We prepared two versions of the Fujaba model: The first one performs incremental validation, the second one resorts to global validation. In contrast to PROGRES, Fujaba does not support incremental re-evaluation of derived data. Thus, the user of Fujaba must explicitly program incremental validation. The additional modeling effort can be determined by comparing the model versions with incremental and global validation, respectively.

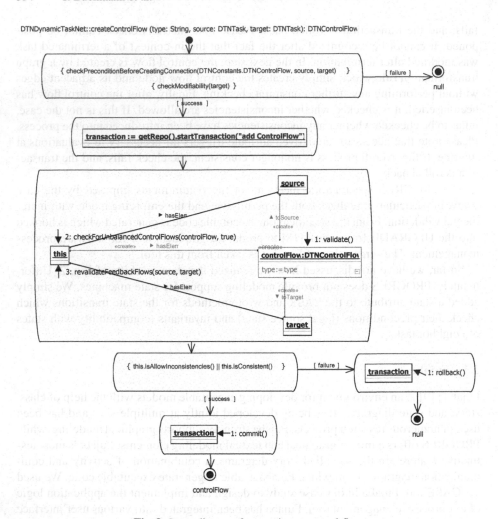

Fig. 8. Story diagram for creating a control flow

Figure 8 shows the story diagram for creating a control flow in the case of *incremental validation*. The story diagram is structured in a similar way as the corresponding PROGRES transaction (see Fig. 7). First, it is checked whether insertion of the control flow would result in a duplicate relationship and whether the dynamic constraint of this operation is violated (the in-context of a terminated task must not be modified). Next, a transaction is started, making use of the Coobra repository services (in PROGRES, the compiler inserts this step automatically due to the transactional semantics of programmed transformations). The story pattern following the start of the transaction inserts the control flow and triggers the required re-validations. Subsequently, it is checked whether inconsistencies have been introduced in enforcing mode. In this case, the transaction is rolled back; otherwise, it is committed.

In the case of incremental validation, it has to be decided for each change which constraints on which graph elements have to be re-evaluated. The story pattern for

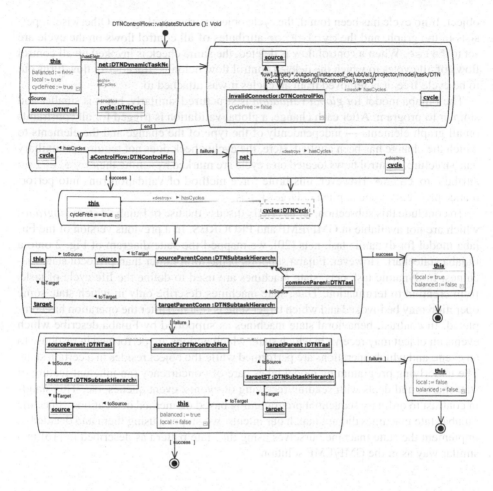

Fig. 9. Story diagram for validating a control flow

creating a control flow triggers validation of all constraints for the new control flow (1). In addition, it has to be checked whether any previously unbalanced control flows are balanced by the new control flow (2). Likewise, feedback flows which did not have a path of opposite control flows have to be re-validated (3). This control logic makes the model for incremental validation both larger (model size) and more difficult to program (modeling effort) than the model for global validation.

For the case of incremental validation, Fig. 9 shows the story diagram for validating static structural constraints for a control flow. The story patterns at the bottom check whether the control flow is local or balanced; they are the same as for global validation. However, the check for cyclic control flows is more complicated than for global validation since it requires the maintenance of auxiliary data structures for efficient re-validation: Control flows which are part of a cycle are attached to a cycle object. When a control flow is inserted, the cycle check is invoked on the new control flow. A cycle object is created tentatively, and control flows on a cycle are attached to the new cycle object. If no cycle has been found, the cycle object is removed again. Otherwise, it persists in the graph, and the `cycleFree` attributes of all control flows on the cycle are set to `false`. When a control flow is deleted, the same check is invoked on all control flows of all cycles to which the deleted control flow belongs. If a control flow turns out to be cycle free, it is removed from all cycles it was attached to.

The Fujaba model for *global validation* is structured similarly, but it is smaller and simpler to program. After each change, a global validation is trigged for all constraints on all graph elements — independently of the type of the change and the elements to which the change has been applied. Here, the cycle check does not require an auxiliary data structure: Control flows located on a cycle are marked by setting their `cycleFree` attribute to `false`. However, this brute force method of validation runs into performance problems when applied to large graphs.

To conclude this subsection, let us briefly discuss the use of Fujaba's *state diagrams*, which are not available in GMF/EMF and PROGRES. In a previous version of the Fujaba model for dynamic task nets [20], we mapped the state diagram of Fig. 2 onto a Fujaba statechart. However, Fujaba supports behavioral rather than protocol state machines. In dynamic task nets, state machines are used to define the life cycle of tasks from creation to termination. Thus, state machines describe only in which state some operation may be invoked and which target state is reached after the operation has completed. In contrast, behavioral state machines as supported by Fujaba describe which events an object may receive in which state, which actions are performed in response to an event, and which operations are performed while the object resides in a certain state. The underlying programming model takes care of concurrency (an inherent feature of statecharts) and deals with sending/receiving of events, event queues, etc. This stands in contrast to ordinary sequential programming based on method invocations. Since the Fujaba state machines did not match our intents, we stopped using them and decided to implement the state machine ourselves using the state pattern as described in [16] in a similar way as in the GMF/EMF solution.

4 Evaluation

Below, the modeling approaches applied in the case study are evaluated with respect to the language features offered, expressiveness of the modeling language, model size, readability, modeling effort, and efficiency. In the latter category, we are interested only in the support for incremental validation — which is crucial for interactive tools with immediate constraint checking. Please note that the evaluation is performed with respect to the case study only. Thus, the findings can be applied only to applications of the same profile as the case study.

Table 1 attempts to collect information on the *model sizes* in terms of the number of model elements classified into different categories. The PROGRES column refers to the specification where derived attributes are defined textually rather than graphically. Furthermore, the Fujaba numbers refer to the models realizing incremental and global validation, respectively (i/g). When a category is not applicable, the table contains the entry "–". Constraints refer to OCL constraints in GMF/EMF, and to evaluation rules for derived attributes in PROGRES. For GMF/EMF, we counted the Java methods which

Table 1. Model size (number of model elements)

	GMF/EMF	PROGRES	Fujaba (i/g)
Classes	15	12	18/16
Attributes	7	5	21/19
Associations	5	6	19/16
Inheritance rel.	10	11	17/15
Constraints	24	15	–/–
Methods	8	34	31/28
Control structures	13	35	36/30
Graph transformation rules	–	5	90/66

were required for implementing the model. For Fujaba, this category refers to story diagrams. In PROGRES, we counted both transactions and functions. In the last row, we counted graph transformation rules in PROGRES and story diagrams in Fujaba (even if they merely describe a graph test rather than a graph transformation). Elementary story patterns (containing one object only) were not included in the numbers.

4.1 GMF/EMF

Language features. GMF/EMF supports the rapid generation of graphical editors from class diagrams and OCL constraints.

Expressiveness. Class diagrams and extended OCL constraints are powerful means for the static model. The dynamic model is not supported at all. In the case study, this restriction was not a severe problem, but it did require to write some Java code.

Model size. The model consists of two small class diagrams, and OCL constraints covering a few pages. In addition, we had to write 8 Java methods covering about 2 pages of source code. Thus, the size of the model is pretty small.

Readability. Class diagrams are widely accepted for the static model. OCL constraints tend to be hard to read and write as soon as complex structural conditions need to be expressed.

Modeling effort. The modeling effort is low as far as it concerns the static model being defined by class diagrams and OCL constraints.

Incremental validation. Basic support for incremental validation is provided, but the set of elements to be re-evaluated is not determined correctly in some cases.

4.2 PROGRES

Language features. PROGRES offers a wide variety of language concepts, but the language does not support state machines. In the case study, we made extensive use of derived attributes and incremental attribute evaluation for checking constraints. Graph transformation rules do not play a dominant role in the case study. Transactions are primarily used for wrapping graph transformations with consistency checks.

Expressiveness. As far as the static model is concerned, PROGRES and GMF/EMF are comparable with respect to expressiveness. PROGRES provides comprehensive and high-level support for specifying graph transformations, but the capabilities of PRO-GRES have not been exploited fully in the case study (only five graph transformation rules were required in the case study).

Model size. The model is larger than the GMF/EMF model, but moderate in size. The variant of the specification where we used textual notation for constraints comprises 13 pages (printed in 10 pt font). The increase of model size compared to GMF/EMF is primarily due to the fact that all operations (create/delete tasks and relationships, perform state transitions, etc.) have to be specified explicitly (while basic operations are generated automatically in GMF/EMF). This explains the number of methods (transactions and functions) plus graph transformation rules (about 40 altogether).

Readability. PROGRES specifications are rather difficult to read (and write) for two reasons: First, PROGRES does not use standard notation the user may be familiar with anyway. Second, the language is complex and offers lots of language constructs. Apart from that, the readability depends on the style in which the specification is written. In particular, we consider graphical notation for constraints easier to read than textual notation in most cases.

Modeling effort. For an experienced user of PROGRES, the modeling effort is moderate. It is possible to write specifications at a high level of abstraction without dealing with operational issues such as pattern matching, consistency maintenance, and rollback of failing transactions.

Incremental validation. PROGRES supports incremental evaluation of derived attributes and relationships.

4.3 Fujaba

Language features. In Fujaba, models are defined in terms of class diagrams, state diagrams, and story diagrams. Fujaba strongly supports graphical modeling and uses textual notation only to a limited extent (e.g., in path expressions).

Expressiveness. By and large, class diagrams, story diagrams, and state diagrams are powerful means for graphical modeling. However, the state diagrams provided by Fujaba were not adequate for our case study. Furthermore, constraint checking has to be performed in a procedural way. The Fujaba models are less declarative than their counterparts.

Model size. The Fujaba model is much larger than the PROGRES model. As in the case of PROGRES, all operations have to be modeled explicitly, while basic operations are generated in GMF/EMF. Constraint checking requires a lot of story patterns, even in the case of global validation.

Readability. Fujaba uses intuitive graphical notation. Therefore, Fujaba models are quite easy to read — as long as they remain small enough. In particular, story diagrams should be decomposed into methods of manageable size and complexity. Otherwise, the reader may easily lose orientation.

Modeling effort. Among the approaches investigated in the case study, Fujaba required the highest effort of modeling. This is due to the size of the model and the handling of algorithmic aspects (which in particular applies to the model for incremental validation).

Incremental validation. Since Fujaba does not support incremental evaluation of derived data, the respective algorithms have to be designed by the Fujaba user for each application anew.

5   Conclusion

In our case study, we have compared GMF/EMF against Fujaba and PROGRES, which are both based on graph transformations, with respect to language features, expressiveness, model size, readability, modeling effort, and efficiency. Since the requirements imposed by our case study match fairly well the support offered by GMF/EMF, a process management tool was developed with the help of GMF/EMF rapidly with small modeling effort. PROGRES is able to compete with GMF/EMF and adds incremental attribute evaluation as a distinctive feature. Finally, the Fujaba model is larger and more procedural than its competitors.

The modeling support by GMF/EMF is confined to graphical editors with basic commands. Further extensions of the case study— e.g., process patterns or data flows— would go beyond the modeling support of GMF/EMF. Please note that building a full-fledged process management system considerably goes beyond building a simple graphical editor. A modeling language like Fujaba provides much more comprehensive modeling support in a single language, but requires further improvements, e.g. with respect to constraint checking and state diagrams. We hope that this case study provides some useful hints and suggestions for further improvements. Graph transformation rules do not play a dominant role in this case study, but they constitute an important building block of a language for model-driven development.

References

1. Schürr, A., Winter, A., Zündorf, A.: The PROGRES approach: Language and environment. In: Ehrig, H., Engels, G., Kreowski, H.J., Rozenberg, G. (eds.) Handbook on Graph Grammars and Computing by Graph Transformation: Application, Languages, and Tools, vol. 2, pp. 487–550. World Scientific, Singapore (1999)
2. Burmester, S., Giese, H., Niere, J., Tichy, M., Wadsack, J.P., Wagner, R., Wendehals, L., Zündorf, A.: Tool integration at the meta-model level: the Fujaba approach. International Journal on Software Tools for Technology Transfer 6(3), 203–218 (2004)
3. Amelunxen, C., Königs, A., Rötschke, T., Schürr, A.: MOFLON: A standard-compliant metamodeling framework with graph transformations. In: Rensink, A., Warmer, J. (eds.) ECMDA-FA 2006. LNCS, vol. 4066, pp. 361–375. Springer, Heidelberg (2006)
4. Taentzer, G.: AGG: A graph transformation environment for modeling and validation of software. In: [10], pp. 446–453
5. Bardohl, R., Ermel, C., Weinhold, I.: GenGED - A visual definition tool for visual modeling environments. In: [10], pp. 413–419
6. Minas, M., Köth, O.: Generating diagram editors with DiaGen. In: [9], pp. 433–440

7. Csertán, G., Huszerl, G., Majzik, I., Pap, Z., Pataricza, A., Varró, D.: VIATRA - visual automated transformations for formal verification and validation of UML models. In: 17th IEEE International Conference on Automated Software Engineering (ASE 2002), pp. 267–270. IEEE Press, Los Alamitos (2002)

8. Agrawal, A.: Graph rewriting and transformation (GReAT): A solution for the model integrated computing (MIC) bottleneck. In: 18th IEEE International Conference on Automated Software Engineering (ASE 2003), pp. 364–368. IEEE Press, Los Alamitos (2003)

9. Münch, M., Nagl, M. (eds.): AGTIVE 1999. LNCS, vol. 1779. Springer, Heidelberg (2000)

10. Pfaltz, J.L., Nagl, M., Böhlen, B. (eds.): AGTIVE 2003. LNCS, vol. 3062. Springer, Heidelberg (2004)

11. Heimann, P., Joeris, G., Krapp, C.A., Westfechtel, B.: Graph-based software process management. Journal of Software Engineering and Knowledge Engineering 7(4), 431–455 (1997)

12. Krapp, C.A.: An Adaptable Environment for the Management of Development Processes. Aachener Beiträge zur Informatik, vol. 22. Augustinus Buchhandlung, Aachen, Germany (1998)

13. Eclipse Foundation: GMF - Graphical Modeling Framework (2006) (last visited, 21/03/2007), http://www.eclipse.org/gmf

14. Eclipse Foundation: The Eclipse Modeling Framework (EMF) Overview (2005) (last visited, 27/10/2006),
    http://dev.eclipse.org/viewcvs/indextools.cgi/checkout/
    org.eclipse.emf/doc/org.eclipse.emf.doc/references/overview/
    EMF.html

15. Warmer, J., Kleppe, A.: The Object Constraint Language, 2nd edn. Addison Wesley, Boston (2003)

16. Gamma, E., Helm, R., Johnson, R., Vlissides, J.: Design Patterns: Elements of Reusable Object-Oriented Software. Addison-Wesley Professional Computing Series. Addison-Wesley, Reading (1994)

17. Kiesel, N., Schürr, A., Westfechtel, B.: GRAS: a graph-oriented software engineering database system. Information Systems 20(1), 21–51 (1995)

18. Böhlen, B., Jäger, D., Schleicher, A., Westfechtel, B.: UPGRADE: A framework for building graph-based interactive tools. Electronic Notes in Theoretical Computer Science 72(2), 113–123 (2002)

19. Zündorf, A.: Rigorous object oriented software development. Technical report, University of Paderborn, Germany (2001)

20. Buchmann, T., Dotor, A.: Building graphical editors with GEF and Fujaba. In: FUJABA Days 2006, Paderborn, Germany, University of Paderborn, pp. 47–51 (2006)

Verification and Synthesis of OCL Constraints Via Topology Analysis*
(A Case Study)

Jörg Bauer[1], Werner Damm[2], Tobe Toben[2], and Bernd Westphal[2]

[1] Technical University of Munich, 85748 Garching, Germany
joerg.bauer@in.tum.de
[2] Carl von Ossietzky Universität Oldenburg, Oldenburg, Germany
{damm,toben,westphal}@informatik.uni-oldenburg.de

Abstract. On the basis of a case-study, we demonstrate the usefulness of topology invariants for model-driven systems development. Considering a graph grammar semantics for a relevant fragment of UML, where a graph represents an object diagram, allows us to apply Topology Analysis, a particular abstract interpretation of graph grammars. The outcome of this analysis is a finite and concise over-approximation of all possible reachable object diagrams, the so-called topology invariant. We discuss how topology invariants can be used to verify that constraints on a given model are respected by the behaviour and how they can be viewed as synthesised constraints providing insight into the dynamic behaviour of the model.

1 Introduction

The Unified Modeling Language (UML) [1,2] is widely employed for model-driven development of systems. A fundamental strategy of UML is to support a separation of concerns by different diagram types, in particular to separate structural from behavioural aspects. By means of classes and associations, class diagrams determine structural aspects as *possible* connections (or links) between system objects. By means of states and transitions, state machine diagrams determine behavioural aspects of system objects, in particular modifications of current links.

In this article, we address the following problem. Given an executable UML model in form of a class and a state machine diagram, compute (an approximation of) all possible system states (or *object diagrams*) reachable during system run-time. Knowledge about these object diagrams is crucial, because class and state-machine diagrams often allow too many, thus many unintended, object diagrams. Even if one is lucky to have a further annotated model, e.g., annotated by OCL constraints, many unintended object diagrams may arise.

* This work was partly supported by the German Research Council (DFG) as part of the Transregional Collaborative Research Centre "Automatic Verification and Analysis of Complex Systems" (SFB/TR 14 AVACS).

A. Schürr, M. Nagl, and A. Zündorf (Eds.): AGTIVE 2007, LNCS 5088, pp. 361–376, 2008.
© Springer-Verlag Berlin Heidelberg 2008

Therefore, we propose a new methodology for computing an over-approximation of *all* reachable object diagrams. While it combines well-established techniques like UML graph grammar semantics and static analysis of graph grammars in a novel manner, it gives the following benefits, on which we shall elaborate in Section 6.

- a *pictorial* overview of all possible object diagrams, whose graphical appeal is one of the major benefits of all graph-based techniques
- the (formal) validation of possibly existing OCL constraints for *every possible* run-time behaviour
- the *synthesis* of OCL constraints, even for non-annotated models (though in few specialised cases only)
- excellent, automatically derivable documentation

We shall now briefly illustrate the problem of unintended object diagrams and its non-triviality with an example. The same example will be used throughout the paper in order to demonstrate the feasibility and usefulness of our methodology.

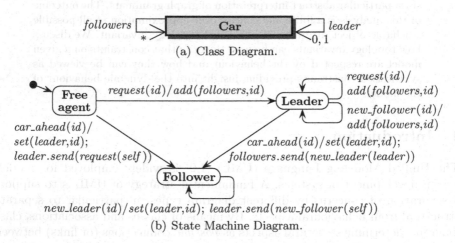

(a) Class Diagram.

(b) State Machine Diagram.

Fig. 1. Structural and Behavioural model of Car Platooning

The Problem Illustrated. Consider the task to design a class structure that describes the associations of cars participating in car platooning, i.e. driving in dynamically established convoys (cf. Section 3 for details). In car platooning, a car assumes one of three roles.

(a) It may be part of the tail of a convoy, a so-called follower, then having a link to the platoon leader,
(b) it may be the first car in a convoy, the so-called leader, then having at least one follower, and
(c) it may drive freely as a so-called free-agent, then having neither followers nor leaders.

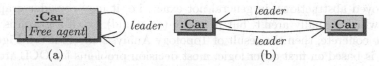

(a)   (b)

Fig. 2. Unintended topologies

A viable solution is the class diagram shown in Figure 1(a), as it supports all of the just named three cases. As cars execute concurrently, we've got to employ two unidirectional links to faithfully model transitional situations. For example, during a merge, a follower may have established the link to its leader while the leader has not yet updated its followers.

What the class diagram doesn't say is that these three cases should be the *only* ones. For example, both object diagrams in Figure 2 are legal according to the class diagram but unintended, as a car shall not be its own leader, and cars shall not consider each other to be the leader. Note that from the behavioural model as given by the tiny state machine shown in Figure 1(b), it is neither obvious whether the system remains in the three cases (a)–(c) nor whether the system reaches one of the particular errors shown in Figure 2.

The issue that the class diagram doesn't precisely *say* which object diagrams are wanted can be solved by adding constraints to the class diagram, most naturally in the form of OCL constraints. For example, the constraint

<u>Car</u>
(Free agent)   (1)
   implies (leader->isEmpty and followers->isEmpty)

formalises case (c) named above, the remaining cases have similar constraints.

But the core problem remains: to analyse whether the system *adheres* to these constraints at run-time. For example, a simple copy-and-paste error during the construction of the state machine could cause *self* to be assigned to the *leader* link in the transition from state *Free agent* to state *Follower.*In this small example, such kind of errors may be excluded by closely considering the actions, but violations of requirements are in general not that obvious.

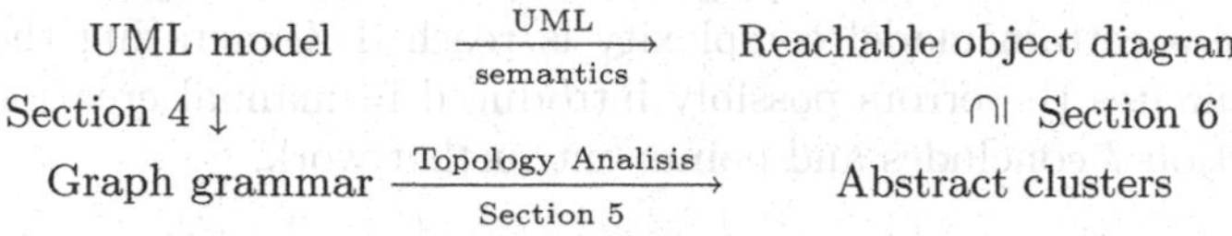

UML model $\xrightarrow[\text{semantics}]{\text{UML}}$ Reachable object diagrams

Section 4 ↓   ∩ Section 6

Graph grammar $\xrightarrow[\text{Section 5}]{\text{Topology Analisis}}$ Abstract clusters

Fig. 3. Approach. A set of abstract clusters is an abstract description of (a superset of) all reachable object diagrams of a UML model. It is obtained by Topology Analysis from a graph grammar representation of the UML model.

The New Methodology. Our proposal is, assuming a graph grammar UML semantics, to employ a technique called Topology Analysis [3] which computes, for a given graph grammar, a concise, finite, abstract description of all graphs possibly reachable by applying the rules of the grammar. The result is, due to the employed abstractions, in general not exact, i.e. it may consider graphs reachable which actually aren't, but it is safe (or sound), i.e. if a graph is reachable in the concrete, then the result of Topology Analysis covers it (cf. Figure 3). As OCL is based on first order logic, most decision problems for OCL are undecidable. On a *finite* characterisation of the reachable object diagrams however, a large fragment of OCL invariants can be evaluated automatically. This does not contradict with the undecidability of OCL as Topology Analysis in general does not compute an exact approximation of the runtime behaviour. Note that neither Topology Analysis nor the specific choice of graph grammar semantics are novel contributions. Rather, our combination and usage of them is unique and beneficial, in particular, in the context of UML/OCL verification. We underpin the usefulness of our methodology by conducting a complex case study.

Structure. Our presentation is structured as follows. Employing the more detailed discussion of the case study in Section 3, we equip a small but relevant fragment of UML with a graph grammar semantics in Section 4. The system described by a UML model is basically a transition system whose states are node and edge-labelled graphs. Objects are nodes which are labelled with the valuation of their attributes and links are edges which are labelled with the association name. The remaining step is then to express actions and event communication in terms of graph grammars. Section 5 recalls the necessary parts of Topology Analysis, in particular the formal definition of topology invariants.

The main contribution of this work is given in Section 6 where we connect topology invariants back to UML models by interpreting them as descriptions of the possible object diagrams. Thereby we gain four things. Firstly, we may evaluate OCL expressions in topology invariants, that is, given a UML model comprising OCL constraints, we can verify that they are satisfied at run-time. Secondly, we can interpret the obtained topology invariant as *synthesised* constraints. A topology invariant may thirdly, in its entirety, provide the developer with an impression of how the system behaves at run-time by giving a concise pictorial overview of reachable object diagrams. This shall in many cases be sufficient to point out subtle design errors. Finally, a subset of the topology invariants may serve for automatically derived documentation. Understanding the intention of data-structures employed in a system necessarily requires object diagrams once a certain model complexity is reached. Generating them automatically eliminates the errors possibly introduced in manual creation of such diagrams. Section 7 concludes and points out further work.

2   Related Work

As far as we are aware, no other abstract interpretation based approach that aims at solving the problem of *computing all possible reachable object diagrams* exists. There are formal verification techniques like [4,5,6] that are able to prove that a given behavioural UML model *always* adheres to properties specified in variants of temporal logic. Due to the complete nature of that approach, it often becomes infeasible in practice. Moreover, it works on symbolic representations of the reachable object diagrams and does not provide direct, graphical access to them; despite the fact that all of these approaches assume finite upper bounds on the number of objects alive at one point in time, that is, only consider under-approximations of the whole system. Abstract interpretation based methods using aggressive abstractions might be a way out. Besides our and the aforementioned methods, there exist tools like UMLAUT [7], VIATRA [8], and USE [9], which allow the interactive or semi-automatic construction of object diagrams from models. However, this exploration is typically not exhaustive.

Apart from computing reachable object diagrams, we are interested in the verification of OCL formulas. USE and VIATRA may be used for evaluating OCL formulas on class and object diagrams, too. However, they are not able to consider *all* possible diagrams for OCL verification. While exhaustive verification techniques are able to do so, they have the well-known scalability issues.

So far, we have summarised related work aiming at the same goal. Below, we take a more technique-centered approach. There is numerous work on graph grammars semantics for UML. The research around the USE tool and graph grammar based UML semantics by Gogolla and others [9,10] is the one we follow for obtaining a graph grammars semantics. Other approaches might be equally well-suited. The technique of Topology Analysis [3] we employ here, has originally been applied in the context of so-called Dynamic Communication Systems [11], which are basically the essence of object-oriented systems, covering dynamic creation and destruction of objects, dynamically changing topology, and asynchronous communication. Just like in the case of UML graph grammar semantics, we have chosen one approach to graph grammars applications. Related to the abstract rule matching in [3], the authors of [12] describe transformation rules for summary nodes (which however do not stem from graph abstraction).

It may be worthwhile to investigate the applicability of other methods to the problem of approximating object diagrams, e.g., [13,14,15], or even the three-valued logic based techniques employed for the analysis of heap manipulating programs, which originate from [16]. Although we will prove the appropriateness of Topology Analysis in this work, the named approaches may be candidates to replace it.

3   Case Study: Car Platooning

We demonstrate our approach on the notably small, but non-trivial and relevant case study of car platooning (cf. Figure 4). Since the late 80's of the last century,

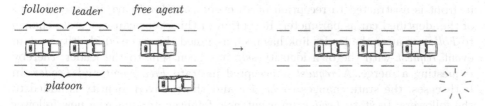

Fig. 4. Car Platooning. A disappearing car and a platoon/free agent merge.

people have investigated systematic ways to improve the throughput of highways and to reduce energy consumption [17]. One particular approach is the so-called car platooning. It assumes that cars are provided with communication equipment supporting a kind of ad-hoc network. Cars are notified about other cars driving in front of them which they may then ask, via the communication network, to form a platoon. If the car in front agrees, the back car becomes a follower in the platoon and reduces the safety distance to a minimum. To remain safe, in particular in case of braking manoeuvres, each platoon has a leader which is responsible for notifying its followers about upcoming braking manoeuvres. In the original design [17], communication happens only between a leader and its followers, but not among followers. We adopt this star-like communication structure in our work.

On a more abstract level, a car can fulfill one of three roles. It can be a *free agent*, a *follower*, or a *leader*. Initially, that is, when entering the highway, a car is a free agent. The roles change along three basic manoeuvres, namely *merge* to join cars into a platoon, *split* to split platoons in half, and *change lane*. In the following, for simplicity, we shall concentrate on the merge manoeuvre; the implementation follows the proposal of [18]. The simplest case of merge involves two cars in role free agent, one approaching the other from the back. If the back car is notified about a car driving in front, it requests a merge by sending an according event with its own identity attached, and accepts the car in front as leader. Its role then changes to follower. On receiving the request, the front car assumes the sender as a follower and changes role to leader. In general, both the front and the back car may actually already be platoons, thereby merging free agents into existing platoons or two platoons into a larger platoon. In case there is a whole platoon in the back instead of only a free agent, the protocol is slightly more complicated as the followers of the back platoon have to change their leader and the new leader has to become acquainted with all new followers. To this end, the back leader sends an event announcing the identity of the new leader to all of its followers. These followers in turn update their leader to the new one and announce themselves as new followers by sending an event carrying their identity to the front leader.

We can capture car platooning on this abstract level in form of UML diagrams as follows. Figure 1(a) shows the rather simple class diagram, comprising only a single, active class *Car* with a possible association *leader* to the leader car and an unbounded, possibly empty association *followers* to the follower cars. The behaviour is given by the state machine shown in Figure 1(b). A newly created car starts off in state *Free agent*, with no links. The identification of cars driving in front is abstracted to reception of an event *car_ahead* carrying the identity of the identified car as parameter. Reception of this event causes a state change to *Follower* after the leader link has been assigned the received identity and an event *request* with the own identity *self* has been sent to the leader, thereby requesting a merge. A *request* is accepted in state *Free agent* and *Leader*. In both cases, the state changes to *Leader* and the received identity is added to the followers. In state *Leader*, an event *new_follower* announces a new follower when a whole platoon approached from the back and requested a merge. The parameter carried by these events is added to the set of followers. If a platoon approaches a car or platoon in front, this is also announced by the environment with a *car_ahead* message. The back leader changes state to *Follower* after it has set its *leader* link and notified all of its followers of the new leader. Here we assume that the *send* method sends a message to all objects linked as followers. Being a follower, the only expected event is *new_leader* which announces a new leader. The state remains *Follower* after the *leader* link has been changed to the received identity and the new leader has been sent a *new_follower* event announcing the own identity as a new follower.

Note that in the following, we assume an environment which non-deterministically chooses to create instances of class *Car* or to destroy them unless they are in state *Leader*. This models that cars may freely enter and leave the highway. In addition, the environment may send *car_ahead* events to the present instances announcing one of the other present instances as having appeared in front of another car. This can explicitly be added to the model in form of an additional class.

4   Ad-Hoc Graph Grammar Semantics of UML

Our approach as sketched in the introduction is based on abstract interpretation of graph grammars, thus we need a graph grammar semantics for a fragment of UML sufficient to cover our case-study.

Using graphs and graph grammars as a semantical domain for UML as such is not new and rather well-studied, cf. for instance the work summarised in [10] and also [19], which is more focused on agents than on UML.

In fact, we employ a simplistic variant of the approach proposed in [10]. It demonstrates that the particular choice of semantics is not the limiting factor of our approach as we discuss the most relevant features of UML. The semantics is ad-hoc in the sense that it is a minimal setting which is suited to present our approach and we don't intend to provide a formal semantics for each and every syntactical feature of the UML 2.0 standard.

UML Model. Principally following [20], for the scope of this paper a UML model is a quadruple $U = (E, C, L, M)$ comprising a finite set E of events, a finite set C of classes, all active, and functions L and M providing classes with associations and state-machines. For each event from E we assume that we're given the information whether it may be sent by the environment or whether it is only used internally in the system, and whether it carries a parameter or not. Given a class $c \in C$, its set of associations $L(c) = \{l_1, \ldots, l_n\}$, $n \in \mathbb{N}_0$, is finite and may be empty. Its state machine $M(c)$ is a quintuple (S, S_0, S_Ω, R, A) comprising a finite set of states S, sets of initial and fragile states $S_0, S_\Omega \subseteq S$, a transition relation $R \subseteq S \times S$, and a transition labelling A assigning each transition $r \in R$ a trigger, a trigger/action pair, or only an action. For the scope of this article, we assume that a trigger is simply an event from E not carrying a parameter, that a trigger/action pair is an event carrying a parameter and an action which manipulates associations and may refer to the parameter, and that plain actions at least comprise association manipulation and event sending. Note that the notion of fragile states is not standard UML, but encodes that cars may non-deterministically be destroyed by the environment we assume (cf. Section 3). For convenience, we assume that states of state machines are disjoint, that is, $S(M(c_1)) \cap S(M(c_2)) = \emptyset$ for classes $c_1 \neq c_2$, which is easily established for any UML model via renaming.

For example, consider the formal representation of the UML model shown in Figure 1. The set of events is $E = \{car\_ahead, request, new\_follower, new\_leader\}$, all carrying parameters and all but car_ahead are only used internally. The set of classes is $C = \{Car\}$. The associations of the only class are $L(Car) = \{leader, followers\}$. Its state machine $M(Car)$ is (S, S_0, S_Ω, R, A) with states

$$S \supseteq \{Free\ agent, Leader, Follower\}, \tag{2}$$

initial state $S_0 = \{Free\ agent\}$, and fragile states $S_\Omega = \{Free\ agent, Follower\}$.

The semantics of a UML model U is an infinite-state transition system where each state is an object diagram, that is, a set of object instances connected via links. In addition, each object has a sequence of events as event queue. Two such states are in transition relation if and only if the destination state is the outcome of applying an action of an according transition in a state machine of U to a single object in the source state. That is, for convenience we consider a strict interleaving semantics as all classes are active (see above).

As discussed in more detail in [20], this simplistic notion of UML models is not a severe restriction of generality of our proposal as it already captures many essential features by appropriate encodings.

In order to fit into our restricted set of actions, the actual set of states is larger than the ones occurring in Figure 1(b) because the sequential compositions of actions has to be split into atomic actions. For example, the transition from *Free agent* to *Follower* would be split into two transitions by adding an auxiliary state to S (cf. Figure 5). The transition to the auxiliary state is annotated by a trigger/action pair, the action assigns the received identity to the *leader* association. The transition from the auxiliary state is annotated by a plain action, which sends an event to the object denoted by the *leader* association. Note that such operations are semantics preserving in the sense that they neither affect the reachability of non-auxiliary states nor liveness, that is, whether non-auxiliary states are finally reached. The operations only increase the number of transitions taken during a run-to-completion step.

Furthermore, hierarchical state machines unfold into the flat ones considered here following the well-known procedures (for an example, consider [20]). Attributes of finite domains can directly be encoded in an enlarged state set.

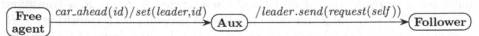

Fig. 5. Splitting transitions with auxiliary states

Similarly, events carrying data of finite domains can be encoded by enlarging the set of events. Methods, unless recursive, can be encoded by "inlining" them into transition annotations. Finally, inheritance can be translated into one class per feature added in a specialisation and a new one-to-one association pointing to the superclass (cf. [20]).

Graphs and Graph Grammars. A *graph* is a quintuple (V, E, s, t, l) featuring sets V and E of *nodes* and *edges*, *source* and *target* functions s and t, and a *labelling* function l. Source and target functions map edges to their respective source and target nodes, the labelling function l maps both, nodes and edges, to a label from a finite set of labels.

A *graph grammar* $\mathfrak{G}$ is a finite set of *graph transformation rules*. A graph transformation rule consists of two graphs, a *left graph L*, a *right graph R*, and a relation between them indicating which nodes and edges in L and R correspond to each other. In the rule shown in Figure 6, this correspondence is given implicitly by graphical position. A rule can be *applied* to a graph G if L is a subgraph of G. The result of an application is the replacement of L's occurrence in G with R. For more details, we refer to the textbook [21].

Graph Grammar-based UML Semantics. According to the paragraph above, a state of the UML model is an object diagram, where each object is additionally equipped with an event queue. That is, states are graphs where each node represents either an object or an event and each edge a link or possession of an event. Object nodes are labelled with the object's state, event nodes with the event name. Recall from above, that we consider attribute valuations to be encoded into state machine states. Edges to object nodes are labelled by association names, edges to event nodes by the special label μ. Note that, on the level of graphs and within the graph transformation rules, there is no explicit distinction between objects and events, they're both nodes. That is, if we were after an even smaller formal representation of UML models than the one presented above, we could even encode events by having a *class* for each category of events; sending and receiving events would then correspond to creating and destroying instances of these artificial classes.

The graph grammar of U is then the set of graph transformation rules obtained for the state machine transitions in U. For example, the rule shown in Figure 6 is actually the rule corresponding to the second half of the transition from state *Free agent* to *Follower*. If there are objects in state *Aux* and *Free agent* and if the former knows the latter by link *leader*, then an event node *request* carrying the identity of the former object as a parameter may be sent to the latter. Note that the latter link is labelled with μ as it points to an event, that is, it can be read as pointing to the head of the message queue.

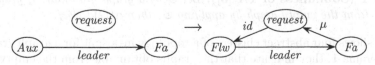

Fig. 6. Graph transformation rule

5   Topology Analysis

The technique we employ to compute the possible object diagrams for a given UML model is called *Topology Analysis* (TA) [3]. The subject of TA are graph grammars for directed node- and edge-labelled graphs, that is, finite sets of graph transformation rules. For a given graph grammar, TA yields a finite over-approximation, called *topology invariant*, which (abstractly) describes all graphs possibly generated by the graph grammar when applied to a finite set of initial graphs. Technically, topology invariants are obtained by an abstract interpretation [22] of graph grammars in the abstract domain of *abstract clusters*. An instance of an abstract cluster is any graph that can be abstracted to it by *partner abstraction*. Partner abstraction of a graph in turn is the quotient graph with respect to *partner equivalence*. Intuitively, two nodes of a graph are partner equivalent if and only if they are similar and if they have similar edges to (sets of) similar nodes, where being similar means having the same label.

More formally, let $G = (V, E, s, t, l)$ be a graph. Two nodes $v_1, v_2 \in V$ are partner equivalent if and only if they have the same label, i.e. $l(v_1) = l(v_2)$, and if for all edge labels a, the nodes reachable from v_1 and v_2 via an edge labelled with a and the nodes reaching v_1 and v_2 via an edge labelled with a have the same label, i.e.

$$out_G(a, v_1) = out_G(a, v_2) \text{ and } in_G(a, v_1) = in_G(a, v_2) \tag{3}$$

where

$$out_G(a, v) = \{l(v') \mid \exists e \in E : (s(e), t(e)) = (v, v') \wedge l(e) = a\} \tag{4}$$

and analogously for incoming edges.

Based on partner equivalence, the partner abstraction $\alpha(G)$ of G is obtained in two steps. Firstly, for each connected component C of G, compute the quotient graph with respect to partner equivalence. Doing so, mark equivalence classes containing more than one node as *summary nodes*. Secondly, summarise isomorphic quotient graphs, that is, keep only one of them. The quotient graphs are called abstract clusters.

As mentioned above, Topology Analysis is an abstract interpretation of a given graph grammar $\mathfrak{G}$ in the domain of abstract clusters. Beginning from the empty abstract cluster, $\mathfrak{G}$ is applied iteratively until a fix-point is reached, which is guaranteed to exist as the abstract domain is finite (cf. [3]). The fix-point is called topology invariant of $\mathfrak{G}$ and denoted by $\mathscr{G}_G$.

Lemma 1 (Soundness of TA [3]). *Let $\mathfrak{G}$ be a graph grammar. If graph G is obtained from the empty graph by applying $\mathfrak{G}$, then $\alpha(G) \subseteq \mathscr{G}_G$.*

Figure 7 shows four abstract clusters of a topology invariant for a graph grammar $\mathfrak{G}$. By Lemma 1, they indicate that the graphs obtainable from the empty graph by applying $\mathfrak{G}$ iteratively may comprise any number of instantiations of abstract

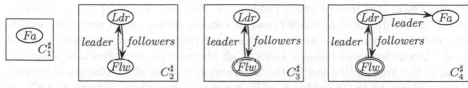

Fig. 7. Abstract clusters. Doubly outlined nodes are summary nodes.

clusters and any combination thereof. An instantiation of an abstract cluster is a concretisation in the sense of abstract interpretation, that is, any graph abstracted to the respective abstract cluster. For example, Figure 7 indicates that there may be any number of nodes labelled "*Fa*" (by abstract cluster $C_1^\sharp$), and any number of connected components with two nodes, one labelled "*Ldr*" and the other one "*Flw*" (by abstract cluster $C_2^\sharp$), and any number of connected components with one node labelled "*Ldr*" and at least two nodes labelled "*Flw*" and connected as indicated by abstract cluster $C_3^\sharp$, etc. That is, a topology invariant is an *over-approximation*. It is an abstract description of the set of all possible graphs obtainable from $\mathfrak{G}$, which doesn't miss an obtainable graph but possibly covers more. This kind of approximation is an inherent feature of abstract interpretation based methods and is the price to pay for efficiency. Due to the high complexity of the original problem, we must lose some information somewhere.

6   Reachable Object Diagrams

The abstract clusters shown in Figure 7 are actually a fragment of the topology invariant of the graph grammar representation of the UML model shown in Figure 1. While the graph grammar has been obtained (and improved) manually for this case study, the computation of topology invariants is completely automatic [3]. To keep the number of abstract clusters well manageable, we've assumed a maximal event queue length of 1 during the analysis, which is not a principal restriction of the approach (cf. [3]).

Recall from Section 4 that graphs are used to represent object diagrams, and a topology invariant is an over-approximation of the reachable object diagrams of the UML model we started from. The information represented by a topology invariant can be exploited in many ways, most prominently the following.

6.1   Constraints Verification

The most sophisticated use is to give OCL expressions a semantics on abstract clusters. As abstract clusters are basically graphs, the starting point for such a semantics will be an OCL semantics on graphs as provided by [9]. The problem with abstract clusters is that they abstract from certain information in order to remain finite, first of all the number of instances. For example, abstract cluster $C_3^\sharp$ doesn't indicate the *number* of followers a leader may have. That is, one has to be careful when evaluating collection comprehension expressions of OCL, for example `self.followers` which yields a set. The size of this set has to evaluate to the indefinite value `oclUndefined` to remain sound, while `notEmpty` evaluates definite on the same set, i.e. a constraint requiring that an object in state *leader* has at least one follower holds in all abstract clusters shown in Figure 7. That is, the information lost by the abstraction has the effect that some expressions evaluate to `oclUndefined`, while some remain definite values. As OCL is a three-valued Kleene logic, the indefinite value is correctly treated through all arithmetical and logical expressions. Table 1 sketches the treatment of OCL concepts; the only untreatable feature are time expressions (see discussion below).

A system-wide OCL expression like (1) from the introduction is then evaluated for all abstract clusters in the topology invariant. For the considered model, we've established constraint (1) by (manual) evaluation in all abstract clusters. In contrast, the following constraint, which explicitly excludes the unintended topology from Figure 2(b), cannot be excluded by topology invariants.

<u>Car</u>
(Leader) implies (leader->leader <> self)   (5)

Close inspection of the model unveils that the state machine is too simple to ensure this property. The reason is that two cars may subsequently be announced to each other as driving in front. As there is no further negotiation, they both continue to set their leader link to each other, ending up in the object diagram shown in Figure 2(b). The error can be eliminated by adding further negotiation employing additional acknowledge events. For the corrected version, the topology invariant, and thus the corrected model, satisfies constraint (5).

Given such an interpretation of OCL in abstract clusters, the constraint verification can be conducted automatically for the constraints found in the model as well as for interactive query of constraints.

However, we cannot prove arbitrary properties to hold for any model. This is related to the *property preservation* properties of Topology Analysis. A property is preserved by an analysis, if the fact, that it evaluates to true on every concrete model, implies that it holds true of any abstract model as well. Property preservation is often used to *exclude* undesired behaviour by applying it in its counterpositive form. Whenever something does not hold for a topology invariant, it will not hold for any object diagram of the model. Topology Analysis, for instance, "preserves graphs". If the abstraction of a certain graph does not occur

Table 1. Abstract semantics of OCL constructs

attribute access ('.')	node label	arithmetic expressions	possibly undefined
association navigation ('.')	possibly undefined	('+', '-')	(indirect)
collection comprehension ('collect')	possibly undefined	logical expressions ('<>', 'and')	possibly undefined (indirect)
collection operations ('->count')	possibly undefined	typing, meta-level ('oclType')	only implicitly
		time expressions ('@pre')	not considered

in the topology invariant, then it will not occur in any object diagram. Topology Analysis doesn't preserve all properties. This is the case for all temporal properties, that is, it won't be possible to support the OCL time expression `@pre`, but also for others. A detailed account of property preservation can be found in [23].

6.2 Constraints Synthesis

In addition to evaluating given OCL expressions in abstract clusters, we can in some cases translate abstract clusters back to OCL. This is tightly related to the *property reflection* properties of the underlying Topology Analysis. Often, property reflection is much harder than property preservation. A property is reflected, if the fact that it holds on a topology invariant implies that it holds on every object diagram represented by it.

Topology analysis reflects only few properties. Again, we refer to [23] for a detailed account. Among the reflected properties are, for instance, edges that do not exclusively involve summary nodes. For example, the abstract clusters in Figure 7 indicate that

$$
\begin{array}{l}
\texttt{\underline{Car}} \\
\texttt{(Follower) implies (leader->followers->includes(self))}
\end{array}
\tag{6}
$$

might be a valid constraint of the considered model.

If some additional and automatically checkable technical requirements are fulfilled as well, then such a constraint can be synthesised (automatically). Constraints obtained by this approach may yield valuable, highly condensed insights into the behaviour of the model, comprehensible for every developer trained in OCL. And even hardly comprehensible constraints, for example due to size or nesting, may serve as indicators for regression if they become violated after changes to the model.

Again, we must stress, that only few properties are reflected and, often, it will not be possible to synthesise constraints. However, the fact that is is possible— sometimes even automatically—seems like an important contribution.

6.3 Graphical Appeal for Debugging and Documentation

One of the major benefits of a graph-based approach like Topology Analysis, is its graphical appeal. Our method lends itself for two major purposes: early error detection (debugging) and documentation.

Given the developer's intuition of how the expected object diagrams look, it should in many cases be possible to identify unwanted object diagrams. Experience with implementing our case study shows, that running Topology Analysis already at early design stages, often reveals subtle mistakes. This is mainly owed to the graphical nature of the outcome.

Finally, abstract clusters could give hints for good object diagrams to be used in a system's documentation. As obvious with the minimal UML model example, the class diagram alone is typically not sufficient to understand a model's behaviour at run-time. To this end, good documentation typically comprises characteristic object diagrams. Given a set of good candidates, the only remaining task is to show that they're not spurious, as Topology Analysis is in general not exact (cf. Section 5). We're confident that this task can efficiently be automated employing formal verification techniques. The observation with formal verification tools, in particular the ones employing search-based techniques similar to the SPIN model-checker [24], is that they're in average orders of magnitude faster for so called "drive to configuration" tasks than for verification tasks. Tasks of the former kind confirm the reachability of certain "good", or desired system states, while verification establishes satisfaction of temporal properties or the absence of "bad" states for the whole state space. Applying SPIN to UML has been demonstrated, for instance, by Schaefer and others in [25].

7   Conclusion

We have proposed a new methodology for approximating all possible object diagrams given a structural and behavioural UML model. Our methodology relies on well-established techniques from the areas of UML graph grammar semantics and graph graph grammar verification. It combines these approaches in a novel fashion. On top of a graphical overview of all possible object diagrams, we expect benefits like OCL constraint verification and synthesis, early error detection, debugging and automated documentation. In fact, the case study presented in this work shows the general feasibility and relevance of the application of Topology Analysis to UML models and fully meets our expectations. Moreover, most of the results were obtained automatically.

As the results presented here are only a case-study, further work clearly consists of fully elaborating this approach. This involves further case studies, thus more experimental results, more automation, and, perhaps, the exploration of other available graph grammar UML semantics and other graph grammar verification methods. In more detail, the formal connection between the specific UML semantics chosen and the specific graph grammars serving as input for Topology Analysis must be established more formally. This may give rise to more automation, too. Furthermore, the abstract interpretation of OCL expressions on abstract clusters has to be fully elaborated. Our first approach as reported in Section 6 clearly indicates the feasibility, but also shows that there is work to be done in order to pass all information from the abstract clusters through to the level of OCL, that is, to obtain a best abstract interpretation.

While we did not experience any scalability problems during our case study, Topology Analysis might be rather costly or imprecise in general, which is not surprising given the complexity of the task. It may thus be beneficial to abstract as early as possible, that is, on an as high language level as possible, for instance, on model level directly rather than on graph grammar level as we propose in our methodology. That is, one should investigate whether there are possibilities to abstract from behaviour of the UML model, for example, certain arithmetics on attributes that don't affect the topology. This will improve the overall scalability of the methodology considerably.

Finally, a promising idea to improve precision was outlined in Section 6: employ formal verification technology but only for the limited (and typically orders of magnitude less expensive) use-case of falsification to confirm the validity of each abstract cluster. This could be conducted after termination of Topology Analysis, on the final topology invariant, or possibly even during the iterative computation constituting the analysis itself. Complementary, the existing criteria for exactness given in [23] can possibly be lifted to the level of UML models.

References

1. OMG: Unified Modeling Language: Superstructure, Version 2.1.1. Technical Report formal/07-02-05 (February 2007)
2. OMG: Unified Modeling Language: Infrastructure 2.1.1. Technical Report formal/07-02-06 (February 2007)
3. Bauer, J., Wilhelm, R.: Static Analysis of Dynamic Communication Systems. In: 14th International Static Analysis Symposium. Springer, Heidelberg (2007)
4. Xie, F., Levin, V., Browne, J.C.: Model Checking for an Executable Subset of UML. In: Feather, M., Goedicke, M. (eds.) Proceedings of ASE-2001: The 16th IEEE Conference on Automated Software Engineering, November 2001. IEEE Computer Society Press, Los Alamitos (2001)
5. Knapp, A., Merz, S., Rauh, C.: Model Checking Timed UML State Machines and Collaborations. In: Damm, W., Olderog, E.-R. (eds.) FTRTFT 2002. LNCS, vol. 2469. Springer, Heidelberg (2002)
6. Schinz, I., Toben, T., Mrugalla, C., Westphal, B.: The Rhapsody UML Verification Environment. In: Cuellar, J.R., Liu, Z. (eds.) Proc. SEFM 2004, Beijing, China, September 2004, pp. 174–183. IEEE, Los Alamitos (2004)
7. Jézéquel, J.M., Ho, W.M., Guennec, A.L., Pennaneac'h, F.: UMLAUT: an Extendible UML Transformation Framework. In: Hall, R., Tyugu, E. (eds.) Proc. ASE 1999. IEEE Computer Society, Los Alamitos (1999)
8. Csertán, G., Huszerl, G., Majzik, I., Pap, Z., Pataricza, A., Varró, D.: VIATRA - Visual Automated Transformations for Formal Verification of UML Models. In: Emmerich, W., Wile, D. (eds.) 17th IEEE International Conference on Automated Software Engineering (ASE 2002), Edinburgh, Scotland, UK, 23-27 September 2002. IEEE Computer Society, Los Alamitos (2002)
9. Gogolla, M., Richters, M.: Development of UML descriptions with USE. In: Shafazand, H., Tjoa, A.M. (eds.) EurAsia-ICT 2002. LNCS, vol. 2510, pp. 228–238. Springer, Heidelberg (2002)
10. Hölscher, K., Ziemann, P., Gogolla, M.: On Translating UML Models into Graph Transformation Systems. Journal of Visual Languages and Computing 17(1), 78–105 (2006)
11. Bauer, J., Schaefer, I., Toben, T., Westphal, B.: Specification and Verification of Dynamic Communication Systems. In: Sixth International Conference on Application of Concurrency to System Design, 2006. ACSD 2006, pp. 189–200. IEEE Computer Society Press, Los Alamitos (2006)
12. Drewes, F., Hoffmann, B., Janssens, D., Minas, M., Eetvelde, N.V.: Shaped Generic Graph Transformation. In: Schürr, A., Nagl, M., Zündorf, A. (eds.) Proc. AGTIVE 2007, pp. 197–212 (October 2007)
13. Rensink, A., Distefano, D.: Abstract Graph Transformation. Electr. Notes Theor. Comput. Sci. 157(1), 39–59 (2006)
14. König, B., Kozioura, V.: Counterexample-guided Abstraction Refinement for the Analysis of Graph Transformation Systems. In: Hermanns, H., Palsberg, J. (eds.) TACAS 2006. LNCS, vol. 3920. Springer, Heidelberg (2006)

15. Becker, B., Beyer, D., Giese, H., Klein, F., Schilling, D.: Symbolic invariant verification for systems with dynamic structural adaptation. In: Osterweil, L.J., Rombach, H.D., Soffa, M.L. (eds.) ICSE, pp. 72–81. ACM, New York (2006)
16. Sagiv, S., Reps, T.W., Wilhelm, R.: Parametric shape analysis via 3-valued logic. ACM Trans. Program. Lang. Syst. 24(3), 217–298 (2002)
17. Varaiya, P.: Smart cars on smart roads: problems of control. IEEE Transactions on Automatic Control 38(2), 195–207 (1993)
18. Hsu, A., Eskafi, F., Sachs, S., Varaiya, P.: The Design of Platoon Maneuver Protocols for IVHS. PATH Research Report UCB-ITS-PRR-91-6, Institute of Transportation Studies, University of California at Berkeley (April 1991) ISSN 1055-1425
19. Depke, R., Heckel, R., Küster, J.M.: Formal agent-oriented modeling with UML and graph transformation. Science of Computer Programming 44(2), 229–252 (2002)
20. Damm, W., Josko, B., Pnueli, A., Votintseva, A.: A discrete-time UML semantics for concurrency and communication in safety-critical applications. Science of Computer Programming 55(1–3), 81–115 (2005)
21. Rozenberg, G. (ed.): Handbook of Graph Grammars and Computing by Graph Transformations. Foundations, vol. 1. World Scientific, Singapore (1997)
22. Cousot, P., Cousot, R.: Abstract interpretation: a unified lattice model for static analysis of programs by construction or approximation of fixpoints. In: Conference Record of the Fourth Annual ACM SIGPLAN-SIGACT Symposium on Principles of Programming Languages, Los Angeles, California, pp. 238–252. ACM Press, New York (1977)
23. Bauer, J.: Analysis of Communication Topologies by Partner Abstraction. PhD thesis, Universität des Saarlandes (2006)
24. Holzmann, G.J.: The Model Checker SPIN. IEEE Transactions on Software Engineering 23(5) (May 1997)
25. Schäfer, T., Knapp, A., Merz, S.: Model Checking UML State Machines and Collaborations. Electr. Notes in Theor. Comput. Sci. 55(3) (2001)

State of the Art of QVT: A Model Transformation Language Standard

Ivan Kurtev

Software Engineering Group, University of Twente, The Netherlands
kurtev@ewi.utwente.nl

Abstract. Query/Views/Transformation (QVT) is the OMG standard language
for specifying model transformations in the context of MDA. It is regarded as
one of the most important standards since model transformations are proposed
as major operations for manipulating models. In the first part of the paper we
briefly summarize the typical transformation scenarios that developers encounter in software development and formulate key requirements for each scenario.
This allows a comparison between the desirable and the formulated requirements for QVT. Such a comparison helps us to initially evaluate the adequacy
of the QVT language.The second part of the paper focuses on the current state
of the standard: the language architecture, specification, paradigm, and open issues. The three QVT sublanguages Operational Mappings, Relations, and Core
are briefly described. Special attention is given to the currently available and
expected tool support.

Keywords: Model transformations, QVT, MDA, MDE.

1 Introduction

Model Driven Engineering (MDE) is an emerging approach for software development
gaining more and more attention by the industry and the academia. MDE emphasizes
the need for thorough modeling of software systems before they are implemented.
The implementation should be derived from the models by applying model transformations, possibly in a fully automated way.

MDE principles may be applied by using different modeling languages, transformation languages, and tools. One example of such an approach is Model Driven Architecture (MDA) initiative proposed by OMG. MDA distinguishes between platform
independent models (PIMs) and platform specific models (PSMs). This classification
is motivated by the constant change in implementation technologies and the recurring
need to port software from one technology to another. Furthermore, MDA proposes
its set of modeling standards: (i) to define models and modeling languages (UML
[12], UML profiles, MOF [14]); (ii) to represent and exchange models (XMI) [11];
(iii) to define model constraints (OCL) [16]; (iv) to specify transformations on models. The last operation is proposed as the main way to manipulate models in MDA.
The important role of model transformations motivates the effort that OMG took to
define a standard language for model transformations aligned with the rest of OMG

A. Schürr, M. Nagl, and A. Zündorf (Eds.): AGTIVE 2007, LNCS 5088, pp. 377–393, 2008.

standards. The result of this effort is the standard QVT MOF 2.0 language [17] which at the time of the writing of this paper is in the final standardization phase.

Transformation technologies are not something new in software engineering. A compiler is actually a transformer that produces an artifact at a lower level of abstraction from another artifact at a higher level of abstraction, possibly expressed in a language that matches the problem domain better. The standardization of XML as an exchange data format gave birth to XSLT, a standard transformation language for XML documents. A similar effort is observed in the domain of Semantic Web. Many more examples may be given from the domain of data engineering, a discipline that is facing hard interoperability and data heterogeneity problems and approaches them by applying data transformations.

In software engineering we witness a stable progress in at least two fields: program transformations and graph transformations. This gives us a valuable insight about the problems we need to tackle and about the advantages and disadvantages of the available techniques.

In the light of this discussion an interesting question emerges. How does OMG derive the QVT standard? What are the transformation scenarios that will be addressed and what kind of properties the language will possess? Unfortunately, a quick look at the QVT Request for Proposals [13] (QVT RFP) document shows that the most important requirements for the language concern its alignment to the existing OMG standards and the software engineering qualities of the language take the role of non-mandatory requirements.

The purpose of this paper is twofold. First we would like to outline a set of transformation scenarios commonly found in software and data engineering. Each scenario naturally poses a set of requirements. They can be compared to the requirements and rationale behind QVT. Second, we present an overview on QVT and the current tool support for this language.

The paper is organized as follows. Section 2 gives a larger context for discussion by considering several well-known transformation scenarios. Section 3 presents the requirements for QVT as described in the QVT RFP. Section 4 explains the overall architecture of the QVT language and briefly describes the three QVT sublanguages: Relations, Core, and Operational Mappings (OM). Section 5 lists the currently available tools for specifying and executing QVT transformations. Section 6 concludes the paper.

2 Transformation Scenarios in Software and Data Engineering

The previous section mentioned that transformations are applied to solve problems in many domains. Those problems, however, generally differ and may pose a set of different requirements. These requirements should be the starting point for the development of a transformation language. In this section we analyze two domains of application of transformations: software development based on the principles of MDE and heterogeneous data translation.

2.1 Model Driven Software Development

Model Driven Software Development (MDSD) applies the principles of MDE in the development of software systems. A system is specified as a set of models that are repetitively refined until a model (models) with enough details to implement the system is obtained. The implementation step should be automated as much as possible by code generation from the models.

When applied in practice, this general scheme of MDSD processes should follow and address some stable general principles and scenarios of software development such as separation of concerns, iterative development, refactoring, reverse engineering, and others. These principles and scenarios take a concrete shape in the context of MDSD and put forward requirements and open questions. In this section we focus on the role of model transformations related to various aspects of MDSD.

Refinement Steps in MDSD. Regardless of the actual development methodology an MDSD process can be seen as a series of refinement steps. More abstract models are transformed into more detailed ones being closer to the actual system. The most important requirement for this refinement process is the semantics preserving property of transformations. Fig. 1 illustrates the process of refinement and the relations of the models to the system.

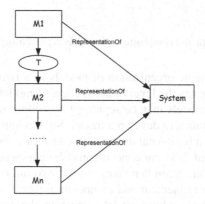

Fig. 1. Refinement of models in MDSD and their relation to the system to be implemented

The vertical dimension denotes the refinement from more abstract to more concrete models. Since all models are representations of the same system every transformation step should preserve the intended meaning of the source model and eventually bring new details. The refinement steps may encode useful design knowledge based on design and architectural patterns, idioms related to a particular implementation technology, and standard transformations such as UML to Java or UML to J2EE. Semantics preservation should ensure that the produced system will behave as it is specified in the models.

Separation of Concerns. The principle of separation of concerns helps in managing the complexity in development of large software systems. The application of this principle in MDSD leads to more than one model of the system developed from different points of interest. These models may be refined independently from each other along a single track as shown in Fig. 2. At a certain moment these models (or code) must be integrated to obtain a complete system.

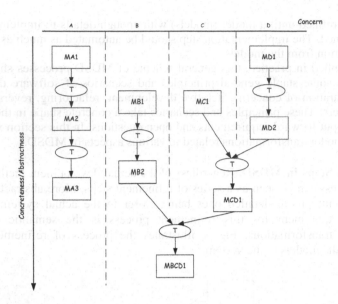

Fig. 2. Refinement and composition of models representing different concerns

Fig. 2 shows an example organization of models in a two-dimensional space. The vertical dimension indicates the level of abstraction of models. The horizontal dimension indicates that the models may be separated according to the problem they solve or the point of interest taken to develop a model. Such points of interest are known as *concerns*. Fig. 2 shows a horizontal dimension with four concerns: *A, B, C*, and *D*. At a certain stage models of different concerns may be composed. Composition of models is treated as a transformation that takes at least two input models and generates an output model. Both the refinement and composition transformations must be semantics preserving since the resulting models represent the same system as the source models.

Two issues arise in relation to the principle of separation of concerns. The first one is the consistency between models belonging to various concerns. Models of different concerns should be treated separately but ultimately they represent the same underlying system. Therefore, the independent changes over the models should not produce inconsistent results.

The second issue is the composition of models which is a special kind of transformation with at least two input models. The composition problems may expose specificities that may require a specialized language optimized for composition tasks [3].

Iterative Development and System Evolution. Contemporary software development methods promote iterative processes to manage complexity and to deal with identification of system inadequacy at an earlier stage of development. Every new iteration changes (adds to) the functionality of the system. Changes may also occur when the system evolves due to changed requirements during the maintenance phase. The impact of a change on a system developed according to the MDE principles requires changes to the existing models and integration of the newly developed models with existing ones. Since the system is developed as a series of transformations over models a change in one model must be propagated through the rest. The propagation may be in two directions: to models derived from the changed model and to models from which the changed model is derived.

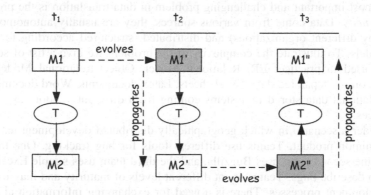

Fig. 3. Evolution and change propagation in MDE

Fig. 3 shows three moments in which models sequentially evolve. After the initial transformation is executed at moment *t1*, subsequent changes of the source and target models (at moments *t2* and *t3*) may require forward and backward change propagation. Two problems arise here: how to identify the required changes and how to apply them on existing models at a low cost.

The first problem is known as *traceability problem*. A trace allows a software artifact to be related to its predecessors that were developed during earlier phases of development. For example, a Java class may be traced back to its design class, analysis class, and ultimately to the requirement that motivates its presence in the system. In the case of model transformations a trace would relate elements in the source model to the created elements in the target model. By transitivity, traces may be detected over the chain of transformations. If a model element is changed, traces help in detecting the changes in the model elements derived from it and ultimately in the system code. Traceability support may not be a property of a transformation language. It may be provided by the transformation engine or the developer may take care of creating and using traces.

The second problem is how to apply the identified changes. One naive solution is to execute again the transformation on the modified model. However, for large models this may be time consuming, especially when there is a long chain of model refinements and compositions. A more efficient solution is to transform only those elements that are modified and to do only incremental changes at the target models.

It should be noted that this scenario does not necessarily call for bidirectional transformation programs. The two directions may be supported by two different transformation programs.

2.2 Data Translation Problems in Data Engineering Domain

Data translation, data mapping, and data integration are among the important sub-fields in data engineering. In this section we consider a real-life scenario that requires solving data translation problems. The scenario is generalized and it is shown that conceptually it exemplifies the classical data and schema translation problem.

The most important and challenging problem in data translation is the problem of *heterogeneity*. Data come from various sources, they are usually autonomous (controlled by different organizations) and distributed, structured according to different data models. To illustrate the complexity of the problem we give a list of some data formats used in practice: ER, Relational Model, Object-Relational Model, XML, SGML, comma-separated data, Excel sheets, Latex documents, Word documents, etc. Even relational data stored in systems coming from different vendors expose some differences.

Consider a scenario in which geographically distributed development teams work on a common product. Teams use different tools for bug tracking. One team uses Mantis, the second team uses Bugzilla, and the third team uses simple Excel spreadsheets to describe bugs. Teams are at different levels of maturity and may use different development processes. There is a need for exchanging information about bugs among the teams. However, every tool uses its own data format for bug description. Moreover, the conceptual models behind every tool used to describe bugs may also differ.

The scenario is illustrated in Fig. 4.

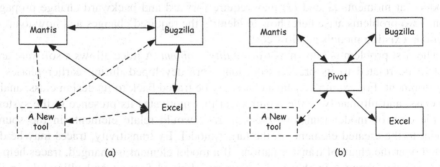

Fig. 4. Tool interoperability problem in bug management

Fig. 4a shows one possible way for interoperability in which there are bridges for every couple of tools. If a new team joins the project a potential new bug tracking system will be used. Then bridges must be built from the new tool to the existing tools. Fig. 4b shows a second way to handle the interoperability: a pivot model is defined that unifies the models used by the tools. Then a bridge is defined between the pivot model and every tool.

The scenario shown above may be generalized to the well known problem of schema and data translation [1]. It is illustrated in Fig. 5. We intentionally use terminology specific to the data engineering domain. We have three levels: *database*,

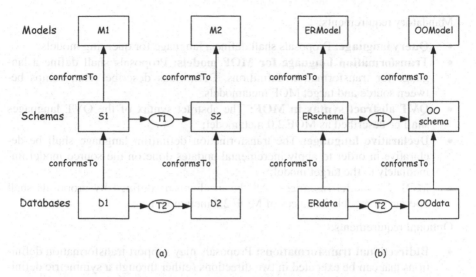

Fig. 5. Schema and data translation problem in data engineering

schema, and *model*. Databases conform to schemas and schemas conform to models. This three-level organization corresponds to the three levels of *model*, *metamodel*, and *metametamodel*.

The schema and data translation problem is formulated as follows. Given two models *M1* and *M2*, a source schema *S1* conforming to *M1*, and a source database *D1* conforming to *S1*, find a translation *T1* that generates a target schema *S2* conforming to the model *M2*, and a translation *T2* that translates the database *D1* to a database *D2* conforming to *S2*. Fig. 5a diagrammatically shows the problem and Fig. 5b gives a concrete example. An interesting question is if it is possible to automatically derive *T2* from *T1*.

The main observation on this problem is that it may involve a large degree of heterogeneity. We also have two possibilities for translations between a pair of models: *lossless* and *lossy* transformations. This depends on the level of compatibility between the schemas/models. In data translation we are interested in preserving the information as much as possible across models and schemas. This requirement is known as *preservation of information capacity* [7, 8].

3   QVT Requirements

After the presentation of two problem domains and the requirements they pose to model transformation systems we present the QVT standard proposed by OMG.

The requirements for the QVT language are described in the formal QVT Request for Proposals (QVT RFP) [13] issued by OMG. Here we briefly summarize the requirements without repeating them in full. QVT requirements are divided into *mandatory* and *optional* requirements.

Mandatory requirements:

- **Query language:** Proposals shall define a language for querying models;
- **Transformation language for MOF models:** Proposals shall define a language for transformation definitions. Definitions describe relationships between source and target MOF metamodels;
- **QVT abstract syntax in MOF:** The abstract syntax of the QVT languages shall be described as MOF 2.0 metamodel;
- **Declarative language:** The transformation definition language shall be declarative in order to apply incremental updates done on the source model immediately to the target model;
- **MOF 2.0 model instances:** All the mechanisms defined by proposals shall operate on models instances of MOF 2.0 metamodels;

Optional requirements:

- **Bidirectional transformations:** Proposals may support transformation definitions that can be executed in two directions (either through a symmetric definition or through a couple of definitions);
- **Traceability between source and target models:** Proposals may support traceability between source and target model elements after transformation execution;
- **Reusable transformations:** Proposals may support mechanisms for reuse of transformation definitions;
- **In-place updates:** Proposals may support execution of transformations where the source and target models are the same;

It should be noted that not all the requirements are listed here. For example, the requirement for view definition is skipped since it is not implemented in the proposed standard.

We also give the definitions of the three concepts that are used in the name of the QVT language (Query, View, and Transformation) as defined by OMG documents.

Query: A query is an expression that is evaluated over a model. The result of a query is one or more instances of types defined in the source model, or defined by the query language.

View: A view is a model which is completely derived from another model (the base model). There is a 'live' connection between the view and the base model.

Transformation: A model transformation is a process of automatic generation of a target model from a source model, according to a transformation definition.

An analysis of the requirements shows that main attention is paid to the alignment of QVT to the rest of the OMG standards, most notably MOF2.0. On the base of the mandatory requirements we may infer the following operational context of the QVT language (Fig. 6).

The operational context is based on the three-level MOF metamodeling architecture. The QVT abstract syntax is defined as a metamodel (*QVT*). QVT transformations are models conforming to the QVT metamodel. Fig. 6 shows an example transformation *Tab*. It is based on the input and output metamodels *MMa* and *MMb*. In general, QVT allows more than one input and output models and their

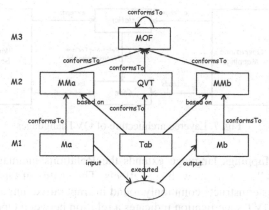

Fig. 6. QVT operational context

corresponding metamodels to be used. For simplicity, we show only single input and output models/metamodels. QVT transformations are executed by taking input models (*Ma*) and producing output models (*Mb*).

The optional requirements correspond to some well-known software quality properties. The RFP does not give any domain analysis and in-depth coverage of possible scenarios in which QVT will be used.

4   QVT Languages

According to Fig. 6, the abstract syntax of QVT is defined as a MOF 2.0 metamodel. This metamodel defines three sublanguages for transforming models. They rely on OCL 2.0 as navigation and query language for models. Creation of views on models is not addressed in the proposal.

4.1   QVT Architecture

QVT languages are arranged in a layered architecture shown in Fig.7. The languages *Relations* and *Core* are declarative languages at two different levels of abstraction. The specification document defines their concrete textual syntax and abstract syntax. In addition, *Relations* language has a graphical syntax. *Operational Mappings* is an imperative language that extends *Relations* and *Core* languages.

Relations language provides capabilities for specifying transformations as a set of relations among models. Core language is a declarative language that is simpler than the Relations language. One purpose of the Core language is to provide the basis for specifying the semantics of the Relations language. The semantics of the Relations language is given as a transformation *RelationsToCore*. This transformation may be written in the Relations language.

Sometimes it is difficult to provide a complete declarative solution to a given transformation problem. To address this issue the QVT proposes two mechanisms for extending the declarative languages Relations and Core: a third language called *Operational Mappings* and a mechanism for invoking transformation functionality implemented in an arbitrary language (*Black Box* implementation).

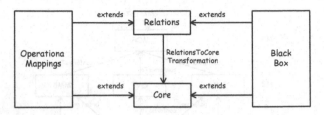

Fig. 7. Layered architecture of QVT languages

Operational Mappings language extends the Relations language with imperative constructs and OCL constructs with side effects. The syntax of Operational Mappings language provides constructs commonly found in imperative languages (loops, conditions, etc.). The QVT specification indicates a relation between Operational Mappings and Core. However, such a relation cannot be identified after inspecting the metamodels of these languages.

Black Box mechanism allows plugging-in and executing external code during transformation execution. This mechanism allows complex algorithms to be implemented in any programming language and enables reuse of already existing libraries. This makes some parts of the transformation opaque, which brings a potential danger since their functionality is arbitrary and is not controlled by the transformation engine.

Fig. 7 does not suggest any particular implementation of a QVT transformation engine. Tool vendors may choose different strategies. For example, the Core language may be supported by an execution engine and the Relations transformations may be transformed to equivalent programs written in Core language. In that way the engine is capable of executing programs written in both languages. Another possibility is that only the Relations and Operational Mappings are supported by a tool.

These implementation options may produce tools with different capabilities. To denote the capabilities of tools, the QVT proposal defines a set of *QVT conformance points* for tools. Conformance points are organized along two dimensions and form a grid with 12 cells. Table 1 shows the dimensions and the possible conformance points.

The *Language Dimension* defines three levels corresponding to the three QVT languages. If a tool conforms to a given level this means that it is capable of executing transformation definitions written in the corresponding language.

Table 1. QVT conformance points for tools

		Interoperability Dimension			
		Syntax Executable	XMI Executable	Syntax Exportable	XMI Exportable
Language Dimension	Core				
	Relations				
	Operational Mappings				

The *Interoperability Dimension* is concerned with the form in which a transformation definition is expressed. It defines four levels:

- **Syntax Executable.** A tool can read and execute transformation definitions written in the concrete syntax given in the QVT proposal;
- **XMI Executable.** A tool can read and execute transformation definitions serialized according to the XMI serialization rules (recall that transformation definitions conform to the QVT metamodel and therefore are XMI serializable);
- **Syntax Exportable.** A tool can export transformation definitions in the concrete syntax of the corresponding language;
- **XMI Exportable.** A tool can export transformation definitions in XMI format;

A requirement states that if a tool is *SyntaxExecutable* or *XMIExecutable* for a given language level, it should also be *SyntaxExportable* or *XMIExportable* respectively.

It should be noted that the QVT specification does not define the term "QVT compliant transformation language". This term tends to be more and more used. However, its meaning is not clear. It is an attractive possibility to attach a standard label to an existing transformation language. The specification gives us only the possibility to claim compliance for tools and not for languages.

4.2 Relations Language

Transformations written in the Relations language consists of declarations of relations among metaelements. Relations are based on an arbitrary number of domains. When a relation is specified no execution direction is assumed. When a transformation is executed an execution direction is chosen. This opens the possibility to specify bidirectional transformations if their logic permits so. The following transformation scenarios are supported by the Relations language:

- **Check-only:** transformation execution checks if given models satisfy the relations specified in the transformation definition. No new models/model elements are created and no changes are made to the existing models. The answer is *yes* or *no* depending if the relations hold;
- **Unidirectional transformation:** the transformation is executed in a given direction. The target model is created according to the relations in the transformation definition. After the transformation execution, the input and output models satisfy the relations in the transformation definition;
- **Model synchronization:** the transformation engine checks if the relations in a transformation definition hold for a given set of models. If a relation is not satisfied the engine makes changes in the models in order to satisfy the relation. This may lead to creation of new elements, deletion, and update of existing elements. This scenario is motivated by the need for handling model updates in an incremental fashion;
- **In-place update:** in this scenario there is only one model that may be changed according to the specified relations;

Every relation contains a set of object patterns. These patterns can be matched against existing model elements, instantiated to model elements in new models, and may be used to apply changes to existing models. The language handles the manipulation of traceability links automatically and hides the related details from the developer. The code snippet below gives an example relation.

```
1.   relation AttributeToColumn {
2.       checkonly domain uml c:Class {};
3.       enforce domain rdbms t:Table {};
4.       primitive domain prefix:String;
5.
6.       where {
7.           PrimitiveAttributeToColumn(c, t, prefix);
8.           ComplexAttributeToColumn(c, t, prefix);
9.           SuperAttributeToColumn(c, t, prefix);
10.      }
11. }
```

In a hypothetical transformation that transforms UML class models to relational schemas there is a relation between UML attributes and columns of relational tables. The relation *AttributeToColumn* specifies this. It consists of three domains: *uml* (line 2), *rdbms* (line 3), and one primitive domain that allows passing strings to the relation in the form of a parameter (line 4). In order to hold, the relation must satisfy the object patterns in the domains and to have the condition in the *where* clause (lines 6-10) evaluated to true. The *where* clause illustrates the possibility for invoking one relation from another one.

The keywords *checkonly* and *enforce* play an important role for the semantics of the transformation. Checkonly indicates that the domain elements (in this case UML classes) cannot be changed (i.e. they are read-only) by the transformation execution. Enforce indicates that the engine should change the elements of the domain to ensure the relation. On the basis of the concrete transformation scenario these keywords have different effect on the domains. For example, if a unidirectional transformation is executed from classes to tables then the *uml* domain will be used for matching and the *rdbms* domain will be created. In this scenario the meaning of *enforce* is creation of new elements. If two models already exist and the transformation is executed to synchronize them, changes are allowed only in the enforced domains.

4.3 Core Language

Core language is a declarative language that is simpler than the Relations language. Transformation definitions written in it tend to be longer than the equivalent definitions written in Relations language. Traceability links are treated as ordinary model elements. The developer is responsible for explicitly creating and using the links. Both languages support the same set of transformation scenarios. The rationale behind Core is to support bidirectional incremental transformations. An ideal execution engine for Core should be event-based: every modification in one model is immediately handled and the required modifications in the other models are performed. The following is a snippet taken from a Core transformation specification.

```
map attributeColumns in umlRdbms {
    check enforce rdbms (t:Table) {
        realize c:Column|
        c.owner := t;
        c.key->size()=0;
        c.foreignKey->size()=0;
    }
    where (c2t:ClassToTable| c2t.table=t;){
        realize a2c:AttributeToColumn|
        a2c.column := c;
        c2t.fromAttribute.leafs->include(a2c);
        default a2c.owner := c2t;
    }
    map{ check enforce rdbms (ct:String) {c.type := ct;}
        where (p2n:PrimitiveToName){
            a2c.type := p2n;
            p2n.typeName := ct;
        }
    }
    map {..........................................................................................}
```

A transformation in Core is a set of *mappings*. Mappings roughly correspond to relations in the Relations language. Mappings can be nested. The concepts of *enforced* and *check* domains are also available.

4.4 Operational Mappings

Operational Mappings language extends the Relations language with imperative constructs and OCL constructs with side effects. The basic idea in this language is that the object patterns specified in the relations are instantiated by using imperative constructs. In that way the declaratively specified relations are imperatively implemented. The syntax of Operational Mappings language provides constructs commonly found in imperative languages (loops, conditions, etc.). Transformations are always *unidirectional*.

```
1.  transformation SimpleUML2FlattenSimpleUML(in source : SimpleUML,
2.                                            out target : SimpleUML);
3.  main() {}
4.  ......................
5.  ...helpers..............
6.  ...mapping operations....
7.  mapping Class::leafClass2Class(in model : Model) : Class
8.  when {not model.allInstances(Generalization)->exists(g | g.general
9.                                                       = self)}
10. {name:= self.name;
11.  abstract:= self.abstract;
12.  attributes:= self.derivedAttributes()->
13.                      map property2property(self);
14. }
```

A transformation in Operational Mappings always has an entry point from which the transformation execution starts. This is the mapping called *main* (line 3). From *main* other mappings may be invoked. The body of the transformation definition contains mappings and helper operations. An example of a mapping is called *leafClass2Class* (lines 7-14). This mapping creates an UML class from every UML class that satisfies the guarding condition specified in the *when* clause (lines 8-9). The properties of the created class are assigned with values in the body of the mapping (lines 10-13). It is possible to invoke other mappings from the body of the current one (the keyword *map* in line 13). In that way the execution order among the mappings is imperatively specified.

4.5 Discussion

In section 2 we outlined several transformation scenarios. We observe a diversity of transformation problems that may require different transformation techniques. A logical question is if it is possible to handle these scenarios by a single transformation language in a satisfactory way. The answer is probably no. This is implicitly supported by the fact that QVT is not a single language. It is a suite of three languages that covers both the imperative and declarative paradigm, and addresses several transformation scenarios. Here we discuss briefly every scenario and how it can be handled by the QVT languages.

Regarding the semantics preservation property of model refinement, the QVT specification and the RFP do not require support for checking this. It is not clear yet what type of reasoning may be performed over QVT programs. We expect that a meaningful reasoning would require a limited version of the languages.

Model composition may be regarded as a transformation from at least two input models to a composed model. From that point of view, QVT supports model composition in general. There are proposals for model composition languages [3] specialized in model composition only.

Performing incremental bidirectional transformations is one of the scenarios in QVT Relations. It is somehow unclear how this scenario is implemented in the current engines. The approach suggested in the specification is to execute the transformation afresh by performing the required pattern matching and to execute only the required changes in the models. More experience is needed to judge if this approach provides satisfactory performance results.

QVT specification does not address data translation problems. Historically, the language is proposed as a solution to software development-related problems. The need for information capacity preservation is not analyzed. Due to the alignment of QVT to the OMG standards we may claim that from the data format point of view QVT transformations operate on XMI data. QVT is applicable in data engineering if suitable translators from and to XMI are available.

We may speculate about the need for domain-specific transformation languages adapted to a specific problem. From that point of view OMG proposes QVT as a general purpose transformation language similar to the role that XSLT plays in the XML domain. Some of the scenarios described in section 2 may require a specialized and eventually less expressive transformation language.

5   QVT Tools

Current tool support for the QVT languages is in its infancy. This is due to several reasons. First, the specification is not officially finalized and still unstable. Second, providing a mature tool requires time and efforts. Most tools do not support all the features of the languages. Once a tool is made available, the feedback from the user community is crucial. Practically all the current tools are dealing with bug fixes and are gaining experience from real life usage. Regardless the stability of the language specification many pragmatics issues are involved ranging from syntax-highlighting and visual syntax editors to the availability of comfortable debug facilities. All these make the current description of the tool support valid for a limited period of time. In this section we report on the tools available at the time of the writing of this paper.

Table 2 summarizes the currently available QVT tools. It is followed by more information on every tool.

Table 2. Tool support per QVT language

QVT Tools per Language	
Core	• A commercial add-on to OptimalJ
Relations	• IKV++ medini QVT
	• Tata Consultancy ModelMorf
	• MOMENT-QVT
	• Eclipse M2M Relations2ATLVM
Operational Mappings	• Borland Together Architect 2006
	• SmartQVT
	• Eclipse M2M OM2ATLVM

Core Language

The Core language is supported by an add-on to the commercial tool OptimalJ provided by Compuware. However, OptimalJ is now in maintenance phase and its future development is questionable. It is expected that an open source implementation of a Core engine may be provided.

Relations Language

Relations currently enjoys the largest tool support. The *medini QVT* [5] developed by IKV++ is an Eclipse based interpreter with syntax highlighting editor, code completion, and debugging facilities. It is available as a part of a commercial suite and as a free downloadable distribution for non-commercial purposes.

One of the original contributors to QVT that proposed the Relations language is Tata Consultancy. They provide a Java-based engine known as *ModelMorf* [9]. Currently ModelMorf is a command line tool. The web site indicates the plan to provide a commercial tool for Relations that implements both textual and visual syntax.

MOMENT-QVT [10] is an MDE project that is based on the term rewriting formalism MAUDE. It plans to provide implementation of OCL and QVT Relations.

Operational Mappings Language

Borland provides both an interpreter and a compiler to Java for one of the earlier QVT OM specifications. It is a part of Borland Together Architect 2006 for Eclipse. 15 days trial is available for download.

SmartQVT [18] is an open source Eclipse-based compiler for QVT Operational Mappings provided by France Telecom, the original initiator of QVT OM.

Both Together Architect and SmartQVT provide a front-end for Operational Mappings that can be used to parse transformation programs and obtain a model conforming to the QVT abstract syntax.

Eclipse M2M Project

M2M [4] is an open source project under Eclipse that aims at providing implementations for QVT and ATL [6]. M2M consists of three components: Procedural QVT (Operational Mappings), Declarative QVT (Relations and Core), and ATL. The committers in this project are: INRIA, Borland, and Compuware. The ATL Virtual Machine is adopted as a basic infrastructure for the project. Compilers from QVT OM and Relations to ATL VM code are under development. This effort is led by Obeo under the umbrella of the ATL industrialization project [1].

6 Conclusions

In this paper we presented QVT – the OMG standard language for model transformations in MDA. QVT is closely integrated with the existing suite of OMG standards, most notably with MOF 2.0 and OCL 2.0.

We believe that the standardization of QVT is a step in the right direction. A software standard has a high chance to attract the attention of a larger user community. This should open the possibility to gain experience with the model transformation technology in real life industrial projects. There are also risks, however. A standard lacking formal ground (as the current QVT specification), not supported by tools with industrial quality may compromise the whole idea behind model transformations. This should encourage the communities working on various transformation technologies to stress the importance of transformation problems in current software engineering practices and to promote alternatives to QVT.

References

1. ATL Pro web site, http://www.atl-pro.com/
2. Atzeni, P., Cappellari, P., Bernstein, P.A.: Model-Independent Schema and Data Translation. In: Ioannidis, Y., Scholl, M.H., Schmidt, J.W., Matthes, F., Hatzopoulos, M., Böhm, K., Kemper, A., Grust, T., Böhm, C. (eds.) EDBT 2006. LNCS, vol. 3896, pp. 368–385. Springer, Heidelberg (2006)
3. Bézivin, J., Bouzitouna, S., Del Fabro, M.D., Gervais, M., Jouault, F., Kolovos, D., Kurtev, I., Paige, R.: A Canonical Scheme for Model Composition. In: Rensink, A., Warmer, J. (eds.) ECMDA-FA 2006. LNCS, vol. 4066, pp. 346–360. Springer, Heidelberg (2006)
4. Eclipse M2M Project, http://www.eclipse.org/m2m/
5. Medini QVT, http://www.ikv.de
6. Jouault, F., Kurtev, I.: Transforming Models with ATL. In: Bruel, J.-M. (ed.) MoDELS 2005. LNCS, vol. 3844, pp. 128–138. Springer, Heidelberg (2006)
7. Miller, R., Ioannidis, Y., Ramakrishnan, R.: The Use of Information Capacity in Schema Integration and Translation. In: Agrawal, R., Baker, S. (eds.) VLDB 1993, pp. 120–133. Morgan Kaufmann, San Francisco (2003)

8. Miller, R., Ioannidis, Y., Ramakrishnan, R.: Schema equivalence in heterogeneous systems: bridging theory and practice. Inf. Syst. 19(1), 3–31 (1994)
9. ModelMorf: A model transformer, http://www.tcs-trddc.com/ModelMorf/
10. MOMENT Project, http://moment.dsic.upv.es/
11. OMG/XMI XML Model Interchange (XMI) OMG document ad/98-10-05 (1998)
12. OMG. OMG Unified Modeling Language Specification v. 1.4. OMG document (2001)
13. OMG. MOF 2.0 Query/Views/Transformations RFP. OMG document ad/2002-04-10 (2002)
14. OMG. Meta Object Facility (MOF) Specification. OMG document formal/02-04-03 (2002)
15. OMG. MDA Guide version 1.0.1. OMG document omg/2003-06-01 (2003)
16. OMG. Object Constraint Language (OCL), OMG document ptc/03-10-14 (2003)
17. OMG. MOF QVT Final Adopted Specification. OMG document ptc/05-11-01 (2005)
18. SmartQVT Project, http://smartqvt.elibel.tm.fr/

Adaptable Support for Queries and Transformations for the DRAGOS Graph-Database

Erhard Weinell

RWTH Aachen University of Technology, Department of Computer Science 3,
Ahornstrasse 55, D-52074 Aachen, Germany
Weinell@cs.rwth-aachen.de

Abstract. The DRAGOS database eases the development of graph-based applications by providing a uniform graph-oriented data storage facility. In this paper, we extend the existing database by a basic Query and Transformation Mechanism, which facilitates the construction of graph transformation systems. Users can therefore access the database by applying structured rules instead of using atomic operations provided before. As result, the development of graph transformation tools is eased by providing a mapping of specific graph languages to the Query and Transformation Language, instead of developing interpreters or code generators. In addition, structured rules offer more optimization potential in the underlying graph storage, which is beneficial for existing graph transformation systems. The presented approach is especially designed for extensibility, so its functionality can be adapted corresponding to the demands of the respective application domain.

1 Introduction

During the past decades, graph transformations have evolved to a mature and well-defined formalism to carry out operations on graph-like data structures. Based on different formal backgrounds, many tools and languages emerged in the community using graph transformations in various application areas. A graph transformation tool (GTT) usually comprises a graph storage facility and a code generator or an interpreter to execute the declarative rules.

Despite all previous standardization efforts, unfortunately, these tools rarely rely on a common basis. Instead, they typically use very different data representation, moreover, both the semantics of their graph transformation language and their execution strategy have differences. As result, developers of GTTs have to implement the required functionality anew for each tool. Furthermore, GTTs are hardly able to interact, e.g. by operating on a common host graph using different specification paradigms.

Graph-oriented database management systems (graph-databases for short) may provide a solution for uniform data representation as they allow to store complex data structures directly in the form of graphs. In contrast, relational

A. Schürr, M. Nagl, and A. Zündorf (Eds.): AGTIVE 2007, LNCS 5088, pp. 394–409, 2008.
© Springer-Verlag Berlin Heidelberg 2008

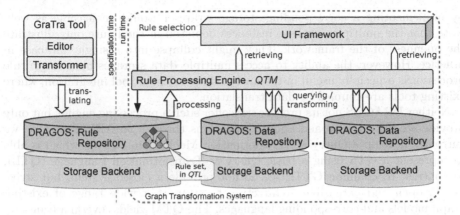

Fig. 1. Applying DRAGOS in graph transformation systems

or object-oriented databases usually require technical helper elements, e.g. additional tables to store many-to-many relations. DRAGOS[1] [1] is the latest representative of this class of databases developed at our department, which supports various back-end databases and model representation formalisms.

However, supporting the interaction between different GTTs is a more difficult challenge, due to semantic mismatches between the languages used by these tools. Exchange formats like GTXL [2] provide a common syntactical representation, but fall short in describing the meaning of a graph transformation rule.

This paper proposes an approach to provide a universal platform which eases the development of GTTs. A coarse-grained overview on the architecture is given in Figure 1. By providing a universal Rule Processing Engine, GTTs can rely on the offered functionality, instead of providing an own code generator or interpreter. The engine is fed by a Rule Repository, which stores the modeled graph transformation system (GTS) in a specialized, low-level graph language. The rule repository actually is a regular DRAGOS instance which stores the GTS in a graph-based form. Graph Transformation Tools *transform* a GTS modeled in their own respective language into the language provided by the processing engine. This transformation step actually maps the semantics of the GTT's language onto the language of the processing engine.

At runtime, the Rule Processing Engine accesses (possibly multiple) DRAGOS instances acting as Data Repository to query and transform the stored graphs. Although, conceptually, this engine acts like a rule interpreter, it might apply code generation techniques internally, depending on its implementation. A UI Framework, which provides a comprehensible representation to the user, selects processing rules from the rule repository, and updates its view structure from the data repositories. Each graph-database uses its own storage backend, which might vary between fast in-memory solutions and relational databases, including transaction support. Providing a graph-based interface to existing applications

---

[1] Database Repository for Applications using Graph-Oriented Storage, previously *Gras/GXL*.

by implementing a corresponding storage wrapper would be feasible as well. Note that the multiple database instances depicted in the figure only illustrate the openness of the framework. They might collapse into a single database in practice. However, the ability to access multiple data storages by a single rule processor is especially useful in the area of data-oriented tool integration, where existing tools are coupled by data translation.

Neither DRAGOS nor its predecessors offer such a processing engine, but only provide atomic retrieval and update operations through an API. Therefore, we currently develop a Query & Transformation Mechanism (QTM) which is able to represent a GTS using a basic Query & Transformation Language (QTL). In contrast to common GTTs, we do not provide a closed system, but strive for an open and extensible architecture to support a wide range of existing graph models and corresponding languages. The QTM yields several advantages from which both existing and newly developed graph transformation tools may benefit:

- Development effort for deriving executable GTS from a declarative specification is reduced, as the "semantic gap" between the specification and the corresponding execution framework is decreased: Instead of generating code based on atomic graph operations, the target domain becomes the DRAGOS QTL, which is considerably closer to a declarative modelling language. Furthermore, the required translation can be conducted based on the abstract syntax graphs of the application-specific graph language and the QTL, essentially making this a matter of model transformation.
- The effort is also reduced for adding additional language constructs to an application-specific graph language, as the QTL is prepared for extensibility itself. Furthermore, such constructs can be transferred to other graph languages by developing an extension of the DRAGOS QTL.
- In case of DRAGOS, evaluating complex queries is significantly more efficient compared to the processing of atomic operations, as conducted by generated code. We will outline this issue towards the end of this paper.
- The set of graph transformation rules can be extended and changed even at runtime of the GTS, thus supporting ad-hoc queries as well.

This paper presents the QTL currently being developed, and discusses its interaction with existing graph languages. In the following Section 2, relevant aspects of the DRAGOS system are introduced. Afterwards, Section 3 introduces the QTL by means of an example. Section 4 then presents the embedding of the QTM into the DRAGOS architecture. Relations to existing approaches are discussed in Section 5 followed by a conclusion in Section 6.

2   DRAGOS Architecture and Graph Model

Unlike its predecessors, DRAGOS does not provide an own graph storage facility. Instead, only a common interface, the so-called core graph model, is defined. Several implementations of this interface exist, which use existing database management systems as storage facility. Implementations are available for various databases accessible through JDBC and for the Java Data Objects framework. For testing purposes, an in-memory storage is provided. Database-specific implementations initialize connections to the database and perform queries and updates corresponding to the operations invoked on the core model.

Figure 2 shows a coarse-grained overview of the DRAGOS architecture. In the middle, the DRAGOS Kernel encapsulates the core graph model and a set of basic services. The responsibility of services include opening and closing of databases as well as transaction and event management.

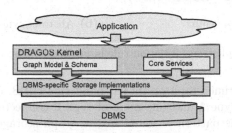

Fig. 2. DRAGOS architecture

Graph model. DRAGOS offers a rich graph model originally inspired by the Graph eXchange Language (GXL) [3]. The model supports hierarchical graphs including graph-crossing connections and n-ary edges (i.e. relations). Nodes, graphs, edges and relations are treated as first-class citizens, and thus can be identified and attributed. This enables flexible connections between entities, e.g. edges connecting edges and the attribution of all entities. All entities need to be typed by some graph entity class. Type hierarchies are supported, including multiple inheritance. As discussed in Section 3, the graph model's overall flexibility however complicates the development of a QTL, as all expressible constructs need to be covered appropriately.

3   Query and Transformation Language

As announced in Section 1, the intended use of the DRAGOS QTL is to provide tool support for existing and novel graph languages. Therefore, the QTL has to be able to cover different graph language approaches appropriately, and to enable an easy translation of the corresponding rules. Furthermore, the QTL should be suited to use the entire DRAGOS graph model, e.g. querying nested graph structures and hyperedges should be supported. This section first examines a transformation rule from an application-specific language, and introduces the QTL by means of this example.

3.1   Application-Specific Graph Language: An Example

Figure 3a shows a transformation rule modeled using the PROGRES graph transformation language. A transformation rule describes a graph structure to

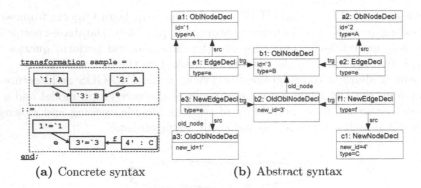

(a) Concrete syntax   (b) Abstract syntax

Fig. 3. Example transformation rule in application-specific language

be found in the runtime graph on its left-hand side (LHS, upper part). In this case, two nodes of type A and one node of type B connected by edges of type e are queried. If this pattern is found in the graph storage, it is transformed corresponding to the rule's right-hand side (RHS, lower part). Here, nodes assigned to '1 and '3 are preserved, as corresponding variables (1' resp. 3') are present on the RHS. The node assigned to '2 is deleted in the course of the transformation, whereas a new node of type C is created and assigned to 4'. As edges are neither identified nor attributed in the PROGRES graph model, they do not need to be preserved explicitly: Removing all edges of the LHS and inserting edges corresponding to the RHS has the same effect as preserving edges if possible.

Figure 3b shows the same transformation rule represented in the abstract syntax model of PROGRES. Objects of type `OblNodeDecl` and `EdgeDecl` represent entities to be retrieved from the database, with the required type stored in the `type` attribute. The class `OldOblNodeDecl` represents objects on the RHS which retain a node during the transformation. Consequently, they have a `OblNodeDecl` assigned via an `old_node` edge. Nodes assigned to an `OblNodeDecl` without such an edge are deleted during the transformation process. `NewEdgeDecl` represents an edge on the RHS. As explained above, there is no explicit correspondence to edges of the LHS. To process this query by the QTM, it needs to be translated into the QTL.

3.2   Language Structure

The Query & Transformation Language should be able to concisely represent rules modeled in an arbitrary application-specific language, and therefore requires a universal basis. We identified the principle of *constraint satisfaction* as such a basis, as it allows a clear distinction between the queried entities, and their desired properties. This idea has been introduced previously, e.g. for efficiently implementing pattern matching algorithms [4] or search-plan generation [5]. As result, distinct properties such as containment within a graph or restriction to a specific type can be modeled by attaching constraints to a variable.

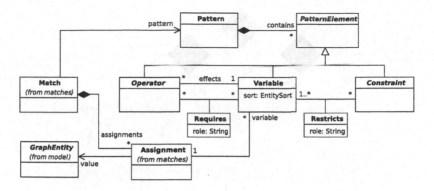

Fig. 4. Core language meta-model (excerpt)

These properties can be neglected by not adding these constraints, e.g. to query connections of an *arbitrary* type between graph entities.

Figure 4 shows an excerpt of the meta-model of the generic core language. A Pattern contains a set of PatternElements, i.e. Variables, Constraints and Operators. Variables are placeholders for entities found during pattern matching. Constraints restrict legal assignment of entities to Variables. Among others, Constraints restrict entities to a specific type, check connectivity between entities, or containment within a graph. The role attribute of the Restricts association distinguishes between Variables a Constraint restricts. For example, the ContainmentConstraint needs to distinguish between Variables holding the parent graph and the child entity, as both may refer to graphs.

An assignment of graph entities to Variables of a Pattern not violating any of its Constraints is called a Match. Each Match aggregates a set of Assignments, which relate a Variable to exactly one GraphEntity. We require that each Variable with an attached Constraint has to be present in a Match, so partial matches are not allowed. Unconstrained Variables are not bound during pattern matching.

Operators define how entities bound to a Match should be transformed. Each Operator effects exactly one entity assigned to a Variable. To do so, the Operator may Requires values of other variables as parameter. Required variables are distinguished by a role name. Creation and deletion of an entity extend and reduce the match by the effected variable, respectively. Operators can be executed only if all required Variables are bound. This indirectly imposes an order on the operator's execution, as required variables need to be bound in advance.

In general, the execution order of operators might influence the result of the transformation. To avoid ambiguities, we require that variables are either bound to an entity, or a new entity is created by a transformation rule. Furthermore, only entities bound to a variable may be deleted. In addition to these restrictions, all operators must act in a single-step manner, i.e. only results of the pattern matching phase may be taken into account when modifying graph entities. For example, computing an attribute value may only be based on the attribute values *before* the first operator invocation. Therefore, the computed result does not depend on other attribute updates within the same transformation.

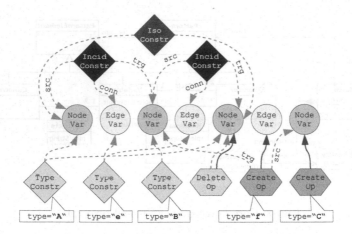

Fig. 5. Example transformation rule in the DRAGOS core language

Figure 5 shows the transformation rule from Figure 3 after translation to the DRAGOS core language. *Circles* represent Variables for each node or edge queried or created by the transformation rule. *Rhombs* depict constraints which a value of a variable has to fulfill. Dashed lines relate constraints to variables, e.g. the IncidenceConstraint puts three variables into relation as source, target and connector. The IsomorphismConstraint ensures that different entities are bound to the attached variables. TypeConstraints restrict the variables' values to entities of the type denoted by the type attribute. *Hexagons* represent operators which denote modifications of the matched graph entities. Here, the entity assigned to the third NodeVariable is deleted and removed from the match. The deletion of an entity also causes the deletion of incident edges and relation ends to prevent dangling connections. Therefore, explicit deletion of the retrieved edge is not required. In contrast, newly created entities are assigned to the two variables on the right, with their type passed via the type attribute of the operator. The variable effected by an operator is attached using a solid line, whereas required variables are connected by a dashed line. To create an edge, its source and target entities are required. The right-most variable is not connected to any constraint, so it is not bound during pattern matching. Hence, creation of the edge is postponed until its designated source node has been created, as the corresponding variable is bound to the new entity afterwards.

This basic representation of the example rule does no longer contain any specifics of the PROGRES language. For example, the implicit condition that distinct entities have to be assigned to the node variables of Figure 3 is explicitly expressed by an IsomorphismConstraint. LHS and RHS are condensed into a single pattern, using operator nodes to express actions. Note, that this pattern could be changed easily to query connections between edges instead of nodes, by changing the variables' sorts. Such queries are not possible in common graph transformation languages.

4   Query and Transformation Mechanism

In this section, we clarify how GTS access the Query & Transformation Mechanism and how the QTM is embedded into the DRAGOS architecture.

4.1   Application Integration

Figure 6 shows how GTS modeled in an application-specific language interact with the DRAGOS QTM. As mentioned in Section 1, the corresponding rules are converted to the DRAGOS core language. This can be achieved by importing the corresponding rules's ASGs into the graph-database, e.g. by parsing a textual representation. Furthermore, we currently implement an import mechanism to access EMF-based model repositories. The translation results in a graph structure representing a set of QTL rules, which are processed by the QTM's language implementation.

In order to map the application-specific graph language to the QTL, a set of *model transformation rules* translate the increments of the GTS' rules to patterns of the QTL. By this translation, the respective language's semantics are mapped to the core language. For example, the two graph transformation languages PROGRES and GROOVE treat rules differently regarding isomorphism: In PROGRES, each node may be bound to only one variable during pattern matching, but allows exceptions using *folding groups*. The default treatment is the other way around in GROOVE, where exceptions are specified using *merge embargo* edges. To cover the former case, an isomorphism constraint is connected to all variables whose values should be pairwise disjoint. For the latter,

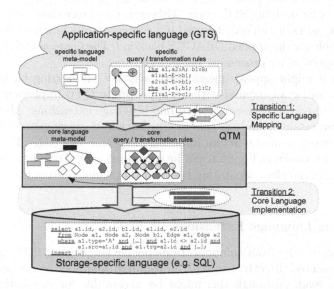

Fig. 6. Application integration with the DRAGOS QTM

isomorphism constraints are simply added between those variable connected by a merge embargo edge.

As the model transformation process operates on the graph-database exclusively, its corresponding rules can again be specified using the QTL. Therefore, a convenient representation of these rules is desirable, which can be achieved by an own application-specific language. Its purpose is to allow a convenient development of application-specific language mappings. Such an integration language is currently being developed, which naturally profits from existing work in the field of model transformations.

4.2   Embedding into the DRAGOS Architecture

The fact that DRAGOS can utilize relational databases as storage backend suggests that the QTM should use their sophisticated query functionality to enable efficient execution. Regarding SQL databases, rules modeled in the QTL can be translated into corresponding SQL queries and update operations, as indicated in the lower part of Figure 6. This transition is currently implemented based on templates. Basically, they create increments in the FROM part of the SQL query for each variable, and increments in the WHERE part for each constraint.

As not all available backend implementations provide database-like functionality, a backend-independent solution is required, too. As the DRAGOS graph model is the common interface of all available implementations, we provide a rule interpreter based on this model. This interpreter is called the Generic Implementation in Figure 7, where the architecture of the QTM is depicted. Gray arrows indicate the approach of processing QTL rules using the Generic Implementation, White arrows show the processing by a backend-specific language implementations, such as by deriving SQL code. Although the latter choice allows a more efficient processing, it can only be used if a corresponding language implementation is available for the applied DRAGOS backend. The Controller Service therefore selects the appropriate processing path at runtime.

Although it might appear questionable why not all existing backend implementations can be augmented with an appropriate QTL implementation, this approach is especially necessary for adding language extensions. Also note that the chosen processing step, e.g. rule interpretation or query generation, is completely independent of the actual application-specific language. Therefore, the two transitions shown in Figure 6 can be combined arbitrarily. In this sense, the QTL acts as an interface separating backend functionality from the application-side GTS.

4.3   Adding Language Extensions

The mapping of rules from an application-specific language to QTL usually cannot be represented directly, causing the required mapping to become complex and hard to read. Although this might be acceptable for supporting a single graph language, the developed mapping cannot be re-used for other application-specific languages. Therefore, we offer to *extend* the core language by additional

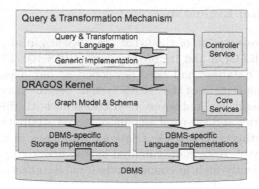

Fig. 7. Extended DRAGOS architecture

language constructs by defining new constraint classes or operator classes. However, the core graph model cannot be extended by additional variable classes, as this would require adaptations to existing constraints and operators. In contrast, constraints and operators only refer to their attached variables, so new types of these elements can be added without effecting existing ones.

Basically, we offer two options to implement added constraint and operator classes: *First*, an extension of the existing backend-specific implementation of the QTL can be provided, e.g. by generating fragments of SQL code. This choice generally yields the more efficient implementation, as backend functionality can be utilized directly. Regarding the architecture in Figure 7, another column is added which allows to bypass the basic QTL and the DRAGOS graph model. However, this approach would require to implement each language extension for all existing storage backends. Even worse, supporting additional storage backends would, the other way around, require to provide variants for all QTL extensions. Obviously, this tight interrelation is not desirable.

As solution for this dilemma, we provide a *second* option for implementing language extensions, which is split into two variants: A QTL extension should *additionally* be implemented by extending the existing Generic Implementation, thus combining the two approaches of Figure 7: If the utilized storage backend does not provide a corresponding extension implementation, the extension's Generic Implementation can always be used. Nevertheless, the backend-specific QTL implementation can be used to process the remaining parts of the query.

In addition, extended language constructs can be *reduced* to basic QTL constructs by providing a corresponding transformation rule. Using this approach, constructs can be implemented in a transformation-based way, in contrast to the programmed approach discussed above. The strictly graph-based representation of query and transformation rules provide a sound basis for such a high-level extension mechanism. As we cannot introduce this aspect of the QTL in detail here, the reader is referred to [6], where the model-based extension mechanism is elaborated in detail.

4.4   Experimental Evaluation

To conclude the presentation of the QTM, we present initial performance comparison against DRAGOS and its predecessor, GRAS [7]. The original GRAS (GRAph Storage) database had been developed at our department since the late eighties. A replacement of the GRAS system became necessary because its tight platform dependency and severe restrictions on both the number of manageable graph entities and the total amount of stored attribute values. As DRAGOS relies on existing solutions like relational databases as graph storage, the amount of manageable data is only limited by the underlying storage backend. This limit is sufficiently high in common relational databases, e.g. PostgreSQL restricts tables to 32 terabytes.

The obvious disadvantage of the DRAGOS approach is the immanent performance penalty, as each atomic graph operation is implemented by at least one SQL statement. Comparisons of real-world examples indicate a factor of around 1 : 12 relating GRAS to DRAGOS operating only on the in-memory storage, which does not provide transactions support. Using PostgreSQL as transactional storage backend, the factor increases up to 1 : 120. The reason for this massive overhead is that the DRAGOS architecture does not allow the adequate use of complex query mechanisms, such as SQL. In fact, only a limited amount of simple statements are used to query the storage facility.

The QTM introduced in this paper, however relieves this architectural disadvantage, as complex graph patterns can be transformed into backend-specific queries. Initial experiments underline this thesis, as shown in Figure 8: We measured the required time to test for circles of a given size (3 resp. 10) in an n-complete graph, comparing the SQL code generated from the QTM, DRAGOS operating on PostgreSQL, and GRAS. All tests were run on a 3 GHz Intel CPU and 2 GB of main memory, showing the median of several test runs.

We can conclude that GRAS outperforms DRAGOS and the QTM for small queries, although results become less clear for larger ones. Interestingly, although DRAGOS and GRAS are controlled by comparably generated (and optimized) code, time consumption behaves differently for these systems: For small queries, the required time remains almost constant with larger graphs for GRAS, whereas

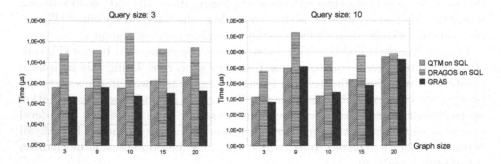

Fig. 8. Timings for querying n-complete graphs (microseconds, logarithmic scale)

it noticeably increases for DRAGOS. The QTM approach performs quite good, given its early stage of development. For larger queries, the PostgreSQL query optimizer does not seem to derive optimal search plans, which needs to be addressed to improve the QTM performance. It should be noted that the specific results of GRAS varied significantly for the large query, so the overall result is less reliable.

Unfortunately, the generation of SQL-code from the QTL is not fully implemented up to now, so that standardized comparisons, e.g. presented in [8], could not be performed. Once the implementation reaches a proper level, we will also evaluate the performance impact on real-world scenarios, such as model transformations.

5   Related Work

This section covers comparisons to existing work, considering model repositories, graph transformations, and related optimization techniques.

Model repositories. Besides being designed as graph-oriented database, DRAGOS can be considered a model repository or data binding tool as well. Both aspects are covered by a wealth of existing standards and tools. An example for such a tool is the Universal Data Model (UDM) [9]. In contrast to DRAGOS, which uses a complex core graph model for data representation, UDM relies on a limited set of base classes. However, UDM is able to generate APIs from provided metadata, such as UML class diagrams, to allow convenient and type-safe use by developers. Such functionality is currently not provided for DRAGOS, although code-generating graph transformation tools can be applied for this purpose. Similar to DRAGOS, the UDM environment provides persistent storage using databases through the Generic Modeling Environment (GME) [10]. UDM does not incorporate a model processing engine, but can be used by the GReAT transformation engine [11].

Graph transformations on relational databases. Implementing GTS on established relational databases has been presented initially by the authors of [12]. Basically, the authors transform a graph schema to a set of database relations, and implement pattern matching by deriving views on these tables. One difference to our approach is the applied meta-level (M1), as the DRAGOS graph model constitutes a common meta model for all applications (thus M2). Furthermore, we apply the basic idea of generating SQL code in a language-independent environment, with the QTL forming a common basis. The separation between variables, constraints, and operators applied in the QTL is indeed closer to the SQL than traditional graph languages considered by [12], which simplifies the translation process for us.

The authors also mention a specialized query optimizer developed for the applied relational databases, which, unfortunately, is not discussed any further. We agree that an optimizer specialized on graph queries is indeed necessary.

Inspection of the internal search plans of the database backend showed that the standard optimizer already prefers table joins with small result sets, e.g. traversing edges instead of global searches over the graph. However, the order of edge traversal is not optimized effectively, which causes inefficient behavior for the larger query discussed above. To relieve this drawback, a specialized query optimizer should adapt results from search-plan driven code generation found in common graph transformation tools.

Optimization techniques. Traditionally, code generated for graph transformation rules is optimized using search plan techniques to find an efficient order of variable assignments. Among others, PROGRES and Fujaba apply this technique in a *static* environment, i.e. code is generated once before the system is run. This only allows to optimize according to the graph schema, as the actual host graph structure is unknown during code generation. Recently, the authors of [13] proposed an approach to generate differently generated variants of code. Depending on the host graph, an appropriate variant is chosen at runtime.

Our approach is not tied to a code generation step, as transformation rules are stored in the database and executed in a backend-specific way. Storage solutions may decide whether to interpret these rules (e.g. the generic implementation follows this approach) or to generate implementation-specific code (e.g. SQL statements). Nevertheless, our approach still requires search-plan based optimization techniques, as common SQL query optimizers do not recognize incident structures.

Graph transformations based on constraint satisfaction. The DRAGOS Query & Transformation Language is based on the theory of *constraint satisfaction problems* (CSP) known from the area of artificial intelligence. CSPs are well-suited to model graph pattern matching by solving the *subgraph-isomorphism problem* [14]. In our work, we aim to implement the Query & Transformation Language based on existing systems, and therefore extensive development of a basic constraint solver is not of crucial importance. This would only improve the generic implementation based on the core graph model, which should be considered as fallback solution only. Instead, we focus on implementations based on sophisticated storage backends like databases.

CSP-like representations of graph transformation rules have also been applied in [5], where search-plan optimization is discussed for such a rule model. As this approach is not concerned with the evaluation of expressions, dynamic aspects such as matches need not to be considered. In contrast, our approach also incorporates matches to model the result of a query. Furthermore, the cited work includes negative application conditions directly into the language, which are treated differently in the QTL [6].

Model transformations. As mentioned in Section 4.1, model transformations are used to map an application-specific language to the DRAGOS Query & Transformation Language. A wide range of languages and tools for model transformations have already been presented in the literature, several of which are compared in

[15]. Available approaches differ with regard to expressiveness, concrete representation (textual vs. visual), usage (batch vs. user-interactive), traceability, and directness (uni- vs. bidirectional).

Currently, we investigate in how far existing solutions can be applied in the DRAGOS system. For our purposes, a very simple batch-oriented uni-directional system suffices. However, we did not collect experiences on the required language constructs yet. In the future, commonly required constructs will form a language specifically tailored for modeling language mappings.

Graph transformations for visual programming. Graph transformation languages like PROGRES and Fujaba provide functionality similar to the presented QTL. In fact, both systems can already generate code to store the runtime data persistently using DRAGOS. As discussed in Section 1, this approach leads to inefficient applications because it is only based on atomic operations. In our approach, DRAGOS executes transformation rules itself, either by interpreting or backend-specific code generation.

Projects at our department recently encountered the need for more advanced language constructs in the PROGRES language. However, extending PROGRES not only requires a visual representation, but also an enhanced code generation. Shortcomings in the architecture of the PROGRES environment caused the authors of [16] to embed new language constructs in a pre-processing phase generating the actual PROGRES specification. Again, executing transformation rules inside DRAGOS and embedding language extension therein would lead to a more concise application development.

In contrast to common graph transformation languages, the DRAGOS core language is not feasible for direct use by a specificator. Due to the very low level of abstraction, even simple queries tend to become quite large and hard to read. Therefore, the presented language should not be considered as competitor to existing languages, but as a common core for existing and new ones to build on.

Unified graph languages. Besides the *GRAph and Rule CEntered specification language* (GRACE) [17] and the *Graph Transformation eXchange Language* (GTXL) [2], little work can be found on providing a common platform for graph transformations. Probably this is caused by the need to establish a standardized unified language, and persuade tool developers to achieve compliance. We therefore do not try to establish such a standard, but offer a flexible and extensible base layer. Graph languages are integrated by transforming the rules' ASGs, which allows to use concepts independent from the QTL.

6   Conclusion

In this paper, we motivated the need for a QTM in the graph-oriented database DRAGOS. Benefits gained from this mechanism comprise easier use by application developers, a high-level integration of application-specific languages, and a more efficient execution.

The newly developed language is especially designed for extensibility regarding two aspects: First, the core language can be extended by adding new language constructs in the form of constraints or operators. Second, the implementation of the core language may use storage-specific functionality for selected language constructs, and refer to a generic implementation otherwise. Therefore, the language's implementation is extensible, too.

Current and Future Work

The core language's expressiveness is currently restricted to graph patterns with a fixed size, hindering its use e.g. for matching path expressions with the Kleene star operator. We therefore offer to dynamically expand a pattern using a template-based mechanism, allowing for *recursive queries.*

In order to model large-scale graph transformation systems, the interaction between different transformation rules needs to be captured. For this purpose, the introduction of *control structures* is necessary, e.g. for iterations or conditional branching. Currently, a minimal amount of control structures is being integrated into the core language to support arbitrary graph transformation systems. This is inspired by the results of [18], where the authors show that a very small set of structures suffices. Extended control structures can be supported by a language extension or by a proper mapping of application-specific languages to the core QTL.

In the future, we will investigate how existing approaches to graph transformations can be mapped to the DRAGOS language, such as the algebraic approach or hyper-edge replacement grammars. This way, DRAGOS can serve as a platform to develop new constructs for graph transformation languages by offering a high-level extension mechanism.

Acknowledgements. I thank Dániel Varró for his many helpful remarks and suggestions during the preparation of the final version of this paper. Thanks also go to the anonymous reviewers for constructive criticism and your ideas for improvement.

References

1. Böhlen, B.: Specific graph models and their mappings to a common model. In: Pfaltz, J.L., Nagl, M., Böhlen, B. (eds.) AGTIVE 2003. LNCS, vol. 3062, pp. 45–60. Springer, Heidelberg (2004)
2. Lambers, L.: A new version of GTXL. In: Graph-Based Tools (GraBaTs 2004). Elec. Notes in Theoretical Comp. Sci., vol. 127. Elsevier Science, Amsterdam (2004)
3. Holt, R., Winter, A., Schürr, A.: GXL: Towards a standard exchange format. In: Proc. of the 7th Working Conference on Reverse Engineering (WCRE), pp. 162–171. IEEE Computer Society Press, Los Alamitos (2000)
4. Rudolf, M.: Utilizing constraint satisfaction techniques for efficient graph pattern matching. In: [19], pp. 238–251

5. Horváth, Á., Varró, G., Varró, D.: Generic search plans for matching advanced graph patterns. In: Ehrig, K., Giese, H. (eds.) Graph Transformation and Visual Modeling Techniques. ECEASST, vol. 6, pp. 57–68 (2007)
6. Weinell, E.: Extending graph query languages by reduction. In: Proc. of the 7th Intl. Workshop on Graph Transformation and Visual Modeling Techniques (GT-VMT) (to appear, 2008)
7. Lewerentz, C., Schürr, A.: GRAS, a management system for graph-like documents. In: Proc. of the 3rd International Conference on Data and Knowledge Bases, pp. 19–31. Morgan Kaufmann, San Francisco (1988)
8. Varró, G., Schürr, A., Varró, D.: Benchmarking for graph transformation. In: Proc. of the 2005 IEEE Symposium on Visual Languages and Human-Centric Computing (VL/HCC), pp. 79–88. IEEE Computer Society Press, Los Alamitos (2005)
9. Magyari, E., et al.: UDM: An infrastructure for implementing Domain-Specific Modeling Languages. In: 3rd OOPSLA Workshop on Domain-Specific Modeling (2003)
10. Davis, J.: GME: the generic modeling environment. In: Companion of the 18th annual ACM SIGPLAN conference on Object-oriented programming, systems, languages, and applications (OOPSLA), pp. 82–83. ACM, New York (2003)
11. Agrawal, A., et al.: The design of a language for model transformations. Software and Systems Modeling 5(3), 261–288 (2006)
12. Varró, G., Friedl, K., Varró, D.: Implementing a graph transformation engine in relational databases. Journal on Software and Systems Modeling 5(3), 313–341 (2006)
13. Varró, G., Friedl, K., Varró, D.: Adaptive graph pattern matching for model transformations using model-sensitive search plans. ENTCS 152, 191–205 (2006)
14. Larrosa, J., Valiente, G.: Constraint satisfaction algorithms for graph pattern matching. Mathematical Structures in Computer Science 12(4), 403–422 (2002)
15. Taentzer, G., et al.: Model Transformation by Graph Transformation: A Comparative Study. In: Proc. of the Intl. Workshop on Model Transformations in Practice (MTiP 2005) (2005)
16. Fuss, C., Tuttlies, V.: Simulating set-valued transformations with algorithmic graph transformation languages. In: Schürr, A., Nagl, M., Zündorf, A. (eds.) AGTIVE 2007. LNCS, vol. 5088. Springer, Heidelberg (2008)
17. Kreowski, H.J., Busatto, G., Kuske, S.: GRACE as a unifying approach to graph-transformation-based specification. In: Ehrig, H., Ermel, C., Padberg, J. (eds.) UNIGRA 2001: Uniform Approaches to Graphical Process Specification Techniques. ENTCS, vol. 44. Elsevier Science, Amsterdam (2001)
18. Habel, A., Plump, D.: A core language for graph transformation. In: Proc. of the APPLIGRAPH Workshop on Applied Graph Transformation, pp. 187–199 (2002)
19. Ehrig, H., et al. (eds.): Theory and Application of Graph Transformations, 6th Intl. Workshop (TAGT). LNCS, vol. 1764. Springer, Heidelberg (2000)

Applying a Grouping Operator in Model Transformations

Daniel Balasubramanian, Anantha Narayanan, Sandeep Neema, Benjamin Ness,
Feng Shi, Ryan Thibodeaux, and Gabor Karsai

Institute for Software Integrated Systems, 2015 Terrace Place, Nashville, TN 37235
{Daniel,Ananth,Sandeep,BNess,FengShi,RThibodeaux,
Gabor}@isis.vanderbilt.edu

Abstract. The usability of model transformation languages depends on the level of abstractions one can work with in rules to perform complex operations on models. Recently, we have introduced a novel operator for our model transformation language GReAT that allows the concise specification of complex model (graph) rewriting operations that manipulate entire subgraphs. In this paper we show how the new operator can be used to implement non-trivial model manipulations with fewer and simpler rules, while maintaining efficiency. The examples were motivated by problems encountered in real-life model transformations.

Keywords: Model Transformation, Graph Transformation.

1 Introduction

Model-based development necessitates the use of model transformations. The cost of setting up a model-based development tool chain depends on how economical it is to implement possibly complex yet necessary model transformations on an ad hoc basis, and whose correctness is often essential for the usability of the toolchain. Thus, higher-level techniques for specifying model transformations have been proposed, and one promising conceptual framework for specifying model transformations is based on graph transformations [1].

The practical application of graph transformation-based model transformation approaches [10] has shown that while the high-level nature of the graph rewriting rules is very powerful, sometimes writing common operations is very tedious. Commonly, graph rewriting operations match a subgraph of a host graph and then create (or remove) nodes and edges in the model graph and possibly modify attributes. Due to the difficulty of performing equivalent operations using Java methods over some primitive graph API, using the graph-based specification has clear advantages.

A matched subgraph typically has a simple structure (pattern nodes and pattern edges are bound to host graph nodes and host graph edges), and it is hard to form closures over such subgraphs. The closure would group together multiple matches of pattern nodes and edges into a graph that is treated as a unit in the context of some subsequent operation, typically un-gluing or gluing this graph with other nodes, copying the graph, or removing the group altogether.

A. Schürr, M. Nagl, and A. Zündorf (Eds.): AGTIVE 2007, LNCS 5088, pp. 410–425, 2008.

In our graph transformation-based model transformation tool, GReAT [1], we have introduced support for such closures over pattern matches. We call it the 'grouping operator', and we extended the semantics of our graph transformation rules with this new operator. This work has been reported in [3]. In this paper we briefly review the semantics of the operator and then give a number of examples —derived from real-life applications— that illustrate the use of the operator. The paper concludes with a review of related approaches and a summary.

2 Recap of Group Operator

In this section we briefly review the fundamentals of GReAT, highlighting the features of the grouping operator, first introduced in [3].

The Graph Rewriting and Transformation Language (GReAT) is a graphical language used for the specification and execution of model transformations defined using elements from the meta-models of the source and target languages. The entire language consists of three sub-languages: a pattern specification language, a transformation rule language, and a control-flow language. The pattern specification language is used to define the patterns matched in the host graph. The transformation rule language allows the creation and deletion of objects in the host graph, along with the modification of object attributes. Finally, the control-flow language allows a transformation to be explicitly sequenced.

The basic rewriting unit of a transformation is a *Rule* that contains two pieces: 1) a pattern to match with the host graph (defined using the pattern specification language), and 2) an action to perform after the matches are found (defined using the transformation rule language). When a *Rule* executes, it first finds all valid matches of the specified pattern in the host graph. After all matches are found, the rule actions are executed. These rule actions can include deleting and creating new elements in the host graph, as well as modifying attributes. Finally, user selected elements are passed to the next rule in the sequence (specified using the control-flow language).

2.1 Motivation for the Group Operator

As described above, the result of the first stage of a rule execution is a set of matches, where each match is a unique binding for the pattern variables in the rule. The limitation with this is that all the matches (of a single pattern) are isomorphic. In other words, all the matches have the same, predetermined number of nodes and edges. It would be useful to form closures over such unique matches, such that more complex sub-graphs can be matched and manipulated using the same rule.

For instance, consider a chain of nodes of arbitrary length, as shown in the graph in Fig. 1. Suppose that we wish to select such chains of arbitrary length and move them to a different container. The pattern shown in Fig. 2 matches two connected nodes at a time. This will result in the matches (a—b), (b—c) and (c—d). While it is possible to use these matches to move the chain to a new container, the description would be cumbersome (especially since moving it in parts would create dangling edges). The group operator allows us to group all these matches together, so that the selected sub-graph is the entire chain, as opposed to pairs of nodes. Using the group operator, the entire chain can be selected and copied in a single rule.

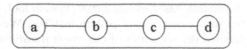

Fig. 1. A chain of arbitrary length

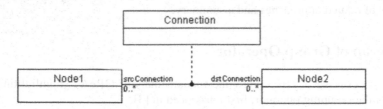

Fig. 2. Graph rule for matching a connection

Consider a container that contains a number of nodes, with a "name" attribute associated with each node. Multiple nodes are allowed to have the same "name", and the container can have any number of nodes, with any number of different "name" attributes. Fig. 3 (a) shows such a container. Suppose that we wish to sort the nodes with the same "name" into a single container, as shown in Fig. 3 (b). This involves creating an arbitrary number of containers (depending upon how many different "name" values are present), and moving an arbitrary number of nodes into each container. The group operator allows us to accomplish this in a single rule, when we use the "name" attribute as the grouping criterion. For the example shown in Fig. 3, the rule produces four matches of different sizes (one match containing four nodes, one with three, and two matches containing two nodes).

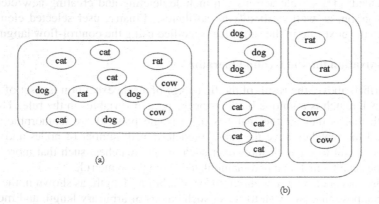

Fig. 3. Sorting items into containers

As shown above, it is useful to specify queries that can produce matches of different, arbitrary sizes in a single rule. The group operator is a new construct introduced into the GReAT language to allow the results of multiple matches to be combined so that larger graph patterns could be specified in a compact manner. In comparison, queries in PROGRES[12] allow the use of complex logic statements to construct a result set, which can contain elements of different and arbitrary sizes. Our approach provides a graphical abstraction that is easier to visualize and use. Similar to GReAT, AGG[14] allows the specification of additional conditions on the attributes of pattern objects in a rule, but the matches are still isomorphic.

In general, a transformation can benefit from the group operator if the user must have the ability to specify a pattern that will match a variable number of objects. This often includes chains of objects with connections between them, such as the first example above, or large groups of objects that need to be separated into smaller groups based on common attributes, as in the second example given above. Also, a group operator should be used if sub-graphs (composed of multiple matches) need to be moved or copied into different containers, as these patterns can be difficult to specify in GReAT without this construct.

Specifying a rule with a group operator is relatively simple. The user adds one group operator to the rule, and then specifies two additional items:

1) Which elements of the overall pattern will be used to form the subgroups that are the subgraphs formed from the individual matches. For instance, in **Fig. 2**, *Connection*, *Node1* and *Node2* must be selected. The purpose of the rule should make the selection of which pattern objects are needed obvious.

2) The Boolean expression that will determine when two matches should be placed into the same subgroup (we use the prefixes "the_" and "other_" to identify the matches). In Fig. 2, this would simply be true, since all the connections form a single group. In Fig. 3, we would use "the_Node.name() == other_Node().name". This step is the crucial part of using the group operator. Matches from individual rules are often inserted into subgroups based on an attribute value of one of the objects, as in the second example above. In cases such as these, the Boolean expression is quite simple, and can even be written by novices who have limited experience with GReAT. Examples of both simple and complex Boolean expressions for subgroup formation are given in the following sections. Detailed information about subgroup formation can be found in [3].

After all matches are found, each match is placed into precisely one subgroup by evaluating the Boolean expression using this match and the matches already placed in subgroups. If the expression evaluates to true, then the current match is placed into the subgroup against which the Boolean expression was evaluated. If the expression yields a "false" for all of the matches in existing subgroups, then the current match is placed in a newly created subgroup. Finally, the rule's action is performed on a per-subgroup basis instead of a per-match basis. In this manner, one can effectively combine several matches into one "larger" match and then perform actions on that larger match. Additionally, the user can also choose to move or copy the elements of the subgroups to another parent container.

The next several sections give examples of the use of the group operator. The examples presented here were derived from actual experience with real-life modeling and model transformations. However, for the sake of brevity they have been simplified to a presentable form. Note also that model transformations are often applied to legacy modeling paradigms that are imperfect, yet cannot be discarded because of the investment in the models.

3 Separating a System into Its Subsystems

A system may be comprised of various subsystems which share common components. For instance, in a building, the electrical, plumbing, and networking subsystems all use rooms as a common component for distribution hubs and endpoints. Because of this, a model for such a system will necessarily have all subsystems represented, overlapping one another on top of their common components. However, at some point it may be necessary to separate the individual subsystems for the purposes of verification, construction, or clarity. GReAT, with its group operator, can be used to specify such a transformation compactly. To demonstrate this, both a "building" meta-model and a building model based on this meta-model, are presented, along with a GReAT transformation rule that makes use of the group operator to separate the model-building's electrical subsystem from its other subsystems.

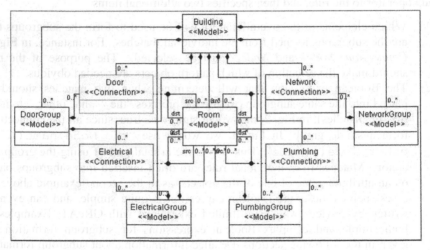

Fig. 4. Building Meta-Model

Fig. 4 shows a meta-model for buildings with electrical, plumbing, networking, and room-connectivity (i.e., door) subsystems. *Room* is the component they share as their infrastructural basis. For instance, *Electrical* connections are between rooms, i.e. between the rooms' sockets and switches, as are *Network* connections, for example, between a server room and other rooms' network ports. Note also that the meta-model has components (*DoorGroup*, *NetworkGroup*, *ElectricalGroup*, and *PlumbingGroup*) that can contain copies each of these subsystems in isolation.

The left side of Fig. 5 shows a simple model based on the building meta-model of Fig. 4. Electrical connections are drawn with dashed lines, while the solid connections represent other types of connections. As can be seen, multiple subsystem types are represented and are overlapping on top of their common *Room* components. For the purposes of building construction, it would be of great utility to be able to separate out these subsystems. For instance, the electrical subsystem (*ElectricalGroup*) in isolation could be given to an electrician for wiring purposes. Similarly, the room-connectivity (*DoorGroup*) subsystem could be presented to an inspector or put through a model checker to make sure the building conforms to certain safety codes.

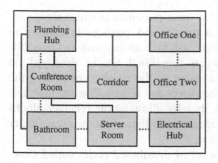
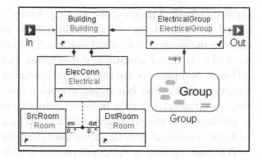

Fig. 5. Building Model (left) and Grouping Rule to Isolate the Electrical Subsystem (right)

The right side of Fig. 5 shows a rule in a GReAT transformation that uses the group operator to separate out the electrical subsystems of the model to its left. The rule creates a new *ElectricalGroup* model that will hold a copy of this subsystem. The group operator contains any *Electrical* connections matched by the rule, along with the rooms connected by these connections. The Boolean expression the group operator uses to group matches together is trivial: it is simply the value "true", indicating that any and all *Electrical* connections and their associated rooms should be included -- this results in a single group that is the entire electrical subsystem. For a more complex setup, the grouping rule could group electrical connections based on the breaker from which they originate, or based on the voltage they carry. Rules for isolating other building subsystems are similar.

Fig. 6 shows the results of applying the GReAT transformation rule in Fig. 5 to the model on its left. The electrical subsystem is successfully separated from the other subsystems. Such a diagram could be useful for an electrician or inspector.

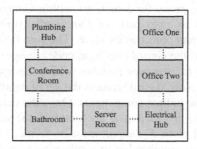

Fig. 6. Building Model's Electrical Subsystem

4   Creating Proxies for Distributed Communication

Models of control systems often consist of dataflow blocks representing mathematical functions that manipulate data obtained from the environment or other input sources to achieve some desired output effect on the controlled system. Control designers initially formulate their controllers with no concern regarding the eventual deployment architecture; however, the implementation is commonly distributed over separate physical nodes (called 'components') that must pass data between their contained functions over a bus infrastructure in a timely and predictable manner to achieve the desired controlled outputs. To facilitate software abstraction and reusability [13][7], direct dataflow connections between functional blocks deployed on different components are often managed using a proxy on the component hosting the receiver blocks. The bus implementation and the proxy are responsible for marshalling and transferring data between components, thereby allowing the receiver blocks to interact with the proxy through an interface identical to that of the original sender without concern of how to access data from the bus.

Assume we have a system deployed across a set of distributed nodes called *Components*. Each component contains a dataflow graph consisting of *Functions* that pass data to and from each other through *Ports*. A connection between two ports is called a *Dataflow*, and it connects only one sending port to one receiving port. Still, one port can send data to multiple receiving ports through multiple dataflows from the port to each receiver. Dataflows can also connect ports of two functions deployed on separate components.

To implement a modeled distributed system described previously, a *Proxy* for a function should be created in all components that receive input from that function. The sending function should be connected to receiver functions through its proxy instead of direct dataflows to the receivers' ports. The *Group* operator provides a means to perform this operation within GReAT by creating a single proxy of a function on other components that use the function's output within their respective dataflow graphs. The proxy inserted into a component will have an input port and an output port for each output port in the sending function connected to inputs of receiving functions on one component. This implements a mirroring of the interface of the sender's ports that concern the functions on the target component.

Fig. 7 shows the Group rule in GReAT for starting this transformation. It is responsible for creating a single proxy for *Function1* within *Component2* if output ports of *Function1* are connected to input ports of *Function2* within *Component2*. The rule takes in the top-level *System* object as its input. The rule first finds all the component objects in the system, and the *Guard* condition code, Component1.uniqueID() != Component2.uniqueId(), removes matches where *Component1* and *Component2* are the same component. Now, the rule returns the set of dataflow connections between function ports within these unique components. Once the dataflows, *DataflowFF*, that connect ports of *Function1* and *Function2* are matched, the subgroups consisting of the sending functions' output ports, *F_Output*, must be formed. The grouping criterion of the group operator restricts membership to a subgroup to unique *F_Output* objects in the same function, *Function1*. A single subgroup holds the output ports needed by a single proxy on a component. According to the Group rule execution semantics, objects with the *CreateNew* action (marked with a checkmark) will be created for each subgroup. This creates a single *Proxy* object within *Component2* for each subgroup, and the Group action of *copy* will copy the ports in the subgroup into the proxy. The output packets of the rule will consist of the ports holding the dataflows across separate components and the components where these ports are located. All *Component2* objects found in the match will now contain appropriate proxies, and each proxy will contain the output ports copied from its representative function, *Function1*.

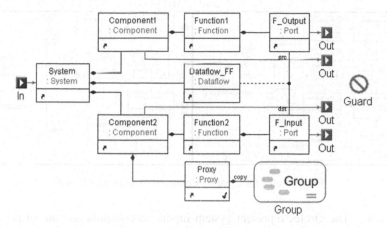

Fig. 7. Group Rule for Creating Proxies with Ports

For each proxy, direct dataflow connections from the original sending function to the receiving functions need to be replaced by the appropriate connections from the proxy to the receiving functions. Also, the same output ports of the sending function must be connected to appropriate input ports of the proxy. The rules to create these dataflows and the input ports of the proxy are shown below in Fig. 8, and they can be executed in parallel.

The left rule of Fig. 8 creates the dataflow connections from a proxy's output ports to the receiver functions' input ports. The output packets from the rule in Fig. 7 contain all of the dataflow connections between *Function1* and *Function2*. The *Guard* condition restricts found matches to those where the output port of the proxy, *P_Output*, has the same name as the output port of *Function1*, *F_Output*. The resulting matches are the correct ports since the output ports copied into the proxy were the output ports of *Function1* in the previous rule, i.e., they will have the same name. Once matched correctly, the connection from the *F_Output* to the input port of *Function2*, *F_Input*, is replaced by the connection from the output of the proxy, *P_Output*, to *F_Input* through a dataflow, *Dataflow_PF*. The procedural code (contained in *AttributeMapping*) renames the proxy object to be "P" plus the name of its corresponding function, *Function1*, to make it identifiable in the resulting model.

The right rule in Fig. 8 matches the sending function's output ports, *F_Output*, to their copied instances within a proxy on another component. The *Guard* condition restricts found matches to those where the output port of the proxy, *P_Output*, has the same name as the output port of *Function1*, *F_Output*. For each match, a new input port, *P_Input*, is created within the proxy. This provides an input interface in the proxy that mirrors its output ports. Each output port of the sending function, *F_Output*, is then connected to its corresponding proxy input port. The procedural code (*Attribute-Mapping*) renames a created input port to be "In_" followed by the name of the output port, *F_Output*, it is now connected to through a dataflow, *Dataflow_FP*.

Fig. 9 shows an example input model that needs proxies included in the components. The boxes labeled C1, C2, and C3 represent components, those labeled F1, F2... F9 represent functions, and arrows within functions represent ports. The arrow indicates the directional flow of data, and directed lines between ports are dataflow

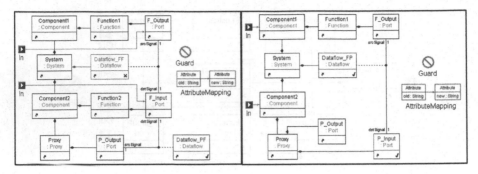

Fig. 8. Rules for Creating Connections to/from a Proxy

connections. The circles represent system inputs and outputs and are of no concern regarding the transformation. The functions F5 and F7 appear twice in components C2 and C3, respectively, as unique instances of the same function block.

Looking at the input model, we see that functions F2 and F3 are the only functions with connections across different components; therefore, proxies must be created for these functions.

Fig. 10 shows the resulting output model of the system after the rules above are applied. During the execution of the first rule, a total of three subgroups would be created for the entire system model. Each subgroup has a corresponding proxy, PF2 and PF3 in this model, where the number identifier for each proxy matches the number identifier for its corresponding function, e.g., PF3 → F3.

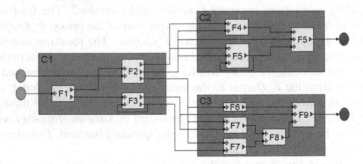

Fig. 9. Sample Input Model

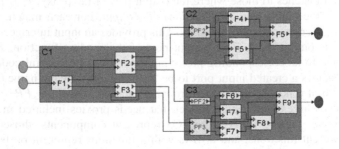

Fig. 10. Sample Output Model

Notice that the proxies' port interfaces are not the same on different components, e.g. PF2 in C2 has a two port interface whereas PF2 in C3 has a one port interface. This occurs since the ports copied into a proxy are the ones explicitly needed by functions on the same component and not the entire set of output ports of the sending function.

5   Shared Variables in a Dataflow Model

A dataflow model consists of *Blocks*, which are connected through *Ports*. Connections between these ports are called *Lines*, which represent flow of data between the blocks through their ports. While the ports may be classified as *input* and *output* ports, the flow of data may be from one input port to another (or one output port to another), as in the case of a hierarchical block, where a top level input port may be passing information along to the lower level blocks.

A single port may be connected to multiple ports through multiple lines. In generating code from such models, we would like to use a single shared variable to represent all such lines. We would also like to make a temporary 'cross-link' association between each line and its shared variable, for specific purposes necessary later in the code generation. The *Group* operator offers a convenient way to achieve this in GReAT. We will see how a Group rule can be used to identify groups of such lines and create a new variable for each such group, and generate the cross-links.

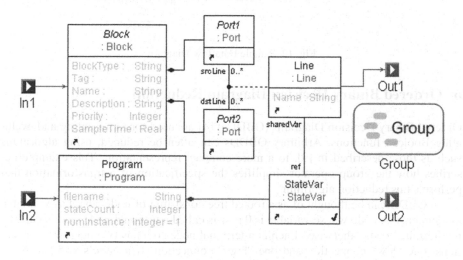

Fig. 11. Group Rule for Creating a Shared Variable

Fig. 11 shows the Group rule in GReAT for creating a single shared variable for a group of lines. For each block, we take the ports contained in that block and group the lines originating from that port. Note that the port may be connected to other ports which are not contained in the same block. *Port1*, *Port2* and *Line* are added to the Group object, and the grouping criterion is set as: the_Port1 == other_Port1. This results in multiple lines originating from a single *Port* object in a *Block* being grouped together. A new variable is then created inside *Program*. Since this is a Group rule, the *CreateNew* action fires once for each subgroup that has been created. This means that a single variable will be created for each set of lines that have been grouped together.

After creating the new variable, we associate it with its *Line*, using a cross-link. This is indicated by the line with the role names *ref* and *sharedVar*. Since the cross-link is a *simple association*, it will be created for each match, between the *Line* in that match, and the *StateVar* created for the group that this match is placed in.

Fig. 12 shows a section of a dataflow diagram. The port *Res* has three *Lines* and the port Con has two Lines coming from it. Let the *Line* connected to port *Pi* be called *Li*. Then, *L1, L2, L3* will be in one subgroup, and *L4* and *L5* will be in another subgroup.

The group rule creates a new shared variable *Var1* for the subgroup {*L1, L2, L3*}, and another shared variable *Var2* for the subgroup {*L4, L5*}. The output packets generated from the group rule are {*L1, Var1*}, {*L2, Var1*}, {*L3, Var1*}, {*L4, Var2*} and {*L5, Var2*}.

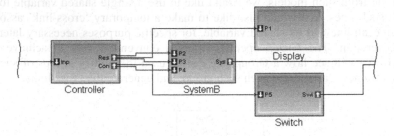

Fig. 12. Sample Dataflow Diagram

6 Ordered Binary Decision Diagram Reduction

Ordered Binary Decision Diagrams (OBDDs) [4] are used for representing and evaluating Boolean functions. Arbitrary OBDDs can often be reduced, using algorithms such as those described in [9], to a more compact representation. This example describes how the group operator simplifies the specification of a transformation that performs this reduction algorithm.

An OBDD can be thought of as a rooted tree consisting of nodes that have variable assignments. A node whose variable is 0 or 1 is called a terminal node, and is called a non-terminal node otherwise. Each non-terminal node contains two outgoing connections: one "low" connection and one "high" connection. If a node's variable is assigned a value of 0, then the low connection tells which node to evaluate next, and if a node's variable is assigned a value of 1, then the high connection tells which node to evaluate next. The value of the function for a particular assignment of values to variables is given when a terminal node is reached.

The reduction algorithm in [9] begins by assigning an integer label to each of the nodes in the diagram in the following manner. The first 0-node that is encountered receives the first label (for instance, #0). All of the other terminal 0-nodes have the same value, so they also received the same label. In the same way, all of the terminal

1-nodes receive the next label (#1). Next, we define two terms: given a non-terminal node n, $lo(n)$ is defined to be the node pointed to by the low connection from n (drawn here using dashed lines), and $hi(n)$ is defined to be the node pointed to by the high connection from n (drawn here using solid lines).

The rest of the algorithm proceeds in a bottom-up manner as follows. To assign a label to each of nodes at level i, we assume that we have already assigned a label to all of the nodes at all levels j such that $j > i$. That is, we assume that all of the nodes on levels below the current level have been labeled. A node n at level i receives its label in one of the following three ways:

1. If the label of the node $lo(n)$ is equal to the label of the node $hi(n)$, n also receives this same label
2. If there is another node m such that n and m have the same variable x_i, and the labels of $lo(n)$ and $lo(m)$ are equal and the labels of $hi(n)$ and $hi(m)$ are equal, n receives the same label as m.
3. Otherwise, n receives the next unused integer as its label.

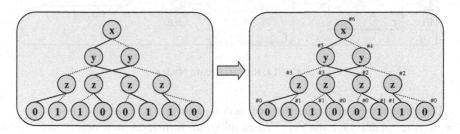

Fig. 13. Unlabeled OBDD (left) and Labelled OBDD (right)

Fig. 13 shows an example OBDD both before and after the labeling algorithm has been applied. In the rest of this example, we assume that the input to our transformation rules is the labeled OBDD on the right of Fig. 13.

After the labeling of the OBDD, the next step of the reduction algorithm of [9], and the transformation we will describe below, removes redundant nodes based on their labels. That is, for each group of nodes with the same label, it creates one new node with that same label and creates the connections between these "reduced" nodes appropriately.

There are two re-writing rules we must write to perform this transformation:

1. Determine which nodes are equivalent based on their labels, and for each set of equivalent nodes, create a new node.
2. Create the low and high connections between the newly created nodes based on the low and high connections that exist between the old nodes.

Fig. 14 shows a rule that performs the first step of our transformation. The incoming context for the rule (the objects bound to the input ports) are the diagrams in which the nodes are found. The diagram named *OldDiagram* is the non-reduced OBDD, and the diagram named *Diagram* will be the reduced OBDD. This rule first finds all of the nodes in *OldDiagram*. A group operator is present, and contains as its only members the nodes found in *OldDiagram*. The subgroups are formed by iterating over each match (which each consist of a single node found in *OldDiagram*) and evaluating the user-specified grouping criteria against matches already in subgroups; in our case, two matches should be inserted into the same subgroup if the values of their labels are equal.

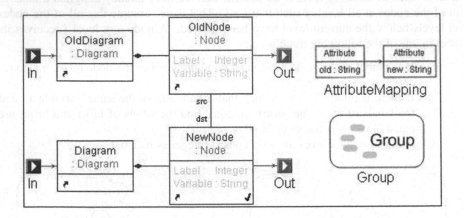

Fig. 14. Rule to Create Nodes

The grouping criteria code that will accomplish this is: `the_OldNode.Label() == other_OldNode.Label()`. After subgroup formation, new objects are created on a per subgroup basis, and new associations are created on a per match basis. Thus, our rule creates one new node in our reduced OBDD (*Diagram*) for each group of nodes that have the same label in the unreduced OBDD, and also creates a temporary association between the newly created nodes and the node in the unreduced OBDD to which the new node corresponds; this temporary association will be matched in the next rule to connect the new states together. Finally, the procedural code (*Attribute-Mapping*) takes care of setting the values of the attributes (the label and variable values) of the newly created nodes.

The next rule in the sequence, shown in Fig. 15, is responsible for connecting the nodes of the reduced OBDD. The incoming context consists of two elements: a node from the unreduced OBDD (labeled *OldNode*) and the corresponding node in the reduced OBDD (labeled *NewNode*). The rule finds all of the connections in the unreduced OBDD such that *OldNode* is the destination of the connection; it then finds the node in the reduced OBDD that corresponds to this "source" node in the unreduced OBDD by matching the association created in the previous rule (labeled with the rolenames *src* and *dst* in both places). Remember that *NewNode* is already the node in the reduced OBDD corresponding to *OldNode* because they are passed from the previous rule together. The *AttributeMapping* block takes care of setting the connection to the proper type, low or high, with the following code: `NewConnection.Type() = OldConnection.Type()`.

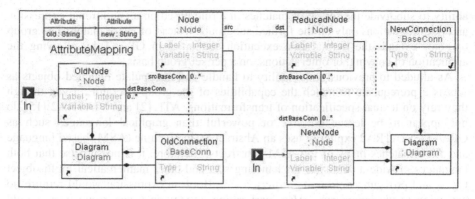

Fig. 15. Rule to Connect States in the Reduced OBDD

The resulting connected and reduced OBDD is shown in Fig. 16.

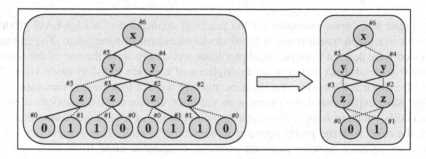

Fig. 16. Connected and (Partially) Reduced OBDD

7 Related Work

Hoffman et al. [5] introduced transformations on frame bounded subgraphs which restrict graph edges from crossing frame boundaries. The copying of such a delimited subgraph permits copying only the nodes and edges contained within a frame. The group operator uses a similar idea when performing actions on grouped objects: only user selected nodes and edges that belong to a group under the membership criterion will have the group action (bind, move, or copy) performed on them. Following the application of the action specified for the group, all edges with an endpoint outside of a subgroup, including those to other formed subgroups in the same rule, will be removed.

Van Gorp et al. [11] implemented the copying of subgraphs in the MoTMoT project [8] using the "copy" and "onCopy" operators. The "copy" and "onCopy" operators provide means to perform deep copies on models and/or copying specified nodes and edges within a rule; however, it is not obvious how a user could implement in MoTMoT transformations presented above using the group operator within the GReAT language. The difficulty for MoTMoT to recreate the same transformations in an equally small number of rules would arise because it does not appear to have the ability to subdivide the set of all matches in a rule based on a conditional expression and perform actions only on the formed subgroups instead of every match. The group operator extends the normal rule execution semantics in GReAT by allowing the application of copying, or other actions, on a per set/group basis.

As alluded to previously, the ability to handle and manipulate matched objects as sets is a prerequisite to match the capabilities of the group operator. Even though they rely on textual specification of transformations, ATL [2] and VIATRA2 [15] do not appear to be less expressive or powerful than graphical languages such as GReAT. VIATRA2 explicitly uses an Abstract State Machine (ASM) based language and ATL matches many of the ASM constructs; therefore, it is no surprise that both languages provide a data type for handling sets and other mathematical multi-object types, and providing a grouping criterion as a Boolean expression would require no extension to the languages. Also, performing actions on a per group basis would involve using the "foreach" command, common to both languages.

8 Summary and Conclusions

This paper has shown examples for the practical application of a high-level grouping operator in a graph-transformation based model transformation language. The examples provided were derived from practical problems and clearly show the use of the operator to allow more abstract and concise descriptions of complex transformation steps. This simplifies the transformation specification, making it easier to write and maintain.

We have implemented the operator in the GReAT interpretive transformation engine (GRE), and we have a prototype implementation of a code generator that compiles the rules with the group operator into executable code. However, it is the topic of further research how to generate efficient executable code from such rewriting rules. Another research topic is related to the restrictions we have placed on the group operator: these restrictions make the implementation of the group-rules straightforward, but it is not clear how well they stand up in practice. We plan to investigate how these restrictions can be weakened while maintaining the powerful properties of the grouping operator.

Acknowledgements

The research described in this paper has been supported by a grant from NSF/CSR-EHS, titled "Software Composition for Embedded Systems using Graph Transformations", award number CNS-0509098, and by NSF/ITR, titled "Foundations of Hybrid and Embedded Software Systems", award number CCR-0225610.

References

1. Agrawal, A., Karsai, G., Neema, S., Shi, F., Vizhanyo, A.: The Design of a Language for Model Transformations. Journal on Software and System Modeling 5(3), 261–288 (2006)
2. ATL Project. An ECLIPSE GMT Subproject,
   http://www.eclipse.org/m2m/atl/

3. Balasubramanian, D., Karsai, G., Narayanan, A., Shi, F., Thibodeaux, R.: A Subgraph Operator for Graph Transformation Languages. In: GT-VMT 2007 Workshop at ETAPS (2007), http://www.cs.le.ac.uk/events/GTVMT07/

4. Bryant, R.E.: Graph Based Algorithms for Boolean Function Manipulation. IEEE Transactions on Computers C-35(8), 677–691 (1986)

5. Drewes, F., Hoffmann, B., Plump, D.: Hierarchical Graph Transformation. Journal of Computer and System Sciences 64, 249–283 (2002)

6. Ehrig, H., Ehrig, K., Prange, U., Taentzer, G.: Fundamentals of Algebraic Graph Transformation. Series: Monographs in Theoretical Computer Science. Springer, Heidelberg (2006)

7. Farcas, E., Farcas, C., Pree, W., Templ, J.: Transparent distribution of real-time components based on logical execution time. In: Proceedings of the 2005 ACM SIG-PLAN/SIGBED Conference on Languages, Compilers, and Tools For Embedded Systems, LCTES 2005, Chicago, Illinois, USA, June 15-17, 2005, pp. 31–39. ACM Press, New York (2005)

8. Van Gorp, P., Schippers, H., Jannsens, D.: Copying Subgraphs within Model Repositories. In: 5th International Workshop on Graph Transformation and Visual Modeling Techniques (GT-VMT), Vienna, Austria (2006)

9. Huth, M., Ryan, M.: Logic in Computer Science: Modeling and Reasoning about Systems. Cambridge University Press, Cambridge (2000)

10. Personal communications with developers and researchers from industrial labs

11. Schippers, H., Van Gorp, P.: Model Driven, Template Based, Model Transformer (MoT-MoT) (2005), http://motmot.sourceforge.net/

12. Schürr, A., Winter, A., Zündorf, A.: Graph grammar engineering with PROGRES. In: Botella, P., Schäfer, W. (eds.) ESEC 1995. LNCS, vol. 989, pp. 219–234. Springer, Heidelberg (1995)

13. Silva, A.R., Rosa, F.A., Gonalves, T., Antunes, M.: Distributed Proxy: A Design Pattern for the Incremental Development of Distributed Applications. In: Emmerich, W., Tai, S. (eds.) EDO 2000. LNCS, vol. 1999, pp. 165–181. Springer, Heidelberg (2001)

14. Taentzer, G.: AGG: A Graph Transformation Environment for Modeling and Validation of Software. In: Pfaltz, J.L., Nagl, M., Böhlen, B. (eds.) AGTIVE 2003. LNCS, vol. 3062. Springer, Heidelberg (2004)

15. VIATRA2 Framework. An ECLIPSE GMT Subproject, http://www.eclsipse.org/gmt

Modeling Successively Connected Repetitive Subgraphs

Anne-Thérèse Körtgen

RWTH Aachen University, Department of Computer Science 3,
Ahornstrasse 55, D-52074 Aachen, Germany
koertgen@i3.informatik.rwth-aachen.de
http://se.rwth-aachen.de/koertgen

Abstract. In this contribution, we introduce an extension of the graph transformation language PROGRES that allows to specify repetitive subgraphs in a compact and comprehensible way. They can be pattern-matched as well as created. Unlike other approaches, the extension supports specifying successively connected repetitive subgraphs, i.e. inter-connections among the repeated instances of the subgraphs are expressed by edges in the graph pattern. The need for this modeling feature arose during a case study with the software company innotec developing tools for data handling in chemical engineering development processes. In this paper, we introduce syntax and semantics of the extension by giving a translation of extended PROGRES transformations into plain PRO-GRES. Furthermore, we show the application of this modeling feature within our project dealing with consistency maintenance.

1 Introduction and Motivation

Model transformation is needed in development processes where a large number of dependent models are created. For example, our research activities are concerned with model transformations in development processes within the chemical engineering domain where flow sheets act as central models. Flow sheets of the chemical plant to be built differ in their level of abstraction and are refined stepwise. Keeping models consistent is a demanding task because of their large number and the iterative character of the development process.

Models can usually be seen as graphs which consist of nodes representing objects and edges representing relationships between these objects. Graphs are well-suited for representing complex data with manifold relationships in a natural way. Model transformations can be applied to graphs using graph rewriting rules. A *graph rewriting rule* describes in a *left-hand side graph pattern* (LHS) how a specific subgraph in a host graph is to be transformed into another subgraph described in a *right-hand side graph pattern* (RHS). Examples for graph rewriting systems are PROGRES[1], GReAT[2] and AGG[3].

In most graph rewriting systems it is possible to specify graph patterns with set semantics, e.g. single nodes or even subgraphs which form a subpattern representing node sets or sets of subgraphs, respectively. The latter pattern construct

A. Schürr, M. Nagl, and A. Zündorf (Eds.): AGTIVE 2007, LNCS 5088, pp. 426–441, 2008.

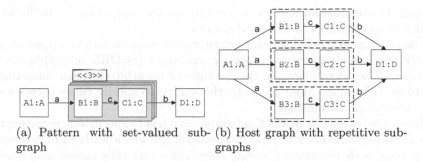

(a) Pattern with set-valued sub- (b) Host graph with repetitive subgraph   graphs

Fig. 1. Example of set-valued subgraphs

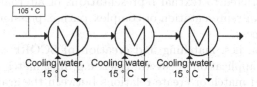

Fig. 2. Example of successively connected repetitive heat exchangers in a flow sheet

is called *set-valued subgraph* in the sequel. For example, in Figure 1(a) a pattern with a set-valued subgraph which contains nodes B1 and C1 is depicted. The size of the set of subgraphs is stated by 3 displayed above the grouping. In addition to the set-valued subgraph, the graph pattern contains nodes A1 and D1 which are connected to the nodes of the set-valued subgraph by edges of type a and b. A host graph matching the pattern from Figure 1(a) is depicted in Figure 1(b). While nodes A1 and D1 appear once, there are three subgraphs matching the set-valued subgraph of the pattern. The subgraphs are surrounded by dashed boxes for illustration purposes. Specified edges of type a and b connecting outer nodes (which are not part of the set-valued subgraph) and inner nodes (which are part of the set-valued subgraph) exist for each instance of the inner node. In Figure 1(b), the nodes A1 and D1 are connected to each of the three subgraphs by a respective edge.

In practice, models often contain objects *repetitively* which are *successively connected*. To give an example from chemical engineering, to optimize the costs of a cooling process, material is cooled down by the use of multiple heat exchangers. Figure 2 shows a flow sheet with three heat exchangers successively connected by a stream which transfers the material. Each of them receives cooling water with an average temperature which is cheaper than to use one heat exchanger which receives extreme cooled down water. The number of heat exchangers depends on the temperature of the material that flows through the heat exchangers, the flow rate, and the aimed temperature. Thus, the number can be determined by computing a formula.

The necessity of modeling successively connected subgraphs is not restricted to the chemical engineering domain. Another example which appears in many domains is searching for paths restricted to certain subgraphs, i.e. paths which consist of repetitively connected subgraphs.

One problem in specifying graph transformations is the lack of a possibility to specify *successively connected repetitive subgraphs* (SCORE subgraphs) as the sequence of heat exchangers in the example or an arbitrary path consisting of repetitive subgraphs. More precisely, the ability to specify edges between set-valued subgraphs is missing.

Up to now, to specify SCORE subgraphs one has to specify one rewriting rule for each possible number of repetitive subgraphs, which leads to unnecessarily many rules with redundancy among these rules and thus causes maintenance problems. Furthermore, the number of repetitive subgraphs is often bound to some attribute value from related objects. Also possibilities to model path expressions are restricted to textual representations of alternatives and quantification. A graphical representation of complex path expressions would facilitate the modeling process.

In other approaches, matching and creation of SCORE subgraphs may be simulated by the application of several rules, e.g. first match or create the subgraphs and second match or create relations between the graphs. This solution requires the specification designer to model exactly these rules, which makes the modeling process more complicated. From the point of view of the specification designer the internal execution should be hidden. Therefore, there is a need for further language constructs.

In this paper, we present a formal but intuitive language construct for graph patterns of PROGRES production rules called *inter-connected set-valued subgraphs* (ICONS subgraphs). In Section 2, the syntax and semantics of ICONS subgraphs are introduced. Section 3 shows how the language construct is translated into plain PROGRES syntax. To show the applicability of the construct, we present several practical example transformations in Section 4. In Section 5, we discuss and compare related work in detail. Besides a short summary, Section 6 gives an outlook to future work in our project also concerning graphical modelling of alternations.

2 Syntax and Semantics of ICONS Subgraphs

A graph pattern may contain, besides nodes and edges, set-valued subgraphs. A set-valued subgraph describes the pattern of subgraphs, which exist repetitively in the host graph. To define SCORE subgraphs, i.e. to define connecting edges between nodes of repetitive subgraphs, the set-valued subgraph is displayed three times. This leads to another pattern item, the so-called ICONS subgraphs. Figure 3(a) shows an example pattern with an ICONS subgraph. Each subgraph of an ICONS subgraph contains the same graph pattern[1]. In the figure, two nodes of type B and C are connected by an edge of type et. Edges between subgraphs define the connections of two successive subgraphs. Note that edges

---

[1] Please note that redundant pattern elements are accepted due to have an appropriate representation of sequences for engineers.

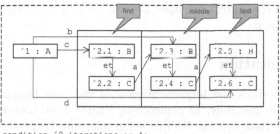

condition '2.iterations := 4;

(a) Pattern with inter-connected set-valued subgraph

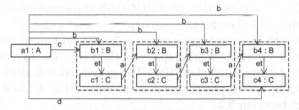

(b) Host graph with SCORE subgraph

Fig. 3. Example of ICONS subgraphs

between the first and the middle and edges between the middle and the last subgraph define the same connections, e.g. edges of type a in the figure.

The cardinality of the ICONS subgraph is determined by its attribute **iterations**. In the example, the attribute is set to the constant 4, but it can be set to any numerical expression. A match of the described pattern of Figure 3(a) is shown in Figure 3(b). While the node a1 appears once, there are four subgraphs matching the pattern of the ICONS subgraphs. The subgraphs are surrounded by dashed boxes for illustration. Two successive subgraphs are connected by an edge of type a as specified in the ICONS subgraph.

Edges from nodes outside an ICONS subgraph to nodes of the middle subgraph have the same semantics as in conventional set-valued subgraphs. In Figure 3(a), the edge of type b connects the outer node '1. It defines edges between the instance of the outer node and each instance of the inner node in the host graph. In the match shown in Figure 3(b), there exists four edges of type b connecting the node a1 to the respective node of type B of a subgraph.

As in SCORE subgraphs there are two subgraphs which constitute the endings of the sequence, connections between the host graph and these two subgraphs can be specified. For this purpose, the first and the last subgraph of the ICONS pattern play each a role of an ending, the first and the last subgraph of the sequence, respectively. In a pattern, the ability to connect an outer node to a node of the first or the last subgraph of an ICONS subgraph leads to two further edge semantics. In the example of Figure 3(a), edges of type c and d are specified connecting the node '1 with nodes of the subgraphs. The corresponding match depicted in Figure 3(b) contains these edges only once (in contrast to the edges of type b) connecting the node a1 with the one ending, particularly the node b1 with edge c, and connecting the node a1 with the other ending, particularly the node c4 with edge d.

3   Implementation

This section describes the implementation of the new language construct in PROGRES. More precisely, as depicted in Figure 4 we transform PROGRES production rules that contain ICONS subgraphs into several plain PROGRES transformations to simulate the creation and matching of SCORE subgraphs. This is done with the help of internal nodes defined in LoopScheme which are presented in the next subsection. A PROGRES transformation containing an ICONS subgraph on either its LHS or RHS is transformed into a PROGRES transformation with the same name which calls several transformations to simulate matching (if the ICONS subgraph is on the LHS) and to simulate creation (if the ICONS subgraph is on the RHS). The generated transformations for the creation of SCORE subgraphs is explained in Subsection 3.2 and the matching is outlined in Subsection 3.3.

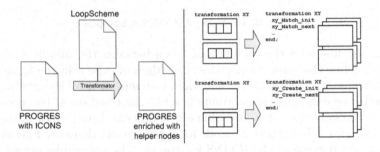

Fig. 4. Overview of the transformation process

The main reason we chose to simulate the new construct and not to really extend the language PROGRES is the pragmatic fact that PROGRES is not easy to extend. A possible performance gain the extension would imply is not focused. The PROGRES implementation of our approach in maintaining consistency of models serves as evaluation environment for our new developed concepts. Furthermore, our PROGRES specification is completely generated whereby no additional effort is caused by the transformation step from enriched PROGRES to plain PROGRES.

3.1   Internal Nodes Used for Matching SCORE Subgraphs

We extended the graph scheme with three node types and several edge types depicted in Figure 5 that mark nodes of a matching subgraph. To group the nodes of a repetitive subgraph, they are referenced by an Iteration node. As subgraphs can be successively connected, an Iteration node refers to a successive grouping by the edge nextIteration to another Iteration node. All

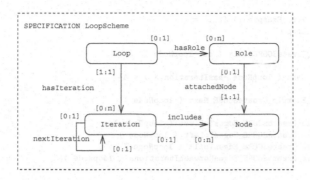

Fig. 5. Graph scheme used for matching repetitive subgraphs

`Iteration` nodes referring to the same SCORE subgraph are grouped by a referencing edge `hasIteration` to a `Loop` node. As matching and creation is divided into multiple steps, it is necessary to add `Role` nodes to refer to nodes which are considered in later execution steps, e.g. nodes of the host graph which are connected to nodes of a SCORE subgraph. How these nodes are applied, is explained in more details in the following subsections.

3.2 Transformation of ICONS Subgraphs on RHS to Create SCORE Subgraphs

In case the ICONS subgraph exists only on the RHS, the generated transformation calls several transformations to iteratively create the subgraphs and after that create the connections between nodes. To illustrate the transformation process, we transform an example PROGRES transformation called `BC_example`, which contains an empty LHS and which contains on his RHS the pattern from Figure 3(a), into the transformation which is shown in Figure 6. The transformations listed there are explained in the following with help of the example.

At first, an initial transformation (`CreateSCORE_Init`) is executed which creates all normal nodes and edges specified on the current RHS. For the example, this is the case for node 1'. Additionally, the transformation creates a loop node and, to identify the node which is to be connected to nodes of the SCORE subgraph, a role node is created which refers to this node. The role node has an attribute `roleName` which is set to the name of the attached node. Its attribute value is determined by the node id of the input transformation. The loop node is returned. In the following, a transformation (`CreateSCORE_Next`) which creates a SCORE subgraph according to the specified pattern is iteratively executed until the cardinality which is specified by the `iterations` attribute is reached. It gets the loop node as input parameter to find the right application point.

In Figure 7, the corresponding transformation `BC_Example_CreateSCORE_Next` is shown. In addition to the loop node, its LHS contains an iteration node '2. The attached restriction of this node ensures that the last created iteration node (which was actually created during the previous execution of this transformation)

432   A.-T. Körtgen

```
transformation + BC_Example () [1:1] =
use loopNode : Loop
  do
    BC_Example_CreateSCORE_Init ( out loopNode )
    & loop
        when (card ( loopNode.-hasIteration-> ) < 4)
        then
            BC_Example_CreateSCORE_Next ( loopNode )
        end
    & BC_Example_CreateSCORE_EdgesToFirst ( loopNode )
    & BC_Example_CreateSCORE_EdgesToLast ( loopNode )
    & BC_Example_CreateSCORE_EdgesToAll ( loopNode )
    & BC_Example_CreateSCORE_EdgesBetweenIterations ( loopNode )
  end
end;
```

Fig. 6. Generated transformation to simulate the transformation BC_example

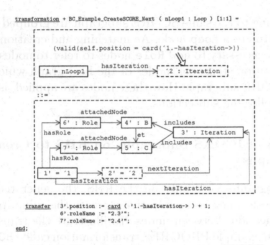

Fig. 7. Transformation to create a SCORE subgraph

is matched. The node is declared as an optional node if the transformation is executed for the first time. On the RHS of the transformation the SCORE subgraph consisting of the nodes 4' and 5' is present. The nodes are referenced by an iteration node 3' to identify their affiliation with a specific subgraph. The iteration node is connected with the previous iteration node by an edge of type nextIteration and its attribute position is set to the number of existing iteration nodes belonging to the current loop node increased by one. Additionally, two role nodes refer to the nodes of the subgraph. The role names are set to the node ids of the input transformation, 2.3' and 2.4', respectively.

The next transformations create edges according to the different edge semantics mentioned in the previous section, namely edges which are to connect nodes of the host graph with nodes of the *first* subgraph, of *all* subgraphs, and of the *last* subgraph, and edges which exist *between* two successive subgraphs. Note that these transformations are only generated in case an edge with the corresponding semantics is specified on the current RHS.

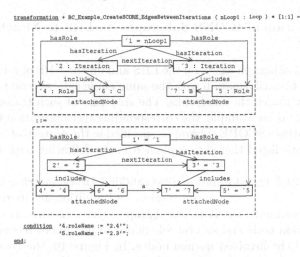

Fig. 8. Transformation to create edges between two successive subgraphs

The transformation (`CreateSCORE_EdgesBetweenIterations`) that adds edges between SCORE subgraphs of the current example is depicted in Figure 8. It gets the loop node as input parameter like the other transformations. On the LHS, two iteration nodes affiliated with the loop node that are connected by an edge of type `nextIteration` are present. As only specific nodes of two successive SCORE subgraphs are to connect, only these have to be obtained. Thus, the example transformation in the figure contains only the nodes '6 and '7 of the preceding and the succeeding subgraph, respectively, which are explicitly matched by role nodes referencing them. The RHS differs from the LHS only in one edge which is added, namely the edge a between the nodes 6' and 7' of two successive subgraphs. As the transformation is to be applied to all subgraphs of this kind and not only to one occurrence, the transformation is applied in parallel to all application points matching the LHS. Parallel execution is achieved by the additional * in the signature of the transformation.

To add edges to all subgraphs, a transformation (`EdgesToAll`) is applied in parallel. Like the previous transformation, it is specified with an additional * and it gets the loop node as input parameter. To add an edge between a specific node of the host graph and a node of a SCORE subgraph, the LHS has to obtain these nodes. They are explicitly matched by role nodes referencing them. The RHS differs from the LHS only in one edge which is added between the nodes.

The transformation to induce edges from the overall graph to the first subgraph (`EdgesToFirst`) is applied only once. For this purpose, the specific nodes of the first subgraph (the position number of their connected iteration node equals one) and the nodes of the overall graph are considered on the LHS and are connected by the edges specified on the RHS. The transformation to induce edges from the overall graph to the last subgraph (`EdgesToLast`) is analogously generated. In this case, the specific nodes of the last subgraph are obtained.

3.3   Transformation of ICONS Subgraphs on LHS to Match SCORE Subgraphs

In case the ICONS subgraph exists on the LHS and on the RHS of a transformation, the generated transformation with the same name calls several transformations to iteratively match the subgraphs. The structure of such transformations is always identical. As an example, the corresponding transformation is shown in Figure 9 which matches SCORE subgraphs specified in the pattern of Figure 3(a). The transformations listed there are explained in the following with help of the example.

At first, an initial transformation (`MatchSCORE_Init`) matches all normal nodes and edges of the input transformation and additionally matches a first subgraph corresponding to the ICONS subgraph. The transformation creates a loop and an iteration node and several role nodes to be able to recover the subgraph's nodes and the involved normal nodes. In Figure 10, the corresponding transformation for the example is depicted. The role nodes' `roleName` attributes are set to the node ids of the pattern, namely '2.3, '2.4 and '1. Note that this transformation is executed in parallel and thus is applied to each application point in the host graph. The application points are obtained from the loop nodes which are returned by the transformation.

The next step considers each loop node returned by the initial transformation. Starting with a matched subgraph, the transitive closure of SCORE subgraphs is matched recursively. For this purpose, a transformation (`MatchSCORE_NextRecur`) shown in Figure 11 invokes recursively a transformation (`MatchSCORE_Next`) which matches a successive subgraph until the specified cardinality is reached. Then the last subgraph which is especially connected with outer nodes is matched (`MatchSCORE_Last`).

Figure 12 shows the transformation (`MatchSCORE_Next`) generated for the example transformation. On the LHS, the attached restriction of the iteration node 8 ensures that the last subgraph of the loop node is obtained. With the help of the role nodes 4 and 5, nodes of this subgraph and the host graph specific to this loop node can be obtained. The successive subgraph is match by the nodes 6 and 7 which are currently not used. On the RHS, a new iteration node 9' refers

```
transformation + BC_Example () [1:1] =
   use loops : loop [0:n]
   do
      BC_Example_MatchSCORE_Init ( out loops )
      & for_all nloop : Loop [1:1] := elem ( loops )
      do
         choose
            BC_Example_MatchSCORE_NextRecur ( nloop )
         else
            GEN_deleteLoop ( nloop )
         end
      end
   end
end;
```

Fig. 9. Generated transformation to simulate the matching of ICONS subgraphs

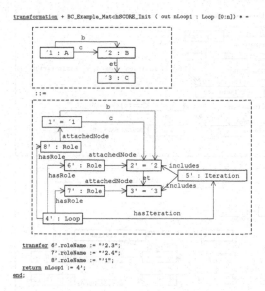

```
transformation + BC_Example_MatchSCORE_Init ( out nLoop1 : Loop [0:n]) * =
```

```
transfer 6'.roleName := "'2.3";
        7'.roleName := "'2.4";
        8'.roleName := "'1";
return nLoop1 := 4';
end;
```

Fig. 10. Initial transformation to match SCORE subgraphs

```
transformation + BC_Example_MatchSCORE_NextRecur ( nLoop1 : Loop [1:1]) [1:1] =
    BC_Example_MatchSCORE_Next ( nLoop1 )
    & choose
        BC_Example_MatchSCORE_NextRecur ( nLoop1 )
        or BC_Example_MatchSCORE_Last ( nLoop1 )
    end
end;
```

Fig. 11. Intermediate transformation

to this successive subgraph matched on the LHS. In the succeeding application of this transformation, this subgraph is obtained as the last found. Additionally, two role nodes 10' and 11' are existent which refer to the nodes of the subgraph.

Sometimes, the last mentioned transformation cannot be applied any further, i.e. another subgraph cannot be found. The number of repetitive subgraphs specified in the ICONS subgraph of the input transformation is checked against the number of subgraphs found. If they are not equal, all transformations applied previously for the current loop node are backtracked. This is a feature of PRO-GRES. The generic transformation (GEN_deleteLoop) which is not restricted to a specific ICONS subgraph deletes all loop, iteration and role nodes that were created in the initial transformation (MatchSCORE_Init).

4   Application

This section is devoted to give application examples of the ICONS subgraphs. In the first subsection, we will give an outlook how to model graphically path expressions with this construct. The second subsection introduces in short our approach using triple graph grammars.

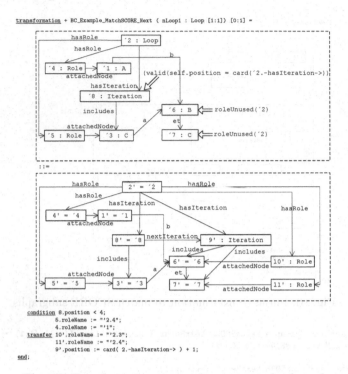

Fig. 12. Transformation to match a connected subgraph

4.1 Application in PROGRES Paths

Modeling alternatives and transitive closures in path expressions is up to now only provided by a textual representation in PROGRES. A visual representation would facilitate the modeling step. The concept of ICONS subgraphs could be used in paths expressions to provide at least the latter.

Figure 13 shows an example of a path expression containing an ICONS subgraph. It computes the set of all successor places '3 of a place '1 in a Petri net. The complex subgraph that can occur repetitively on this path consists of a transition and another place. As this subgraph is part of a path the interconnections among the repetitive subgraphs have to be specified. Therefore, an ICONS subgraph is suitable.

However, the feature's implementation is ongoing. Furthermore, we plan to add also an alternative construct for LHS of transformation rules as well as for path expressions.

4.2 Application in Triple Graph Grammar Rules

We developed an approach for the realization of consistency maintaining tools which are currently being used in the chemical engineering domain. In this subsection, we only give a short summary of the approach to be able to show how ICONS subgraphs are used within our project. In [4], a more detailed description

```
path successor: PLACE [0:n] -> PLACE [0:n] =
'1 => '3 in
```

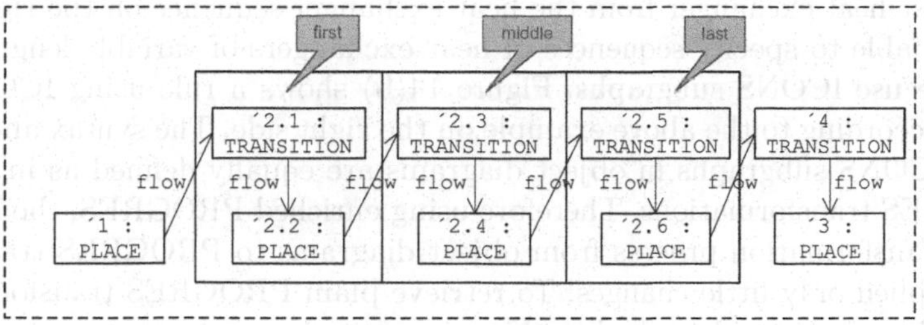

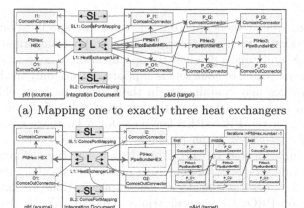

Fig. 13. Example of an ICONS subgraph used in a path expression

(a) Mapping one to exactly three heat exchangers

(b) Mapping one to arbitrary many heat exchangers

Fig. 14. Example of a rule mapping a heat exchangers

of the approach can be found. Further implementation details of our tools are sketched in [5].

The approach is based on Triple Graph Grammars (TGG) [6]. The core idea is to define graph-based rules which specify the relationships that have to be established or maintained between graph patterns of source and target models. Relationships are also based on a graph model and are described by a third graph pattern within a rule. To edit such rules, we introduced in [7] the underlying rule model based on UML object diagrams and a rule editor.

As an introducing example, we pick up the example from Figure 2 showing three successively connected heat exchangers. A rule specifying the correspondence of a single heat exchanger modeled in a pfd (process flow diagram) and three connected heat exchangers modeled in a p&id (piping and instrumentation diagram) is depicted in Figure 14(a). The integration document part shows the pattern describing the relationships of the source and the target model pattern. The heat exchangers on the right side are inter-connected by edges between their out and in connectors. The in and out connectors of the single heat exchanger on the left side are mapped to the in connector of the first and to the out connector of the last heat exchanger from the heat exchanger sequence on the right.

To be able to specify sequences of heat exchangers of variable length within rules, we use ICONS subgraphs. Figure 14(b) shows a rule using ICONS subgraphs according to the above example on the right side. The syntax and semantics of ICONS subgraphs in object diagrams are equally defined as in enriched PROGRES transformations. Therefore using enriched PROGRES, the adaption of the transformation process from object diagrams to PROGRES transformations implied only little changes. To retrieve plain PROGRES transformations, we use the generator described in this paper.

5   Related Work

In this section, similar modeling constructs for the specification of repetitive subgraphs in related work are discussed. The graph transformation languages PROGRES [1,8] and Fujaba [9] allow the specification of node sets in production rules. Only the matching of node sets is supported, thus, only the left hand sides of production rules may contain sets in their graph patterns. The right hand sides may copy node sets defined on the left hand sides of the production rule.

An extension of the PROGRES language for a language construct that allows to specify *set-valued* graph patterns in production rules, is presented in [10] and was implemented by [11]. The ideas follow the theoretical results of [12]. As with node sets, only the matching of set-valued subgraphs is supported and maximal matches are considered. Such specifications are internally translated to common PROGRES specifications. The core idea is that productions with set-valued patterns define equivalence classes of common production rules which obtain explicitly different numbers of equal subpatterns. Dependent on the number of matches in a working graph, a common production rule is selected at runtime and executed. It is not possible to specify edges between set-valued graph patterns, i.e. it is not possible to match successive subgraphs. Furthermore, creation of repetitive subgraphs is not implemented. Our extension of the PROGRES language is based on the extending strategy of this project.

Another possibility to address the matching of repetitive subgraphs are *amalgamated graph transformations* [13] introduced for the tool AGG [3]. At runtime productions are constructed by merging previously defined subproductions. The construction is dependent on a specific application point in the working graph. Repetitive subgraphs may be matched by specifying the subpattern in a subproduction. As in [10], matching successive subgraphs and creation of repetitive subgraphs are not implemented.

In [14], extended UML object diagrams are introduced to specify mappings between UML models, establishing automatic model transformations. Within this extension, repetitive object models may be specified for creation purposes during the transformation step. A stereotype for packages named *ForEach* is developed. Such stereotyped packages may contain parameterized object models, which may be linked to other objects outside the package. For this kind of link, each repetitive object created during transformation will be linked to the outer object. However, relations between instances of repetitive object models cannot be specified or created.

The graph transformation language GReAT is enriched with constructs in [2] to establish matching and creation of set-valued subgraphs. For this purpose, subpatterns grouping nodes may be used in larger patterns. Edges from nodes outside of the subpattern to nodes which are included in the subpattern are allowed. Additionally, the subpatterns have cardinalities, i.e. the cardinality determines the number of created or matched subgraphs according to the subpattern. However, edges between instances of repetitive subgraphs cannot be specified or created.

With *shaped generic graph transformations* [15] a compact notation of complex graph transformations is introduced. Placeholders for node sets as well as subgraphs can be added to graph transformations. At runtime complex transformations are evaluated and equivalent ordinary transformations are constructed and applied. However, the syntax of the complex graph transformations is not intuitive. But simplicity is a hard requirement in our transfer project which aims to transfer our solutions into practice.

6   Conclusion and Future Work

We presented a new language construct, the inter-connected set-valued (ICONS) subgraphs, for the specification of successively connected repetitive (SCORE) subgraphs. The need for this new language construct arose while doing a case study with the software company innotec developing tools for data handling in chemical engineering development processes. In a previous section, we showed the application of ICONS subgraphs in our project which is concerned with incremental model transformation to establish model consistency.

Future work will further investigate the case study, and when needed, we will define the semantics of edges between ICONS subgraphs and their generation in plain PROGRES transformations. Additionally, we would follow up variants of the specification of the cardinality of ICONS subgraphs, e.g. the parametrization of transformations such that the cardinality of subgraphs to create or match is determined at runtime by user input. As in our scenario the integrated application is able to determine attribute values by the evaluation of complex expressions, we will not follow up evaluation of complex expressions and hold on using constants or attribute values.

As explained by innotec, the need for fuzzy rules which do not precisely state certain structures is given. Particularly, it is often the case that the detailed structure of a subgraph is queried. Therefore, similar to regular expressions we plan to support basic operations like alternatives and quantification of graph patterns in order to restrict the set of possible matches. Quantification is already realized by the concept of ICONS subgraphs.

Furthermore, our project is a two-year transfer project which aims at transferring the achieved results in document integration into practice. As PROGRES transformations as well as UML object diagrams are not suitable for engineers, we are currently working on a user-friendly transformation rule editor which provides ICONS subgraphs.

Acknowledgments

This work was in part funded by the CRC 476/TC 61 of the Deutsche Forschungs-gemeinschaft (DFG). Furthermore, the author gratefully acknowledges the fruitful cooperation with innotec.

References

1. Schürr, A.: PROGRES: A Visual Language and Environment for PROgramming with Graph REwrite Systems. In: Aachener Informatik Bericht 94-11, RWTH Aachen University, Germany, Fachgruppe Informatik (1994)
2. Agrawal, A., Karsai, G., Shi, F.: Graph Transformations on Domain-Specific Models. Technical report, Vanderbilt University, Institution for Software Integrated Systems, Nashville, Tennessee (2003) ISIS-03-403
3. Taentzer, G.: AGG: A Tool Environment for Algebraic Graph Transformation. In: Nagl, M., Schürr, A., Münch, M. (eds.) AGTIVE 1999. LNCS, vol. 1779, pp. 481–488. Springer, Heidelberg (2000)
4. Becker, S.M., Haase, T., Westfechtel, B., Wilhelms, J.: Integration tools supporting cooperative development processes in chemical engineering. In: Proc. of the 6th World Conf. on Integrated Design & Process Technology (IDPT 2002), SDPS, p. 10 (2002)
5. Körtgen, A., Becker, S.M., Herold, S.: A Graph-Based Framework for Rapid Construction of Document Integration Tools. In: Proc. of the 11th World Conf. on Integrated Design & Process Technology (IDPT 2007), SDPS, p. 13 (2007)
6. Schürr, A.: Specification of Graph Translators with Triple Graph Grammars. In: Proc. of the 20th Intl. Workshop on Graph-Theoretic Concepts in Computer Science (WG 1994), Herrsching, Germany. LNCS, vol. 903, pp. 151–163. Springer, Heidelberg (1995)
7. Becker, S.M., Westfechtel, B.: UML-based Definition of Integration Models for Incremental Development Processes in Chemical Engineering. In: Proc. of the 7th Intl. Conf. on Integrated Design and Process Technology (IDPT 2003), SDPS, p. 10 (2003)
8. Schürr, A., Winter, A.J., Zündorf, A.: Visual Programming with Graph Rewriting Systems. In: Proc. of the 11th Intl. IEEE Symposium on Visual Languages (VL 1995), Washington, DC, USA. IEEE Computer Society Press, Los Alamitos (1995)
9. Fischer, T., Niere, J., Torunski, L., Zündorf, A.: Story Diagrams: A new Graph Rewrite Language based on the Unified Modeling Language. In: Ehrig, H., Engels, G., Kreowski, H.-J., Rozenberg, G. (eds.) TAGT 1998. LNCS, vol. 1764, pp. 296–309. Springer, Heidelberg (2000)
10. Fuss, C., Tuttlies, V.E.: Simulating Set-Valued Transformations with Algorithmic Graph Transformation Languages. In: AGTIVE 2007. LNCS, p. 16. Springer, Heidelberg (2008)
11. Tuttlies, V.E.: Further Language Constructs for Rule-based Model Transformation. Diploma Thesis, Department of Computer Science 3, RWTH Aachen University (2006)

12. Speulmanns, A.: Visuelles Programmieren mit Graphersetzungsregeln. Diploma Thesis, Department of Computer Science 3, RWTH Aachen University (1995)
13. Taentzer, G., Beyer, M.: Amalgamated Graph Transformations and Their Use for Specifying AGG - an Algebraic Graph Grammar System. In: Proc. of the Intl. Workshop on Graph Transformations in Computer Science, London, UK, pp. 380–394. Springer, Heidelberg (1994)
14. Milicev, D.: Automatic Model Transformations Using Extended UML Object Diagrams in Modeling Environments. IEEE Trans. Softw. Eng. 28(4), 413–431 (2002)
15. Drewes, F., Hoffmann, B., Janssens, D., Minas, M., Van Eetvelde, N.: Shaped Generic Graph Transformation. In: AGTIVE 2007. LNCS, p. 16. Springer, Heidelberg (2008)

Simulating Set-Valued Transformations with Algorithmic Graph Transformation Languages

Christian Fuss and Verena E. Tuttlies

RWTH Aachen University, Computer Science 3 (Software Engineering)
Ahornstr. 55, 52074 Aachen, Germany
{fuss,verena}@i3.informatik.rwth-aachen.de

Abstract. PROGRES is one of the most mature graph transformation languages currently available. It offers many language features, also some for non-homomorphic transformations, e.g. set-nodes. Nevertheless, the language does not offer a comfortable possibility to work with complex set-valued structures. However, these are often useful when modeling complex systems, e.g. simulation systems, models-of-computation, or product lines using multiplicity variation points. We introduce the notion of set-valued transformations to PROGRES, define their syntax and semantics and show how they can be simulated using basic language constructs offered by most algorithmic graph transformation languages with a rich set of control structures.

1 Introduction

Today's model-driven development processes require the transformation of one model into another along the process. Most up-to-date models, like all MOF (Meta Object Facility) models, have an underlying graph structure, and thus model transformations are only a special form of graph transformations. The recent standardization of QVT (Query, View, and Transformation), a transformation language for the MOF, endorses this need and has brought much new attention to the field of graph transformations. Graph transformation languages, e.g. PROGRES, AGG, GReAT, or Fujaba can offer good means to define model transformations as rule-based automated or semi-automatic tasks [24]. Applying graph transformation languages to real life model-driven development of complex systems, e.g. simulation systems, models-of-computation, or product lines, demands easy handling of complex graph structures.

The above mentioned graph transformation languages all compete in their means to specify inherently difficult and complex transformation rules as easy as possible. PROGRES [20] is an algorithmic approach and one of the most mature and feature-rich graph transformation languages currently available, it is being developed since the early 90s and offers many language features not offered by other languages (comprehensive comparisons of the languages can be found in [4,12,25]). Although PROGRES offers some language features for non-homomorphic transformations, e.g. set nodes, it lacks a comfortable possibility

A. Schürr, M. Nagl, and A. Zündorf (Eds.): AGTIVE 2007, LNCS 5088, pp. 442–455, 2008.

to work with complex set-valued structures. In order to be applicable to the above-mentioned domains.

In this paper, we will introduce a language feature for complex set-valued transformations in PROGRES. The problem solved is that of defining an intuitive and comprehensive language feature, that fits into the paradigm of sequential graph rewriting lanuages. We also outline the implementation by simulation, using existing control structure language features. This approach of using existing constructs, which are also available in other languages, makes the concept also applicable to algorithmic graph transformation approaches offering a rich set of control structures and underlines their expressive power.

The remainder of this work is structured as follows: Section 2 describes related work. Section 3 gives an outline of existing possibilities to deal with set-valency in PROGRES. Section 4 introduces syntax and semantics of the new language element *set-valued transformations*. Section 5 sketches the implementation using existing PROGRES language elements and outlines how the results can be transferred to other algorithmic graph transformation languages. Section 6 summarizes the results and gives an outlook, how the approach could be extended, e.g. for recursive transformations.

2   Related Work

The topic of set-valued transformations is not new to graph transformation approaches, but got a lot new attention lately. At a recent workshop three publications were presented covering some form of set-valued graph transformations. [17] proposes a star operator similar to the star operator in Kleene Algebra for a model query language. Actually, the proposed operator resembles the star operator long-known from PROGRES path queries, which does not suffice to transform complex set-valued graph structures, as will be shown in the next section. [13] establishes means to define recursive rules within the double pushout approach [6]. Although this problem is related to set-valued structures as well, the semantics and concepts are different to the ones behind parallel graph transformations. In Section 6 we give an outlook, how our simulation approach could be used for recursive rule definitions. [3,2] defines a subgraph operator for the GReAT language [14]. Motivated by the demand to apply the same action across multiple matches, the papers introduce a notion of a group operator, which can be assigned one of four group actions (bind, move, copy, or delete). There is previous work on set-valued transformations related to GReAT; [1] states some common problems encountered when working with set-valued graph patterns, e.g. the issue of set- or tree-like semantics, which will be discussed in Section 4.2.

Most influences on the ideas in this paper have come from another concept developed for the double pushout approach, namely *amalgamated graph transformations* [23,21]. Amalgamated rules are used in AGG [22] to define parallely executed synchronized rules very similar to our understanding of set-valued transformations. Using amalgamated transformations, one can construct a so-called operational production set by amalgamating the elementary production and the given subproductions. The amalgamated production can finally be applied just like a regular production.

3 PROGRES and Set-Valued Rule Elements

PROGRES [20] is a rule-based graph transformation language that uses a formalism very similar to algebraic approaches like [5,7] to define a sequential graph rewriting system similar to algorithmic graph rewriting approaches like [19,9,16]. The calculus used to describe the language formally is based on first order logic; it allows the specification of a graph transformation system as a set of logic formulae. The formalism is explained in more detail only as necessary. For detailed definition of the calculus see [20, Ch. 3] and for detailed definition of the basic language constructs see [20, Ch. 4].

From the user perspective, simple PROGRES rules, so-called productions, look very similar to single-pushout rules or double-pushout rules when omitting the common interface part. Figures 2 and 3 show examples of PROGRES rules. They consist of a left-hand side (LHS, above the ::=) and a right-hand side (RHS, below the ::=), each defining a subgraph, and a morphism between both (mappings are denoted in the RHS, e.g. by 2'='2). During rule execution, nodes and edges from the working graph are matched to the LHS subgraph. If all rule elements can be matched (and all other conditions evaluate to true), the matching elements are replaced by the according elements of the RHS. The standard matching is injective, i.e. one node from the working graph can only be mapped to one LHS node, but with the folding construct one working graph node can be matched to multiple rule nodes.

With *set nodes* and *star qualifier* PROGRES productions also offer some possibilities to handle set-valency, i.e. non-homomorphic matching of multiple working graph nodes to one rule element. But these means are not sufficient to handle complex set-valued structures, as we will show for the following simple example: We want to specify a production for firing an arbitrary transition in an arc-constant Petri Net. The net is modeled by nodes of type Place, Transition and Token, and edges of type arc and placedAt (pointing to the place of a token). For the sake of brevity we leave out the edge labels (edge types can be inferred from the connected nodes). Fig. 1 shows a small Petri Net model using this schema with transitions T1 to T3, places P1 to P6 and some tokens.

For firing a transition, we have to match an enabled transition, i.e. a transition where all places in the preset have at least one token. When executing, we have to delete one token from each place in the preset and create a new token for each place in the postset. Preset and postset of the transition may be empty.

Set Nodes

Set nodes, available as obligatory and optional set nodes, offer non-homomorphic matching, i.e. multiple nodes from the working graph can be mapped to a single set node from the production. Set nodes are sufficient, if only one element in a rule is set-valued, but fall short with complex set-valency, where relationships

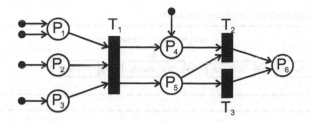

Fig. 1. Petri Net modeled according to the simple graph schema

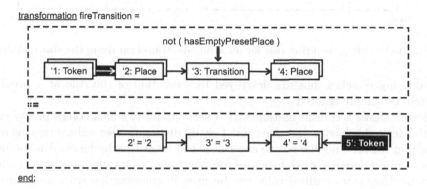

Fig. 2. Modeling the firing rule for an arbitrary transition using set nodes (invalid syntax elements are highlighted)

between sets of nodes have to be expressed, because there is no general and intuitive way to define edges between sets. Fig. 2 shows an imaginable way to declare a production for firing a transition, using only set nodes. The transition (node '3) is restricted to enabled transitions by the application restriction **not** (hasEmptyPresetPlace), which is declared outside the production. Additionally, it contains sets for preset and postset places as well as tokens.

But this declaration is not valid. Invalid elements are highlighted: PROGRES cannot match edges between set nodes, thus the edge between node '1 and '2 is invalid. Also it cannot create sets of nodes, hence node 5' is marked invalid. PROGRES can create edges between sets of nodes, but it creates an edge from each node of the source set to all nodes of the target set. Of course, this is not desired for the relation between places and tokens.

Star Qualifier

Another possibility to cover set-valency with productions is the star qualifier, which was introduced into PROGRES to execute productions in parallel. All PROGRES productions have a qualifier, determining the number of potential matches expected for this rule, nevertheless, the rule is executed only once. The star qualifier breaks this convention and causes the left-hand side to be matched to *all* potential matches in the working graph in parallel. The matching is then followed by (sequential) application of the right-hand side to all matches.

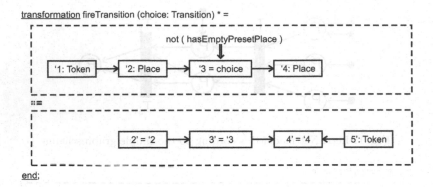

Fig. 3. Modeling the firing rule for an arbitrary transition using the star qualifier

Conflicting matches that are destroyed by execution of the rule at a previous match are simply ignored.

Fig. 3 shows a transformation with a star qualifier, which comes pretty close to the desired behavior, but one cannot easily distinguish set-valued regions from common regions and one has to determine the transition by hand. Additionally, this solution does not work for more complex rules, containing nested set-valued regions. How star-qualified rules can be used in combination with programmed rules to define complex patterns is described in Section 5.

Programmed Rules

However, besides productions, PROGRES offers programm d rules[1], so-called transactions[2]. For the programming of sequential or pseudo-parallel rules execution, one can use many different control structures. Besides conditional statements, there are loop statements (for_all and while) suited to deal with set-valency. Applying these statements allows complete handling of complex set-valued structures. Nevertheless, programming seemingly simple and intuitive rules containing set-valued structures, e.g. the firing of Petri Nets, turns out to be a complex and consequently error-prone task.

Thus when discussing about a specification, we ended up drawing rules like Fig. 4 by hand, using a notation resembling set nodes, but with internal structure. The meaning, denoting a production with arbitrary big sets of the marked structures, could be grasped easily as illustrated in Fig. 5. However, we always had to specify complicated transactions, which simulated the matching and parallel execution of the sketched rule.

Knowing amalgamated rules from algebraic approaches and the power of algorithmic transformation languages with a rich set of control structures, we will define a language construct similar to amalgamated transformations, which can be simulated with existing language elements.

---

[1] Programmed rules gave PROGRES its name: PROgrammed Graph REwriting System.

[2] The execution of programmed rules is transactional, hence their name.

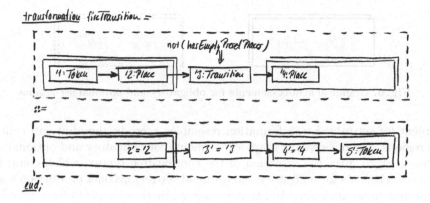

Fig. 4. Hand-drawn rule from our discussions about a set-valued transformation, sketching the firing of a Petri Net transition

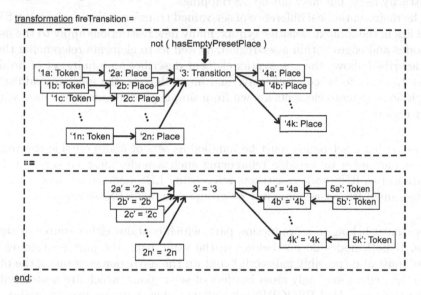

Fig. 5. Meaning of the rule from Fig. 4 with set-valued regions expanded

4   Syntax Definition and Semantics

In this section, we will introduce the notion of set-valued transformations, like the one presented in Fig. 4. A set-valued transformation defines an infinite set of productions that share some commonalities. The commonalities and differences should be easily identifiable.

4.1   Syntax

The syntax should allow easy and compact declaration of set-valued transformations in a production-like manner as sketched in Fig. 4. The new syntax

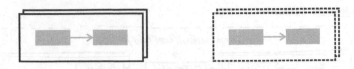

Fig. 6. Graphical syntax elements for obligatory and optional set-regions

element for set-valued transformation resembles a production, but can contain set-regions. Fig. 6 shows the graphical elements for obligatory and optional set-regions. Fig. 7 gives the extension of the context-free syntax, which comprises four new elements for obligatory and optional set-regions on a production's left-hand and right-hand side. Additionally, all syntactical elements from standard PROGRES that can contain the four new elements have to be redefined to reflect the addition. As the syntax definition implies, set-regions can be nested arbitrarily deep, but may not be overlapping.

The main syntactical difference of set-valued transformation declaration SVT-Decl lies in the context-sensitive syntax; many new restrictions apply to the usage of nodes and edges within a set-region, as well as to elements referencing them. As described above, the new syntax element describes an infinite set of productions. In order to be comprehensive and unambiguous, the following additional restrictions apply to elements known from simple productions, when used within a set-region.

Nodes within a set-region must be handled as sets of nodes outside the region, thus a parameter or variable referencing such a node, must be set-valued. In addition, two RHS node constructs referencing LHS node constructs contained in the same LHS set-region, must be grouped in one RHS set-region.

Edges must belong to a production part, which contains either source or target node. If both nodes do not belong to the same part, the part containing one node, must also (possibly indirectly) contain the set-region containing the other node. I.e., edges may only cross borders of set-regions, which are nested within each other. Standard PROGRES also allows edges between two set-nodes, but only on the RHS, creating edges from each node of the one set to all nodes of the other set (yielding an unambiguous *set semantics* according to [1]). Such a definition is not (yet[3]) supported by our implementation and prohibited with this constraint. Nevertheless, this constraint still allows the definition of tree structures using nested set-regions, which are unambiguous due to the concrete nesting.

---

[3] We have considered edges between hierarchically not related sets of nodes and it would be possible to define unambiguous (nevertheless non-deterministic) set-semantics for these edges and implement that with our simulation approach. But the semantics would not be intuitively understandable and the structure of the (non-deterministically) matched set of nodes, would be very dependent on the chosen matching strategy. Thus we decided to prohibit this kind of edges.

OblSetRegionDecl ::=   "set_region" "="
                            OptSVTLeftSideList
                         "end" ";" ;
OptSetRegionDecl ::=   "opt_set_region" "="
                            OptSVTLeftSideList
                         "end" ";" ;

OblOldSetRegionDecl ::= "set_region" "="
                            OptSVTRightSideList
                         "end" ";" ;
OptOldSetRegionDecl ::= "opt_set_region" "="
                            OptSVTRightSideList
                         "end" ";" ;

SVTDecl ::=   "setvalued_transformation" DeclSVTId FormParPart "="
                            SVTBody
                         "end" ";" ;
SVTBody ::=   [**SVTGraphPart**] [OptAttCondList] [OptEmbList]
                         [OptAttTransferList] [OptReturnList] ;
SVTGraphPart ::=   **OptSVTLeftSideList** "::=" **OptSVTRightSideList** ;

OptSVTLeftSideList ::=   {**SVTLeftSideClause**} **SVTLeftSideClause** ;
SVTLeftSideClause ::=   NodeDecl | EdgeDecl | SetNodeDecl | · · ·
                         | **OblSetRegionDecl** | **OptSetRegionDecl** ;
OptSVTRightSideList ::= {**SVTRightSideClause**} **SVTRightSideClause** ;
SVTRightSideClause ::=   OldNodeDecl | NewNodeDecl | NewEdgeDecl
                         | **OblOldSetRegionDecl** | **OptOldSetRegionDecl** ;

Fig. 7. Context-free syntax extension for set-valued transformations

4.2 Semantics

A set-valued transformation describes a set of productions that can be constructed from the description by extending the minimal contained production
by arbitrarily multiplying the set-regions. We will not formally define the construction of this set, because the set is infinite and thus cannot be constructed
in advance; we will only outline the construction.

A PROGRES specification is formally defined by a set of first order logic
formulae, which can be divided into subsets belonging to different syntactical
regions according to the syntactical element defining the formulae, i.e. if a syntactical element is internally structured by other syntactical elements, the set of
formulae can be divided into subsets according to the syntactical structure.

In order to construct a production from the set, the formulae from the set-
regions can be multiplied. While multiplying the formulae, the ones defining
the element names have to be rewritten to give each element a distinct name.
The edges crossing region borders are called the region's *interface*. In addition
to the elements from the set-region, the formulae for the region's interface also

have to be multiplied, obeying the above mentioned renaming of the elements within the region.

The execution semantics of a set-valued transformation is defined as the semantics of the maximum production applicable to a subgraph containing a non-deterministically chosen match of the minimum production.

The maximum production out of the set is defined as follows: The production P ∈ SVT is maximal with respect to an initial match M, if P matches a subgraph covering M and if there is no other matching production in SVT covering M, which can be constructed out of P using the extension from SVT.

This definition is quite similar to the semantics definition of the existing PROGRES set nodes and guarantees a maximum match while maintaining the desired non-determinism. E.g., when firing a Petri Net transition, the expected behavior of the transformation is to remove a token from each place in the preset and put a new token into each place of the postset for a non-deterministically chosen enabled transition, thus the defined execution semantics.

5   Implementation

Because the set of productions defined by a set-valued transformation is infinite, the set cannot be generated completely in advance. Instead, the adequate maximum production has to be generated at execution time according to the initial match for the minimal production. Once the maximum production is generated according to the description from Section 4.2, it can be applied just like a regular production. This idea is very similar to the concept of amalgamated graph transformations as proposed for double-pushout approaches in [21].

This approach can be implemented for the PROGRES interpreter fairly straight-forward, but on the one hand is the monolithic PROGRES application not well extensible and on the other hand adapting the interpreter would leave most prototype editors specified with PROGRES without the new construct, because they run on generated code.

Thus we decided to implement the new construct with the help of a preprocessor, which converts a PROGRES specification containing the new construct for set-valued transformations into a specification using only standard constructs. As proclaimed in Section 3, PROGRES with its rich set of control structures, has already all language features to handle set-valency sufficiently. Hence it should be possible to replace each set-valued transformation by a transaction, which simulates the desired behavior.

The transactions simulating set-valued transformations all work in two phases, in a first phase, the matching of a maximum production is simulated, in the second phase the rule application is simulated.

Matching

The matching is done by marking partial matches for the nodes within set-regions. New markers are inserted, until no more extending partial matches can be found. The markers are structured according to the nesting structure of the

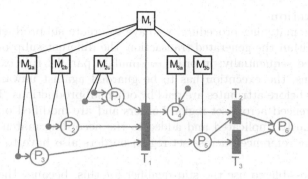

Fig. 8. Matching structure of the set-valued transformation from Fig. 4 applied to the Petri Net example from Fig. 1

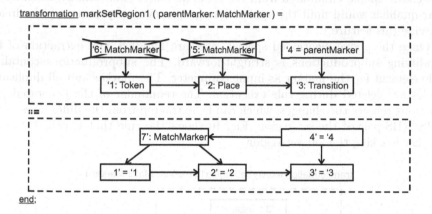

Fig. 9. Marking production for the left set-region from Fig. 4

set-regions. Fig. 8 shows an example matching of the set-valued transformation from Fig. 4 applied to the Petri Net example from Fig. 1.

For the sake of an easy and well-understandable implementation, we insert the markers temporarily into the working graph. For this we have to amend the graph schema and introduce a MatchMarker node type. In order to avoid changing the working graph, one would have to create a data structure for the matches, which is local to the generated transaction and supports the desired injective matching.

For each set-region we have to create one marking rule. The marking rules can easily be extracted from the set-valued transformation. Fig. 9 shows the marking rule for the left set-region from Fig. 4. Besides the contents of the set-region itself, it contains the nodes belonging to the regions interface (edges crossing the regions borders) and the marker of the embedding transformation part, which is inserted as input parameter to the matching production. This rule is applied within a loop until no more matches can be found.

Rule Application

Similar to the matching procedure, we have to create subproductions for each set-region. Within the generated transaction, the different subproductions have to be executed sequentially; in order to simulate parallel rule execution of all subproductions, the execution has to be guarded against unwanted attribute modifications before attributes are read by other subproductions. Thus all nodes that are referenced across set-region borders and are modified or deleted have to be temporarily duplicated and added to the according match marker. New nodes that are referenced across set-region borders also have to be created in advance.

It is not possible to use the star-qualifier for this, because the execution of star-qualified rules in PROGRES is only pseudo-parallel and previously found matches that are altered by the execution of the rule for another simultaneous match are simple eliminated from the set of matches. Additionally, usage of the star-qualifier would limit the approach to graph rewrite systems, which already provide this feature.

Once the above-mentioned special cases are handled, the extraction of the modifying subproductions is straight-forward. The subproductions contain a rule element for the marker as input parameter. The marker and all duplicated nodes are deleted during rule execution. The remainder of the generated productions reflects the changes, which can be extracted from the differences of the LHS/RHS-pair of the set-region. Fig. 10 shows the rule that is called for each marker marking the left set-region.

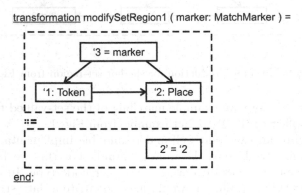

transformation modifySetRegion1 (marker: MatchMarker) =

'3 = marker

'1: Token ———→ '2: Place

::=

2' = '2

end;

Fig. 10. Production executing the modifications for the left set-region from Fig. 4

A similar implementation could be used to implement a language construct for set-valued transformations in other graph transformation languages offering a rich set of control structures, e.g. Fujaba [10,11].

The above preprocessor implementation together with analyzes for the syntax directed editor is not yet incorporated into the standard PROGRES application, but can be run externally. The resulting specifications look very similar to the previous specifications, which contained hand-coded set-valued transformations. The performance of the generated transformations could be improved by not changing the working graph for the matching procedure, but rather generating a local data structure to hold the match. In a similar way it would be possible to eliminate the temporary duplication of modified nodes, which are referenced external to the modifying region. With this implementation the simulation approach would perform similar to a native implementation in the PROGRES interpreter and generator. Because we use PROGRES mainly for the specification of complex editing commands in interactive model editor prototypes, performance is not really an issue. Thus we settled for the better understandable solution, rather than the better performing one. The main drawback of the simulation approach at the moment is, that it is not seamlessly integrated in the PROGRES specification editor and that debugging a generated specification using the interpreter is not well supported.

6   Conclusion

We have introduced a notion of set-valued transformations for algorithmic graph transformation languages by defining their syntax and semantics. The syntax was chosen to be very similar to that of simple productions. But a set-valued transformation can contain a new syntax element, *set regions* that mimic the use of set nodes, known from the PROGRES syntax, but have an internal structure. The semantics was defined as infinite set of simple productions, which can be constructed from the transformation definition by arbitrarily multiplying the set regions. We also showed, how this behavior can be simulated by a PROGRES transaction generated from the transformation definition.

The approach proved to be viable and should also be applicable to other algorithmic graph transformation languages that offer a rich set of control structures. An implementation for Fujaba should be possible without many problems.

As future extension, a region construct solely for a rules right-hand side, comparable to a NewNodeDecl, creating a new set-valued pattern could be interesting, but the binding of the set size remains an issue. Also the definition of a general region construct seems interesting, it could then be easily used for further extensions like recursive transformation rules, that are urgently required in related fields [15]. Since PROGRES already offers recursive transformation calls within transactions, it would be no problem to simulate the semantics of a new syntactical element for recursive transformations very similar to the approach shown in this paper.

References

1. Agrawal, A., Karsai, G., Neema, S., Shi, F., Vizhanyo, A.: The design of a language for model transformations. Journal on Software and System Modeling 5(3), 261–288 (2006)
2. Balasubramanian, D., Narayanan, A., Neema, S., Ness, B., Shi, F., Thibodeaux, R., Karsai, G.: Applying a grouping operator in model transformations. In: Schürr, A., Nagl, M., Zündorf, A. (eds.) AGTIVE 2007. LNCS, vol. 5088. Springer, Heidelberg (2008)

3. Balasubramanian, D., Narayanan, A., Neema, S., Shi, F., Thibodeaux, R., Karsai, G.: A subgraph operator for graph transformation languages. In: Margaria, et al. (eds.) [18], pp. 95–106
4. Bardohl, R., Taentzer, G., Minas, M., Schürr, A.: Application of Graph Transformation to Visual Languages, vol. 2, pp. 105–180. World Scientific, Singapore (1999)
5. Bauderon, M., Courcelle, B.: Graph expressions and graph rewritings. Technical report, University Bordeaux, Department of Mathematics and Informatics, TR 8525 (1985)
6. Corradini, A., Ehrig, H., Heckel, R., Korff, M., Löwe, M., Ribeiro, L., Wagner, A.: Algebraic Approaches to Graph Transformation – Part I: Basic Concepts and Double Pushout Approach, vol. 1, pp. 163–245. World Scientific, Singapore (1997)
7. Courcelle, B.: A representation of graphs by algebraic expressions and its use for graph rewriting systems. In: Ehrig, et al. (eds.) [8], pp. 112–132
8. Ehrig, H., Nagl, M., Rosenfeld, A., Rozenberg, G. (eds.): Graph Grammars 1986. LNCS, vol. 291. Springer, Heidelberg (1987)
9. Engels, G., Lewerentz, C., Schäfer, W.: Graph grammar engineering: A software specification method. In: Ehrig, et al. (eds.) [8], pp. 186–201
10. Fischer, T., Niere, J., Torunski, L., Zündorf, A.: Story Diagrams: A new graph rewrite language based on the Unified Modeling Language. In: Ehrig, H., Engels, G., Kreowski, H.-J., Rozenberg, G. (eds.) TAGT 1998. LNCS, vol. 1764, pp. 296–309. Springer, Heidelberg (2000)
11. Fujaba – From UML to Java and Back Again (1999), http://www.fujaba.de/
12. Fuss, C., Mosler, C., Ranger, U., Schultchen, E.: The jury is still out: A comparison of agg, fujaba, and progres. In: Margaria, et al. (eds.) [18], pp. 183–195
13. Guerra, E., de Lara, J.: Adding recursion to graph transformation. In: Margaria, et al. (eds.) [18], pp. 107–120
14. Karsai, G., Agrawal, A., Shi, F., Sprinkle, J.: On the use of graph transformation in the formal specification of model interpreters. Journal of Universal Computer Science 9(11), 1296–1321 (2003)
15. Körtgen, A.-T.: Modeling successively connected repetitive subgraphs. In: Schürr, A., Nagl, M., Zündorf, A. (eds.) AGTIVE 2007. LNCS, vol. 5088. Springer, Heidelberg (2008)
16. Lewerentz, C.: Interaktives Entwerfen großer Programmsysteme. PhD-Thesis, RWTH Aachen, IFB 194 (1988)
17. Lindqvist, J., Lundkvist, T., Porres, I.: A query language with the star operator. In: Margaria, et al. (eds.) [18], pp. 69–80
18. Margaria, T., Padberg, J., Taentzer, G. (eds.): Proc. of the 6th International Workshop on Graph Transformation and Visual Modeling Techniques (GT-VMT 2007), Braga, Portugal. Electronic Communications of the EASST, vol. 6 (March 2007)
19. Nagl, M.: Graph-Grammatiken: Theorie, Anwendungen, Implementierung. Vieweg Verlag (1979)
20. Schürr, A.: Operationales Spezifizieren mit programmierten Graphersetzungssystemen. Deutscher Universitätsverlag, Wiesbaden, Doctoral Dissertation (1991)
21. Taentzer, G.: Parallel and distributed graph transformation: Formal description and application to communication-based systems. Doctoral dissertation, Technische Universität Berlin (1996)
22. Taentzer, G.: AGG: A tool environment for algebraic graph transformation. In: Münch, M., Nagl, M. (eds.) AGTIVE 1999. LNCS, vol. 1779, pp. 481–488. Springer, Heidelberg (2000)

23. Taentzer, G., Beyer, M.: Amalgamated graph transformations and their use for specifying agg - an algebraic graph grammar system. In: Dagstuhl Seminar on Graph Transformations in Computer Science, pp. 380–394 (1993)
24. Taentzer, G., Ehrig, K., Guerra, E., de Lara, J., Lengyel, L., Levendovszky, T., Prange, U., Varró, D., Varró-Gyapay, S.: Model Transformation by Graph Transformation: A Comparative Study. In: Proceedings of the International Workshop on Model Transformations in Practice, MTiP 2005 (Satellite Event of MoDELS 2005), Montego Bay, Jamaica (2005)
25. Varró, G., Schürr, A., Varró, D.: Benchmarking for graph transformation. In: 2005 IEEE Symposium on Visual Languages and Human-Centric Computing (VL/HCC), pp. 79–88. IEEE Computer Society, Los Alamitos (2005)

Recursive Graph Pattern Matching*

(With Magic Sets and Global Search Plans)

Gergely Varró[1], Ákos Horváth[2], and Dániel Varró[2]

[1] Department of Computer Science and Information Theory
Budapest University of Technology and Economics
gervarro@cs.bme.hu
[2] Department of Measurement and Information Systems
Budapest University of Technology and Economics
{ahorvath,varro}@mit.bme.hu

Abstract. We present core data structures and algorithms for matching graph patterns with general recursion. Our approach uses magic sets, a well-known technique from deductive databases, which combines fixpoint-based bottom-up query evaluation with top-down handling of input parameters. Furthermore, this technique is enhanced with the global search plans, thus non-recursive calls are always flattened before elementary pattern matching operations are initiated in order to improve performance. Our approach is exemplified using VIATRA2.

1 Introduction

Graph transformation (GT) [1] is a frequently used means to capture model transformations in the context of model-driven software development. Graph transformation rules provide a declarative, rule and pattern-based language for specifying both interlanguage and intra-language model manipulations for model analysis, refactoring or simulation.

GT rules consist of a left-hand side (LHS) and a right-hand side (RHS) graph pattern. The LHS specifies contextual conditions which should hold as a precondition for applying the rule, which is checked by graph pattern matching. Then the model is manipulated by calculating the difference of the RHS and the LHS in the model.

However, in order to design complex transformations, the core GT formalism has been extended to address reusability or maintainability. For instance, graph transformation units [2], modules [3] or programs [4, 5] have been introduced where elementary GT rules are enriched with control structures.

An alternate, and more declarative way for reusability has also been introduced (in systems like VIATRA2 [6] or Tefkat [7]) where graph patterns are stand-alone concepts, which can be assembled into more complex patterns and/or transformation rules by pattern composition (or pattern call). This concept is quite similar to other popular

---

* This work was partially supported by the SENSORIA European IP (IST-3-016004), the Hungarian National Research Fund and the National Office for Research and Technology (grant No. 67651, OTKA), and the János Bolyai scholarship.

A. Schürr, M. Nagl, and A. Zündorf (Eds.): AGTIVE 2007, LNCS 5088, pp. 456–470, 2008.

declarative formalisms in logic programming or deductive database systems (like Prolog or Datalog), where basic facts and complex predicates are treated identically when evaluating a query. A key performance issue when matching graph patterns in case of pattern composition is to generate a single global search plan for the flattened pattern, which is discussed in [8].

A natural extension for pattern-level reuse is to allow recursive calls in case of pattern composition, i.e., when a predefined graph pattern may call itself or other patterns recursively. Investigating recursion in graph transformation rules has recently become very popular with several approaches [9, 10] targeting mainly its specification aspects. However, these approaches mostly assume simple recursion where a pattern may call itself only once in a single execution branch.

In the current paper, we make only a single, very general assumption on recursion, namely, parameters of negative application conditions must be bound at the time of their invocation , but otherwise arbitrary recursive calls are allowed. As the main contribution, we define data structures and sketch core algorithms how recursive graph patterns can be matched based upon *magic sets* [11], a well-known technique from deductive databases, which combines fixpoint-based bottom-up query evaluation with top-down handling of input parameters. Furthermore, this technique is enhanced with the global search plans of [8, 12] thus non-recursive calls are always flattened before elementary pattern matching operations are initiated to improve performance.

The remainder is structured as follows. First, Section 2 briefly introduces a combined graph-based representation for models and metamodels used in the paper (and in the VIATRA2 framework). Then Section 3 describes the overview of our approach, while Section 4 and Section 5 propose our data structures and algorithms used in the compile and run-time phases of the recursive pattern matcher, respectively. Related work is discussed in Section 6, while Section 7 concludes our paper.

2 Background

First we informally introduce models, metamodels and graph patterns used in the paper, using the object-relational mapping defined in the model transformation contest of [13] as a running example. This transformation was captured by graph transformation rules using recursive patterns in [7, 14].

2.1 VIATRA Models and Metamodels

Metamodeling provides the structural definition (i.e., abstract syntax) of modeling languages.

In the paper, we use a unified directed graph representation [6] which stores metamodels and models in a combined model space. Intuitively, the morphisms from instance nodes (and edges) to their respective node (edge) types are stored explicitly in our graph model. As a summary, nodes represent basic concepts of a (modeling) domain, while edges represent the relationships between model elements. This unified graph representation serves as the underlying model of the VIATRA2 framework.

This way, graph nodes (called entities in VIATRA2, depicted as a rectangle in Fig. 1) uniformly represent MOF packages, classes, or objects on different metalevels, while graph edges with identities (called relations in VIATRA2, depicted as a solid line in Fig. 1) denote MOF association ends, attributes, link ends, and slots in a uniform way. Nodes are arranged into a strict containment hierarchy to denote model element containment either on the metamodel or model-level.

Example 1. Figure 1 presents the joint representation of a simplified UML metamodel and an instance model. The metamodel is depicted on the right side. Both the classes of the metamodel (such as cls, assoc, etc.) and the objects of the instance model (such as car, plt) uniformly appear as nodes (entities), while relations between nodes are illustrated by solid edges.

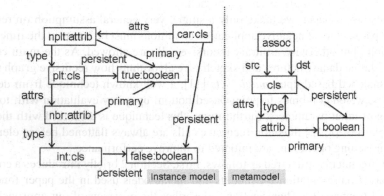

Fig. 1. Sample instance model and metamodel

2.2 Graph Patterns

Graph transformation (GT) is a rule and pattern-based paradigm frequently used for describing model transformations. A graph transformation rule contains a left-hand side graph LHS (or graph pattern) and a right-hand side graph RHS, and (one or more) negative application condition graphs (NAC) connected to LHS. Graph patterns (precondition pattern) consist of the LHS pattern, the NAC pattern, and the mapping between them. They are describe by pattern bodies consist of a set of constraints that have to be fulfilled by a model to apply graph transformation rule. In order to define recursive pattern we allow alternate (OR) *pattern bodies* for a pattern, with a meaning that the pattern is fulfilled if at least one of its bodies is fulfilled.

As different graph transformation languages allow different language constraints (e.g., containment between model elements), in the following we use the constraints of the VIATRA2 framework containing (i) *structural constraints* prescribing the existence of nodes and edges of a given type, (ii) *check constraints* capturing term evaluation over the attributes of the matched elements (using the check keyword), and (iii) *pattern invocation constraints* allowing pattern composition (invocation) of other patterns supported in a declarative way (using the find keyword). The semantics of this reference is similar to that of the declarative Horn clauses, where the caller pattern can be fulfilled only if their local constructs can be matched, and if the pattern invoked with the *actual parameters* is also fulfilled.

Example 2. The graphical and VIATRA2 textual representation of the graph patterns of the object-relational mapping are depicted in Fig. 2, 3, and 4. Both `classHasAttr` and `classHasIncludedAttr` contain all recursive features offered by VIATRA2, from which we use `classHasAttr` as our running example. The meaning and purpose of the `classHasAttr` that a `Cls` "has" an `Attr` for the purpose of the mapping if, (i) it is directly owned and a primitive type, or (ii) a referenced `Cls` (via an `Attr` or an `Assoc`) "has" the `Attr`, or (iii) the children of the `Cls` "have" the `Attr`. Informally the meaning of the `classHasIncludedAttr` to map additional attributes along references and inheritance, while `classHasReference` is a helper pattern for matching "references" (attributes and associations) between classes.

The *pattern* `classHasAttr` contains three *formal parameters*: `Cls`, `Attr` and `Key`, and it consists of three pattern bodies. The first body prescribes that there exists a `Cls` class with an `Attr` attribute, which has a `Boolean` value `Key` denoting whether attribute `Attr` is a primary key. The second prescribes the `classHasIncludedAttr` pattern invocation with formal parameters (`Cls`, `Attr`, `Key`) of the caller pattern as actual parameters (depicted by grey boxes on the invoked pattern). The last body prescribes three constraints: (i) there exists two classes `SubCls` and `Cls` with a parent relation between them, (ii) the `classHasAttr` pattern invocation where the first parameter is the local `SubCls` element (depicted by dashed line), while the two other (`Attr` and `Key`) are the formal parameters of the caller pattern, and (iii) that the value of `Key` is false.

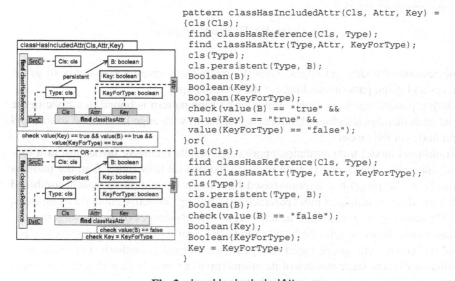

```
pattern classHasIncludedAttr(Cls, Attr, Key) =
{cls(Cls);
 find classHasReference(Cls, Type);
 find classHasAttr(Type,Attr, KeyForType);
 cls(Type);
 cls.persistent(Type, B);
 Boolean(B);
 Boolean(Key);
 Boolean(KeyForType);
 check(value(B) == "true" &&
 value(Key) == "true" &&
 value(KeyForType) == "false");
}or{
 cls(Cls);
 find classHasReference(Cls, Type);
 find classHasAttr(Type, Attr, KeyForType);
 cls(Type);
 cls.persistent(Type, B);
 Boolean(B);
 check(value(B) == "false");
 Boolean(Key);
 Boolean(KeyForType);
 Key = KeyForType;
}
```

Fig. 2. classHasIncludedAttr pattern

2.3   Graph Pattern Matching

The most critical step of graph transformation is graph pattern matching, i.e., to find a matching of the LHS pattern in the model, that is not invalidated by a matching of the negative application condition graph NAC, which prohibits the presence of certain

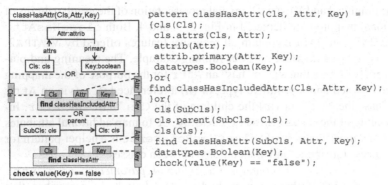

```
pattern classHasAttr(Cls, Attr, Key) =
{cls(Cls);
 cls.attrs(Cls, Attr);
 attrib(Attr);
 attrib.primary(Attr, Key);
 datatypes.Boolean(Key);
}or{
find classHasIncludedAttr(Cls, Attr, Key);
}or{
 cls(SubCls);
 cls.parent(SubCls, Cls);
 cls(Cls);
 find classHasAttr(SubCls, Attr, Key);
 datatypes.Boolean(Key);
 check(value(Key) == "false");
}
```

Fig. 3. classHasAttr pattern

```
pattern classHasReference(SrcC, DstC) =
{cls(SrcC);
 cls.attrs(SrcC, A);
 attrib(A);
 attrib.type(A, DstC);
 cls(DstC);
}or{
 assoc(Assoc);
 cls(SrcC);
 assoc.src(Assoc, SrcC);
 cls(DstC);
 assoc.dest(Assoc, DstC);
}
```

Fig. 4. classHasReference pattern

combinations of nodes and edges. Thus we restrict our investigations only to graph patterns and graph pattern matching for the current paper.

During pattern matching each variable of a graph pattern is bound to a node in the model such that this matching (binding) is consistent with edge labels, and source and target nodes of the model.

Traditional model transformation approaches handle recursive invocation in a top-down imperative way, usually integrated into the control flow rather than the patterns themselves. We propose a fixpoint-based bottom-up evaluation approach combined with a top-down handling of input parameters following deductive database techniques. As [11] states, such a technique benefits from the advantages (e.g., convergence detection, strong focus on relevant facts) of both the semi-naive bottom-up and the traditional top-down style, queue-based rule/goal tree expansion methods. Furthermore, it terminates after the same number of iterations (up to a constant factor), and it provenly produces [11] the same results as the others.

3   Overview of the Approach

The proposed workflow of implementing recursive graph pattern matching is summarized in Fig. 5.

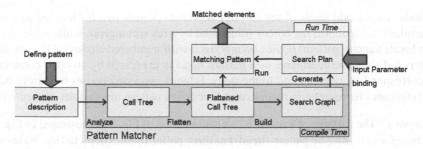

Fig. 5. Overview of the recursive pattern matching approach

We separate compile time parts from run-time parts, where each part consists of the following steps:

- At compile time each step is calculated once for each pattern description.
    - First, for each pattern description a *call tree* is generated capturing how patterns call other patterns.
    - Then for each *call tree flattened patterns* are generated. The use of flattened patterns allows the optimization of pattern matching in a global scope (e.g., edges that are defined in different patterns can be traversed one after the other).
    - For each *flattened pattern* a corresponding *search graph* is generated. The search graph is glued from the patterns of the flattened pattern body according to the passed parameters of the calls.
- After initializing the previous data structures at compile time, run-time steps have to be calculated for each separate pattern invocation.
    - *Search plan* is generated from the *search graph* based on the parameter binding to drive the pattern matching process.
    - Then matchings are calculated by an iterative bottom-up recursion evaluation using magic sets, helping the pattern matcher to focus only on matches relevant to the input parameter binding.

4   Compile Time Steps of the Recursive Pattern Matcher

In this section we briefly introduce the data structures and algorithms needed for the compile time tasks of the recursive pattern matcher.

4.1   Call Tree

A *call tree* is a directed bipartite tree describing the structural dependencies of a given pattern. It is constructed by a traversal process, which explores the possible body alternatives of a pattern and all the pattern invocations in a depth first manner.

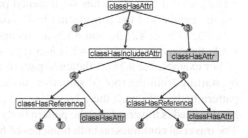

Fig. 6. Call tree of the classHasAttr graph pattern

Nodes on the odd levels of the call tree represent *pattern heads* (denoted as simple rectangles) and (pattern) *references* (illustrated by grey rectangles), while nodes on the even levels denote (pattern) *bodies* (symbolized with numbered circles). The fact that a *body* is a disjunctive alternative of a *pattern head* is expressed by an edge connecting the corresponding *pattern head* to the *body*. Edges connecting bodies to pattern heads and references represent non-recursive and recursive pattern invocations, respectively.

Example 3. The call tree of pattern classHasAttr of Fig. 3 is illustrated in Fig. 6.

The classHasAttr pattern (head) has three pattern bodies depicted by circles with numbers 1, 2 and 3. Pattern body 2 invokes the classHasIncludedAttr pattern head which has pattern bodies 4 and 5. Both of these bodies have similar sub-trees, as they differ only in the check constraint. The classHasReference contains two pattern bodies, and contained twice in the *call tree* as it is invoked separately from 4 and 5.

4.2 Flattening

In order to provide better performance for pattern matching, we use search plan optimization techniques, where optimization can be considered as a process that orders constraints to provide an efficient evaluation plan for their run-time execution.

As current optimization techniques [4, 12, 8] have been developed for non-recursive use, they operate on the scope of pattern bodies, which means that a separate optimization procedure is executed for the set of constraints defined by a given body. This approach often results in poor search plans for a recursive pattern matcher due to the lack of global view for the optimizer on the overall set of structural constraints.

In order to get better search plans, the operation scope of the optimizer module is increased by flattening the call tree and by merging pattern bodies and recursive invocations resulting in a larger set of constraints to be processed by the optimizer.

In the flattening process each pattern body or pattern reference node is recursively merged to the closest ancestor pattern body and mapped to *flattened pattern bodies* (FPB). As a result, a *flattened call tree* is obtained in which the new flattened pattern bodies are direct children of the root pattern head node.

Example 4. The flattened version of the call tree of Fig. 3 is depicted in Fig. 7. The classHasAttr pattern has six flattened pattern bodies denoted by vectors, containing the numbers of the constituting body nodes. The flattened pattern bodies (#2460, #2470, #2580, #2590 and #30) are recursive as depicted by grey square with circle, while flattened pattern body #1 is non-recursive.

For example the #2460 flattened pattern is constructed by starting from the root (disjunctive) node selecting the pattern body 2. From 2 the classHasIncludedAttr pattern head is traversed and the pattern body 4 is selected. The traversal continues on both branches of body 4 adding pattern body 6 and classHasAttr pattern call to the flattened pattern.

Fig. 7. Flattened patterns

4.3 Search Graph

Informally a *search graph* is a common representation of constraints (e.g., there is a relation between two elements) that drives the pattern matching process. For each flattened pattern body a separate *search graph* is generated, where a search graph is built by merging the constraint of the contained pattern bodies of a flattened pattern body, i.e., all formal parameters of the invoked pattern head are substituted with the corresponding actual parameters of the caller.

Example 5. For easier readability an extract of the search graph — without all constraints — of #2460 from Fig. 7 is depicted on the left side of Fig. 8, with the simplified VIATRA2 textual representation on the right hand side.

The search graph created from the combination of pattern bodies 2, 4, 6 and the pattern reference classHasAttr contains 7 entities all denoted as rectangles. Relations are captured by solid lines (e.g., attrs relation source is Cls), while binding between the actual and formal parameters of the recursive invocation are highlighted by dashed lines between the corresponding elements (e.g., Type is the actual parameter of the Cls formal parameter). While passing the formal parameter Attr of the caller pattern is denoted by a dotted box.

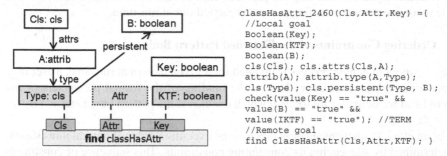

```
classHasAttr_2460(Cls,Attr,Key) ={
  //Local goal
  Boolean(Key);
  Boolean(KTF);
  Boolean(B);
  cls(Cls); cls.attrs(Cls,A);
  attrib(A); attrib.type(A,Type);
  cls(Type); cls.persistent(Type, B);
  check(value(Key) == "true" &&
  value(B) == "true" &&
  value(IKTF) == "true"); //TERM
  //Remote goal
  find classHasAttr(Cls,Attr,KTF); }
```

Fig. 8. Search graph of classHasAttr flattened pattern #2460

In order to present our concepts, we use an intuitive database like notation, where *search graphs* are defined as a set of natural joins over tables formed by the structural and invocation constraints of the FPB, while check constraints are mapped to filters on matching candidates. Tables defined for entities and relations (structural constraints) are illustrated with tables of one and two columns, respectively, while pattern references and heads are captured by tables containing a column for each formal and actual parameter of the pattern. Note that, pattern references and heads of the same pattern are mapped to the same table.

This representation allows to define the matching process as a least-fix point evaluation $(table of matchings = lfp(structural constraints \bowtie pattern reference))$ over the joined tables, where the $table of matchings$ holds the matchings of the invoked pattern head.

As a result this representation pin-points the crucial parts of recursive pattern matching, namely (i) optimized ordering of natural joins, and (ii) effective evaluation of least-fix points for which our solutions are introduced in Sec. 5.

Example 6. The extract database like representation of Fig. 8 is depicted in Fig. 9. Structured constraints (boxed in dashed line) are illustrated by tables of one and two columns, where the first row holds the type of the element, while the second represents the corresponding name of the involved search graph elements (e.g., the attrs table with two columns represent the attrs relation between the Cls and A entities). While the classHasAttr pattern recursive invocation is captured by a table of rows Type, Attr, and KFT. Finally, the search graph described as a least-fix point evaluation is $classHasAttr = lfp(structuralconstraints \bowtie classHasAtrr)$.

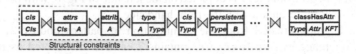

Fig. 9. Natural join representation of the classHasAttr pattern

5 Run-Time Behavior of the Recursive Pattern Matcher

After calculating and initializing the previous data structures at compile time, the rest of the recursive pattern matching process is carried out at run-time.

5.1 Ordering Constraints of the Flattened Pattern Body

When a pattern matching process is initiated for a given pattern at run-time, a user may supply input parameters. Depending on the binding of the formal parameters of the pattern head we define an *adornment* which denotes if the pattern parameter is bound (B) or free (F).

For an efficient query evaluation process, the execution order of natural joins should be determined by sequencing its constituting constraints. This sequence of constraints in a flattened pattern body is called a *search plan*, and it is produced by the algorithms of [12, 8], which also use the adornment information during the generation process.

5.2 Recursion Evaluation Techniques

Approaches for efficiently calculating the fix-point for the table of matchings can be categorized as follows.

The queue-based top-down recursion evaluation technique performs a breadth-first traversal for collecting matchings by alternately using the flattened call tree and navigating along pattern invocation constraints to explore the recursion in depth. As an advantage, this technique is able to focus only on exactly those "relevant" matchings that can provide solution for the actual binding of the pattern head at the topmost recursion level. On the other hand, as the matchings found in a deeper level of recursion are always immediately propagated upwards by performing a series of natural joins, this approach requires the proper maintenance of the pattern heads that have actually been invoked during the traversal including one local copy for their actual bindings and one for their matchings resulting in a decentralized solution.

The bottom-up recursion evaluation technique directly follows the fixpoint calculation approach, and in this sense, it iteratively extends one global table of matchings by repeatedly evaluating the query of each flattened pattern body. As a consequence, compared to the top-down approach, queries are executed fewer times and on larger blocks of data resulting in a faster solution. On the other hand, the bottom-up technique always calculates all matchings independently of the initial bindings, which unavoidably produces a table of matchings that is significantly larger than the final result set.

5.3 Magic Sets

In order to preserve the fast and centralized bottom-up evaluation technique and to simultaneously minimize the gap between the number of calculated matchings and the size of the final result set, the concept of magic sets is introduced, which helps avoiding the generation (and temporary storage) of irrelevant matchings by restricting calculations only on such input parameters that might be produced during the actual pattern matching process.

For each pattern head, a *magic set (MS) table* is allocated, which stores such tuples of the bound parameters of the pattern head that have ever been passed downwards (i.e., to a deeper level of recursion) as input parameters during the evaluation. Note that the adornment (or binding pattern) of the pattern head determines, which columns must be contained by the magic set.

A *magic set transformation* is performed to introduce the MS table in the query calculation by placing it into the first (i.e., leftmost) position. Additionally, queries for extending the MS table are defined. As it is difficult to give a short and intuitive explanation for specifying these queries, the process of MS table extension is only exemplified in the current paper.

5.4 Execution

Recursive graph pattern matching is an iterative process, in which a fix-point is calculated for each MS table and each table of matchings.

Tuples can be classified based on the number of iterations passed since they got into a given table. Based on this categorization, tuples that joined just before the current iteration are called *recent*. All other tuples already contained by the tables are referred as *old*. Tuples being calculated in the current iteration are called *new*.

The exact process of fix-point calculation is as follows.

– **Initialization.** The table of matchings is initially empty, and the MS table is initialized with a single recent tuple containing the input parameters of the original pattern invocation.
– **Calculation tasks of each iteration.** In each iteration, all queries are executed once to possibly generate new tuples for the MS table and the table of matchings, which, in turn, represent new input parameters passed downwards and new matchings passed upwards, respectively. In order to avoid unnecessary recalculations on old tuples, only recent tuples of the MS table and the table of matchings are involved in the natural joins. The tuples calculated by the natural joins are filtered

by check constraints. If all the constraints are fulfilled, then the result tuple is projected on the formal parameters of the pattern head, and scheduled to be added to the corresponding table as a new tuple.

- **Synchronization after each iteration.** Synchronization is performed after each iteration by an ageing process, which (i) keeps old tuples, (ii) makes all recent tuples old, (iii) collects new tuples from flattened pattern bodies, (iv) adds these new tuples to the corresponding table, if they are not yet contained, and (v) marks all the collected new tuples recent.
- **Termination.** Pattern matching is terminated when neither the MS table, nor the table of matchings is extended during an iteration. Based on analogy to [15], termination can be guaranteed, if negative application condition checks are invoked only with bound parameters, which is typically fulfilled in graph transformation approaches.
- **Postprocessing.** Finally, in a postprocessing phase, the table of matchings is filtered by checking whether the result tuples in the bound parameter positions match the input parameters passed at the original pattern invocation.

Example 7. The iterative pattern matching process is illustrated in Fig. 10. It calculates such matchings for pattern head `classhasAttr`, in which formal parameters `Cls` and `Key` are bound to `car` and `true`, respectively.

Each subfigure shows (i) the table of matchings for the pattern head `classhasAttr` in its top-right corner together with the corresponding MS table beneath, (ii) the detailed search plans of flattened pattern bodies #1 and #2460 in the middle, and (iii) the flattened pattern bodies (#30, #2590, #2580 and #2470) not involved in the calculations on the left.

Fig. 10(a) illustrates the state of the runtime execution after the calculation tasks of the first iteration, during which (i) the MS table is initially loaded with recent tuple (car, true), (ii) the query of non-recursive flattened pattern body #1 is evaluated by natural joining all its tables to the recent tuple (car, true) of the MS table producing a new matching (car, nplt, true), and (iii) a new tuple (plt, true) of input parameters to be passed downwards later is generated by calculating natural joins of tables up to (but excluding) the recursive invocation constraint in flattened pattern body #2460.

At the second iteration in Fig. 10(b), the previously matched tuples (car, nplt, true) and (plt, true) appear as recent tuples in the table of matchings and the MS table, respectively. In this iteration, the query of flattened pattern body #1 produces a new matching (plt, nbr, true) for the pattern head `classHasAttr`, while queries of flattened pattern body #2460 fail on checking constraints as the natural joins produce such results by starting from either recent tuple, in which the value in column B is false.

In the third iteration (shown by Fig. 10(c)), the table of matchings for pattern head `classHasAttr` is extended by a new matching (plt, nbr, true) produced by the query of flattened pattern body #2460, which uses the recent tuple (plt, nbr, true) for performing the natural joins.

The fixpoint calculation algorithm terminates after the fourth iteration (depicted in Fig. 10(d)) as neither the MS table, nor the table of matchings is further extended.

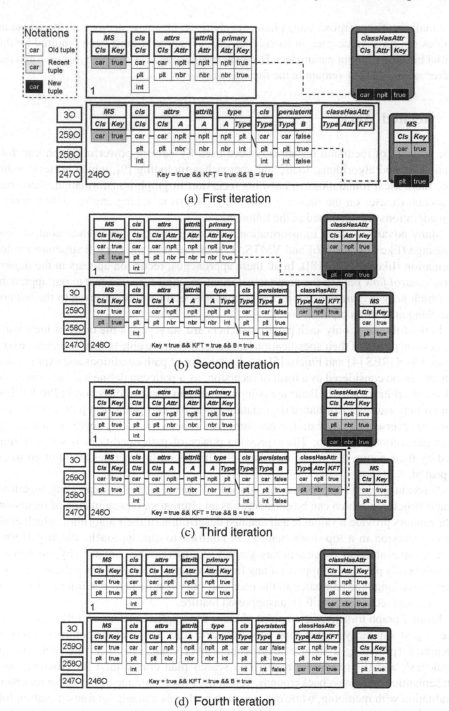

Fig. 10. Runtime iterations of the classHasAttr pattern

Finally, in the postprocessing phase, matching (plt,nbr,true) is filtered out as it does not have value car in its column Cls as it would have been required by the initial binding of input parameters. However, matchings (car,nplt,true) and the (car,nbr,true) remain in the final result set.

6 Related Work

The concept of recursion has already been used by several powerful, graph transformation related algorithms, tools, and approaches including [9], which presents valuable theoretical foundations of handling recursion in graph transformation. Since our approach focuses on the *implementation* of a pattern matching engine, only practical considerations are examined in the following.

Many advanced graph transformation tools support recursion in their control flow language (like GReAT [16] and VMTS [17]) or use it in the control structure implementation (like MOLA [18]). In all these approaches, recursion appears in the *imperative control flow part* of the graph transformation engine, in contrast to our approach, in which *fully declarative and recursive pattern* specifications are given to the *pattern matching module* as input.

In the following, only such pattern matchers are surveyed in the order of increasing expression power of their specification language, which are able to handle recursive patterns. PROGRES [4] and Fujaba [5] use the concept of path conditions and expressions, which can be considered as a form of recursion, as a path can define a set of connected edges of arbitrary length. Paths are computed only in forward direction in PROGRES, which may cause performance degradation when the end point of a path condition is fixed as reverse path navigation is not part of the otherwise, highly sophisticated search plan generation algorithm. The expression power of path conditions is strongly limited by their nature due to the fact that only linear graph structures are allowed to be repeated.

A recent paper [10] presents the concept of star regions for expressing repetitive graph structures, which can be considered as an alternative representation of recursion. The authors provide a valuable and detailed description of their algorithm, which evaluates recursion in a top-down manner, in contrast to our approach, which performs bottom-up evaluation. Since arbitrary graph structures can be contained by star regions (undoubtedly providing support for any form of simple recursion) this indicates a more expressive language compared to the ones that only handle path conditions. However, e.g., mutual recursion is still an unsupported feature.

From a graph transformation point of view, the implementation of Tefkat [7] shows the largest similarity to our approach. Both are able (i) to handle complex forms of recursion (providing a stronger expression power compared to all the previous approaches), and (ii) to reorder terms (i.e., search plan constraints) for efficiency and on semantic correctness backgrounds. Tefkat uses the technique of top-down recursion evaluation with memoing, while our approach performs a magic set transformation followed by a bottom-up evaluation. Additionally, our approach provides support for flattening, which allows an inter-pattern search plan optimization for such patterns that can be evaluated by a single non-recursive pattern matching algorithm.

The technique of combining bottom-up evaluation with magic set transformation [11] is well-known in the knowledge-base system community for over a decade. This technique is intentionally used by our approach as several important theorems (including statements about algorithm termination) have already been proven. Arguments for preparing an own implementation include (i) the lack of support for flattening by any existing general-sense knowledge-base systems, and (ii) a vision to build further runtime optimizations by using graph pattern matching specific knowledge.

The popularity of recursive graph pattern matching has been demonstrated at the AGTIVE workshop by several contributions discussing its specification issues. [19] proposed query support for the DRAGOS graph database, and mentioned the handling of recursive queries by nested subgraph as future work. [20,21] examined different aspects of set-valued graph transformation by using the PROGRES tool. Note that these contributions can be considered as application domains for our approach as it (over)fulfills their specification criteria by providing a larger expression power.

7 Conclusion

In the current paper we proposed a pattern matching framework for matching recursive patterns by using fixpoint-based bottom-up query evaluation with top-down handling of input parameters. The essence of the matching process is to flatten non-recursive pattern compositions for global optimization and execute recursive invocations in an iterative manner by using magic set transformation.

Finally, it is worth pointing out that the proposed approach has been fully implemented, and it will be part of the upcoming VIATRA2 release.

References

1. Rozenberg, G. (ed.): Handbook of Graph Grammars and Computing by Graph Transformation. Foundations, vol. 1. World Scientific, Singapore (1997)
2. Kreowski, H.J., Kuske, S.: Graph transformation units and modules. In: Ehrig, H., Engels, G., Kreowski, H.J., Rozenberg, G. (eds.) Handbook of Graph Grammars and Computing by Graph Transformation. Applications, Languages and Tools, vol. 2, pp. 607–638. World Scientific, Singapore (1999)
3. Heckel, R., Ehrig, H., Engels, G., Taentzer, G.: Classification and comparison of module concepts for graph transformation systems (1999)
4. Zündorf, A.: Graph pattern-matching in PROGRES. In: Cuny, J., Engels, G., Ehrig, H., Rozenberg, G. (eds.) Graph Grammars 1994. LNCS, vol. 1073, pp. 454–468. Springer, Heidelberg (1996)
5. Nickel, U., Niere, J., Zündorf, A.: The FUJABA environment. In: Proc. of the 22nd International Conference on Software Engineering, pp. 742–745. ACM Press, New York (2000)
6. Balogh, A., Varró, D.: Advanced model transformation language constructs in the VIATRA2 framework. In: Proc. of the 21st ACM Symposium on Applied Computing, Dijon, France, pp. 1280–1287. ACM Press, New York (2006)
7. Lawley, M., Steel, J.: Practical declarative model transformation with Tefkat. In: Bézivin, J., Rumpe, B., Schürr, A., Tratt, L. (eds.) Proc. of the International Workshop on Model Transformation in Practice (MTiP 2005), October 3rd (2005)

8. Horváth, Á., Varró, G., Varró, D.: Generic search plans for matching advanced graph patterns. In: Proc. of the Sixth International Workshop on Graph Transformation and Visual Modeling Techniques (GT-VMT 2007). March 31- April 1 2007, Braga, Portugal, March 31- April 1 2007. Electornic Communications of the EASST, pp. 57–68 (2007)

9. Guerra, E., de Lara, J.: Adding recursion to graph transformation. In: Proc. of the Sixth International Workshop on Graph Transformation and Visual Modeling Techniques (GT-VMT 2007), Braga, Portugal, March 31- April 1 2007. Electornic Communications of the EASST, pp. 107–120 (2007)

10. Lindqvist, J., Lundkvist, T., Porres, I.: A query language with the star operator. In: Proc. of the Sixth International Workshop on Graph Transformation and Visual Modeling Techniques (GT-VMT 2007), Braga, Portugal, March 31- April 1 2007. Electornic Communications of the EASST, pp. 69–80 (2007)

11. Ullman, J.D.: Principles of database and knowledge-base systems, vol. II. Computer Science Press, Inc., New York (1989)

12. Varró, G., Varró, D., Friedl, K.: Adaptive graph pattern matching for model transformations using model-sensitive search plans. In: Karsai, G., Taentzer, G. (eds.) Proc. of Int. Workshop on Graph and Model Transformation (GraMoT 2005), Tallinn, Estonia. ENTCS, vol. 152, pp. 191–205 (September 2005)

13. Bézivin, J., Rumpe, B., Schürr, A., Tratt, L.: Challenge of the model transformations in practice workshop (October 3rd 2005)

14. Ehrig, K., Guerra, E., de Lara, J., Lengyel, L., Levendovszky, T., Prange, U., Taentzer, G., Varró, D., Varró-Gyapay, S.: Model transformation by graph transformation: A comparative study. In: MTiP 2005, International Workshop on Model Transformations in Practice (Satellite Event of MoDELS 2005) (2005)

15. Ullman, J.D.: Principles of Database and Knowledge-Base Systems. The New Technologies, vol. II. Computer Science Press (1989)

16. Agrawal, A., Vizhanyo, A., Kalmar, Z., Shi, F., Narayanan, A., Karsai, G.: Reusable idioms and patterns in graph transformation languages. In: Mens, T., Schürr, A., Taentzer, G. (eds.) Proc. of the International Workshop on Graph-Based Tools, Rome, Italy. ENTCS, vol. 127, pp. 181–192. Elsevier, Amsterdam (2004),
http://tfs.cs.tu-berlin.de/grabats/

17. Lengyel, L., Levendovszky, T., Mezei, G., Charaf, H.: Model transformation with a visual control flow language. International Journal of Computer Science 1(1), 45–53 (2006)

18. Kalnins, A., Celms, E., Sostaks, A.: Model transformation approach based on MOLA. In: Bézivin, J., Rumpe, B., Schürr, A., Tratt, L. (eds.) Proc. of the International Workshop on Model Transformation in Practice (MTiP 2005) (October 2005),
http://sosym.dcs.kcl.ac.uk/events/mtip05/

19. Weinell, E.: Adaptable support for queries and transformations for the DRAGOS graph-database. In: Schürr, A., Nagl, M., Zündorf, A. (eds.) Proc. of the 3rd International Workshop and Symposium on Applications of Graph Transformation with Industrial Relevance, Kassel, Germany (October 2007)

20. Fuss, C., Tuttlies, V.E.: Simulating set-valued transformations with algorithmic graph transformation languages. In: Schürr, A., Nagl, M., Zündorf, A. (eds.) Proc. of the 3rd International Workshop and Symposium on Applications of Graph Transformation with Industrial Relevance, Kassel, Germany (October 2007)

21. Körtgen, A.T.: Modeling successively connected repetitive subgraphs. In: Schürr, A., Nagl, M., Zündorf, A. (eds.) Proc. of the 3rd International Workshop and Symposium on Applications of Graph Transformation with Industrial Relevance, Kassel, Germany (October 2007)

A First Experimental Evaluation of Search Plan Driven Graph Pattern Matching

Gernot Veit Batz, Moritz Kroll, and Rubino Geiß

Universität Karlsruhe (TH), 76131 Karlsruhe, Germany
batz@ira.uka.de, {moritz,rubino}@ipd.info.uni-karlsruhe.de

Abstract. With graph pattern matching the field of graph transformation (GT) includes an NP-complete subtask. But for real-life applications it is essential that graph pattern matching is performed as fast as possible. This challenge has been attacked by the approach of search plan driven, host-graph-sensitive (also known as model-sensitive) graph pattern matching. To our knowledge no experimental evaluation of this approach has been published yet. We performed first experiments regarding the runtime performance using the well-known GT benchmark introduced by Varró et al. as well as an example from compiler construction. Moreover we present an improved cost model and heuristics for search plans and their generation.

Keywords: Graph transformation, graph pattern matching, subgraph isomorphism problem, search plan driven, host-graph-sensitive, model-sensitive, heuristic optimization, experiment.

1   Introduction

In graph transformation (GT) [1] declarative rules are used to specify the alteration of graphical structures. The application of those transformations requires *graph pattern matching*[1] which is an NP-complete problem (see Garey and Johnson [2], problem GT48). However, real-life applications demand that transformation steps are done within a reasonable amount of time. For this reason efficient graph pattern matching is one of the important issues in GT.

This challenge has been attacked by the heuristically optimizing approach of *search plan driven, host-graph-sensitive*[2] graph pattern matching [3,4,5,6,7]. The key idea of this method is to represent possible matching strategies by so-called *search plans*, which are sequences of *primitive matching operations* dealing with single graph elements. A cost model assigns costs to all matching operations and search plans. This makes search plan generation an optimization problem and allows the generation of matching strategies at runtime depending on the current *host graph*. The required statistical information about the host graph can

---

[1] Also known as "subgraph matching" or the "subgraph isomorphism problem".
[2] In the following, we omit the term "host-graph-sensitive" (which is also referred to as "model-sensitive") for conciseness.

A. Schürr, M. Nagl, and A. Zündorf (Eds.): AGTIVE 2007, LNCS 5088, pp. 471–486, 2008.

be obtained by an analysis of the host graph in linear time. The actual graph pattern matching is performed by *executing* the generated search plan.

However, no experimental evaluation of this approach has been published yet. In this paper we present a first experimental case study on search plan driven graph pattern matching using our GT tool GRGEN.NET [8,9,10,11] (see Section 3). As test cases we utilize the well-known GT benchmark invented by Varró et al. [12] (see Section 3.1) as well as an example taken from compiler construction (see Section 3.2).

Additionally we present an improved version of cost model and heuristics (Section 2): The old cost model and heuristics only consider the backtracking that might occur during the execution of the primitive operations. The new cost model and heuristics deal with the effort raised by the operations themselves as well. So, in our experiments we evaluate the old cost model and heuristics as well as the new ones. At least for our two test cases it becomes apparent that

- the execution times of the possible search plans vary greatly (otherwise, there would be no room for optimization at all),
- the new cost model yields a reasonable picture of the real execution times,
- the search plans generated by the improved heuristics are quite good,
- the old cost model and heuristics perform partly worse (but still tolerable).

2   Search Plan Driven Graph Pattern Matching

In this section we give a brief introduction to search plan driven graph pattern matching. Other and partly more detailed discussions that describe different flavors of the approach have been provided by Batz [4], Varró et al. [5], and Horváth et al. [7]. Here, we present an improved version of the approach, which has not been published before.

Given a GT rule $L \rightsquigarrow R$ and a host graph H, we want to find a *match* (i.e. an occurrence) of L in H. We do this in three major steps:

1. To obtain the statistical information needed by the cost model we perform an analysis of the host graph H (this might be avoided by using domain-specific knowledge).
2. Using the information provided by the analysis, we generate a search plan P of preferably low cost.
3. We perform the actual graph pattern matching by executing P.

2.1   Search Plans and Their Execution

Primitive Matching Operations. A search plan $P = \langle o_1, \ldots, o_k \rangle$ is a sequence of primitive matching operations o_i, which are atomic search actions binding exactly one pattern element to an appropriate[3] unbound element of the host graph. We distinguish five kinds of primitive matching operations:

---

[3] In this context "appropriate" means that nodes are bound to nodes, edges to edges, and that the types of the participants are compatible.

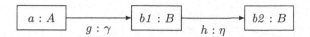

Fig. 1. A simple pattern graph

1. A *lookup operation* lkp(x) binds the pattern element x to *any* appropriate element of the host graph.
2. An *incoming edge operation* in(v, e) binds the pattern edge e, that must be an incoming edge of the already bound pattern node v, to an appropriate unbound edge of the host graph, that is incoming on the current host graph partner of v.
3. An *outgoing edge operation* out(v, e) works analogously to in(v, e) but deals with an *outgoing* edge.
4. A *get source operation* src(e) binds the source node of an already bound pattern edge e to the source node of the current host graph partner of e.
5. A *get target operation* tgt(e) works analogously to src(e) but deals with the *target* node.

Search Plans. Now we are able to give an exact definition of search plans: A sequence $P = \langle o_1, \ldots, o_k \rangle$ of primitive matching operations is called a *valid search plan* for L if the following two conditions hold:

1. Every element of the pattern graph L is treated exactly once.
2. If an operation o_i requires, that a pattern element is already bound, then this element must be bound by one of the preceding operations $o_1, \ldots, o_{i-1}$.

Consider, for example, the small pattern graph shown in Figure 1. Then the operation sequences

$$P_1 := \langle \mathsf{lkp}(b2), \mathsf{in}(b2, h), \mathsf{src}(h), \mathsf{in}(b1, g), \mathsf{src}(g) \rangle ,$$
$$P_2 := \langle \mathsf{lkp}(h), \mathsf{tgt}(h), \mathsf{src}(h), \mathsf{lkp}(a), \mathsf{out}(a, g) \rangle$$

are valid search plans for this pattern graph.

Executing a Search Plan. Given a valid search plan $P = \langle o_1, \ldots, o_k \rangle$, we can perform the actual graph pattern matching by *executing* P. This means, that a match of L in H is stepwise constructed by executing one primitive operation of P after another. Whenever a primitive operation o_i is executed successfully, the current partial match is extended by a new binding of the pattern element the operation o_i refers to. When the whole search plan P is executed successfully, a full match of L in H is found.

When we execute a primitive operation that deals with a pattern element x, it might happen that x can be bound to more than one appropriate element of the host graph. In this case we choose only one of the possible elements. The alternatives can be processed later by backtracking, if necessary. This, of course, may lead to an execution time that is exponential in the number of pattern elements.

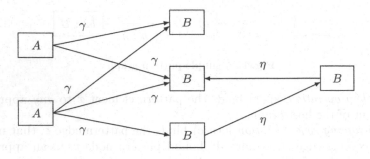

Fig. 2. A simple host graph

Implicit Checks. Consider, for example, the following two operation sequences, which are—according to the above definition—both valid search plans:

$$P_3 := \langle \mathsf{lkp}(b2), \mathsf{in}(b2, h), \mathsf{lkp}(b1), \mathsf{lkp}(a), \mathsf{lkp}(g) \rangle$$
$$P_4 := \langle \mathsf{lkp}(a), \mathsf{lkp}(b2), \mathsf{out}(a, g), \mathsf{in}(b2, h), \mathsf{src}(h) \rangle$$

While executing P_3 the operation $\mathsf{lkp}(b1)$ is performed *after* h is already bound by a previous operation. As a consequence, the only remaining choice to bind $b1$ is the source node of the current host graph partner of h. But as a lookup operation chooses *any* appropriate element, a chosen node is probably not that very same source node. Thus, an appropriate check must be performed implicitly during the execution of a lookup operation. This applies analogously to the operation $\mathsf{src}(h)$ in P_4 as well as to edge lookups like $\mathsf{lkp}(g)$ in P_3. More precisely, if a primitive operation binds a pattern element x to a partner y in H, it must be checked implicitly, whether the current partners of all already bound pattern elements incident to x are correctly linked to y[4].

2.2 The Cost Model

As exponential execution time is a consequence of backtracking, the cost model must assign a higher cost to a search plan whose execution requires more backtracking. But in some cases the running time of an operation (without considering backtracking) may be even more siginficant.

The Cost of Primitive Matching Operations. For a primitive operation o we define two different cost measures $b(o)$ and $t(o)$ that estimate the *backtracking* and the execution *time* raised by o itself, respectively. Backtracking is caused by primitive operations that involve multiple possible bindings. Accordingly, $b(o)$ estimates the number of choices that are possible during the execution of o.

---

[4] Of course, P_3 and P_4 are quite stupid search plans. But allowing such awkward situations and performing implicit checks simplifies the theory a lot in the sense that the set of valid operation selections directly corresponds to the set of directed spanning trees (DSTs) in the plan graph and in the sense that all enumerations of such a DST are valid search plans (see Section 2.3).

To predict the time spent during the execution of o itself, $t(o)$ estimates the number of host graph elements processed during the execution of o. Both measures should reflect the underlying data structures, of course. In this paper we define b and t in a way that they are suited to the implementation provided by our tool GRGEN.NET. Note that in the following $b(o) \leq t(o)$ always holds for any operation o by definition.

Before going on we define some notation first: For any pattern element x let $\#_x$ be the number of elements in H having a type compatible with x. For a pattern edge e, let M_e be the number of edges in H having a compatible edge type as well as compatibly typed source and target nodes. Lastly, let S_e and T_e be the number of edges in H having a compatible edge type as well as a compatibly typed source node or target node, respectively (thus, in case of S_e and T_e "the other" node may have an incompatible type). Of course, $\#_e \geq S_e \geq M_e$ and $\#_e \geq T_e \geq M_e$ always holds.

Node Lookups. Consider an operation $\mathsf{lkp}(v)$ for a pattern node v. Then the number of choices raised by $\mathsf{lkp}(v)$ as well as the number of host graph elements processed during the execution of $\mathsf{lkp}(v)$ is at most $\#_v$. Accordingly, we assign $t(\mathsf{lkp}(v)) := b(\mathsf{lkp}(v)) := \#_v$ as costs. For the pattern graph of Figure 1 and the host graph of Figure 2 we have $t(\mathsf{lkp}(b1)) = b(\mathsf{lkp}(b1)) = 4$, for example.

Edge Lookups. An edge lookup $\mathsf{lkp}(e)$ for a pattern edge e works analogously to a node lookup $\mathsf{lkp}(v)$. But sooner or later, the source and target node of e must also be matched. This further reduces the number of possible choices for e. For example, if an edge f in H has a compatible edge type, but an incompatible typed source node, an appropriate operation $\mathsf{lkp}(e)$ will be executed successfully but a subsequent operation $\mathsf{src}(e)$ will fail. So, we assign $t(\mathsf{lkp}(e)) := \#_e$ and $b(\mathsf{lkp}(e)) := M_e$. As a consequence src and tgt should occur as early as possible in a search plan of course.

Incoming and Outgoing Edge Operations. We define $b(\mathsf{out}(v,e)) := M_e/\#_v$, which is the average number of appropriate incident to the current host graph partner of v. In contrast, we set $t(\mathsf{out}(v,e)) := S_e/\#_v$, which is the average number of outgoing edges incident to the current host graph partner regardless whether they are appropriate or not. Analogously, we assign $b(\mathsf{in}(v,e)) := M_e/\#_v$ and $t(\mathsf{in}(v,e)) := T_e/\#_v$. So, for the pattern graph of Figure 1 and the host graph of Figure 2 we have $b(\mathsf{in}(b1,g)) = 5/4 = 1.25$ and $t(\mathsf{in}(b1,g)) = 7/4 = 1.75$, for example.

Get Source and Get Target Operations. Primitive Operations of the form $\mathsf{src}(e)$ and $\mathsf{tgt}(e)$ do *not* raise multiple choices during the matching process and process exactly one graph element during their execution. So, we assign $t(\mathsf{src}(e)) := t(\mathsf{tgt}(e)) := b(\mathsf{src}(e)) := b(\mathsf{tgt}(e)) := 1$ as costs.

The Cost of a Search Plan. The cost model should estimate the time needed for the execution of a search plan $P = \langle o_1, \ldots, o_k \rangle$. So, we use the cost function

$$t(P) := t_1 + b_1 t_2 + b_1 b_2 t_3 + \cdots + b_1 \cdots b_{k-1} t_k \qquad (1)$$

with $b_i := b(o_i)$ and $t_i := t(o_i)$. This is in fact a weighted sum of the estimated execution times $t_1, \ldots, t_k$ of the operations $o_1, \ldots, o_k$. The weights $b_1 \cdots b_{i-1}$ with $2 \leq i \leq k$ multiplicatively accumulate the estimated backtracking that arises during the matching process. So, under the assumption that $b_1, \ldots, b_{i-1}, t_i$ are stochastically independent[5] for $1 < i \leq k$, the expected execution time is in $O(t(P))$. In the context of our second experiment (see Section 3.2) the cost function $t(P)$ does a far better job than the "traditional" cost function $b(P)$ that is defined as

$$b(P) := b_1 + b_1 b_2 + \cdots + b_1 \cdots b_k \tag{2}$$

and only estimates the backtracking raised by P. So, we claim that with the cost function $t(P)$ we have an improved cost model.

2.3   Generating a Search Plan

As we do not know efficient algorithms that construct search plans that are optimal according to $t(P)$ or $b(P)$, we have to settle for heuristic methods. Here, we consider two heuristic methods which we call BACKTRACKINGONLY and BACKTRACKINGLOOKUP. The first of the two only minimizes the backtracking, which actually addresses the cost function $b(P)$. The second tries to minimize the backtracking *and* the execution time of the operations themselves and, hence, addresses the cost function $t(P)$. However, the second one works exactly as the first one except for a little modification. So, we firstly describe the BACKTRACKINGONLY heuristics and characterize the modifications done by BACKTRACKINGLOOKUP afterwards.

2.4   The BacktrackingOnly Heuristics

The BACKTRACKINGONLY heuristics works in two phases: the *operation selection* and the *operation ordering*. But before these two phases can be performed, we have to generate a structure that we call *plan graph* first.

The Plan Graph. For a pattern graph L the plan graph $\tilde{L}$ is defined as follows:

1. For every element x of L the plan graph $\tilde{L}$ contains a node v_x representing x. All these nodes are labeled with the name of the pattern element they represent. Additionally, $\tilde{L}$ contains a special *root* node.
2. For every element x of L the plan graph $\tilde{L}$ contains an edge f_x that leads from the root node to the node that represents x in $\tilde{L}$. It is labeled with lkp and represents the operation $\mathsf{lkp}(x)$.
3. For every edge e in L let v_e be the node representing e in $\tilde{L}$. Then $\tilde{L}$ contains four further edges incident to v_e:
   - An edge labeled with tgt leading from v_e to the node representing the target node t of e and an edge in reverse direction labeled with in. These edges represent the operations $\mathsf{tgt}(e)$ and $\mathsf{in}(t, e)$, respectively.

---

[5] Stochastic independence might not hold, but it provides a good intuition of what is happening.

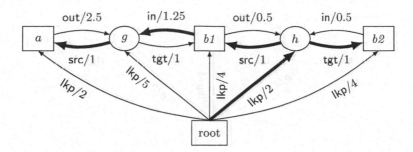

Fig. 3. The plan graph for the pattern graph of Figure 1 with estimated backtracking costs induced by the host graph of Figure 2. A multiplicative MDST is denoted by thick edges. It has a total cost of $2 * 1 * 1 * 1.25 * 1 = 2.5$.

- An edge labeled with src leading from v_e to the node representing the source node s of e and an edge in reverse direction labeled with out. These edges represent the operations $src(e)$ and $out(s, e)$, respectively.

As every edge of the plan graph represents a primitive matching operation o, we can assign the estimated backtracking $b(o)$ as a cost to the corresponding edge. In this way the plan graph becomes a weighted directed graph. Figure 3 shows the plan graph for the pattern graph of Figure 1 while the edge weights represent the estimated backtracking induced by the host graph of Figure 2.

Operation Selection. Looking at the cost function $b(P)$ in equation (2) we see that $b_1 b_2 \cdots b_k$ is the most significant term. By minimizing this term, the BACK-TRACKINGONLY heuristics tries to minimize $b(P)$. As every cost b_i appears in $b_1 b_2 \cdots b_k$ exactly once, this corresponds to finding a *minimal operation selection*[6] $S = \{o_1, \ldots, o_k\}$. This is not a trivial task but luckily there is a one-to-one correspondence between the set of valid operation selections and the set of directed spanning trees (DSTs) in the plan graph[7]. Moreover, the corresponding DST of a *minimal* operation selection is just a *minimum* directed spanning tree (MDST) according to multiplicatively[8] computed total costs. Such an MDST can be computed in polynomial time by the Edmonds/Chu-Liu algorithm [13,14]. In Figure 3 an example of a multiplicative MDST is denoted by thick edges.

Operation Ordering. Having found a minimal operation selection S we have to build a valid search plan from the operations in S. This can be done very simply by traversing[9] the corresponding MDST starting from the root node.

---

[6] Minimal in terms of the backtracking.

[7] This has been shown by Batz [4].

[8] Typically, the cost of a MDST is computed in terms of a sum, but it can also be computed in terms of a product. As logarithms are strictly increasing functions from $\mathbb{R}_{>0}$ to $\mathbb{R}$ and $\log(ab) = \log a + \log b$ holds, the computation of a multiplicative MDST can be reduced to the computation of an additive MDST using the logarithm.

[9] A traversal of a directed graph is an enumeration of its edges where an edge must not be visited unless its source node is a given start node or the target node of an already visited edge.

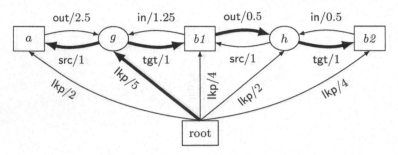

Fig. 4. The same plan graph as the one of Figure 3. But here another multiplicative MDST which involves edge costs between 0 and 1 is shown. Its total cost is computed by $5 * 1 * 1 * 0.5 * 1 = 2.5$.

During the traversal we successively emit the operation represented by each edge. All operation sequences generated in this way are valid search plans.

However, we do not only want *some* valid search plan but a "good" one. Therefore, we traverse the plan graph in a *best-first* manner. That means that we prefer edges of minimal cost. To understand this, look at equation (2). Obviously an operation has more impact on the overall cost the earlier it occurs in a search plan. So, we place the cheap operations possibly early and the expensive ones possibly late. Moreover, all operations of kind src and tgt are placed *as soon as possible*. This is because src and tgt operations rise costs next to no expense but a pretended match might be exposed earlier.

Non-Forgetful Operation Selection. As the cost of an operation selection $S = \{o_1, \ldots, o_k\}$ we could assign the product $b_1 b_2 \cdots b_k$. However, this would make the selection process "forgetful": As a plan graph may contain edge costs between 0 and 1 and as the total cost of a DST is computed in terms of a product[10] each such edge *reduces* the total cost of a DST. As a result, information about intense intermediate backtracking may be destroyed. Consider for example, the MDST shown in Figure 4: Though the cost $b(\mathsf{lkp}(g)) = 5$ indicates that intense backtracking may arise, the cost $b(\mathsf{out}(b1, h)) = 0.5$ taints the result as $5 * 0.5 = 2.5$ holds. So, we assign

$$\mathrm{BO}_*(S) := \prod_{o \in S} \max\{1, b(o)\} \tag{3}$$

as the cost of an operation selection S. If we use this "non-forgetful" cost function, the DST shown in Figure 4 has no longer minimal cost.

Varró et al. [5] use a different cost function for the operation selection, namely

$$\mathrm{BO}_+(S) := \sum_{o \in S} b(o). \tag{4}$$

---

[10] In the context of the corresponding, additive MDST problem, we obtain by logarithmizing, a multiplicative edge cost between 0 and 1 becomes a negative edge cost.

Obviously, BO_+ is also a "non-forgetful" cost function minimizing backtracking. But using BO_+ the operation selection does not directly minimize the product $b_1 \cdots b_k$ anymore, which might distort the result. On the other hand, by BO_+ costs between 0 and 1 are *not* lifted to 1. In this way the first-fail principle is included in the operation selection, which is the pro of this technique.

So, there are two variants of the BACKTRACKINGONLY heuristics: The first one uses the function BO_* on the operation selection and the second one BO_+ instead.

2.5   The BacktrackingLookup Heuristics

Unlike BACKTRACKINGONLY, the BACKTRACKINGLOOKUP heuristics not only minimizes backtracking but also deals with estimated execution times. This is achieved only by a little modification of BACKTRACKINGONLY: Go back to the plan graph as defined in Section 2.4 and consider all edges that correspond to an operation $o := \mathsf{lkp}(e)$ for a pattern edge e. For all these edges replace the cost $b(o)$ by $t(o)$. Having done this we proceed exactly as in case of BACKTRACKINGONLY with cost function BO_*. So, the operation selection of BACKTRACKINGLOOKUP minimizes a cost function $BL(S)$ which is a modified version of $BO_*(S)$: For edge lookups we minimize the estimated execution time instead of the backtracking. At least for our second test case (see Section 3.2) this is a real step forward. For our first test case (see Section 3.1) both methods behave similar well.

3   Experimental Results

The essential idea of our experiments is to generate *all* search plans possible for a pattern graph L while measuring the execution time for each search plan. This way we experimentally validate our cost model and our heuristics. Additionally we consider the heuristics proposed by Varró. As test cases we use the well-known STS Mutex benchmark introduced by Varró et al. [12] (see Section 3.1) as well as an example taken from compiler construction (see Section 3.2). All measurements are carried out using our GT tool GRGEN.NET [9,10,11], which implements the BACKTRACKINGLOOKUP heuristics described in Section 2, as well as our benchmarking tool SPBENCH which is included in the 1.3 release of GRGEN.NET. The underlying platform is an AMD Athlon XP 3000+ with 1 GByte main memory that runs with Windows XP and .NET 2.0.

Displaying the Results. In each diagram we relate the different cost measures $(b(P), t(P), BO_*(S), BO_+(S)$, and $BL(S))$ with the execution time each. On the horizontal axis we display the cost, on the vertical axis the detected execution time. Note that we use a logarithmic scale for both axes; for technical reasons both axis show the logarithmized values.

However, some points occur in the data set very often. Under these circumstances scatter plots loose very much of their expressiveness. For this reason, we do not chart every single point. Instead, we divide the plane into hexagons and draw only those hexagons that contain at least one point. The more points a hexagon contains, the darker we draw it.

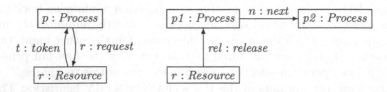

Fig. 5. The pattern graph of the *takeRule* (left) and the *giveRule* (right)

Goal. We are primarily interested in the quality of a heuristics: It is good, if and only if plans with low costs actually have low execution times, i.e., we want to see that the leftmost points in the diagram have low execution times. Besides this primary goal it would be nice to have a good overall correlation between costs and execution time—both for a heuristics and for a cost model.

3.1 First Experiment: The STS Mutex Benchmark

Background. The *STS Mutex benchmark* models a mutual exclusion scenario of N processes trying to access a single resource (in this experiment we choose $N = 10,000$). The N processes are represented by N nodes of type *Process*, which are connected by N edges of type *next* such that the processes form a ring. The single resource is represented by a node of type *Resource*. This structure is built first by certain rules. Afterwards other rules insert and delete edges of different types all over the graph. More details can be found in a technical report by Varró et al. [12].

Experimental Setup. In this experiment we perform an exhaustive exploration of all search plans only for the *takeRule* and the *giveRule*. Figure 5 shows the pattern graphs of these rules.

In a first pass we execute the whole benchmark for every search plan that is possible for the *takeRule* and measure the execution time with a timeout of 10 seconds each. For the *giveRule* we use a fixed search plan, namely the one provided by the heuristics. The results are displayed in Figure 6. The plot on the right, which relates BL(S) with the execution time, shows the desired behavior: Points in the far left have low execution time. Hence, BACKTRACKINGLOOKUP chooses one of the most fast executing plans possible. In the plot on the left we see that the actual cost function $t(P)$ shows a little more diversified behavior than BL(S). However, due to the very simple structure of the STS benchmark the figures only show a simple level-wise distribution.

In a second pass we performed the analogous experiment by checking all possible search plans for the *giveRule*. The resulting plots are similar and hence omitted.

3.2 Second Experiment: Finding Loop Counters

Background. In compiler construction internal intermediate representations (IRs) are used for programs. Modern IRs are graph based and represent programs

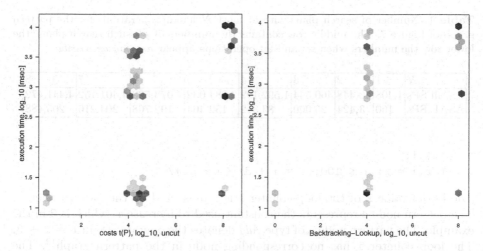

Fig. 6. Plotted results for all search plans possible for the *takeRule*

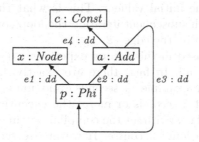

Fig. 7. A pattern graph that specifies data dependencies typical for a loop counter

as dependency or flow graphs. In this experiment we use an adoption of an IR called FIRM [15] for our GT tool GrGen.NET. FIRM uses dependency graphs, and fulfills the so-called SSA[11] property. IRs with this property represent programs in a way that each variable has exactly one occurrence as a left-hand-side of an assignment. This requires the so-called Φ-*operation* that models alternative dataflows as they occur in the context of conditions and loops, for example.

Experimental Setup. The essential idea of this second experiment is to find loop counters in C programs. As a host graph we use the IR graph of the C function `RenderTiles()` in `RenderWorld.c` (revision 1328) taken from the open source project JAGGED ALLIANCE 2 – STRACCIATELLA [16]. The function `RenderTiles()` has 1,418 lines of code; the corresponding IR graph consists of 4,705 nodes and 16,714 edges. As a pattern graph we use the one shown in Figure 7, which shows a pattern typical for a loop counter. To understand this, consider the following code fragment written in C:

---

[11] SSA stands for *static single assignment*.

Table 1. Number of search plans with at most N lookup operations for the pattern graph of Figure 7. The middle row contains the numbers of *all* such search plans, the lower row the numbers when src and tgt operations appear *as soon as possible*.

N	1	2	3	4	5	6	7	8
all SPs	1,408	56,448	460,544	1,592,192	3,084,032	4,078,592	4,401,152	4,441,472
ASAP SPs	160	3,424	25,000	83,312	152,464	192,768	204,216	205,488

```
int i;
for(i = x; i < 100; i = i + 3) { /*...*/ }
```

The initial value x of the loop counter i is represented by the pattern node x. The pattern node c represents the constant used to increase i, which is 3 in the example. The pattern node a of type *Add* denotes the operator '+' in i = i + 3. The loop counter i has no corresponding node in the pattern graph[12]. The pattern node p of type *Phi* denotes the Φ-operation mentioned above. It is needed because a loop induces alternative control paths: When the loop is entered for the first time, i has the initial value x. This is what the edge *e1* stands for. At the beginning of each subsequent iteration the loop counter i is incremented by c, which is expressed by the edge *e2*.

The pattern graph used in this second experiment has far too many search plans to execute them all. In fact, there are exactly 4,441,472 search plans. With a timeout of, for example, 5 seconds (and under the assumption that most search plans need 5 seconds or more) the execution of the search plans would take about 250 days (without the compilation time needed for the search plans) which is far too long of course. However, we reduce the set of search plans dramatically by restricting ourselves to search plans where src and tgt operations are scheduled as soon as possible—every sensible search plan should be like that (see Section 2.3). Moreover, we only consider search plans with a limited number of lookup operations. Table 1 shows the number of search plans with at most N lookup operations for $N \in \{1, 2, \ldots, 8\}$—as the pattern graph has eight elements, at most eight lookups are possible.

In this experiment we choose $N \leq 2$ and perform an exhaustive search for *all* matches for each of the 3,424 search plans (repeated a 50 times each). The timeout in this second experiment is also 10 seconds. The results are displayed in Figure 8. The two plots at the top show the behavior of $b(P)$ and $t(P)$. Both cost functions exhibit a visible correlation between costs and execution time. However, $b(P)$ reveals a great weakness: Several search plans with low cost have comparatively high execution time. At this regard $t(P)$ is much better. This is also reflected by the corresponding heuristic methods (see the two plots in the middle): In the plot on the left (BACKTRACKINGONLY) there are leftmost points with comparatively high execution times, too. In contrast, the plot on the right (BACKTRACKINGLOOKUP) shows the desired behavior that minimal cost corresponds to quite low execution times.

---

[12] In graph based SSA, variables have no explicit representation in general.

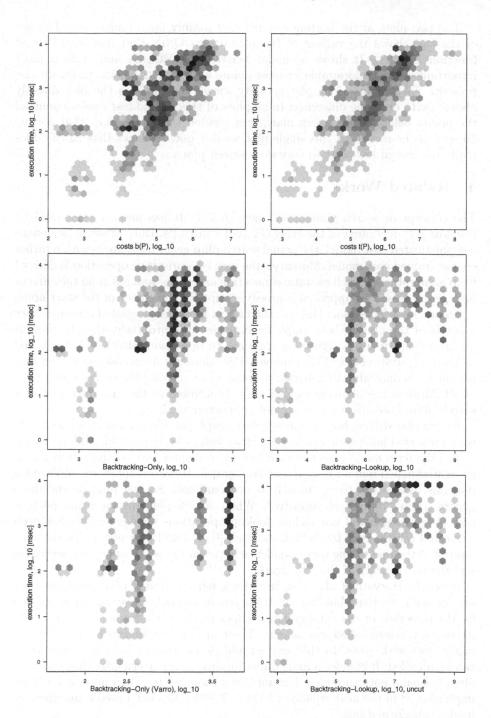

Fig. 8. Plotted results for our second test case "Finding Loop Counters"

The two plots at the bottom are included mainly for completeness. The left of the two shows the variant of BACKTRACKINGONLY that uses Varró's cost function $BO_+(S)$. It shows a similar behavior as $BO_*(S)$ and—this is most important—those undesirable leftmost points with high execution times are also present. The bottom right plot actually shows the same as the plot directly above—with only one difference: In all plots of this second test case we omitted the points belonging to search plans that yielded a time-out (i.e., that needed 10 seconds or more). In this single plot we did not. It shows that $BL(S)$ does really not assign low costs to very slow search plans.

4   Related Work

The concept of search plans is not new in GT. It has already been used by Zündorf [17] in context of the early GT tool PROGRES. But, although he defines a sophisticated cost model, the actual search plan generation works with a rather coarse grained cost model. Moreover, the cost of a primitive operation is derived from assumptions as well as static connection assertions and not from the current host graph. Also, his approach is greedy except for the choice of the start node.

To our knowledge Dörr [18] was the first in GT who suggested a preparatory analysis of the present host graph for bunches of appropriate edges to prevent backtracking. He also suggests an approach to operation selection that is based on the computation of a DST. However, Dörr does not use a cost model. For this reason he is only able to generate a linear time search plan or no search plan at all. Moreover, lookup operations are only allowed as the first operation of a search plan. Lookups of edges are not supported at all.

Search plan driven, host-graph-sensitive graph pattern matching has originally been presented independently by Batz [3] as well as by Varró et al. [5]. Varró et al. coined the term *model-sensitive search plans* to emphasize that the search plan is generated depending on the present host graph. However, there are application domains, where the term "model" is not common. So, we propose the more general term "host-graph-sensitive". When search plan driven graph pattern matching arose, it did not include lookup operations for edges. This has been suggested a little later by Geiß, Batz et al. [6,4]. The latter paper also contains a proof of the one-to-one correspondence between the set of operation selections and the set of DSTs of the plan graph.

Recently, Horvath et al. [7] suggested a generalization of plan graphs as they are defined here. Here, binding constraints on in and out operations are expressed by the direction of the corresponding edges in the plan graph. Horvath et al., in contrast, use so called adornments. These are annotations that relate binding constraints with costs. In this way an additional kind of primitive operations can be handled: It enables a more direct binding of a pattern edge that connects already bound pattern nodes. The authors announce that their approach will be implemented in the next release of VIATRA2 which is a GT based framework for model transformations.

An implementation of the BACKTRACKINGLOOKUP heuristics as described in Section 2 is included in our GT tool GRGEN.NET [9,10,11].

5   Conclusions

In this paper we presented a first experimental evaluation of search plan driven graph pattern matching (using our GT tool GRGEN.NET) as well as an improved cost model and heuristics. As test cases we used the well-known GT benchmark introduced by Varró et al. as well as an example taken from compiler construction. At least for the two test cases it became apparent that

- the execution times raised by the possible search plans vary greatly, so there is room for optimizations,
- the improved cost model reasonably reflects the real execution times,
- the search plans generated by the improved heuristics are quite good,
- the old cost model and heuristics perform partly worse.

For the future it is interesting whether better heuristic methods for the generation of search plans can be developed and how we can deal with NACs[13]. Moreover, the development of more GT benchmarks—particularly with bigger pattern graphs—would be highly desirable.

Acknowledgements. We want to thank all the students and researchers at IPD Goos for the creative atmosphere. Especially we want to thank Christoph Mallon. Also we want to thank Jakob Blomer, Edgar Jakumeit, Jens Müller, and Katja Weisshaupt who helped us on the preparation of this work. Moreover we thank our Professors Gerhard Goos and Peter Sanders for supporting this work. Last but not least, we want to thank the anonymous reviewers for their useful hints and suggestions.

References

1. Heckel, R.: Graph Transformation in a Nutshell. In: Bézivin, J., Heckel, R. (eds.) Language Engineering for Model-Driven Software Development. Dagstuhl Seminar Proceedings, Internationales Begegnungs- und Forschungszentrum für Informatik (IBFI), Schloss Dagstuhl, Germany, vol. 04101(2004)
2. Garey, M.R., Johnson, D.S.: Computers and Intractability; A Guide to the Theory of NP-Completeness. W. H. Freeman & Co., New York (1990)
3. Batz, G.V.: Graphersetzung für eine Zwischendarstellung im Übersetzerbau. Master's thesis, Universität Karlsruhe (2005)
4. Batz, G.V.: An Optimization Technique for Subgraph Matching Strategies. Technical Report 2006-7, Universität Karlsruhe, Fakultät für Informatik (2006)
5. Varró, G., Varró, D., Friedl, K.: Adaptive Graph Pattern Matching for Model Transformations using Model-sensitive Search Plans. In: Karsai, G., Taentzer, G. (eds.) Proc. of Int. Workshop on Graph and Model Transformation (GraMoT 2005), Tallinn, Estonia. ENTCS, vol. 152, pp. 191–205. Elsevier, Amsterdam (2005)

---

[13] A negative application condition (NAC) is a graph associated with the pattern graph. An appropriate occurrence of a NAC in H prevents the application of a GT rule.

6. Geiß, R., Batz, G.V., Grund, D., Hack, S., Szalkowski, A.M.: GrGen: A Fast SPO-Based Graph Rewriting Tool. In: Corradini, A., Ehrig, H., Montanari, U., Ribeiro, L., Rozenberg, G. (eds.) ICGT 2006. LNCS, vol. 4178, p. 383. Springer, Heidelberg (2006)
7. Ákos Horváth, G.V., Varró, D.: Generic Search Plans for Matching Advanced Graph Patterns. In: Proc. of the Sixth International Workshop on Graph Transformation and Visual Modeling Techniques (GT-VMT 2007), Braga, Portugal, Electornic Communications of the EASST, pp. 57–68 (2007)
8. Geiß, R., Kroll, M.: GrGen.NET: A Fast, Expressive, and General Purpose Graph Rewrite Tool. In: Schürr, A., Nagl, M., Zündorf, A. (eds.) AGTIVE 2007. LNCS, vol. 5088. Springer, Heidelberg (2008)
9. Kroll, M.: GrGen.NET: Portierung und Erweiterung des Graphersetzungssystems GrGen, Studienarbeit, IPD Goos, Universität Karlsruhe (2007)
10. Geiß, R.: GrGen.NET homepage (2008), http://www.grgen.net
11. Blomer, J., Geiß, R.: The GrGen.NET User Manual. Technical Report 2007-5, Universität Karlsruhe, IPD Goos (2007)
12. Varró, G., Schürr, A., Varró, D.: Benchmarking for Graph Transformation. Technical report, Department of Computer Science and Information Theory, Budapest University of Technology and Economics (2005)
13. Edmonds, J.: Optimum Branchings. J. Res. Natl. Bureau Standards 71B, 233–240 (1967)
14. Chu, Y.J., Liu, T.H.: On the shortest arborescence of a directed graph. Science Sinica 14, 1396–1400 (1965)
15. Trapp, M., Lindenmaier, G., Boesler, B.: Documentation of the Intermediate Representation FIRM. Technical Report 1999-14, Universität Karlsruhe, Fakultät für Informatik (1999)
16. Mallon, C., Gantert, W.C.: Jagged Alliance 2 - Stracciatella (A port of the game Jagged Alliance 2 using SDL) (2007), http://ja2.dragonriders.de/
17. Zündorf, A.: Graph Pattern Matching in PROGRES. In: Cuny, J., Engels, G., Ehrig, H., Rozenberg, G. (eds.) Graph Grammars 1994. LNCS, vol. 1073, pp. 454–468. Springer, Heidelberg (1996)
18. Dörr, H.: Efficient Graph Rewriting and Its Implementation. LNCS, vol. 922. Springer, Heidelberg (1995)

AGTIVE 2007 Graph Transformation Tool Contest

Arend Rensink[1] and Gabriele Taentzer[2]

[1] University of Twente, The Netherlands
rensink@cs.utwente.nl
[2] Philipps-Universität Marburg, Germany
taentzer@mathematik.uni-marburg.de

Abstract. In this short paper we describe the setup and results of a new initiative to compare graph transformation tools, carried out as part of the AGTIVE 2007 symposium on "Applications of Graph Transformation with Industrial Relevance". The initiative took the form of a contest, consisting of two rounds: the first round was a call for cases, the second round a call for solutions. The response to both rounds was very good, leading to the conclusion that this is an initiative worth repeating. There are, however, a number of lessons to be learned; these are summarised here, in order to improve the organisation and the eventual benefits of this type of contest.

1 Introduction

Tools are crucial for the promotion of graph transformation in industry. It is only with the ready availability of reliable, easy-to-use tools that the attractions and benefits of graph transformation can ever become clear to anyone not having a prior education in this field. Furthermore, given the inherent complexities of the method, tool performance is an important issue. As a community we should be constantly working to improve tool support in all these aspects.

A variety of tool environments exists, supporting different graph transformation approaches and to some degree serving different purposes. There are some examples of tool comparisons, e.g., [5, 3, 2]; furthermore, Varro et al. [9] propose some benchmarks to be used for such purposes. Nevertheless, having a certain application in mind, it is difficult for newcomers to decide the right graph transformation tool to use. Moreover, even for most of the tool experts it is true that they know much about one or two tools but little about the others.

To stimulate both the continued improvement of tools and the wider dissemination of knowledge about existing tools, we have organised a *tool contest* as part of the AGTIVE 2007 symposium. The aim of this event was to compare the expressiveness, the usability and the performance of graph transformation tools, along a number of selected case studies. The desired outcome was twofold:

- To learn about the pros and cons of each tool considering different applications. A deeper understanding of the relative merits of different tool features will help to further improve graph transformation tools and to indicate open problems.
- To instill a sense of challenge and competition that will motivate tool developers to continue their efforts. There is nothing like seeing, and being inspired by, the features supported by other tools to stimulate progress in one's own development.

A. Schürr, M. Nagl, and A. Zündorf (Eds.): AGTIVE 2007, LNCS 5088, pp. 487–492, 2008.
© Springer-Verlag Berlin Heidelberg 2008

The case studies were selected from the entries received after an open call for cases, which was distributed among the graph transformation tool providers. The call and selection procedure are outlined in Sect. 2. This was followed by a call for solutions, distributed more widely through the usual channels for calls for papers. Since the response exceeded our expectations, it was not possible to demonstrate all solutions at the contest session, as we had originally planned. The setup eventually chosen for this session is described and evaluated in Sect. 3. In Sect. 4 we draw conclusions from the experience gained in this way, and we give recommendations for next instances of the contest.

As a final word, let us repeat the motto that we stated on the call for solutions. Tool improvement is what we seek, and this contest was a means of achieving it. To paraphrase a famous saying (see [7]):

't Is better to have competed and lost, then never to have competed at all.

2 Call for Cases

Although the idea for the tool contest has arisen at ICGT 2006, in September 2006, it took some time to put it into practice. The call for cases (constituting, in fact, the first announcement of the tool contest) was issued only three months in advance of the event, and contained a deadline of a mere two weeks for case descriptions. The call was very broad, merely asking for case studies of any kind, from which a "small but representative" subset was to be selected.

The response far exceeded our expectations: we received 13 case descriptions, of varying size and amount of detail. Since we wanted to select at most 3, we had to set up a ranking system. The following criteria were used:

Nature. What is being modelled; in other words, what is the application area? Among the cases received, the application areas were: real-world systems (a game and a biological system, respectively), semantics, model transformations of various kinds, and algorithms.

Size. What is the expected size of the solution? This can be expressed in terms of the expected number of rules (order of magnitude), the expected complexity of the meta-model and the rules. In general, the best measure is the effort to create a correct solution.

Challenge. What is (or are) the core problem(s) in solving the case? Some of the more specific challenges identified were: showing confluence and termination, verifying correctness, offering sufficient (space and time) performance, allowing human interaction. For most of the cases, however, the main challenge was to come up with a "good" model – where, of course, it is not at all easy to define the "quality" of a model in the first place.

Detail. What is the detail of the case description? Some of the submissions were quite detailed, clearly constituting cases that had already been carried out by the submitters — which is in fact something we very much encouraged in our communications, believing it to be the only way to ensure fast response. Clearly, a fair amount of detail is an advantage in a case description, in particular if this includes a good indication of the challenges (see above). On the other hand, a too precise description of the case runs the danger of leaving too little room for different solutions and creativity. In particular, a case description should describe *what* is to be done, and not *how*.

On all these dimensions, the submissions received were quite diverse. In the end we identified a partitioning from which we selected three representative cases:

Category. On a certain level of abstraction, the following three categories could be distinguished (as a mixture of the nature and the challenge of the case):

1. *General graph transformation cases.* These are real world applications, as well as algorithms, for which the main challenge lies in actually providing a model.
2. *Model transformation cases.* This is a very important application area on its own, to which much tool development has been devoted.
3. *Performance cases.* These are cases inspired by algorithms and decision problems in which the speed of transformation and/or memory consumption are the main challenges.

In each of these categories there were case submissions with a sufficient amount of detail to be usable. In the end we made the following selection:

1. *Ludo game.* This case was actually submitted by two teams, in slightly different form. It involved modelling a (fairly simple) board game, i.e., a real-world application. The challenges of this game are in modelling, visualisation and (human) interaction, and to a minor degree in analysis. This case is reported in [4].
2. *UML-to-CSP model transformation.* This is a non-trivial model transformation case, which had in fact already been studied before (see [1]). The challenges are the ease of definition and understandability of the rules, as well as the ability to read and write models in common formats. This case is reported in [8].
3. *Sierpinski triangles.* This case involves the fast and efficient generation of very large graphs, based on a simple transformation. Challenges are time and memory performance. This case is reported in [6].

It should be noted that none of these categories addresses analysis or verification issues, and indeed this was perceived as an omission in the contest. Similarly, the chosen case studies have little or no need for backtracking — which is an important element when modelling NP-complete problems using graph grammars. We will come back to this in Sect. 4.

3 Solutions

The call. The call for solutions was issued just before the summer holidays, two-and-a-half months before the workshop. The deadline for submissions was one month before the event, with notification promised ten days later. The danger with such tight deadlines obviously is that attendance may depend upon acceptance, and so late notifications can give rise to late registrations.

In the call for solutions, we merely asked that submissions should

- Contain a description of the chosen case study variant (if any);
- Present the chosen solution, including a discussion of design decisions.

As a guideline this is rather weak. In response to queries we added that submissions should

- Not exceed 5 pages in length;
- Include enough information so that readers should be able to reconstruct the solution.

As with the call for cases, the response was very good: we received 30 solutions altogether, reasonably well divided over the cases:

Case	Solutions
Ludo	8
UML-to-CSP	11
Sierpinski triangles	13

Given the absence of strict guidelines, submissions were quite diverse and, as a consequence, hard to judge and compare. For that reason we accepted all of them to the contest session. In turn, this meant we could not allow all solutions to be demonstrated during the workshop, as we had originally planned: not only would the available time be too short, but also an over-long demonstration session would not be attractive.

The event. Because of the relatively large number of submissions, the actual contest session was held in two stages, the first of which was split in three parallel meetings, one for each case. During these case meetings, a small number of submissions were demonstrated; these were selected by the organisers on the basis of the diversity of the approaches involved. The demonstrations were followed by a discussion on the aspects identified in the case, and the various solutions offered for those aspects by the different tools.

In the second (plenary) stage, after a brief report on the case meetings, a more global discussion took place on the setup and principles of the contest, the manner in which the outcome was to be published, suggestions for case studies and recommendations for future editions. For inspiration to future organisers, we include the outcome of this discussion in the form of a list of suggestions.

- Distinguish between the transformation language and the transformation tool. Criteria for the language are (among others): naturality for the domain, ease of modelling. Criteria for the tool are (among others): efficiency, usability.
- Include test suites in the case description.
- Ideas for types of case studies:
  - Large matches in irregular graphs (e.g., compiler construction problems). The main challenge is performance.
  - Refactoring. An important challenge in this context if *copying* graphs (in particular trees).
  - Comparison of different matching strategies, along the lines of the benchmarks provided in [9].

- Algorithmic problems with well-known solutions, involving backtracking
- Complex text-to-model and model-to-text transformations. A challenge is the flexibility and adaptability of the tools for this (important, and often ignored) type of transformation.
- Cases involving formal analysis/correctness proofs. Challenges are the power to address certain types of problems, and the performance in producing results.
- Ideas for organisation:
  - Throw a bunch of students at a problem, using different tools
  - Present all solutions and let the audience judge them, using a questionnaire
  - Set up a central server for a fair comparison of execution performance
  - Produce solutions under time constraints
- Set up a repository of case studies and solutions. (This has in the meanwhile been put into practice: see gtcases.cs.utwente.nl.)

4   Evaluation and Recommendations

In the following, we draw some conclusions from the past tool contest and give recommendations for the next contest round.

4.1   Evaluation

Strong points. The response to this tool contest far exceeded our expectations. It shows us that the time is ripe to initiate competition for graph transformation tools. Each part of this contest was borne by a remarkable enthusiasm of the participants. In the run-up of the tool contest, there was already remarkable stimulus for further tool development. The positive experience with this tool contest leads to enough excitement for a next edition of such a contest.

Weak points. However, the first round of this tool contest had less contest character, since we did it without any ranking. Although general challenges have been identified, they were not precisely given and could not be used to judge and to rank. Furthermore, we did not have enough time for everyone to demonstrate their solution. The tool contest could have been a workshop by its own. The time restriction led to a shift of discussions among tool builders into the preparation phase of papers [4, 6, 8] which report on the tool contest in detail.

4.2   Recommendations

For the next round of tool contests we like to give some recommendations. For truly creating a contest, a ranking should be possible. This starts with the identification of case categories and the submission of cases within these categories. Besides categories mentioned in Section 2, further categories are needed to cover all kinds of challenges for graph transformations tools. For example, a category "NP-complete problem" could be an interesting new category to test the efficiency of rule matching. Furthermore, verification issues should be covered by case studies.

All challenges should be included in case descriptions. They need to be formulated precisely enough to allow comparison. Performed experiments should be repeatable by outsiders. This requirement includes a detailed experiment description mentioning all tool specialities used. In general, the comparability of solutions has to be increased such that a ranking system can be set up.

Assuming the enthusiasm for graph transformation tool contests will hold on, the next contests should be organised as some kind of workshop which offer enough time for demonstrating all solutions, including live-demos of experiments. Since tool contests are an important incitement for tool improvements, deadlines should be less tight. Continuous comparisons and improvements of tools should be possible and supported, to keep the lively contest going on. A wiki for this purpose has been set up at gtcases.cs.utwente.nl

References

[1] Engels, G., Heckel, R., Küster, J.M.: The Consistency Workbench: A tool for consistency management in UML-based development. In: Stevens, P., Whittle, J., Booch, G. (eds.) UML 2003. LNCS, vol. 2863, pp. 356–359. Springer, Heidelberg (2003)

[2] Fuß, C., Mosler, C., Ranger, U., Schultchen, E.: The jury is still out: A comparison of AGG, Fujaba, and PROGRES. In: Graph Transformation and Visual Modeling Techniques (GT-VMT). Electronic Communications of the EASST, vol. 6 (2007)

[3] Geiß, R., Batz, G.V., Grund, D., Hack, S., Szalkowski, A.: GrGen: A fast SPO-based graph rewriting tool. In: Corradini, A., Ehrig, H., Montanari, U., Ribeiro, L., Rozenberg, G. (eds.) ICGT 2006. LNCS, vol. 4178, pp. 383–397. Springer, Heidelberg (2006)

[4] Rensink, A., Dotor, A., Ermel, C., Jurack, S., Kniemeyer, O., de Lara, J., Maier, S., Staijen, T., Zündorf, A.: Ludo: A case study for graph transformation tools. In: Schürr, A., Nagl, M., Zündorf, A. (eds.) AGTIVE 2007. LNCS, vol. 5088. Springer, Heidelberg (2008)

[5] Rensink, A., Schmidt, V.D.: Model checking graph transformations: A comparison of two approaches. In: Ehrig, H., Engels, G., Parisi-Presicce, F., Rozenberg, G. (eds.) ICGT 2004. LNCS, vol. 3256, pp. 226–241. Springer, Heidelberg (2004)

[6] Taentzer, G., Biermann, E., Bisztray, D., Bohnet, B., Boneva, I., Boronat, A., Geiß, R., Horvath, Á., Kniemeyer, O., Mens, T., Ness, B., Plump, D., Vajk, T.: Generation of Sierpinski triangles: A case study for graph transformation tools. In: Schürr, A., Nagl, M., Zündorf, A. (eds.) AGTIVE 2007. LNCS, vol. 5088. Springer, Heidelberg (2008)

[7] Tennyson, A.: In memoriam (1850)

[8] Varró, D., Asztalos, M., Bisztray, D., Boronat, A., Dang, D.H., Geiß, R., Greenyer, J., Van Gorp, P., Kniemeyer, O., Narayanan, A., Rencis, E., Weinell, E.: Transforming UML models to CSP: A case study for graph transformation tools. In: Schürr, A., Nagl, M., Zündorf, A. (eds.) AGTIVE 2007. LNCS, vol. 5088. Springer, Heidelberg (2008)

[9] Varró, G., Schürr, A., Varró, D.: Benchmarking for graph transformation. In: IEEE Symposium on Visual Languages and Human-Centric Computing (VL/HCC), pp. 79–88. IEEE Computer Society, Los Alamitos (2005)

Ludo: A Case Study for Graph Transformation Tools

Arend Rensink[1], Alexander Dotor[2], Claudia Ermel[3], Stefan Jurack[4], Ole Kniemeyer[5], Juan de Lara[6], Sonja Maier[7], Tom Staijen[8], and Albert Zündorf[9]

[1] Universiteit Twente, The Netherlands
rensink@cs.utwente.nl
[2] Universität Bayreuth, Germany
alexander.dotor@uni-bayreuth.de
[3] Technische Universität Berlin, Germany
Claudia.Ermel@tu-berlin.de
[4] Philipps-Universität Marburg, Germany
sjurack@Mathematik.Uni-Marburg.de
[5] BTU Cottbus, Germany
okn@informatik.tu-cottbus.de
[6] Universidad Autónoma de Madrid, Spain
juan.delara@uam.es
[7] Universität der Bundeswehr München, Germany
sonja.maier@unibw.de
[8] Universiteit Twente, The Netherlands
staijen@cs.utwente.nl
[9] Universität Kassel, Germany
zuendorf@uni-kassel.de

Abstract. In this paper we describe the *Ludo case*, one of the case studies of the AGTIVE 2007 Tool Contest (see [22]). After summarising the case description, we give an overview of the submitted solutions. In particular, we propose a number of dimensions along which choices had to be made when solving the case, essentially setting up a *solution space*; we then plot the spectrum of solutions actually encountered into this solution space. In addition, there is a brief description of the special features of each of the submissions, to do justice to those aspects that are not distinguished in the general solution space.

1 Introduction

The field of graph transformation was set up over 30 years ago, but the development of supporting tools started with considerable delay. Currently, a number of tool environments for different graph transformation approaches is available and the activity in tool development has increased considerably. Thus, a comparison of tools with respect to both functional and non-functional issues is becoming more and more important.

This paper describes one of the three case studies chosen for the tool contest outlined in [22], based on a (children's) game that in English goes under the name *Ludo*. The motivation for choosing this case was that it provides the following tool challenges:

1. Modelling the rules of the game in an easy and understandable way;
2. Allowing the specification of different player strategies;

A. Schürr, M. Nagl, and A. Zündorf (Eds.): AGTIVE 2007, LNCS 5088, pp. 493–513, 2008.

3. Simulating, storing and replaying different games in a flexible manner;
4. Visualising the game and allowing user interaction;
5. Offering high performance in simulating games.

The case was actually proposed by two different parties: Hölscher [14] and Kroll and Geiß [19], with somewhat different emphases: the former stresses the issue of different player strategies, the latter concentrates on some modelling aspects. The case descriptions are combined and summarised in Sect. 2 below.

The case received 8 solution submissions, with a fair diversity of approaches and choices for the different aspects of the case. In the remainder of this paper, after describing the case itself, in Sect. 3 we propose a number of dimensions or criteria along which one can distinguish solutions, and we match the submitted solutions against those criteria, thus setting up a *solution space*. Subsequently, Sect. 4 contains a short description for each of the submitted solutions, highlighting those aspects that are insufficiently covered by the general criteria. Sect. 5 ends with a conclusion, evaluation and recommendation for future cases.

2   Ludo Case Description

In this section we describe the original case, by combining the original descriptions in [14, 19] and clearing up some ambiguities.

The goal of this case is to model the "Mensch ärgere dich nicht" game, the German variant of the Ludo game. The following is adapted from Wikipedia:

"Mensch ärgere dich nicht" is a German board game, by Joseph Friedrich Schmidt (1907/1908). It is a Cross and Circle game, similar to the Indian game Pachisi, the American game Parcheesi, and the English game Ludo, though as with Ludo the circle is collapsed onto the cross.

2.1   The Game

The Ludo board consists of a directed 40 field ring in form of a cross (see Fig. 1).
    The rules are as follows:

1. There are four *players*: traditionally, red, blue, yellow and green. Every player has four *pawns*, which are not in the game initially (they are "*at home*").
2. Every 10th field serves as *entry field* for a player. Note that this imposes a cyclic order over the players. In addition, directly preceding each entry field is a junction to four consecutive *goal fields* of the same player.
3. At every point in time, it is the *turn* of one of the players. Turns rotate according to the cyclic order of players.
4. The player whose turn it is throws a *six-sided die*, and moves one of his pawns according to one of the following rules, if any is applicable. If no rule is applicable, no pawn is moved.

    Entry: If the die shows a six and the player still has pawns at home, and the player's entry field is not already occupied by a pawn of his own, he must put one pawn from his home to his entry field.

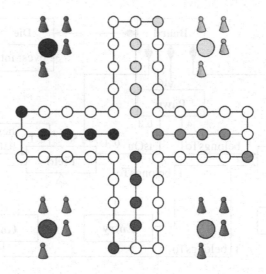

Fig. 1. The Ludo playing board

Forward: If no entry move is possible, the player must select one of his pawns
on the board and move it forward by the exact number of eyes on the die. In
doing so he may not pass (i.e., overtake) or end on his own entry field (instead
he must take the junction to his goal fields) and may not end on a field that is
already occupied by a pawn of his own. Moreover, a forward move may not
pass any pawn already on a goal field.

If there is already a pawn (of another player) on the target field of a move, then this
pawn is *kicked* and returns to the other player's home.

5. If the die roll was a six, the same player takes another turn; otherwise, the next
player (in the given order) gets his turn.

The game ends when one of the players has occupied all his goal fields. This player
has won the game.

2.2 Strategies

As with any game, an interesting question from the point of view of formal analysis
is to determine strategies for playing that are likely to win the game. Without going
into game theory, for the particular case of Ludo one can easily identify several global
strategies (global in the sense that they do not change during the game).

Aggressive: Give preference to a move that kicks a pawn;
  Cautious: Give low priority to a move that kicks a pawn (so as not to anger the other
            player);
  Defensive: Give preference to a move to a target field where the pawn cannot be
            kicked;
Move-first: Give preference to moving the foremost pawn;
  Move-last: Give preference to moving the hindmost pawn.

More sophisticated strategies can be defined by taking the moves (or the strategies) of
other players into account.

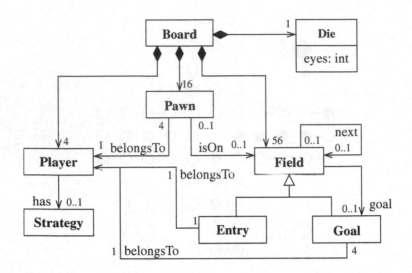

Fig. 2. Expalantory type graph for the Ludo case

3 Solution Space

In this section, we discuss some dimensions along which choices have to be made while modelling the game, and which therefore serve as a basis for distinguishing solutions. We end with a table in which all the solutions received are positioned along those dimensions.

3.1 Elements of the Model

First of all, let us describe the essential elements of any graph transformation-based Ludo model. This comes down to selecting the concepts from the case description that are turned into node and edge types. The concepts are collectively displayed in Fig. 2 in a simple type graph. (Note that this was *not* part of the case description and does not necessarily have any connection with the type graphs or meta-models used in the solutions; it is just provided for explanatory purposes.)

Player. This is modelled by a node type. Players can have an identifier or colour to distinguish them. The cyclic order of players is typically modelled explicitly (through edges).

Pawn. This is modelled by a node type. Each pawn *belongs* to a certain player; this is typically modelled by an edge, or in some cases by an attribute.

Field. This is modelled by a node type. Entry and goal fields are special kinds of fields, typically modelled by subtypes, or in some cases marked by special self-loops. The same may be done for home fields, although these are not essential for the game (we left them out of Fig. 2). Entryand goal (and home) fields belong to a player; this is typically modelled by an edge. The position of a pawn (on a field) is likewise modelled by an edge.

Board. This consists of all the fields and their interconnections, i.e., the next fields and the junctions to the goal fields. The interconnections may be turned into nodes, but typically will be modelled by edges. The board itself does not necessarily need a special node, since all fields already implicitly belong to it.

Die. This is modelled by a (singleton) node, possibly of a special type but optionally integrated with some existing node. The outcome of a die roll is then typically an attribute of the die node.

Strategy. This is modelled by a node or an attribute value; a player can then be assigned a strategy by adding an edge or attribute.

3.2 Game Rules

It is natural to turn the game rules into graph transformation rules. An important issue here is the *granularity* of the transformation rules: a rule can capture either a small part of a turn, on the level of a single step in the description of Sect. 2.1 or even smaller, or combine several such steps into an atomic whole.

The game rules impose restrictions in selecting the pawn to move, and also in executing the move. Some of these restrictions, such as the one that forbids passing a pawn on a goal field, are not straightforward to specify. An important choice is therefore whether the Ludo model indeed enforces all the game rules. There are at least the following four options:

- *A priori enforcement.* In this case, only moves that are according to the rules are ever enabled. This typically requires that the move itself is modelled by a single rule, which moves the pawn immediately to the target field.
- *A posteriori enforcement.* In this case, a move is tried out, and discarded if it leads to an illegal state, either by backtracking or marking the pawn als immovable. The actual move is then selected among the pawns that are not immovable.
- *No enforcement.* Depending on the underlying graph transformation tool, game rule enforcement may be out of scope altogether. In particular, this may be true of the solutions based on diagram editor generators: although they may offer complex editing operations that actually model a valid move, the simpler operations that result in "cheating" cannot always be turned off.

3.3 Modelling Choices

The description above already indicates that there are a number of choices to be made in the model. We list the most interesting choice points and the possible options, below.

Randomness. Die rolls are supposed to be random, but graph transformation rule application is deterministic by design (once a rule match is established). It is therefore a choice point how to obtain the non-determinism, and even more difficult, the randomness needed here. On the other hand, the Ludo case is relatively benign in that there is an a priori fixed, small number of outcomes. (This would even allow an exhaustive enumeration of all possible outcomes using 6 different rules. However, none of the submitted solutions took this "ad hoc" approach.)

Options for implementing die rolls are:

- Calling a *system function* for a random number. This means that the graph transformation is not "pure" any more, but, on the other hand, randomness is guaranteed (insofar the underlying system guarantees it). The solution also works for more general random selections.

- *User query* for the outcome. Rather than asking the underlying system, a graph transformation rule may ask the user for a "random" value. This does result in non-determinism, but not in randomness (humans are notoriously bad at randomness). Since at the point of interaction all values are still possible, a case can be made that this solution is more "pure" than the first. It also works for more general random selections.
- *Match selection.* This solution also relies on human selection of a value, but here the potential outcomes are pre-determined as part of the start graph, resulting in six different matches; a choice among the resulting rule applications is offered to the user. This has the same disadvantages as the previous solution regarding randomness, and will only work as long as the number of values is finite (and preferably small); on the other hand, it falls entirely within the graph transformation formalism.
- *Random exploration.* In this solution, like the previous, all potential rule applications are pre-computed; one is then automatically chosen, as part of the state space exploration. In this case, randomness is once more guaranteed, but like the previous solution, it will only work if the outcomes can indeed be pre-determined.

In the solutions we have seen that the first option is favoured, whereas the last option also occurs once. The second and third do not occur.

Counting. The forward move involves counting fields. In other words, the length of the path that a pawn has to traverse is determined by a number in the graph itself, namely, the outcome of the die roll. There is a choice point in how to achieve this. Additional difficulties are: (i) the pawns must go to the goal fields rather than pass again to the entry field; and (ii) pawns on the goal field may not be overtaken. Leaving aside the obvious *ad hoc* solution of specifying one rule per die roll, which was (fortunately) not chosen in any of the solutions, viable options are:

- *Numbering the fields.* By numbering the fields consecutively, the target field of a pawn can be calculated by addition modulo the number of fields. In order to ensure the additional constraints, however, quantification is needed over the intermediate fields, which requires a more powerful notion of transformation rule.
- *Single-step rules.* The granularity of the rules can be made smaller, so that each rule application only moves the pawn by one step, at the same time decreasing a counter. There are then distinct rules for intermediate steps and for the last step (when the counter decreases to zero): only in the last case a test has to be included for the presence of pawns on the target field. Since the legality of a move can sometimes only be decided later on (for instance, a move is not legal if its final field is occupied by a pawn of the same player), this solution also requires some form of backtracking.
- *System functionality* for determining the correct target location. This means that the rules interact with the underlying system to invoke dedicated code; in other words, this part of the problem is not solved within the graph transformation formalism.

Strategies. To implement a player strategy, one has to select between allowed moves on the basis of a ranking: first try out the best (kind of) move, then (if that is not possible) a less preferable one, etc. Ideally, this selection should be orthogonal to the moves themselves, i.e., the rules describing the moves should not have to be adapted in order to take strategies into account. This, however, is not easy to realise, given the fact that the strategies impose a complex ranking. In fact, there are two types of ranking: position-based and result-based.

The foremost and hindmost strategies are position-based, in that they select a move on the basis of the position of the pawn that moves. Note that it is not enough to simply require that the fore- or hindmost pawn must move, since if this pawn *cannot* move (because one of the other constraints would be violated) then the next one (from the front or back) should be selected instead, and so forth.

The aggressive, cautious and defensive strategies are result-based, in that they select a move on the basis of the outcome. This is in a sense easier than the former type of ranking, since such a condition on the outcome is essentially a right application condition in the rule, which can typically also be translated to a left application condition. In combination with rule priorities or some other form of control, this has the desired effect.

3.4 Graph Formalism

Regarding the graph transformation formalism, we distinguish the following dimensions of choice. (Note that these choices are made on the level of the graph transformation tool, and not the Ludo model.)

- The *typing* available for the graphs. All but one of the tools have a built-in notion of typing, which usually is given in the form of a type graph. In some cases these type graphs conform to an existing (standardised) meta-model, namely EMF. In one case the typing is actually determined by the underlying programming language.
- The *language* in which the rules are formulated. For most (in fact all but one) submissions this is a visual format; only one submission requires a textual input of the rules. If rules are specified visually, there is still a choice between the abstract graph or concrete syntax level; see Sect. 3.5 below.
- The *control* that is imposed on top of the graph transformation rules. The amount of control that a tool offers is an important factor in the ease with which complex game rules can be easily specified and enforced (see above). Control can range from none to a full-fledged language in which rule applications can be specified, including hints about their matchings. An intermediate option is *prioritised*, meaning that the rules have fixed global priorities. In practice we have encountered two kinds of control languages: *imperative* (programming language-style) and *storyboarded*, which is the FuJaBa speciality (see Sect. 4.1).

3.5 Visualisation

From a "lay user's" (rather than a tool developer's) perspective, one of the most important features of a graph transformation tool is surely its ability to show the graphs in a nice, easily comprehensible manner. There is a wide range of capabilities among the submitted solutions.

- *Plain graphs.* The base level, which all tools offer, is to show the abstract graphs that constitute the model. This means, for instance, that the order of the players, the numbering of the fields, etcetera, which are only there for the model and do not provide useful information for the game player, are nevertheless visible. Typically, moreover, on this level no extensive layouting support is available — and even if available, the layout information is not considered to be part of the model.
- *Concrete syntax.* A much more sophisticated visualisation is achieved if a concrete, domain-specific syntax can be defined on top of the abstract graphs. This makes for solutions that really offer something looking like a Ludo game board.
- *3D Rendering.* By far the most attractive visualisation, which only one of the solutions can offer, is a 3D view of the board. This requires a rendering mechanism that is much more sophisticated even than the concrete syntax solution described above.

3.6 Interaction

The unit of interaction between user and Ludo model is in principle a single rule application — which is indeed the obvious choice given the setting of graph transformation. However, the way applications are selected can differ, as well as the degree to which rule selection can be automated. Possible options are:

- *GUI-based interaction.* If the visualisation offers a concrete, Ludo-specific GUI view, then it may also offer functionality for selecting moves by interacting directly with this view, meaning that the rules become completely invisible. In other words, the model can have the look-and-feel of a mature game application.
- *Match selection.* Most of the tools work on the basis of pre-computed matches. The interaction is then typically through a user-guided selection of the rule to be applied, including the match if there is more than one (which is the case if there is more than one pawn that can move, or in some cases also in order to select the die roll, see Sect. 3.3).
- *Match construction.* For tools that do not rely on pre-computed matches, the user must *construct* the match by hand. A rule is executed once a legal match has been selected.
- *Partially automatic.* If there is only a single applicable rule, and the tool is able to detect this (meaning that it does not rely on user-guided match construction), then there is the possibility of executing this rule straight away, without requiring user interaction. Alternatively, some rules may always be executed automatically, whereas others (the human player's moves) always wait for user input.
- *Fully automatic.* A further step towards automation consists of automatic rule selection and execution even in the case of non-determinism. This means that a tool can play a game all on its own, without user interaction.

3.7 Analysis

A final choice point in the solutions is the amount of analysis that has been done regarding different player strategies. In particular, by letting different strategies play against one another, one may attempt to determine the best strategy experimentally. For this to be possible, the tool must first of all support fully automatic game play (see Sect. 3.6), and secondly have a performance good enough to play a reasonable number of games.

Table 3. Solution space

	FuJaBa	FuJaBa/GMF	DiaMeta	XL	AGG/ROOTS	AToM3	Groove	Tiger	
Game rules									
A priori	X	X	X	X		X	X	X	
A posteriori					X				
Cheats possible		X	X					X	
Granularity	T	T	P	T	P	P	P	S	Turn / Phase / Small step
Randomness									
System function	X	X	X	X	X	X	X	X	
Exploration					X	X	X		
Counting									
Numbered fields	X	X	X		X	X		X	
Small steps								X	
System function	X	X	X	X	X	X	X		
Strategies									
Position-based	X	X	X	X	X	X	X		
Result-based	X	X	X	X	X	X	X		
Formalism									
Typing	T	M	M	P	T	T		T	Type graph / Metamodel / Program types
Rule language	A	A	A	T	A	C	A	C	Concrete visual / Abstract visual / Textual
Control	S	S	–	–	A	P	P		Prioritised / Storyboarded / Imperative
Visualisation									
Rendered	X	GMF	X	X	X	Python	X	X	
Concrete syntax				X	X	X	X		
Abstract syntax	X	X	X		X	X	X	X	
Interaction									
GUI-based	X		X	X	X	X	X		
Match selection					X				
Match construction		X				X			
Partially automatic					X				
Fully automatic	X	X	X	X	X	X	X		
Analysis									
Performance	50	50	2600	290			1500		ms/game, rough average
Experiments	X						X		

3.8   Overview

In Table 3 we show the resulting table of choice points for the solutions received; see
also [8, 10, 20, 17, 15, 5, 2, 1].

4   Individual Solutions

4.1   Fujaba

At the University of Kassel we use the
Ludo game as an exercise for our courses
in object oriented modeling with Fujaba (see [13]) for about 4 years now.
We have also used it within highschool
courses in computer science as an example for beginners. Thus, we have many
experiences with this example and it was
easy for us to come up with a case
study for the Agtive tool contest. Our
case study addresses all the topics mentioned in the Ludo tool contest: we have
modeled the game rules. We have developed a graphical user interface for interactive playing. For this contest, we
have developed automatic player strategies and a driver for automatic simulations. Note, seeding our random number
generator results in deterministic game
simulations.

The first part of the challenge is the
modelling of the rules of the game. For
instance, Fig. 4 shows the move method
of class Stone which is invoked when
the user clicks on a pawn during the
game. This kind of diagram is called a
storyboard. The activity comment starts
with an identifer that we use for reference. Activity A1 uses a reaches
link to look up the target field that is
reached in the current situation. Note,
if method getReaches returns null,
this lookup fails and accordingly, activity A1 would fail. The rest of the story-

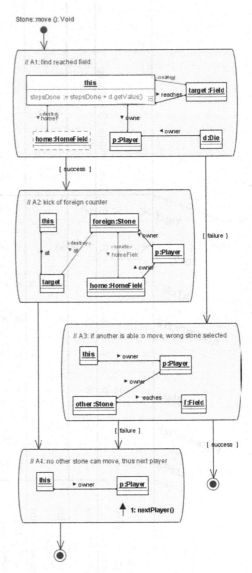

Fig. 4. Example storyboard

board implements the complete move. As a simple GUI framework we use the White-
Socks library, cf. [9]; see Fig. 5. This is created by turning the Ludo model elements
into WS objects, and by assigning appropriate icons and labels. One may play the game

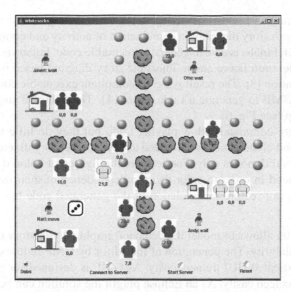

Fig. 5. Ludo game built with Fujaba and Whitesocks

by clicking on the die; this will compute a new die value and update the die icon, accordingly. Then, the player may click on one of his pawns. This will move the icon above the reached field and the die will be forwarded to the next player.

To simulate and rerun games, one may just store the start situation and then start the game with automatic players on. If one seeds the die correctly, the game will rerun similar to previous runs with the same seed.

As an example for a simulation, we have run 100 games with 2 level 7 automatic players positioned at 12 and at 3 o'clock at the board. As expected, the player at 3 o'clock has a little disadvantage because pawns waiting at the entry field of the 12 o'clock player may kick his pawns just before they enter the last lane before its goal fields. However, it was 57 wins for the 12 o'clock player and 43 for the 3 o'clock player. To simulate one game we need about 50 milliseconds where 60% of the time is devoted to the computation of priorities for the automatic players.

From our point of view, Fujaba is well suited for modelling the rules of the Ludo game and for the development of automatic player strategies. With the help of the White-Socks framework, it was easy to build a graphical user interface for the game. There may be multiple human and or automatic players at one computer or with the help of the Coobra environment mutliple player may play over the net. While the simulation performance is reasonable, we have once again recognized that our intensive usage of Java exceptions is a bottleneck for the generated code. We plan to improve this soon.

4.2 Fujaba and GMF

The following solution uses Fujaba [13] as well as the Eclipse Modelling Framework (EMF) [11] and the Graphical Modelling Framework (GMF) [12] to generate an automatic Ludo player and a Ludo editor to create, display and play the game.

First the structure of Ludo is modelled as UML class diagram. Second the behaviour is modeled with story diagrams, a combination of activity and communication diagrams, from which Fujaba is able to generate executable code. Fujaba is able to map the Fujaba-Metamodel onto Ecore and to inject the story diagram based methods into the EMF code generation [3]. The result is Ecore-compliant executable code which serves as input for the GMF to generate a Ludo editor [4]. This editor is used to create the initial board setup (see Fig. 6).

The basic editor commands allow playing Ludo but they do little to enforce valid moves. Buttons and context menus are added to execute the story diagram based methods which allow valid moves only. Furthermore the figures of colored game elements have to be enhanced in order to color them in dependency of their owner [12]. Both enhancements do not require manipulation of the generated code but are loaded in a separate plugin.

Highlights: Fujaba allows to model the behavior graphically in story diagrams which increases the readability. The generation of the editor by GMF reduces the implementation of a sophisticated GUI tremendously. As GMF is designed for extensibility the editor can be enhanced easily. As an Eclipse plugin the solution can be deployed platform independently. See [4] for more details.

Open issues: The Ludo editor intermingles both editing the game board and playing the game, so it is possible to cheat by editing the board during play. Also the mapping between Ecore-model and graphical model is limited and requires manual coding (in case of the colored elements). The missing backward trace from compiler (and runtime) errors to Fujaba diagram elements makes debugging a tedious task.

4.3 DiaMeta

We used the diagram editor generator framework DIAMETA [21] to specify the board game Ludo. The generated editor offers the possibility to specify a board and to play the game.

Specification. To create an editor for a specific diagram language with DIAMETA [21], the editor developer has to provide two specifications: First, the abstract syntax of the diagram language in terms of its model (EMF model). Second, the Designer specification that primarily contains the visual appearance of diagram components, the interaction specification and the structured editing operations. Additionally, a layouter had to be programmed since DiaMeta does not yet support automatically generating a layouter.

Functionality. The generated editor makes it easy to create different boards, e.g., varying the number of fields or pawns. Fig. 7 shows a board that was created with the editor. A board consists of a die and some connected fields. For each player, we need a certain number of pawns, home fields, entry fields and goal fields.

To play the game, the editor offers two possibilities: Having a human player that rolls a die and then moves a pawn by hand, or choosing a strategy to play the game automatically.

A human player can either operate in free-hand editing mode, or in structured editing mode. In the first case, the editor user rolls the die and then grabs a pawn with the mouse and moves it somewhere on the board. It is not checked whether the move is allowed or

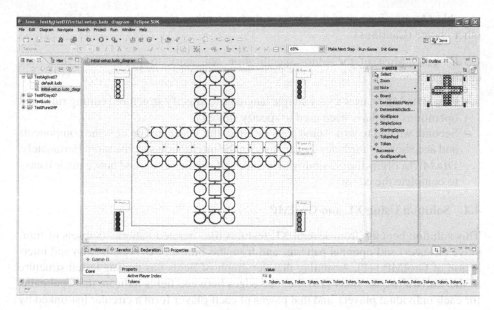

Fig. 6. GMF Ludo editor with initial board setup

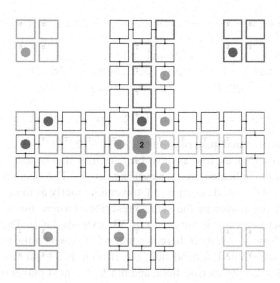

Fig. 7. Ludo board created with DiaMeta

not. In the second case, he rolls the die and then moves the pawn by clicking a button. In this case, it is checked whether the move is allowed or not.

Besides that we have the option to use a strategy, either for a single step, or to play the complete game. We can move the pawn that is nearest to the goal fields (Move-last), or we can move the pawn that is farthest from the goal fields (Move-first). Another criterion is to choose whether a player always tries to kick other players' pawns when possible (Aggressive), or if the player only kicks other players' pawns if left with no other choice (Cautious).

Challenges. Most of the editor specification was easy to write. Two parts were challenging:

- First, DIAMETA uses a very simple language to specify structured editing rules and operations that have been used to specify strategy.
- Second, we had to write some parts by hand: the visualization of some components and accessors to attributes that are used in the interaction specification. Fortunately, DIAMETA offers the possibility to include self-written code, and hence made it easy to complete the editor.

4.4 Solution Using XL and GroIMP

This solution benefits from several XL features like iterated patterns (subsets of transitive closures) and optional patterns, and from the built-in 3D visualization and interaction of GroIMP [18]. Assuming that our graph of fields has the suggested structure of the Karlsruhe case study [19] (i.e., the edges between fields indicate the legal paths for each individual player), and that pawns of each player form a circular list linked by `next` edges, the pawn movement for the Karlsruhe variant can be implemented by a single rule:

```
(* d:Die < p:Player *) -tryNext-> (* Pawn *)(-next->){0,3}:
(
    (* f:Pawn [-next-> n:Pawn] *)
    <+ (* a:Field *) (-edges[p.index]->){d.score()} b:Field
    (? +> g:Pawn(gp,h)), ((g == null) || (gp != p))
)
==>> b [f], if(g != null) (h [g]), p -tryNext-> n;
```

It makes use of an iterated pattern `(-next->){0,3}` : `(...)` which traverses 0 to 3 `next` edges (but as few as possible) to find the actually moved pawn `f`, starting at the pawn indicated by a `tryNext` edge. The second iterated pattern `(-edges[p.index]->){d.score()}` traverses exactly as many edges of the distinct edge type of the player as the score prescribes (where the implementation of the random number generator is very easy as XL extends Java). The optional pattern `(? +> g:Pawn(gp,h))` tests if there is some other pawn on the potential new field `b`. For a match of the whole left-hand side, i.e., if there is a legal move, the rule is applied and moves `f` to `b`, `g` to its base field, and marks the next player to be tried. On a 3 GHz computer using an initial seed of 98754321, the complete sequence of 460 moves takes about 290 milliseconds.

A visualization can be obtained easily within GroIMP by using predefined geometric classes as superclasses for our nodes:

```
module Field extends Cylinder(0.001, 0.4);
```

For the pawns, we may also use an interactively modelled spline curve to create a surface of revolution. As each field defines its own local coordinate system, a pawn is

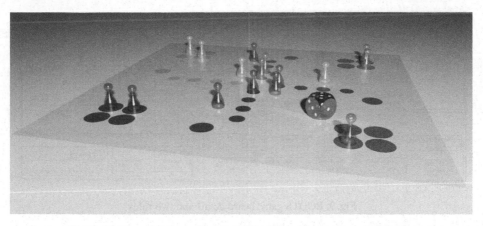

Fig. 8. 3D Visualization using GroIMP, rendered by integrated raytracer

automatically moved in 3D space from one field to another by simply redirecting its incoming edge as it is done by the movement rule. If we interactively design shaders (definitions of optical properties), we arrive at Fig. 8.

The extension of the rules to the complete set of Sect. 2.1 was also done with the exception of the interdiction to pass pawns at goal fields (but the latter could be integrated as a condition in the iterated pattern). Likewise, several strategies as well as human players were implemented. The latter can be controlled by hot-keys, but a mouse-based selection of the pawn to be moved would be possible without great effort, too.

4.5 ROOTS

The Rule-based Object-oriented Transformation System (ROOTS) is a plug-in for Eclipse, which is based on the graph transformation engine AGG following the algebraic approach. For further information on this tool see [16]. The basis of this Ludo implementation is a type graph including all elements of the game, e.g., pawn, die, fields, strategies etc. These are represented in an object-oriented manner i.e. by attributed classes, associations and inheritance. The virtual game board (clipping shown on the left of Fig. 9) is constituted by an instance of this type graph arranged analogously to the original board layout. In contrast to other solutions presented in this volume, ROOTS does not generate/compile any concrete syntax editors but directly shows the abstract syntax and allows detailed tracing of graph transformation steps.

The implemented rules define the game rules. They can be distinguished according to three different concerns: (1) starting phase e.g. negotiating the first player, (2) general game play e.g. moving a pawn, and (3) strategy-specific decisions (e.g., which pawn to move). The rule 'Roll Die' related to the first concern is exemplarily depicted on the right of Fig. 9. It demonstrates the capability of exploiting Java expressions, in particular in this case to throw the die at random. Since the strategy-relevant decisions are separated, common operations benefit from reuse and flexibility in strategy usage (during game play), by simply associating a strategy object (cp. game board graph in Fig. 9), or even omitted enabling a human player. Four different automated strategies

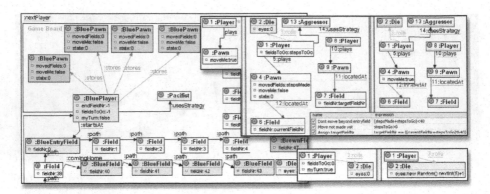

Fig. 9. ROOTS game board detail and two rules

are realized: Pacifist, Shepherd, Runner and Aggressor. The rule 'Aggressor: Mark valid move' is shown in the right corner of Fig. 9.

Our solution is purely rule-based, i.e. we use graph elements and especially attributes to control the application of rules. To support a good understanding ROOTS provides the possibility to put descriptions on almost every element.

4.6   AToM³

AToM³ [7] is a tool for the generation of modelling environments for Domain Specific Visual Languages (DSVLs). It allows describing the DSVL abstract syntax by means of a meta-model with constraints (specified in Python). The concrete syntax is specified by assigning icon-like entities to classes and arrow-like elements to associations. It is possible to define model manipulations by graph transformations. These can be customized to work under the double or single pushout approaches [23]. Rules may use the inheritance relations defined in the meta-model [6], can have application conditions of the form $p \rightarrow q$ and have a priority, so that these with higher priority are tried first. Transformations can be executed in interactive mode (the user chooses the match), or batch (rules are executed until the grammar finishes). A delay can be assigned to the rules so that the rule execution can be animated. Starting from the meta-model and the concrete syntax specifications, AToM³ generates a customized modelling environment for the DSVL. The user interface of the environment is also a model, and can be customized, e.g. adding buttons to execute transformations.

A generalization of the Spanish Ludo (called *Parchis*) has been modelled, allowing some degree of parameterization regarding the board topology, and the number of: players and their colours, pawns per player, fields to be counted when kicking pawns, and when a pawn reaches the finish. The resulting environment is shown in Fig. 10.

The game dynamics were specified using Double Pushout rules. A button was added in the final user interface to execute the transformation. The grammar runs in interactive mode, so the user selects a match for a rule if more than one is available (thus he selects the pawn to be moved). The rules moving the pawns of computer players usually produce unique matches, so no decisions have to be made (however sometimes two "equivalent" moves have to be chosen, e.g., when two pawns are the first ones, or when

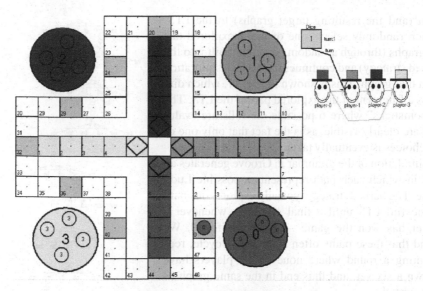

Fig. 10. The AToM³ Generated Environment

several pawns can be eaten). Regarding the visualization, rules moving pawns take care of placing them inside the target cells by means of Python code.

4.7 GROOVE

Our solution of the Ludo case is a specification of the game using the Groove tool set. Groove is a tool for graph transformations that uses directed, edge labelled simple graphs and the SPO approach. Given a graph grammar (G, P), composed of a start graph G and a set of production rules P, the tool allows to compute a labelled transition system (LTS) corresponding to all possible derivations in this grammar.

For the Ludo case, a graph is specified that models the Ludo board and the four players with their pawns. The actions of the players, including the constraints imposed by the rules of the game, are modelled as a set of nine graph transformation rules. These rules are applied in four steps: rolling the die, moving a pawn, kicking another players' pawn and selecting the player to have the next turn.

While modelling the game, we tried to keep the graph as simple and straightforward as possible (for both memory and visualisation reasons) while still being able to specify pawn-movement in a single rule, to minimize the size of the generated transition system. This is achieved by flagging the player nodes with a colour. Fields are either connected by *next* edges or by edges labelled with these colours, indicating which players are allowed to move between the fields. Groove's feature to match regular expressions (over labels on edges connecting nodes) allows to simply specify rules that move pawns into the players home and that disallow pawns to stay on the board more then a single lap.

One of the challenges was to have random results for rolling a die. The *die-roll* rule always has six possible derivations: one for each possible value of the die. We use Groove's *barbed exploration strategy* to achieve randomness. For a given state in the LTS, this strategy determines all possible rule applications and adds them (and the resulting target graphs) to the LTS. It then randomly selects one of the unexplored target graphs (through a random generator built into the barbed strategy) and continues the barbed exploration from that graph. This is shown in Fig. 11, which displays a fragment of the explored part of the LTS. The "broomsticks" where 6 possible die rolls are evaluated are clearly visible, as is the fact that only one of the choices is eventually taken.

Simulation of the grammar in Groove generates an LTS in which each path represents a possible Ludo game. The barbed strategy typically explores one path of the full LTS until a final graph — whenever a player has won the game — has been found. We found that these paths often start with a cycle, representing a round where none of the players have thrown a six yet, and thus end in the same graph as they started.

Player strategies are implemented by adding strategy-rules with a higher priority than the *move* rule, replacing it in specific cases. Example strategies implemented in this way are *foremost* and *aggressive* as discussed in Sect. 2.2. To apply a strategy to a player, the *Player* node can be tagged with the name of the strategy, which is required by the rule. This allows different players to use distinct strategies.

4.8 Tiger Plays Ludo

The TIGER project (transformation-based generation of environments) [24] aims at generating visual editors as plug-ins for ECLIPSE from a visual language specification which is based on a typed graph grammar. The TIGER *Designer* allows a language designer to define concrete visual graphics for language elements and to use this concrete syntax to define editor operations as graph rules.

The TIGER *Generator* generates visual editors where all defined editor operations are provided in the palette. In order to perform an editor operation (e.g. insert a symbol), the user has to select a rule from the palette, and, if required, to click on match objects in the editor panel where the rule should be applied.

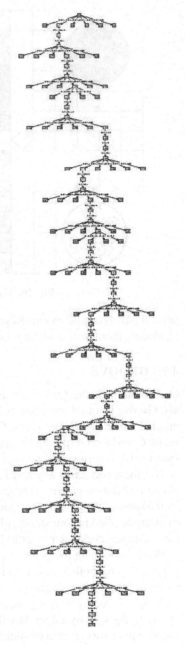

Fig. 11. Partial state space in GROOVE

Since editor usage is highly interactive (i.e. each editor operation is an action evoked by the user), TIGER does not provide means to control rule applications.

In our Ludo specification, the board with tokens in their initial position was defined as a start graph. Each graph rule for game simulation represents a phase in the game, like selecting the first player, throwing the die, moving forward, or kicking out another player's token (see the rule palette of the generated Ludo tool to the right). The only strategic choices we allow the player to make are the following: who will be the first player of the game, which token shall move (in case there is more than one token of the player's color on the field), and which token shall go to the start place (if a six has been thrown). Hence, strategies are interactive user decisions, e.g., selecting from different applicable rules or choosing one of several possible matches. In the cases where there is no choice left, only one rule will be applicable at one match to go on with the game. Due to TIGER's nature, this rule still has to be selected from the palette instead of being applied automatically.

Specifying Ludo using the TIGER Designer, rules are edited using the concrete syntax, see e.g. rule *moveOneStep* in Fig. 12 (a). Note that this rule has a set of negative application conditions (not depicted), forbidding e.g. that the next field is the entry field of the active player. Fig. 12 (b) shows the generated Ludo game environment with the Ludo board in the editor panel besides the game rule palette. The four colored fields around the die control the turns of the players. The current player and his currently selected pawn are marked by colored rings around the respective fields. Please note that due to TIGER being an editor generator, the palette may easily be extended by editing rules for drawing the game board, thus adding a flexibility of designing user-specific Ludo boards as part of the game simulation.

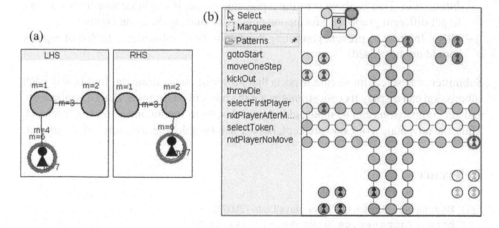

Fig. 12. TIGER rule *moveOneStep* (a) and Ludo Game Environment (b)

5 Conclusions

The response to the Ludo case has been a quite diverse set of solutions. We refer again to Table 3 for an overview and comparison along the established choice points. This multitude of solutions is, of course, very positive: clearly, many tool developers have been challenged to show what they can achieve when modelling this well-known application. Indeed, the Ludo case descriptions have left a lot of room for different interpretations and special features.

The same observation also has a negative connotation: given this diversity, there is no very objective basis for comparing, let alone ranking, the submissions. Although in Table 3 we did manage to set up a number of "choice dimensions", largely inspired by the solutions that we actually received, it would in fact be preferable to identify beforehand what the expected modelling challenges are, and in some cases perhaps also how we want them to be addressed. An example of one aspect that, in our opinion, could have been worked out to greater effect, is the analysis of the player strategies.

We recommend that a next tool contest again includes a case that is essentially about modelling a system, with at least the complexity of the Ludo game. In fact, we would favour another game-related application, since, as we have seen, this offers scope for many different tool approaches. However, we also recommend that a list of case aspects is provided beforehand, with for each aspect a description of what should be addressed. Example aspects can be found among the choice dimensions in Table 3:

– *Modelling.* This concerns particular game characteristics that are expected to be hard to model.
– *Analysis.* This concerns investigating actual game runs, comparing player strategies, etc. Possibly some performance criteria could be identified. Alternatively, correctness issues such as termination may be identified.
– *Visualisation.* This concerns creating an appealing or understandable visual model environment for the game application.
– *Interaction.* This is about creating a playable game. It might be worthwhile trying to get different graph transformation engines to play against one another.
– *Other.* In order to prevent restricting the creativity of submitters, the list of aspects should not be closed.

Submitters can select those case aspects that they will concentrate on. In this way each submission can display its own strengths, on the basis of a common, shared application, and yet comparisons can be made, along lines that were set out and known beforehand. Thus, the advantages of Ludo are kept, but we will be able to draw more value out of it.

References

[1] Biermann, E., Ermel, C.: Tiger plays Ludo (2007), http://gtcases.cs.utwente.nl/wiki/Ludo
[2] Boneva, I., Kastenberg, H., Staijen, T., Rensink, A.: The Ludo Game with the Groove Tool Set (2007), http://gtcases.cs.utwente.nl/wiki/Ludo
[3] Buchmann, T., Dotor, A., Geiger, L.: Emf codegeneration with fujaba. In: FujabaDays 2007 conference (submitted, 2007)
[4] Buchmann, T., Dotor, A., Westfechtel, B.: Model driven development of graphical tools: Fujaba meets gmf. In: Proceedings of the 2nd International Conference on Software and Data Technologies (ICSOFT 2007), INSTICC, pp. 425–430 (July 2007)

[5] de Lara, J.: Generating a Tool to Play Ludo with AToM³ (2007),
    http://gtcases.cs.utwente.nl/wiki/Ludo

[6] de Lara, J., Bardohl, R., Ehrig, H., Ehrig, K., Prange, U., Taentzer, G.: Attributed graph transformation with node type inheritance. Theoretical Computer Science 376, 139–163 (2007)

[7] de Lara, J., Vangheluwe, H.: Atom³: A tool for multi-formalism modelling and meta-modelling. In: Kutsche, R.-D., Weber, H. (eds.) FASE 2002. LNCS, vol. 2306, pp. 174–188. Springer, Heidelberg (2002)

[8] Diethelm, I., Geiger, L., Zündorf, A.: Implementing Ludo with Fujaba (2007),
    http://gtcases.cs.utwente.nl/wiki/Ludo

[9] Diethelm, I., Jubeh, R., Koch, A., Zündorf, A.: Whitesocks - a simple GUI framework for Fujaba. In: International FujabaDays 2007, Kassel, Germany (2007)

[10] Dotor, A., Buchmann, T.: Building Ludo with Fujaba and the Graphical Modeling Framework (GMF) (2007), http://gtcases.cs.utwente.nl/wiki/Ludo

[11] Eclipse Foundation: The Eclipse Modeling Framework (EMF) Overview. (2005),
    http://www.eclipse.org/modeling/emf

[12] Eclipse Foundation: GMF - Graphical Modeling Framework (2006),
    http://www.eclipse.org/gmf

[13] The fujaba toolsuite (2006), http://www.fujaba.de

[14] Hölscher, K.: Case proposal: Don't get angry (2007),
    http://gtcases.cs.utwente.nl/wiki/uploads/ludo_bremen.pdf

[15] Jurack, S., Taentzer, G.: Realizing Ludo by ROOTS (2007),
    http://gtcases.cs.utwente.nl/wiki/Ludo

[16] Jurack, S., Taentzer, G.: ROOTS: An Eclipse Plug-in for Graph Transoformation Systems based on AGG. In: Schürr, A., Nagl, M., Zündorf, A. (eds.) AGTIVE 2007. LNCS, vol. 5088. Springer, Heidelberg (2008)

[17] Kniemeyer, O.: Ludo — Solution using XL (2007),
    http://gtcases.cs.utwente.nl/wiki/Ludo

[18] Kniemeyer, O., Kurth, W.: The modelling platform GroIMP and the programming language XL. In: Schürr, A., Nagl, M., Zündorf, A. (eds.) AGTIVE 2007. LNCS, vol. 5088. Springer, Heidelberg (2008)

[19] Kroll, M., Geiß, R.: A Ludo Board Game for the AGTIVE 2007 Tool Contest (2007),
    http://gtcases.cs.utwente.nl/wiki/uploads/ludo_karlsruhe.pdf

[20] Maier, S., Minas, M.: Ludo meets DiaMeta (2007),
    http://gtcases.cs.utwente.nl/wiki/Ludo

[21] Minas, M.: Generating meta-model-based freehand editors. In: Proc. of 3rd Intl. Workshop on Graph Based Tools. Electronic Communications of the EASST (2006)

[22] Rensink, A., Taentzer, G.: AGTIVE 2007 graph transformation tool contest. In: Schürr, A., Nagl, M., Zündorf, A. (eds.) AGTIVE 2007. LNCS, vol. 5088. Springer, Heidelberg (2008)

[23] Rozenberg, G. (ed.): Handbook of Graph Grammars and Computing by Graph Transformations. Foundations, vol. 1. World Scientific, Singapore (1997)

[24] Tiger Project Team, Technical University of Berlin: Tiger: Generating Visual Environments in Eclipse (2005), http://www.tfs.cs.tu-berlin.de/tigerprj

Generation of Sierpinski Triangles: A Case Study for Graph Transformation Tools

Gabriele Taentzer[1], Enrico Biermann[2], Dénes Bisztray[3], Bernd Bohnet[4],
Iovka Boneva[5], Artur Boronat[3], Leif Geiger[6], Rubino Geiß[7], Ákos Horvath[8],
Ole Kniemeyer[9], Tom Mens[10], Benjamin Ness[11], Detlef Plump[12],
and Tamás Vajk[8]

[1] Philipps-Universität Marburg, Germany
taentzer@mathematik.uni-marburg.de
[2] Technische Universität Berlin, Germany
enrico@cs.tu-berlin.de
[3] University of Leicester, UK
{dab24,aboronat}@mcs.le.ac.uk
[4] Universität Stuttgart, Germany
bohnet@informatik.uni-stuttgart.de
[5] University of Twente, The Netherlands
bonevai@cs.utwente.nl
[6] Kassel University, Germany
leif.geiger@uni-kassel.de
[7] Universität Karlsruhe, Germany
rubino@ipd.info.uni-karlsruhe.de
[8] Budapest University of Technology and Economics, Hungary
ahorvath@mit.bme.hu, tamas.vajk@aut.bme.hu
[9] BTU Cottbus, Germany
okn@informatik.tu-cottbus.de
[10] University of Mons-Hainaut, Belgium
tom.mens@umh.ac.be
[11] Vanderbilt University, US
bness@isis.vanderbilt.edu
[12] The University of York, UK
det@cs.york.ac.uk

Abstract. In this paper, we consider a large variety of solutions for the generation of Sierpinski triangles, one of the case studies for the AGTIVE graph transformation tool contest [15]. A Sierpinski triangle shows a well-known fractal structure. This case study is mostly a performance benchmark, involving the construction of all triangles up to a certain number of iterations. Both time and space performance are involved. The transformation rules themselves are quite simple.

1 Introduction

The field of graph transformation was set up over 30 years ago, but the development of supporting tools started with considerable delay. Currently, a number of

A. Schürr, M. Nagl, and A. Zündorf (Eds.): AGTIVE 2007, LNCS 5088, pp. 514–539, 2008.

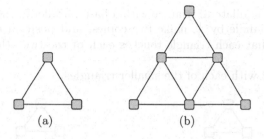

Fig. 1. Initial and first generation of the Sierpinski triangle

tool environments for different graph transformation approaches is available and the activity in tool development has increased considerably. Thus, a comparison of tools with respect to both functional and non-functional issues is becoming more and more important.

Graph transformation tools can serve very different purposes. The case study we consider in this paper allows us to compare the efficiency of graph representations and the performance of repeated rule applications. For this comparison we have chosen the generation of Sierpinski triangles. Due to its exponential nature, the problem involves graphs which are getting huge within a few generation steps. Theses graphs need not be typed and attributed; hence very simple graph models may be used. Furthermore, the generation process is very regular and can be performed with only a few rules.

In the context of the AGTIVE tool contest, the response to the call for this case study has been impressive. Twelve solutions with variants have been submitted, differing heavily in the underlying graph transformation approaches and tools, the graph representation, and the application control for rules. At the end of this paper, we categorize the given solutions and compare their runtime performance.

This paper is structured as follows: The case study used for competition is presented in Section 2. It comprises the generation of Sierpinski triangles. Section 3 gives an overview on the dimensions of solutions, while Section 4 presents a variety of concrete solutions. In Section 5, we briefly compare the presented solutions and draw some conclusions.

2   Case Study "Generation of Sierpinski Triangles"

The goal of this case study is to measure the performance of graph transformation tools constructing Sierpinski triangles. The Sierpinski triangle is a fractal named after Waclaw Sierpinski who described it in 1915. Originally constructed as a mathematical curve, this is one of the basic examples of self-similar sets, i.e. it is a mathematically generated pattern that can be reproduced at any magnification or reduction.

An algorithm for obtaining arbitrarily close approximations to the Sierpinski triangle is as follows:

1. Start with an equilateral triangle with a base parallel to the horizontal axis.
2. Shrink the triangle by $\frac{1}{2}$, make two copies, and position the three shrunk triangles so that each triangle touches each of the two other triangles at a corner.
3. Repeat step 2 with each of the smaller triangles.

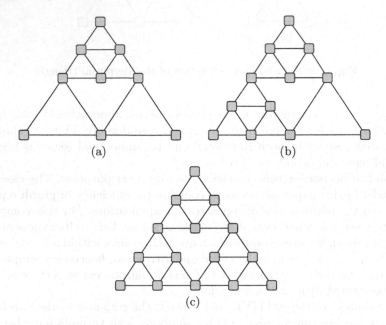

(a)   (b)

(c)

Fig. 2. Second generation of the Sierpinski triangle

2.1 Sierpinski Triangle as a Graph

For the purpose of the case study the Sierpinski triangle has to be represented as a (mathematical[1]) graph, and the construction rules have to be restated in the context of graph transformation. As an initial step a triangle has to represented as a graph: Three nodes connected by three edges (see Figure 1(a)).

Next, an elementary "Sierpinski step" is defined: On every edge of a triangle a node is placed. These new nodes are connected by edges (see Figure 1(b) in comparison to 1(a)). This forms a triangle consisting of four smaller triangles. The inner of the four triangles is considered "dead" and no further "Sierpinski steps" will be performed there. The other three triangles are candidates for further steps. (See Fig. 2 for the next elementary Sierpinski steps.) If all elementary steps are done for a certain graph (without reconsidering newly created triangles), we call this a generation (Figure 1(a) shows generation zero, Figure 1(b) shows generation one, and Figure 2(c) shows generation two). It is required for this case study that a generation is completed before any transformation for the next generation takes place.

---

[1] A mathematical graph has no immediate representation on a two dimensional plane—though embeddings may be computed.

2.2   Goals of the Case

This case study is pretty easy to implement: It uses only small pattern graphs, simple graph rewrites, and only a few rules. The generated graphs get huge fast. The number of nodes is equal to $\frac{3}{2}(1+3^n)$ and the number of edges is $3^{(n+1)}$ with n being the number of generations. So it tests the ability of a tool to represent large graphs efficiently, and to perform simple rewrites, fast. With growing number of generations it is possible to sample memory usage and computation time. Last but not least, we can see how the tools are capable of enabling adequate meta models, rule sets, and rule applications.

3   Overview on Solutions

The solutions presented in the following differ heavily. For getting a better overview, we discuss those dimensions of modelling that play a role for this case study.

3.1   Modelling Choices

The solutions presented below differ heavily concerning the representation of graphs and modelling of Sierpinski steps. In the following, we list the main alternatives.

Graph representation. In most solutions, graph nodes and edges are typed and carry information important for the generation process, i.e. they mostly guide the generation process. Some solutions also use additional nodes or edges to store data about intermediate steps of the Sierpinski triangle generation. Moreover, also node attributes are used for storing additional information. Clearly, additional graph elements and attributes may affect the efficiency of graph representation.

Modelling of Sierpinski steps. All solutions contain one or more rules for performing an elementary Sierpinski step. All generation steps, except the first one, consist of several applications of the elementary step. The solutions show different kinds of controlling rule applications. Basically, we can distinguish parallel from sequential rule application.

The generation of Sierpinski triangles is well suited for parallel rule application and means that the basic Sierpinski step is performed on all triangles being "alive" simultaneously (compare Sec. 2.1).

Sequential rule application necessarily leads to intermediate graphs where some atomic triangles of the current generation step are already refined, while others still have to be considered. For not refining an already refined triangle again in the same generation step, some application control has to be added which can be done in different ways. Some solutions add further graph elements holding information about the generation process and/or add application conditions to their generation rules or even add further rules, while others rely on external control which is formulated by e.g. regular expressions. Besides just controlling the selection of rules, some solutions even control the rule matching explicitly and thus eliminate any kind of non-determinism in rule application.

3.2 Graph Transformation Approaches

A number of different graph transformation approaches are used to perform the generation of Sierpinski triangles. The solutions proposed differ also according to offered graph transformation features. In the following, we sketch the most important features for this case study:

- Nearly all solutions use typed graphs, sometimes even with node type inheritance.
- Some solutions are based on attributed graphs. In these cases simple attribute computations are performed only.
- The approaches differ in the ability to visually or textually represent graph rules.
- While most approaches offer sequential rule application only, there are some approaches which support parallel rule application (in addition). Here, a rule is applied to all possible matches in parallel. Note, that parallel refers to simultaneous rewriting semantics; it has not necessarily to be implemented by parallel threads of any kind. In fact almost all tools do not support thread-based or distributed rewriting.
- To further control sequential rule application, additional application conditions for rules are offered by several approaches. These include negative application conditions, attribute conditions, and type conditions.
- Another form of application control is to put control on top of rules by using concepts from regular expressions, abstract state machines, activity diagrams, Java programs, and recursive rule application. Some of these forms allow to control rule matches in addition.

4 Solutions

In the following, twelve different graph transformation solutions for the generation of Sierpinski triangles are presented. These solution are available with all details at the following newly created Web site for graph transformation cases: http://gtcases.cs.utwente.nl/

4.1 Tiger EMF Transformation Framework

The Tiger EMF Transformation Framework (EMT) [16] is a tool for modeling and applying graph transformation rules. The solutions consist of a set of graph transformation rules on EMF [8] models, that are designed using the Visual Editor of EMT. The production rules are defined by rule graphs, namely a left-hand side (LHS) and a right-hand side (RHS). The rule set is compiled to Java code and run by the Eclipse development platform [7]. This enables the implementation of control structure to perform the specified changes to the given model instance.

Two solution were implemented, a deterministic and a non-deterministic one.

Deterministic solution. This solution uses a programmed control flow to apply rules.

For our solution we first define an EMF model and an initial Sierpinski triangle as shown on the right. This can be defined by using any editor for EMF models, for example the EMF tree editor.

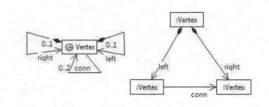

Afterwards we define two rules for transforming a Sierpinski instance such that we reach a new Sierpinski generation. This can be done by using the graphical rule editor which is part of EMT. The defined rules are translated to Java code that changes a given Sierpinski triangle as described by the rules *AddTriangle1* and *AddTriangle2*. In our case we need two rules because EMF requires a containment hierarchy between all classes and a class can only be contained in exactly one other class. Rule *AddTriangle1* refines left triangles where the upper vertex contains both lower vertices, while *AddTriangle2* refines right triangles. Here, the upper vertex contains the lower right vertex only.

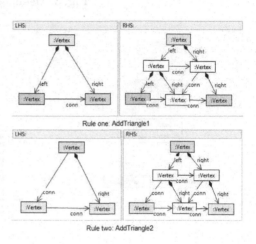

In the next step we define a control structure for the application of our two rules. AddTriangle1 should be applied to the uppermost vertex and if possible to all left children. AddTriangle2 should be applied to all right children if possible. Both rules are no longer applicable when attempting to apply AddTriangle1 or AddTriangle2 to the vertices at the bottom of the containment hierarchy. After the control structure terminates, the resulting model instance is a new Sierpinski generation.

Non-Deterministic Approach. The non-deterministic solution uses the algorithm from [12] to generate the Sierpinski triangles.

The metamodel shown in Figure 3 was used. There are two types of nodes. The *NormalNode* is an ordinary node in the Sierpinski structure, while the *CentralNode* is used to mark those triangles that needs unfolding in the next Sierpinski step. The *Alive* property of *CentralNode* indicates if that triangle is alive in that step.

The Sierpinski step is implemented with the rule depicted in Figure 4. A triangle that has an *alive CentralNode* gets unfolded. The generated triangles

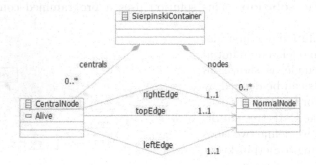

Fig. 3. Metamodel

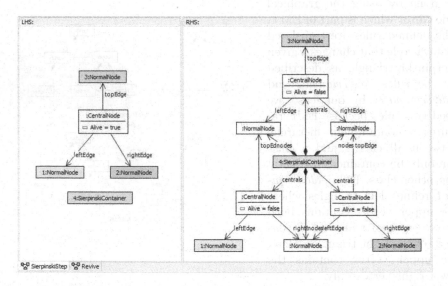

Fig. 4. Sierpinski Step

are not *alive*. When all alive triangles have been unfolded, a second *aliveRule* revives them for the next step. These two phases form the Sierpinski step.

4.2   Graph Transformation Using Two Tapes

Using two tapes in graph transformation has many advantages since the rule interpreter can apply rules in parallel. During the rule application, the input graphs stay unchanged while the rule interpreter builds up new graphs. Therefore, rules can access the input graphs as well as the graphs created so far. In the case that rules need the result of other rules they form a sequence. Later applied rules might apply in parallel with other rules in the same state. The context (conditions) determines the application order of these rules and not an explicit specification of the order.

We originally developed the approach for Natural Language Processing (NLP) where we use it for instance to generate texts by mapping text plans to semantic graphs, semantic graphs to syntactic graphs, and syntactic graphs to topological graphs, cf. [5]. The demands for the graph transformation language come from the area of NLP where the rule interpreter can do much in parallel because of the nature of the application, but not everything. An example for this is the mapping of syntactic graphs to topological graphs that we apply to determine the word order. The words for example of all noun phrases (such as 'the blue car') can be ordered independently of other noun phrases and therefore in parallel whereas distinct complete phrases of German sentences are ordered depending on the position of the main verb. These rules determine first the position of the verb and depending on the result, the position of the other parts. Within the same graph transformation approach, we could easily describe the mapping of the Sierpinski triangle with one rule. The rule interpreter applies rules in four steps. (1) First, it searches with a parallel matching algorithm all occurrences of the left-hand side in the input graph and evaluates the conditions. (2) Then the rule interpreter clusters the rules, which are applicable together. In the case of the Sierpinski triangle, the rule interpreter builds only one cluster since no alternative rules are specified. (3) After that, the rule interpreter creates the right-hand sides of the rules for each matched rule in parallel. (4) Finally, the rule interpreter glues the graph fragments together.

The approach works very well and fast for the problem of the Sierpinski triangle. It builds the thirteenth generation with one core of a CPU in 18.9 seconds and the speed nearly doubles to 10.3 seconds with four cores of the same CPU. Looking at the figures, the question comes up, why does the processing speed not increase even more? Partially essential is that the gluing step is not performed in parallel and compared with the gluing the parallel matching works in this application on a three times smaller data set, therefore it contributes much less to the processing time. Another part of the answer seems related with the used CPU itself due to a test, which identified the memory bandwidth as a problem. The cause could be that the CPU is a first generation quad core, which is blamed as a not 'native' quad core. Nevertheless, the parallel approach is very promising since in future CPUs with many more cores will become standard and many applications such as the evolution of plants or Natural Language Processing fits very well to parallel approaches, which are capable to compute, like our brain, solutions in parallel.

4.3 The Groove Tool

Groove is a graph transformations tool-set based on the SPO approach for untyped, edge-labelled, simple graphs. The tool-set comes with a GUI allowing to easily define transformation rules and graphs, and to apply graph transformation either interactively, or automatically using so called exploration strategies. Strategies can also be used without the graphical interface. Although Groove is a general purpose graph transformation tool, it is optimised for generating (a finite portion of) all possible derivations in a graph grammar and allows to verify properties on the set of derived graphs and on the derivation paths. Groove is Java-based, so platform independent. The tool, as well as the solution presented here, can be downloaded at [1].

Let us now explain the main characteristics of our modelling of the Sierpinski triangles in the Groove framework.

Modelling the triangles and the rules. Fig. 5 represents an intermediary graph met while computing the second generation.[2] The bottom part represents the Sierpinsky fractal itself encoded by a set of triangles in a very straightforward way. The top part is additional control structure present in the graph. It is composed by generation nodes numbered from 0 to 4 (for computing the fourth generation), and a "current" marker indicating the currently computed generation. Each elementary triangle "belongs" to the generation on which it was constructed, encoded as an additional edge from its top node to the corresponding control node. On Fig. 5, the two big elementary triangles belong to the first generation, and the three small elementary triangles belong to the current, second generation. This is used to ensure that a particular generation is completed before the computation of the next one starts. Transformation is ensured by two small and simple rules. The first one performs an elementary step: a triangle belonging to the previous generation is replaced by three new triangles of the current iteration. On Fig. 5, such elementary step was just performed on the bottom right triangle. The second rule is with lower priority, thus applicable only if the first one does not match. It simply moves the "current" marker to the control node corresponding to the next generation. None of the rules uses negative application conditions.

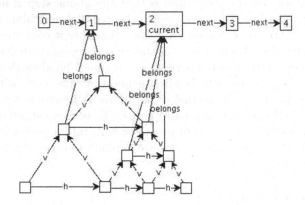

Fig. 5. Intermediary graph while computing the second iteration

Computing the fractal. Transformations in Groove are fully non-deterministic, on purpose. However, in the case of the Sierpinski triangles, rule applications are confluent. We used the existing *Linear exploration strategy* to ensure that

---

[2] Node labels on that figure are just another representation of self-edges.

only a single derivation path is computed, thus avoiding superfluous rule transformations. Moreover, the tool allows to specify in which order edge labels should
be matched, thus guided finding of matches. In the case of the Sierpinski triangles
this allowed to avoid the computation of any superfluous matches.

Performance. Memory is a critical resource in Groove. As mentioned previously, the tool computes the set of all graphs derivable in a graph grammar
and stores all intermediate results. Different memory-saving mechanisms are in
place, as for instance sharing nodes and edges between graphs. They showed
quite efficient, as we managed to compute the twelfth iteration of the Sierpinski
fractal on a desktop machine with 1,5 GB of memory and in 45 seconds.

Alternative solution using quantified transformations. Since its last version, Groove implements so called quantified transformation rules. Roughly
speaking, and among other things, quantified rules allow to make atomic the
application of a rule for all of its matches in the host graph. In the case of
the Sierpinski triangles, one can define a single, quite compact rule that is responsible for the computation of one generation. This results in slightly better
performance, but the main improvement is the increased expressiveness of transformation rules. More information on quantified transformations can be found
in the Groove documentation accessible at [1].

4.4   MOMENT2-GT

MOMENT2-GT is a graph transformation tool based on the SPO approach.
Graphs are provided as EMF-based models so that their nodes are attributed
and typed, taking inheritance into account. Graph transformation definitions
are constituted by a set of production rules, which are defined in a QVT-based
textual format, where OCL expressions can be used either as guards in (possibly
negative) application conditions or as attribute value manipulation expressions.
In MOMENT2-GT, a graph transformation definition is compiled into a rewrite
theory in Maude [6]. MOMENT2-GT permits defining production rules as deterministic (production equations) or non-deterministic (production rules). The
inclusion of this explicit difference allows performing model checking of graph-
based systems where states are algebraically defined by means of a metamodel
and production equations, and transitions between such states are defined as
production rules. In EMF, bidirectional and containment edges can be defined.
MOMENT2-GT takes into account such features to avoid the generation of inconsistent EMF models with dangling edges. This consistency checking can be
disabled if dangling edges are explicitly avoided in the transformation definition.
The tool and the solution presented here are available at [3].

In this solution, we have based ourselves on the transformation that is provided in [12], also implemented with the Tiger EMF Transformer (see the non-
deterministic solution in Section 4.1). Our transformation definition consists in
two simple rules: *a)* a first rule computes the division of a triangle and *b)* a
second rule ensures that the following iteration in the fractal generation process

is not performed until all triangles have been split. The second rule contains a negative application condition.

In MOMENT2-GT, the input graph is represented as a term of a specific sort that is defined in a rewrite theory, and the execution of a graph transformation is handled by Maude's algorithm for term rewriting modulo associativity and commutativity. Maude finishes the graph rewriting process when it achieves a normal form. The resulting term is parsed by MOMENT2-GT and projected as an EMF model again.

Although our tool is based on the reuse of Maude's term matching algorithm without taking into account optimized rewriting strategies, we have shown that MOMENT2-GT can be used to rewrite reasonably big graphs but efficiency needs to be improved still. The advantage of our approach relies on the reuse of Maude-based formal verification techniques [6] for graph transformations together with modeling standards.

4.5 Fujaba Solution

This section reports on our case study with the Fujaba environment, cf. [2], on building Sierpinsky triangles. It turned out, that the key bottleneck for building Sierpinski triangles is the memory usage. Thus, we exploited Fujaba's code generation features for the implementation of unidirectional to-one associations. Our model uses objects for the vertices of triangles with only three unidirectional to-one associations to refer to the horizontal right neighbor and to the vertical left and right neighbor. This models the triangles, appropriately, with a small memory footprint. Actually, we found out that two outgoing edges per node are sufficient. Thus, our model can even be reduced by one edge. But the rules for this solution are a bit more complex, so we won't explain this solution here due to space constraints.

We have decided to use a recursive approach for building the triangles. Figure 6 shows that recursive rule. The rule has to be executed on the top node of a triangle. This node is represented by the `this` node in our rule. From that node the `left` edge is traversed to get the left node of the triangle and the `right` edge to get the right node. To represent the triangle structure the `horizontal` edge is checked as well. Note, this could be omitted for further performance tuning. Now a new triangle is created into the one found before. This is indicated by the elements marked with ≪create≫. Since we use to-one links creating a new link automatically destroys the old link. So we left out the ≪destroy≫ markers for performance reasons. When the current triangle has been refined, we initiate the refinement of the left and the right underlying triangles. This is specified using a recursive call on the `left` and the `right` object. Note that, if the lookup for the triangle in this rule is not successful, the modifying operations are not executed. That results in termination of the recursion if the bottom triangles have been refined.

To initialize the algorithm an initial triangle has to be created. On the top node of the triangle the `refine` method described above can be called several times depending on the number of iterations one wants to calculate. This

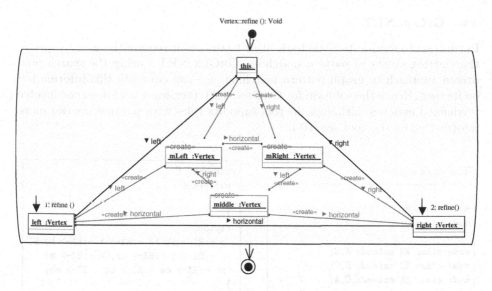

Fig. 6. Refining Rule for Sierpinski triangles

execution is modeled by a second rule not shown here. From these rules Fujaba now generates standard Java code which can be used for performance measuring.

Measurement Data. We have done our measurements on a 64-bit quad core AMD processor with 32GB memory using Java6. 15 iterations take about 1.4 seconds. Each additional iteration takes about three times longer until the memory is full. On our machine this works up to iteration 17 (12 seconds). We found that in our model the runtime consumption for graph pattern lookup is neglectable since we use a recursive approach that passes the important handle elements to the next rule application. Thus runtime is dominated by creating new objects and assigning pointer values. Since our approach seemed fast enough for us, we tried to optimize the memory footprint to be able to do some more iterations. Fujaba uses objects to represent nodes and fields of those objects to represent edges. So only the objects need memory. On a 32-bit machine, each of our nodes has three pointers which take 4 bytes each. A Java object has an additional pointer to its class and a unique ID which are both again 4 bytes each. So one node costs 20 bytes. On our 64-bit system the memory usage doubles. To get rid of the 16 bytes of Java internal memory usage, we wrote a C++ code generation for Fujaba. C++ objects do not have the unique ID and if all methods are declared final also no pointer to their class. That way we were able to reduce the memory usage to 12 bytes per node. So, using C++ one more iteration fits into our memory. But the generated C++ code was a bit slower than the Java code. 17 iterations took 22 seconds and 18 took 1:08 minute. Using the algorithm mentioned above which needs only two pointers per node, we were even able to reduce the memory footprint to 8 bytes per node for the C++ code. The rules needed here just need one additional distinction of cases which does not make them measurably slower.

4.6 GrGen.NET

In contrast to semi-automatic tools like FUJABA, that require the user to specify the starting points of pattern matching, GRGEN.NET—using the search plan driven approach to graph pattern matching [4]—can compute this information on its own. Hence the solution for GRGEN.NET (version 1.3.1) does not involve predefined matches, although the tool supports rules with parameters (for more information on the tool see [10]).

The meta model:

```
node class A;
node class B;
node class C;

node class AB extends A,B;
node class BC extends B,C;
node class CA extends C,A;

edge class E0;
edge class E1;
```

The rules:

```
rule init {
  pattern {
  }
  replace {
    a:A -:E0-> b:B -:E0-> c:C -:E0-> a;
  }
}
```

```
rule gen0 {
  pattern {
    a:A -:E0-> b:B -:E0-> c:C -:E0-> a;
  }
  replace {
    a -:E1-> ab:AB -:E1-> b -:E1-> bc:BC
      -:E1-> c -:E1-> ca:CA -:E1-> a;
    ab -:E1-> ca -:E1-> bc -:E1-> ab;
  }
}
```

```
rule gen1 {
  pattern {
    a:A -:E1-> b:B -:E1-> c:C -:E1-> a;
  }
  replace {
    a -:E0-> ab:AB -:E0-> b -:E0-> bc:BC
      -:E0-> c -:E0-> ca:CA -:E0-> a;
    ab -:E0-> ca -:E0-> bc -:E0-> ab;
  }
}
```

Fig. 7. The meta model and all rules for the GRGEN.NET-based solution

As a first step we generate an initial triangle with the rule `init` (see Figure 7). Afterwards we use two almost identical rules (`gen0`, `gen1`) in an alternating fashion. Each rule is applied as long as possible, thus computing a whole generation. The graph rewrite sequence `init & (gen0* gen1*)[5]+` produces the 10th generation (see [10]).

The edge types E0 and E1 are used for distinction of generations, i.e. the rule `gen0` replaces E0 edges with E1 edges and vice versa. The node types together with the orientation of the edges ensure that only appropriate (not dead) triangles are matched; in particular node types encode the positions. We use multiple inheritance to cope with the situation, where one node occurs in two triangles in different positions.

We also experimented with parallel rewriting semantics. This way only one rule is needed to refine the initial triangle, because the interlocking of steps is done automatically. Analogous to the graph rewrite sequence above, we get `init & [gen][10]`. Due to the overhead of temporarily storing all matches, this approach takes 20% more time.

Because GRGEN.NET always supports all features like multi-edges, complex type hierarchies as well as attributed nodes and edges, performance-wise suboptimal code is produced. Note that the information present in a meta model (like *connection assertions*) is rich enough to automatically generate a stripped down and therefore more efficient implementation (see LIMIT in Section 5.2).

4.7   Viatra2

The current section highlights the concepts used to implement the Sierpinski triangles example in the VIATRA2 [9] (VIsual Automated model TRAnsformations) framework. VIATRA2 is a general-purpose model transformation engineering framework that aims at supporting the entire life-cycle, i.e. the specification, design, execution, validation and maintenance of transformations within and between various modeling languages and domains in the MDA.

Metamodel and Transformation. From the programmers point of view, the most difficult part of implementing the Sierpinski triangle generator is to create the correct triangle *"finder mechanisms"*. In our solution, we tried to adhere to the typing scheme found in the problem description by taking advantage of the multiple-inheritance support of the VIATRA2 framework resulting the metamodel depicted in Fig. 8.

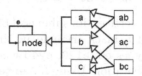

Fig. 8. The metamodel of the Sierpinski triangles

This representation allowed us to create a very simple and elegant pattern – used in VIATRA2 to describe the *precondition* (LHS and the NACS) of a GT rule – illustrated in Fig. 9, where the right and left side describe the Viatra Textual Command Language (VTCL) representation and the graphical notation, respectively. Capital letters stand for variables, normal letters denote direct references to modelspace elements. For instance the expression `a(A)` declares that the variable `A` is of type `a`. On the other hand, the expression `node.e(ECA,C,A)` means that the variable `ECA` refers to an edge of type `node.e` that points from the entity in `C` to `A`. The pattern in Fig. 9 matches a triangle with vertices type `a,b,c`, respectively. The order is granted by the direction of the arrows.

As for the model manipulation part, instead of using *GT rules* for the triangle generations we were utilizing *graph patterns* to match the corresponding model parts and then performing the model manipulation by built in ASM rules. This resulted in overall better memory consumption and a slightly faster runtime performance.

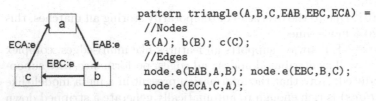

```
pattern triangle(A,B,C,EAB,EBC,ECA) =
//Nodes
a(A); b(B); c(C);
//Edges
node.e(EAB,A,B); node.e(EBC,B,C);
node.e(ECA,C,A);
```

Fig. 9. Sierpinski pattern

Conclusion. Note that, we also used the example for profiling the upcoming VIATRA2 release and it pointed out that the most critical part in the pattern matching process is the *model manager* as it took more than 99 percent of the total execution time. As for the overall performance, we were happy to see that our current *interpretation* based engine can handle up to 800000 model elements (level 11) within reasonable time.

4.8   Solution Using XL

The XL solution [11] is very simple as rules are applied in parallel by default, which exactly matches the Sierpinski construction. The complete rule is:

```
a:LLVertex -e0-> b:Vertex -e120-> c:Vertex -e240-> a ==>>
    a -e0-> ab:LLVertex -e0-> b -e120-> bc:Vertex -e120-> c
        -e240-> ca:LLVertex -e240-> a,
    ca -e0-> bc -e240-> ab -e120-> ca;
```

The class **Vertex** represents vertices, its subclass **LLVertex** those vertices which are the lower left vertex of a black triangle in the usual 2D representation. Furthermore, we use edge types e0, e120, e240 where the number is the angle of the edge in the 2D representation. Using **LLVertex** speeds up matching since a match for the pattern exists if and only if a is a lower left vertex of a black triangle. Thus, we exclude dead ends of pattern matching as soon as possible.

We tested the performance of our solution in four different settings. The simplest one uses the graph model of the modelling environment GroIMP [11]. This introduces some amount of memory overhead as nodes store additional book-keeping information and all changes to the graph are logged in a protocol. On a 3 GHz computer with 2 GB RAM we were able to execute 13 steps, the last step took 17.3 seconds on average. But logging can be deactivated which is our second setting and allowed an additional step. This setting is also used for the benchmark in Figure 15. A significant improvement concerning memory consumption and speed (roughly factor 3 in both respects) is achieved by the third setting where we use our own minimal graph model whose nodes only store three pointers to adjacent nodes, thus indirectly representing the edges (which can no longer be traversed bidirectionally). On 32-bit Java virtual machines, such a node requires 20 bytes. We were able to execute 15 steps, the last step took 54.7 seconds on average. The fourth setting reduces the memory consumption to 8.25 bytes (66 bits) for lower-left vertices and 0 bytes for the other ones on both 32- and 64-bit machines: at first, we dispense with the e120 edge so that only a subgraph of the Sierpinski graph is generated (but which can be extended to the true graph by local operations). Furthermore, we address vertices by unique `long` values which in case of lower-left vertices are indices into a list of pairs of 33-bit values which hold the addresses of the neighbours. 33 bits are sufficient for up to 20 steps, the final graph then consumes nearly 27 B of memory. On a 2.6 GHz computer with 32 GB RAM (thanks to Andreas Hotho, University of Kassel) we were able to execute 20 steps where the last step took 2 hours on average, resulting in a graph with 5,230,176,603 nodes and 6,973,568,802 edges.

Being able to use XL for any given graph structure, even exotic ones as in the last setting, is certainly a highlight. We have to admit that the last setting is very tricky and requires temporary proxy objects in order to be accessible for XL.

4.9 AGG

The graph transformation tool *AGG* was developed at TU Berlin to explore advanced graph transformation properties for doing formal analysis. Performance was not one of its main design criteria. *AGG* can be used in two different modes: (a) via its built-in GUI to specify and execute graph transformations visually; (b) via its API to write Java programs that use AGG's underlying graph transformation engine. We explored both ways to implement the Sierpinski triangle.

GUI with rule sequences and NACs. Our first implementation resorts to *AGG*'s ability to define *rule sequences*, i.e., a predefined composition of graph transformation rules. We used the following rule sequence:

(FindMatch{*} ApplyToMatch{*}){n}

where integer value n represents the desired number of iterations, and {*} denotes that each rule is applied as long as possible. The two transformation rules

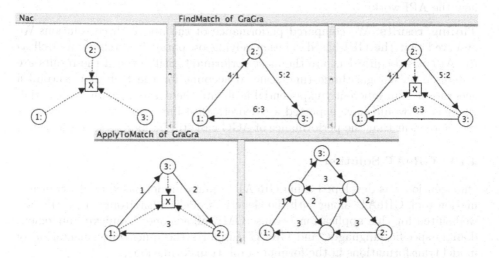

Fig. 10. Implementation of Sierpinski in AGG with NACs and rule sequences

in this rule sequence are shown in Figure 10. `FindMatch` identifies and annotates all triangles that need to be expanded. It uses a negative application condition to avoid applying the rule more than once to the same occurrence. `ApplyMatch` performs the actual transformation on the found matches. This solution has two shortcomings. First, it requires an auxiliary, somehow artificial, node X. Second, the timing results are not very promising.

GUI with parallel matching. To improve performance, Olga Runge extended the *AGG* engine with a mechanism of *parallel matching*, enabling the computation of all possible matches of a given rule at once, and then repeatedly applying the desired transformation to all of these matches. For the Sierpinski example, this feature allowed us to simplify the solution by using only one rule (Figure 11), while simultaneously improving the timing results.

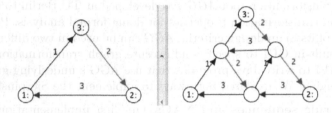

Fig. 11. Implementation of Sierpinski in AGG using parallel matching

API-based solution. For our third and final implementation, we wrote a simple Java program that calls AGG's API to execute the graph transformations. This solution also relied on a single rule (Figure 11) using parallel matching, but was more complex to implement since one needs to write a Java program and know how the API works.

Timing results. We compared performance of the above three solutions. We observed that the GUI-based solution relying on parallel matching, as well as the API-based equivalent are the most performant. Still, even if the results are visualised on a logarithmic time scale to account for the fact that Sierpinksi generation is an inherently exponential problem, the curves remain exponential, whereas we would have expected a (theoretically) linear increase instead. It is therefore clear that the performance of AGG can still be increased considerably.

4.10   GReAT Solution

One solution was developed using GReAT, a meta-model based model transformation tool. GReAT, along with the Generic Modeling Environment, GME, are well-suited for this application because GME allows one to quickly implement domain-specific languages, and GReAT supports the quick implementation of model transformations in the form of graph transformations.

The overall process we used was the following. We started by defining a meta model in GME to describe models of Sierpinski Triangles. Next, we created an instance model of this meta-model that contained one triangle. We then created a GReAT transformation that performed the Sierpinski Triangle-generation algorithm on this instance model using simple graph rewriting rules that are explicitly sequenced.

The meta model consisted of a base object, SierpinskiTriangleModel. This object serves as the root container of the model as well as the container for all other objects. The "Generations" attribute on this object indicates the number of times the Sierpinski algorithm is to be performed on the input graph. The "DecrementGeneration" attribute is used during the transformation to determine when the "Generations" attribute is ready to be decremented. "Node" objects are used to represent triangle vertices, and "Connection" objects are used to represent the edges between triangles.

Using GReAT, a simple graph transformation was written to generate the Sierpinski triangle graph. The transformation takes an input graph containing a single triangle and produces the corresponding Sierpinski generation as a separate output file.

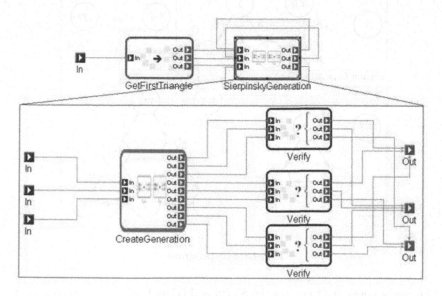

Fig. 12. GReAT rules

The transformation consists of several simple rules that are organized into hierarchical blocks. The first rule, "GetFirstTriangle" (see Figure 12), locates the triangle in the input model. The next block, "SierpinkiGeneration", is a sequence of rules that, when executed, will rewrite the graph into the next Sierpinski generation. "DecrementRule" (a rule contained inside the "CreateGeneration" block) is executed once per generation rather than once per triangle. After every execution of the "CreateGeneration", the number of generations remaining is compared to zero in the Verify test case. Once the "Generations" attribute equals zero, the Verify test case will fail, and the transformation will end.

Using GME and GReAT to perform this transformation provided a very simple, graphical approach that was very easy to implement and execute while still achieving an acceptable level of performance. In addition, smaller generations are very easy to visualize using the GME interface.

4.11   Generating Sierpinski Triangles with GP

The graph programming language GP is based on conditional rule schemata [14]. The program in Figure 13 consists of three rule-schema declarations and the main command sequence following the key word main. It expects as input a graph consisting of a single node labelled with the generation number of the Sierpinski triangle to be produced.

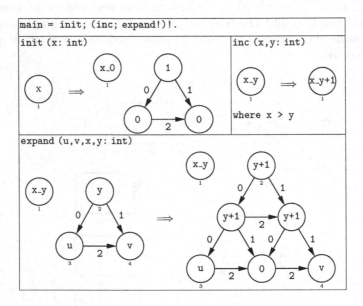

Fig. 13. GP program

The rule schema init creates the Sierpinski triangle of generation 0 and turns the input node into a unique "control node" whose label is of the form x_y. The underscore operator allows to hold the required generation number x and the current generation number y in a common node.

After init has been applied, the nested loop (inc; expand!)! is executed. Intuitively, the operator ! executes a subprogram as long as possible. In each iteration of the outer loop, the rule schema inc increases the current generation number if it is smaller than the required number. The latter is checked by the condition where x > y. If the test is successful, the inner loop expand! performs a Sierpinski step on each triangle whose top node is labelled with the current generation number: the triangle is replaced by four triangles such that the top nodes of the three outer triangles are labelled with the next higher generation number. The test x > y fails when the required generation number has been reached. In this case the application of inc fails and hence the outer loop terminates and returns the current graph. The resulting graph is the Sierpinski triangle of the required generation.

The GP compiler translates the program of Figure 13 into bytecode that can be executed by the York abstract machine [14]. The execution times shown in Figure 15 have been obtained on a PC with an Intel Pentium 4 processor with a clock rate of 2.80GHz and 512MB of main memory. For these executions, the backtracking mechanism of the abstract machine has been switched off because the program's input/output behaviour is deterministic.

Most of the execution time is used to create the elements of the triangles while matching the left-hand sides of the rule schemata is fast due to the uniqueness of the control node labelled with x_y. In general, matching starts at the rarest node or edge and then proceeds to find other elements of the left-hand side of the rule schema. In the case of expand, clearly the rarest element is the control node. Next the variable y is bound, and so the root of the triangle labelled with y is found. Matching then extends over the 1- or 2-edge outgoing from the y-node, and finds the remainder of the structure in a unique way.

4.12   VMTS Solution

In Visual Modeling and Transformation System (VMTS) [18], we have created a metamodel that defines two types; the *Vertex* type is used to represent the nodes of the Sierpinski triangle, while the *DepthLimit* node helps to set the actual magnification (the depth level used in the transformation). The edges of the triangles are represented at meta level by a loop edge connected to the *Vertex*. Both types have an attribute *Level*. In case of a *Vertex* the attribute shows on which level (in which generation) the vertex has been created, while in case of the *DepthLimit*, *Level* means the depth that we would like to reach during the transformation.

The main idea behind our transformation is that at every step, we match all possible triangles in the complete Sierpinski triangle and we transform each triangle into four sub-triangles. There is only one exception: we do not process triangles in which the *Level* attributes of the forming nodes are equal. This

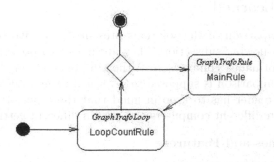

Fig. 14. Control flow diagram of the transformation in VMTS

exception is required to skip the inner triangles. There are two important comments on the procedure: (i) We do not match triangles for which the vertices are not direct neighbors; (ii) on the first (0th) level, when we have only one triangle, the *Level* attributes of the nodes are the same. We can handle this as an initial step and avoid applying the exception rule in this case. The transformation stops if there is a node in the triangle for which the *Level* attribute is equal to the level set by the *DepthLimit* object. The input model of the transformation is an initial triangle having three vertices and a *DepthLimit* object.

In VMTS, we use an activity diagram-like specification [13] to define the steps of graph transformations. Our Visual Control Flow Language supports processes (transformation rules), start/end states, decisions, fork and join constructs. The utilized control flow, shown in Fig. 14, forms a pretest loop, which is executed until we reach the configured depth limit. The loop consists of two rewriting rules and a decision node. The first rule, named *LoopCountRule* in the control flow model, references the *GraphTrafoLoop* transformation which checks whether the *Level* attribute of *DepthLimit* is 0. If so, the rule deletes the object, which makes the decision element select the end state of the transformation. Inside the loop, the main transformation rule is executed (*MainRule*, *GraphTrafoRule*). Matching is based on graphical rule definition, while rewriting uses Imperative OCL [17] code. The main rule is set to apply matching in a *MultipleMatch* mode, thus, the matching algorithm finds not only the first match, but all possible matches. This means that rewriting is applied once on the complete list of matches, which can dramatically improve performance according to our experiences. Moreover, this way the rule is executed only once for each iteration, which makes handling the *Level* attribute much simpler.

Our initial solution matched each triangle three times with different orientation and the filtering was applied after the matching process. With an improved matching which checks for multiplicity, we have achieved processing times of 23220ms on the 9th level and 211750ms on the 10th. It is important to note that our transformation framework applies the transformation steps in a strict order, defined by the control flow, and it does not compile control flows, but interprets them. Therefore, the processing times achieved can be considered as raw values without any optimization specific to this task.

5 Lessons Learned

For a rough comparison of the solutions presented, we give some key characteristics in the following subsection. They are meant to provide a basis for the subsequent performance comparison. Although concrete numbers are set into relations, this comparison is supposed to give just a rough idea of runtime performances. The reader has to keep in mind that these performance tests have been executed on different computers and within different settings.

5.1 Approaches and Features

Even for a rough performance comparison of graph transformation tools it is important to know the degree of non-determinism used within the given solution.

We distinguish the following kinds of rule matching and application to characterize the given graph transformation solutions:

1. Selection of rules and matches by the tool
2. The order of rule application is (partly) given, but matches are selected by the tool.
3. The order of rule application as well as their matches are (partly) given.
4. The order of rule application is (partly) given and rules are allowed to be matched and applied as often as possible in parallel.

In addition, we provide some information on the kind of graph representation used within the presented solutions. Some tools allow a custom graph representation to perfectly adapt to the case. In certain cases, graph features such as attributes, are not needed. Custom graph representations allow to adapt to such special cases.

To get a rough idea of the graph size in memory, we collected figures for the size of one elementary triangle, i.e. the size of three nodes glued together to a triangle produced in an elementary step of the Sierpinski generation.

A further information which seems to be significant for performance comparisons of graph transformations is the representation of edges. Here we look for double linked edges such that it is possible to traverse the edges in $O(1)$ in both directions by just knowing an adjacent node. (Note: This feature has nothing to do with directed or undirected edges in the meta model.)

Table 1. Some special solution characteristics

tool	kind	custom graph	size of triangle	edges doubly linked
TIGER EMF	1/3	no		
MOMENT2-GT	1	no		no
GROOVE	1	no		yes
TWO TAPES	1	partially	240 bytes	yes
FUJABA	3	yes	60 bytes	no
GRGEN.NET	2	in v2.0	312 bytes	yes
VIATRA	2	yes		yes
XL (GroIMP graph)	1	possible	336 bytes	yes
AGG	1/4	no		yes
GREAT	2			
GP	2	no	410 bytes	yes
VMTS	2	no	3396 bytes	yes
LIMIT	3	yes	6 pointers	no

5.2   Runtime Performance

Comparing the performance of the solutions we can see a widespread distribution from milliseconds to hours for the same task—even spreading over several complexity classes (see Figure 15). To investigate how fast the fastest solutions really are, Mallon and Geiß developed a hand-coded solution called LIMIT. This artificial solution is roughly 2.6 times faster and 2.5 times more memory efficient than

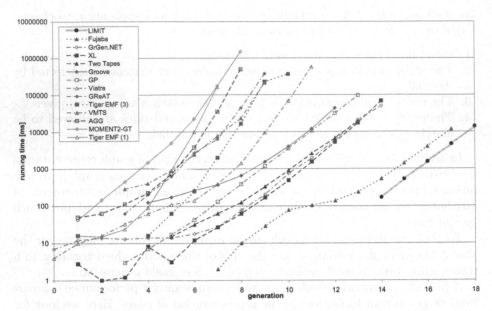

Fig. 15. Running times of the solutions shown in logarithmic scale. All measurements were carried out on different machines, so this figure has a deviation of a factor of about 3. The line style is selected according to the kind of matching and rule application of the solution: Kind 1 ⇒ solid line, kind 2 ⇒ dash-dot line, kind 3 ⇒ dotted line, and kind 4 ⇒ dashed line.

the fastest semi-automatic tool (FUJABA)(kind 3). The fastest fully automatic tools, i.e. GRGEN.NET (kind 2) and parallel tools (XL, TWO TAPES)(kind 4), are even two orders of magnitude slower than LIMIT. One of the differences between semi and fully automatic tools is that the semi-automatic ones require the developer to specify the starting points of pattern matching, whereas automatic tools can compute this information on their own. However, LIMIT uses only knowledge automatically deducible from a meta model. Hence it should be possible to tune tools to generate such efficient code automatically.

LIMIT is based on a compressed memory representation. Each node is represented by its (at most two) outgoing edges; the node itself uses no memory. The edges are stored in, and refer to, a single array. The Sierpinski triangles can be generated using only few types. Therefore, LIMIT uses a few bits of the indices to encode the types of the respective nodes. This way edges can only be traversed in one direction with $O(1)$ the other direction possibly needs the inspection of the whole graph. The pattern matching is done by extracting just the right edges with the right direction from memory. The rewrite step just adds more nodes, i.e. edges.

5.3 Concluding Remarks

The generation of Sierpinski triangles is well suited to measure the memory footprint of a solution approach and therefore, well suited for tuning tools with respect to graph representation. It is pleasant to note, that there are tools capable of handling millions of nodes and edges in very little time; reasonable hand-coded solutions are only one order of magnitude faster and more memory efficient. Tools which allow custom graph representations can be well adapted to given problems which leads to usually better runtime performances than built-in representations. However, it would be preferable to deduce a very efficient host graph implementation directly from the meta model. Considering Table 1 again, we have to stress that the motivations for building graph transformation tools have been very diverse. Dependent on intended application domains, quality criteria such as performance, usability, correctness, validation facilities, etc. are considered with intensity of varying degree. Hence, only some tools allow for custom graph representations.

In the process of preparing contest solutions, a large part of the tool builders started to improve the performance of their tools. For several tools this case study has been the first application which creates huge graphs. That quickly showed that graph representations have to be very economic regarding memory. Some tool builders immediately started to reduce memory consumption significantly, others will follow in the next time. Improvements regarding time seem to be possible concerning the graph matching algorithms used. Often, simple patterns can be handled more efficiently than currently done.

The considered tools offer a wide range of features enabling developers to provide elegant solutions. However, although the case study is pretty small, missing features have been identified. E.g. the graphical layout of Sierpinski triangles was often not optimal. Furthermore, this case study led the interest especially to parallel matching and application of rules.

All solutions of kinds 1 and 2 allow some kind of non-determinism in the selection of matches and/or rules. However, this case study does not need any kind of non-determinism and Fig. 15 shows that solutions of kinds 3 and 4 tend to show a better performance. Due to this diversity of solution approaches, Figure 15 does not really provide an objective comparison of the tools' runtime performance. Note that many participants did provide more than one solution, in order to provide more elegant and more performant solutions. For more precise measurements, it would be preferable to choose one solution approach beforehand. Even if doing so, this case study does not measure well the matching time for patterns, since the patterns used are small. Moreover, the (non-deterministic) application of many different rules and rule interaction are not considered. Hence, further case studies need to be considered in future.

References

1. Graphs for Object Oriented Verification, http://groove.cs.utwente.nl/
2. Fujaba-Homepage (2007), http://www.fujaba.de/
3. Boronat, A.: The MOMENT2-GT web site (2008),
   http://www.cs.le.ac.uk/people/aboronat/tools/moment2-gt

4. Batz, G.V., Kroll, M., Geiß, R.: A First Experimental Evaluation of Search Plan Driven Graph Pattern Matching. In: Schürr, A., Nagl, M., Zündorf, A. (eds.) AGTIVE 2007. LNCS, vol. 5088. Springer, Heidelberg (2008)
5. Bohnet, B.: Textgenerierung durch Transduktion linguistischer Strukturen. In: DISKI 298, AKA, Berlin (2006)
6. Clavel, M., Durán, F., Eker, S., Meseguer, J., Lincoln, P., Martí-Oliet, N., Talcott, C.: All About Maude. LNCS, vol. 4350. Springer, Heidelberg (2007)
7. Eclipse Consortium. Eclipse – Version 3.3 (2007), http://www.eclipse.org
8. Eclipse Consortium. Eclipse Modeling Framework (EMF) – Version 2.3 (2007), http://www.eclipse.org/emf
9. VIATRA2 Framework. An Eclipse GMT Subproject, http://www.eclipse.org/gmt/
10. Geiß, R., Kroll, M.: GrGen.NET: A Fast, Expressive, and General Purpose Graph Rewrite Tool. In: Schürr, A., Nagl, M., Zündorf, A. (eds.) AGTIVE 2007, vol. 5088. Springer, Heidelberg (2008)
11. Kniemeyer, O., Kurth, W.: The modelling platform GroIMP and the programming language XL. In: Schürr, A., Nagl, M., Zündorf, A. (eds.) AGTIVE 2007. LNCS, vol. 5088. Springer, Heidelberg (2008)
12. Kreowski, H.-J., Klempien-Hinrichs, R., Kuske, S.: Some essentials of graph transformation. In: Esik, Z., Martin-Vide, C., Mitrana, V. (eds.) Recent Advances in Formal Languages and Applications. Studies in Computational Intelligence, vol. 25, pp. 229–254. Springer, Heidelberg (2006)
13. Lengyel, L., Levendovszky, T., Mezei, G., Charaf, H.: Control Flow Support in Metamodel-Based Model Transformation Frameworks. In: EUROCON 2005, Proceedings of the IEEE, Belgrade, Serbia and Montenegro, pp. 595–598 (2005)
14. Manning, G., Plump, D.: The GP programming system. In: Proc. Graph Transformation and Visual Modelling Techniques (GT-VMT 2008). Electronic Communications of the EASST (to appear, 2008)
15. Rensink, A., Taentzer, G.: AGTIVE 2007 Graph Transformation Tool Contest. In: Schürr, A., Nagl, M., Zündorf, A. (eds.) AGTIVE 2007. LNCS, vol. 5088. Springer, Heidelberg (2007)
16. Tiger Developer Team. Tiger EMF Transformer (2007), http://www.tfs.cs.tu-berlin.de/emftrans
17. Vajk, T., Levendovszky, T.: Imperative OCL Compiler Support for Model Transformations. In: 7th International Symposium of Hungarian Researchers on Computational Intelligence, Budapest, Hungary, pp. 166–178 (November 2006)
18. VMTS website (2007), http://vmts.aut.bme.hu/

Appendix

Table 2. Comparison of the different approaches regarding the running time. Please note, that all measurements were conducted on different computers; hence only the tendency of the figures is significant (see Figure 15). To make the figures more accessible, we ordered the columns comparing their running times referring to the highest common available generation.

Tool → Gen. ↓	LIMIT'	Fujaba	GrGen .NET	XL	Two Tapes	GP	Groove	Viatra	VMTS	Tiger EMF (3)	GReAT	AGG	Tiger EMF (1)	MOMENT 2-GT
0			7					4						
1			12	3				10		16		50	16	42
2			14	1				16				63	15	144
3			13	1		3		33	290			111	24	453
4			14	8	15	7	125	62	406	16	62	224	91	1.475
5			14	3	32	17	172	108	920	62	204	729	906	4.928
6			18	12	63	43	265	141	2.450	250	624	3.788	9.870	22.284
7		2	27	27	125	130	375	388	7.630	2.000	2.688	34.724	162.427	172.868
8		10	77	62	334	390	656	1.413	23.220	16.500	6.344	495.059		1.511.668
9		29	206	169	907	1.183	1.547	9.474	211.750	227.250	43.906			
10		78	749	489	2.600	3.520	4.000	67.593		364.984	373.781			
11		104	1.930	1.542	6.700	10.619	11.969	568.589						
12		138	5.876	5.252	18.900	31.471	43.672							
13		238	20.872	17.321	96.474									
14	170	537	49.919	68.061										
15	531	1.417												
16	1.562	4.022												
17	4.687	11.778												
18	14.015													

Transformation of UML Models to CSP: A Case Study for Graph Transformation Tools

Dániel Varró[1], Márk Asztalos[1], Dénes Bisztray[2], Artur Boronat[2],
Duc-Hanh Dang[3], Rubino Geiß[4], Joel Greenyer[5], Pieter Van Gorp[6],
Ole Kniemeyer[7], Anantha Narayanan[8], Edgars Rencis[9], and Erhard Weinell[10]

[1] Budapest University of Technology and Economics, Hungary
`varro@mit.bme.hu, asztalos@aut.bme.hu`
[2] Leicester University, UK
`{dab24,aboronat}@mcs.le.ac.uk`
[3] Universität Bremen, Germany
`hanhdd@informatik.uni-bremen.de`
[4] Universität Karlsruhe, Germany
`rubino@ipd.info.uni-karlsruhe.de`
[5] University of Paderborn
`jgreen@uni-paderborn.de`
[6] University of Antwerp, Belgium
`pieter.vangorp@ua.ac.be`
[7] BTU Cottbus, Germany
`okn@informatik.tu-cottbus.de`
[8] Vanderbilt University, TN, USA
`ananth@isis.vanderbilt.edu`
[9] University of Latvia, Latvia
`Edgars.Rencis@lumii.lv`
[10] RWTH Aachen University of Technology, Germany
`Weinell@cs.rwth-aachen.de`

Abstract. Graph transformation provides an intuitive mechanism for capturing model transformations. In the current paper, we investigate and compare various graph transformation tools using a compact practical model transformation case study carried out as part of the AGTIVE 2007 Tool Contest [22]. The aim of this case study is to generate formal CSP processes from high-level UML activity diagrams, which enables to carry out mathematical analysis of the system under design.

1 Introduction

Graph transformation provides an intuitive graphical mechanism for capturing model transformations. Many tools have been developed in the past which implemented different graph transformation principles and introduced new extensions to address specific practical requirements. For example, some tools allow to specify a control structure over their transformation rules whereas others remain purely declarative. Also, different tools provide a different degree of expressive power in what kind of graph structures and attribute values they can handle. In

A. Schürr, M. Nagl, and A. Zündorf (Eds.): AGTIVE 2007, LNCS 5088, pp. 540–565, 2008.

the AGTIVE Tool Contest [22], 17 different tools participated and competed on problems of different nature in order to document and classify their strengths and weaknesses.

This case study represents a typical (exogenous) model-to-model transformation from UML activity diagrams [21] to Communicating Sequential Processes [17]. As the de-facto standard for software design, UML [21] activity diagrams are used to describe low level behavior of software components or to represent business-level workflows. In both cases, verification of the behavior can be important to guarantee the quality of service for the components. The purpose of verification can run from a simple liveness or termination check to the verification of refinement between model instances of different levels of abstraction. To verify any aspect of behavior, the activity diagrams have to be provided with a formal semantics. We are using CSP as a semantic domain, defining the mapping from activity diagram to CSP by means of graph transformation.

In this case study, the transformation tools shall support metamodel-based transformation or any equivalent notion of type graphs. Also, support for attribute handling is required, the various names and properties of elements should be dealt with. The ability to define any kind of control structure for rule application and attribute conditions may be an important issue to guarantee that the transformation is deterministic or to improve its performance. However, the transformation problem also gives space to purely declarative solutions. Due to the large variety of solutions, these solutions will now be compared based upon the model transformation-specific features provided by their corresponding tools.

The rest of the paper is structured as follows. Section 2 provides a brief introduction to the model transformation problem serving as this case study. In Sec. 3, we discuss which criteria are important for specifying and executing transformations of UML models to CSP. Moreover, we overview what kind of tools are used to perform the case study, and in what dimensions the solutions differ from each other. Section 4 presents a one-page summary for each individual solution. Finally, Section 5 provides a high-level comparison of the solutions.

2   Case Study "UML to CSP Transformation"

2.1   Metamodels

First, we introduce the source and target metamodels of the UML2CSP problem. A metamodel formalizes the abstract syntax of a modeling language in the form of UML class diagrams. Classes of the metamodel capture the main concepts of the language together with its attributes. The interrelation of such concepts are captured by associations. Finally, classes can be arranged into a generalization (inheritance) hierarchy.

UML Activity Metamodel. The source language is captured by a simplified metamodel for activity diagrams based on [21] (shown in Fig. 1).

Figure 2 shows a simple example activity diagram (taken from [16]) containing two *ActivityEdges* which connect an *InitialNode* with an *Action* and an *Action*

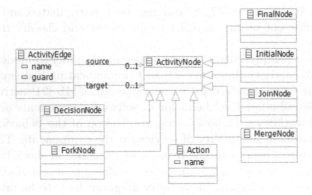

Fig. 1. Activity Diagram Metamodel

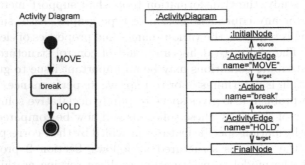

Fig. 2. Simple Activity Model (Concrete and abstract syntax)

with a *FinalNode*. The object diagram on the right shows how this concrete syntax is represented according to the metamodel shown in Fig. 1.

CSP metamodel. The metamodel for CSP, as far as required for the case study, is shown in Figure 3. A *Process* is the behavior pattern of an object with an alphabet of a limited set of events. Processes are defined using recursive process equations (*ProcessAssignment*) with guarded expressions.

The syntax of the process equations is the following.

$$P ::= F \mid event \rightarrow E \mid E \parallel F \mid E \setminus F \mid E \nless b \ngtr F \mid SKIP \mid STOP$$

The abstract class *ProcessExpression* represents a guarded expression. It can be either a simple *Process P*, a *Prefix* operator, a *BinaryOperator* combining two expressions or can be associated with a set of events (*ProcessWithSet*).

The interpretation of the process expressions is as follows. The *Prefix* operator $x \rightarrow E$ performs an *Event* x and then behaves like expression E. If E and F are expressions, *Concurrency* yields their synchronous parallel composition $E \parallel F$ (*performing E and F simultaneously by synchronizing of shared events*). According to [17], the operator $E \nless b \ngtr F$ is a *Condition* operator, which means, if the boolean *expression b* is true then it behaves like E, else it behaves like

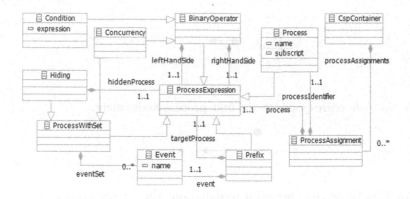

Fig. 3. CSP Metamodel

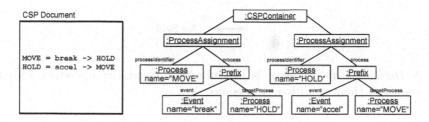

Fig. 4. Simple CSP Model (Concrete and abstract syntax)

F (*if b then E else F*). If F is a set of *Events* and E is an expression, *Hiding* $E \setminus F$ behaves like E except that all occurrences of events in F are hidden. Finally $SKIP$ represents successful termination, while the $STOP$ process is a deadlock.

Figure 4 (from [16]) shows an example CSP document containing two process assignments. The object diagram on the right shows how the abstract syntax graph of the two statements is built up according to the CSP metamodel show in Fig. 4. In particular, note that there is a Process object for every occurrence of a process in the CSP text.

2.2 Overview of the Transformation

In this section, we provide an overview of the transformation by showing intuitive correspondences between UML and CSP models. The idea behind the mapping is to relate an Edge in the activity diagram to a Process in CSP. The correspondences are the followings.

1. An *ActivityEdge* corresponds to a *ProcessIdentifier* while an *Action* to an *Event*. Without loss of generality we restrict Action nodes to have only one incoming and one outgoing edge.

A = action → B

2. *InitialNode* corresponds to the first process assignment.

A = ...

3. An *FinalNode* is a successful termination, thus it corresponds to a $SKIP$ process.

A = SKIP

4. A *DecisionNode* corresponds to embedded *Condition* operators with the *guards* as their condition *expressions*.

$$A = B \nleq x \ngeq (C \nleq y \ngeq D)$$

Note that this correspondence, which creates non-determinism at the syntactic level, leads to semantically equivalent processes. According to [21], *the order in which guards are evaluated is undefined* and *the modeler should arrange that each token only be chosen to traverse one outgoing edge, otherwise there will be race conditions among the outgoing edges.* Hence, if guard conditions are disjoint, syntactically different nestings are semantically equivalent.

5. The *MergeNode* is mapped to an equation identifying the processes corresponding to the two incoming edges.

A = C
B = C

6. The *ForkNode* corresponds to the *Concurrency* binary operator. Since $P \parallel$ $(Q \parallel R) = (P \parallel Q) \parallel R$, the different possible matches are equivalent.

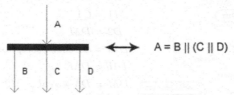

$$A = B \parallel (C \parallel D)$$

7. *JoinNode* represent the most complex cases. Before describing the mapping, we discuss some observations. If in an activity diagram the names of Action nodes are unique, the intersection of the alphabets of the corresponding processes is empty. This is partly intended because in this way the processes will not get stuck while waiting for some random other process that accidentally has events with similarly names. On the other hand we need synchronization points in order to implement the joining of processes. Thus we add an event *processJoin* to the alphabet of every participating processes. Since events that are in the alphabets of all participating processes require simultaneous participation, this fact is used to join concurrent processes by blocking them until they can perform the synchronization event.

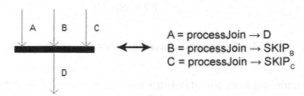

$$A = processJoin \rightarrow D$$
$$B = processJoin \rightarrow SKIP_B$$
$$C = processJoin \rightarrow SKIP_C$$

In the concrete mapping the first edge that meets the *JoinNode* is chosen to carry the continuation process, while the others terminate in a *SKIP*. The choice of the first node to be processed in a *JoinNode* is arbitrary, thus we can create multiple, but semantically (i.e. trace, failure and divergence) equivalent set of CSP expressions.

A sample activity diagram and its CSP equivalent (up to process equivalence) is presented in Fig. 5, which was used as a test case for validating the solutions.

The scenario captured by the UML activity diagram describes an autonomous service reacting to an alert issued in case of a car accident. First the driver's cell phone is called to ask if any help is required. If the alert is confirmed by the driver, then the location of the accident (and other service-specific parameters) are sent to the appropriate service provider (e.g. ambulance or tow truck service). This automotive case study is taken from the SENSORIA European Project [25].

2.3   Challenges for the Approach

In this case study, transformation tools should support metamodels or any equivalent notion of type graphs for model management. Metamodels (or type graphs)

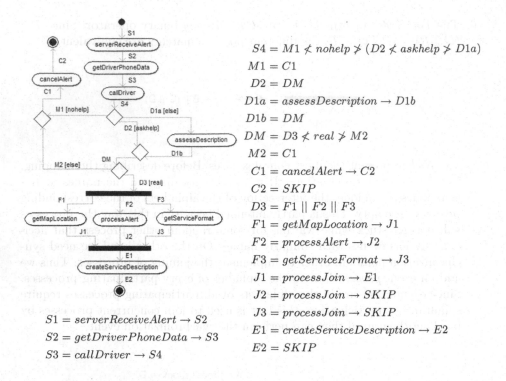

$$S4 = M1 \nless nohelp \ngtr (D2 \nless askhelp \ngtr D1a)$$
$$M1 = C1$$
$$D2 = DM$$
$$D1a = assessDescription \rightarrow D1b$$
$$D1b = DM$$
$$DM = D3 \nless real \ngtr M2$$
$$M2 = C1$$
$$C1 = cancelAlert \rightarrow C2$$
$$C2 = SKIP$$
$$D3 = F1 \parallel F2 \parallel F3$$
$$F1 = getMapLocation \rightarrow J1$$
$$F2 = processAlert \rightarrow J2$$
$$F3 = getServiceFormat \rightarrow J3$$
$$J1 = processJoin \rightarrow E1$$
$$J2 = processJoin \rightarrow SKIP$$
$$J3 = processJoin \rightarrow SKIP$$
$$E1 = createServiceDescription \rightarrow E2$$
$$E2 = SKIP$$

$$S1 = serverReceiveAlert \rightarrow S2$$
$$S2 = getDriverPhoneData \rightarrow S3$$
$$S3 = callDriver \rightarrow S4$$

Fig. 5. Sample source and target models

should also provide support for attribute handling. Control structures and control conditions may provide significant help in specifying the transformation, although their use is not explicitly required.

While performance was not the critical aspect for this case study, it is very important from a practical point of view that a transformation should be executed preferably in a few seconds so that transformation designers may immediately observe and validate the result of their transformation.

Finally, the use of some validation techniques is also desirable, although not required. More specifically, termination and determinism up to process equivalence are probably the most relevant questions to be verified for this transformation.

3   Overview on Solutions

In this case study, our primary focus was put on assessing the *expressiveness of different transformation languages* including the expressiveness of the *rule language* itself, as well as the richness of *control structures*, which aim at restricting the applicability of the transformation rules.

Furthermore, solution providers also presented those *advanced features* of their tools, which significantly improved their productivity when creating the solutions. These features included *advanced graphical user interface functionality* (e.g.

graphical rule editors) as well as *advanced model transformation features* (such as higher-order transformations, or bidirectionality). Various solution providers highlighted *analysis capabilities* of their tools to pinpoint flaws in the models or the transformation itself. Finally, most of the solutions relied upon an *advanced underlying metamodeling framework* supporting model manipulation and language design.

While the actual solutions were quite different, we identified *common subproblems for all solutions*. One subproblem is how different solutions prevent the applicability of a transformation rule on the same match multiple times. This is a typical problem in many model transformations, thus it offers some comparison specific to the graph transformation problem itself. Another interesting case is the proper handling of outgoing *ActivityEdges* on *Decision* and *ForkNodes*, since in the CSP domain, the outgoing *ActivityEdge* handled last would cause the recursive nesting of *Condition/Concurrency*-expressions to be ended. In the current paper, we will put more emphasis on the former subproblem as all the different solutions demonstrate this issue in a compact way.

The UML2CSP case study has been solved altogether by 11 tools, which are categorized (and then presented) below by the overall nature (strategy) of the solution.

- *Pure GT solutions.* Some solutions (like Tiger/EMF in Sec. 4.1 and TGGs in Sec. 4.2) build purely upon core graph transformation formalism with implicit (or minimal) control structure. These solutions demonstrate how model transformations can be formulated in a purely declarative way using graph transformation.
- *Solutions with control structures.* However, most of the solutions rely upon the use of some control structures to restrict the non-determinism of transformations. The underlying tools offer either some *textual language* (like in case of PROGRES in Sec. 4.3 or GRGEN.NET in Sec. 4.4), or some *graphical syntax*, typically with a UML flavour as in case of VMTS (Sec. 4.6), USE (Sec. 4.7), MoTMoT (Sec. 4.8), and GrTP (Sec. 4.9). In GReAT (Sec. 4.5), the control language is mostly dataflow based.
- *Solutions with a host framework / language.* There are two solutions, which rely upon a host framework not particularly designed for model / graph transformations. In the solution developed in MOMENT2-GT (Sec. 4.10), the transformation rules are translated into the Maude rewriting framework [11], while XL (Sec. 4.11) uses native Java as its control language.

4   Solutions

In this section, each solution individually describes the principles of the approach with the main settings and highlights of the used tool. Each solution is demonstrated by an example, which gives a brief insight to the look-and-feel of the transformation language or the tool itself.

4.1   Solution Using Tiger EMF Transformer

The solution is a set of graph transformation rules on EMF [12] models, that are designed using the Visual Editor of Tiger EMF Transformer [26], and run in the Eclipse development platform. The production rules are defined by rule graphs, namely a left-hand side (LHS), a right-hand side (RHS) and possible negative application conditions (NACs).

Transformation Mechanics. As the case study is presented with a list of intuitive correspondences between the source and target metamodels, the transformation rules are also in groups that resemble the correspondences. These rules are the implementation of the transformation concept introduced in [10].

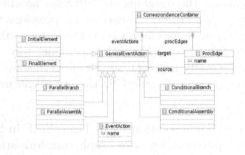

Fig. 6. Correspondence Metamodel

The rules also use a third, correspondence metamodel shown in Figure 6. For example the corresponding element between an *Edge* of activity diagram and a *Process* of CSP is the *ProcEdge*. The role of this metamodel is similar to correspondence structures used by Triple Graph Grammar [23] rules.

The benefits of using it are twofold. Firstly, it is used to mark the procession of the nodes in the source model. This way, we refrain from deleting any nodes in our rules. Secondly, all the possible NACs refer to elements from the correspondence model, as these elements are created during the transformation, never deleted. In [10] it is shown that these properties are important to make the transformation compositional.

The transformation consists of 11 rules within 7 groups. To show the background mechanics of the transformation, we introduce one rule in detail, the transformation of an *Action*.

Rule Descriptions. The transformation starts with the application of the **Initial** rule that transforms the *InitialNode*. The rule processes the only outgoing edge from the *InitialNode* by creating an empty process assignment, and also a corresponding *ProcEdge*, to track that this edge has been processed. The NAC guarantees that no edge has been processed in the model before.

The **Action Rule** depicted in Figure 7 is the essential transformation rule. The definition of the previously processed edge *A* is completed, and the new

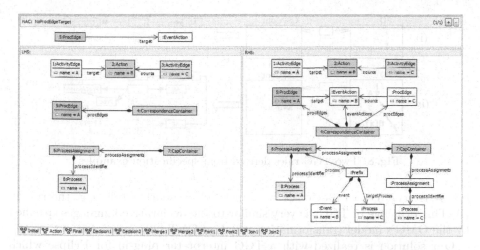

Fig. 7. Action Rule

edge C is indicated as processed and an empty definition is opened for it. The
definition of process A is a prefix operator from *Event B* to target process C.

Remaining Rules. The **Final** rule processes a *FinalNode* and fills the previous
empty process definition with a *SKIP* process. **Merge1** and **2** rules process
the *MergeNode* and connect the empty process definitions with the process that
corresponds to the outgoing edge of the *MergeNode*. **Fork1** and **2** transform
the *ForkNode* to a 2-regular tree of *Concurrency* operators the similar way the
DecisionNode tree is built. And finally **Join1** and **2** process the *JoinNode* by
creating the synchronization event and related processes. The entire set of rules
is available in [9].

4.2   Solution Using Triple Graph Grammars

The transformation from UML Activity Diagrams to CSP given in this case
study is a typical application for Triple Graph Grammars (TGGs) [23]. Their
main advantage over other (single) graph rewriting approaches is that TGG rules
reflect the relation between model patterns. This relation can be interpreted in
different ways: To translate models in a forward or backward direction, or to
maintain their consistency.

The representation of corresponding model patterns is furthermore quite intuitive. In fact, the transformation rules can often be derived from examples in
the transformation specification, such as given for this case study. Fig. 8 shows
how rules are derived from the information that an *ActivityEdge* corresponds
to a *Process* in a *ProcessAssignment* (i) and that an *Action* relates to a *Prefix-
Expression* (ii), compare the specification given in Sec. 2. The elements marked
green (and with $++$) are those essentially related by a rule. Their relationship
holds when a certain structural context (b/w nodes) is given. This context implies dependencies to other rules. For example, the second rule in Fig. 8 requires

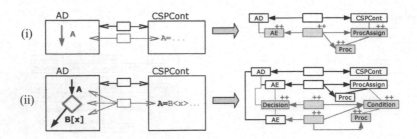

Fig. 8. Two TGG rules derived from specification examples

two *ActivityEdges* to previously be translated by another rule, e.g. the rule in (i). This principle of TGGs is very similar to the declarative languages specified by the OMG's model transformation standard QVT [20] as pointed out in [15].

Our solution is realized with a TGG interpreter plug-in for Eclipse which transforms EMF models. The rules can be modeled in a graphical editor generated with GMF. For details of our solution, refer to [16]. For this example and many others, the interpreter performs very well. For bigger models, the matching algorithm could still be improved, or we would want to compile the rules into executable code. This is done in other TGG transformation engines, like implemented in Fujaba [28] or MOFLON [4].

Concluding, we see the particular advantage of our solution in the straightforward and declarative way of specifying a transformation. We require no additional control structure nor priorities on rules. This greatly improves the maintainability and comprehensibility of the transformations. Furthermore, it is possible to bidirectionally interpret the relational rules.

4.3   Solution Using PROGRES

The *Programmed Graph REwrite System* [24] is a general-purpose graph rewriting language. Its expressive graph language and the mature environment (including static analyzers, a debugger and code generator) encouraged its application in the tool contest. However, PROGRES does not explicitly support model transformation features like automated traceability management or bidirectionality.

The PROGRES-based solution comprises a single graph schema for both meta-models, plus a single interconnecting edge type to store traceability links. Model transformation rules are roughly structured as follows: The left-hand side (*LHS*) queries subgraphs of both (source and target) models connected by traceability edges, forming the transformation's *context*. In addition, an *increment* of the source model, which should be transformed by the current rule, is connected to the LHS's context. Non-recursive processing is guaranteed by negative application conditions (*NACs*), which ensure that no element in the target model exists for the given source increment. On the right-hand side (*RHS*) of rules, a corresponding element is created in the target model and connected to the processed source increment.

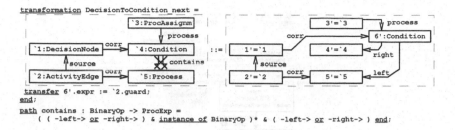

Fig. 9. PROGRES transformation rule & textual path expression

Special handling is required for correspondences mapping n-ary source increments to binary target increments. As an example, the handling of DecisionNodes
is split into two. First, an initial transformation rule maps their respective else-
branch and an arbitrary other branch to a corresponding Condition. Afterwards,
the rule depicted in Figure 9 is applied as long as possible to remove the Condition ('4) of ProcessAssignment from its container and to add it as right child to a
newly created Condition (6'). The termination of the transformation is guaranteed in this case by the negated path condition contains. This condition (depicted
textually in the figure) ensures that the candidate Process '5 is not reachable
from node '4 via left or right edges.

The PROGRES-based solution does not explicitly model control-flow, but
relies on a non-deterministic rule application following an as-long-as-possible
manner. Therefore, no dataflow passing "current" elements along with rule invocations is necessary. Termination is guaranteed by the guards discussed above,
and by the fact that a traceability link is created by each rule application.

From the created specification, an executable prototype can be generated
which is able to visually present UML activity diagrams and the resulting CSP
expressions. Besides, GXL-based graph exchange and a textual output for CSP
expressions is available. Activity diagrams can be edited using a set of consistency-
preserving graph transformation rules.

4.4   Solution Using GrGen.NET

The basic idea of our approach is to process the UML graph in a topological
order. The working set is determined by specially marked edges (by type) and
negative application conditions (NACs). During the transformation process each
piece of the UML graph is removed as the according CSP graph elements are
created.

As GRGEN.NET provides all the necessary primitives, the UML and CSP
meta models can be expressed directly (see [13]). Especially the ActivityEdge
can be modeled by an edge type (as opposed to nodes in the given UML meta
model) because the type system allows attributed edges.

Moreover, GRGEN.NET provides basic support for the transformation of
models to text (unparsing). However, more expressive support could alleviate
the user from the overhead of specifying rules and control flow for unparsing.

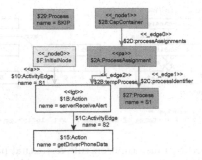

Fig. 10. The TFInitial rule applied to the example graph

Figure 10 shows a screenshot of the debugger of GRGEN.NET during a rewrite step, which removes UML elements and builds up the according CSP elements. The red (dark grey) graph elements have just been created, whereas the light grey graph elements will be deleted. The names of the rule elements are given in angle brackets.

Using the standard settings of GRGEN.NET, the transformation including the text output only takes about 100 ms. This even includes the overhead for just-in-time compilation, which accounts for about 99% of the execution time.

4.5   Solution Using GReAT

GReAT [3] is a metamodel based transformation tool implemented within the framework of GME [19]. GReAT offers several features that make designing and implementing transformations intuitive and simple. The metamodels of the source and target languages are specified using UML class diagrams, with the additional capacity to define cross metamodel entities and temporary global objects which can be accessed in any rule of the transformation. A data-flow like model is used for sequencing transformation rules, added with conditional execution of rules (using a boolean *Guard* condition) and conditional branching. The GReAT solution for this case study illustrates the use of some of these options.

An interesting part of the UML to CSP case study was the transformation of **Decision** and **Fork** nodes. The challenge was to construct a binary tree structure from a list of arbitrary length, such that the last Condition node has two Process type children. The strategy adopted for transforming **Decision** nodes is: (1) When encountering a **Decision** node, take the first outgoing edge. Create a **Condition**, whose *lhs* is the associated **Process**, and the *rhs* is a new **Condition**; (2) For the next **Activity Edge**, create an *lhs* for the associated **Process** on the last **Condition**, and a new **Condition** as *rhs*. This is repeated for all the edges that are not marked "else" in the **Decision** node; (3) Finally, when only the edge marked "else" is left, the last remaining empty *rhs* **Condition** is replaced with a **Process** corresponding to the last edge. This requires collecting all the **Decision** nodes in the input model, and performing a sequence of operations for

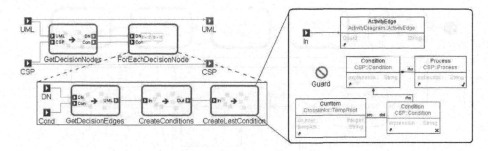

Fig. 11. Rule Sequencing and Rule Detail in GReAT

each Decision node. The layout of the transformation rules in GReAT is shown in Figure 11.

The rule *CreateConditions* is executed conditionally, for Activity Edges that do not have an "else" guard. This creates a binary tree of Condition nodes in the output, with each node having a Process as its *lhs* child, and another Condition node as its *rhs* child. When the "else" edge is encountered, the last *rhs* Condition node child is replaced with a Process. This is done by the rule *CreateLastCondition* as shown in Figure 11. *CurrItem* is a global object, which is used to track the last Condition node in the current binary tree. The rule *CreateLastCondition* deletes the last *rhs* Condition and creates a new Process in its place.

In addition to these features, GReAT comes with a code generator to generate more efficient transformations in C++, and an interactive debugger. A complete overview of the GReAT toolkit can be found in [7].

4.6   Solution Using VMTS

In VMTS environment [1], we have created the metamodels of the activity diagrams and the CSP diagrams according to the specification of the case study. Metamodel based modeling and validation is supported: metamodels are used during the whole transformation process to describe models and to validate them in each transformation step.

The transformation is defined with a control flow (using the notation of the UML activity diagrams), which consists of separate transformation steps as depicted in Fig. 12.

Each transformation step is a graph rewriting rule defined with a left hand side and a right hand side graph. The transformation control flow describes the order of the transformation steps with directed edges between the nodes; it receives an input model (an instance of the activity diagram metamodel) and produces a newly created output model (an instance of the CSP metamodel). The most important properties of the transformation control flow are the following:

1. Some rules are exhaustive rules, which means that before we proceed to the next rule, we apply the current rule repeatedly while the input model can be matched.

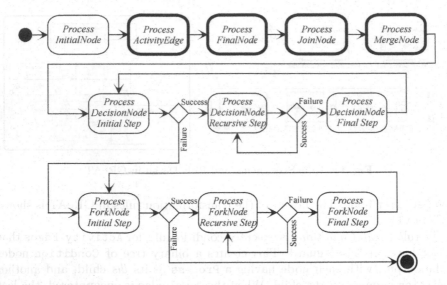

Fig. 12. The control flow of the transformation in VMTS

2. By changing the value of a special attribute (*IsProcessed*) owned by each element belonging to the input activity diagram, we guarantee to process each element at most once during the transformation rules, hereby the transformation process surely terminates.
3. Each branch node of the control flow is left by two edges, the processing flow follows one of them if the previous rule was successfully applied, or the other one if the previous rule could not be applied.
4. With internal causalities, it is possible to identify an element on the left hand side of a rule with an element on the right hand side of the same rule.
5. With external causalities (also known as parameter passing), we can identify an element on the right hand side of a rule with the element of the left hand side of the next rule in the control flow.

The Traversing Processor (TP) is part of VMTS tool. In the first step, it generates a C# API based on a chosen metamodel. Using TP we can execute the code by providing an instance model of the current metamodel as an input. By modifying the generated source code, any processing algorithm can be easily realized. In this case we use TP to produce the CSP expressions in a plain text format from a successfully created CSP model.

The result of the transformation is deterministic and the termination of the transformation process is guaranteed, because of the special attributes that ensure that each rule can be applied only finite number of times during the transformation.

4.7   Solution Using USE

This section presents a solution with USE (UML-based Specification Environment) [14], which combines UML and OCL for specifying transformations.

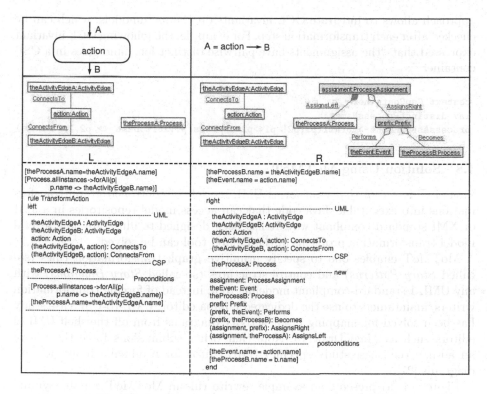

Fig. 13. Realizing the rule TransformAction with USE

For the case study, the metamodels of UML activity diagrams and CSP processes are directly expressed in USE as class diagrams attached with OCL invariants. The host graphs are presented as object diagrams.

The figure 13 shows a formulation of the rule TransformAction with USE. Matching a rule is carried out by evaluating OCL queries on the source object diagram. These queries are captured by the precondition of the operation corresponding to the rule. In this case, we obtain objects for the nodes on the left-hand side as the input of the operation. Applying the rule by USE commands realizing the rule, we create objects and links for the right-hand side. After each rule application, one may check the postconditions of the rule for an on-the-fly verification of the transformation. The sequence of rule applications can be presented by a sequence diagram.

Rules in USE are captured in a dedicated language, which are then automatically translated into USE command sequences and OCL pre- and postconditions by the OCL generator of USE.

The example transformation is always checked after each rule application. By that, USE detects that the original metamodels from the case study had to be adjusted: some composition relationships had to be changed to aggregation relationships. Otherwise the object diagram representing the CSP process of the case study is not a well-formed instance of the CSP metamodel. In addition, our approach allows to integrate OCL invariants on the metamodels, which can be checked after each transformation step. For example, the following OCL invariant expressed that "the assignments have pairwise distinct left hand sides in a CSP container ":

```
context CspContainer
inv distinctProcessNames:
processAssignment->forAll(p1,p2| p1<>p2 implies p1.left.name <> p2.left.name)
```

4.8   Solution Using MoTMoT

MoTMoT is a tool that transforms UML models of controlled graph transformations into executable Java code that can access model repositories in a JMI or XMI standard compliant way. It has been designed to illustrate how several model transformation problems of the Fujaba tool can be solved.

MoTMoT enables one to specify primitive graph transformation rules (so-called *Story Patterns*) and control structures (so-called *Story Diagrams*) with any UML 1 standard-compliant modeling tool, instead of forcing transformation writers/maintainers to use the dedicated Fujaba editor. UML-to-CSP case study has been solved for mapping input activity diagrams from off-the-shelf UML 2 editors such as MagicDraw 10. Note that other submissions force the use of an ad-hoc (i.e., case-study specific) UML editor for producing input activity diagrams [27].

Figure 14 (a) presents an example rewrite rule in MoTMoT/Fujaba syntax. Remark that ≪*bound*≫ node variables either represent nodes that have already been bound by previously executed rules (e.g., *topProcess*), or nodes that are available as method parameters (e.g., *fork, out*). Node and edge variables marked with ≪*create*≫ are created by the rewrite rule. Finally, nodes and edges without such markers need to be matched in the host graph. With this semantics in mind, Figure 14 (a) shows the rule for mapping an input *Fork* node to an output CSP expression.

Figure 14 (b) shows how the MoTMoT transformation ensures that each input node is transformed exactly once: the Story Diagram models that after the creation of the output CSP container, the transformation should match each input node exactly once (using the iterative ≪*loop*≫ construct). For each match, a *transform(inputElement, outputContainer)* method is called. This method is implemented for each type of activity node and is modeled by diagrams such as Figure 14 (a).

A first strength of the MoTMoT submission is the utilization of colors and layout patterns to improve the readability of a transformation model. Secondly, complex transformation rules are decomposed into manageable units by means of views on such rewrite rules. For example, Figure 14 (a) only shows the core mapping concerns for mapping a UML *Fork* node to a CSP *Process Assigment*.

More technical concerns are modeled by another view on the same rewrite rule. A third strength of MoTMoT is its conformance with OMG's MDA standards. For the UML-to-CSP case study specifically, we have illustrated how input from

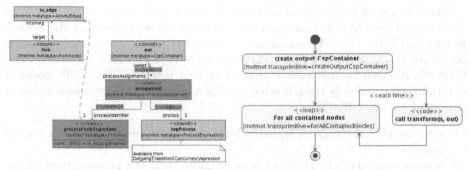

(a) Out-place rewrite rule for Fork nodes   (b) Control flow: transform each input node

Fig. 14. Story Driven Modeling: Story Pattern and Story Diagram examples

non-standard tools can be consumed as well, using in-place transformation rules. Finally, the submission illustrates MoTMoT's extensibility by applying language constructs that are realized by means of higher-order transformations.

The first drawback is the limited "out-of-the-box" usability: when only specializing a generic UML editor with the UML profile for Story Diagrams, some domain-specific editor features (such as advanced auto-completion) are not available. In practice, one may therefore want to extend one's favorite UML tool with a (small) plugin for such features. As a second drawback, the submission illustrates that some platform specific details cannot (yet) be hidden from a MoTMoT transformation model.

4.9   Solution Using GrTP

The aim of this case study is to build a model transformation which takes a UML activity diagram as an input and gives a list of CSP processes as an output. The initial activity diagram can be produced by means of transformation-based Graphical Tool-building Platform called GrTP [8]. The platform (regardless of other facilities) allows users to make an activity diagram based on the UML activity diagram meta-model and execute the transformation called *UMLtoCSP* which transforms the UML model to a CSP model and then verifies it upon termination and determinism up to process equivalence.

The result of the transformation consists of several parts:

1. a CSP model - an instance of the CSP meta-model;
2. a text file containing the list of CSP processes together with their assignments according to the textual syntax of CSP;
3. an answer to the question "Does the CSP model execution terminate?";
4. an answer to the question "Is the CSP model deterministic?".

For the GrTP platform to be able to work efficiently, a novel model transformation language L0 [2] has been implemented with a highly efficient compiler. The transformation *UMLtoCSP* is also written in the language L0. The language L0 is very simple and completely procedural, and it has only a textual syntax.

The solution of the problem is mainly based on rules given in Section 2. In addition, a rule containing information about conditions without an else branch is added (Figure 15). The termination is verified partly - it is only possible to assure the CSP model execution terminates if it contains no cycles. The CSP determinism in this case is defined in this manner - the CSP model is deterministic if and only the following condition holds for each process expression starting from the initial process:

1. every symbol of the given alphabet leads to at most one process from a given state;
2. if some symbol of the alphabet leads to more than one process, then bisimulation holds between such processes.

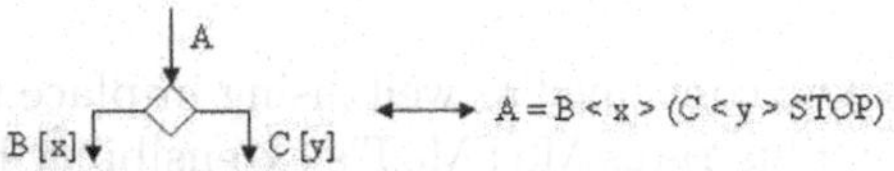

Fig. 15. Extra rule - a condition without an else branch

The advantage of the tool used to solve the task is in its simplicity from the view point of an end user: no installation is required, no complicated instructions need to be learned, — although, obviously, a new language has to be learned. However, since the tool allows user to make arbitrary UML activity diagrams, the result of the *UMLtoCSP* transformation cannot be predicted in some (erroneous) cases.

4.10   Solution Using MOMENT2-GT

MOMENT2-GT [5] is a graph transformation tool where graphs are provided as MOF-based models and production rules are defined in a QVT-based textual format. In MOMENT2-GT, a graph transformation definition is compiled into a rewrite theory in Maude [11], the input graph is represented as a term of a specific sort that is defined in this theory, and the execution of a graph transformation is handled by Maude's algorithm for term rewriting modulo associativity and commutativity. Graph transformations are performed by following the *Single Pushout* approach.

In our solution, we process the objects that constitute the input activity model generating objects in the resulting CSP model. The idea behind the transformation definition is to delete activity nodes whenever they have been processed. We have studied two solutions for the case study by taking into account dangling edges implicitly or explicitly. In the first case, MOMENT2-GT takes care of possibly generated dangling edges. In the second case, the user must avoid their generation in the transformation definition. Both solutions can be downloaded from [5].

```
eq 'rule2-ActivityEdge-->ProcessIdentifier
{
    lhs 'source {
        '1 : 'ActivityEdge {
            'name = 'inEdgeName:String
        }
        '2 : 'CspContainer { }
    };

    rhs 'source {
        '1 : 'ActivityEdge {
            'name = 'inEdgeName:String
        }
        '2 : 'CspContainer {
            'processAssignments = 'pa : 'ProcessAssignment {
                'processIdentifier = 'sp : 'ProcessIdentifier {
                    'name = 'inEdgeName:String
                }
            }
        }
    };

    nac 'source 'noProcess {
        'sp : 'ProcessIdentifier {
            'name = 'inEdgeName:String
        }
    };
}
```

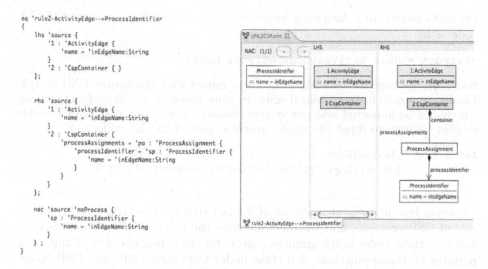

Fig. 16. Production rule in MOMENT2-GT and Tiger

We provide an average of the time measurements that have been obtained during 10 experiments[1]. The transformation that can produce dangling edges was performed in an average time of 1431.2 ms by Maude. The transformation that was designed to avoid dangling edges was performed in an average time of 885.4 ms by Maude.

MOMENT2-GT is based on a Maude algebraic specification of Essential MOF that is provided as a plugin to EMF. This means that EMF models can be directly used as formal entities in the algebraic framework, where they can be treated as graphs or as terms. Therefore, we can apply Maude-based formal analysis techniques [11], such as model checking of invariants or LTL model checking, to model-based systems in a straightforward way.

A disadvantage in our approach is that it lacks of graphical concrete syntax. Comparing a production rule in Tiger and in MOMENT2-GT (as illustrated in Fig. 16) shows, at a first glance, that our approach is not the most appropriate for communication purposes. However, for expert users, a textual-based syntax may offer editing facilities that are difficult to achieve in a graphical approach: copy & .paste, text replacement, etc. In addition, MOMENT2-GT constitutes a framework that is defined at a high level of abstraction in Maude. Therefore it is ideal for experimenting with new model transformation features, keeping in mind a realistic approach in terms of efficiency.

4.11   Solution Using XL

The case study can be implemented easily using the textual programming language XL on the basis of the graph of GroIMP [18]. At first, we have to translate

---

[1] The experiments have been performed on a Core DUO 2Ghz with 2Gb RAM, using Ubuntu 7.04.

the meta models to a Java class hierarchy which can be done as part of the XL code as in

```
abstract module ActivityNode extends Node;
```

Secondly, we have to instantiate the meta model with the source UML graph. Ideally, we would use a graphical editor or some common graph exchange format which can be imported into our system. Unfortunately, this is not yet possible so that we have to input the source graph as part of the XL code, too:

```
Axiom ==>> ^ InitialNode
           -ActivityEdge("S1")-> Action("serverReceiveAlert")  ...;
```

Thirdly, we have to specify the transformation rules and to control their application. For the rules we make use of the fact that UML activity edges play the role of CSP processes and UML actions play the role of CSP events. Thus, we can keep these nodes in the graph as context for the gluing of the SPO approach, perform all transformations as if these nodes were both UML and CSP nodes, and replace them with their actual CSP nodes as a final step. As an example, the rule for an action

```
a:ActivityEdge -o-> x:Action -i-> b:ActivityEdge ==>>
    ^ -processAssignments-> ProcessAssignment [-identifier-> a]
      -process-> Prefix [-event-> x] -targetProcess-> b;
```

already creates some CSP nodes and edges, but keeps the UML nodes of the left-hand side. Only after the final step we have a valid CSP graph:

```
a:ActivityEdge ==>> p:Process(a.getName()) moveIncoming(a, p, -1);
a:Action ==>> e:Event(a.getName()) moveIncoming(a, e, -1);
```

Concerning the control of rule application, we make use of XL extending Java: a rule is executed simply when it is reached (as a statement) by the usual control flow of Java. Furthermore, we may set the mode of rule application, either parallel or sequential. It turns out that most rules can be applied in parallel in an initial step with the exception of the creation of binary expression trees for UML decision and fork nodes which has to be done sequentially afterwards.

Among the three case studies of AGTIVE 2007, the UML-to-CSP case study was least related to the principal application domain of XL. Nevertheless, it was easily possible to implement the transformation. However, our system does not provide means for verification.

5   Lessons Learned

According to the categories discussed in Sec. 3, we can draw the following conclusions, which are summarized also in Table 1.

Table 1. Comparison of solutions and tools

Solution	Metamodeling	Rule language	Control structure (in the solution)	Handling each match once	Analysis support (in the tool)	Advanced transf. features
Tiger	EMF	graphical GT rules	none	reference metamodel & NAC	–	compiled GT rules
TGG	EMF	TGGs (graphical)	none	implicitly handled by TGG semantics	–	bidirectionality
PROGRES	graph schema	visual GT rules	non-det. rule appl., as long as possible	NAC	graph constraints	path expressions, backtracking
GrGen.NET	custom domain-specific	textual GT rules	sequential composition of rules	deconstruct the source graph	connection assertions, interactive debugger	transactions
GReAT	UML Class Diagrams	Graphical, UML-like notation with Boolean Guards	Explicit sequencing of rules with Dataflow like syntax	Implicit	Interactive Debugger	Closure over matches to form groups
VMTS	domain independent, n-level metamodeling framework	graphical rules with OCL	activity diagram with parameter passing	helper attributes and OCL constraints	run-time validation of OCL constraints	explicit traceability
USE	MOF and EMF can be explicitly modeled	textual GT rules	scripting and redex computation	with NACs	checking of (pre- and post) conditions and invariants	bidirectionality possible
MoTMoT	standards compliant (MOF, UML, JMI)	graphical GT rules	Story diagrams	helper structures	–	higher-order transformations
GrTP	UML	textual model transformation language L0	textual structures (foreach etc.)	using foreach construct	verif. of termination and determinism (of the target model)	–
MOMENT2-GT	EMF (compiled to Maude)	textual QVT-based GT rules	none	NAC, OCL constraints	formal analysis provided by Maude	–
XL	Java class hierarchy	textual, extends Java	parallel, seq., as long as possible, Java	removal of used UML nodes	–	–

- **Modeling (metamodeling) framework:** Each tool offers an underlying model manipulation and metamodeling framework to support transformations. Supported features frequently included standards-compliant metamodels (like EMF or GXL) well-formedness constraints for a modeling language (typically expressed in OCL), edge attributes, etc. Several solutions used UML diagrams for capturing metamodels and model. Furthermore, some transformations were built above a full-fledged domain-specific modeling framework.
- **Rule language.** Solutions used either a textual or a graphical language for capturing transformation rules. Some tools integrated relied on standards-compliant languages in transformation design such as OCL (as in case of USE or VMTS) or QVT (in case of MOMENT2 GT). Interestingly, none of the tools provided *both* a graphical and a textual language for capturing rules.
- **Control structures.** Control structures used in at least one of the solutions included parameter passing (e.g. GReAT and VMTS), parallel rule execution (e.g. XL), as long as possible rule application, topological (hierarchical) ordering enforced by rules and rewrite sequences (in GRGEN.NET), a dataflow-based language (in GReAT), and traditional programming constructs like conditional branching or loops. XL used native Java constructs as control structures for the transformation. The TIGER, the TGG and the MOMENT2-GT solutions were purely declarative, i.e., they did not use any control structure.
- **Handling each match once.** In order to process each match only once, different solutions used either some explicit helper data structure (such as a reference model or a helper attribute), negative application conditions for rules, and control structures like *foreach*. The TGG solution automatically maintains all instances of the applied rules to remember the matched nodes. Finally, some solutions (such as GRGEN.NET, GReAT or XL) removed some (or all) elements of the source model one by one to prevent multiple application of rules on the same match.
- **Advanced GUI features.** Advanced features of the graphical user interface of different tools included graphical editors (e.g. in case of TIGER, TGGs or GrTP), different views of rules (e.g. in MoTMoT), and editors of the source and target models (e.g., in PROGRES, VMTS, GrTP). Online and interactive layout of the host graph is present in GRGEN.NET.
- **Underlying run-time transformation platform.** Most of the tools were implemented in Java, several of them above industrial modeling platforms like EMF (in case of e.g TIGER or TGG) or JMI (in case of MoTMoT). The exceptions include VMTS and GRGEN.NET, which used .Net as underlying platform. PROGRES transformations can be compiled into C, GReAT and GrTP transformations can be compiled into C++. Finally, MOMENT2-GT transformations are executed within the Maude rewriting framework.
- **Analysis support.** Some tools provided support for analyzing the models or the transformations. OCL-based validation of models were reported in USE and VMTS, where the latter also supports the run-time validation of constraints during transformation. An interactive debugger is available in

GReAT and GRGEN.NET. Formal analysis of transformation specifications is available in MOMENT2-GT as provided by the underlying Maude engine.

- **Advanced model transformation features.** Some advanced model transformation constructs have also been used in different solutions. The TGG solution was the only solution supporting the bidirectionality of transformations. Higher-order transformations were used in MoTMoT.

As a concluding remark, let us identify some areas where existing tool support is not as extensive. Interestingly, none of the tools supported *implicit traceability* when all correspondence structures are derived automatically when applying the transformation rules. Such a solution is present in model transformation frameworks like ATL [6]. Instead, all solutions used some kind of explicit traceability (i.c. manually introduced correspondence structure) information to represent the interconnection of source and target models. Furthermore, incremental transformations were not supported by any of the tools, which is also a key issue in the design of model transformations. Existing analysis support available in the presented tools can only guarantee some correctness criteria for specific runs of a transformation, while there is a lack of support for *reasoning on the transformation (rule) level.* Finally, solutions did not emphasize the *reusability support* available in the corresponding tools, which is a critical aspect when developing complex transformations.

References

1. Visual Modelling and Transformation System (VMTS), http://vmts.aut.bme.hu
2. The Lx transformation language set (2007), http://Lx.mii.lu.lv
3. Agrawal, A., Karsai, G., Ledeczi, A.: An end-to-end domain-driven software development framework. In: 18th Annual ACM SIGPLAN Conference on Object-Oriented Programming, Systems, Languages, and Applications (OOPSLA), Anaheim, California (2003)
4. Amelunxen, C., Königs, A., Rötschke, T., Schürr, A.: MOFLON: A Standard-Compliant Metamodeling Framework with Graph Transformations. In: Rensink, A., Warmer, J. (eds.) ECMDA-FA 2006. LNCS, vol. 4066, pp. 361–375. Springer, Heidelberg (2006)
5. Boronat, A.: The MOMENT2-GT web site (2008), http://www.cs.le.ac.uk/people/aboronat/tools/moment2-gt
6. ATLAS Group. The ATLAS Transformation Language, http://www.eclipse.org/gmt
7. Balasubramanian, D., Narayanan, A., van Buskirk, C., Karsai, G.: The graph rewriting and transformation language: GReAT. In: 3rd International Workshop on Graph Based Tools (GraBaTs 2006), Natal, Brazil (2006)
8. Barzdins, J., Zarins, A., Cerans, K., Kalnins, A., Rencis, E., Lace, L., Liepins, R., Sprogis, A.: GrTP: Transformation based graphical tool building platform. In: MDDAUI 2007: Workshop on Model Driven Development of Advanced User Interfaces (Satellite event of MODELS 2007) (2007)
9. Bisztray, D.: Verification of architectural refactoring rules. Tech. rep., Department of Computer Science, University of Leicester (2008), http://www.cs.le.ac.uk/people/dab24/refactoring-techrep.pdf

10. Bisztray, D., Heckel, R.: Rule-level verification of business process transformations using CSP. In: Proc. of 6th International Workshop on Graph Transformations and Visual Modeling Techniques (GTVMT 2007) (2007)
11. Clavel, M., Durán, F., Eker, S., Lincoln, P., Martí-Oliet, N., Meseguer, J., Talcott, C.: All About Maude - A High-Performance Logical Framework. LNCS, vol. 4350. Springer, Heidelberg (2007)
12. Eclipse Consortium. Eclipse Modeling Framework (EMF) – Version 2.3 (2007), http://www.eclipse.org/emf
13. Geiß, R., Kroll, M.: GrGen.NET: A fast, expressive, and general purpose graph rewrite tool. In: Schürr, A., Nagl, M., Zündorf, A. (eds.) AGTIVE 2007. LNCS, vol. 5088. Springer, Heidelberg (2008)
14. Gogolla, M., Büttner, F., Richters, M.: USE: A UML-Based Specification Environment for Validating UML and OCL. Science of Computer Programming 69, 27–34 (2007)
15. Greenyer, J., Kindler, E.: Reconciling TGGs with QVT. In: Engels, G., Opdyke, B., Schmidt, D.C., Weil, F. (eds.) MODELS 2007. LNCS, vol. 4735, pp. 16–30. Springer, Heidelberg (2007)
16. Greenyer, J., Kindler, E., Rieke, J., Travkin, O.: TGGs for Transforming UML to CSP: Contribution to the ACTIVE 2007 Graph Transformation Tools Contest. Tech. Rep. tr-ri-08-287, Software Engineering Group, Dept. of Computer Science, Univ. of Paderborn (2008), http://www.uni-paderborn.de/cs/ag-schaefer/Veroeffentlichungen/Quellen/Papers/2008/tr-ri-08-287.pdf
17. Hoare, C.A.R.: Communicating Sequential Processes. Prentice Hall International Series in Computer Science. Prentice-Hall, Englewood Cliffs (1985)
18. Kniemeyer, O., Kurth, W.: The modelling platform GroIMP and the programming language XL. In: Schürr, A., Nagl, M., Zündorf, A. (eds.) AGTIVE 2007. LNCS, vol. 5088. Springer, Heidelberg (2008)
19. Ledeczi, A., Bakay, A., Maroti, M., Volgyesi, P., Nordstrom, G., Sprinkle, J., Karsai, G.: Composing domain-specific design environments. Computer 34(11), 44–51 (2001)
20. Object Management Group (OMG). MOF QVT Final Adopted Specification (2007), http://www.omg.org/cgi-bin/apps/doc?ptc/07-07-07.pdf
21. OMG. Unified Modeling Language, version 2.1.1 (2006), http://www.omg.org/technology/documents/formal/uml.htm
22. Rensink, A., Taentzer, G.: AGTIVE 2007 Graph Transformation Tool Contest. In: Schürr, A., Nagl, M., Zündorf, A. (eds.) AGTIVE 2007. LNCS, vol. 5088. Springer, Heidelberg (2007)
23. Schürr, A.: Specification of Graph Translators with Triple Graph Grammars. In: Mayr, E.W., Schmidt, G., Tinhofer, G. (eds.) WG 1994. LNCS, vol. 903, pp. 151–163. Springer, Heidelberg (1995)
24. Schürr, A., Winter, A.J., Zündorf, A.: The PROGRES approach: Language and environment. In: Ehrig, H., Engels, G., Kreowski, H.-J., Rozenberg, G. (eds.) Handbook on Graph Grammars and Computing by Graph Transformation: Applications, Languages, and Tools, vol. 2, pp. 487–550. World Scientific, Singapore (1999)
25. SENSORIA: Software Engineering for Service-Oriented Overlay Computers, http://www.sensoria-ist.eu
26. Tiger Developer Team. Tiger EMF Transformer (2007), http://www.tfs.cs.tu-berlin.de/emftrans

27. Van Gorp, P., Muliawan, O., Keller, A., Janssens, D.: Executing a platform independent model of the UML-to-CSP transformation on a commercial platform. In: AGTIVE 2007 Tool Contest (2007),
http://gtcases.cs.utwente.nl/wiki/UMLToCSP/MoTMoT
28. Wagner, R.: Developing Model Transformations with Fujaba. In: Giese, H., Westfechtel, B. (eds.) Proc. 4th International Fujaba Days 2006, Bayreuth, Germany, vol. tr-ri-06-275. Techn. Rep., pp. 79–82. Univ. of Paderborn (2006)

The EMF Model Transformation Framework

Enrico Biermann[1], Karsten Ehrig[2], Claudia Ermel[1], Christian Köhler[3], and
Gabriele Taentzer[4]

[1] Institut für Softwaretechnik und Theoretische Informatik, TU Berlin, Germany
[2] Department of Computer Science, University of Leicester, UK
[3] Department of Software Engineering, CWI Amsterdam, The Netherlands
[4] Fachbereich Mathematik und Informatik, Universität Marburg, Germany
emftrans@cs.tu-berlin.de
http://tfs.cs.tu-berlin.de/emftrans

Abstract. We present the EMF Model Transformation framework
(EMT), which supports the rule-based modification of EMF models.
Model transformation rules are defined graphically and compiled into
Java code to be used in model transformation applications.

Introduction. The ECLIPSE Modeling Framework (EMF)[1] provides a modeling and code generation framework for ECLIPSE applications based on structured data models. The goal of the *EMF Model Transformation framework (EMT)* is to support the modification of EMF models based on graphical EMF model transformation rules. EMT currently consists of three components: a graphical editor for EMF model transformation rules, a compiler, generating Java code from these rules to be used in further projects, and an interpreter for the execution of the rules using AGG [2], a graph transformation tool environment.

Definition of EMF Model Transformations. Transformations of EMF models are defined by transformation rules. Each rule consists of a left-hand side (LHS), a right-hand side (RHS), possible negative application conditions (NACs) and mappings between these object structures. An object structure consists of a number of possibly linked objects conforming to the EMF models for which the transformation is defined. Each of these structures is visualized in the graphical editor by a diagram that contains a number of object nodes which can be connected and/or attributed.

The left-hand side of a rule formulates the structural preconditions that must be fulfilled to apply the rule. Accordingly, a right-hand side describes the result (or postconditions) of a rule. Negative application conditions are defined in the same way and describe structural conditions that must not be fulfilled for rule application. Furthermore it is possible to define a layer for each rule. Rules on lower layers are applied prior to those on higher layers. Attributes of an object can be calculated using Java. Each expression may contain variables defined in the context of the rule the expression is used in.

Fig. 1 shows a screenshot of EMT where a model transformation from activity diagrams to Petri nets is defined. The loaded EMF models are shown in the lower center, while a three-pane rule editor is depicted above. Corresponding objects

A. Schürr, M. Nagl, and A. Zündorf (Eds.): AGTIVE 2007, LNCS 5088, pp. 566–567, 2008.

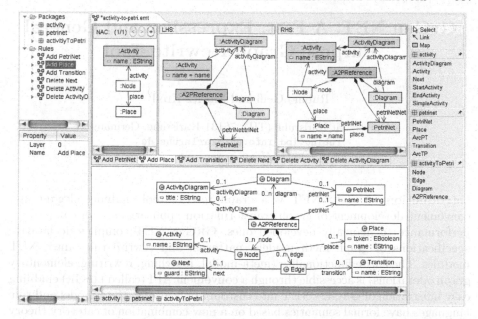

Fig. 1. EMF model transformation perspective

in these panes are colored equally to visualize rule mappings. The EMT compiler generates a Java class for each defined rule. Such a class contains methods for setting rule parameters, checking applicability, as well as performing and undoing rule applications which change models in-place.

Applications of the EMT framework so far include endogenous model transformations such as the extension of Eclipse GMF-generated editors by complex editor commands [3], as well as refactoring of EMF models [4,5], and exogenous model transformations from class diagrams to relational date bases, from activity diagrams to Petri nets and from UML to CSP.

References

1. Eclipse Consortium: Eclipse Modeling Framework (EMF) – Version 2.2.0 (2006), http://www.eclipse.org/emf
2. Taentzer, G.: AGG: A Graph Transformation Environment for Modeling and Validation of Software. In: Pfaltz, J.L., Nagl, M., Böhlen, B. (eds.) AGTIVE 2003. LNCS, vol. 3062, pp. 446–456. Springer, Heidelberg (2004)
3. Taentzer, G., Crema, A., Schmutzler, R., Ermel, C.: Generating Domain-Specific Model Editors with Complex Editing Commands. In: Schürr, A., Nagl, M., Zündorf, A. (eds.) AGTIVE 2007. LNCS, vol. 5088. Springer, Heidelberg (2008)
4. Biermann, E., Ehrig, K., Köhler, C., Kuhns, G., Taentzer, G., Weiss, E.: EMF Model Refactoring based on Graph Transformation Concepts. In: Proc. Software Evolution through Transformations (SETra 2006), EC-EASST, vol. 3 (2006)
5. Biermann, E., Ehrig, K., Köhler, C., Kuhns, G., Taentzer, G., Weiss, E.: Graphical Definition of In-Place Transformations in the Eclipse Modeling Framework. In: Nierstrasz, O., Whittle, J., Harel, D., Reggio, G. (eds.) MoDELS 2006. LNCS, vol. 4199, pp. 425–439. Springer, Heidelberg (2006)

GrGen.NET: A Fast, Expressive, and General Purpose Graph Rewrite Tool

Rubino Geiß and Moritz Kroll

Universität Karlsruhe (TH), 76131 Karlsruhe, Germany
rubino@ipd.info.uni-karlsruhe.de
http://www.grgen.net

Introduction. GRGEN.NET is a graph rewrite tool enabling elegant and convenient development of graph transformation applications with comparable performance to manually developed ones. GRGEN.NET compiles declarative specifications of graph meta models, patterns, and rewrite rules into .NET modules. The entire functionality (meta-model, matching, rewriting, elementary graph operations) is accessible through a convenient API (called LIBGR) enabling easy integration of GRGEN.NET into custom applications. Meta-model and rule languages have formal semantics based on a new combination of category theory and denotational semantics [1].

The general purpose graph rewrite tool GRGEN.NET is a descendant of GR-GEN [2], initially developed for transformations in compiler construction [3]. GRGEN.NET is published under LGPL along with a user manual.

Meta Model Language. GRGEN.NET uses typed and directed multigraphs with multiple inheritance on node and edge types. These types can be equipped with typed attributes (primitive types, enums and C#-objects). The type hierarchies in GRGEN.NET are similar to those in common OO-languages.

Pattern and Rewrite Language. A set of rewrite rules can be specified referring to graph meta models. The pattern matcher is able to perform plain isomorphic subgraph matching (injective mapping) as well as homomorphic matching for a selectable set of nodes and edges. The language has special support for typical use cases like finding induced subgraphs and exact patterns (i.e., all the incident edges in the host graph are specified in the pattern) by pattern modifiers. Matches can further be restricted by arithmetic and logical conditions on the attributes and types (including powerful instanceof-like type expressions). Nested negative application conditions—i.e., subpatterns whose existence forbids the matching—are supported, too.

The task of rewriting is internally implemented as an extension to SPO semantics. However, the user is able to specify rules in well-known DPO semantics, too. The rewrite language offers an extensive set of useful graph operations, including recalculation of node and edge attributes and retyping (a more general version of type casts) of nodes and edges. In addition to rules in algebraic style, extended graph rewrite sequences (XGRS) and emit text can be applied in the rewrite part of a rule. This way we successfully performed MOF model transformation with automatic generation of XMI files[4].

A. Schürr, M. Nagl, and A. Zündorf (Eds.): AGTIVE 2007, LNCS 5088, pp. 568–569, 2008.

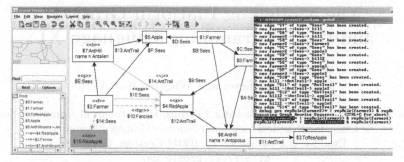

Fig. 1. Screenshot of GRSHELL and YCOMP in debug mode (colors optimised for print)

Usability. Because GRGEN.NET works on pure text files, handling of large meta models and rule sets as well as the integration with code generation tools is easy. A .NET shell application (GRSHELL) is shipped, capable of interactive and batched execution of the graph rewrite functionalities. This includes commands for creation, deletion, input, and output of graphs, nodes, and edges as well as application of rewrite rules. Several rules can be composed with logical and iterative sequence control to an XGRS, resulting in its Turing-completeness. Moreover, XGRS may contain nested transactions.

By accessing the match and rewrite facility through LIBGR, instead of using GRSHELL, custom algorithmic rule applications are possible. Graphical and stepwise debugging integrated into the GRSHELL complements the feature highlights of GRGEN.NET (see Figure 1).

Performance. According to all available benchmarks GRGEN.NET is among the fastest graph rewrite tools, with a feature set being superior to most of the other tools. In contrast to FUJABA (competing in speed with our tool) GR-GEN.NET is fully automatic: The user does not have to (partly) specify how the tool should search for a pattern graph. To automatically optimize the performance for a given (class of) host graphs, GRGEN.NET implements the search plan based approach to graph pattern matching [5] as the first tool.

References

1. Geiß, R.: Graphersetzung mit Anwendungen im Übersetzerbau. PhD thesis, Universität Karlsruhe, approved, to appear (2007)
2. Geiß, R., Batz, G.V., Grund, D., Hack, S., Szalkowski, A.: GrGen: A Fast SPO-Based Graph Rewriting Tool. In: Corradini, A., Ehrig, H., Montanari, U., Ribeiro, L., Rozenberg, G. (eds.) ICGT 2006. LNCS, vol. 4178, pp. 383–397. Springer, Heidelberg (2006)
3. Schösser, A., Geiß, R.: Graph Rewriting for Hardware Dependent Program Optimizations. In: Schürr, A., Nagl, M., Zündorf, A. (eds.) AGTIVE 2007. LNCS, vol. 5088. Springer, Heidelberg (2008)
4. Gelhausen, T., Derre, B., Geiß, R.: Customizing GrGen.NET for Model Transformation. In: GraMoT 2008 (accepted, 2008)
5. Batz, G.V., Kroll, M., Geiß, R.: A First Experimental Evaluation of Search Plan Driven Graph Pattern Matching. In: Schürr, A., Nagl, M., Zündorf, A. (eds.) AGTIVE 2007. LNCS, vol. 5088. Springer, Heidelberg (2008)

The Modelling Platform GroIMP
and the Programming Language XL

Ole Kniemeyer and Winfried Kurth

Brandenburgische Technische Universität Cottbus, Department of Computer Science,
Chair for Practical Computer Science/Graphics Systems,
Ewald-Haase-Straße 12/13, 03044 Cottbus, Germany
http://www.grogra.de/

Abstract. We present the open-source modelling platform GroIMP and the rule-based programming language XL. The underlying representation of data within GroIMP is a graph, which can be transformed by rules specified in XL. The principal field of application is modelling of virtual plants, but the system can also be used for a lot of other applications.

Introduction. The GroIMP software (growth-grammar related interactive modelling platform) has been developed as an integrated modelling environment for the specification of plant models. Thus, special importance had to be attached to the 3D representation of modelled structures as well as to a concise specification language. For the latter, the success of L(indenmayer)-systems for plant modelling [1] proved that the rule-based paradigm is most suitable, but the simple string data structure of L-systems turned out to be too poor to reflect the increasing biological knowledge and demands on modelling software. So we chose to use graphs as the underlying data structure of GroIMP, and graph grammars as the rule-based formalism. As specification language, we implemented the language XL, extending Java and incorporating rules and graph queries.

The Programming Language XL. The definition of XL as an extension of the imperative programming language Java is a distinguished feature: XL inherits several properties from Java, which in combination are seldom present in other graph-grammar tools: typing system with inheritance, the possibility to declare own classes, control flow, modularization of large systems into types and packages, huge run-time library, standard representation of compiled code, platform-independence. XL adds *queries* and *rules* to Java: a query is an expression which specifies a graph pattern and finds all matches of this pattern in the host graph, and a rule consists of a query as left-hand side and *production statements* as right-hand side. These statements may have the shape of a graph as in the following rule which inserts a new `Node` in a list linked with `next` edges

```
a:Node -next-> b:Node ==>> a -next-> Node -next-> b;
```

but may also contain control flow statements to dynamically construct the replacement for the current match:

A. Schürr, M. Nagl, and A. Zündorf (Eds.): AGTIVE 2007, LNCS 5088, pp. 570–572, 2008.

```
a:Node -next-> b:Node ==>> a if (some condition) (-next-> Node) -next-> b;
```

Queries may contain advanced patterns like optional patterns or transitive closures of path expressions or subsets thereof (e. g., `(-next->){n}` for exactly n iterations of a `next` edge). Queries operate on the host graph via a general data model interface which allows XL to be used not only for GroIMP, but for almost any given structured data. Imperative and rule-based code can be mixed freely:

```
void step(boolean delete) {
    if (delete) [s:Sphere ==>> {System.out.println("Deleted " + s);};]
    ... }
```

This distinguished feature is very useful from a practical point of view, especially for programmers familiar with Java who want to have a more suitable language for the access and modification of graph-like structures of any kind.

The Modelling Platform GroIMP. GroIMP is implemented in Java and available as open-source software. It contains a comfortable source code editor for XL programs. The integrated compiler compiles them into executable code which can immediately be run within GroIMP. The data of a project is represented as a graph, with nodes being instances of Java classes. The library of GroIMP provides a rich set of predefined node classes, most of which stand for 3D-geometric objects like spheres, boxes, spline surfaces, or coordinate transformations. The typical interpretation of a graph is that of a 3D scene graph, in which case the built-in 3D view displays instances of 3D classes using their intrinsic 3D meaning. There is also a 2D view which shows the topology of a graph. GroIMP implements the XL interfaces such that rule application conforms to relational growth grammars [2] which extend the single-pushout approach.

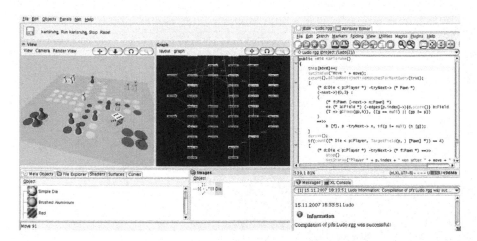

Fig. 1. Screenshot of GroIMP displaying 3D visualization, graph structure and source code editor of the Ludo game example (contained in the GroIMP release)

References

1. Prusinkiewicz, P., Lindenmayer, A.: The Algorithmic Beauty of Plants. Springer, New York (1990)
2. Kniemeyer, O., Barczik, G., Hemmerling, R., Kurth, W.: Relational growth grammars – a parallel graph transformation approach with applications in biology and architecture. In: Schürr, A., Nagl, M., Zündorf, A. (eds.) AGTIVE 2007. LNCS, vol. 5088. Springer, Heidelberg (2008)

Metamodeling with MOFLON

Carsten Amelunxen, Alexander Königs, Tobias Rötschke, and Andy Schürr

Darmstadt University of Technology, Real-Time Systems Lab
{amelunxen,koenigs,rotschke,schuerr}@es.tu-darmstadt.de
http://www.moflon.org

Abstract. The metamodeling tool MOFLON provides an integrated approach for the specification of a modeling language's abstract syntax, static and dynamic semantics especially for means of tool integration and further applications.

The Real-Time Systems Lab at the Darmstadt University of Technology develops the metamodeling tool MOFLON [1] which addresses the issues of metamodeling in general and especially the issue of metamodel-based integration of development tools by bringing together the latest OMG standards with graph transformations and their formal semantics. Using MOFLON, developers are able to generate code for specific metamodels needed to perform the integration of development tools or other tasks like guideline checking, creation of metrics or for the classical scenario of building CASE-tools.

Since, tool integration is also a matter of metamodeling, MOFLON is designed to meet especially the demands of metamodeling. As such MOFLON implements the latest OMG metamodeling standard MOF 2.0. It provides graphical editing facilities for MOF 2.0 compliant class diagrams created from scratch by the application of MOFLON's editor or imported via XMI from commercial modeling tools like Rational Rose or Enterprise Architect. The integrated code generation machinery enables MOFLON to generate repository implementations which are compliant to SUN's metadata standardization approach JMI. Hence, MOFLON is able to transform a MOF 2.0 compliant metamodel into executable Java code which can be used for the before mentioned tasks.

A MOF 2.0 compliant metamodel in MOFLON can also be completed by OCL statements in the form of invariants, derivation rules, etc. which are integrated into the generated repository implementation. Due to the integration of OCL, metamodels can be modeled much more precisely. Furthermore, beside OCL, MOFLON also integrates the technique of story driven modeling (SDM) which is implemented by MOFLON's base framework Fujaba. Thus, MOF 2.0 metamodels act as graph schema, which, in turn, allows to specify any kind of behavior based on graph transformation rules. Fig. 1 gives an idea how the different parts of MOFLON interact.

Especially for the task of tool integration, MOFLON provides an implementation of triple graph grammars [2]. With the technique of triple graph grammars, integration rules between two MOF 2.0 compliant metamodels can be specified.

A. Schürr, M. Nagl, and A. Zündorf (Eds.): AGTIVE 2007, LNCS 5088, pp. 573–574, 2008.

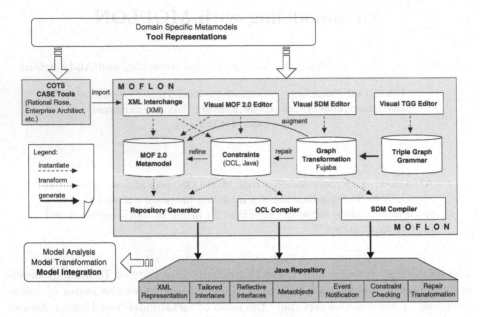

Fig. 1. Overview MOFLON architecture

Integration rules can first be transformed into common SDM graph transformations and than be further transformed by MOFLON's code generator into executable integration code. The generated integration code can be executed within a generic integration component. In combination with tool adapters for the involved commercial tools, the integration can be executed during the tools' runtime. Find further details and a demonstration of the mentioned integration scenario at **www.moflon.org**

References

1. Amelunxen, C., Königs, A., Rötschke, T., Schürr, A.: MOFLON: A Standard-Compliant Metamodeling Framework with Graph Transformations. In: Rensink, A., Warmer, J. (eds.) ECMDA-FA 2006. LNCS, vol. 4066, pp. 361–375. Springer, Heidelberg (2006)
2. Königs, A., Schürr, A.: Tool Integration with Triple Graph Grammars - A Survey. In: Heckel, R. (ed.) Proceedings of the SegraVis School on Foundations of Visual Modelling Techniques. Electronic Notes in Theoretical Computer Science, vol. 148, pp. 113–150. Elsevier Science Publ., Amsterdam (2006)

The Graph Rewriting Language and Environment PROGRES

Ulrike Ranger and Erhard Weinell

RWTH Aachen University of Technology
Department of Computer Science 3 (Software Engineering)
Ahornstraße 55, D-52074 Aachen, Germany
{Ranger,Weinell}@cs.rwth-aachen.de
http://se.rwth-aachen.de/progres

Introduction. PROGRES (PROgrammed Graph REwriting Systems) [1] has been developed since the late 1980s, and thus constitutes one of the eldest implemented graph rewriting languages and environments. It is based on the logic-oriented approach to graph grammars. The PROGRES language allows to model the structure and the behavior of software applications in a visual and declarative way. Thereby, it is not tied to a specific application domain, but may be used for arbitrary software applications (see [2] for a simple example). Besides an extensive language, PROGRES offers an integrated modeling environment, including a syntax-directed editor, an interpreter, and a debugger. Furthermore, the environment supports rapid prototyping by generating executable source code from a specification. The code can be embedded into a visual prototype.

The Graph Language PROGRES. PROGRES offers language constructs for defining graph schemas and graph transformation rules. Thereby, it uses directed, attributed, node and edge labeled graphs as underlying data model.

Graph Schema. A PROGRES graph schema consists of node types and edge types where the edge types model relations between the node types. Following the object oriented programming paradigm, attributes and graph transformation rules may be defined for every node type. For modeling complex navigations through a host graph, paths may be defined in the schema describing such navigations by using operators like the Kleene star. Furthermore, a schema may contain integrity constraints imposing advanced restrictions on valid host graphs.

Graph Transformation Rules. In PROGRES, graph transformation rules are distinguished into *simple rules* and *combined rules*. A simple rule describes a graph transformation in a visual way, consisting of a left-hand side (LHS) and a right-hand side (RHS). The LHS specifies a graph pattern for which an according match has to be found in the host graph. If such a match could be found, it is transformed according to the RHS. For modeling variable coherences, rules may contain optional, negative or even set-valued nodes and negative edges. Furthermore, embedding clauses may be used for integrating the transformed sub graph into the remaining host graph. In contrast to a simple rule, a combined rule composes several rules by textual control structures, e. g. loops and conditions. Thus, a complex

A. Schürr, M. Nagl, and A. Zündorf (Eds.): AGTIVE 2007, LNCS 5088, pp. 575–576, 2008.

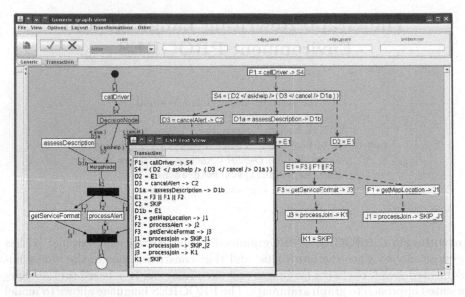

Fig. 1. Screenshot of a generated prototype

transformation may be modeled by a combined rule. PROGRES also comprises an OCL-like language for formulating constraints in transformation rules or paths.

Environment. As example for the extensive PROGRES environment, the rapid prototyping framework UPGRADE is sketched here. Using the code generated from a PROGRES specification, UPGRADE is able to display host graphs and to invoke the specified transformation rules on them. As host graphs tend to become too incomprehensible for inspection, UPGRADE offers a display mechanism which is highly user-configurable: *Filters* allow to hide instances of node and edge types not relevant to the user. They also allow to collapse edge-node-edge constructs into a single attributed edge. *Display attributes* modify colors, fonts, and shapes of nodes and edges. All attributes can be refined by conditions, e.g. to mark a node red if one of its attributes exceeds a certain threshold. *Label attributes* assign labels to the displayed graph entities, such as type information or node attributes. All of these attributes can be assigned to each type, or the type's hierarchy.

Figure 1 shows a prototypical editor created for the case study presented in [2]. Besides the graphical representation, a textual view window displays contents derived from the according nodes labels. UPGRADE supports the development of such customized views by a set of extendable base classes.

References

1. Schürr, A., et al.: The PROGRES approach: Language and environment. In: Ehrig, H., et al. (eds.) Handbook on Graph Grammars and Computing by Graph Transformation, 1st edn., vol. 2, pp. 487–550. World Scientific, Singapore (1999)
2. Varró, D., et al.: Graph Transformation Tools Contest on the Transformation of UML Models to CSP. In: Schürr, A., Nagl, M., Zündorf, A. (eds.) AGTIVE 2007. LNCS, vol. 5088. Springer, Heidelberg (2008)

Algorithm and Tool for Ontology Integration Based on Graph Rewriting

Thomas Heer, Daniel Retkowitz, and Bodo Kraft

Department of Computer Science 3, RWTH Aachen University,
Ahornstr. 55, 52074 Aachen, Germany
{heer,retkowitz}@i3.informatik.rwth-aachen.de,
bodo.kraft@amb-informatik.de
http://www-i3.informatik.rwth-aachen.de

Abstract. Ontologies are often used to define concepts of certain application domains. Using knowledge from several different subdomains then requires the integration of the defined ontologies. Since ontology integration is a difficult task, there is a need for adequate tool support. In the ConDes project, we developed a knowledge-based support for the conceptual design phase in building engineering. Thereby the problem of ontology integration had to be solved. In this paper, we describe these tools and demonstrate how they support the integration task.

1 Introduction

The first phase in the process of designing a new building is the conceptual design phase. The CAD tools currently available do not support this early stage adequately. In the ConDes project [1] we developed new concepts for software tools to support this conceptual design phase. On the one hand, the tools enable the architect to create conceptual sketches, and on the other hand they allow for the specification of conceptual design knowledge. The tools we develop allow for a consistency analysis of conceptual sketches against the respective design knowledge [2].

The term *ontology* can be used with several semantics [3]. In our case, we use this term to denote a *light-weight ontology*, which consists of several taxonomies of concepts. Ontologies form the basis for the above mentioned consistency analysis. Domain-specific conceptual design knowledge is specified by a knowledge engineer at tool runtime in the form of rules. These rules define for example the possible arrangements of rooms and their dimensions as well as the the maximal length of escape routes. Before the definition of knowledge in the form of rules, the concepts used in this knowledge specification have to be specified in a domain-specific ontology. All domain-specific ontologies are based on a static, predefined *top-level ontology*, which comprises certain basic concepts, that are common to all building designs. One ontology and the according knowledge rules together constitute a knowledge module for a certain subdomain.

To check a specific design sketch, in most cases knowledge from different subdomains has to be considered. The relevant knowledge modules have to be integrated before the analysis can be performed. To integrate the knowledge, a prior

A. Schürr, M. Nagl, and A. Zündorf (Eds.): AGTIVE 2007, LNCS 5088, pp. 577–582, 2008.

integration of the respective ontologies is required. Different types of ontology integration can be distinguished [4]. We use integration in terms of *merging* in our approach, i. e. unifying two or more ontologies into a single one. In the remainder of this paper, we present the tools we developed for the integration task.

In [5] a survey over existing approaches to ontology alignment is presented. This work gives an overview over theoretic frameworks and several current research projects. The surveyed works range from formal over heuristic approaches to approaches, which use machine learning to automate the process of ontology alignment. However, most of the presented works more or less neglect the issues involved with the interactive part of the integration process, which is always necessary, because a completely automatic approach is not feasible.

2   Tool Support for Ontology Reuse and Integration

Our tools enable the definition, reuse and integration of light-weight ontologies, i. e. classifications of concepts. Figure 1 shows the three software tools used for these tasks: the ontology editor (1), the modules browser (2) and the ontology integration tool (3).

The *ontology editor* (1) is used to define domain ontologies. During the definition of a new ontology, parts of previously defined ontologies can be reused. Ontology elements can be copied from a concept hierarchy of an existing ontology into the corresponding concept hierarchy of the new ontology. These elements can be hooked into the new concept hierarchy as specializations of existing elements. Thereby, several consistency constraints are enforced by the tool. For example, if a concept and one of its specializations are copied, then these concepts have to be in the same generalization relation in the new ontology. By enforcing constraints of this type the tool prohibits, that the semantics of copied ontology elements get implicitly changed. In figure 1, concept hierarchies from three different ontologies are shown. Edges of type CopyOf indicate, which ontology elements have been copied from another ontology.

Domain ontologies are used as a basis for the formalization of domain knowledge. This domain knowledge is defined in form of design rules. Knowledge modules can be managed with the help of the *modules browser* (2). This tool provides an overview over all defined knowledge modules and their dependencies. Dependencies between knowledge modules result from ontology reuse. When ontology elements are copied from one knowledge module to another, the latter module depends on the former. This is the case, because design rules from the former knowledge module, which apply to the copied elements, also apply to the copies, when the latter module is used to check a conceptual building sketch. The modules browser as well as the ontology editor support the versioning of knowledge modules and their storage in the file system. In figure 1, three user-defined modules are represented as nodes in a graph, and their dependencies are indicated by edges of type uses. A fourth module node represents the result of the integration of the three user-defined modules. It is connected to the modules it integrates via edges of type integrates.

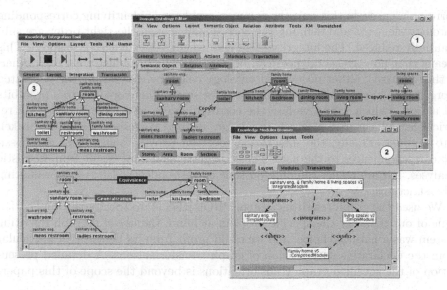

Fig. 1. Tools for ontology definition, reuse and integration

The integration of knowledge modules is supported by the *integration tool*. It supports the task of merging domain ontologies from different knowledge modules into one unified ontology. Besides that, it allows for resolving conflicts between knowledge rules. The ontologies to be integrated have to be aligned [4], so that they can be merged into one ontology. The alignment is performed by a knowledge engineer with the help of our integration tool. Thereby, he defines semantic correspondences between the elements of the ontologies.

During the interactive alignment of ontologies, several problems have to be solved [6]. For example, how can a knowledge engineer identify corresponding ontology elements, and how can it be assured, that he defines the correspondences in the right order. An important issue is, how to ensure the integrity of all defined correspondences. Furthermore, possible mismatches between the ontologies, like synonymous terms or different modeling conventions, have to be resolved during the alignment process.

The alignment of the ontologies relies on the definition of semantic correspondences between their elements. Like in [7], four different types of semantic correspondences are used: *equivalence*, *generalization*, *overlap* and *disjointness*. While the semantic correspondences are defined manually by the knowledge engineer, the merged ontology is generated automatically from the defined correspondences and the source ontologies. The knowledge engineer is supported by the integration tool in many ways. Alignment and merging steps alternate throughout the integration process. After each definition of a correspondence, the intermediate result of the integration is immediately updated. That way, the effects of defined correspondences on the integration result become directly visible. The knowledge engineer is guided through the merged ontology, and his attention is focused on small parts of the ontology, where he has to define new correspondences. In this way, the common problems of identifying corresponding ontology elements and defining the correspondences in the right order are substantially reduced. The integrity of all defined correspondences is ensured. This means that no correspondences can be defined, which conflict with each other. If this occurred, either no merged ontology could be created, or the generated merged ontology would be in an inconsistent state. Therefore, the tool prohibits all actions, which would violate the correspondence integrity. Thereby, all restrictions, which arise through previously defined correspondences, are taken into account. Finally, the integration tool can provide suggestions for possible correspondences to the user. These suggestions do not result from heuristic analyses, but are rather the only possible correspondences left, after evaluating all restrictions.

We used the graph rewriting system PROGRES [8] to specify the application logic of our tool. For the specific problem at hand, the use of a graph rewriting system was a natural choice, and we could profit from its benefits, in particular from the declarative specification of graph transformations. A detailed presentation of the specified graph transformations is beyond the scope of this paper.

3 Running the Integration Procedure

The graphical user interface of the integration tool is divided into two views. During the integration process, one view shows a part of the intermediate merged ontology. In this view, the user can select highlighted ontology elements, and he can define correspondences between these. The second view of the integration tool shows the original source ontologies together with the correspondences, which have been defined between their elements.

Several different ontologies can be integrated into one. Thereby, the ontologies are successively integrated one by one into a merged ontology. In each run, concept hierarchies of the intermediate result and the next ontology have to be aligned. The concept hierarchies of the merged ontology are traversed in an adapted breadth-first order. The traversing is steered by previously defined correspondences. At any time, the currently relevant elements of the merged ontology are highlighted, and the user is asked to define correspondences for these elements.

We will now describe the integration procedure by example. In figure 2, the integration tool is depicted in a state during the integration of three ontologies. In a first run of the integration procedure the ontologies living spaces and family home were merged into one ontology. After that, the ontology sanitary engineering has to be merged with the intermediate integration result. The correspondence Equivalence (1) has been established by an automatic top-level grounding [9]. In the first run the correspondences Overlap and Generalization (2) were defined by the user. This resulted in a merged ontology, in which family room is a specialization of dining room and living room (3). In the second run the user has already defined the correspondence Generalization (4) between toilet and sanitary room. Because of this correspondence the former ontology element has become

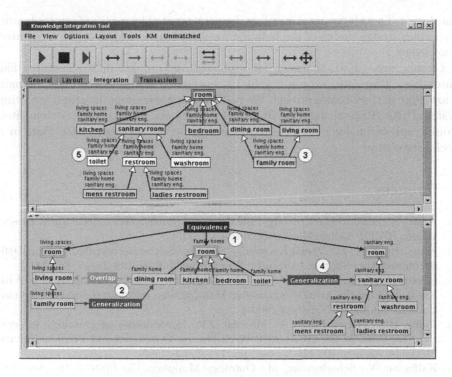

Fig. 2. Alignment during integration of three ontologies

a specialization of the latter, and the elements toilet, restroom and washroom are highlighted in the merged ontology (5). The user is now asked to define appropriate correspondences between these marked elements. He will define an equivalence relation between the ontology elements toilet and restroom. In this state, the user cannot define any correspondence for elements, which are not highlighted. The equivalence relation is only allowed, because the considered elements have the same relations with all highlighted elements and their parent elements. Many similar integrity constraints are checked by the tool, whenever the user attempts to define a new correspondence. If any constraint is violated, the tool prohibits the definition of the correspondence.

4   Conclusion

In this paper, we presented tools for an interactive, incremental integration of ontologies. In contrast to other approaches to ontology integration, we focused on providing substantial support for the interactive part of the integration process. The user is guided through the merged ontology. His actions have an immediate effect on the integration result. The integrity of all defined correspondences is assured.

For the evaluation of our tools, conceptual knowledge relevant for the design of the university hospital Aachen has been formalized in several domain specific ontologies. These large ontologies have been integrated by means of our tools, and a complex design sketch of the building has been checked against the integrated knowledge.

Graphs are a natural means for representing complex data structures like ontologies. Therefore, we use graphs to represent both ontologies and domain knowledge in the ConDes project. We realized our tools using the graph rewriting system PROGRES [8] and the UPGRADE framework [10]. Thereby, we benefited from graph technology, as we could visually specify the application logic in a declarative way.

References

1. Kraft, B.: Semantische Unterstützung des konzeptuellen Gebäudeentwurfs. Dissertation, RWTH Aachen University, Aachen (2007)
2. Kraft, B., Nagl, M.: Visual Knowledge Specification for Conceptual Design: Definition and Tool Support. Advanced Engineering Informatics 21, 67–83 (2007)
3. Gómez-Pérez, A., Fernández-López, M., Corcho, O.: Ontological Engineering: With Examples from the Areas of Knowledge Management, e-Commerce and the Semantic Web. Springer, Heidelberg (2004)
4. Pinto, H.S., Gómez-Pérez, A., Martins, J.P.: Some Issues on Ontology Integration. In: Proc. of the IJCAI 1999 Workshop on Ontologies and Problem-Solving Methods, Aachen, RWTH Aachen, pp. 7/1–7/12 (1999)
5. Kalfoglou, Y., Schorlemmer, M.: Ontology Mapping: The State of the Art. The Knowledge Engineering Review 18(1), 1–31 (2003)
6. Klein, M.: Combining and Relating Ontologies: An Analysis of Problems and Solutions. In: [11], pp. 53–62
7. Hakimpour, F., Geppert, A.: Resolving Semantic Heterogeneity in Schema Integration: an Ontology Based Approach. In: Proc. of the 2nd Intl. Conf. on Formal Ontology in Information Systems, pp. 297–308. ACM Press, New York (2001)
8. Schürr, A., Winter, A., Zündorf, A.: The PROGRES approach: Language and environment. In: Ehrig, H., Engels, G., Kreowski, H.J., Rozenberg, G. (eds.) Handbook on Graph Grammars and Computing by Graph Transformation: Applications, Languages, and Tools, vol. 2, pp. 487–550. World Scientific, Singapore (1997)
9. Wache, H., Vögele, T., Visser, U., Stuckenschmidt, H., Schuster, G., Neumann, H., Hübner, S.: Ontology-Based Integration of Information – A Survey of Existing Approaches. In: [11], pp. 108–117
10. Böhlen, B., Jäger, D., Schleicher, A., Westfechtel, B.: UPGRADE: A Framework for Building Graph-Based Interactive Tools. In: Corradini, A., Ehrig, H., Kreowski, H.-J., Rozenberg, G. (eds.) ICGT 2002. LNCS, vol. 2505, pp. 270–285. Springer, Heidelberg (2002)
11. Gómez-Pérez, A., Gruninger, M., Stuckenschmidt, H., Uschold, M. (eds.): Proc. of the IJCAI 2001 Workshop on Ontologies and Information Sharing. AAAI Press, Menlo Park (2001)

Generating Eclipse Editor Plug-Ins Using Tiger

Enrico Biermann[1], Karsten Ehrig[2], Claudia Ermel[1], and Gabriele Taentzer[3]

[1] Institut für Softwaretechnik und Theoretische Informatik, TU Berlin, Germany
[2] Department of Computer Science, University of Leicester, UK
[3] Fachbereich Mathematik und Informatik, Universität Marburg, Germany
tigerprj@cs.tu-berlin.de
http://tfs.cs.tu-berlin.de/tigerprj

Abstract. We present TIGER, a visual environment to design visual
language (VL) specifications based on meta models, graph grammars
and layout definitions. A VL specification serves as basis to generate a
visual editor for VL diagrams as ECLIPSE plug-in.

Introduction. Domain specific modeling languages are of growing importance
for software and system development. Meta tools are needed to support the
rapid development of domain-specific visual editors. A visual language (VL) definition based on a meta model in combination with a rule-based specification of
editor commands is used in TIGER *(Transformation-based Generation of Environments)* to generate a corresponding visual editor.

TIGER combines the advantages of precise VL specification techniques using
graph transformation concepts with sophisticated graphical editor development
features offered by the Eclipse Graphical Editing Framework (GEF) [1]. Using
graph transformation at the abstract syntax level, an editor command is modeled
in a rule-based way. The application of such syntax rules to the underlying syntax graph of a diagram is performed by the graph transformation engine AGG
[2]. TIGER extends AGG by means for concrete syntax definition. From the VL
definition, Java source code is generated, implementing an ECLIPSE visual editor
plug-in based on GEF. Thus, the generated editors appear in a timely fashion,
conforming to the ECLIPSE standard for graphical tool environments.

Tiger Architecture and User Interface. The two major parts of the TIGER
environment are the *Designer* [3] and the *Generator* [4]. A VL is specified by the
Designer providing the following four parts: the abstract syntax, the concrete syntax of the corresponding abstract elements, the start graph, and the syntax rules
which define the VL editing operations. After defining the VL in the *Designer* the
Generator is evoked to generate an editor as ECLIPSE plug-in based on GEF.

The TIGER user interface makes extensive use of the standard elements provided by the ECLIPSE workbench paradigm. Fig. 1 shows a few sample designer
views and editors arranged in the Tiger perspective defining a VL for automata:
the tree view 1 shows the hierarchical structure of a VL alphabet, a visual
editor 2 is used to define the layout for a symbol type, and a properties view
3 allows to change values for graphical layout properties of the selected ellipse

A. Schürr, M. Nagl, and A. Zündorf (Eds.): AGTIVE 2007, LNCS 5088, pp. 583–584, 2008.

584   E. Biermann et al.

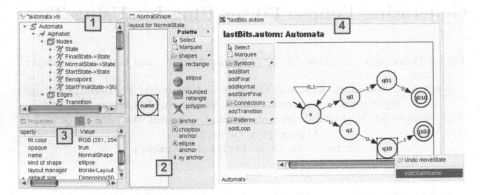

Fig. 1. The TIGER perspective in ECLIPSE and the generated automata plug-in

figure. Screenshot 4 shows the generated editor plug-in for automata. The editor palette contains VL-specific creation operations, grouped into categories *Symbols* (for creating symbols), *Connections* (for creating connections between two symbols) and *Patterns* (for modifying patterns consisting of more than one symbol). Dialogs are used for the definition of input parameter and for edit operations which can be evoked in the context menu of a selected symbol.

Note that graph transformation-based editors like TIGER, in contrast to related meta-model-based editors like GMF [5] and AToM³ [6] or MetaEdit+ [7], do not only offer basic editor commands, but also support complex editing commands which insert or manipulate larger model parts consisting of a number of elements. With complex editing commands, model optimizations, such as model refactoring, as well as model simulation may be performed.

References

1. Eclipse Consortium: Eclipse Graphical Editing Framework (GEF) – Version 3.2 (2006), http://www.eclipse.org/gef
2. Taentzer, G.: AGG: A Graph Transformation Environment for Modeling and Validation of Software. In: Pfaltz, J.L., Nagl, M., Böhlen, B. (eds.) AGTIVE 2003. LNCS, vol. 3062, pp. 446–456. Springer, Heidelberg (2004)
3. Ermel, C., Ehrig, K., Taentzer, G., Weiss, E.: Object Oriented and Rule-based Design of Visual Languages using TIGER. In: GraBaTs 2006, vol. 1. EC-EASST (2006)
4. Ehrig, K., Ermel, C., Hänsgen, S., Taentzer, G.: Generation of visual editors as Eclipse plug-ins. In: Proc. ASE 2005, pp. 134–143. IEEE Computer Society, Los Alamitos (2005)
5. Eclipse Consortium: Eclipse Graphical Modeling Framework (GMF)(2007), http://www.eclipse.org/gmf
6. de Lara, J., Vangheluwe, H., Alfonseca, M.: Meta-Modelling and Graph Grammars for Multi-Paradigm Modelling in AToM³. Software and System Modeling 3(3), 194–209 (2004)
7. Tolvanen, J., Rossi, M.: MetaEdit+: Defining and Using Domain-Specific Modeling Languages and Code Generators. In: Proc. Object-oriented programming, systems, languages, and applications (OOPSLA 2003), pp. 92–93. ACM Press, New York (2003)

From Graph Transformation to OCL Using USE

Martin Gogolla, Fabian Büttner, and Duc-Hanh Dang

Universität Bremen, Fachbereich 3, AG Datenbanksysteme, D-28334 Bremen
http://www.db.informatik.uni-bremen.de/projects/USE/

With the tool USE, UML class diagrams[1] with additional OCL constraints can be validated and properties can be formally checked. Constraints may be class invariants and operation pre- and postconditions. USE builds system states with object diagrams[2] and expresses system evolution with operations employing basic state manipulations by creating and destroying objects (nodes) and links (edges) and by modifying attributes[3].

A graph transformation system is expressed in USE by modeling the working graph with an object diagram and by expressing the graph transformation rules with operations modifying the working graph[4]. These operations encapsulate an executable sequence of basic state manipulations[5] and are additionally characterized by pre- and postconditions in which application conditions of the graph transformation rules can be expressed[6]. The graph transformation rules are formulated in a special language permitting to describe left and right hand side of rules as well as their application conditions. This language is automatically translated into USE command sequences and OCL pre- and postconditions. The rules may be executed interactively through operation calls[7]. The current working graph and its properties may be inspected on a graphical user interface and through evaluation of OCL expressions, e.g., for determining the rule redexes in the current working graph[8]. Additionally, OCL invariants may be used to restrict the permitted working graphs[9].

---

[1] Figure 1 pictures in the lower third a class diagram with class **Person** having a civil status property **civstat** which is modified by events like **birth** or **marry**.

[2] Figure 1 shows an object diagram with five **Person** objects and one **Marriage** link.

[3] The class **RuleCollection** includes the operations **birth** for creating a new person and **marry** for establishing a marriage. **RuleCollection** is a singleton class.

[4] In the top, the graph transformation rule for a marriage is shown as it is specified currently. On the right, a possible graphical representation is captured. Left and right hand side of rules consist of objects, links, and OCL assertions. The rule **marry** is the origin of the operation **marry** in the class **RuleCollection**.

[5] A call of **marry** will introduce a **Marriage** link and will modify the participating **civstat** attributes as described in the rule **marry**.

[6] The precondition of **marry** will assert that only unmarried living people with the correct gender can be involved as specified in the rule **marry**.

[7] The sequence diagram shows the executed operations leading from the empty working graph to the shown object diagram.

[8] The two OCL expressions compute the names of unmarried people and the redexes of rule **marry**, i.e., the possible meaningful substitutions for the **marry** parameters.

[9] As shown in the class invariants window, all invariants are valid in the reached system state, for example, the displayed invariant **femaleNoWife**.

A. Schürr, M. Nagl, and A. Zündorf (Eds.): AGTIVE 2007, LNCS 5088, pp. 585–586, 2008.

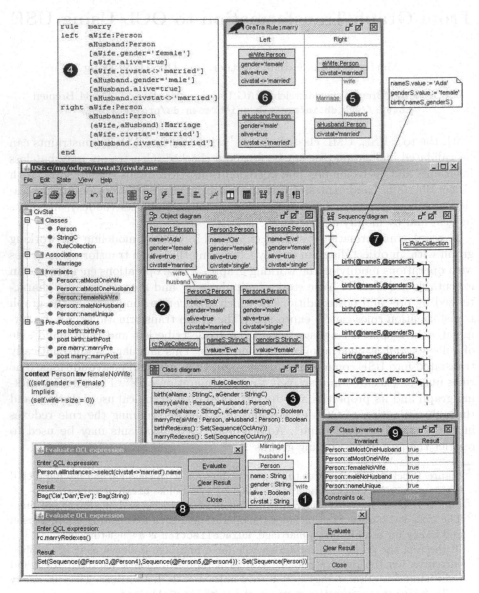

Fig. 1. Example Graph Transformation and USE Screenshot

References

[1] USE Team. USE: A UML-based Specification Environment (2008),
http://www.db.informatik.uni-bremen.de/projects/USE/

[2] Büttner, F., Gogolla, M.: Realizing Graph Transformations by Pre- and Post-
conditions and Command Sequences. In: Corradini, A., Ehrig, H., Montanari,
U., Ribeiro, L., Rozenberg, G. (eds.) ICGT 2006. LNCS, vol. 4178, pp. 398–412.
Springer, Heidelberg (2006)

Introducing the VMTS Mobile Toolkit

Tihamér Levendovszky, László Lengyel, Gergely Mezei, and Tamás Mészáros

Budapest University of Technology and Economics,
Goldmann György tér 3.
1111 Budapest, Hungary
{tihamer,lengyel,gmezei,mesztam}@aut.bme.hu

Abstract. Developing software for mobile devices requires special attention, and it is still a larger effort compared to the development for desktop computers and servers. With the introduction and the popularity of wireless devices, the diversity of the platforms has also been increased. There are different platforms and tools from different vendors such as Microsoft, Sun, Nokia, SonyEricsson and many more. Therefore, generative techniques underpinned by model-driven development can be applied extensively in this field. This paper introduces the Mobile Toolkit for the tool Visual Modeling and Transformation System (VMTS). This toolkit provides a bridge between the different mobile platforms with respect to the user interface and network communication development.

Keywords: Metamodeling, model-driven development, development for mobile platforms, domain-specific modeling.

1 Introduction

Developing software for different mobile devices requires more and more time and work investment because of the diversity of the increased number of mobile platforms and the development style required by embedded systems.

Currently, Symbian [1] is one of the most popular mobile platforms. There are several versions of Symbian OS. The Symbian v9.5 is the latest of all. Symbian provides a robust architecture and API to support development. There are two important ways to develop applications for Symbian platform. The first choice is to choose C++, which is the native language of the Symbian OS and the second option is to use Java which runs on top of the OS layer. Recently, the OS can be programmed in Python as well, which is an emerging direction.

The Microsoft .NET Compact Framework [2] (.NET CF) is a subset of the full Microsoft .NET Framework [3]. The full .NET Framework was downscaled to fit resource-constrained devices without compromising user scenarios in such a way that the developers would experience enhanced performance with majority of the functionality at a reduced size. The most significant benefit is that the programming model for .NET Compact Framework devices is identical to that used .NET to build applications for desktop PCs and servers.

The Java 2 Micro Edition (J2ME) [4] is also a popular platform for developing applications for mobile devices. J2ME is a smaller version of Java 2 Standard Edition targeted towards consumer end embedded and small devices.

A. Schürr, M. Nagl, and A. Zündorf (Eds.): AGTIVE 2007, LNCS 5088, pp. 587–592, 2008.

The Visual Modeling and Transformation System [5] is a metamodel-based modeling environment and a model transformation system. VMTS has been written in C# and it is bound to the .NET environment. The aim of VMTS Mobile Toolkit is two-fold: (i) to provide an easy-to-use development environment for mobile developers and (ii) unify the development for different mobile platforms on the modeling level. This paper elaborates on the first aspect only.

2 A Modeling Environment for Wireless Devices

In general purpose application development for mobile devices, there are two frequently appearing domain: (i) the user interface development, and the (ii) network communication. Accordingly, these are the two supported area of mobile development in VMTS Mobile Toolkit. Other functionalities such as graphics and animation support are not provided by the toolkit.

The organization of this section is as follows. Firstly, we present the modeling environments for the user interface development. There are three domain-specific languages (DSLs) developed for this purpose: one for each supported environment, namely, for the Java, Symbian, and .NET CF-based mobile devices. Secondly, we outline the model transformation for Symbian platform. Thirdly, we introduce a DSL describing protocols and network communication for mobile devices. Finally, we give a brief description of the code generator for .NET CF.

Fig. 1 depicts the metamodels for the three supported platforms. These metamodels illustrate the fundamental differences between the user control libraries of the target platforms. Although the difference between the naming conventions of the controls can be resolved by defining the correspondence between the appropriate metamodel elements, the conceptual differences cannot be handled in such a way. For instance, the user interface libraries for the Symbian operating systems require a tab page-based form, which is not a requirement in the other two cases. This observation underpins the existence of three different DSLs as a design decision of the environment.

An example instance model for each of these DSLs is depicted in Fig. 2. In VMTS, it is possible to define a concrete syntax for the appearance of a metamodel instance. The tool offers a plugin-based architecture, which means that each instance is attached to three components in a plugin, according to the Model/View/Controller pattern [6]. These components specify the appearance and the behavior of the model item. The WYSIWG ("What You See Is What You Get") characteristic of the model presented in Fig. 2 is facilitated by this architecture.

The next component of the user interface-related part of the environment is the generator. Fig. 3 outlines the code generation process for the Symbian platform. The generator was built using a visual modeling processor offered by VMTS. This is a model transformation method on the basis of graph rewriting [7]. The transformation takes the metamodel of the input and output models, the input model itself, a set of transformation rules together with a control flow definition.

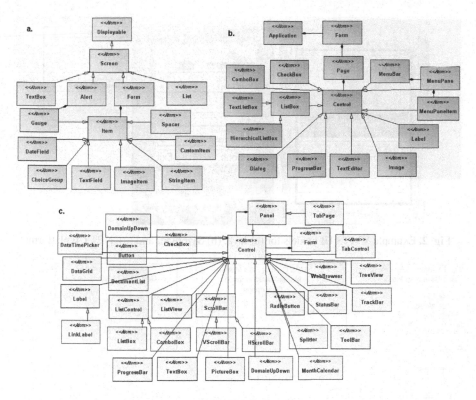

Fig. 1. The VMTS resource metamodels for (a) Java, (b) Symbian, and (c) .NET CF mobile platforms

In our case the metamodel of the input model is depicted in Fig. 1b. Moreover, the Symbian code generator supports data binding and database generation [8], thus, a database metamodel is also provided as an input. VMTS uses the Microsoft Code-DOM technology [3] for code generation. The CodeDOM consists of classes representing the syntactic elements of the .NET languages, such as C# and managed C++. The .NET framework has a code generator for these elements that generates syntactically correct code. VMTS has a CodeDOM metamodel, and there is a built-in code generator for the instance models. Thus, the metamodel of the output model is the CodeDOM metamodel.

The input model of the transformation is a Symbian user interface model accompanied with a database model. The output model of the transformation is a CodeDOM model from which VMTS automatically generates the appropriate C++ code. The transformation consists of a control flow specification and the related transformation rules. The rules have a left-hand-side (LHS) and a right-hand-side (RHS). Both LHS and RHS are specified in terms of metamodel elements. The input model of a rule is referred to as a host model. The execution of a transformation rule is as follows: (i) an instantiation of LHS must be found in the host model, and it is replaced with an instance of RHS. The instance of the RHS is retrieved from an attribute transformation specified in XML or imperative OCL.

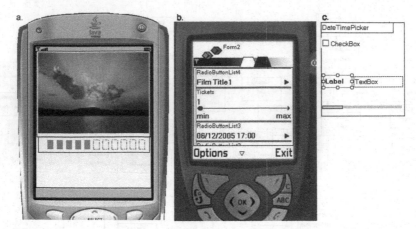

Fig. 2. Example VMTS UI models for (a) Java, (b) Symbian, and (c) .NET CF platforms

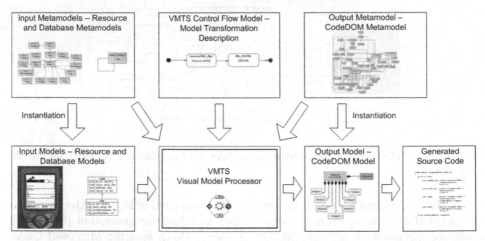

Fig. 3. The transformation process for Symbian-based wireless devices

We illustrate the transformation with another feature of the toolkit. Fig. 4 depicts an overview of the transformation process that generates source code from mobile protocol models (*Filter* models). Source code generation is again based on the Code-DOM technology. The *Filter* metamodel and an example for its instance model is presented in Fig. 5. From each *Filter*, the transformation builds a separate class which inherits from the *Filter* base class. Each class has a *Process* method with a *byte[]* and an *int* parameter and a *byte[]* return type: Data exchange between *Filter*s is based on byte arrays. This method is intended to define the logic of the protocol.

An example transformation rule is depicted in Fig. 6. This rule is part of the transformation for mobile network communication systems. The result of the transformation uses a state machine to parse the packet structure modeled by the protocol. The rule *BuildFSM* is used to build the skeleton of the state machine implemented by the generated source code, namely creating the *if* clauses for every control flow node, and connecting the nodes and the belonging *if* statements with a helper edge for later processing. Thus, the control flow graph is transformed into a semi-interpreted Finite State Machine. This state machine consists of an infinite loop, and the states are defined with *if-then* clauses in the loop for examining actual status and perform the action ordered to them. The only exit point from this infinite loop is a return statement contained by the state of the *Stop* element. States are identified with unique numbers

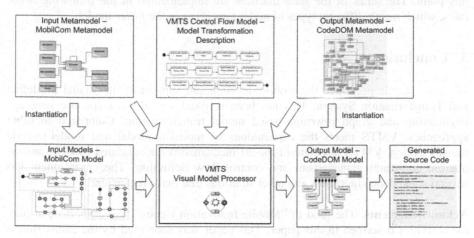

Fig. 4. Code generation process for .NET CF-based mobile devices

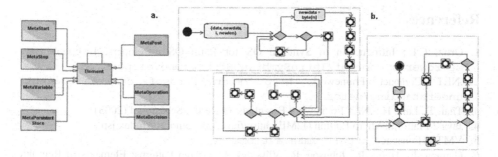

Fig. 5. (a) *Filter* metamodel and (b) an example model describing protocol

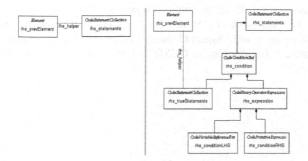

Fig. 6. Transformation rule *BuildFSM*

and the actual state is stored in the __*state* (*int*) variable inherited from the *Filter* base class. This member field can be advanced with the help of the *Next(state)* inherited method. The first five rules of the control flow model have the general purpose of creating the skeleton of the *Filter* including the complete class hierarchy, constructor, methods and state-conditions. However, the content of the states is not generated at this point. The states of the state machine are implemented in the following seven rules, which match different types of nodes appearing in the *Filter* model.

3 Conclusions

We have shortly presented the mobile development support of the Visual Modeling and Transformation System. This has been realized with domain-specific language engineering and graph rewriting-based model transformation. Compared to other approaches, VMTS meets the expectations of model-to-model and model-to-code transformation. VMTS has state-of-the-art mechanisms for validated model transformation, constraint management and control flow definition. The environment has several standalone algorithms and other solutions that make it efficient.

Acknowledgments. The fund of "Mobile Innovation Centre" has supported, in part, the activities described in this paper. This paper was supported by the János Bolyai Research Scholarship of the Hungarian Academy of Sciences.

References

1. Ortiz, C.E.: Introduction to Symbian OS for Palm OS developers, http://www.metrowerks.com/pdf/IntroSymbianOSforPalmDevelopers.pdf
2. .NET Compact Framework, http://msdn.microsoft.com/smartclient/understanding/netcf/
3. Thai, T., Lam, H.: .NET Framework Essentials. O'Reilly, Sebastopol (2003)
4. Java 2 Platform, Micro Edition (J2ME), http://java.sun.com/j2me/index.jsp
5. VMTS Homepage, http://vmts.aut.bme.hu
6. Gamma, E., Helm, R., Johnson, R., Vlissides, J.: Design Patterns: Elements of Reusable Object-Oriented Software. Addison-Wesley Professional Computing Series, Reading (1995)
7. Rozenberg, G. (ed.): Handbook on Graph Grammars and Computing by Graph Transformation. Foundations, vol. 1. World Scientific, Singapore (1997)
8. Lengyel, L., Levendovszky, T., Mezei, G., Forstner, B., Charaf, H.: Metamodel-Based Model Transformation with Aspect-Oriented Constraints. In: International Workshop on Graph and Model Transformation, GraMoT, Tallinn, Estonia, September 28 (accepted, 2005)

Author Index

Lecture Notes in Computer Science

Sublibrary 2: Programming and Software Engineering

For information about Vols. 1– 4680
please contact your bookseller or Springer